CONCEPTS AND CHALLENGES

# LIFE ❖ SCIENCE

**Fourth Edition**

Leonard Bernstein ◆ Martin Schachter ◆ Alan Winkler ◆ Stanley Wolfe

Stanley Wolfe
*Project Coordinator*

PEARSON

***About the Cover:*** Life science is the study of living organisms and their life processes. The images on the cover represent a couple of the subjects that you will be learning about in this book. The polar bears' white fur and thick insulation are adaptations that have evolved over time to help them survive in a harsh environment. Among the six characteristics of living things is the ability of organisms to produce more organisms of their own kind. In addition to the parent-child relationship shown here, polar bears interact with other species. The inset photograph is of a peacock's feathers. The male peacock uses his colorful feathers to attract a mate during a courting ritual. What do you think are some other things that you will study in life science?

***Staff Credits:*** Amanda Aranowski, Doug Bauernschmidt, Melania Benzinger, Karen Blonigen, Sarah Brandel, Katie Colón, Barbara Drewlo, Daren Hastings, Helen Higgins, Mariann Johanneck, Becky Johnson, Mary Kaye Kuzma, Vivian Lemanowski, Charles Luey, Mary Lukkonen, Paul Ramos, Dan Ray, Marie Schaefle, Christopher Tures, Mike Vineski, Sue Will



ISBN-13: 978-0-7854-6768-7
ISBN-10: 0-7854-6768-8

1 2 3 4 5 6 7 8 9 10 12 11 10 09 08

PEARSON

**1-800-321-3106**
**www.pearsonschool.com**

# Acknowledgments

## *Science Consultant*

**Dr. Richard Lowell**
Ramapo College of New Jersey
Mahwah, NJ

## *Laboratory Consultants*

**Sean Devine**
*Science Teacher*
Ridge High School
Basking Ridge, NJ

**Vincent R. Dionisio**
*Science Teacher*
Clifton High School
Clifton, NJ

## *Reading Consultant*

**Sharon Cook**
*Consultant*
Leadership in Literacy

## *Internet Consultant*

**Janet M. Gaudino**
*Science Teacher*
Montgomery Middle School
Skillman, NJ

## *ESL/ELL Consultant*

**Elizabeth Jimenez**
*Consultant*
Pomona, CA

## *Content Reviewers*

**Dr. Vincent Adamo, M.D.**
(pp. 322, 323, 370, 371, 394, 395, 436, 437, 460, & 461)
Parsippany, NJ

**Dr. Daniel Bush** (Ch. 8)
*Professor*
USDA-ARS and Department of Plant Biology
University of Illinois at Urbana-Champaign
Urbana, IL

**Sharon Danielsen** (Ch. 3)
*Site Manager*
Darrin Fresh Water Institute
Rensselaer Polytechnic Institute
Troy, NY

**Scott Denny** (pp. 146 & 147)
*Food Services Manager*
Denville, NJ

**Ivan Dmochowski** (pp. 348 & 349)
*Helen Hay Whitney Postdoctoral Scholar*
California Institute of Technology
Pasadena, CA

**Dr. Steven R. Hill** (Ch. 7)
*Associate Research Scientist*
Center for Biodiversity, Illinois Natural History Survey
Champaign, IL

**Tana M. Hoban-Higgins** (Ch. 9–10)
University of California, Davis
Davis, CA

**Sukamol Jakobsson, Ph.D.** (Ch. 11–12)
*Visiting Scholar*
University of California, San Diego
La Jolla, CA

**Rusty Lansford** (Ch. 15, 17, & 18)
*Senior Scientist*
Division of Biology
California Institute of Technology
Pasadena, CA

**Dr. Charles Liu, Astrophysicist** (pp. 28, 29, 112, & 113)
Department of Astrophysics and Hayden Planetarium
American Museum of Natural History
New York, NY

**Helen McBride, Ph.D.** (Ch. 5 & 6)
*Postdoctoral Scholar*
California Institute of Technology
Pasadena, CA

**Terry Moran** (pp. 166, 167, 412, & 413)
Moran Research Service
Harvard, MA

**Sandra Nierzwicki-Bauer** (Ch. 1–4)
*Professor of Biology*
Director, Darrin Fresh Water Institute
Rensselaer Polytechnic Institute
Troy, NY

**Alyssa Perz-Edwards, Ph.D.** (Ch. 14 & 19)
*Lecturer*
Duke University
Durham, NC

**Xanthia Samaropoulos, M.S., M.S.** (Ch. 13 & 16)
*Laboratory Assistant Professor, Department of Biology*
Georgetown University
Washington, DC

**Hugh P. Taylor, Jr.** (pp. 218, 219, 272, 273, 300, & 301)
*Robert P. Sharp Professor of Geology*
Division of Geological and Planetary Sciences
MS 100-23
California Institute of Technology
Pasadena, CA

**Dr. Raymond C. Turner** (pp. 180, 181, 244, & 245)
*Alumni Distinguished Professor Emeritus of Physics*
Department of Physics and Astronomy
Clemson University
Clemson, SC

## Teacher Reviewers

**Jennifer L. Salmon**
Belleville Middle School
Belleville, NJ

**Robert L. Fincham**
Keithley Middle School
Tacoma, WA

# Contents

## Scientific Skills and Investigations Handbooks



## UNIT 1 THE BASICS OF LIFE

### Chapter 1 Characteristics of Living Things . . . . . 15

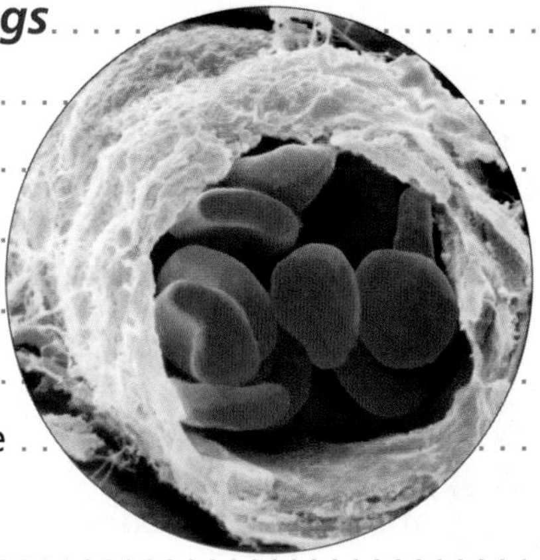



### Chapter 2 Cell Structure and Function . . . . . 37

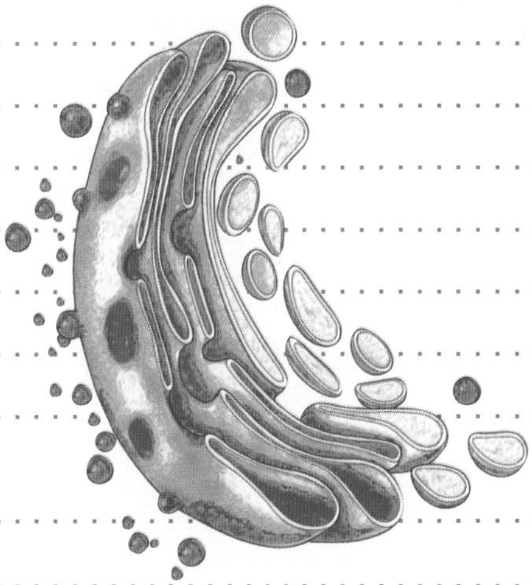

## UNIT 2 The Variety of Life



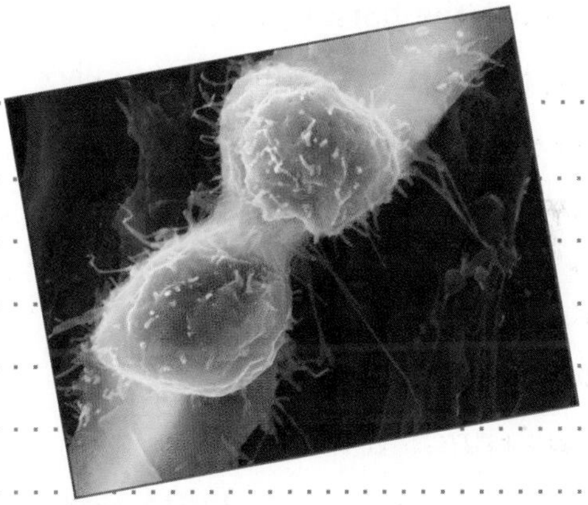

## UNIT 3 The Plant Kingdom

## Chapter 8 Plant Structure and Function ..... 171



# UNIT 4 THE ANIMAL KINGDOM

## Chapter 9 Animals Without Backbones ..... 199

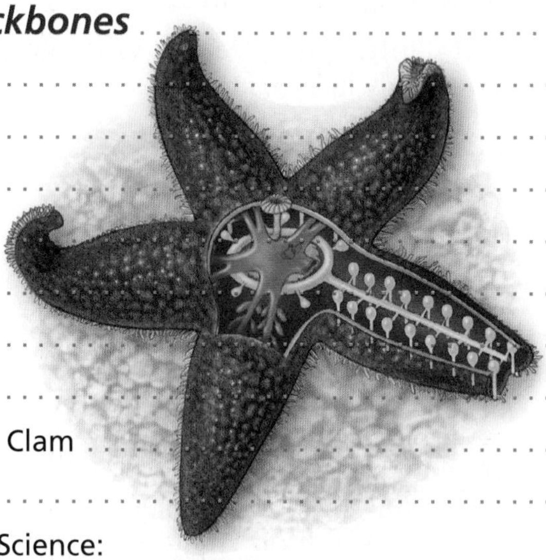

## Chapter 10 Animals With Backbones ........ 227

# UNIT 5 ECOLOGY

## Chapter 11 Living Things and the Environment ........ 255

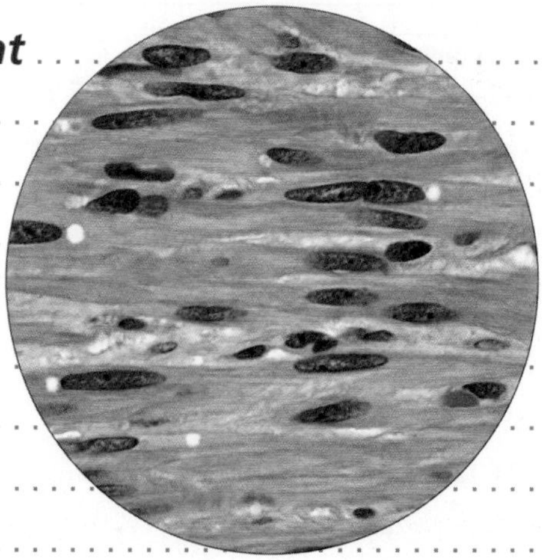

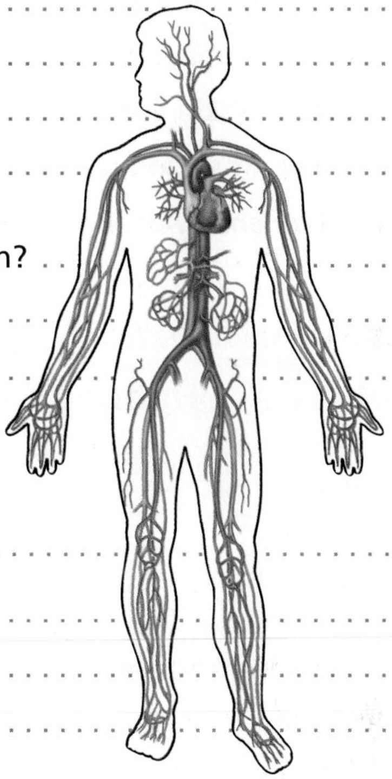

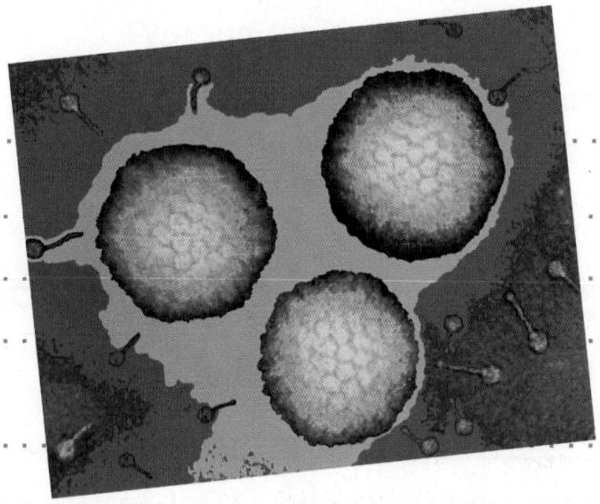

## Chapter 18 Control and Regulation ... 417



## Chapter 19 Reproduction and Development ... 445



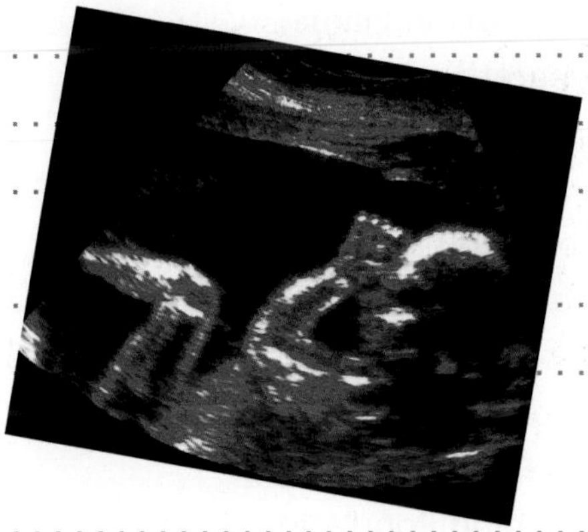

## Appendices

# Life Science Features

## Hands-On Activity



## How Do They Know That?



## Integrating the Sciences

## People in Science



## Real-Life Science



## Science and Technology

# INVESTIGATE



## Web InfoSearches

# What are scientific skills?

People are naturally curious. They want to understand the world around them. They want to understand what makes flowers grow and how their own bodies work. The field of science would probably not exist if it were not for human curiosity about the natural world.

People also want to be able to make good guesses about the future. They want to know when it will rain again and which nutrients in soil grow the best crops.

Scientists use many skills to explore the world and gather information about it. These skills are called science process skills. Another name for them is science inquiry skills.

Science process skills allow you to think like a scientist. They help you identify problems and answer questions. Sometimes they help you solve problems. More often, they provide some possible answers and lead to more questions. In this book, you will use a variety of science process skills to understand the facts and theories in life science. Science process skills are not only used in science. You compare prices when you shop and you observe what happens to foods when you cook them. You predict what the weather will be by looking at the sky. In fact, science process skills are really everyday life skills that have been adapted for problem solving in science.

1 **NAME:** What is the name for the skills scientists use to solve problems?

▲ **Figure 1** Scientists use science process skills to understand what makes trees grow, what attracts bees to flowers, and how the human digestive system works.

## Contents

# 1 Observing and Comparing

**Making Observations** An important part of solving any problem is observing, or using your senses to find out what is going on around you. The five senses are sight, hearing, touch, smell, and taste. When you look at the petals on a flower or touch the hard shell of a hermit crab, you are observing. When you observe, you pay close attention to everything that happens around you.

Scientists observe the world in ways that other scientists can repeat. This is a goal of scientific observation. It is expected that when a scientist has made an observation, other people will be able to make the same observation.

2 **LIST:** What are the five senses?

**Comparing and Contrasting** Part of observing is comparing and contrasting. When you compare data, you observe the characteristics of several things or events to see how they are alike. When you contrast data, you look for ways that similar things are different from one another.

▲ **Figure 2** Crocodiles and alligators are alike in many ways. They also have many differences.

3 **COMPARE/CONTRAST:** How are a crocodile and an alligator similar? How are they different?

**Using Tools to Observe** Sometimes an object is too small to see with your eyes alone. You need a special tool to help you make observations. One tool that life scientists use to observe things is a microscope. A microscope magnifies, or makes objects appear larger than they actually are.

▲ **Figure 3** Scientists use microscopes to observe very small objects.

4 **INFER:** What are some things that scientists might need a microscope to see?

## *Hands-On Activity*

### MAKING OBSERVATIONS

*You and a partner will need 2 shoe boxes with lids, 2 rubber bands, and several small objects.*

1. Place several small objects into the shoe box. Do not let your partner see what you put into the shoe box.
2. Cover the shoe box with the lid. Put a rubber band around the shoe box to keep the lid on.
3. Exchange shoe boxes with your partner.
4. Gently shake, turn, and rattle the shoe box.
5. Try to describe what is in the shoe box without opening it. Write your descriptions on a sheet of paper.

**Practicing Your Skills**

6. IDENTIFY: What science process skill did you use?
7. IDENTIFY: Which of your senses was most important to you?
8. ANALYZE: Direct observation is seeing something with your eyes or hearing it with your ears. Indirect observation involves using a model or past experience to make a guess about something. Which kind of observation did you use?

## 2 Classifying Data

### *Key Term*

**data:** information you collect when you observe something

**Collecting and Classifying Data** The information you collect when you observe something is called **data**. The data from an experiment or from observations you have made are first recorded, or written down. Then they are classified.

When you classify data, you group things together based on how they are alike. This information often comes from making comparisons as you observe. You may classify by size, shape, color, use, or any other important feature. Classifying data helps you recognize and understand the relationships between things. Classification makes studying large groups of things easier. For example, life scientists use classification to organize the different types of living things.

5 **EXPLAIN:** How can you classify data?

### *Hands-On Activity*

#### ORGANIZING LIVING THINGS

*You will need 15 index cards with photographs of living things taped to them.*

1. Look at the pictures on the index cards. Classify the photographs into two categories, *Plants* and *Animals*.
2. Look at the pictures you classified as *Plants*. Choose a general characteristic, such as if they have flowers or not. Divide the plants into two groups based on that specific characteristic.
3. Repeat Step 2 for the pictures you classified as *Animals*.
4. Divide these four groups into smaller groups.

**Practicing Your Skills**

5. **ANALYZE:** How did you classify the pictures?
6. **EXPLAIN:** Why is a classification system useful?

## 3 Modeling and Simulating

### *Key Terms*

**model:** a tool scientists use to represent an object or process

**simulation:** a computer model that usually shows a process

**Modeling** Sometimes things are too small to see with your eyes alone. Other times, an object is too large to see. You may need a model to help you examine the object. A **model** is a good way to show what a very small or a very large object looks like. A model can have more details than what may be seen with just your eyes. It can be used to represent a process or an object that is hard to explain with words. A model can be a three-dimensional picture, a drawing, a computer image, or a diagram.

6 **DEFINE:** What is a model?

**Simulating** A **simulation** is a kind of model that shows a process. It is often done using a computer. You can use a simulation to predict the outcome of an experiment. Scientists use simulations to study everything from the insides of a frog to the development of an embryo.

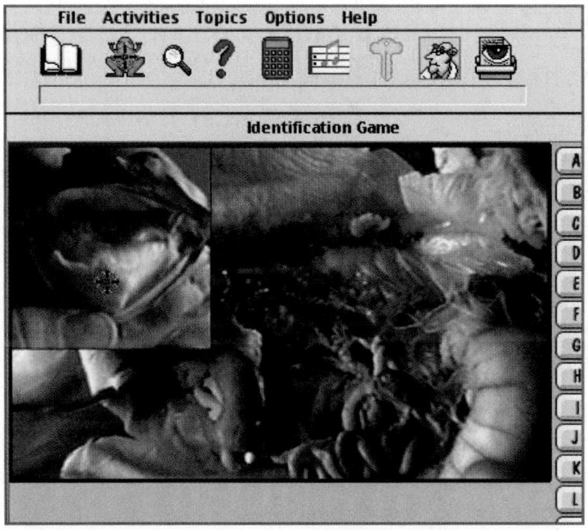


▲ **Figure 4** Some schools use a computer simulation program instead of dissecting a preserved frog.

7 **DEFINE:** What is a simulation?

# 4 Measuring

## Key Terms

**unit:** amount used to measure something

**meter:** basic metric unit of length or distance

**mass:** amount of matter in something

**gram:** basic metric unit of mass

**volume:** amount of space an object takes up

**liter:** basic metric unit of liquid volume

**meniscus:** curve at the surface of a liquid in a thin tube

**temperature:** measure of the amount of heat energy something contains

**Two Systems of Measurement** When you measure, you compare an unknown value with a known value using standard units. A **unit** is an amount used to measure something. The metric system is an international system of measurement. Examples of metric units are the gram, the kilometer, and the liter. In the United States, the English system and the metric system are both used. Examples of units in the English system are the pound, the foot, and the gallon.

There is also a more modern form of the metric system called SI. The letters *SI* stand for the French words *Système International.* Many of the units in the SI are the same as those in the metric system.

The metric and SI systems are both based on units of 10. This makes them easy to use. Each unit in these systems is 10 times greater than the one before it. To show a change in the size of a unit, you add a prefix to the unit. The prefix tells you whether the unit is larger or smaller. For example, a centimeter is 10 times bigger than a millimeter.

| PREFIXES AND THEIR MEANINGS | |
|---|---|
| kilo- | one thousand (1,000) |
| hecto- | one hundred (100) |
| deca- | ten (10) |
| deci- | one-tenth (1/10) |
| centi- | one-hundredth (1/100) |
| milli- | one-thousandth (1/1,000) |

◀ Figure 5

**8 IDENTIFY:** What are two measurement systems?

**Units of Length** Length is the distance from one point to another. In the metric system, the basic unit of length or distance is the **meter.** A meter is about the length from a doorknob to the floor. Longer distances, such as the distances between cities, are measured in kilometers. A kilometer is 1,000 meters. Centimeters and millimeters measure shorter distances. A centimeter is 1/100 of a meter. A millimeter is 1/1,000 of a meter. Figure 6 compares common units of length. It also shows the abbreviation for each unit.

| SI/METRIC UNITS OF LENGTH | |
|---|---|
| 1,000 millimeters (mm) | 1 meter (m) |
| 100 centimeters (cm) | 1 meter |
| 10 decimeters (dm) | 1 meter |
| 10 millimeters | 1 centimeter |
| 1,000 meters | 1 kilometer (km) |

▲ Figure 6

Length can be measured with a meter stick. A meter stick is 1 m long and is divided into 100 equal lengths by numbered lines. The distance between each of these lines is equal to 1 cm. Each centimeter is divided into 10 equal parts. Each one of these parts is equal to 1 mm.

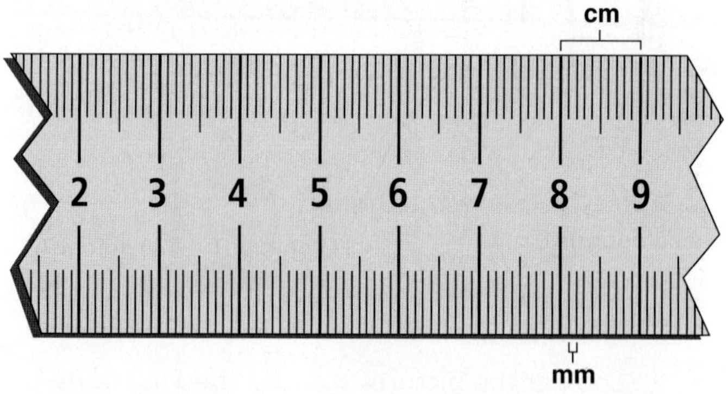


▲ Figure 7 A meter stick is divided into centimeters and millimeters.

**9 CALCULATE:** How many centimeters are there in 3 m?

**Measuring Area** Do you know how people find the area of the floor of a room? They measure the length and the width of the room. Then they multiply the two numbers. You can find the area of any rectangle by multiplying its length by its width. Area is expressed in square units, such as square meters ($m^2$) or square centimeters ($cm^2$).

Area = length × width

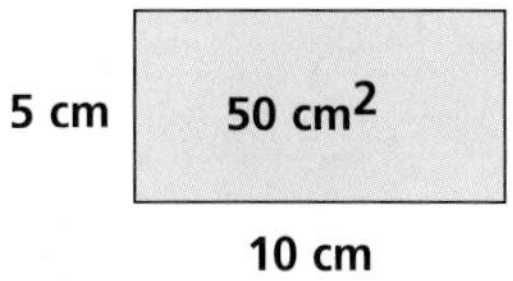


◀ **Figure 8** The area of a rectangle equals length times width.

**10 CALCULATE:** What is the area of a rectangle 2 cm × 3 cm?

**Mass and Weight** The amount of matter in something is its **mass.** The basic metric unit of mass is called a **gram (g).** A paper clip has about 1 g of mass. Mass is measured with an instrument called a balance. A balance works like a seesaw. It compares an unknown mass with a known mass.

One kind of balance that is commonly used to measure mass is a triple-beam balance. A triple-beam balance has a pan. The object being measured is placed on the pan. The balance also has three beams. Weights, called riders, are moved along each beam until the object on the pan is balanced. Each rider gives a reading in grams. The mass of the object is equal to the total readings of all three riders.

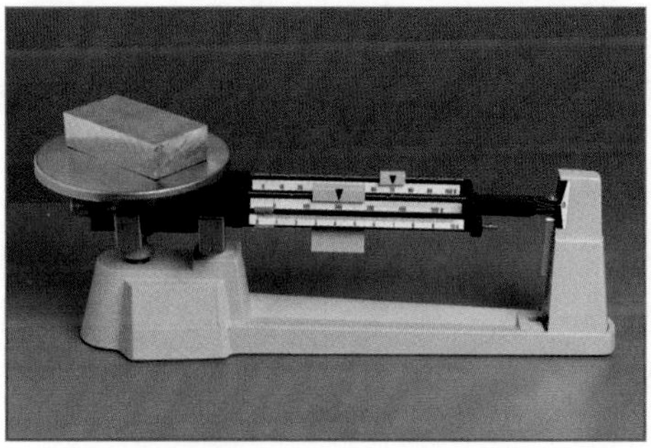

◀ **Figure 9** A triple-beam balance

Mass and weight are related; however, they are not the same. The weight of an object is a measure of Earth's pull of gravity between Earth and that object. Gravity is the force that pulls objects toward the center of Earth. The strength of the pull of gravity between two objects depends on the distance between the objects and how much mass they each contain. So, the weight changes as its distance from the center of Earth changes.

**11 IDENTIFY:** What instrument is used to measure mass?

**Volume** The amount of space an object takes up is its **volume.** You can measure the volume of liquids and solids. Liquid volume is usually measured in **liters.** Soft drinks in the United States often come in 2-liter bottles.

A graduated cylinder is used to measure liquid volume. Graduated cylinders are calibrated, or marked off, at regular intervals. Look at Figure 10. It shows a graduated cylinder. On this graduated cylinder, each small line is equal to 0.05 mL. The longer lines mark off every 0.25 mL up to 5.00 mL. However, every graduated cylinder is not calibrated in this manner. They come in different sizes up to 2,000 mL, with different calibrations.

Always read the measurement at eye level. If you are using a glass graduated cylinder, you will need to read the mark on the graduated cylinder closest to the bottom of the meniscus. A **meniscus** is the curve at the surface of a liquid in a thin tube. A plastic graduated cylinder does not show a meniscus.

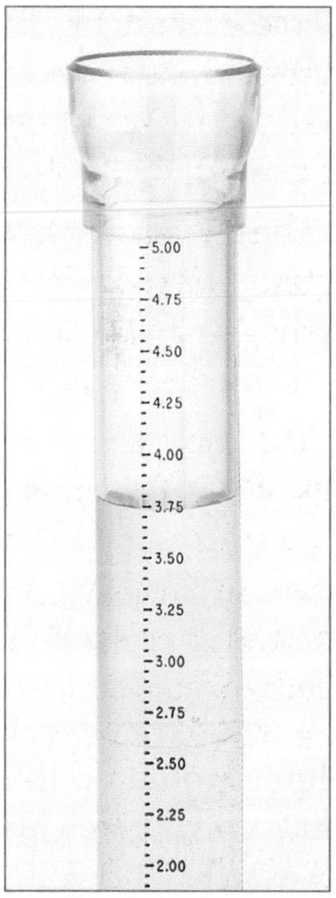


▲ **Figure 10** This glass graduated cylinder shows a meniscus.

The volume of solid objects is often measured in cubic centimeters. One cubic centimeter is the same as 1 milliliter (mL).

Look at Figure 11. Each side of the cube is 1 cm long. The volume of the cube is 1 cubic centimeter ($cm^3$). Now, look at the drawing of the box in Figure 12. Its length is 3 cm. Its width is 2 cm. Its height is 2 cm. The volume of the box can be found by multiplying length by width by height. In this case, volume equals $3 \times 2 \times 2$. Therefore, the volume of the box in Figure 12 is 12 $cm^3$.

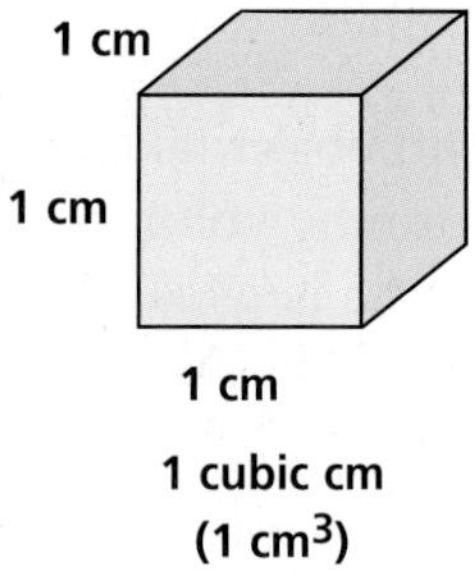


◀ **Figure 11**
A cube

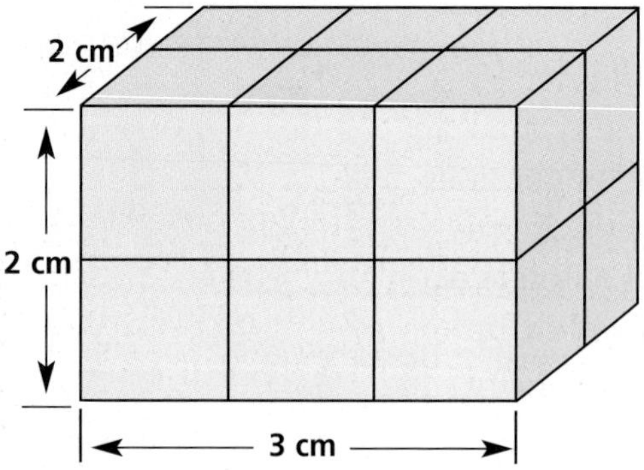


▲ **Figure 12** The volume of a box equals length by width by height.

$$V = l \times w \times h$$

If you have a box that is 10 cm on each side, its volume would be 1,000 $cm^3$. A liter is the same as 1,000 $cm^3$. One liter of liquid will fill the box exactly.

12 **CALCULATE:** How many milliliters of water would fill a 12-$cm^3$ box?

## *Hands-On Activity*

### CALCULATING AREA AND VOLUME

*You will need 3 boxes of different sizes, paper, and a metric ruler.*

1. Measure the length, width, and height of each box in centimeters. Record each measurement in your notes.
2. Calculate the volume of each box. Record each volume in your notes.
3. Find the surface area of each box. Record each area in your notes.

**Practicing Your Skills**

4. **ANALYZE:** Which of the three boxes has the largest volume?
5. **CALCULATE:** How many milliliters of liquid would fill each box?
6. **ANALYZE:** What is the surface area of the largest box?

**Temperature** **Temperature** is a measure of the amount of heat energy something contains. An instrument that measures temperature is called a thermometer.

Most thermometers are glass tubes. At the bottom of the tube is a wider part, called the bulb. The bulb is filled with liquid. Liquids that are often used include mercury, colored alcohol, or colored water. When heat is added, the liquid expands, or gets larger. It rises in the glass tube. When heat is taken away, the liquid contracts, or gets smaller. The liquid falls in the tube. On the side of the tube is a series of marks. You read the temperature by looking at the mark on the tube where the liquid stops.

Temperature can be measured on three different scales. These scales are the Fahrenheit (F) scale, the Celsius (C) scale, and the Kelvin (K) scale. The Fahrenheit scale is part of the English system of measurement. The Celsius scale is usually used in science. Almost all scientists, even in the United States, use the Celsius scale. Each unit on the Celsius scale is a degree Celsius (°C). The **degree Celsius** is the metric unit of temperature. Water freezes at 0°C. It boils at 100°C.

Scientists working with very low temperatures use the Kelvin scale. The Kelvin scale is part of the SI measurement system. It begins at **absolute zero,** or 0K. This number indicates, in theory at least, a total lack of heat.

| COMPARING TEMPERATURE SCALES | | | |
|---|---|---|---|
| | Kelvin | Fahrenheit | Celsius |
| Boiling point of water | 373K | 212°F | 100°C |
| Human body temperature | 310K | 98.6°F | 37°C |
| Freezing point of water | 273K | 32°F | 0°C |
| Absolute zero | 0K | −459.67°F | −273.15°C |

▲ **Figure 13**

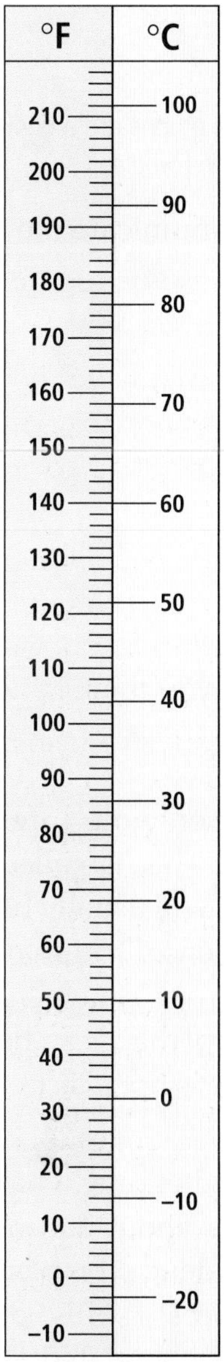


◀ **Figure 14** The Fahrenheit and Celsius scales

**13 ▶ NAME:** What are the three scales used to measure temperature?

## *Hands-On Activity*

### READING A THERMOMETER

*You will need safety goggles, a lab apron, 2 beakers, a heat source, ice water, a wax pencil, a ruler, and a standard Celsius thermometer.*

1. Boil some water in a beaker. ⚠CAUTION: Be very careful when working with heat. Place your thermometer in the beaker. Do not let the thermometer touch the sides or bottom of the beaker. Wait until the mercury rises as far as it will go. Record the temperature.
2. Fill a beaker with ice water. Place the unmarked thermometer into this beaker. Wait until the mercury goes as low as it will go. Record the temperature.

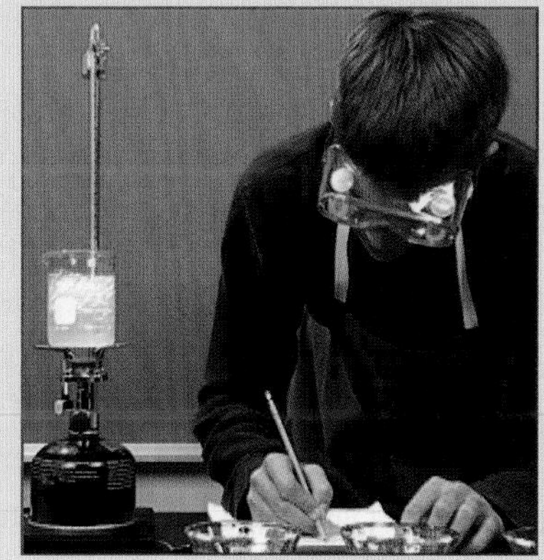

▲ **STEP 1** Record the temperature of the boiling water.

### Practicing Your Skills

3. **IDENTIFY:** What is the temperature at which the mercury rose as high as it would go?
4. **IDENTIFY:** What is the temperature at which the mercury went as low as it would go?

# 5 Analyzing Data and Communicating Results

*Key Term*

**communication:** sharing information

**Analyzing Data** When you organize information, you put it in a logical order. In scientific experiments, it is important to organize your data. Data collected during an experiment are not very useful unless they are organized and easy to read. It is also important to organize your data if you plan to share the results of your experiment.

Scientists often organize information visually by using data tables, charts, graphs, and diagrams. By using tables, charts, graphs, and diagrams, scientists can display a lot of information in a small space. They also make it easier to compare and interpret data.

Tables are made up of rows and columns. Rows run from left to right. Columns run up and down. Tables usually show numerical data. Information in a table can be arranged in time order. It can also be set up to show patterns or trends. A table showing the number of endangered species born over a period of time, for example, can reveal a pattern of extinction rates. Figure 15 shows a table of elements in animals.

| ELEMENTS FOUND IN ANIMALS | |
|---|---|
| **Element** | **Percentage (%)** |
| Oxygen | 64.5 |
| Carbon | 18 |
| Hydrogen | 10 |
| Sulfur, phosphorus, and others | 4.5 |
| Nitrogen | 3 |

▲ **Figure 15**

Graphs, such as bar graphs, line graphs, and circle graphs, often use special coloring, shading, or patterns to represent information. Keys indicate what the special markings represent. Line graphs have horizontal ($x$) and vertical ($y$) axes to indicate such things as time and quantities.

**14** **EXPLAIN:** How do tables and graphs help you analyze data?

**Sharing Results** When you talk to a friend, you are communicating, or sharing information. If you write a letter or a report, you are also communicating but in a different way. Scientists communicate all the time. They communicate to share results, information, and opinions. They write books and magazine or newspaper articles. They may also create Web sites about their work. This is called written **communication.**

Graphs are a visual way to communicate. The circle graph in Figure 16 is showing the same information as Figure 15. The circle graph presents the information in a different way.

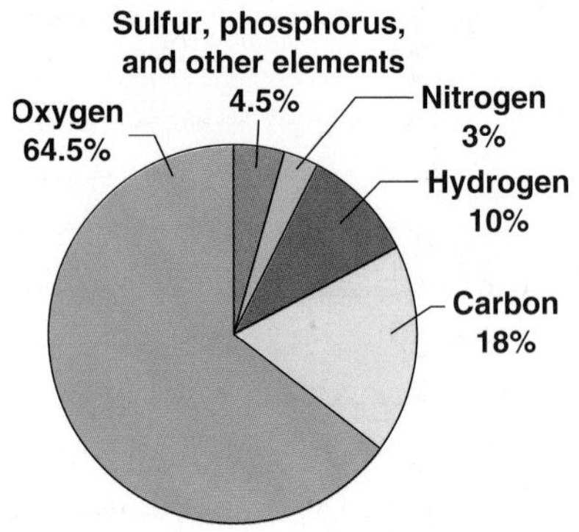


▲ **Figure 16** Circle graphs are a good way to show parts of a whole.

**15** **LIST:** What are some ways to communicate the results of an experiment?

# 6 Making Predictions

*Key Terms*

**infer:** to form a conclusion

**predict:** to state ahead of time what you think is going to happen

**Thinking of Possibilities** When you **infer** something, you form a conclusion. This is called making an inference. Your conclusion will usually be based on observations or past experience. You may use logic to form your statement. Your statement might be supported by evidence and perhaps can be tested by an experiment. An inference is not a fact. It is only one possible explanation.

When you **predict,** you state ahead of time what you think will happen. Predictions about future events are based on inferences, evidence, or past experience. The two science process skills of inferring and predicting are very closely related.

**16** **CONTRAST:** What is the difference between inferring and predicting?

# How do you conduct a scientific investigation?

By now, you should have a good understanding of the science process skills. These skills are used to solve many science problems. There is also a basic procedure, or plan, that scientists usually follow when conducting investigations. Some people call this procedure the scientific method.

The scientific method is a series of steps that can serve as a guide to solving problems or answering questions. It uses many of the science process skills you know, such as observing and predicting.

Not all experiments use all of the steps in the scientific method. Some experiments follow all of them, but in a different order. In fact, there is no one right scientific method. Each problem is different. Some problems may require steps that another problem would not. However, most investigations will follow the same basic procedure.

1 **DESCRIBE:** What is the scientific method?

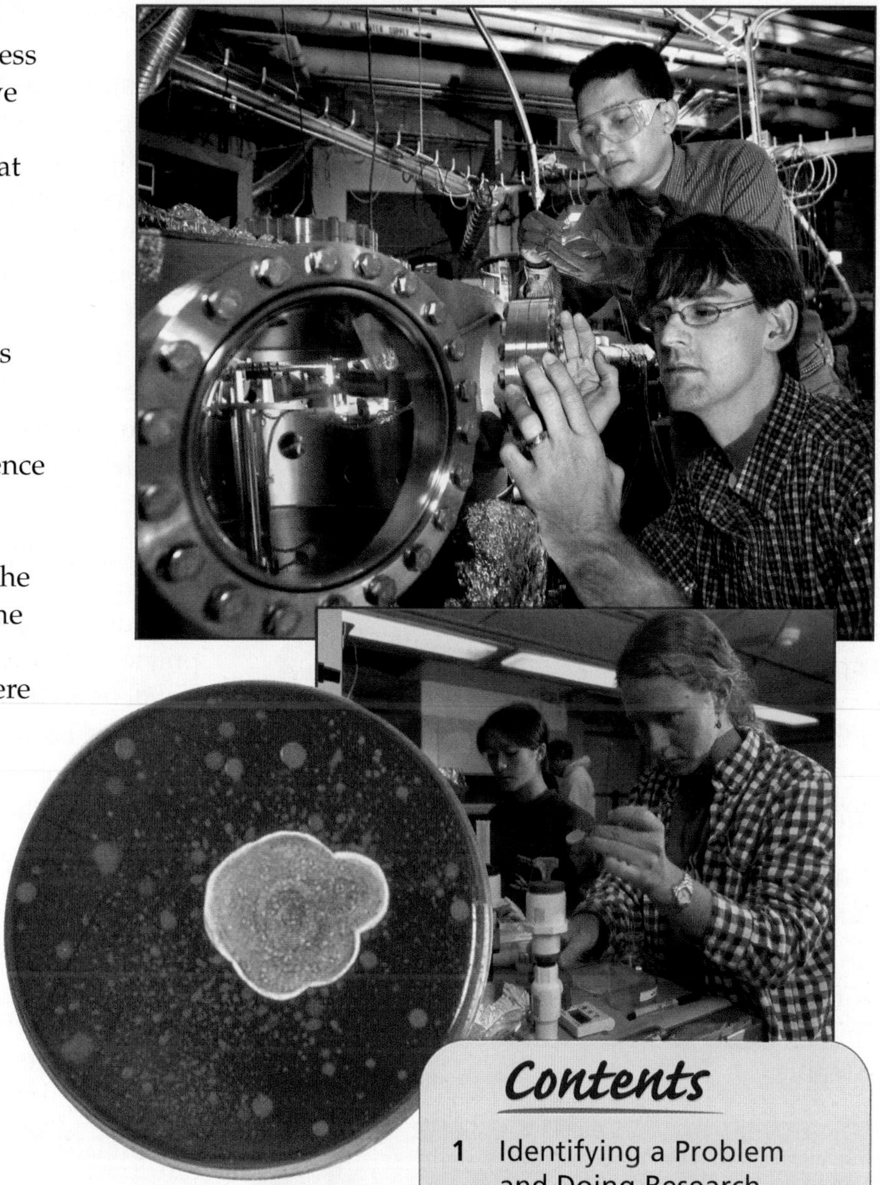

▲ **Figure 1** Scientists use the scientific method to guide experiments.

## Contents

## 1 Identifying a Problem and Doing Research

**Starting an Investigation** Scientists often state a problem as a question. This is the first step in a scientific investigation. Most experiments begin by asking a scientific question. That is, they ask a question that can be answered by gathering evidence. This question is the reason for the scientific investigation. It also helps determine how the investigation will proceed.

Have you ever done background research for a science project? When you do this kind of research, you are looking for data that others have already obtained on the same subject. You can gather research by reading books, magazines, and newspapers, and by using the Internet to find out what other scientists have done. Doing research is the first step of gathering evidence for a scientific investigation.

2 **IDENTIFY:** What is the first step of a scientific investigation?

### BUILDING SCIENCE SKILLS

***Researching Background Information*** Suppose you notice that there is moss growing in your backyard. You also notice that the moss in the shady area of your backyard seems to grow faster and look healthier than the moss that grows in sunlight. You wonder if sunlight affects moss growth.

To determine if sunlight affects moss growth, look for information on moss in encyclopedias, in botany books, or on the Internet. Put your findings in a report.

▲ **Figure 2** Moss grows best in shady areas.

## 2 Forming a Hypothesis

### Key Terms

**hypothesis:** suggested answer to a question or problem

**theory:** (THEE-uh-ree) set of hypotheses that have been supported by testing over and over again

**Focusing the Investigation** Scientists usually state clearly what they expect to find out in an investigation. This is called stating a hypothesis. A **hypothesis** is a suggested answer to a question or a solution to a problem. Stating a hypothesis helps to keep you focused on the problem and helps you decide what to test.

To form their hypotheses, scientists must think of possible explanations for a set of observations or they must suggest possible answers to a scientific question. One of those explanations becomes the hypothesis. In science, a hypothesis must include something that can be tested.

A hypothesis is more than just a guess. It must consider observations, past experiences, and previous knowledge. It is an inference turned into a statement that can be tested. A set of hypotheses that have been supported by testing over and over again by many scientists is called a **theory.** An example is the theory that explains how living things have evolved, or changed, over time.

A hypothesis can take the form of an "if…then" statement. A well-worded hypothesis is a guide for how to set up and perform an experiment.

3 **DESCRIBE:** How does a scientist form a hypothesis?

### BUILDING SCIENCE SKILLS

***Developing a Hypothesis*** If you are testing how sunlight affects moss growth, you might write down this hypothesis:

*Moss that grows in the shade is healthier than moss that grows in sunlight.*

However, what do you mean by healthier? Is the moss greener? Does it grow faster? You need to make your hypothesis specific. Revise the hypothesis above to make it more specific.

## 3 Designing and Carrying Out an Experiment

### *Key Terms*

**variable:** anything that can affect the outcome of an experiment

**constant:** something that does not change

**controlled experiment:** experiment in which all the conditions except one are kept constant

**Testing the Hypothesis** Scientists need to plan how to test their hypotheses. This means they must design an experiment. The plan must be a step-by-step procedure. It should include a record of any observations made or measurements taken.

All experiments must take variables into account. A **variable** is anything that can affect the outcome of an experiment. Room temperature, amount of sunlight, and water vapor in the air are just some of the many variables that could affect the outcome of an experiment.

4 **DEFINE:** What is a variable?

**Controlling the Experiment** One of the variables in an experiment should be what you are testing. This is what you will change during the experiment. All other variables need to remain the same. In this experiment, you will vary the amount of sunlight.

A **constant** is something that does not change. If there are no constants in your experiment, you will not be sure why you got the results you did. An experiment in which all the conditions except one are kept constant is called a **controlled experiment.**

Some experiments have two setups. In one setup, called the control, nothing is changed. In the other setup, the variable being tested is changed. Later, the control group can be compared with the other group to provide useful data.

5 **EXPLAIN:** Explain how a controlled experiment is set up.

**Designing the Procedure** Suppose you now want to design an experiment to determine if sunlight affects moss growth. You have your hypothesis. You decide your procedure is to grow moss. Your procedure will be to grow one moss plant in sunlight and the other in shade. You will then check your plants after a few days to see if your hypothesis was correct.

Suppose you water the moss that is growing in the sunlight but forget to water the moss in the shade? The moss in the sunlight might grow faster than the moss in the shade. Is the difference caused by the sunlight or by the water? You would have no way of knowing if your experiment had more than one variable.

In designing your experiment, you need to identify the variables. The amount of water you give the mosses, temperature, and the type of soil are all variables that could affect the outcome of your experiment. Everything about growing the mosses needs to be the same except the amount of sunlight each receives.

Finally, you should decide on the data you will collect. How will you measure the "health" of the moss? In this case, you might want to record the thickness of the moss, its color, and whether it reproduces.

The hands-on activity on page 12 is an example of an experiment you might have designed.

6 **LIST:** How do constants and variables affect an experiment?

## *Hands-On Activity*

### CARRYING OUT AN EXPERIMENT

*You will need 4 clumps of fresh moss, 4 medium-sized paper cups, soil, a hand lens, a metric ruler, water, and safety goggles.*

1. Fill the four paper cups with the soil and plant a clump of moss in each cup. Label cups 1 and 2 *Sunlight*. Label cups 3 and 4 *Shade*.
2. Examine each moss plant with a hand lens. Measure the heights of each sample. Record your observations in your notes.
3. Place cups 1 and 2 in an area where the moss plants will receive sunlight for most of the day. Place cups 3 and 4 where the moss plants will be in shade for most of the day.
4. Water the moss plants each day. Be sure to give the same amount of water to each plant.
5. After a week, examine the moss plants with a hand lens. Describe the moss plants in each cup.

▲ **STEP 1** Plant a clump of moss in each cup.

#### Practicing Your Skills

6. **COMPARE:** Compare the color of the moss plants grown in direct sunlight with the color of the moss plants grown in indirect sunlight.
7. **MEASURE:** Measure the heights of each sample. Is there a relationship between height and sunlight?

## 4 Recording and Analyzing Data

**Dealing With Data** During an experiment, you must keep careful notes about what you observe. For example, you might need to note down the time of day that you made your observations. Was there any change of temperature or color? This is important information that might affect your conclusion.

At the end of an experiment, you will need to study the data to find any patterns. Much of the data you will deal with is written text, such as a report or a summary of an experiment. However, scientific information is often a set of numbers or facts presented in other, more visual ways. These visual presentations can make the information easier to understand. Tables, charts, and graphs, can help you understand a collection of facts on a topic.

After your data have been organized, you need to ask what the data show. Do they support your hypothesis? Do they show something wrong in your experiment? Do you need to gather more data by performing another experiment?

7 **LIST:** What are some ways to display data?

### BUILDING SCIENCE SKILLS

***Analyzing Data*** You made the following notes during your experiment. How would you display this information?

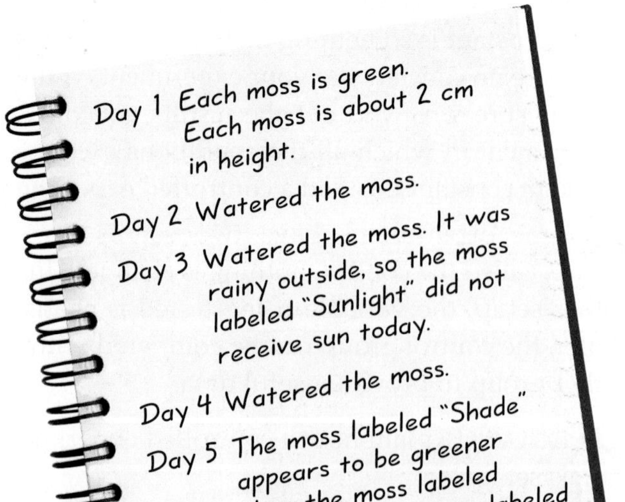


▲ **Figure 3** Possible notes

## 5 Stating a Conclusion

**Drawing Conclusions** A conclusion is a statement that sums up what you have learned from an experiment. When you draw a conclusion, you need to decide whether the data you collected supported your hypothesis. You may need to repeat an experiment several times before you can draw any conclusions from it. Conclusions often lead you to ask new questions and plan new experiments to answer them. Sometimes a scientist's conclusion is to find that his or her hypothesis was incorrect. This will then lead to a new hypothesis.

8 **EXPLAIN:** Why might it be necessary to repeat an experiment?

### BUILDING SCIENCE SKILLS

***Stating a Conclusion*** Review your hypothesis statement regarding the effect of sunlight on moss plants. Then review the data you obtained during your experiment.

- Was your hypothesis correct? Use your observations to support your answer.
- Which moss plants grew best? What type of light is best for the growth of moss plants?

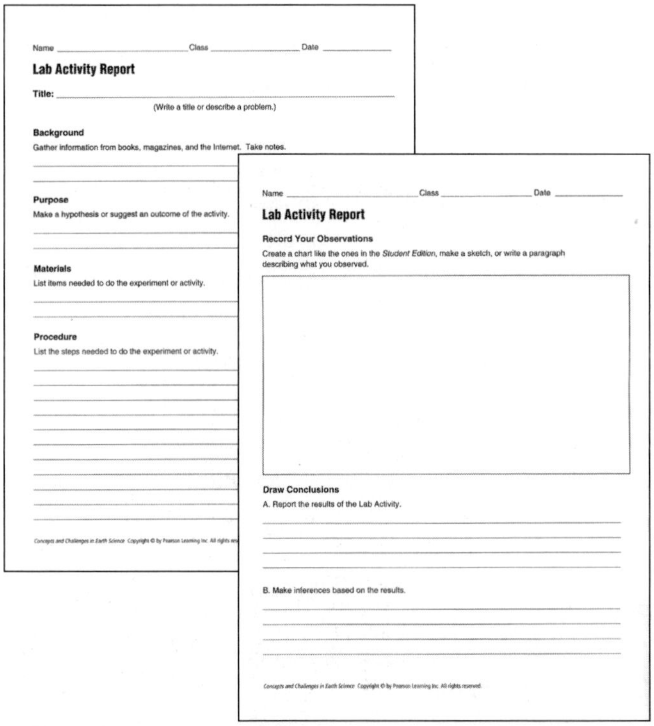
Name ____ Class ____ Date ____

**Lab Activity Report**

**Title:** ____
(Write a title or describe a problem.)

**Background**
Gather information from books, magazines, and the Internet. Take notes.

**Purpose**
Make a hypothesis or suggest an outcome of the activity.

**Materials**
List items needed to do the experiment or activity.

**Procedure**
List the steps needed to do the experiment or activity.

*Concepts and Challenges in Earth Science* Copyright © by Pearson Learning Inc. All rights res

Name ____ Class ____ Date ____

**Lab Activity Report**

**Record Your Observations**
Create a chart like the ones in the *Student Edition*, make a sketch, or write a paragraph describing what you observed.

**Draw Conclusions**
A. Report the results of the Lab Activity.

B. Make inferences based on the results.

*Concepts and Challenges in Earth Science* Copyright © by Pearson Learning Inc. All rights reserved.

▲ **Figure 4** Throughout this program, you may use forms like these to organize your lab reports.

## 6 Writing a Report

**Communicating Results** Scientists keep careful written records of their observations and findings. These records are used to create a lab report. Lab reports are a form of written communication. They explain what happened in the experiment. A good lab report should be written so that anyone reading it can duplicate the experiment. It should contain the following information:

- Title
- Purpose
- Background information
- Your hypothesis
- Materials used
- Your step-by-step procedure
- Your observations
- Your recorded data
- Your analysis of the data
- Your conclusions

Your conclusions should relate back to the questions you asked in the "purpose" section of your report. Also, the report should point out any experimental errors that might have caused unexpected results. For example, did you follow the steps in the correct order? Did an unexpected variable interfere with your results? Was your equipment clean and in good working order? This explanation of possible errors should also be part of your conclusions.

9 **EXPLAIN:** Why is it important to explain possible errors in your lab report?

### BUILDING SCIENCE SKILLS

***Writing a Lab Report*** Write a lab report to communicate to other scientists your discoveries about the effect of sunlight on moss plants. Your lab report should include a title, your hypothesis statement, a list of materials you used, the procedure, your observations, and your conclusions. Try to include one table of data in your report.

# LAB SAFETY

**Working in a science laboratory can be both exciting and meaningful. However, you must always be aware of safety precautions when carrying out experiments. There are a few basic rules that should be followed in any science laboratory:**

- Read all instructions carefully before the start of an experiment. Follow all instructions exactly and in the correct order.
- Check your equipment to make sure it is clean and working properly.
- Never taste, smell, or touch any substance in the lab that you are not told to do so. Never eat or drink anything in the lab. Do not chew gum.
- Never work alone. Tell a teacher at once if an accident occurs.

**Experiments that use chemicals or heat can be dangerous. The following list of rules and symbols will help you avoid accidents. There are also rules about what to do if an accident does occur. Here are some rules to remember when working in a lab:**

1. Do not use glass that is chipped or metal objects with broken edges. Do not try to clean up broken glassware yourself. Notify your teacher if a piece of glassware is broken.
2. Do not use electrical cords with loose plugs or frayed ends. Do not let electrical cords cross in front of working areas. Do not use electrical equipment near water.
3. Be very careful when using sharp objects such as scissors, knives, or tweezers. Always cut in a direction away from your body.
4. Be careful when you are using a heat source. Use proper equipment, such as tongs or a ring stand, when handling hot objects.
5. Confine loose clothing and hair when working with an open flame. Be sure you know the location of the nearest fire extinguisher. Never reach across an open flame.
6. Be careful when working with poisonous or toxic substances. Never mix chemicals without directions from your teacher. Remove any long jewelry that might hang down and end up in chemicals. Avoid touching your eyes or mouth when working with chemicals.
7. Use extreme care when working with acids and bases. Never mix acids and bases without direction from your teacher. Never smell anything directly. Use caution when handling chemicals that produce fumes.
8. Wear safety goggles, especially when working with an open flame, chemicals, and any liquids.
9. Wear lab aprons when working with substances of any sort, especially chemicals.
10. Use caution when handling or collecting plants. Some plants can be harmful if they are touched or eaten.
11. Use caution when handling live animals. Some animals can injure you or spread disease. Handle all live animals as humanely as possible.
12. Dispose of all equipment and materials properly. Keep your work area clean at all times.
13. Always wash your hands thoroughly with soap and water after handling chemicals or live organisms.
14. Follow the ⚠ **CAUTION** and safety symbols you see used throughout this book when doing labs or other activities.

# Chapter 1 Characteristics of Living Things

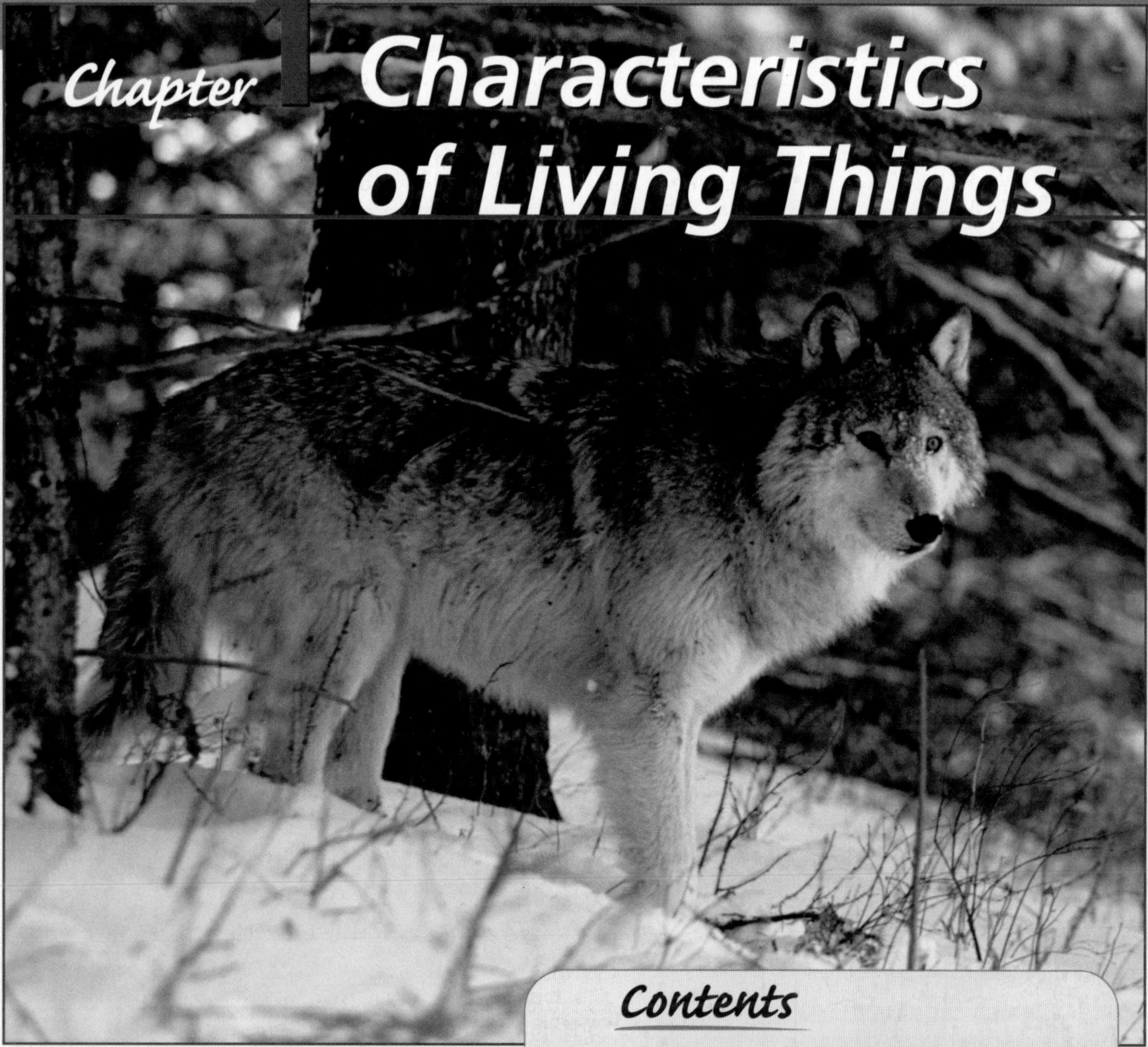

▲ **Figure 1-1** Many living things, such as this gray wolf, can survive in the cold temperatures of Alaska.

Living things are everywhere. Some are easy to identify. Humans and other animals are living. Trees and other plants are also living. Some living things are not so easy to identify. They may be so small that we need special tools to see them. No matter their size, all living things have certain characteristics in common. In life science, we study all living things to learn how they are alike, how they are different, and how they interact.

►How many different kinds of living things can you identify in Figure 1-1?

## Contents

# 1-1 What is life science?

## *Objective*

Identify and describe what is studied in some of the branches of life science.

## *Key Term*

**specialization** (spehsh-uhl-ih-ZAY-shuhn): studying or working in only one part of a subject

**Studying Life Science** Science is an organized collection of knowledge about the world. It is a way of finding out why things happen as they do. Scientists try to solve problems by testing possible answers to see if they work. Science knowledge is based on testing and observations.

The scientific study of the areas of science that deal with living things is called life science. Life science is divided into many different branches. One branch is anatomy, or the study of the parts of the body. Another branch is physiology, or the study of how the whole body functions. Some of the other branches of life science are described in Figure 1-2.

1 **LIST:** What are two branches of life science?

**Specialization** As more and more is learned about the world, people can choose specific subjects to study. This is called **specialization.** A person who studies or works in one part of a subject is called a specialist. There are many life science specialists. For example, some zoologists study only one group of animals. Some scientists study diseases that affect only animals. Other scientists study diseases in plants.

2 **DESCRIBE:** What is specialization?

**Importance of Life Science** The study of living things affects your life in many ways. The medicine you might use for acne was developed through scientific study. The causes and warning signs of cancer were learned from scientific research. Doctors can perform operations because they know about the parts of the human body and how they work.

Some of the foods you eat were grown by using information about plants. The making of some foods also uses knowledge of life science. Many cheeses could not be made without molds. Yogurt could not be made without bacteria. People had to learn about bacteria and molds to use them to make these foods.

3 **EXPLAIN:** How is life science part of your life?

**BRANCHES OF LIFE SCIENCE**

**Botany**
Botanists study plants. Some careers in botany are plant geneticist and horticulturalist.

**Zoology**
Zoologists study animals. Marine biologist and veterinarian are two of the careers in zoology.

**Microbiology**
Microbiologists study viruses and very small living things. Two careers in microbiology are cell biologist and epidemiologist.

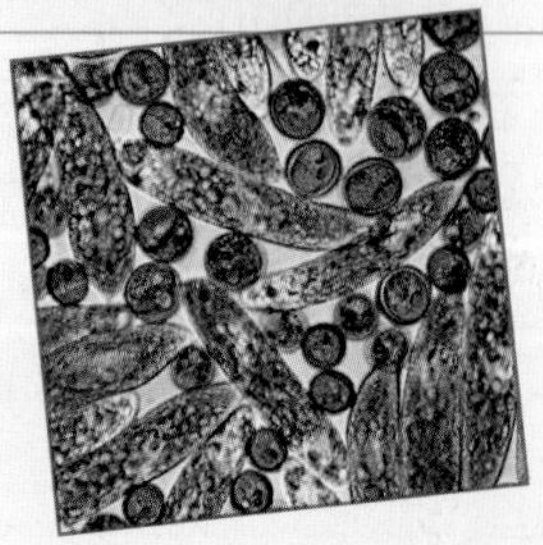

**Ecology**
Ecologists study the way living things interact with their environment. Park ranger and environmentalist are careers in ecology.

▲ **Figure 1-2**

## ✓ CHECKING CONCEPTS

1. The knowledge of science is based on __________.
2. Life science is made up of many different __________.
3. Anatomy and __________ are branches of life science.
4. A scientist who studies only one small branch of life science is a __________.
5. Ecology is the study of the way living things interact with their __________.

## THINKING CRITICALLY

6. INFER: What area of life science would you need to know about to study the problem shown in Figure 1-3?

▲ **Figure 1-3** Why do you think this sign was posted?

7. CLASSIFY: In which branch of life science would you study each of the following?
   **a.** whales and birds
   **b.** corn and barley
   **c.** the rain forest
   **d.** bacteria

## Web InfoSearch

**A Career in Life Science** Most careers in life science require a four-year college degree in one of the following subjects: biology, botany, zoology, or ecology.

**SEARCH:** Use the Internet to find out more about becoming a life scientist. Choose a career and write about why you might want to do that job. Start your search for information at www.conceptsandchallenges.com. Some key search words are **marine biology, zoology,** and **botany.**

## *People in Science*

### MARINE BIOLOGIST

Marine biologists are scientists who study life in the oceans. They study the ways living things are adapted for life in the ocean. They study how forms of marine life interact with each other and their environment. Some marine biologists study the behavior of ocean animals such as dolphins and whales. One career in marine biology is marine mammal trainer.

▲ **Figure 1-4** Some marine biologists work with dolphins in aquariums.

Marine mammal trainers work with dolphins, whales, and other marine mammals. They are responsible for the physical well-being of the animals in their care. They make sure the animals are well fed and that their pool water is kept clean and at the proper temperature. Occasionally, marine mammal trainers join the animals in the pool and swim with them.

A marine biologist needs at least a bachelor of science degree in marine biology or a related science field. Some jobs require a graduate degree in marine science. If you are interested in becoming a marine biologist, you may want to consider volunteering at a fish and wildlife agency, aquarium, zoo, or wildlife rescue center.

**Thinking Critically** What qualities do you think are needed for a career in marine biology?

# 1-2 What are living things?

## INVESTIGATE

### *Observing Living Things and Nonliving Things*

HANDS-ON ACTIVITY

1. Observe a cup of sand. Record the characteristics of the sand.
2. Observe an earthworm. Record the characteristics of the earthworm.
3. Compare your findings with those of a classmate. Then work together to determine which is living and which is not. Be sure to support your hypothesis with evidence.

**THINK ABOUT IT:** Do all living things share the same characteristics?

### *Objective*

Describe the six characteristics of living things.

### *Key Terms*

**organism** (AWR-guh-nihz-uhm): any living thing

**characteristic:** quality or property that defines or classifies something

**cell:** basic unit of structure and function in living things

**response:** reaction to a change

**Organisms** The world around you is made up of many different things. Some things, such as dogs and trees, are living. Living things are called **organisms.** Other things, such as cars and radios, are nonliving.

1 DEFINE: What is an organism?

**Characteristics of Organisms** It is not always easy to decide if something is living or nonliving. Nonliving things may do some of the same things as organisms. For example, a robot may move and speak like a person. A robot, however, is not living. Plants and animals grow, or get larger. Icicles also grow, but icicles are not living.

Biologists use six **characteristics,** or qualities, to classify something as a living thing. All organisms have these six characteristics.

- Organisms are made up of one or more **cells.** A cell is the basic unit of structure and function in living things. Cells often are called the building blocks of life.
- Organisms use energy. Energy is the ability to do work or cause change. Sunlight is the source of energy for most organisms. Plants use the energy in sunlight to make food. Animals get energy from the Sun by eating plants or other animals that have eaten plants.
- All organisms have features that help them adapt to their surroundings. For example, chameleons change color to help blend in with their environment. This protects them from predators.

▲ **Figure 1-5** A chameleon survives by changing colors to hide itself from predators.

- Organisms react to changes in their surroundings. Any reaction to a change is called a **response.** You might respond to the honking of a car's horn by jumping. A bright light may cause you to close your eyes.
- Organisms change, or develop, during their lifetimes. One way organisms change is by growing. They may also change in appearance.

▲ **Figure 1-6** An elephant produces more elephants.

- Organisms can produce more organisms of their own kind. For example, pine trees produce more pine trees. The production of new organisms allows each kind of organism to continue living on Earth.

**2 IDENTIFY:** What is the source of energy for most living things?

**Matter** Do you know what everything around you has in common? Everything around you is made up of matter. **Matter** is any substance that has mass.

Some substances can be broken down into simpler substances. For example, water is made of hydrogen and oxygen. However, hydrogen and oxygen cannot be broken down. These substances are called elements. The smallest part of an element is called the **atom.** Most living things are made up of the elements carbon, hydrogen, oxygen, nitrogen, sulfur, and phosphorus. Different organisms contain different percentages of these elements.

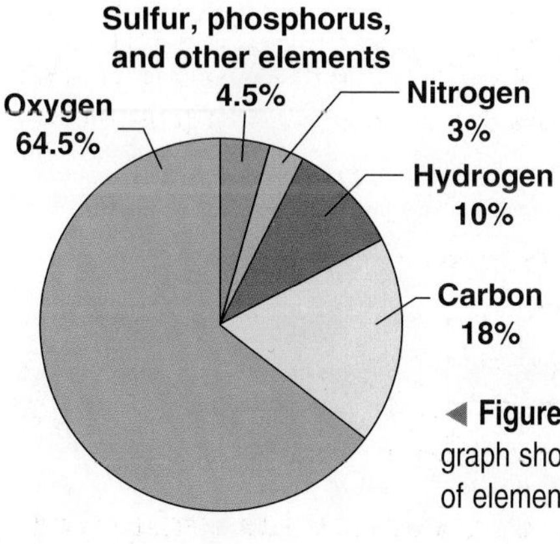


◀ **Figure 1-7** This circle graph shows percentages of elements in humans.

**3 NAME:** What are four elements found in most organisms?

**Compounds** When two or more atoms from different elements join, they form a compound. Most compounds found in living things are called organic compounds. Organic compounds contain carbon. There are four main types of organic compounds found in all organisms. They are carbohydrates, lipids, proteins, and nucleic acids.

**Carbohydrates** are made up of carbon, hydrogen, and oxygen. Sugars and starches are types of carbohydrates. Organisms use carbohydrates for energy. **Lipids**, or fats, are made up mostly of carbon and hydrogen. Organisms use lipids to store energy. **Proteins** are made up of carbon, hydrogen, oxygen, and nitrogen. They help organisms repair their bodies. **Nucleic acids** are a combination of sugars, nitrogen, and other elements. They contain important information about the organism.

**4 HYPOTHESIZE:** What kind of information do you think nucleic acids contain about an organism?

## CHECKING CONCEPTS

1. Organisms use __________ to store energy.
2. Organisms __________ to changes in their surroundings.
3. Plants use the energy in __________ to make food.

## THINKING CRITICALLY

4. **APPLY:** How do you get energy from sunlight?
5. **HYPOTHESIZE:** Could an ant be the offspring of a fly? Explain your answer.
6. **CLASSIFY:** Flashlights and cars both use energy to work. Use the characteristics of organisms to explain why cars and flashlights are not classified as living things.

## DESIGNING AN EXPERIMENT

*Design an experiment to solve the following problem. Include a hypothesis, variables, a procedure, and a type of data to study.*

PROBLEM: You have just come home from being on vacation for a week. All of your houseplants are leaning to one side. Design an experiment to discover what happened to your houseplants.

# 1-3 What are the needs of organisms?

***Objective***

Identify and describe the needs of living things.

***Key Terms***

**autotroph** (AW-toh-trahf)**:** organism that can make its own food

**heterotroph** (HEHT-uh-roh-trahf)**:** organism that cannot make its own food

**homeostasis** (hoh-mee-oh-STAY-sihs)**:** process of keeping conditions inside a body constant, no matter the conditions outside the body

**Energy** All organisms need energy to grow. Organisms obtain energy from the foods they eat. Some organisms make their own food. They are called **autotrophs.** Plants are an example of autotrophs. Other organisms cannot make their own food. They are called **heterotrophs.** Humans are heterotrophs.

1 APPLY: Why is a lion called a heterotroph?

**Water** Organisms also need water. Without water, all plants and animals would die. Plants use water to make food. About two-thirds of your body is water.

Most substances dissolve in water. These dissolved substances can then be transported throughout a living thing. Most chemical changes in living things need water to take place.

▲ **Figure 1-8** This prickly pear cactus stores water to use during long desert droughts.

2 ANALYZE: What is the most common substance in your body?

**Air** Without oxygen, most living things would die in minutes. Air is a mixture of gases. Oxygen is one of the gases in air. Oxygen is needed by most living things to change food into energy. Land organisms get oxygen from the air. Water organisms get oxygen from the water. The oxygen is dissolved in the water.

Carbon dioxide is another gas found in air. Animals release carbon dioxide when they breathe. Plants use carbon dioxide to make their own food.

3 ANALYZE: How does a fish get oxygen?

**Temperature** The temperature of the environment is important to living things. Organisms need a proper temperature to live. Most organisms could live only within a small temperature range if it were not for **homeostasis.** Homeostasis is the process of keeping conditions inside an organism constant, no matter the conditions outside. When changes in temperature or other parts of the environment occur, homeostasis keeps things working properly inside a living thing.

Cold-blooded animals do not have a constant body temperature. Their body temperatures change as the temperatures of their surroundings change. To maintain homeostasis, cold-blooded animals must change their surroundings. A lizard is an example of a cold-blooded animal. When a lizard gets cold, it must warm itself in the Sun. When it gets too warm, it must cool down in the shade.

▲ **Figure 1-9** Cold-blooded organisms, such as this collared lizard, keep their body temperatures regulated by changing their surroundings.

**Warm-blooded animals** have a constant body temperature. When temperatures in the environment change, a warm-blooded animal's body temperature stays about the same. This happens automatically, without the animal having to think about it.

4 **DEFINE:** What is homeostasis?

**Living Space** All organisms need a place to live, or living space. In order for an organism to survive, its living space must provide all of its needs. These include food, water, air, and shelter. The living space also has to be at the proper temperature.

In any environment, living space is limited. All the organisms in the environment compete for resources in their living space. They compete for food, water, sunlight, and shelter.

5 **NAME:** List four things a living space must provide.

## CHECKING CONCEPTS

1. Most chemical changes in living things cannot take place without ___________.
2. In any environment, ___________ is limited.
3. ___________ can make their own food.
4. Fish get oxygen from ___________.
5. ___________ keeps conditions constant inside a living thing.

## THINKING CRITICALLY

6. **INFER:** How do you think shivering and perspiring are related to homeostasis?
7. **HYPOTHESIZE:** What might happen to an organism when its living space is destroyed?

## BUILDING SCIENCE SKILLS

***Modeling*** Research an organism and its living space. Then using materials such as paper, cardboard, markers, and glue, create a model of the organism in its living space. Present your model to the class.

## *Real-Life Science*

### COOKING FOOD

▲ **Figure 1-10** Cooking foods kills harmful organisms.

The human body does not create its own energy. Instead, humans eat plants and other animals to get energy. Most of the foods humans eat need to be cooked. Cooking helps kill some of the harmful organisms that can live inside or on food. It also makes some food taste better.

When cooking, you should plan healthy, balanced meals. A balanced meal includes carbohydrates, proteins, and fats. The carbohydrates and fats that are found in foods give us energy. Proteins help us build up and repair our bodies.

For some people, cooking is more than a way to get energy. It is a relaxing activity. You can learn how to cook by observing an experienced cook at work. You can also try family recipes or recipes from a cookbook.

**Thinking Critically** What might be the danger in eating raw foods?

# 1-4 How do organisms use energy?

## Objective

Name and describe the life processes.

## Key Terms

**nutrient** (NOO-tree-uhnt)**:** chemical substance that is needed to carry out life processes

**ingestion** (ihn-JEHS-chuhn)**:** process of taking in food

**digestion** (dih-JEHS-chuhn)**:** process of breaking down food so that it can be used by living things

**cellular respiration** (rehs-puh-RAY-shuhn)**:** process by which a cell releases energy from food molecules

**byproduct:** something produced in addition to the main product

**excretion** (ehks-KREE-shuhn)**:** process of getting rid of wastes

**transport:** process of moving nutrients and wastes in a living thing

**Life Processes** All organisms carry out life processes. Life processes are the things an organism must do to stay alive. They are also features of organisms. Being alive means carrying out all the life processes.

1 DEFINE: What are life processes?

**Ingestion and Digestion** Living things need food because it provides them with **nutrients.** Nutrients are chemical substances that are needed for growth and energy. Animals take food into their bodies. Taking in food is called **ingestion.** Plants make their own food. Plants also take in some nutrients from the soil.

Food needs to be changed before an organism can use the nutrients in food. The process of changing food into a useable form is called **digestion.** You have an organ system that digests your food. It is your digestive system. Some parts of your digestive system are your mouth, stomach, and intestines.

2 DEFINE: What is digestion?

▲ **Figure 1-11** Animals, such as this Alaskan brown bear, take in nutrients through the foods they eat.

**Cellular Respiration** Organisms get energy from food by a process called **cellular respiration.** The cell uses food in the form of sugar. During cellular respiration, sugar molecules break apart. This process releases energy. Carbon dioxide and water also are produced. These are **byproducts** of cellular respiration.

oxygen + food = energy, water, and carbon dioxide

▲ **Figure 1-12** In cellular respiration, food molecules are broken down to release energy.

3 NAME: What are the byproducts of cellular respiration?

**Excretion** During life processes, an organism makes many waste products. Some waste products are formed during digestion. Others are formed during cellular respiration. All organisms must get rid of the waste products formed by the life processes. Getting rid of waste products is called **excretion.**

4 NAME: Name two life processes that produce waste products.

**Transport** Once food is digested, nutrients must be carried to all parts of a living thing. Waste products must be carried away and excreted. The moving of nutrients and waste products through an organism is called **transport.**

5 **INFER:** What materials are transported inside an organism?

## CHECKING CONCEPTS

1. ___________ are needed for growth and energy.
2. ___________ take in some nutrients from the soil.
3. Taking in food is called ___________.
4. During cellular respiration, sugar molecules are ___________.
5. Two byproducts of ___________ are carbon dioxide and water.
6. The moving of waste products and nutrients through an organism is called ___________.

## THINKING CRITICALLY

7. **INFER:** Why does being alive mean carrying out all the life processes?
8. **SEQUENCE:** Describe what happens to food after it is ingested by an animal. Include a discussion of digestion, respiration, excretion, and transport in your description.

## HEALTH AND SAFETY TIP

Food provides you with the nutrients you need for energy, growth, and repair of body tissues. Proper nutrition is important for staying healthy. The Recommended Dietary Allowance is a set of nutrient standards established by the Food and Nutrition Board of the National Academy of Science. Use the Internet to find out how much of each nutrient you need each day. Organize your findings in a chart.

## *How Do They Know That?*

### TRANSPORT IN HUMANS

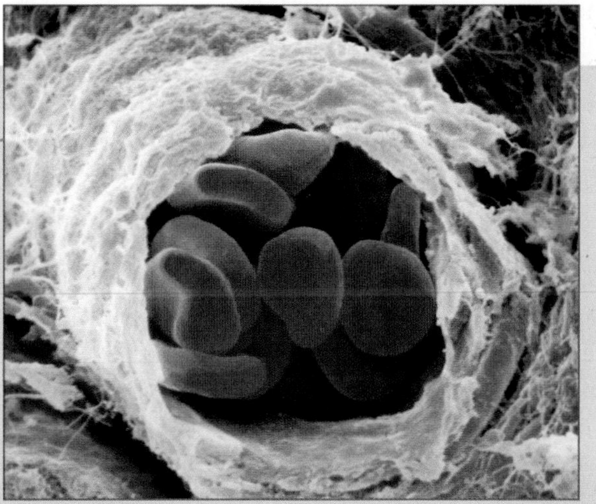

▲ **Figure 1-13** Blood cells in a blood vessel

Today, scientists know that blood is transported through blood vessels. The blood vessels are connected and form a circular path. In the fourth century B.C., however, people believed that blood vessels carried both air and blood.

In the 2nd century, a Greek physician named Galen proved that arteries carried only blood. He still believed that air entered the body from the right side of the heart. Galen did not know the blood moved in a circular path. Galen and others thought that blood mixed with air in the lower parts of the heart. They thought there were holes in the dividing walls of the heart.

In the 16th century, scientists began to think that blood was transported through the heart and lungs in a circular path. In 1628, William Harvey, an English physician, explained how blood was transported in the human body. He proved that the heart did not have a wall with holes in it. Harvey could not show that the large blood vessels were connected by smaller blood vessels called capillaries. He did not have a microscope that was powerful enough to see capillaries. Thirty-three years later, an Italian physician named Marcello Malpighi (mahl-PEE-gee) used a microscope to identify a network of capillaries.

**Thinking Critically** The heart and blood vessels are part of the circulatory system. Is this an accurate name for the system? Explain.

# 1-5 How do organisms respond to change?

## *Objectives*

Explain how stimuli and responses are related. Identify some kinds of behavior.

## *Key Terms*

**stimulus** (STIHM-yuh-luhs), *pl.* **stimuli:** change that causes a response

**behavior:** way in which living things respond to stimuli

**migration** (my-GRAY-shuhn)**:** seasonal movement of animals from one place to another and back

**hibernation** (hy-buhr-NAY-shuhn)**:** inactive state of some animals during winter months

**Stimulus and Response** Organisms respond to their environments. In the morning, your alarm clock rings. You respond by waking. The ringing alarm clock is a **stimulus.** A stimulus is a change that causes a response.

Organisms respond to stimuli in different ways. If you turn a plant so that its leaves face away from the Sun, in a few days, the leaves of the plant will turn back toward the Sun. The movement of the plant's leaves is a response. Plant responses are usually slower than animal responses.

**Figure 1-14** ▶ This plant's leaves have responded to the sunlight coming from a new direction.

**1** **IDENTIFY:** A flower slowly turns to face the Sun. What is the stimulus and response for this action?

**Behavior** The way in which an organism responds to stimuli is called **behavior.** A behavior that an organism is born with is called an instinct. Nest building is an instinct in some kinds of birds. Birds do not have to be shown how to build nests. Other behaviors have to be learned. Tying your shoelaces is a learned behavior. You have many learned behaviors.

**2** **ANALYZE:** Foxes are taught how to hunt by other foxes. Is hunting a learned behavior or an instinct in these animals?

**Animal Behaviors** The seasonal movement of animals from one place to another and back again is called **migration.** Animals often migrate to warmer places during the cold months to find food. Animals also migrate to find a safe place to reproduce and raise their young.

▲ **Figure 1-15** Every winter, monarch butterflies migrate from Canada to southern California and Mexico.

Some animals spend the winter months in a sleeplike state called **hibernation.** During hibernation, an animal is not active. The body temperature of the animal lowers. The heartbeat of the animal slows. The animal does not need to use as much energy. As a result, the animal can live off the fat stored in its body. Chipmunks and squirrels are two kinds of animals that hibernate.

**3** **DEFINE:** What is hibernation?

## CHECKING CONCEPTS

1. A change that causes a response is a __________.
2. The ways in which living things respond to stimuli is called __________.
3. Behaviors that an animal is born with are called __________.
4. The seasonal movement of animals from one place to another and back again is __________.
5. The inactive state of some animals during the winter months is called __________.
6. During hibernation, an animal's activities __________.

## THINKING CRITICALLY

7. INFER: What happens to a squirrel's breathing rate during hibernation?
8. CLASSIFY: Identify each action described as learned behavior or as instinct.
   **a.** reading a book **c.** blinking
   **b.** a newborn crying **d.** going to school

### Web InfoSearch

**Bird Migration** Many kinds of birds migrate during the winter and summer months. Year after year, birds follow the same migration routes. Scientists are not completely sure how birds do this. Some scientists think the birds use the Sun as a landmark. Others think birds use wind currents or Earth's magnetic field.

**SEARCH:** Use the Internet to find out about the migration routes of some birds in your state. Write about the bird you chose and draw a map of its migration route. Start your search for information at www.conceptsandchallenges.com. Some key search words are **migration** and **migration routes.**

## *Hands-On Activity*

### TESTING PUPIL RESPONSES TO LIGHT

*You will need a penlight or flashlight.*

1. Work with a partner. Look at the pupil of your partner's eye. The pupil is the dark circle in the middle of the colored part of the eye. Note the size of the pupil.
2. Quickly shine the penlight in your partner's eye. Observe what happens to the size of the pupil.
3. Take the light away. Observe what happens to the size of the pupil.

▲ **STEP 2** Observe the pupil.

**Practicing Your Skills**

4. OBSERVE: What happened to the size of the pupil when the light was shone on it?
5. EXPLAIN: What was the stimulus, and what is the response?
6. OBSERVE: What happened to the size of the pupil when you took the light away? INFER: Why do you think this happened?
7. HYPOTHESIZE: What would happen if the pupil never changed its size?
8. PREDICT: Under what conditions would the size of the pupil be the largest?

# LAB ACTIVITY
# Investigating Stimulus and Response

**Materials**
Gloves, apron, safety goggles, 8 earthworms, 1 sheet of black construction paper, 1 sheet of white construction paper, spray bottle with water, clock or stopwatch, data table

### *BACKGROUND*

A stimulus is any condition in the environment that causes a response by an organism. Earthworms react to daily changes in their environment. They live in soil that changes its condition depending on the weather. Moist soil is good, but very wet soil may drown them. Earthworms cannot live in extremely dry soil either.

Temperature also affects an earthworm's habitat. If it is too hot or too cold, an earthworm will move to better conditions.

⚠ The earthworms you will use in this experiment are alive. They should be kept in moist soil and cared for properly.

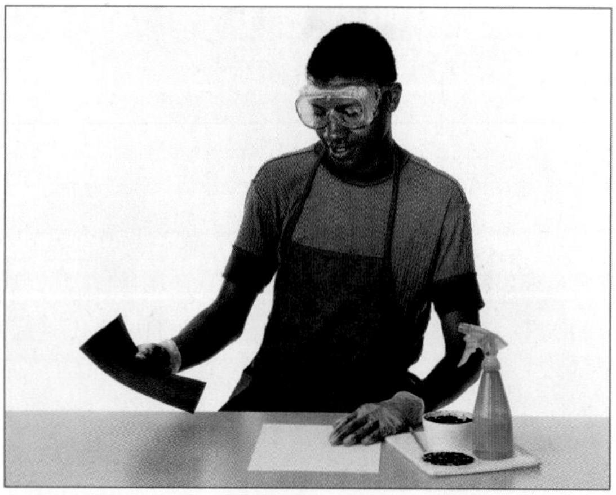

▲ **STEP 1** Place the paper on a flat surface.

### *PURPOSE*

In this activity you will observe how earthworms respond to changes in their environment.

### *PROCEDURE*

1. Place a sheet of black construction paper next to a sheet of white construction paper on a flat surface.
2. Copy the chart in Figure 1-16.
3. Thoroughly spray each sheet of construction paper with water.
4. Place two worms on each sheet of paper. Wait five minutes. Observe which paper the worms move toward.
5. Record your observations.

▲ **STEP 3** Spray the paper with water.

6. Repeat Steps 3 through 5 with four different worms.

7. Put the worms back into their container. Wash your hands thoroughly with soap and water.

▲ **STEP 4** Gently place the worms on the paper.

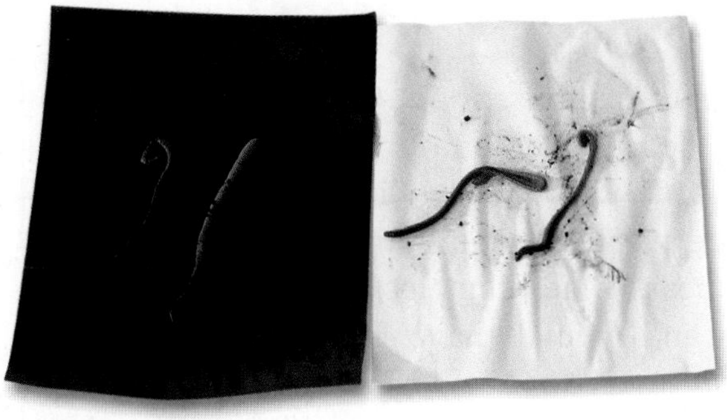

▲ **STEP 5** Observe the worms.

**Observations**

| Environment | Trial 1 | Trial 2 |
|---|---|---|
| Black | | |
| White | | |

▲ **Figure 1-16** Copy this chart onto your paper. Leave enough space in each row to record your observations.

### *CONCLUSIONS*

1. **ANALYZE:** How did the worms respond to changes in their environment?

2. **MODEL:** What does the white construction paper represent? What does the black paper represent?

3. **INFER:** What kind of environment do you think worms prefer? Explain.

4. **PREDICT:** What other living things do you think will respond to changes in the environment such as darkness and wet weather? Explain.

# THE Big IDEA

## How do organisms adapt to changes of the seasons?

All organisms must adapt to changes in their living space. One important factor in an organism's living space is climate, or the average weather conditions of an area over many years. Many climates have four seasons. Plants and animals have features that allow them to survive in harsh climates and respond to seasonal changes.

The seasons are caused by the tilt of Earth's axis and the movement of Earth around the Sun. The axis is an imaginary line through the center of Earth on which Earth rotates. For part of the year, Earth's axis is tilted toward the Sun. The part that is tilted toward the Sun gets more hours of sunlight each day. The result is warmer weather. This is summer. Meanwhile, the other half of Earth is tilted away from the Sun. This half gets fewer hours of sunlight each day. The result is colder weather. This is winter. As Earth revolves around the Sun, the seasons change in each half of Earth.

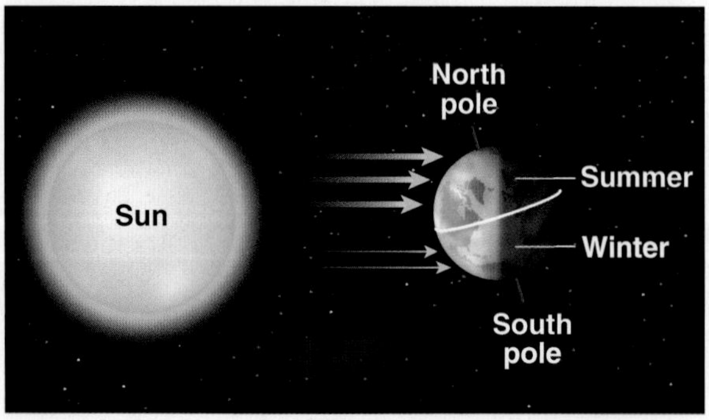


▲ **Figure 1-17** The tilt of the Earth causes seasons.

Look at the photos, illustrations, and boxes of text that appear on these two pages. Then follow the directions in the Science Log to find out more about "the big idea."✦

**Reproduction**
All living things come from other living things of the same kind. Like many animals, elk reproduce in the spring when there are warm temperatures and plenty of food. This allows their offspring a chance to grow and develop before the harsh winter arrives.

**Energy**
All living things use energy. Plants use energy from the Sun to make their own food. The energy in sunlight is changed into food energy. The plant can then use this energy to carry out its life processes such as growing, developing, and reproducing.

### Cells

All living things are made of cells. The cells inside the needles of this pine tree survive through the winter because they are covered with a waxy coating. This coating protects them from the severe temperatures of winter.

### Response

All organisms respond to changes in their surroundings. The Columbian ground squirrel hibernates in a closed-off area of its burrow for seven to eight months.

### Adaptations

All organisms adapt to their surroundings. The fur of a snowshoe hare changes to white in winter. This ability to blend into the environment helps protect the snowshoe hare from predators.

### Growth and Development

All living things grow and develop. Humans, along with most animals, grow and develop over a period of time. Many plants only have one growing season. This means that the plant begins its life in the spring and dies in the winter.

**WRITING ACTIVITY**

### Science Log

Look at the scene on these two pages. Which of these living things would you like to know more about? In your science log, research and write about one of these living things and the features that help it survive in its environment. Explain why you find it interesting. Start your search at www.conceptsandchallenges.com.

# 1-6 Where do organisms come from?

## *Objective*

Recognize that all life comes from existing life.

## *Key Term*

**spontaneous generation** (spahn-TAY-nee-uhs jehn-uhr-AY-shuhn)**:** idea that living things come from nonliving things

**Spontaneous Generation** Do you believe that organisms can grow from straw? Hundreds of years ago, people believed that mice came from straw. They also believed that maggots and flies grew from rotting meat. Maggots are a stage in the life cycle of a fly. The idea that living things come from nonliving things is called **spontaneous generation.** In the 1600s, most people believed in spontaneous generation.

Francesco Redi was an Italian doctor. He lived during the 17th century. Redi did not think that living things came from nonliving things. He thought that organisms could come only from other organisms. To test his hypothesis, Redi performed an experiment.

**1 IDENTIFY:** Who was Francesco Redi?

**Redi's Experiment** Redi performed two experiments. First, he put different kinds of meat into several jars. He left half of the jars uncovered. He covered the other jars with lids. The setups for Redi's experiments are shown in Figure 1-18.

After a few days, Redi observed wormlike animals on the meat in the uncovered jars. There were no wormlike animals in the jars with lids.

Redi did a second experiment to test if fresh air was needed. He left half of the jars uncovered again. The other half were covered with mesh. After a few days, the uncovered jars had the wormlike animals. The meat in the jars with mesh did not have the wormlike animals. The uncovered jars (labeled *A* and *C* in Figure 1-18) were Redi's controls in both experiments.

The wormlike animals that Redi observed were maggots. The maggots hatched from eggs that flies had laid on the meat. Redi showed that maggots did not come from the meat. Today, scientists know that flies often lay eggs on spoiled meat. The meat is food for the maggots. Scientists know that all organisms come from other organisms of the same kind.

**2 INFER:** Why did maggots not appear in the covered jars?

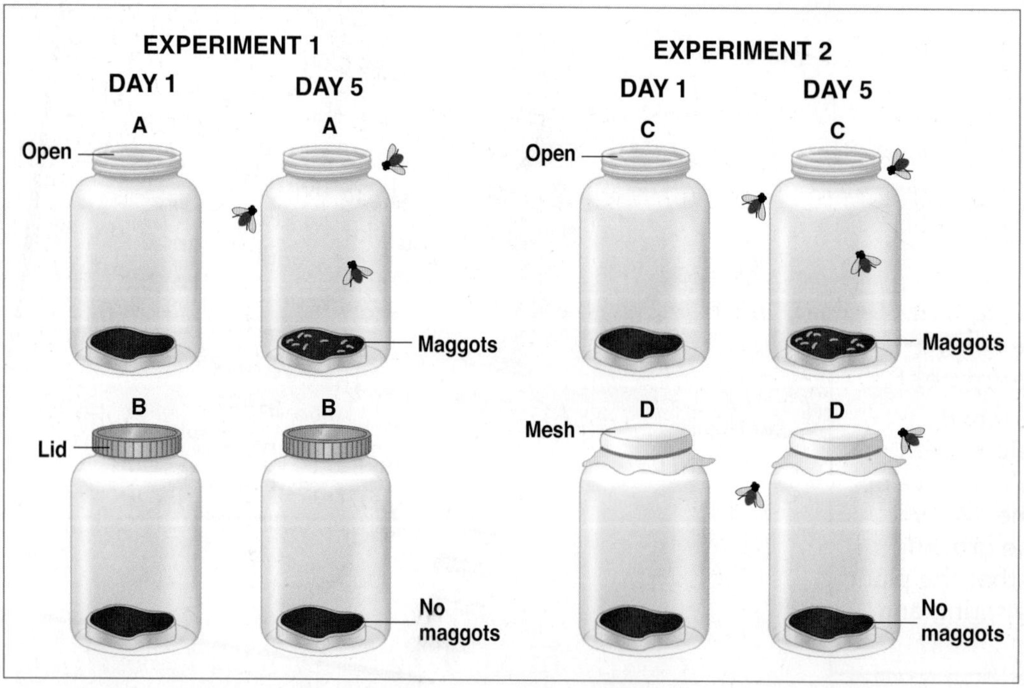


Go Online **active art**
**For:** Redi's and Pasteur's Experiments activity
**Visit:** PHSchool.com
**Web Code:** cep-1011

◀ **Figure 1-18** Redi's experiment helped scientists realize that all organisms come from other organisms of the same kind.

**Pasteur's Experiment** Louis Pasteur was a French microbiologist. He performed an experiment in the mid 1800s that disproved spontaneous generation.

▲ **Figure 1-19** Pasteur's experiment proved that organisms do not spontaneously generate.

In his experiment, Pasteur poured a broth into curved-necked flasks. The necks prevented microorganisms from entering the flasks. He boiled the flasks to kill any microorganisms in the broth. After several days, Pasteur saw no microorganisms growing in the flasks. He then tipped the flasks, allowing microorganisms living in the air to enter the broth. In a few days, microorganisms were growing in the flasks. Pasteur demonstrated that living things did not arise spontaneously from the broth. They grew from microorganisms in the air.

3 **EXPLAIN:** What did Pasteur disprove?

## ✓ CHECKING CONCEPTS

1. What is spontaneous generation?
2. Who was Francesco Redi?
3. Why do flies often lay eggs on spoiled meat?
4. What was the control for Redi's experiment?

## THINKING CRITICALLY

5. **EXPLAIN:** Why is it important to use a control in an experiment?
6. **ANALYZE:** What did Pasteur's experiment show?

## DESIGNING AN EXPERIMENT

*Design an experiment to solve the following problem. Include a hypothesis, variables, a procedure, and a type of data to study.*

PROBLEM: Mark finds flies swarming on the inside of his garbage can. The garbage can has been completely sealed since he took it outside two days ago. Mark wonders how the flies got there.

## *Integrating Earth Science*

**TOPIC: atmosphere**

### MILLER'S EXPERIMENT

Stanley Miller, an American scientist, performed an experiment to try to find an answer to the question, "How did life begin on Earth?"

To begin, Miller filled a glass chamber with chemicals that were present in early Earth's atmosphere. These included hydrogen, water, and ammonia. He used an electrical spark to model lightning in the glass chamber. At the end of a week, Miller discovered that the chamber contained several organic compounds, including amino acids. Organisms use amino acids to make proteins.

Miller's experiment did not prove how life began. However, it gave many scientists reason to believe that 4 billion years ago, Earth's atmosphere had the right compounds in it to support the beginning of life. Space scientists look for the same ingredients on other planets that may be able to support life.

**Thinking Critically** Why was Miller's experiment important?

▲ **Figure 1-20** Miller tried to re-create Earth's atmospheric conditions from 4 billion years ago.

# 1-7 How do organisms make more of their own kind?

## INVESTIGATE

### *Modeling Budding*

HANDS-ON ACTIVITY

1. Roll a piece of clay into a ball. Then divide it in half. How are the two pieces similar?
2. Put the two pieces back together. Again, form a ball with the clay.
3. Squeeze a small piece of clay so that a small ball is formed on one side of the ball.
4. Break the smaller ball of clay off the larger ball. How are the two pieces similar?

**THINK ABOUT IT:** How might your model represent the way new organisms are formed?

STEP 3

### *Objective*

Describe the two kinds of reproduction.

### *Key Terms*

**reproduction** (ree-pruh-DUHK-shuhn)**:** process by which living things produce new organisms like themselves

**offspring:** new organism produced by a living thing

**asexual** (ay-SEHK-shoo-uhl) **reproduction:** reproduction needing only one parent

**sexual** (SEHK-shoo-uhl) **reproduction:** reproduction needing two parents

**Reproduction** Organisms do not live forever. Before many organisms die, they produce new organisms like themselves. The process by which organisms produce new organisms is called **reproduction.** Reproduction does not keep individual organisms alive. Reproduction only continues each kind of living thing by producing new organisms called **offspring.**

**1 DEFINE:** What is reproduction?

**Asexual Reproduction** Simple organisms and some plants produce offspring by **asexual reproduction.** Asexual reproduction is reproduction that requires only one parent. In asexual reproduction, each new offspring is an exact copy of its parent. A simple form of asexual reproduction is called **fission** (FIHSH-uhn). In fission, new organisms are produced when the parent organism splits in two. Bacteria reproduce by fission.

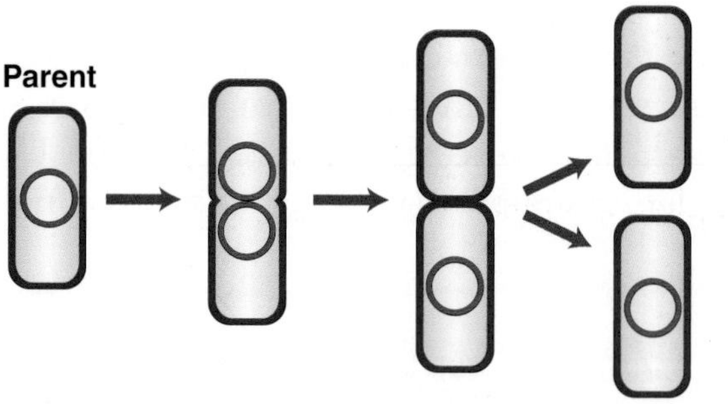


▲ **Figure 1-21** Bacteria reproducing

Another type of asexual reproduction is **budding**. Budding is the growth of a new organism from the parent organism. Yeasts and some coral reproduce by budding.

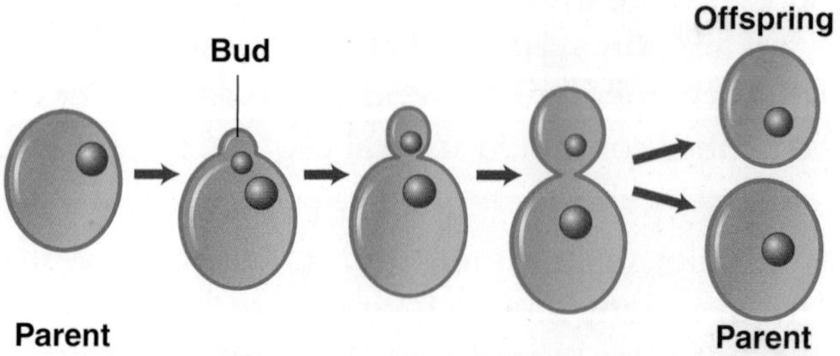


▲ **Figure 1-22** Budding requires only one parent.

**2 NAME:** What are two forms of asexual reproduction?

**Sexual Reproduction** Most types of living things reproduce by **sexual reproduction.** Sexual reproduction is reproduction needing two parents. During sexual reproduction, cells from two parents join.

A new organism develops from the joined cells. This new organism is not exactly like either of its parents. Instead, the offspring has some features of each parent and may have features of neither parent.

▲ **Figure 1-23** A lion cub may have some features of both its parents.

3 **CONTRAST:** How is sexual reproduction different from asexual reproduction?

## CHECKING CONCEPTS

1. New living things produced by organisms are called ___________.
2. Asexual reproduction involves only ___________ parent.
3. Two forms of asexual reproduction are fission and ___________.
4. During fission, the parent organism ___________ in two.
5. Sexual reproduction needs two ___________.

## THINKING CRITICALLY

6. **PREDICT:** What might happen to a kind of organism that produces few offspring?
7. **MODEL:** Draw a diagram showing the process of budding. Label your drawing.

## INTERPRETING VISUALS

*Use Figure 1-21 to answer the following questions.*

8. **OBSERVE:** What process is being shown?
9. **ANALYZE:** Is this a type of asexual or sexual reproduction?

## *Science and Technology*

### BACTERIA AND THE ENVIRONMENT

Most bacteria reproduce by fission. Under ideal conditions, a bacterial cell can divide every 20 minutes.

Because bacteria have such a quick reproduction rate, scientists often use helpful bacteria in making foods and medicines. They also use bacteria to help clean Earth of pollutants. For example, some bacteria feed on oils. They turn the harmful substances in oil into harmless substances. If there are oil spills in the oceans, these bacteria can be used to clean them up. Scientists are working on finding bacteria that will clean up oil spills more quickly.

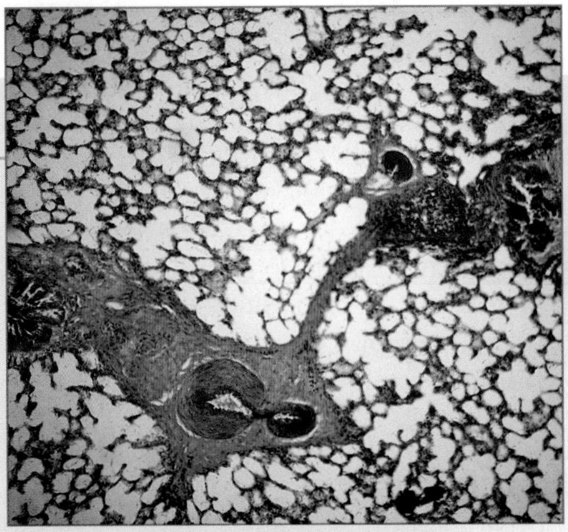

▲ **Figure 1-24** Bacterial cells can split every 20 minutes.

**Thinking Critically** Why do you think scientists want to find quicker oil-eaters?

# Chapter 1 Challenges

## Chapter Summary

### Lesson 1-1

- The study of the areas of science that deal with living things is called life science. Six branches of life science are anatomy, physiology, botany, zoology, microbiology, and ecology.

### Lesson 1-2

- Living things are called **organisms.**
- All organisms have six characteristics. Organisms are made up of **cells,** use energy, are adapted to their surroundings, produce more of their own kind, respond to changes, and grow and develop.
- Most organisms contain the elements carbon, hydrogen, oxygen, nitrogen, sulfur, and phosphorus.

### Lesson 1-3

- Organisms need food, water, and oxygen.
- Organisms need a proper temperature to carry out life processes.
- All organisms need living space.

### Lesson 1-4

- All organisms carry out life processes. Taking in food is called **ingestion.** The process of changing food so it can be used is **digestion.** Organisms get energy from food by **cellular respiration.**
- Organisms get rid of waste products by the process of **excretion.** The moving of nutrients and waste products is called **transport.**

### Lesson 1-5

- Organisms respond to **stimuli** in different ways. The way in which organisms respond to stimuli is called **behavior.**
- **Migration** and **hibernation** are animal behaviors.

### Lesson 1-6

- Francesco Redi and Louis Pasteur performed experiments that disproved the idea of **spontaneous generation.**

### Lesson 1-7

- **Reproduction** is the process by which living things produce new organisms like themselves.
- Reproduction that needs only one parent is called **asexual reproduction. Sexual reproduction** requires two parents.

## Key Term Challenges

asexual reproduction (p. 32)
autotroph (p. 20)
behavior (p. 24)
byproduct (p. 22)
cell (p. 18)
cellular respiration (p. 22)
characteristic (p. 18)
digestion (p. 22)
excretion (p. 22)
heterotroph (p. 20)
hibernation (p. 24)
homeostasis (p. 20)
ingestion (p. 22)
migration (p. 24)
nutrient (p. 22)
offspring (p. 32)
organism (p. 18)
reproduction (p. 32)
response (p. 18)
specialization (p. 16)
sexual reproduction (p. 32)
spontaneous generation (p. 30)
stimulus (p. 24)
transport (p. 22)

MATCHING **Write the Key Term from above that best matches each description.**

1. the ability of an organism to keep conditions inside its body constant
2. the inactive state of some animals during winter months
3. the idea that living things come from nonliving things
4. the process by which a cell releases energy from food molecules
5. reproduction needing two parents
6. new organisms produced by a living thing
7. studying or working in only one part of a subject
8. chemical substance that is needed to carry out life processes

IDENTIFYING WORD RELATIONSHIPS **Explain how the words in each pair are related. Write your answers in complete sentences.**

9. ingestion, digestion
10. heterotroph, autotroph
11. behavior, migration
12. stimulus, response

## Content Challenges TEST PREP

**MULTIPLE CHOICE Write the letter of the term or phrase that best completes each statement.**

1. Two kinds of animals that hibernate are
   - **a.** chipmunks and squirrels.
   - **b.** birds and chipmunks.
   - **c.** bears and birds.
   - **d.** birds and squirrels.
2. Offspring that are not exactly like either parent are produced by
   - **a.** budding.
   - **b.** sexual reproduction.
   - **c.** asexual reproduction.
   - **d.** fission.
3. All of the following are nonliving except
   - **a.** sand.
   - **b.** sunlight.
   - **c.** trees.
   - **d.** water.
4. The source of energy for most living things is
   - **a.** oxygen.
   - **b.** soil.
   - **c.** water.
   - **d.** sunlight.
5. All living things
   - **a.** make their own food.
   - **b.** hibernate.
   - **c.** migrate.
   - **d.** are made up of cells.
6. Getting rid of waste products is called
   - **a.** transport.
   - **b.** excretion.
   - **c.** response.
   - **d.** ingestion.
7. A change that causes a response is
   - **a.** a stimulus.
   - **b.** behavior.
   - **c.** an adaptation.
   - **d.** a reaction.
8. Behaviors that organisms are born with are called
   - **a.** learned behaviors.
   - **b.** stimuli.
   - **c.** instincts.
   - **d.** adaptations.
9. The process keeping conditions inside an organism's body constant is called
   - **a.** homeostasis.
   - **b.** hibernation.
   - **c.** migration.
   - **d.** reproduction.
10. The idea that living things can be produced from nonliving things is called
    - **a.** asexual reproduction.
    - **b.** Redi's theory.
    - **c.** spontaneous generation.
    - **d.** Pasteur's theory.

**TRUE/FALSE Write *true* if the statement is true. If the statement is false, change the underlined term to make the statement true.**

11. Animals often <u>hibernate</u> to find a safe place to reproduce.
12. In <u>fission</u>, new organisms are produced when the parent organism splits in two.
13. When changes in temperature occur, <u>homeostasis</u> keeps conditions stable inside a living thing.
14. Biologists use six characteristics to classify something as a <u>nonliving thing</u>.
15. During <u>hibernation</u>, animals live off fat stored in their bodies.
16. During hibernation, the body temperature of an animal <u>rises</u>.
17. Budding and fission are two types of <u>sexual</u> reproduction.
18. Pasteur <u>proved</u> the theory of spontaneous generation.

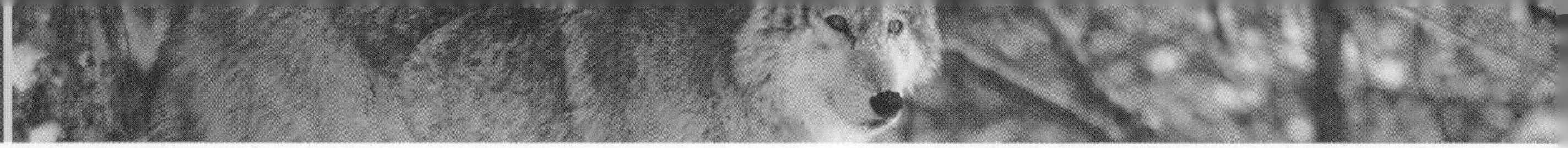

## Concept Challenges TEST PREP

WRITTEN RESPONSE **Answer each of the following questions in complete sentences.**

1. EXPLAIN: Is a robot an organism? Explain.
2. COMPARE: How are growing and developing related?
3. IDENTIFY: What are three byproducts of cellular respiration?
4. ANALYZE: How do living things compete with each other?
5. INFER: Why does sexual reproduction produce offspring that are not exactly like either of their parents?

INTERPRETING A VISUAL **Use Figure 1-25 to answer the following questions.**

6. OBSERVE: Which jars attracted flies?
7. ANALYZE: Which jars are the controls?
8. EXPLAIN: Why did maggots not grow in all the jars?
9. ANALYZE: Where did the maggots come from?
10. DISCUSS: How did the results of this experiment disprove spontaneous generation?

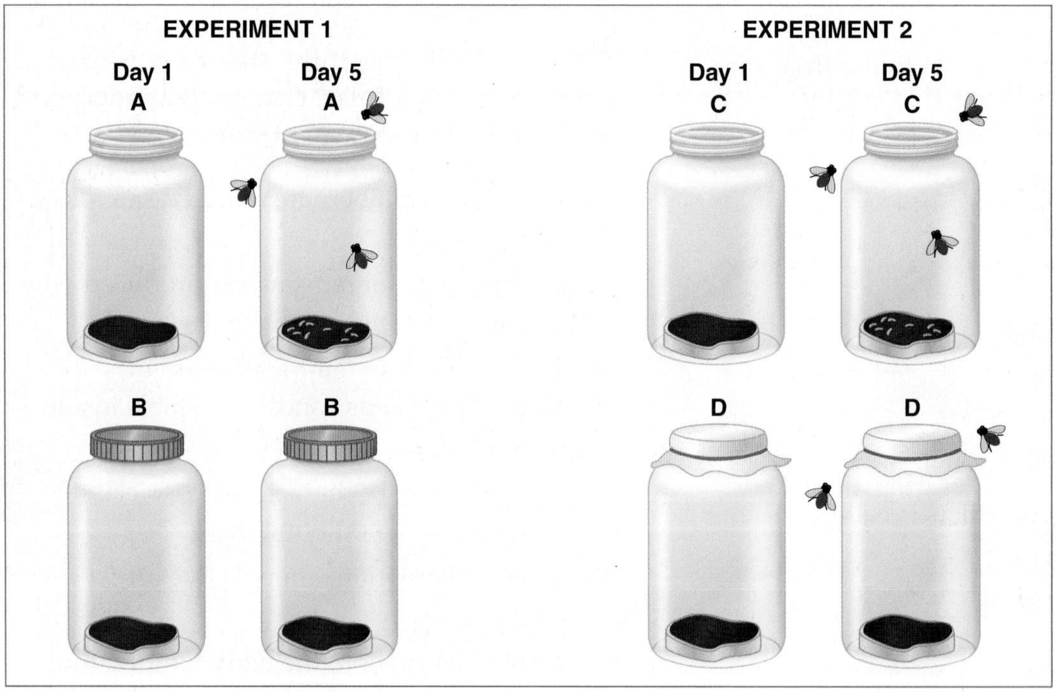


▲ **Figure 1-25** Redi's experiment

# Chapter 2 Cell Structure and Function

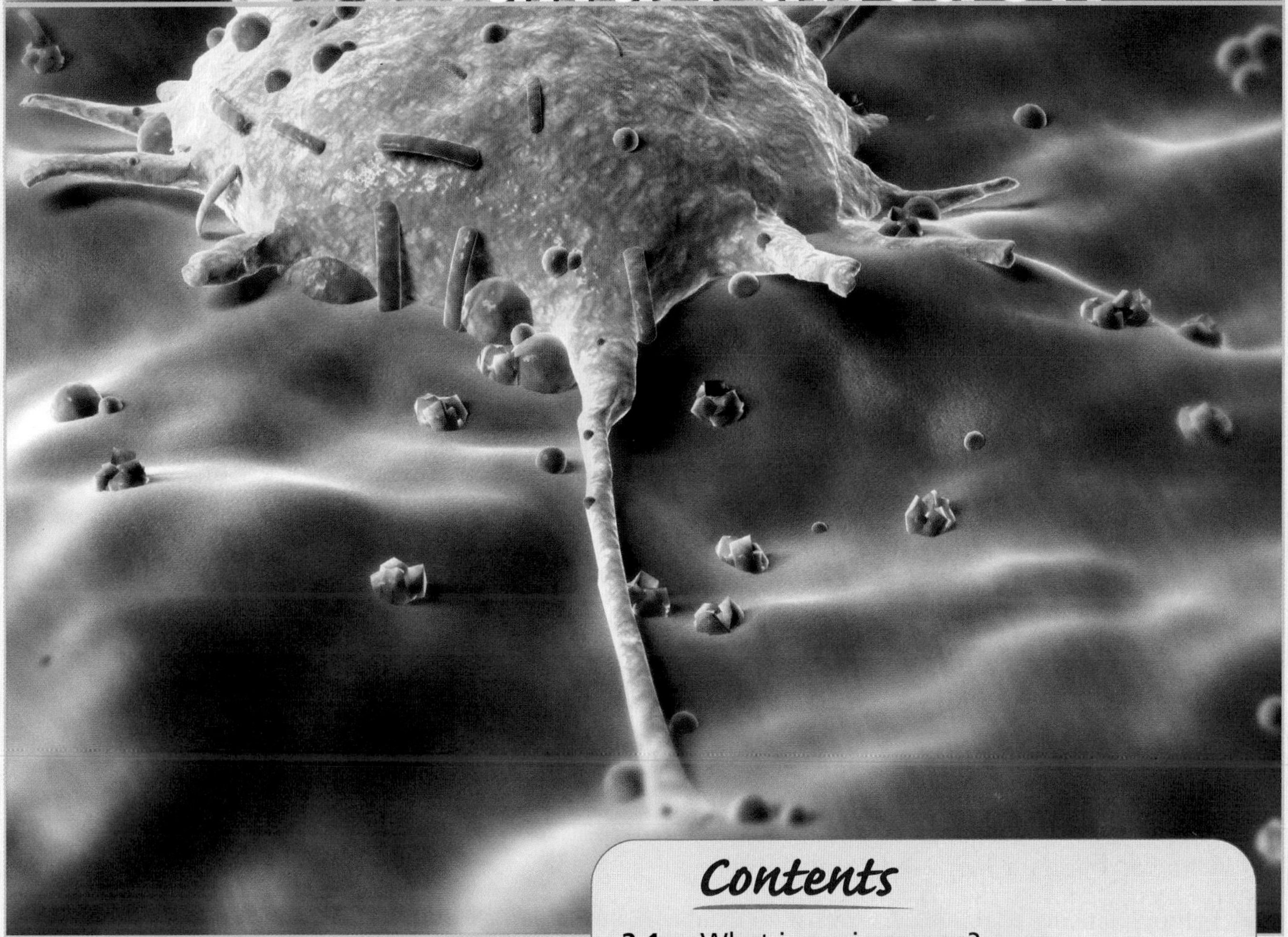

▲ **Figure 2-1** A white blood cell (green) attacks disease-causing organisms (brown).

All living things are made of microscopic structures called cells. Different cells have different functions, or jobs. In many cases, the shape and structure of a certain cell is related to its function. The cell shown in green in Figure 2-1 is a white blood cell. White blood cells are part of your immune system. They travel through the bloodstream of your body, defending you from unknown invaders such as bacteria.

►Why do you think it is important for white blood cells to be able to move on their own and change shape?

## Contents

# 2-1 What is a microscope?

## INVESTIGATE

### *Making a Simple Microscope*

**HANDS-ON ACTIVITY**

**1.** Dip the hole in a key into a glass of water. Make sure that a drop of water stays in the hole.

**2.** Look through the drop of water to read the small print in a book.

**3.** Move the key up and down very slowly. What happens?

**THINK ABOUT IT:** How did the drop of water change the way the text appears?

### *Objective*

Describe microscopes and their parts.

### *Key Terms*

**microscope:** tool that makes things look larger than they really are

**lens:** piece of curved glass or other clear material that causes light rays to come together or spread apart as they pass through

**Microscopes** One of the most important tools used to study living things is the **microscope.** *Micro-* means "very small." *Scope* means "to look at." A microscope is a tool used to make things look larger than they really are.

**1 DEFINE:** What is a microscope?

**Lenses** A **lens** is a piece of curved glass or other clear material. Some lenses have one curved surface and one flat surface. Others have two curved surfaces. A lens brings light rays together or spreads them apart. Light that passes through a lens is bent. The bending of the light rays causes the object to look either larger or smaller. To make an object look larger than it is, you can magnify it by using a lens.

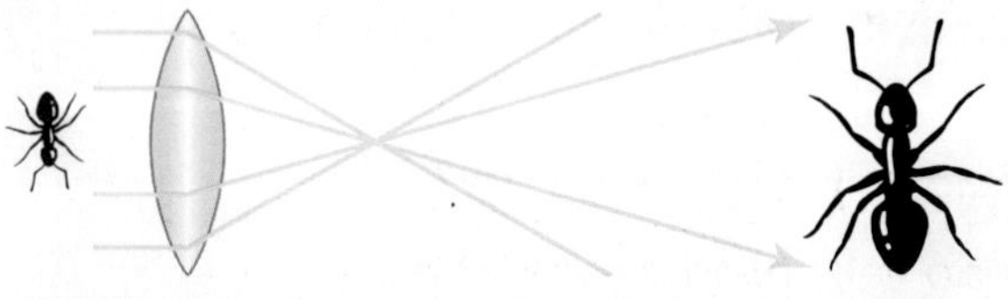

▲ **Figure 2-2** This lens has magnified an ant's image.

**2 INFER:** Why might you magnify an object?

**Parts of a Microscope** All microscopes have the same basic parts. Look at Figure 2-3 to learn about each part of a microscope.

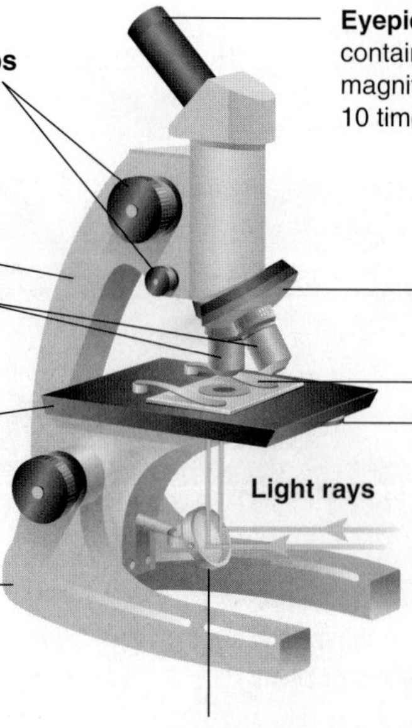


▲ **Figure 2-3** A compound light microscope

A microscope's parts are fragile. You need to take care of your microscope. Use only lens paper to clean the lenses and specimen slides. Be careful not to break a slide when you focus using the coarse adjustment. To carry a microscope properly, use one hand to hold the arm and one hand under the base.

**3 DESCRIBE:** How do you carry a microscope properly?

**Types of Light Microscopes** Have you ever used a magnifying glass? If you have, you have used a simple microscope. A simple microscope has only one lens. A compound microscope has two or more lenses. Using two lenses makes things look even larger than using one lens.

The first compound microscope was developed in the 1590s by two Dutch eyeglass makers, Hans and Zacharias Janssen. Since then, many scientists have made and used microscopes. Much of what is known about living things would not have been discovered without the microscope.

The microscopes you use in the classroom are compound light microscopes. Light microscopes have one or more lenses in them. These microscopes use light and lenses to magnify things.

4 DESCRIBE: How many lenses does a compound microscope have?

## CHECKING CONCEPTS

1. What is a lens?
2. What causes an object to look larger or smaller than it actually is?
3. Where on a microscope do you place the object you want to view?
4. What is the difference between a simple microscope and a compound microscope?

## THINKING CRITICALLY

5. **INFER:** Which of your senses is helped by using a microscope?
6. **EXPLAIN:** How would changing the objective lenses affect what is seen through the microscope?
7. **ANALYZE:** Why do you think it is more important to get a clear, less magnified image than a fuzzy image that is greatly magnified?

## BUILDING MATH SKILLS

***Calculating*** To find the total magnification power of a microscope, you multiply the number found on the eyepiece lens by the number found on the objective lens. Find the magnification for the following microscopes.

| Eyepiece | Objective |
|---|---|
| 8. 3× | 40× |
| 9. 5× | 10× |
| 10. 10× | 100× |

## *Science and Technology*

### ELECTRON MICROSCOPES

Most cells can be seen using a light microscope. However, with a power of 1,000× or more the images get fuzzy. An electron microscope can be used to clearly see the smaller structures inside a cell. Electron microscopes use electrons to form images of objects. An electron microscope can magnify objects up to 300,000 times their normal size.

One kind of electron microscope is the transmission electron microscope, or TEM. A TEM sends beams of electrons through the object that is being viewed. The image that you see is two-dimensional. The TEM is used to study cell parts.

▲ **Figure 2-4** SEM image of fly head

Another type of electron microscope is the scanning electron microscope, or SEM. The SEM sends a beam of electrons over the surface of an object to produce realistic, three-dimensional images. However, only the surface can be viewed. Small organisms such as insects or single-celled organisms are often studied using SEM images.

**Thinking Critically** When might you want to use an SEM instead of a TEM?

# 2-2 What are cells?

## INVESTIGATE

### *Looking at Onion Cells*

**HANDS-ON ACTIVITY**

1. Peel off a very thin layer of onion tissue with a pair of tweezers.
2. Carefully place a small piece of onion tissue on a clean slide. Try to keep the onion tissue very flat. Then, put a drop of stain on top of it.
3. Place a cover slip on the slide.
4. Place the slide on the microscope. Use the low power of the microscope to observe the onion tissue. Draw a picture of what you see.

**THINK ABOUT IT:** What part of the onion tissue does the microscope help you see?

*Objective*

Explain the cell theory.

*Key Term*

**cell:** basic unit of structure and function in living things

**Cells** A brick house is made up of many bricks. A brick is the basic unit of structure of a brick house. The basic unit of structure in living things is a **cell.** All living things are made up of one or more cells.

Cells carry out all life processes. For example, a cell takes in and breaks down food. It breaks down a simple sugar called glucose (GLOO-kohs) to produce energy. This life process is called cellular respiration.

1 **DEFINE:** What is a cell?

**Discovery of Cells** The first person to observe and describe cells was Robert Hooke, an English scientist. He used a light microscope to look at thin slices of cork. Cork is found in some plants. The cork seemed to be made up of many small boxes. Hooke named the structures that made up the cork "cells." In 1665, he published his drawings of cork cells in his book, *Micrographia.*

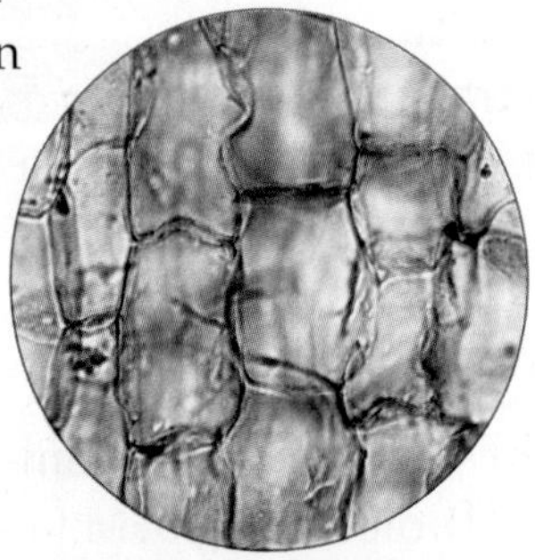

▲ **Figure 2-5** Robert Hooke saw cork cells like these.

Hooke saw only dead plant cells in the cork. Antoine van Leeuwenhoek (van LAY-vuhn-huk) was the first person to observe and describe living cells. Van Leeuwenhoek was a Dutch lensmaker. In 1674, he saw single-celled organisms swimming in a drop of pond water. These living things were microscopic. They could not be seen without a microscope.

▲ **Figure 2-6** Microscopic organisms like these volvox live in pond water.

2 **NAME:** Who was the first person to see cells?

**Cell Theory** By 1800, inventors were developing more advanced microscopes. These microscopes allowed scientists to see plants and animals in more detail. Scientists developed many ideas about cells.

Matthias Schleiden (SHLY-duhn) was a German botanist. Schleiden studied many plants in order to learn more about living things. In 1838, Schleiden stated that all plants are made up of cells.

Theodor Schwann (SHVAHN) was a German zoologist. He studied many animals. Schwann said the cell is the basic unit of structure in animals. Schwann published his ideas in 1839.

Rudolph Virchow (FUR-koh) was a doctor in Germany. He also studied cells. In 1855, Virchow said that new cells come from cells that already exist. In other words, he said that cells divide to create new cells.

In the mid-1800s, these ideas were put together as a theory. The ideas in a theory are supported by observations and data again and again. The theory that was developed is called the cell theory. The cell theory states that

- all living things are made up of one or more cells.
- cells are the basic units of structure in living things, and cells carry on all life processes.
- cells come only from other living cells.

3 **RESTATE:** What does the cell theory state?

## ✓ CHECKING CONCEPTS

1. What is the basic unit of structure in living things?
2. What did Anton van Leeuwenhoek see in a drop of pond water?
3. Where do cells come from?
4. Whose ideas make up the cell theory?

## THINKING CRITICALLY

5. **RELATE:** How did improved microscopes lead to more discoveries about cells?
6. **ANALYZE:** Why did the cell theory include the research of Schleiden, Schwann, and Virchow?

### Web InfoSearch

**SEARCH:** Use the Internet to write a report about one of the scientists who contributed to the **cell theory.** Start your search at www.conceptsandchallenges.com. Some key search words are **Theodor Schwann, Matthias Schleiden,** and **Rudolph Virchow.**

## *People in Science*

### CELL BIOLOGISTS

Cell biologists study how cells work, grow, and reproduce. Many cell biologists study cells to find out more about diseases. They examine healthy cells and sick cells. They hope that by studying cells, they will be able to find cures for diseases such as cancer and AIDS.

Donella Wilson is a cell biologist who studies red blood cells. Red blood cells carry oxygen to all the cells in the body. Wilson's research about red blood cells may lead to a cure for sickle-cell anemia. Sickle-cell anemia is an inherited blood disease that prevents red blood cells from carrying oxygen to the organs. Without oxygen, the organs cannot function properly. As a result, people with sickle-cell anemia can die.

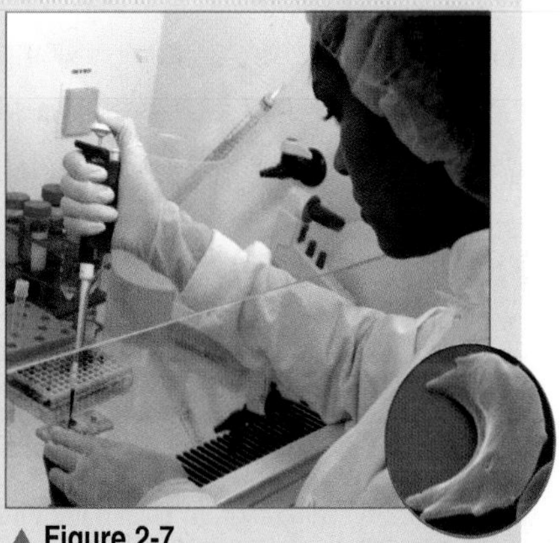

▲ **Figure 2-7** Cell biologists' research may help people with abnormal red blood cells like the one shown.

To become a cell biologist, Wilson studied chemistry and biology. She earned a degree in immunology, which is the study of how the body fights diseases. She has received many awards for her research, including the National Science Foundation Research Opportunity Award.

**Thinking Critically** Why do you think Dr. Wilson has received awards for her research?

# 2-3 What are the main cell parts?

*Objective*

Identify the main parts of a cell and describe their functions.

*Key Terms*

**cell membrane** (MEHM-brayn)**:** thin structure that surrounds a cell

**cytoplasm** (SYT-oh-plaz-uhm)**:** gel-like substance inside the cell where most of the cell's activities take place

**nucleus** (NOO-klee-uhs), *pl.* **nuclei:** control center of a cell

**nuclear membrane:** thin structure that surrounds and protects the nucleus

**Three Main Parts** Most cells have three main parts. The three main parts of the cell are shown in Figure 2-8. They are the cell membrane, the cytoplasm, and the nucleus. Each of these main cell parts has a special and important job to do.

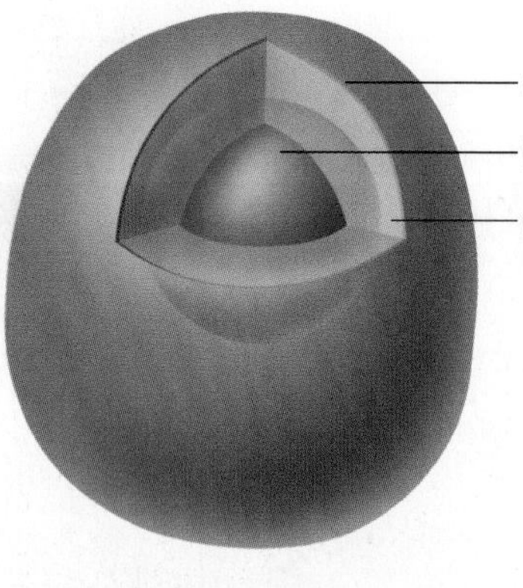


▲ **Figure 2-8** This diagram shows the three main parts of a cell.

**1 NAME:** What are the three main parts of a cell?

**Cell Membrane** The **cell membrane** is a thin structure that surrounds a cell. Sometimes it is called the plasma (PLAZ-muh) membrane. The cell membrane has three important jobs. It protects the inside of a cell. It supports and gives a cell its shape. The cell membrane also controls the movement of materials into and out of a cell. Food, water, and oxygen move through the cell membrane into the cell. Wastes move out of the cell through the cell membrane. Look at Figure 2-9. Notice that the cell membrane surrounds the cell.

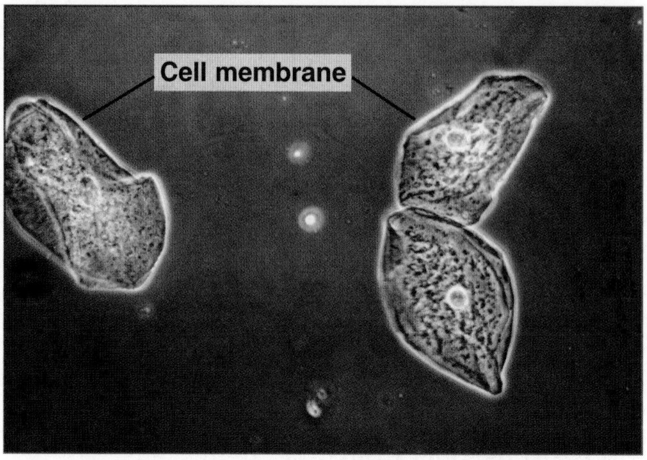


▲ **Figure 2-9** A cell membrane surrounds each of these cells.

**2 LIST:** What are the jobs of the cell membrane?

**Cytoplasm** Most cell parts are located in the cytoplasm. The **cytoplasm** is a gel-like substance that is constantly moving. Most of the activities in the cell take place in the cytoplasm.

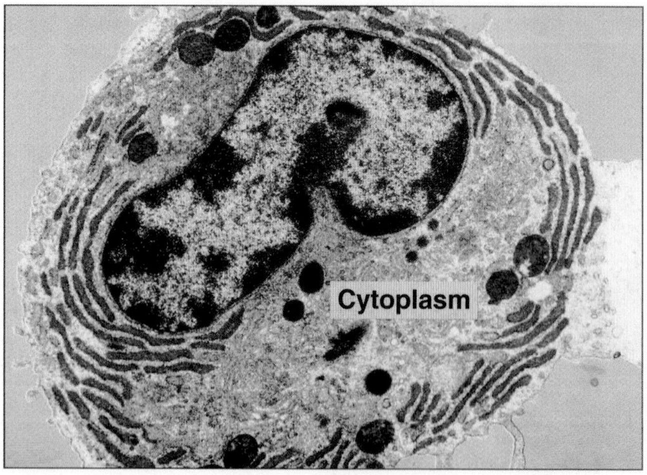


▲ **Figure 2-10** The cytoplasm is colored gold in this photo.

**3 DESCRIBE:** What takes place in the cytoplasm?

**Nucleus** The **nucleus** of a cell is round or egg-shaped. Most cells have a nucleus. The nucleus is the control center of a cell. It controls all the life processes of a cell. The nucleus also controls cell reproduction. The nucleus is separated from the cytoplasm by the **nuclear membrane.** It is a thin structure that surrounds and protects the nucleus. The nuclear membrane also controls the movement of materials into and out of the nucleus.

Inside the nucleus there are blueprints called DNA. DNA contains the instructions for how the cell is supposed to function.

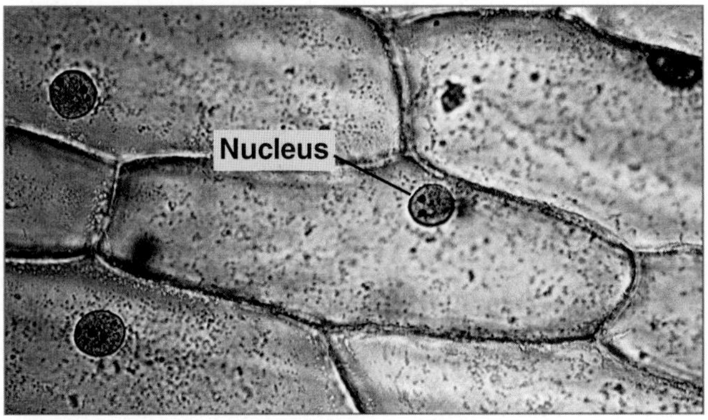


▲ **Figure 2-11** The nucleus of a cell can be seen by using a microscope.

4 INFER: What might happen to a cell if the nucleus were taken out?

## CHECKING CONCEPTS

1. All the life processes of a cell are controlled by the __________.
2. The three main parts of the cell are the nucleus, the cell membrane, and the __________.
3. The cell membrane controls the __________ of materials into and out of a cell.
4. Most cell parts are located in the __________.

## THINKING CRITICALLY

5. APPLY: What cell part controls reproduction?
6. COMPARE: How are the cell membrane and nuclear membrane similar?
7. MODEL: Draw a diagram of a cell. Label the three main parts of the cell.

## BUILDING READING SKILLS

***Using Vocabulary*** A prefix is a word part at the beginning of a word. The meaning of a prefix usually remains the same. Look up the meaning of the prefix *cyto-*. Write the definition, and then list and define five words that begin with it.

## Hands-On Activity

### OBSERVING CELLS

*You will need a clean microscope slide, stain, a popsicle stick, an eyedropper, a cover slip, gloves, and a microscope.*

1. Hold the edge of the popsicle stick against the inside of your cheek. Using an up-and-down motion, gently rub the inside of your cheek. ⚠ CAUTION: Do not share or touch each others' samples.
2. Rub the edge of the popsicle stick back and forth on the microscope slide.
3. Add a drop of the stain to the material on the slide.
4. Place the cover slip carefully on the slide. Then place the slide on the stage of the microscope.
5. Use the microscope to observe the cells. Begin by focusing the low-power lens with the coarse adjustment knob, then switch to the high-power lens. ⚠ CAUTION: Do not use the coarse adjustment knob to focus the high-power lens.

▲ **STEP 5** Observe the cells.

**Practicing Your Skills**

6. MODEL: Draw a picture of the cells you see. Label the parts.

# 2-4 What are other cell parts?

## *Objective*

Describe the functions of the parts of a cell.

## *Key Terms*

**organelle** (awr-guh-NEHL)**:** small structure in the cytoplasm that does a special job

**mitochondrion** (myt-oh-KAHN-dree-uhn), *pl.* **mitochondria:** structure that releases energy for a cell

**endoplasmic reticulum** (ehn-doh-PLAZ-mihk rih-TIHK-yuh-luhm)**:** small network of tubes inside a cell that substances move along

**ribosome** (RY-buh-sohm)**:** small, round structure that makes proteins

**Golgi** (GOHL-jee) **body:** organelle that packages and sends materials to other places in the cell

**vacuole** (VAK-yoo-ohl)**:** space in the cytoplasm that stores the different substances a cell needs to survive

**lysosome** (LY-soh-sohm)**:** small, round structure that breaks down nutrient molecules and old cell parts

**Organelles** A cell is like a factory. Each machine in a factory has a special job. The machines work together to keep the factory working. The "machines" of a cell are its **organelles.** Organelles are small structures that are suspended in the cytoplasm. Most organelles are so small that they can only be seen with an electron microscope. Each organelle has a special job to do. Organelles work to produce energy, transport materials, and get rid of waste. They keep the cell working properly. As you read about each organelle, look at Figure 2-13.

1 **DEFINE:** What are organelles?

**Mitochondria** One kind of organelle is the **mitochondrion.** Mitochondria are known as the "powerhouses" of the cell. They release energy that the cell can use. The energy is used by the cell to carry out its life processes.

2 **EXPLAIN:** Why does a cell need energy?

**Endoplasmic Reticulum** The **endoplasmic reticulum** is a very small network of tubes inside the cell. The tubes are like a tiny highway system for the cell. Substances move along these tubes from one organelle to another. The endoplasmic reticulum is also known as the ER.

3 **DESCRIBE:** What is the job of the ER?

**Ribosomes** **Ribosomes** are small, rounded structures located within the cell. Ribosomes make proteins. The proteins are needed for growth and are involved in all cell processes. Some ribosomes appear as small bumps attached to the ER. Not all ribosomes are attached to the ER. Some are scattered throughout the cytoplasm.

4 **INFER:** Why is "protein factory" a good name for a ribosome?

**Golgi Bodies** Cells contain many flattened and folded sacs called **Golgi bodies.** The Golgi bodies are like a post office for the cell. Proteins and other materials are sent to the Golgi bodies through the endoplasmic reticulum. Then, the Golgi bodies package and distribute the materials to other parts of the cell. They also send materials to the outside of the cell.

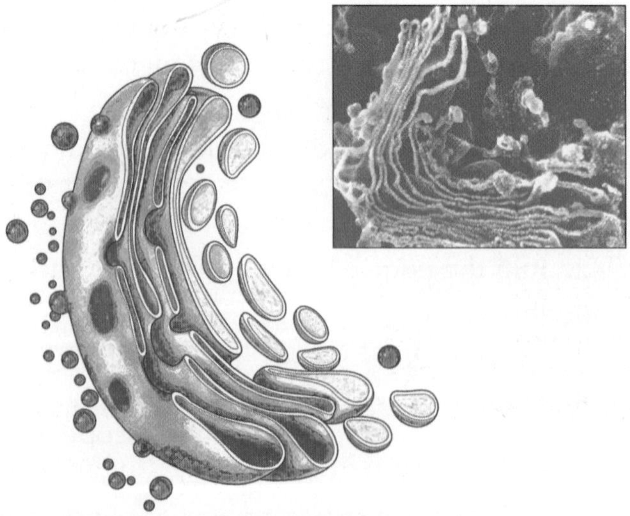

▲ **Figure 2-12** The photo shows a Golgi body in a cell. The diagram of a Golgi body shows packages of materials being made.

5 **DESCRIBE:** How are Golgi bodies like a post office?

Go Online
active art

For: Plant and Animal Cells activity
Visit: PHSchool.com
Web Code: cep-3012

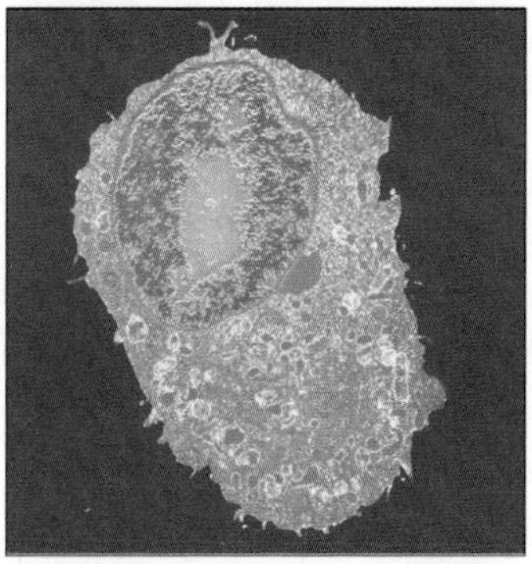

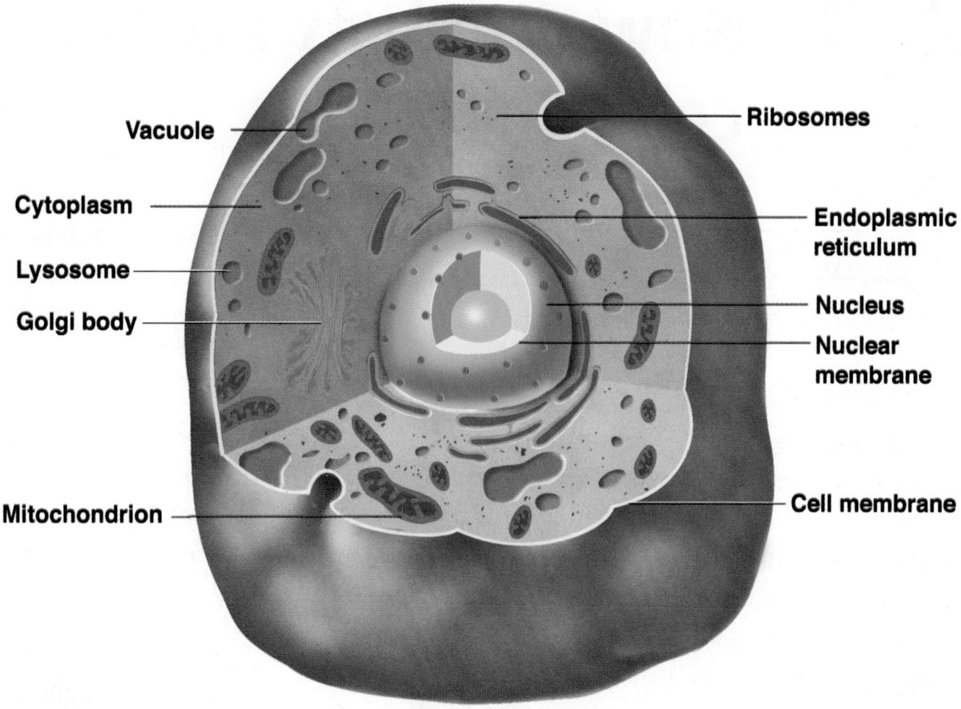


▲ **Figure 2-13** The photo shows an animal cell. The diagram shows some of the basic parts in the cell.

**Vacuoles** The **vacuoles** of a cell are small storage spaces in the cytoplasm. The spaces are surrounded by a membrane. Vacuoles are like storage bins. They store food and waste. Some vacuoles store extra water. They pump extra water out of a cell. Plant cells usually have one large vacuole. Animal cells may have many small vacuoles.

6 **LIST:** What are two things that are stored in vacuoles?

**Lysosomes** Cells also contain small, round organelles called **lysosomes.** Lysosomes are the cleanup crew of the cell. Lysosomes contain powerful chemicals that digest nutrient molecules in the cell.

When other organelles in the cell stop working properly, the lysosomes break down and recycle the old cell parts so they can be used again. The chemicals in the lysosomes only break down unhealthy cell parts. In a healthy cell, a membrane surrounds the lysosomes. This membrane prevents the lysosomes from destroying the entire healthy cell.

7 **EXPLAIN:** What is the job of the lysosomes?

## CHECKING CONCEPTS

1. What are organelles?
2. Why are the mitochondria called the "powerhouses" of the cell?
3. What are the small storage spaces in a cell called?
4. What is the job of the Golgi bodies?
5. How are the lysosomes like a cleanup crew?

## THINKING CRITICALLY

6. **COMPARE:** Name the organelle that has a job similar to each of these objects: railroad, cabinets, post office, electric company.
7. **INFER:** Think about the jobs performed by your muscles and your skin. Do you think there are more mitochondria in muscle cells or in skin cells? Explain.
8. **MODEL:** Draw a diagram of a cell that includes all the organelles you have learned about. Label the parts of your diagram.

## Web InfoSearch

**SEARCH:** Use the Internet to write a report about one of the organelles you just learned about. Start your search at www.conceptsandchallenges.com. Some key search words are **organelles, mitochondria,** and **ribosomes.**

# 2-5 How do plant and animal cells differ?

## *Objective*

Compare plant cells and animal cells.

## *Key Terms*

**cell wall:** thick outer layer that surrounds the cell membranes of plants and some simple organisms

**cellulose** (SEHL-yoo-lohs)**:** carbohydrate, made up of many sugar molecules, that forms most of the cell wall of a plant cell

**chloroplast** (KLAWR-uh-plast)**:** organelle in a plant cell that contains chlorophyll

**chlorophyll** (KLAWR-uh-fihl)**:** green material in chloroplasts that is needed by plants to make food

**Cell Wall** All plant cells have a **cell wall**. Animal cells do not have a cell wall. The cell wall surrounds the cell membrane of a plant cell. The cell wall is made up of a hard material called **cellulose**. Wood is made up mostly of cellulose.

The cell wall has three jobs: it protects the plant cell, it gives the cell its shape, and it gives the plant cell support. Find the cell wall in Figure 2-14.

**1 NAME:** What does the cell wall surround?

**Vacuoles** The number and size of vacuoles are different in plant and animal cells. Plant cells have only one or two very large vacuoles. Animal cells may have many small vacuoles. Look at Figure 2-14 and compare the vacuoles in each cell.

Most of the water in a plant cell is stored in the vacuoles. When it rains, plants store water in the vacuoles to use at a later time. When there is a lot of water in vacuoles, the plant is healthy. When there is little water in the vacuoles, the plant wilts.

**2 OBSERVE:** How many vacuoles does a plant cell usually have?

**Chloroplasts** Most plant cells have roundish organelles called **chloroplasts.** They contain a material called **chlorophyll.** Chlorophyll gives a plant its green color. Plants use chlorophyll to

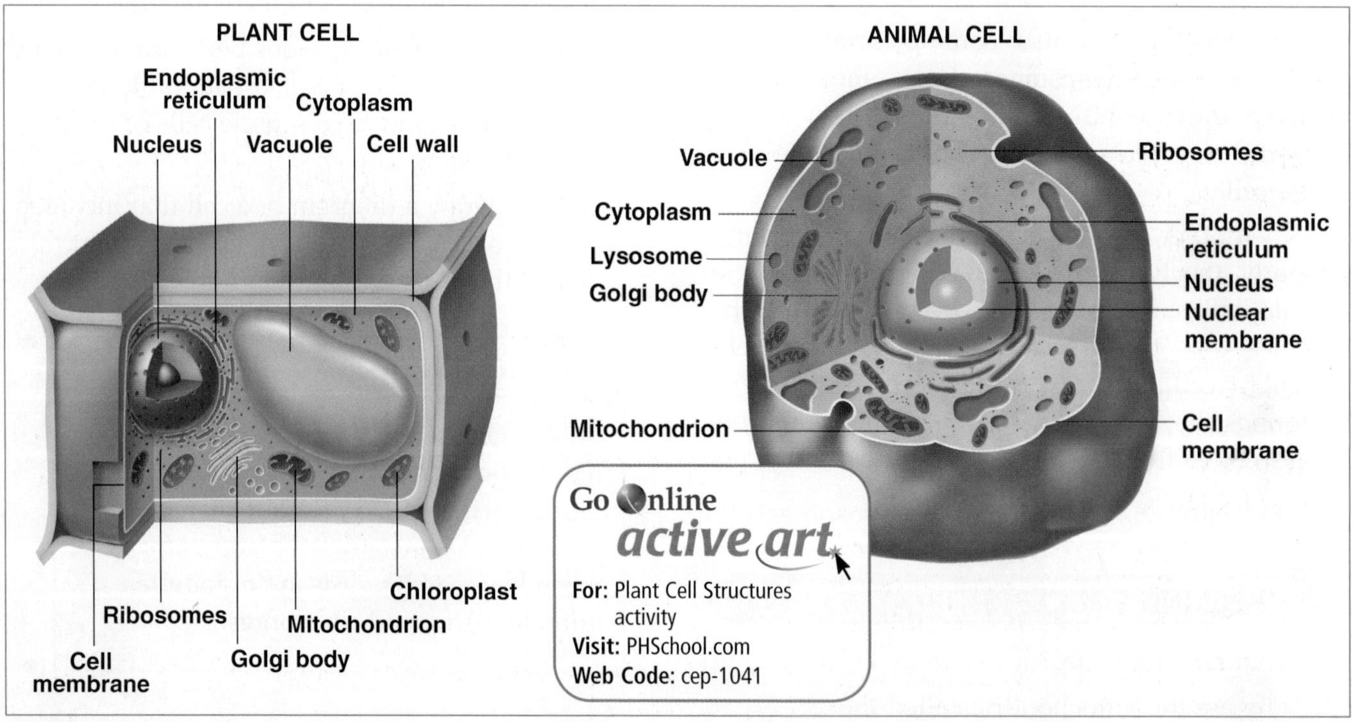


Go Online
*active art*
**For:** Plant Cell Structures activity
**Visit:** PHSchool.com
**Web Code:** cep-1041

▲ **Figure 2-14** Plant and animal cells have many of the same organelles but they are not exactly alike.

make food. Animal cells do not have chloroplasts or chlorophyll.

3 **EXPLAIN:** Why are most plants green?

## CHECKING CONCEPTS

1. What are the three jobs of a cell wall?
2. What is cellulose?
3. How do the vacuoles in animal cells differ from those in plant cells?
4. What are chloroplasts?

## THINKING CRITICALLY

5. **COMPARE:** How are plant and animal cells alike? How do plant and animal cells differ?
6. **ANALYZE:** Which of the following organisms contain cellulose: a pine tree, a cow, a rabbit, a fern, a grass, a goldfish?
7. **INFER:** Large plants do not have a skeleton, or frame. How can large plants stand up without skeletons?

## INTERPRETING VISUALS

*Use Figures 2-15 and 2-16 to answer the following questions.*

8. Which figure has chloroplasts? Why is that structure missing from the other figure?
9. What structures do the cells in both figures have in common?
10. Why do you think plant cells often have a rectangular shape?

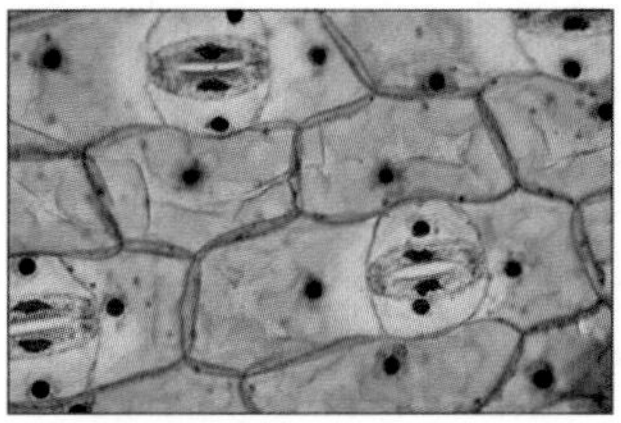

▲ **Figure 2-15**

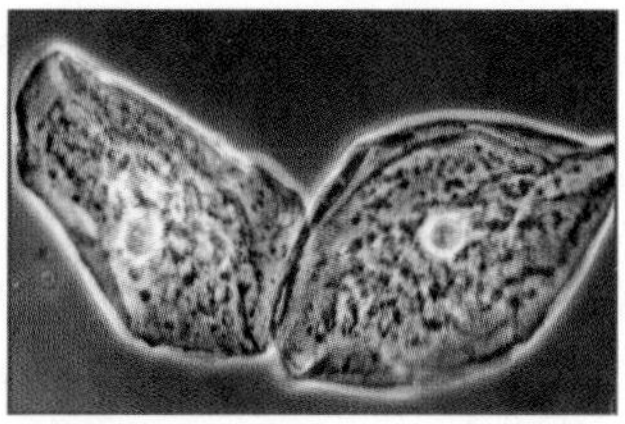

▲ **Figure 2-16**

## *Integrating Physical Science*

**TOPICS: light, color**

### PLANT PIGMENTS

Most light sources give off visible light. Visible light is made up of seven colors of light: red, orange, yellow, green, blue, indigo, and violet. When visible light strikes an object, the object appears a certain color. The object absorbs all the colors except the color it reflects. The pigments in a blue shirt will absorb all the colors except blue. Pigments are substances that absorb light.

Sunlight is made up of visible light. When sunlight strikes the leaf of a plant, it is absorbed by a special pigment called chlorophyll. Chlorophyll is the main pigment in plants. It absorbs large amounts of red, orange, and violet light. It reflects yellow and green light. Because chlorophyll reflects yellow and green light, the leaf looks green.

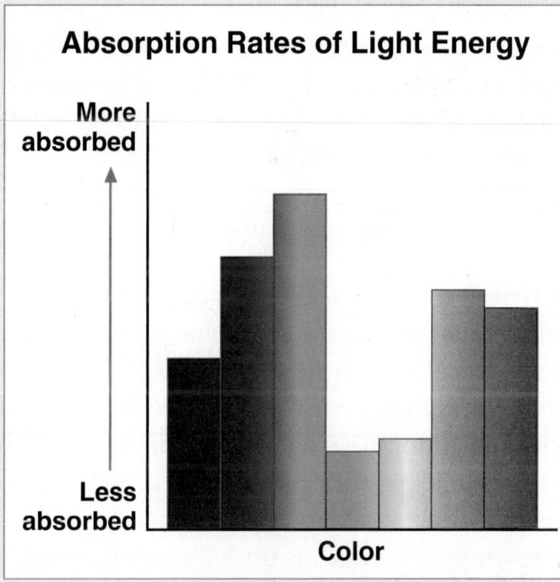


▲ **Figure 2-17** The chlorophyll found in plants absorbs red and blue colors of light and reflects green and yellow.

Figure 2-17 is a bar graph showing the absorption rate of chlorophyll in a leaf. The lowest rate of absorption is the color green. This means that the leaf reflects green light.

**Thinking Critically** Carotene is a plant pigment that reflects red and orange light. What color do you think a leaf filled with carotene is?

# 2-6 Why do cells have different shapes?

## *Objective*

Describe and relate the structures and functions of different kinds of cells.

## *Key Terms*

**unicellular:** containing only one cell

**multicellular:** containing more than one cell

**pseudopod:** (SOO-doh-pahd): fingerlike extension of the cytoplasm

**guard cell:** cell that controls the size of a stoma

**stoma** *pl.* **stomata:** tiny opening in the upper or lower surface of a leaf

**Cell Size and Shape** Some organisms are made of only one cell. They are called **unicellular.** In unicellular organisms, all of the life processes are carried out by the same cell. Most organisms you are familiar with have more than one cell. These organisms are called **multicellular.** The cells of these organisms are not all the same. They have different sizes and shapes. Different kinds of cells have different jobs. The shapes of most cells help them to do their jobs.

1 **EXPLAIN:** Why do cells have different shapes?

**Amoeba** An amoeba (uh-MEE-buh) is a unicellular organism that lives in water. Amoebas have the ability to change shape. These organisms use temporary, fingerlike extensions of the cytoplasm to move and get food. These extensions are called **pseudopods.** An amoeba uses its pseudopods to surround food particles. Then, the pseudopod closes around the food particle and digests it.

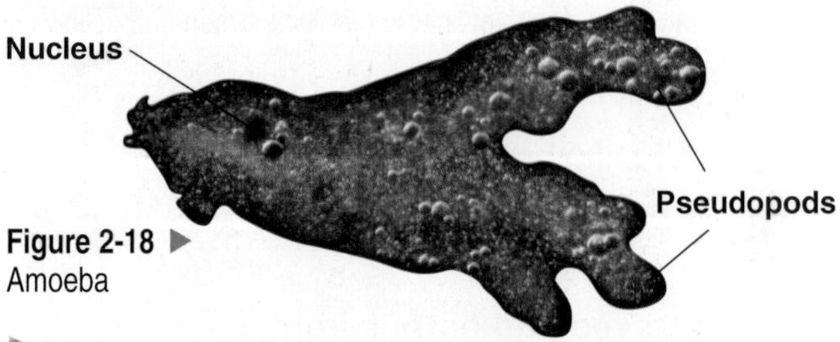


Figure 2-18 ▶ Amoeba

2 **EXPLAIN:** How does an amoeba use its pseudopods?

**Red Blood Cells**
Your blood contains round, flexible cells called **red blood cells.** Red blood cells do not have a nucleus, thus they can easily bend and fold. The job of a red blood cell is to carry oxygen. Because they are flexible, the red blood cells can fit through very small tubes in your body called capillaries.

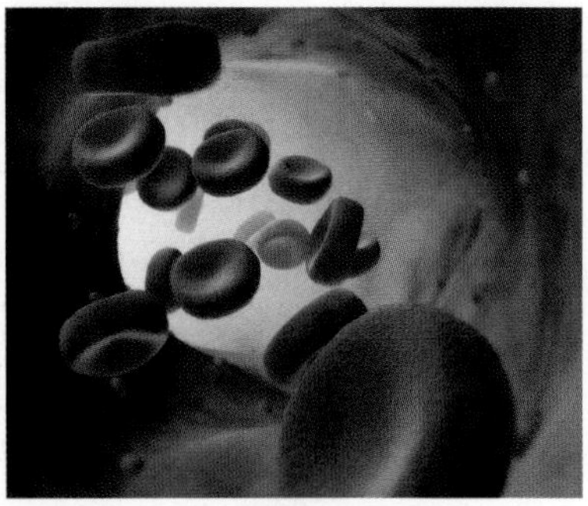

▲ **Figure 2-19** Red blood cells

3 **INFER:** Do you think red blood cells can reproduce themselves? Why or why not?

**Nerve Cells** Nerve cells store or transfer information. There are different types of nerve cells. The nerve cells in the brain store information. Other kinds of nerve cells carry messages from one part of the body to another. These messages are called impulses. Nerve cells that carry information are usually long and very thin. Some nerve cells are the longest of all the cells in your body.

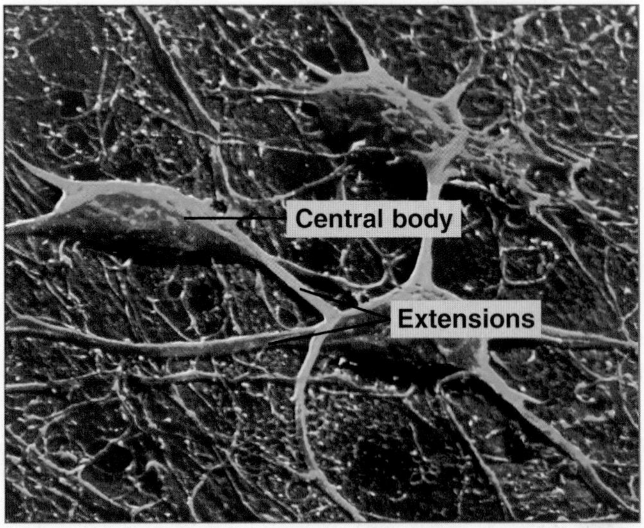


▲ **Figure 2-20** Most nerve cells have a central body and several long, thin extensions.

4 **INFER:** Why do you think some nerve cells are long and thin?

**Guard Cells** Two bean-shaped cells called **guard cells** surround a tiny opening on the outer surface of a plant leaf. This opening is called a **stoma.** A stoma lets carbon dioxide into the leaf and releases oxygen and water into the air. Guard cells control the size of the stoma. When the guard cells swell, the stoma opens. When the guard cells shrink, the stoma closes.

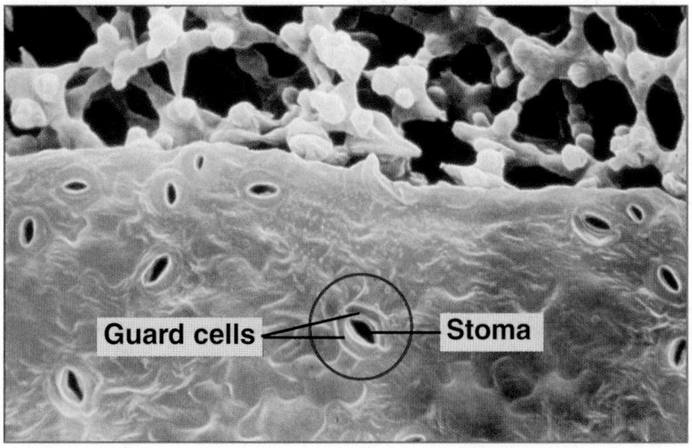


▲ **Figure 2-21** Most guard cells and stomata are located on the underside of a leaf.

5 PREDICT: Does carbon dioxide enter a plant when the guard cells swell or when they shrink?

## CHECKING CONCEPTS

1. Organisms with one cell are __________.
2. Amoebas use __________ to capture food.
3. The job of a __________ is to carry oxygen.
4. A __________ is a tiny opening on the underside of a plant leaf.
5. The __________ control the size of the stoma.

## THINKING CRITICALLY

6. RELATE: How is the size and shape of a nerve cell related to its function?
7. CONTRAST: How do red blood cells differ from most other kinds of cells?

## BUILDING SCIENCE SKILLS

***Modeling Cells*** Make a model of one of the cells in this lesson. Make sure that the model you make clearly represents the shape of the cell you chose. Answer the following questions about your cell model: How is the shape of the cell related to its function, or purpose? What would happen if the cell's shape was different?

## *Hands-On Activity*

### OBSERVING GUARD CELLS AND STOMATA

*You will need a broad leaf, clear nail polish, scissors, a glass slide, a microscope, and safety goggles.*

1. Put on the goggles. Cover the underside of the leaf with three coats of nail polish. Allow each coat to dry for at least two minutes before applying another coat.
2. Allow the nail polish to dry for 30 minutes. Then, carefully peel the nail polish from the leaf. (Remember which side was touching the leaf.)
3. Cut the nail-polish sheet into small squares. ⚠CAUTION: Be careful when using scissors.
4. Place one square on a clean slide. Make sure that the side of the nail-polish square that was touching the leaf is facing up.
5. Observe the slide under the microscope.

▲ **STEP 1** Apply nail polish to the leaf.

### Practicing Your Skills

6. DESCRIBE: What shape do you see? How many stomata can you count?
7. EXPLAIN: Were the guard cells on this leaf swollen or not?
8. INFER: Based on your observations, do you think this leaf was actively exchanging gases?

# 2-7 How do materials move in and out of cells?

## INVESTIGATE

### *Observing Diffusion*
HANDS-ON ACTIVITY

1. Fill a small glass or beaker with water.
2. Add 4 to 5 drops of food coloring to the water. Observe what happens.
3. Wait a few minutes, and observe the water again.

**THINK ABOUT IT:** What happened when the food coloring was added? Did a change take place immediately or after a few seconds? What do you think caused the water to change color?

### *Objective*
Describe how materials can move in and out of cells.

### *Key Terms*
**diffusion** (dih-FYOO-zhuhn)**:** movement of material from an area where molecules are crowded to an area where they are less crowded

**passive transport:** movement of materials through a membrane without the use of energy

**osmosis** (ahs-MOH-sihs)**:** movement of water through a membrane

**active transport:** movement of materials through a membrane using energy

**Diffusion** A molecule is the smallest part of a substance that still has the characteristics of that substance. Molecules are always moving. Most molecules move from places where they are crowded to places where they are less crowded. The movement of molecules from crowded areas to less crowded areas is called **diffusion.**

1 EXPLAIN: Where do most molecules move to?

**Passive Transport** Diffusion also takes place through cell membranes. A cell membrane has very tiny holes through which some molecules can move. These molecules will move through the cell membrane until the same number of molecules is on both sides of the cell membrane. This is called **passive transport.** Passive transport does not require energy.

2 DEFINE: What is passive transport?

**Osmosis** The movement of water through a membrane is called **osmosis.** Osmosis is a special kind of diffusion. Many substances dissolve in water. Molecules of water usually move across a membrane to each area with more dissolved substances.

3 PREDICT: What would happen if water constantly entered a cell and none left it?

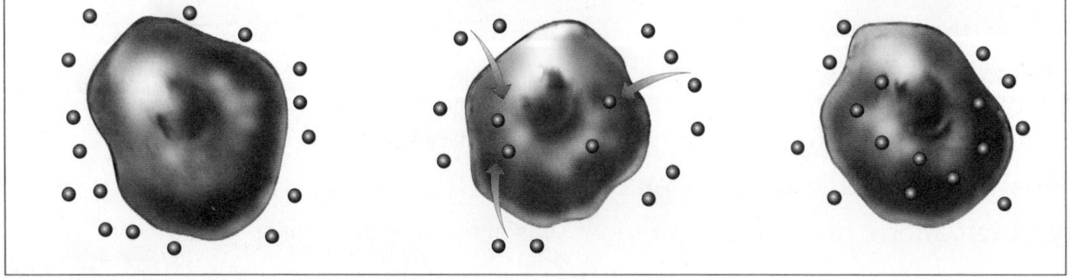


◀ **Figure 2-22**
The process of diffusion and passive transport

**Active Transport** Usually, a cell needs to have more molecules of a certain substance inside it than outside it. In this situation, the molecules have to move toward an area where they would be more crowded. This is the opposite direction of the way molecules move naturally. This type of movement is called **active transport.** Active transport needs energy to take place.

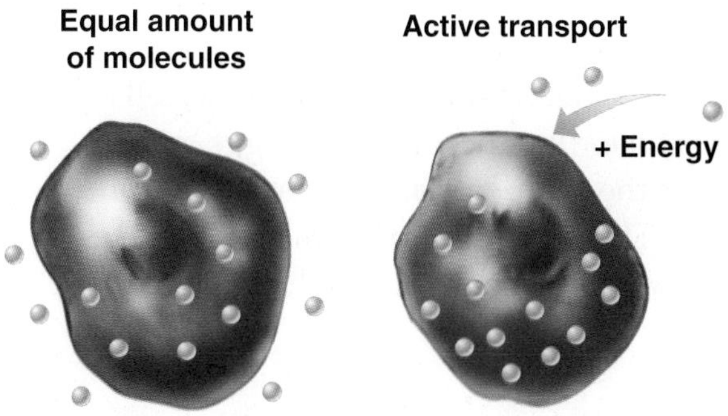


▲ **Figure 2-23** Active transport allows molecules to continue moving into a cell, even if there is an equal amount of molecules inside and out.

4 **COMPARE:** How is active transport different from passive transport?

## CHECKING CONCEPTS

1. The movement of molecules from crowded areas to less crowded areas is called __________.
2. The movement of water through a membrane is called __________.
3. The __________ controls what molecules pass in and out of a cell.
4. Many substances dissolve in __________ before entering a cell.
5. Active transport requires __________.

## THINKING CRITICALLY

6. **HYPOTHESIZE:** Will a teaspoon of salt dissolve more quickly in a glass of fresh water or a glass of salt water? Explain.
7. **EXPLAIN:** Why might the smell of freshly baked bread eventually fill an entire house?

*Real-Life Science*

## HYPOXIA AND MOUNTAIN CLIMBING

▲ **Figure 2-24** Mountain climbers must make sure they are getting enough oxygen into the cells of their bodies.

When you inhale air into your lungs, molecules of oxygen move into your red blood cells by diffusion. The red blood cells then carry the oxygen molecules to all the cells in your body. The cells in your body need oxygen to carry out cellular respiration.

Hypoxia is a dangerous condition that occurs when your cells do not get enough oxygen. The symptoms of hypoxia include headache and nausea. Sometimes your body tries to help by breathing rapidly and deeply. Mountain climbers often suffer from hypoxia when they hike at high altitudes where the amount of oxygen molecules in the air is lower. This means fewer oxygen molecules are able to get into the cells of the body by diffusion.

To prevent hypoxia, mountain climbers should move up the mountain at a slow pace. This allows the body to adjust to the lower levels of oxygen in the air. Experts recommend that climbers should stop often. In addition, mountain climbers should always bring an altimeter, a device that measures altitude, so they know exactly how high up they are at all times. They should also carry tanks of oxygen.

**Thinking Critically** What other activities do you think could cause hypoxia?

# LAB ACTIVITY
# Measuring Diffusion in Eggs

**Materials**

Apron and goggles, 3 eggs, 3 large plastic cups, vinegar, vegetable oil, water, a metric ruler, plastic wrap, a marker, a pan, a small dish, a balance or scale, a measuring cup or graduated cylinder, string

▲ **STEP 2** Measure the weight of the egg.

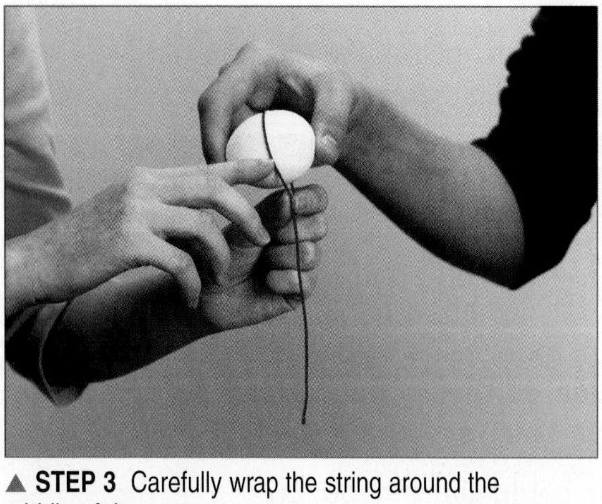

▲ **STEP 3** Carefully wrap the string around the middle of the egg.

### *BACKGROUND*

A bird's egg is a large single cell. The shell has tiny pores, or openings. Just inside the shell is the cell membrane. Diffusion can occur in bird eggs when molecules enter the cell pores and move through the cell membrane. This process allows important gases to get to the developing chick inside the egg cell.

### *PURPOSE*

In this activity, you will be measuring diffusion in eggs to see which common substances can move through the cell membrane of an egg by passive transport.

### *PROCEDURE*

1. First, copy the data table in Figure 2-25 onto your own paper.

2. Place the small dish on the balance. Record the weight. Bring the balance to zero, place the first egg in the dish and record the combined weight. To find the weight of the egg, subtract the weight of the dish from the combined weight of the dish and egg. Record the egg's weight on your chart in the first row marked "Vinegar," under the heading marked "Day 1 Observations."

3. Now determine the circumference of the same egg. Wrap a piece of string around the middle of the egg. Measure the length of the string. Record the circumference in the first row marked "Vinegar," under the heading marked "Day 1 Observations."

4. Put on your safety goggles. Fill a cup with 250 mL of vinegar. Fill another cup with 250 mL of vegetable oil. Fill the last cup with 250 mL of water. Label the cups with the name of the liquid each contains. Then record the volume of the liquid in each cup on your chart under the heading marked "Day 1 Observations." Using the spoon, place the first egg in the cup of vinegar.

▲ **STEP 4** Carefully lower the egg into the cup using the spoon.

▲ **STEP 7** After three days, remove and measure the eggs again.

5. Repeat Steps 2 and 3 for the second egg. Record all the measurements in the row marked "Oil." Place the second egg in the cup of oil.

6. Repeat Steps 2 and 3 again for the third egg. Record all the measurements in the row marked "Water." Place this third egg into the cup of water.

7. Cover each cup with plastic wrap. After three days, use the spoon to remove your eggs. Use a graduated cylinder to find the volume of liquid remaining in each container. Measure the weight and circumference of each egg. Record these measurements under the heading "Day 3 Observations." Note any other observations on your paper about how the eggs look or feel.

*Measuring Diffusion in Eggs*

| | Day 1 Observations | | | Day 3 Observations | | |
|---|---|---|---|---|---|---|
| | Liquid Volume | Egg Circumference | Egg Weight | Liquid Volume | Egg Circumference | Egg Weight |
| Vinegar | | | | | | |
| Oil | | | | | | |
| Water | | | | | | |

▲ **Figure 2-25** Copy this chart onto your paper. Leave enough space in each row to record your measurements.

### *CONCLUSIONS*

1. **OBSERVE:** In which cup did the volume of the liquid change the most?
2. **CALCULATE:** How much did the volumes change?
3. **COMPARE:** How did the sizes of the eggs change compared with the change in the volume of liquid?
4. **INFER:** Which substance's molecules are able to pass through an egg's shell and membrane?

# 2-8 How do cells obtain energy?

## *Objective*

Describe the processes that cells use to get energy.

## *Key Terms*

**energy:** the ability to do work or cause change

**photosynthesis** (foht-oh-SIHN-thuh-sis)**:** food-making process in plants and other organisms that uses sunlight

**glucose:** a simple type of sugar

**fermentation:** process by which a cell releases energy from food without using oxygen

**Cells and Energy** Cells perform many important activities such as growing, repairing structures, creating new cell parts, and reproducing. All of these activities require **energy.** Energy is the ability to do work or cause change. Energy can be found in many forms. The Sun provides energy in the form of light. The food you eat provides energy in the form of nutrients.

1 **DEFINE:** What is energy?

**Photosynthesis** Plant cells have the ability to use the energy from the Sun to make food. This process is called **photosynthesis.** Photosynthesis occurs in the chloroplasts. During photosynthesis, plants take in carbon dioxide and water. The Sun's energy is used to change these molecules into food and oxygen. The food produced by the chloroplasts is sugar. It can be stored in a plant and used later as a source of nutrients for the plant. Only organisms that have chloroplasts can perform photosynthesis.

▲ **Figure 2-26** Chloroplasts use sunlight to make food.

2 **DEFINE:** What is photosynthesis?

**Cellular Respiration** When a plant needs to use some of its stored sugar, it breaks it down into a simple sugar called **glucose.** The glucose is used in a process called cellular respiration. Cellular respiration takes place in the mitochondria of the cell. During cellular respiration, glucose is broken down into hydrogen and carbon molecules. These molecules then combine with oxygen to form carbon dioxide and water. This process releases energy for use by the cell.

Cells that do not contain chloroplasts cannot make their own food. They must take in energy from their environment. Animal cells are examples of this kind of cell. For example, an elephant gets energy from the plant material it eats. You get energy from the foods that you eat. After the food is digested, nutrient molecules enter the cell. The nutrients are sent to the mitochondria, and they are used to release energy during cellular respiration.

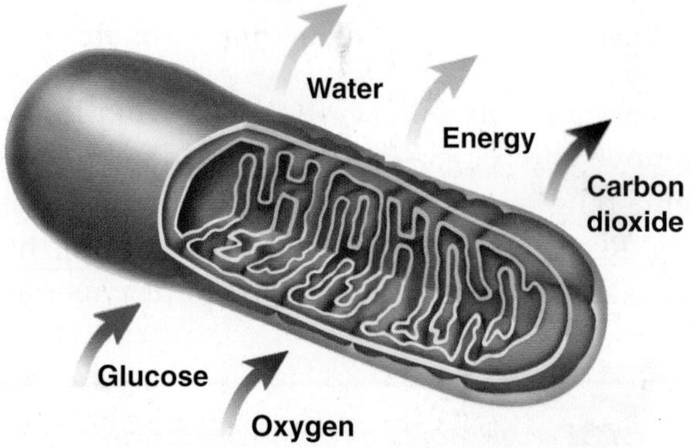


▲ **Figure 2-27** In cellular respiration, glucose and oxygen combine to release energy. Carbon dioxide and water are the byproducts.

3 **EXPLAIN:** How is oxygen used to release energy?

**Fermentation** Sometimes respiration must take place when there is no oxygen available. Certain plants and other organisms called yeast have the ability to carry out respiration without using oxygen. This process is called **fermentation.**

During fermentation, cells break down sugar and give off carbon dioxide and alcohol molecules in the process. Fermentation is used in baking to help make bread rise. When yeast cells are mixed in with the dough, bubbles of carbon dioxide are produced during fermentation. These carbon dioxide bubbles actually force the dough to expand. As a result the dough rises.

**4** **INFER:** What are the byproducts of fermentation?

## CHECKING CONCEPTS

1. Plants make food during __________.
2. Food is turned into energy during __________.
3. Animals must get their energy from __________.
4. The process of fermentation does not use __________.

## THINKING CRITICALLY

5. **INFER:** Why are animals unable to perform photosynthesis?
6. **PREDICT:** What might happen if plants could not perform photosynthesis?
7. **RELATE:** How is fermentation different from cellular respiration?

## DESIGNING AN EXPERIMENT

*Design an experiment that solves the following problem. Include a hypothesis, variables, a procedure, and the type of data to collect and study.*

PROBLEM: Yeast performs the type of respiration called fermentation. During fermentation, carbon dioxide and alcohol are released. How could you prove that live yeast cells in a mixture of sugar water are alive?

## *Integrating Earth Science*

**TOPIC: atmosphere**

### BALANCE IN THE ATMOSPHERE

Oxygen and carbon dioxide are very important gases in Earth's atmosphere. Look carefully at the diagrams for photosynthesis and cellular respiration in Figures 2-26 and 2-27. You will find that some materials on the left side of one diagram can be found on the right side of the other diagram. This is not just by chance.

▲ **Figure 2-28** The life processes of plants and animals maintain a balance in the atmosphere.

The oxygen that plants produce during photosynthesis is used by animals during cellular respiration. At the same time, the carbon dioxide given off by animals during cellular respiration is needed by plants to do photosynthesis. You cannot have one process without the other. This relationship allows the gases in the atmosphere to remain in balance.

The atmosphere is a layer of gases that surrounds Earth. This layer supplies all of the living things on Earth with the gases they need to survive. Earth's atmosphere is composed mainly of nitrogen, oxygen, carbon dioxide, and water vapor. The cellular relationship between photosynthesis and respiration allows these gases to recycle themselves. Plants, animals, and other living things can use these gases again and again. This helps to keep all organisms on Earth supplied with the materials necessary for life.

**Thinking Critically** What do you think would happen to animal life on Earth if there were no plants?

# 2-9 How do cells produce new cells?

*Objective*

Describe how cells reproduce.

*Key Terms*

**chromosome** (KROH-muh-sohm)**:** cell part that determines what traits a living thing will have

**chromatin** (KROH-muh-tihn)**:** threadlike material that makes up a chromosome

**mitosis** (my-TOH-sihs)**:** division of the nucleus

**daughter cell:** new cell produced by cell division

**Cell Division** You have grown a great deal since you were born. This growth did not happen because your cells got larger. It happened because the total number of cells in your body increased. The cells of most organisms, including humans, are able to reproduce and make new cells. This process is called **cell division.**

1 **DEFINE:** What is cell division?

**Chromosomes** The nucleus controls cell division. Inside the nucleus are **chromosomes.** Chromosomes are made up of a threadlike material called **chromatin.** Chromosomes control cell processes and determine the traits of the entire organism. During cell division, each chromosome makes an exact copy of itself.

2 **IDENTIFY** Where are chromosomes located?

**Mitosis** After chromosomes make copies of themselves, the nucleus divides. This is called **mitosis**. There are five phases in mitosis: prophase, prometaphase, metaphase, anaphase, and telophase.

During prophase, the chromosomes group tightly together, and the nuclear membrane disappears. Two identical copies of each chromosome are formed. During prometaphase spindle fibers form from the region of the centrioles and attach to the chromosomes. In metaphase, all the copied chromosomes line up across the center of the cell. During anaphase, the chromosome copies separate and move to opposite ends of the cell. Special organelles called centrioles and spindle fibers help with this process. During telophase, the cell membrane pinches together in between the two nuclei. Finally, the cell splits apart, forming two identical cells. Look at Figure 2-29.

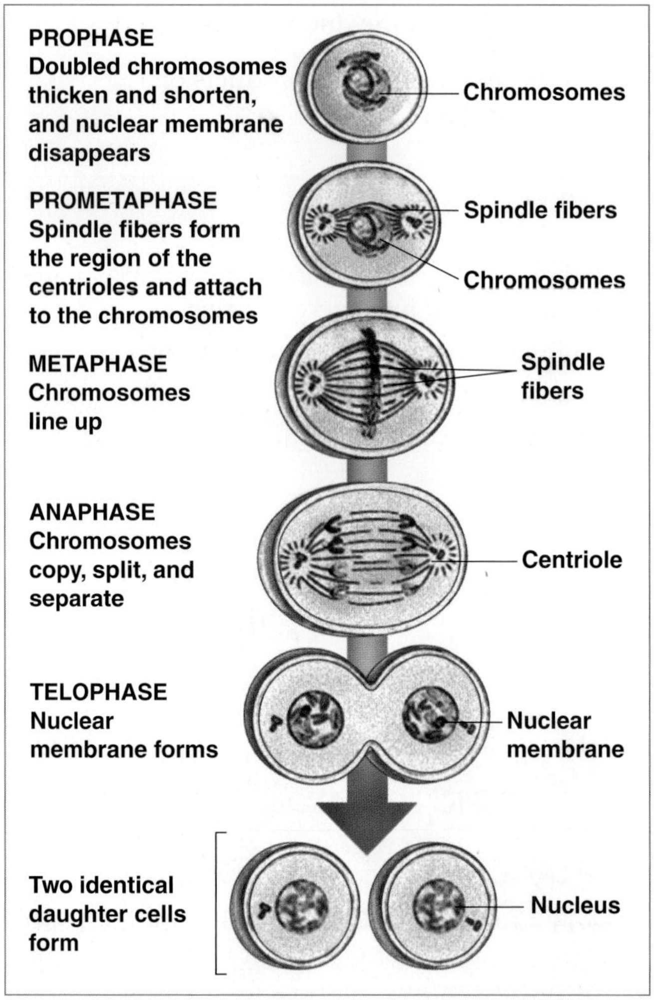


▲ **Figure 2-29** After mitosis, two new identical cells are created.

The two identical cells formed by cell division are called **daughter cells.** The nuclei of the two daughter cells are exactly alike. Each daughter cell is about half the size of the original cell. In time, each of the daughter cells will grow and divide to form two new daughter cells.

3 **LIST:** What are the five phases of mitosis?

**Cell Division in Plants** Plant cells also reproduce by cell division. Like animal cells, plant cells make copies of their chromosomes and carry out mitosis. However, in plant cells, the cell membrane does not pinch together to form two daughter cells. In plant cells, a new cell wall and new cell membrane form

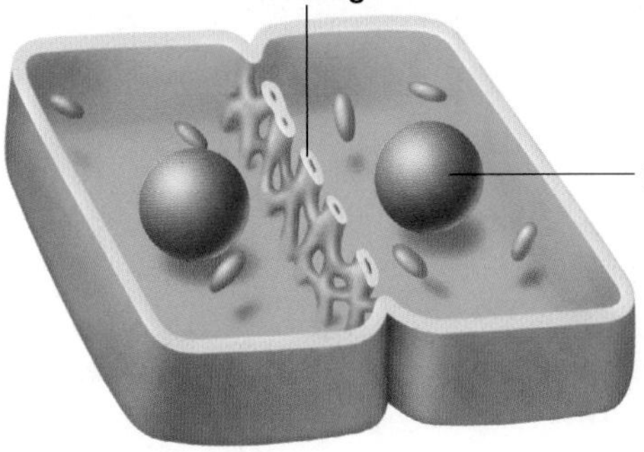


◄ **Figure 2-30** Plant cells form a new cell wall during mitosis.

down the middle of the cell. They form a wall between the two new nuclei. Two daughter cells are formed, one on each side of the new cell wall.

**4** **IDENTIFY:** What forms down the middle of a dividing plant cell?

## ✓ CHECKING CONCEPTS

1. What is mitosis?
2. What controls cell division?
3. What are chromosomes?
4. What are daughter cells?
5. How is cell division in plants different from cell division in animals?

## THINKING CRITICALLY

6. **INFER:** Why do you think chromosomes are copied during cell division?
7. **ANALYZE:** Is cell division a form of reproduction? Explain.
8. **SEQUENCE:** Place the phases of mitosis in the correct order: **a.** anaphase **b.** metaphase **c.** prophase **d.** telophase **e.** prometaphase

## BUILDING MATHEMATICS SKILLS

***Calculating*** Cell division can occur very rapidly in many organisms. If you start with one cell and it splits every 5 minutes, how many cells will there be at each of the time intervals listed below?

At 0 minutes _____ After 10 minutes _____
After 5 minutes _____ After 30 minutes _____

## *Hands-On Activity*

### MODELING CELL DIVISION IN AN ANIMAL CELL

*You will need four red and four black pipe cleaners or twist ties to represent chromosomes, a sheet of white paper, and a drawing compass.*

1. Use the compass to draw a large circle on a sheet of white paper. Draw a small circle in the middle of the first circle. Place four "chromosomes" in the inner circle.
2. Twist a second "chromosome" around each of the original ones, forming an X shape. Erase the inner circle. What phase of cell division does this represent?
3. Line up each X-shaped pair in the middle of the large circle. Make sure the red "chromosomes" are on one side and the black "chromosomes" are on the other side. What phase of cell division does this represent?

▲ **STEP 3** Line up the "chromosomes."

4. Now, untwist the X shapes and separate them by an inch. What phase does this represent?
5. Move each set of "chromosomes" to opposite ends of the circle. What phase of cell division does this represent?

**Practicing Your Skills**

6. **IDENTIFY:** In your model, what does each circle represent?
7. **EXPLAIN:** How could you show the formation of daughter cells in your model?

Integrating Chemistry

# THE Big IDEA

## How are elements and compounds part of living things?

All living things like the people, plants, and dog in this photo are made of cells. Cells carry out many important processes. All of the processes that go on inside a cell involve elements and molecules.

An **element** is a simple substance that cannot be broken down into another substance. Elements are made of tiny particles called atoms. Carbon, hydrogen, nitrogen, oxygen, phosphorus, and sulfur are the most common elements in all living things.

When atoms combine, they form **molecules.** A water molecule is made of hydrogen and oxygen. Molecules can be represented by chemical formulas. For example, the chemical formula for water is $H_2O$. The small "2" after the "H" means that there are two atoms of hydrogen in this molecule. There is no number after the "O." This means that there is only one oxygen atom in a molecule of water. The chart to the right shows some other chemical formulas.

Molecules can become very large. The sugar called glucose is represented by the formula $C_6H_{12}O_6$. When sugars link together, they form carbohydrates, such as starches and cellulose. Cells use sugars and starches for energy. Cellulose gives a plant cell strength and support.

Proteins are long chains of molecules called amino acids. Amino acids are made mostly of carbon, hydrogen, oxygen, and nitrogen. Proteins are created in the ribosomes of the cell. Proteins are used for growth and repair of cells.

Look at the photo and illustrations that appear on these two pages. Then, follow the directions in the Science Log to find out more and write about "the big idea."✦

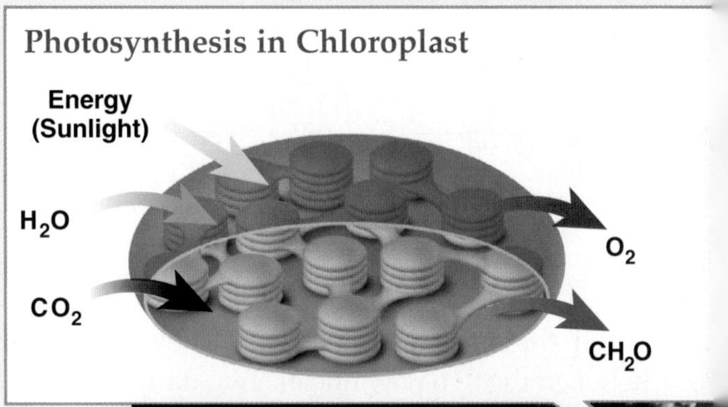


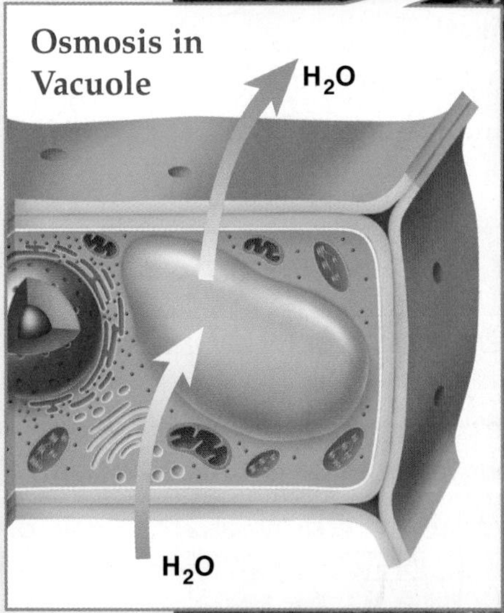

| Chemical Formula | Molecule |
|---|---|
| $H_2O$ | Water |
| $O_2$ | Oxygen |
| $CO_2$ | Carbon Dioxide |
| $C_6H_{12}O_6$ | Glucose |
| $C_2H_5O_2N$ | Amino Acid (Glycine) |
| $CH_2O$ | Carbohydrate |

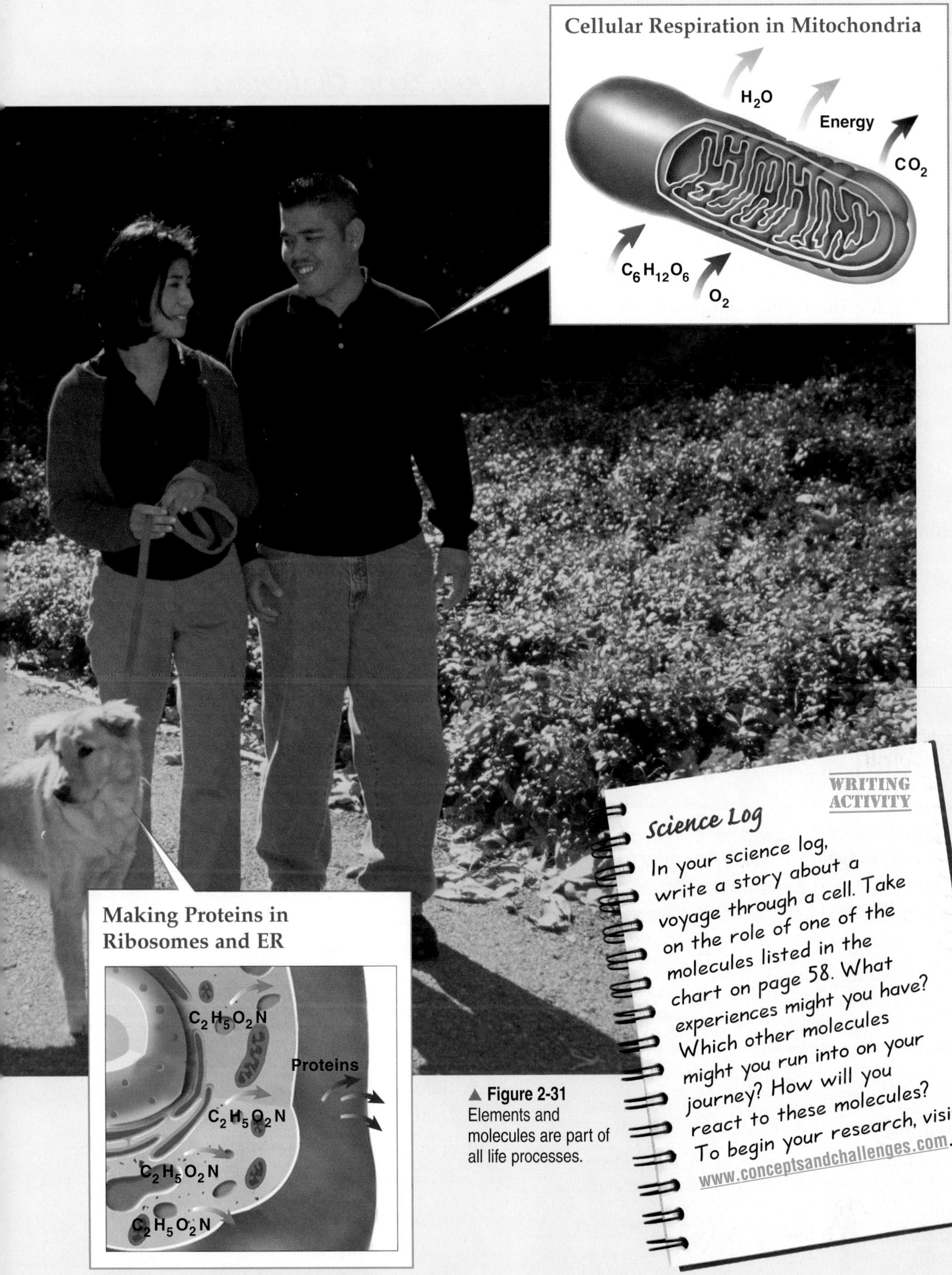


▲ **Figure 2-31** Elements and molecules are part of all life processes.

**WRITING ACTIVITY**

## Science Log

In your science log, write a story about a voyage through a cell. Take on the role of one of the molecules listed in the chart on page 58. What experiences might you have? Which other molecules might you run into on your journey? How will you react to these molecules? To begin your research, visit www.conceptsandchallenges.com.

# Chapter 2 Challenges

## Chapter Summary

**Lesson 2-1**

- A **microscope** is a tool that uses lenses to magnify images.

**Lesson 2-2**

- The cell theory states that all living things are made up of **cells**. Cells are basic units of structure and function. Cells only come from other living cells.

**Lessons 2-3 and 2-4**

- The three main parts of the cell are the **cell membrane,** the **nucleus,** and the **cytoplasm.**
- **Organelles** are small structures in the cytoplasm. Each organelle has a special job to do, such as releasing energy, transporting or packaging materials, storing nutrients, or making proteins.

**Lesson 2-5**

- Plant cells have a **cell wall,** whereas animal cells do not. Plant cells usually have a larger vacuole than animal cells do. Plant cells contain **chloroplasts.**

**Lesson 2-6**

- **Unicellular** organisms have only one cell. **Multicellular** organisms are made of more than one cell.
- Cells come in different sizes and shapes. The shape of a cell is usually related to its job or function.

**Lesson 2-7**

- Materials can move in and out of cells by **passive transport** or **active transport.**
- **Diffusion** and **osmosis** are both forms of passive transport.

**Lesson 2-8**

- During **photosynthesis,** plants use light energy to make food.
- During **cellular respiration,** oxygen is used to release the energy found in food. **Fermentation** is a type of cellular respiration that does not require oxygen.

**Lesson 2-9**

- Cells reproduce by a process called cell division. During cell division, each chromosome makes an exact copy of itself.
- **Mitosis** occurs before cell division.

## Key Term Challenges

active transport (p. 50)
cell (p. 40)
cell membrane (p. 42)
cellulose (p. 46)
cell wall (p. 46)
chlorophyll (p. 46)
chloroplast (p. 46)
chromatin (p. 56)
chromosome (p. 56)
cytoplasm (p. 42)
daughter cell (p. 56)
diffusion (p. 50)
endoplasmic reticulum (p. 44)
energy (p. 54)
fermentation (p. 54)
glucose (p. 54)
Golgi body (p. 44)
guard cell (p. 48)
lens (p. 38)
lysosome (p. 44)
microscope (p. 38)
mitochondrion (p. 44)
mitosis (p. 56)
multicellular (p. 48)
nuclear membrane (p. 42)
nucleus (p. 42)
organelle (p. 44)
osmosis (p. 50)
passive transport (p. 50)
photosynthesis (p. 54)
pseudopod (p. 48)
ribosome (p. 44)
stoma (p. 48)
unicellular (p. 48)
vacuole (p. 44)

MATCHING **Write the Key Term from above that best matches each description.**

1. cell part that makes proteins
2. control center of a cell
3. structure found in plant cells that carries out photosynthesis
4. outer part of a plant cell
5. storage spaces found in the cytoplasm
6. material that makes up the cell wall

FILL IN **Write the Key Term from above that best completes each sentence.**

7. The organelles are suspended in the ___________ of the cell.
8. Osmosis is a special type of ___________.
9. Before mitosis, the ___________ duplicate themselves.
10. If an organism is not unicellular, it must be ___________.

## Content Challenges TEST PREP

**MULTIPLE CHOICE Write the letter of the term or phrase that best completes each statement.**

1. The first person to observe cells was
   - **a.** Theodor Schwann.
   - **b.** Matthias Schleiden.
   - **c.** Anton van Leeuwenhoek.
   - **d.** Robert Hooke.
2. The main parts of a cell are the cell membrane, the nucleus, and the
   - **a.** plasma.
   - **b.** cytoplasm.
   - **c.** mitochondria.
   - **d.** ribosomes.
3. Cell structures that act as "storage bins" are
   - **a.** mitochondria.
   - **b.** ribosomes.
   - **c.** vacuoles.
   - **d.** organelles.
4. A microscope that uses two or more lenses is called a
   - **a.** magnifying glass.
   - **b.** simple microscope.
   - **c.** compound microscope.
   - **d.** telescope.
5. One of the functions of the cell wall is to
   - **a.** get rid of oxygen.
   - **b.** give the cell its shape.
   - **c.** give the cell its color.
   - **d.** move water through the cell.
6. Cells only come from
   - **a.** the air.
   - **b.** other cells.
   - **c.** oxygen.
   - **d.** cork.
7. When a cell divides, each chromosome makes a copy that is
   - **a.** identical to the original.
   - **b.** slightly different from the original.
   - **c.** very different from the original.
   - **d.** a mutation of the original.
8. Cells that carry messages from one part of the body to another are
   - **a.** guard cells.
   - **b.** blood cells.
   - **c.** nerve cells.
   - **d.** muscle cells.
9. During cellular respiration, glucose and oxygen combine to release energy and to form
   - **a.** water and carbon dioxide.
   - **b.** cellulose.
   - **c.** chlorophyll.
   - **d.** carbon and nitrogen.
10. Diffusion and osmosis are both examples of
    - **a.** replication.
    - **b.** mitosis.
    - **c.** passive transport.
    - **d.** active transport.

**TRUE/FALSE Write *true* if the statement is true. If the statement is false, change the underlined term to make the statement true.**

11. The cell membrane surrounds the nucleus of the cell.
12. The Golgi bodies package and send materials throughout the cell.
13. The organelles responsible for releasing energy from food inside a cell are the mitochondria.
14. Chlorophyll is the material that makes food in animal cells.

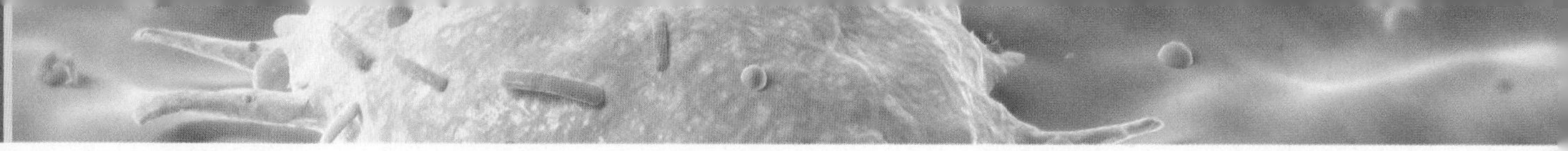

## *Concept Challenges* TEST PREP

**WRITTEN RESPONSE** **Answer each of the following questions in complete sentences.**

1. **INFER:** Why do you think little was known about cells before the invention of the microscope?
2. **RELATE:** Why do you think that organelles can be compared to machines in a factory?
3. **CONTRAST:** What are three differences between plant cells and animal cells?
4. **EXPLAIN:** What makes osmosis a special kind of diffusion?
5. **CONTRAST:** How does plant-cell division differ from animal-cell division?

**INTERPRETING A DIAGRAM** **Use the diagram in Figure 2-32 to complete the following questions.**

6. What are the names of the structures that are identified *A–F* in the diagram?
7. What is the function of the structure labeled *A*?
8. In which structure does cellular respiration take place?
9. In which structure are chromosomes located?
10. What is the function of the structure labeled *C*?
11. What substances are contained in the structure labeled *B*?
12. Is this a plant cell or an animal cell? How can you tell?

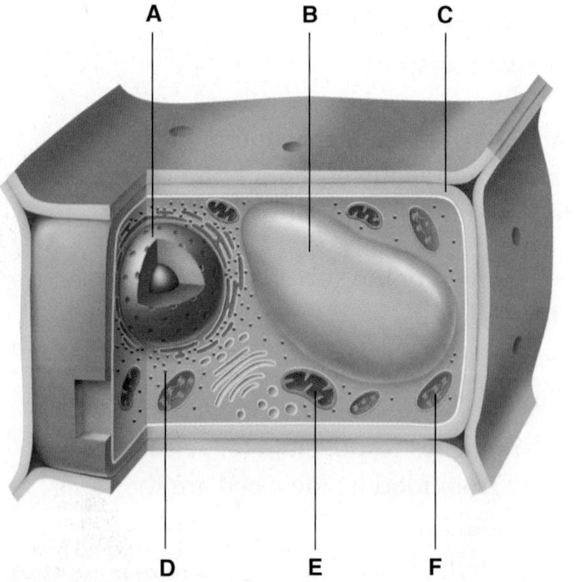


▲ **Figure 2-32** You can tell if this is a plant cell or an animal cell by looking at its organelles.

# Chapter 3 Heredity and Genetics

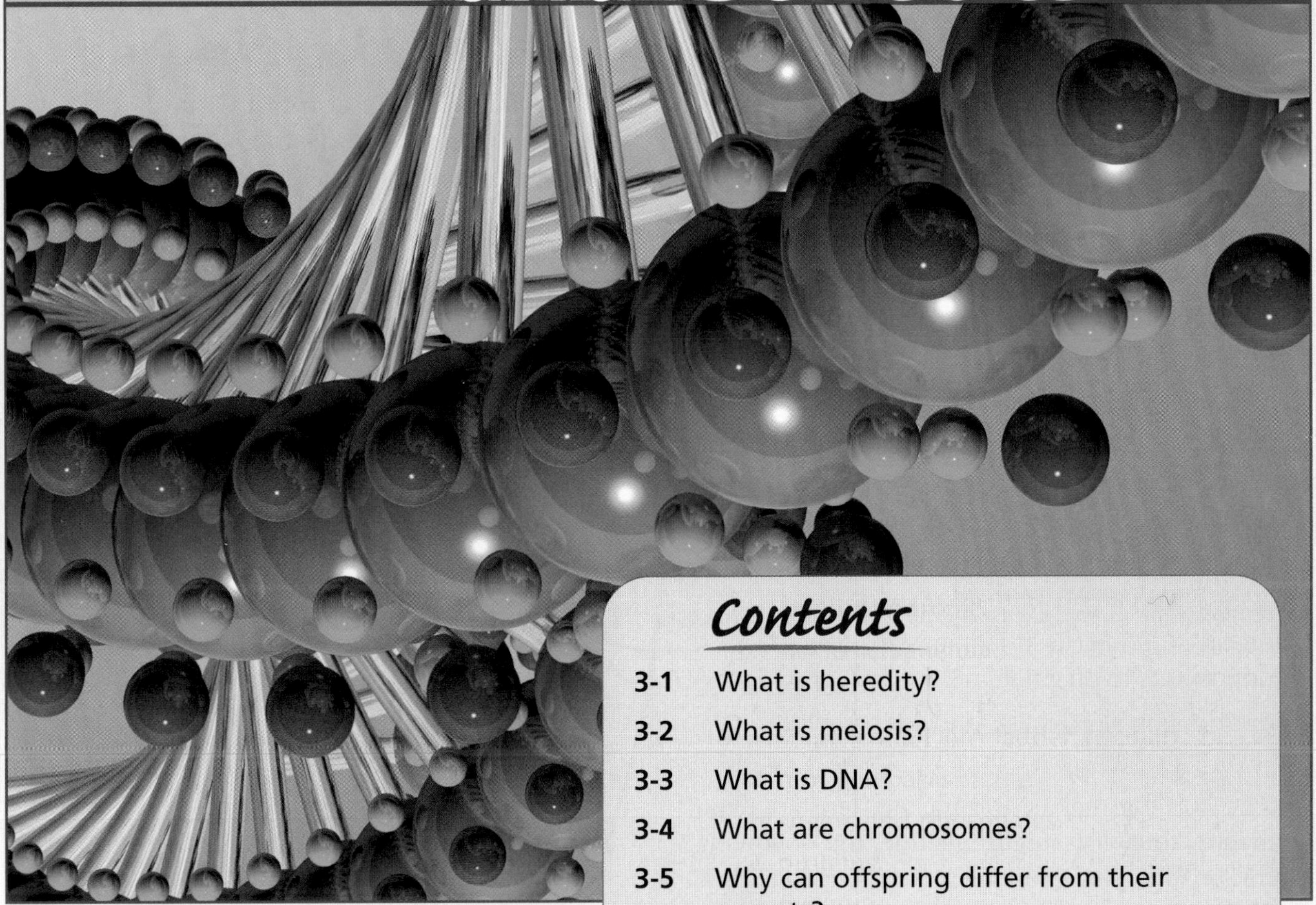

▲ **Figure 3-1** Computer-generated image of DNA molecule

DNA is found in all living things. This large molecule stores genetic information. In 1953, scientists made a model to show the structure of DNA. The shape of DNA is like a twisted ladder and is called a double helix. One molecule of DNA can contain millions of atoms. When unraveled, there are about 6 feet of DNA in each of your body's cells. The discovery of DNA is said to be one of the greatest advances in science.

▶What kind of information do you think is stored in DNA?

## Contents

# 3-1 What is heredity?

## INVESTIGATE

### *Comparing Your Traits*

HANDS-ON ACTIVITY

1. Work in groups of 3 to 5 students.
2. Make a list of about five characteristics that describe your appearance. Include characteristics such as hair color, eye color, and height in your list.
3. Compare your list with those of the rest of your group.

**THINK ABOUT IT:** Do you have any characteristics in common with the rest of your group? Was your list identical to that of another student?

### *Objective*

Explain why offspring have some of the traits of their parents but not all.

### *Key Terms*

**trait:** characteristic

**inherited** (ihn-HEHR-ih-tuhd) **trait:** trait that is passed from parents to their offspring

**heredity** (huh-REHD-ih-tee)**:** passing of traits from parents to offspring

**genetics** (juh-NEHT-ihks)**:** study of heredity

**Traits** You can make a list of characteristics about yourself. Your list might include the following characteristics: blue eyes, black hair, 5 feet tall. It is unlikely that another student would list the same exact characteristics. This is because each person is unique. The characteristics you might include on your list are called **traits**. Traits are the characteristics of an organism.

1 **DEFINE:** What are traits?

**Identifying Traits** You may look like your mother, your father, or a mixture of both your parents. Children often look like their parents or grandparents in some way.

There is a reason for this. During fertilization, male and female sex cells join together. Each of these sex cells contains material that affects the development of the offspring. Traits that are passed from parents to their offspring are called **inherited traits**. Eye color is an example of an inherited trait.

▲ **Figure 3-2** These children have inherited traits from each parent.

2 **INFER:** How was your eye color determined?

**Heredity** When living things produce offspring, they pass on traits to them. The passing of traits from parents to their offspring is called **heredity**. The field of biology that studies heredity is called **genetics**.

▲ **Figure 3-3** The kittens in this picture show a variety of traits, such as their different markings.

One of the first people to study heredity was Gregor Mendel, an Austrian monk. Mendel studied how traits in pea plants are passed from one generation to the next. Gregor Mendel often is called the Father of Genetics.

**3** **RELATE:** What is the relationship between traits and genetics?

## CHECKING CONCEPTS

1. The characteristics of an organism are called __________.
2. An example of an inherited trait is __________.
3. Inherited traits are passed from __________ to their offspring.
4. One of the first people to study inherited traits was __________.
5. The field of biology that studies heredity is called __________.

## THINKING CRITICALLY

6. **INFER:** Why do brothers and sisters often have similar traits?
7. **EXPLAIN:** Why is Gregor Mendel called the Father of Genetics?
8. **INFER:** Why do you think the study of genetics is important?

## INTERPRETING VISUALS

*Use Figures 3-2 and 3-3 to answer the following questions.*

9. **IDENTIFY:** What traits do the mother and daughter in Figure 3-2 have in common?
10. **ANALYZE:** Which of the offspring in Figure 3-2 most resembles the father?
11. **IDENTIFY:** Identify three traits of the cats shown in Figure 3-3.
12. **PREDICT:** What traits do you think the father of the kittens might have?

## *Real-Life Science*

## THE HEREDITY OF TWINS

Twins are siblings that are born at the same time. There are two types of twins, identical and fraternal (fruh-TER-nuhl). Identical twins develop from one egg, fertilized by a single sperm cell. After the egg is fertilized, it splits in two. These two cells become two identical embryos. Because identical twins develop from one original cell, they are genetically identical. They inherit the exact same traits. They are always both girls or both boys. It can be very difficult to tell identical twins apart.

▲ **Figure 3-4** Identical twins have the same genetic material.

Fraternal twins are more common than identical twins. These twins develop from two separate eggs that have been fertilized by two separate sperm cells. Each embryo develops on its own. Fraternal twins are genetically different from each other. They may even be brother and sister. Fraternal twins are no different than siblings born at different times.

**Thinking Critically** Why do you think fraternal twins are more common than identical twins?

# 3-2 What is meiosis?

## *Objectives*

Define gamete. Describe the type of cell division called meiosis.

## *Key Terms*

**sperm cell:** male reproductive cell

**egg cell:** female reproductive cell

**gamete** (GAM-eet)**:** reproductive cell

**meiosis** (my-OH-sihs)**:** type of cell division that produces gametes

**Gametes** Every body cell of an animal contains the same number of chromosomes. **Sperm cells** and **egg cells** are reproductive cells. Reproductive cells are also called **gametes**. Gametes develop from special cells in the body. During the formation of gametes, the number of chromosomes changes. It is cut in half. Each gamete contains only half as many chromosomes as a body cell. The process by which gametes form is called **meiosis**. The cells formed by meiosis have half the number of chromosomes as body cells.

| Number of Chromosomes in Various Organisms | | |
|---|---|---|
| **Organism** | **Body Cells** | **Gametes** |
| Fruit fly | 8 | 4 |
| Bull frog | 26 | 13 |
| Human | 46 | 23 |

▲ **Figure 3-5** Gametes contain half the number of chromosomes as body cells.

**1** **COMPARE:** What is the relationship between the number of chromosomes in body cells and gametes?

**Meiosis** The process of meiosis occurs in two parts, meiosis I and meiosis II. The phases of each part are similar to those in mitosis. The difference is that meiosis includes two cell divisions instead of one. Look at the stages shown in Figure 3-6.

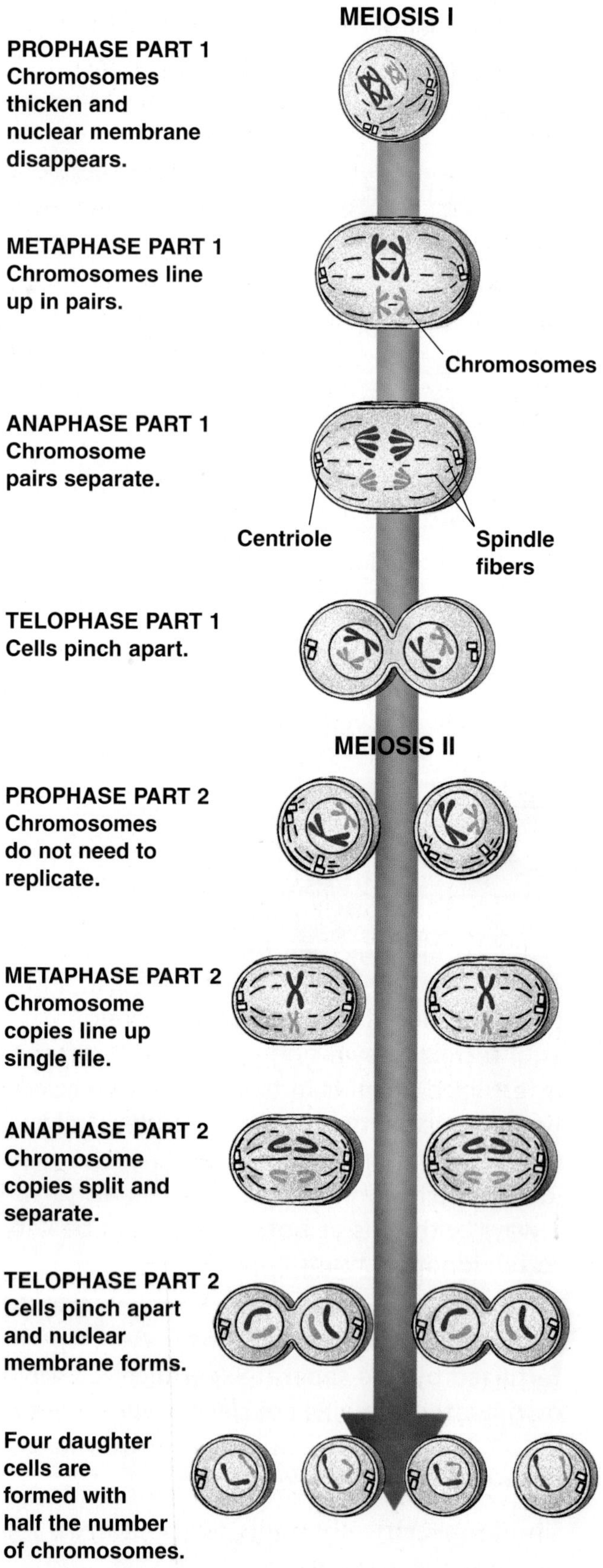


▲ **Figure 3-6** The phases of meiosis

Meiosis I is similar to mitosis except that the chromosome copies do not split. Instead, the paired chromosomes separate. The result is still two daughter cells. However, each daughter cell contains a set of chromosomes that is different from the other.

The stages of meiosis II are the same as meiosis I, but the end result is different. The daughter cells formed from meiosis II contain only half the number of chromosomes compared to the number of chromosomes in normal body cells. These new cells become gametes.

The body cell of a fruit fly contains eight chromosomes. After meiosis, there are only four chromosomes in each gamete. Your body cells contain 46 chromosomes. After meiosis, there are only 23 chromosomes in each gamete that forms.

2 **EXPLAIN:** Why do gametes contain half the number of chromosomes as body cells?

## CHECKING CONCEPTS

1. All human body cells contain __________ chromosomes.
2. Sperm cells and egg cells are __________.
3. The process that reduces the number of chromosomes in a cell by one-half is __________.
4. Meiosis occurs only in the formation of __________.

## THINKING CRITICALLY

5. **INFER:** How many chromosomes does a human egg cell contain? Explain.
6. **PREDICT:** What would happen if the chromosomes did not move to opposite sides of the nucleus before the cell pinched apart?
7. **EXPLAIN:** Why is it important for gametes to have half as many chromosomes as normal body cells?
8. **COMPARE:** How are mitosis and meiosis similar?
9. **CALCULATE:** How many chromosomes would the gametes of an organism with 14 chromosomes in its body cells have?

*Real-Life Science*

## NONDISJUNCTION

During meiosis, chromosome pairs separate to form gametes. Usually, a gamete receives one chromosome from each pair. Sometimes, however, the chromosome pairs do not separate correctly. This condition is called nondisjunction (nahn-dihs-JUHNK-shuhn).

When nondisjunction occurs, both chromosomes in a pair go to the same gamete. As a result, one gamete has too many chromosomes and the other gamete has too few. If either of these gametes unites with a normal gamete during fertilization, the organism does not develop properly.

There are several conditions that result from nondisjunction. One of these conditions is Down syndrome. The body cells of a person with Down syndrome contain 47 chromosomes instead of 46. People with Down syndrome can lead productive lives, but they usually have some degree of mental disability.

▲ **Figure 3-7** A Special Olympian with Down syndrome

**Thinking Critically** Would a person with 45 chromosomes in his body cells have nondisjunction? Explain.

# 3-3 What is DNA?

***Objectives***

Describe the molecular makeup of DNA. Explain the role of DNA in living organisms.

***Key Terms***

**DNA:** large molecule contained in chromosomes

**replication:** (rehp-lih-KAY-shuhn): process by which DNA is duplicated

**protein synthesis:** process by which proteins are made

**RNA:** molecule used in the making of proteins

**Discovery of DNA** After the discovery that chromosomes contain hereditary information, scientists wondered what molecules make up chromosomes. Scientists found that chromosomes are made of large molecules called **DNA**. DNA stands for deoxyribonucleic (dee-AHKS-ee-ry-boh-noo-KLAY-ihk) acid.

The structure of DNA was discovered in 1953 by an American scientist, James Watson, and a British scientist, Francis Crick. Watson and Crick built a model of a DNA molecule. Their model, shown in Figure 3-8, was based on the research of other scientists as well as their own discoveries. The model created by Watson and Crick is considered one of the greatest contributions to the field of genetics.

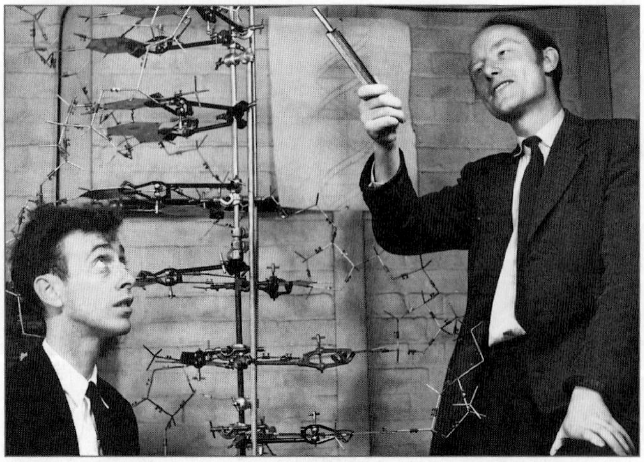

▲ **Figure 3-8** James Watson and Francis Crick

1 **DEFINE:** What is DNA?

**Structure of DNA** Watson and Crick's model showed that a molecule of DNA looks like a twisted ladder. They found that the sides of this ladder are made up of sugars and other molecules called phosphates. The model also showed that the steps of the ladder are made up of nitrogen bases. There are four kinds of nitrogen bases. Each base always pairs with another specific base to form the steps of the ladder. Look at the key shown in Figure 3-9. It shows the four nitrogen bases and each base's pair.

2 **DESCRIBE:** How are nitrogen bases arranged in a DNA molecule?

**Replication** During mitosis, new body cells are created. The new daughter cells that are formed need to have the same number of chromosomes as the parent. Therefore, each chromosome must double to form two identical chromosomes. To do this, the DNA molecule in the chromosome must make a copy of itself. This process is called **replication**. The DNA ladder breaks between the nitrogen bases in the steps. This is like unzipping a zipper. Then, the new nitrogen bases pair up and attach to each half of the ladder. The result is two new DNA strands that are exact copies of the original DNA molecule.

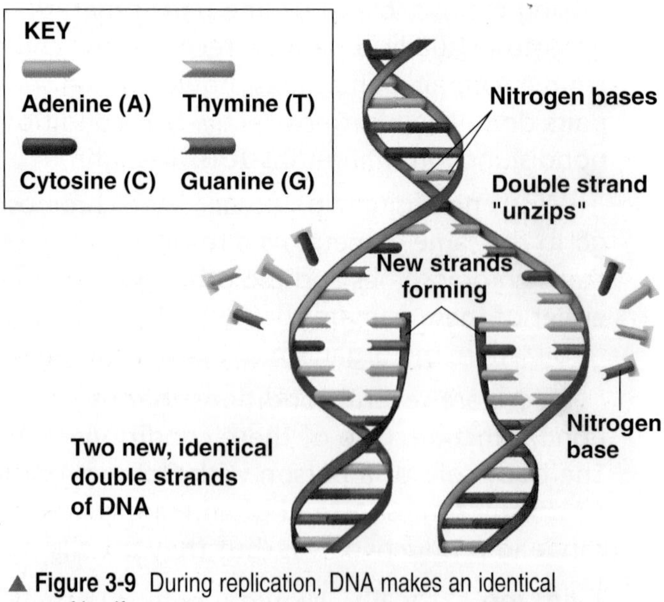


▲ **Figure 3-9** During replication, DNA makes an identical copy of itself.

3 **DEFINE:** What is replication?

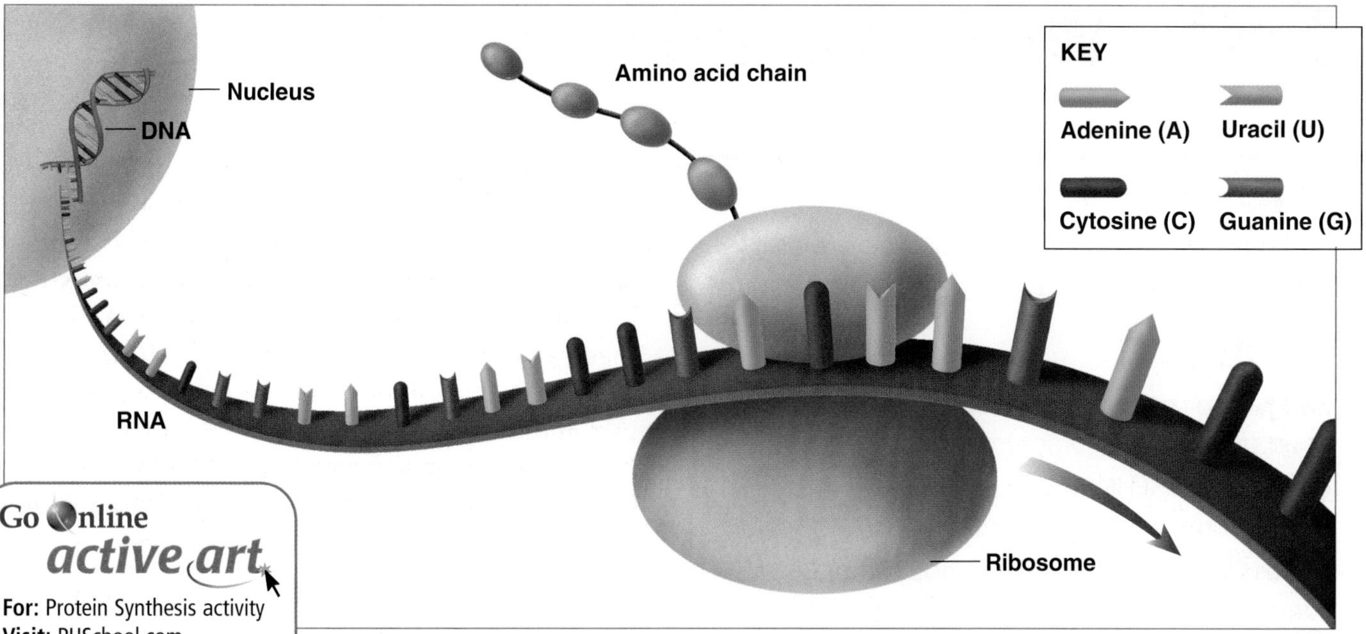


Go Online
*active art*
**For:** Protein Synthesis activity
**Visit:** PHSchool.com
**Web Code:** cep-3034

▲ **Figure 3-10** Protein synthesis occurs at the ribosomes of the cell.

**The Role of DNA** A single DNA molecule, or ladder, can have thousands of steps, or base pairs. The number and arrangement of these steps form a genetic "code." This code determines the kind of gene that forms. Different genes determine the different kinds of inherited traits of an organism.

4 **EXPLAIN:** What determines the inherited traits of an organism?

**Protein Synthesis** A DNA molecule controls an organism's traits by producing certain proteins at certain times. This process is called **protein synthesis**. Proteins are composed of molecules called amino acids. They are made by the ribosomes of cells. The DNA code is located inside the nucleus of the cell. A special molecule is needed to carry the code from the nucleus to the ribosome. That molecule is called **RNA**, or ribonucleic (ry-boh-noo-KLAY-ihk) acid.

RNA differs from DNA in several ways. RNA has only one side of the ladder shape. It also contains the nitrogen base uracil instead of thymine. RNA copies the code from the DNA strand and then carries it to the ribosome. Then, the RNA acts as a pattern on which the proteins can be built. The ribosome reads the RNA strand and attaches the correct amino acids. The amino acids link together, forming a protein. This process is shown in Figure 3-10.

5 **CONTRAST:** How is RNA different from DNA?

## ✓ CHECKING CONCEPTS

1. What is the basic molecule in chromosomes?
2. What is protein synthesis?
3. With which base does guanine always pair?
4. By which process does DNA duplicate itself?

## THINKING CRITICALLY

5. **PREDICT:** Suppose the DNA in the chromosomes of a cell did not replicate. What effect would this have on the daughter cells?
6. **HYPOTHESIZE:** A plant has a mistake in its DNA code for a certain protein that makes up the cell membrane. What effect might this have on the plant?

### Web InfoSearch

**Rosalind Franklin** Watson and Crick were not the only scientists working with DNA. They based their discovery on the work of another British scientist, Rosalind Franklin.

**SEARCH:** Use the Internet to find out more about Rosalind Franklin. Write a short biography of her. Start your search at www.conceptsandchallenges.com. Some key search words are **DNA** and **Rosalind Franklin.**

# 3-4 What are chromosomes?

### *Objective*

Describe how genes and chromosomes are involved in heredity.

### *Key Terms*

**karyotype** (KAIR-ee-oh-typ)**:** organized display of an organism's chromosomes

**centromere** (SEHN-troh-meer)**:** point of a chromosome where two parts meet

**genes** (JEENZ)**:** parts of a chromosome that control inherited traits

**allele** (uh-LEEL)**:** one of two or more forms of a particular gene

**Chromosomes** Fine, threadlike structures called chromosomes are located in a cell's nucleus. They control heredity. Scientists often study chromosomes by looking at a **karyotype.** A karyotype is a display of an organism's chromosomes, organized by size and shape. Sometimes the chromosomes in a karyotype are numbered.

1 **DEFINE:** What are chromosomes?

**Chromosome Structure** Every chromosome is composed of material called chromatin. Chromatin is made of very long, thin strands of DNA. These strands are wrapped around special proteins that help to keep the chromatin wrapped tightly together in an X shape. Each part, or side, of the X-shaped chromosome is called a chromatid. Chromatids are exact copies of each other. They are held together at a region called the **centromere.** Chromatin is not usually found in this form. It only forms into tightly coiled chromosomes when the cell is about to divide.

2 **DESCRIBE:** What is the structure of a chromosome?

**Genes** A **gene** is a part of the chromosome that controls inherited traits. Each gene is located at a certain place on the chromosome. Each gene affects a different trait. Genes determine your eye color, hair color, and many other characteristics. Genes also control the life processes of your cells.

3 **DEFINE:** What are genes?

**Chromosome Pairs** In organisms that carry out sexual reproduction, chromosomes exist in pairs. Chromosomes come in pairs because a version of

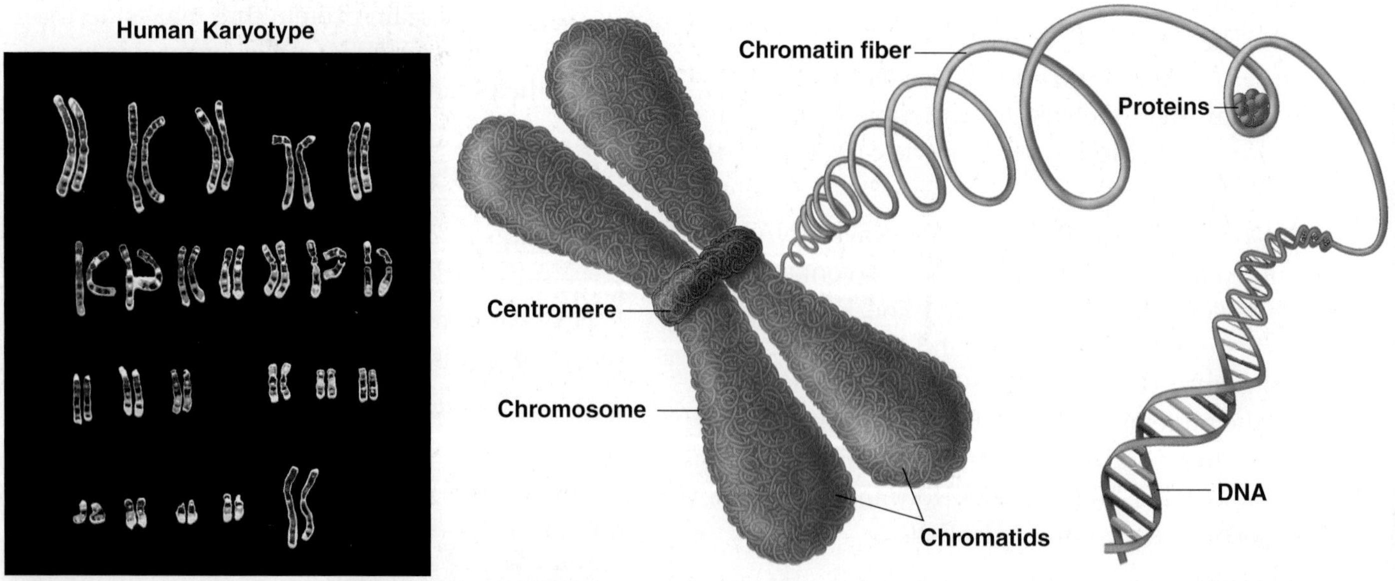


▲ **Figure 3-11** Chromosomes are made of strands of DNA coiled together. A karyotype shows the size and shape of all an organism's chromosomes.

the same chromosome is contributed by each parent to the offspring. For example, humans usually have 23 pairs, or 46 chromosomes all together. Look back at Figure 3-11. Notice that the chromosomes are arranged in pairs. Also notice the similar size between two chromosomes of the same pair.

**4 EXPLAIN:** Why do chromosomes come in pairs?

**Alleles** Because chromosomes come in pairs, most genes have two or more forms for each trait. **Alleles** are different versions of the same gene. For example, plants may have an allele for pink flowers or an allele for white flowers. The gene for eye color in humans has several different alleles. In animals, one allele may produce black fur while another produces brown fur. Alleles for a specific gene are always found in the same location on the same chromosome. The matching allele for a certain trait will be in the same location on the other chromosome in the pair.

**5 INFER:** What do you think are the possible alleles for eye color in humans?

## CHECKING CONCEPTS

1. Where are chromosomes located?
2. When does chromatin form into chromosomes?
3. Where are genes located?
4. What controls the life processes of cells?
5. What are alleles?

## THINKING CRITICALLY

6. **RELATE:** What is the relationship between genes and alleles?
7. **INFER:** Why do you think a doctor would be interested in looking at a person's karyotype?

## BUILDING LANGUAGE ARTS SKILLS

***Writing*** Fold a sheet of paper in half. On one side, list as many of your own traits as you can. On the other side, list the traits of a brother, sister, or parent. Use this information to write a report about your family. Include similarities and differences within your family. Explain why these similarities and differences may have occurred.

## *How Do They Know That?*

### JUMPING GENES

▲ **Figure 3-12** Barbara McClintock discovered the genes that cause the speckled kernels in this ear of corn.

Barbara McClintock was an American plant geneticist. For more than 60 years, she studied the inherited traits of corn. Dr. McClintock was especially interested in the color of corn kernels. She identified the genes that control this trait.

In 1931, Dr. McClintock made a startling discovery. She found that some genes "jump," or change position on a chromosome. The "jumping" gene caused changes in the traits controlled by the genes next to the place where it landed. For example, when a "jumping" gene landed next to the gene that controlled kernel color, the corn grew speckled kernels.

Dr. McClintock announced her results in 1951. Most scientists at this time did not take her work seriously. They thought genes always remained in a definite position on a chromosome. It was not until the 1970s that other scientists began to take note of her conclusions. In 1983, more than 50 years after she made her discoveries, Dr. McClintock received the Nobel Prize.

**Thinking Critically** How could Dr. McClintock tell where "jumping" genes occurred?

# 3-5 Why can offspring differ from their parents?

## *Objective*

Explain the difference between dominant and recessive traits.

## *Key Terms*

**homozygous** (hoh-moh-ZY-guhs)**:** having two like genes for the same trait

**heterozygous** (heht-uhr-oh-ZY-guhs)**:** having two unlike genes for the same trait

**dominant gene:** gene whose trait always shows itself

**recessive** (rih-SEHS-ihv) **gene:** gene of a trait that is hidden when the dominant gene is present

**Genes and Traits** Gregor Mendel hypothesized that inherited "factors" produced certain traits. These factors are now called genes. Mendel based his hypothesis on the pea plants he was studying. Some of the plants were tall. Others were short. Mendel decided there must be a gene for tallness and another gene for shortness. The trait of height for a pea plant is determined by two genes, one from each parent. Each trait of an organism is determined by at least one gene from each parent.

▲ **Figure 3-13** Gregor Mendel

**1 DESCRIBE:** How are traits determined?

**Homozygous Plants** Mendel found that one kind of tall pea plant always had tall offspring. These plants have two tall genes, one from each parent. Mendel called these plants **homozygous** tall. An organism is homozygous if it has two like genes for a given trait. Mendel found that some short pea plants always have short offspring. These plants have two short genes. Mendel called these plants homozygous short.

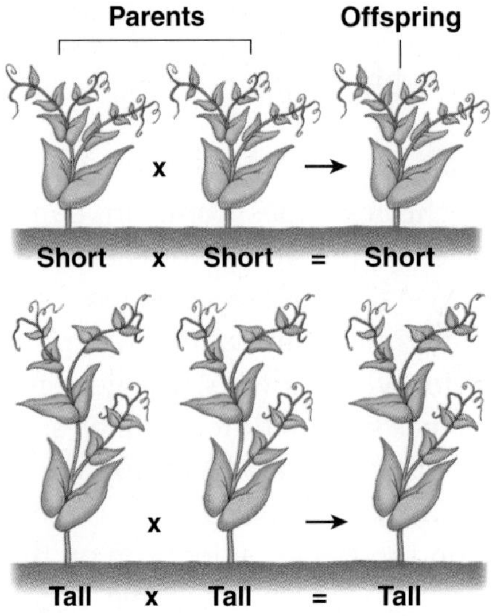


◀ **Figure 3-14** Homozygous plants have two of the same genes for a trait.

**2 IDENTIFY:** What genes does a homozygous short pea plant always have?

**Heterozygous Plants** Mendel wondered what the offspring of one homozygous tall parent and one homozygous short parent would look like. He crossed a homozygous tall pea plant with a homozygous short pea plant. All of the offspring were tall. They had received a tall gene from the tall parent and a short gene from the short parent. They had one tall gene and one short gene but grew up tall. Mendel called these plants **heterozygous.** Organisms that have two unlike genes for a trait are heterozygous for that trait.

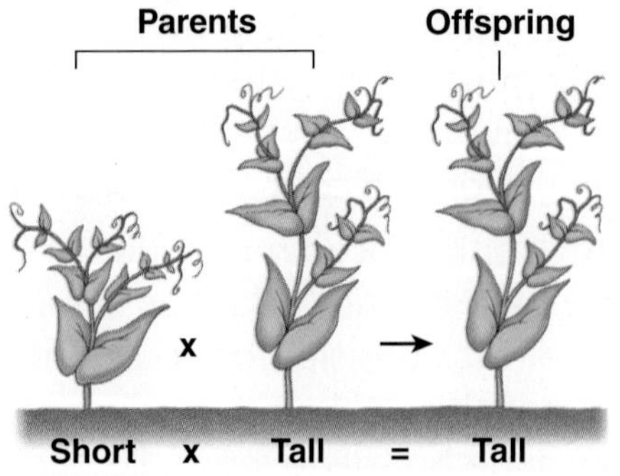


◀ **Figure 3-15** Heterozygous plants have two different genes for a trait.

**3 CONTRAST:** What is the difference between a homozygous and a heterozygous plant?

**Dominant Genes** Mendel found that in a heterozygous organism, one gene always shows its trait. The other gene is hidden. Mendel called the gene that always shows itself the **dominant gene.** He called the hidden gene a **recessive gene.** The tall gene is dominant in pea plants. The short gene is recessive. That is why plants with one tall gene and one short gene are always tall. Only plants with two short genes will be short.

4 **COMPARE:** What is the difference between a dominant and a recessive gene?

## CHECKING CONCEPTS

1. A pea plant with two tall genes is called __________.
2. A heterozygous tall pea plant has one tall gene and one __________ gene.
3. The gene whose trait always shows itself is called the __________ gene.
4. The recessive gene for height in pea plants is __________.
5. A homozygous short pea plant has two __________ genes.

## THINKING CRITICALLY

6. **RELATE:** What combinations of genes could a tall pea plant have?
7. **PREDICT:** Could a short pea plant be heterozygous? Explain your answer.
8. **PREDICT:** One pea plant is homozygous for yellow seeds. The other pea plant is homozygous for green seeds. Yellow is the dominant color of seeds. What color seeds will the offspring have?
9. **RELATE:** The prefix hetero means "different." How does this relate to the term heterozygous?

## BUILDING SCIENCE SKILLS

***Researching*** Gregor Mendel often is called the Father of Genetics. Use library references to find information about Gregor Mendel's life. Find out what other traits Mendel studied besides the ones you learned about in this lesson. Make a poster that illustrates Mendel's work. Present your poster to the class.

## *Hands-On Activity*

### IDENTIFYING DOMINANT GENES IN CORN

*You will need four ears of hybrid corn, a marker, a pencil, and paper.*

▲ **STEP 2** Count the number of kernels of one color.

1. Observe an ear of hybrid corn. On your paper, list the different colors of kernels present.
2. Begin counting the number of kernels of the first color. Use the marker to mark which corn kernels you have already counted. This will prevent you from counting a kernel twice. Record the number on your paper.
3. Repeat Step 2 for the second color.
4. Work with a partner to find the total number of each kernel color for three more ears of corn. Record the numbers on your paper.

### Practicing Your Skills

5. **IDENTIFY:** Which kernel color occurred more frequently?
6. **CALCULATE:** Using the results of the entire class, determine the percentage that each color occurs. (Hint: Add the numbers of one color and divide by the total number of kernels.)
7. **HYPOTHESIZE:** Which color do you think is dominant in this type of corn?

# 3-6 How do genes combine in offspring?

## INVESTIGATE

### Modeling Chance in Heredity

**HANDS-ON ACTIVITY**

1. Place a piece of tape on both sides of a penny and a nickel.
2. Use a small piece of paper to label one side of each coin with an "E" to represent the dominant gene. Label the other side of each coin with an "e" to represent the recessive gene.
3. Flip the two coins together 50 times. Record the gene combinations that result from each flip.
4. Organize your results into a chart showing the number of "EE," "ee," and "Ee" results.

**THINK ABOUT IT:** What percentage of the flips represent heterozygous offspring?

### *Objective*

Identify what causes differences in the traits of parents and their offspring.

### *Key Term*

**Punnett square:** chart that shows possible gene combinations

**Gene Symbols** Organisms have at least two genes for most traits. They usually receive at least one gene from each parent. Symbols are used to represent the combinations of genes. An uppercase letter represents a dominant trait. A lowercase letter represents a recessive trait. In humans, the gene for black hair is dominant. The symbol for this gene is B. The gene for brown hair is recessive. The symbol for this gene is b.

**1 EXPLAIN:** What does a capital letter show about a gene?

**Predicting Traits** Suppose a father is homozygous for black hair. His genes are BB. Suppose a mother is homozygous for brown hair. Her genes are bb. What color hair will the offspring have? One way to predict the hair color trait is to use a **Punnett square**. A Punnett square is a chart used to show possible gene combinations and the probability of each combination occurring.

You can use a Punnett square to predict the hair color of the offspring in the previous example. Draw a box with four squares in it, as shown in Figure 3-16. In Step 1, write the genes for black hair (BB) from the father across the top. In Step 2, write the genes for brown hair (bb) from the mother down the side. In Step 3, fill in each square with a gene from the father. In Step 4, fill in each square with a gene from the mother. All the offspring are heterozygous dominant.

**2 OBSERVE:** What color hair will all the offspring shown in Figure 3-16 have?

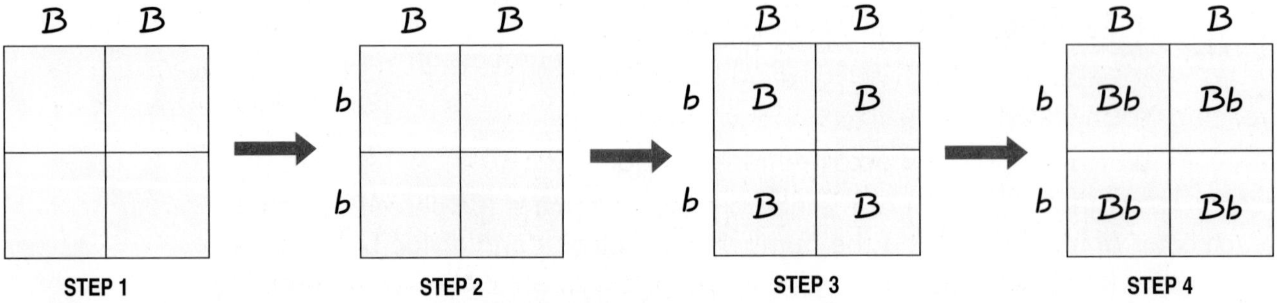


▲ **Figure 3-16** A Punnett square is used to show possible gene combinations.

**Combining Heterozygous Genes** Figure 3-17 shows what happens when both parents are heterozygous for a trait. The Punnett square can be used to predict the possible genetic makeup of their offspring. There is a 1 out of 4, or 25 percent, chance the offspring will be homozygous dominant (BB). There is a 2 out of 4, or 50 percent, chance they will be heterozygous dominant (Bb). There is a 1 out of 4, or 25 percent, chance they will be homozygous recessive (bb). This means that there is a 25 percent chance the offspring will have brown hair.

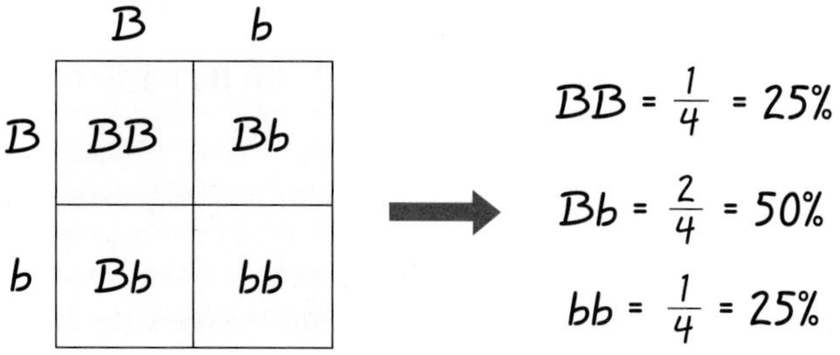


▲ **Figure 3-17** A cross between two heterozygous parents

3 **LIST:** What are three possible gene combinations that the offspring of heterozygous parents can have?

## CHECKING CONCEPTS

1. A capital letter always represents a __________ gene.
2. The recessive gene for brown hair in humans is shown by the symbol __________.
3. When one parent is homozygous dominant and the other parent is homozygous recessive, their offspring are all heterozygous __________.
4. If both parents are heterozygous, then there is a 50 percent chance their offspring will have __________ traits.

## THINKING CRITICALLY

5. **ANALYZE:** Why is it impossible for parents with the genes Bb and BB for hair color to have a child with brown hair?
6. **PREDICT:** A homozygous white (bb) guinea pig is crossed with a homozygous black (BB) guinea pig. Predict the possible colors of their offspring.

## *Science and Technology*

### HUMAN GENOME PROJECT

In June 2000, scientists completed a draft sequence of the Human Genome. Many scientists consider this one of the biggest milestones in scientific history. The goal of this project was to identify all of the nearly 30,000 genes found in human chromosomes. Another goal was to find the sequence of the millions of base pairs that make up the genes.

The Human Genome map provides detailed DNA information to biologists, genetic counselors, and doctors. This information includes the location of genes that either cause disease or make a person more likely to get a disease. The information may help researchers find cures for genetic diseases, such as cancer and diabetes.

It has been said that the information found by this project would take up the space of 200 telephone books of 1,000 pages each. A computer database has been developed to keep track of all the information gained by the various scientists who contributed to the project.

**Thinking Critically** Why do you think the completion of the Human Genome Project was considered such an important accomplishment?

| Chromosome Number | Diseases Linked to Chromosome |
|---|---|
| 3 | Ovarian cancer<br>Night blindness<br>Heart disease |
| 6 | Dyslexia<br>Asthma<br>Obesity |
| 11 | Deafness<br>Osteoporosis<br>Diabetes |
| 18 | Myopia<br>Parkinson's disease |
| X | Migraine<br>Hemophilia<br>Heart disease |

▲ **Figure 3-18** Scientists have discovered the approximate location of many disease-causing genes.

# LAB ACTIVITY
# Modeling Inheritance

## *BACKGROUND*

Genes are passed on to offspring from their parents. Genes determine many of the traits of offspring. In many cases, the traits an organism has depends on which genes it happens to get from its parents. Some parents may be homozygous for a given trait, while others may be heterozygous for that trait. The gene that any particular offspring receives from its parents depends on chance.

## *PURPOSE*

In this activity, you will be making gene models for fur color in rabbits. In most rabbits, the allele for black fur is dominant over the allele for brown fur. You will use the models to explore the chances of rabbit offspring having black or brown fur.

▲ **STEP 1** Label the index cards.

▲ **STEP 4** Take a card from each bag to make a gene combination.

## *PROCEDURE*

1. Write an uppercase *B* on two index cards. Write a lowercase *b* on the other two index cards. Copy the tables in Figure 3-19 onto a sheet of paper.

2. Label one of the paper bags *male.* Place two *B* cards in the bag. This will represent a male parent that is homozygous for black fur color.

3. Label the other paper bag *female.* Place two *b* cards in the bag. This will represent a female parent that is homozygous for brown fur color.

4. Working with a partner, take one card out of each bag without looking at them. Put the two cards together on your desk to represent the gene combination of the first offspring.

5. Record the results in Table 1. Place a tally mark in the row for the gene combination you pulled from the bags.

6. Repeat Steps 4 and 5 ten times. Record how many times you draw each possible gene combination in your table.

7. Empty both bags. Place a *B* and a *b* card in the male bag. Place a *B* and a *b* in the female bag.

8. Repeat Step 4 ten times. Observe how many times you draw each possible gene combination. Record your results in Table 2.

9. Calculate the percentage that each gene combination has a chance of occurring by using the following formula:

$$\frac{\text{number of times gene combination is drawn}}{\text{total number drawn}} \times 100 = \text{percentage chance}$$

▲ **STEP 8** Observe how many times you draw each combination.

**Table 1: Inherited Fur Color with Parents BB and bb**

| Inherited Fur Color | Tallies | Total |
|---|---|---|
| Homozygous black (BB) | | |
| Heterozygous black (Bb) | | |
| Homozygous brown (bb) | | |

**Table 2: Inherited Fur Color with Parents Bb and Bb**

| Inherited Fur Color | Tallies | Total |
|---|---|---|
| Homozygous black (BB) | | |
| Heterozygous black (Bb) | | |
| Homozygous brown (bb) | | |

▲ **Figure 3-19** Copy the tables onto a sheet of paper.

## CONCLUSIONS

1. **CALCULATE:** In Table 1, what percentage of offspring had black fur? What percentage had brown fur?

2. **CALCULATE:** In Table 2, what percentage of offspring had black fur? What percentage had brown fur?

3. **ANALYZE:** What are the chances of two parents, both of whom are homozygous for brown fur, having offspring with brown fur?

4. **INFER:** Can a male parent with the genes BB and a female parent with the genes Bb have any offspring with brown fur? Explain your answer.

# 3-7 What are incomplete dominance and codominance?

*Objective*

Describe incomplete dominance and codominance.

*Key Terms*

**incomplete dominance:** pattern of inheritance in which alleles from both parents are blended

**codominance:** pattern of inheritance in which both alleles of a gene are expressed

**Incomplete Dominance** Usually if an allele is dominant over another allele, the dominant trait is the only one that shows in the offspring. Sometimes there is no completely dominant trait. This type of inheritance is called **incomplete dominance.** In cases of incomplete dominance, offspring will show a blending of traits from each parent.

Incomplete dominance can be seen in many organisms. In four o'clock flowers, red and white are possible flower colors. Neither allele is completely dominant over the other. Homozygous red plants are given the symbol RR. Homozygous white plants are given the symbol WW. The capital letter R stands for red petal color. The capital letter W stands for white petal color. Figure 3-20 shows what can happen when homozygous red-flowering plants are crossed with homozygous white-flowering plants.

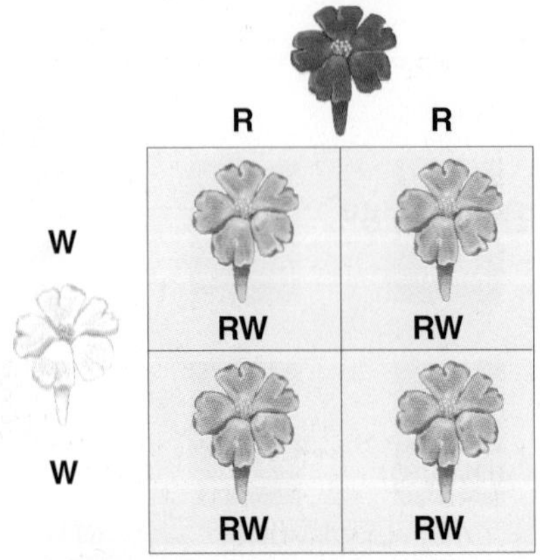


▲ **Figure 3-20** Incomplete dominance occurs in four o' clock plants.

**1 EXPLAIN:** What is incomplete dominance?

**Codominance** A different type of inheritance pattern occurs when both alleles of a certain trait appear in the offspring. This is called **codominance.** As in the case of incomplete dominance, neither allele is dominant over the other. However, codominance is different from incomplete dominance because it does not involve blending. The alleles from each parent both appear in the offspring.

**2 CONTRAST:** How is codominance different from incomplete dominance?

**Codominance in Chickens** There is a kind of chicken that has a gene for black feathers and a gene for white feathers. Neither of these genes is dominant over the other. The capital letter B stands for black feathers. The capital letter W stands for white feathers. A chicken that is homozygous for black feathers has the symbol BB. A chicken homozygous for white feathers has the symbol WW. When a homozygous black chicken and a homozygous white chicken are mated, all of the offspring have the gene combination BW. These heterozygous offspring have both black and white feathers.

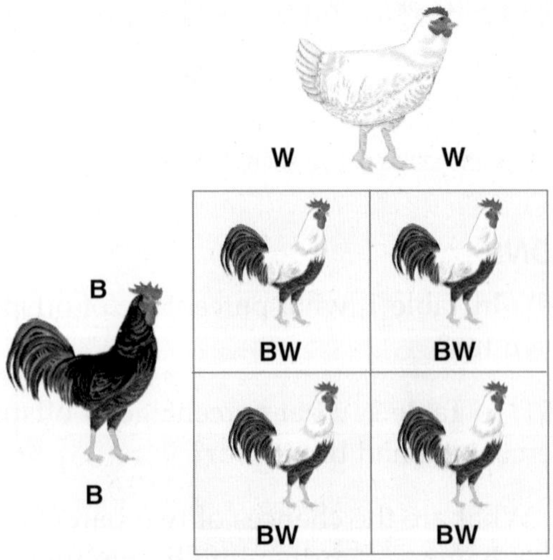


▲ **Figure 3-21** The alleles for feather color are codominant in Erminette chickens.

**3 DESCRIBE:** What causes a chicken to have both black and white feathers?

**Heterozygous Crosses** Recessive genes do not disappear. They show up again when heterozygous organisms are mated. If two heterozygous black and white chickens are mated, there will be a 25 percent chance of the offspring being BB, or homozygous black. There will be a 50 percent chance of the offspring being BW, or heterozygous black and white. There will be a 25 percent chance of the offspring being WW, or homozygous white.

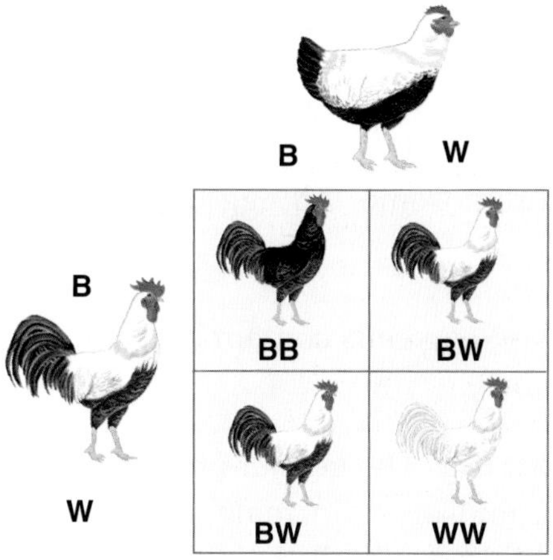


▲ **Figure 3-22** A cross between two heterozygous chickens

4 **LIST:** List the possible gene combinations that can occur when two heterozygous chickens are crossed.

## CHECKING CONCEPTS

1. What gene combination do pink four o'clock flowers have?
2. What is the result of a cross between homozygous red and homozygous white four o'clock flowers?
3. What color feathers will a chicken with the gene combination WW have?
4. What is the gene combination for a chicken with black and white feathers?
5. What gene combination will have a 50 percent chance of occurring if two heterozygous black and white chickens are mated?

## THINKING CRITICALLY

6. **INFER:** Why are capital letters used to represent all the genes for feather color in certain types of chickens?
7. **HYPOTHESIZE:** Why does blending occur only in organisms that are heterozygous for a certain trait?

## *Hands-On Activity*

### SOLVING PUNNETT SQUARES

*You will need a sheet of paper, a ruler, and a pencil.*

1. Copy the Punnett squares shown in Figure 3-23 onto your paper.
2. Write the appropriate gene symbols in the four empty boxes of the Punnett square. Round is the dominant seed shape trait in pea plants. List all of the possible gene combinations and the probability they will occur next to your Punnett square.
3. Repeat Step 2 for the Punnett square on color in four o'clock flowers.

**Practicing Your Skills**

*Make your own Punnett squares to answer the following questions.*

4. The allele for purple flowers, P, is dominant over the allele for white flowers, p, in pea plants. What are the possible gene combinations for a cross between two pea plants heterozygous for flower color?
5. In some horses, the allele for white hair, W, is codominant with the allele for red hair, R. What is the chance of offspring with only red hair resulting from a cross between two heterozygous parents?

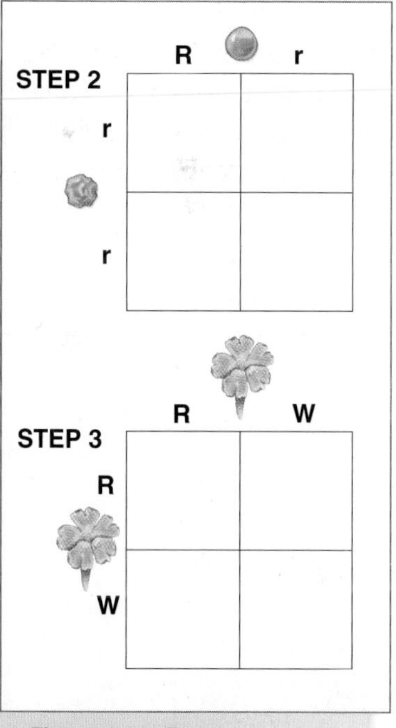


▲ **Figure 3-23** Punnett squares can be used to determine the possible traits in offspring.

# 3-8 How is gender determined?

### *Objective*

Explain how chromosomes in a sperm cell determine the gender of offspring.

### *Key Term*

**gender:** sex of a person or other organism

**X and Y** All human traits are determined by 23 pairs of chromosomes. Look at the 23 pairs of chromosomes shown in the karyotype in Figure 3-24. In females, all pairs of chromosomes look identical. In males, the chromosomes of the 23rd pair are not alike. These different chromosomes are called X and Y. Male cells have one X chromosome and one Y chromosome. The Y chromosome is smaller than the X chromosome. Female cells have two X chromosomes in the 23rd pair. The X and Y chromosomes determine the **gender** of an organism. Gender is the sex of an organism.

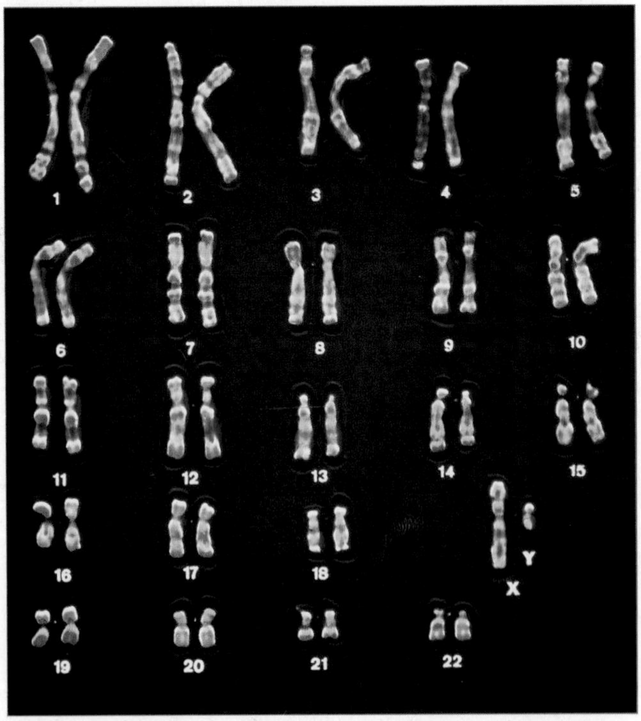


▲ **Figure 3-24** This karyotype shows the chromosomes of a human male.

**1** ▶ **IDENTIFY:** Which chromosomes determine gender?

**Gametes** Male gametes have an XY pair of chromosomes. During meiosis, each sperm cell receives only one chromosome from each pair. Half of the sperm cells receive an X chromosome. The other half receive a Y chromosome. Every sperm contains either an X or a Y chromosome. Female cells have an XX pair of chromosomes. During meiosis, each egg cell receives one chromosome from each pair of chromosomes. Therefore, each egg cell receives one X chromosome. All egg cells contain X chromosomes.

**2** ▶ **RELATE:** Why do egg cells contain only one X chromosome?

**Gender of Offspring** The gender of offspring is controlled by chromosomes in male sperm cells. As a result, all children inherit their gender from their fathers. During fertilization, if the egg cell is fertilized by a sperm cell carrying an X chromosome, the fertilized egg will have two X chromosomes (XX). It will develop into a female.

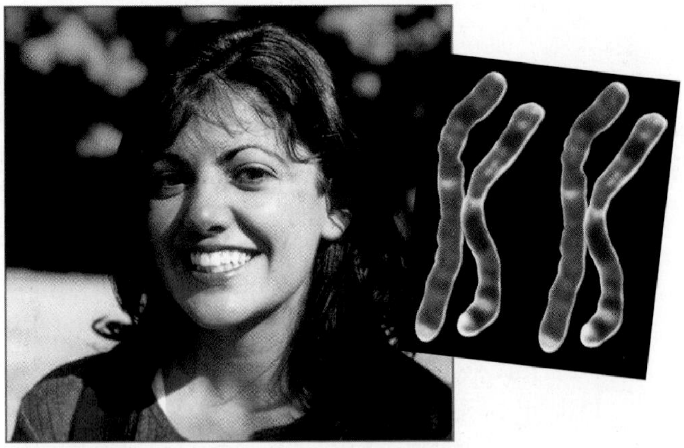

▲ **Figure 3-25** Females have two X chromosomes.

If the sperm is carrying a Y chromosome, the fertilized egg will have one X chromosome and one Y chromosome (XY). It will develop into a male.

Half the sperm cells carry the X chromosome. The other half carry the Y chromosome. Therefore, each new offspring has a 50 percent chance of being a girl and a 50 percent chance of being a boy.

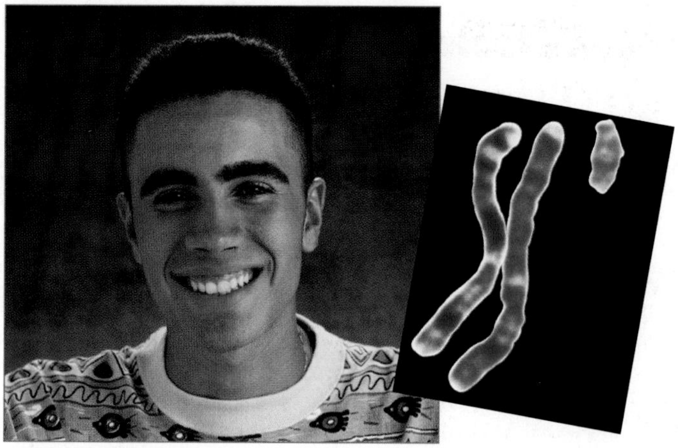

▲ **Figure 3-26** Males have an X and a Y chromosome.

**3** IDENTIFY: Which parent is responsible for the gender of the offspring?

## CHECKING CONCEPTS

1. The gender of offspring is controlled by chromosomes in the __________.
2. A female body cell contains two __________.
3. A __________ cell can contain either an X or a Y chromosome.
4. A fertilized egg that has two X chromosomes will develop into a __________.
5. A fertilized egg that has an X and a Y chromosome will develop into a __________.

## THINKING CRITICALLY

6. **CALCULATE:** Last year, 250 babies were born at a certain hospital. Estimate the number of males born there during the year. Explain.
7. **PREDICT:** What might happen if an egg cell received two X chromosomes during meiosis instead of one?

### Web InfoSearch

**Gender in Other Animals** In birds, moths, and some fish, the gender chromosomes are the reverse of human gender chromosomes. In these animals, the male has two identical chromosomes (XX) and the female has two different ones (XY).

**SEARCH:** Use the Internet to find out more about gender in other animals. Write a report on one of these animals. Start your search at www.conceptsandchallenges.com. Some key search words are **gender, chromosomes,** and **X and Y.**

## *Science and Technology*

### AMNIOCENTESIS

Amniocentesis (am-nee-oh-sehn-TEE-sis) is a test performed during a woman's pregnancy. A needle is inserted through the woman's abdomen and into her uterus. Some of the fluid that surrounds the fetus is removed through the needle. The fluid contains cells that have been shed by the fetus. Doctors can study the chromosomes found in fetal cells. They can also learn about structures and enzymes found in the cells.

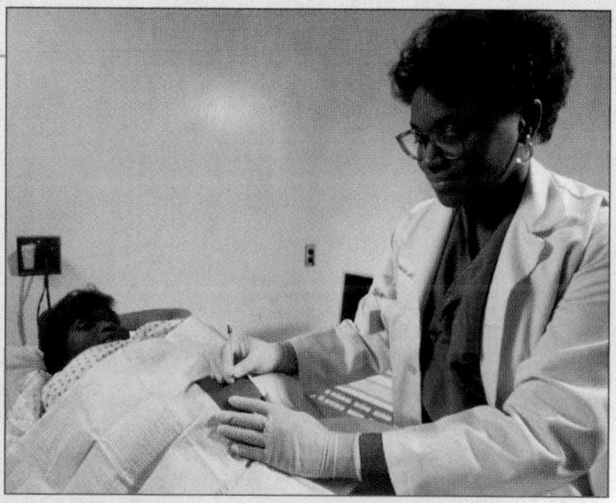

▲ **Figure 3-27** Amniocentesis can predict the health of unborn babies.

More than 50 different genetic disorders can be identified by amniocentesis. The test also reveals the gender of the fetus. Doctors can use this information when looking for certain disorders that occur more often in one gender, such as hemophilia (hee-moh-FIHL-ee-uh) and Duchenne muscular dystrophy.

An advantage of determining if a developing fetus has an inherited disease is that treatment can begin early—sometimes even before the baby is born. Doctors are developing techniques for replacing faulty genes with normal genes before birth.

**Thinking Critically** Why is amniocentesis performed?

# 3-9 What are sex-linked traits?

## *Objective*

Describe how certain traits are inherited along with sex chromosomes.

## *Key Terms*

**sex-linked traits:** traits that are controlled by the sex chromosomes

**carrier:** an organism that has a recessive gene for a trait but does not show the trait

**pedigree:** chart that shows inheritance of certain traits over several generations

**Inherited Traits** Some traits are inherited along with gender. These traits are controlled by the X and Y gender chromosomes. Traits that are inherited along with gender are called **sex-linked traits**.

Like all other chromosomes, the sex chromosomes carry genes. The X chromosome carries many genes, but the Y chromosome carries few genes. Most of the genes for sex-linked traits are found on the X chromosome.

1 **DEFINE:** What are sex-linked traits?

**Sex-Linked Disorders** Some hereditary disorders are controlled by the sex chromosomes. Two sex-linked disorders are hemophilia and color blindness. Hemophilia is a disorder in which the blood does not clot properly. Color blindness is a disorder in which a person cannot see the difference between certain colors.

Sex-linked disorders are found more often in men than in women. This occurs because the genes for most sex-linked disorders are recessive. In women, there are two X chromosomes. Both X chromosomes contain genes for these traits. While one of these chromosomes may have the allele for the disorder, the other X chromosome usually has a normal allele. Because the gene for the disorder is recessive, a female with each type of gene still appears normal.

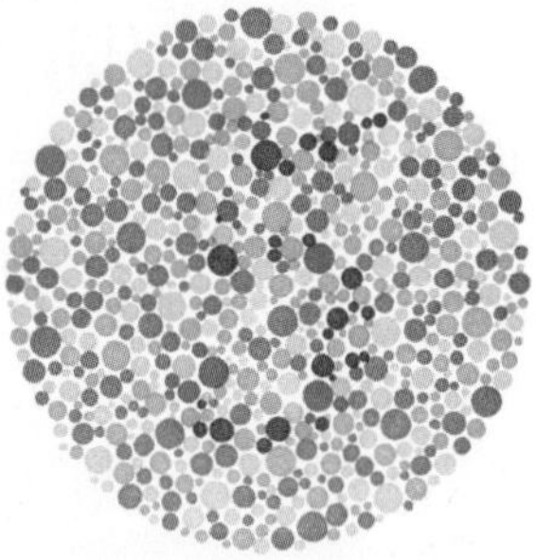

▲ **Figure 3-28** People who are colorblind cannot distinguish between the colors in this image.

2 **EXPLAIN:** Why does a female with a gene for a sex-linked disorder usually appear normal?

**Carriers** Women who have one normal gene and one gene for a sex-linked disorder are said to be **carriers** of the disorder. Although they do not show the disorder, they can pass the gene for it to their children.

When the sex chromosomes of a female carrier separate during meiosis, half the eggs get the normal chromosome and half get the chromosome for the disorder. If an egg cell containing the $X^C$ chromosome for the disorder is fertilized by a sperm containing the normal X chromosome, the daughter will be a carrier. If an egg containing the $X^C$ chromosome for the disorder is fertilized by a sperm with a Y chromosome, the son will have the disorder.

| | X | $X^C$ |
|---|---|---|
| X | Normal XX | Carrier $XX^C$ |
| Y | Normal XY | Color-blind $X^CY$ |

◄ **Figure 3-29** Color blindness is carried on the X chromosome.

3 **EXPLAIN:** Why do more men have sex-linked disorders?

**Hemophilia** Hemophilia is a sex-linked disorder. A person with hemophilia lacks a special protein that allows blood to clot. This can cause serious health problems should the person suffer a cut or bruise. Because it is a recessive trait, males generally have the disease. Females generally are carriers who do not show the disease.

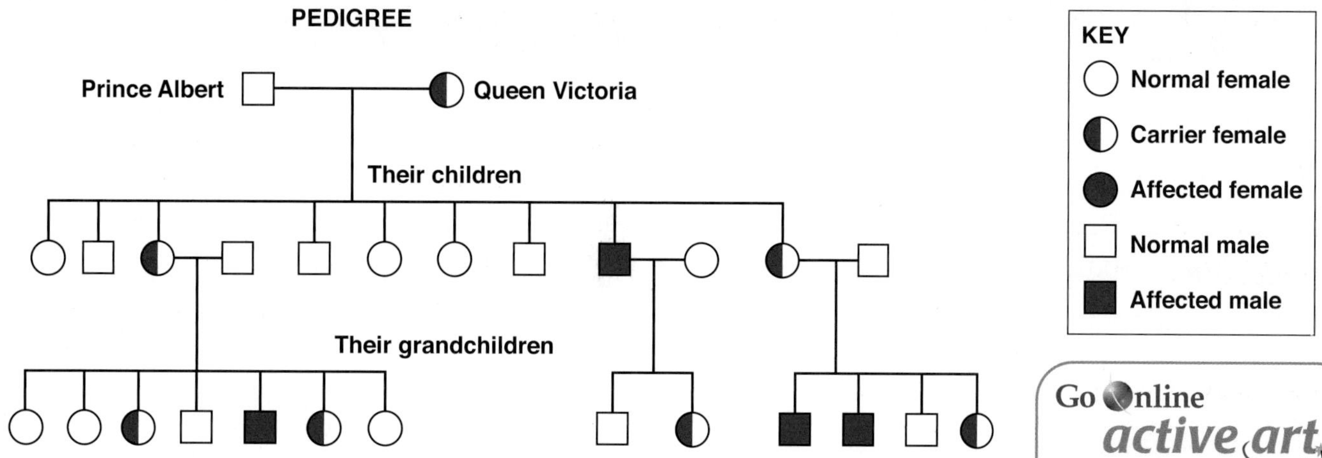


▲ **Figure 3-30** Hemophilia was common in the family of Queen Victoria.

Go Online
*active art*
For: Pedigree activity
Visit: PHSchool.com
Web Code: cep-3042

A famous carrier of hemophilia was Queen Victoria of England. Her husband, Prince Albert did not have hemophilia. Three out of nine of Queen Victoria and Prince Albert's offspring inherited the gene for hemophilia. Two of Queen Victoria's daughters were carriers of hemophilia. One of her sons had hemophilia. These offspring passed the trait along to some of their own children.

Several of Queen Victoria's granddaughters were carriers. Some of her grandsons had hemophilia. In those days, it was quite common for members of royal families to marry members of other royal families in Europe. As her grandchildren married members of other royal families, the disorder continued to spread. As a result, hemophilia was quite common among European royalty during the 19th century.

4 **INFER:** Why can't a male be a carrier for hemophilia?

**Pedigrees** Scientists often study the traits of past generations in order to predict the traits of offspring. One way they can do this is by making a **pedigree**. A pedigree is a chart that is similar to a family tree. It shows how a certain trait is passed down from generation to generation. Pedigrees identify which members of a family are carriers of a trait and which have the disease. Figure 3-30 shows a pedigree of Queen Victoria's family.

5 **EXPLAIN:** What is the purpose of a pedigree?

## CHECKING CONCEPTS

1. Traits that are inherited along with gender are called __________ traits.
2. Most of the genes for sex-linked traits are found on the __________ chromosome.
3. The genes for most sex-linked disorders are __________.
4. A female who has a gene for a sex-linked disorder but does not show the disorder is a __________.
5. A male who has a normal Y chromosome and an X chromosome for a sex-linked disorder __________ have the disorder.

## THINKING CRITICALLY

6. **INFER:** How can a female have the sex-linked disorder of hemophilia?
7. **DESCRIBE:** What kind of gene pair is found in the female carrier of a sex-linked disorder?

## INTERPRETING VISUALS

*Use the pedigree in Figure 3-30 to answer the following questions.*

8. **IDENTIFY:** How many children did Queen Victoria have that were carriers for hemophilia?
9. **IDENTIFY:** How many of Queen Victoria's grandchildren had the disease hemophilia?
10. **ANALYZE:** Why do you think none of the Queen's daughters had hemophilia?

# 3-10 What are some inherited diseases?

*Objective*

Identify some inherited diseases.

*Key Term*

**inherited disease:** disease caused by an inherited gene

**Inherited Diseases** Sometimes a gene is defective, or abnormal. The abnormal gene stops the body from working properly. An abnormal gene can be passed from the parents to their offspring. The gene can cause disease in the offspring. A disease that is caused by an inherited abnormal gene is called an **inherited disease**.

1 **DEFINE:** What is an inherited disease?

**Sickle-Cell Anemia** Sickle-cell anemia is an inherited disease that mainly affects people of African descent. Some of the red blood cells of a person with sickle-cell anemia have an abnormal shape. Rather than being rounded, these red blood cells are shaped like a sickle or crescent. Because of their abnormal shape, sickle cells are easily trapped in blood vessels. They clog the blood vessels and block the flow of blood. The clogged blood vessels may cause severe pain and, in some cases, an early death.

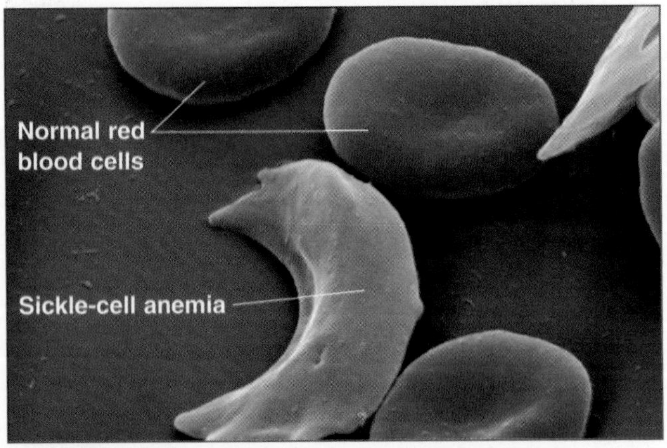


▲ **Figure 3-31** Sickle-cell anemia affects the shape of red blood cells.

The gene for sickle-cell anemia is recessive (s). The gene for normal red blood cells is dominant (S). People who inherit two recessive genes (ss) for the trait have the disease. People who inherit one dominant and one recessive gene (Ss) for the trait are carriers of the disease.

2 **EXPLAIN:** Why do people with one recessive gene for the sickle-cell anemia trait not show the disease?

**PKU** Phenylketonuria (fehn-uhl-keet-uh-NOOR-ee-uh), or PKU, is another kind of inherited disease caused by a recessive gene. People with PKU are missing an important enzyme that is needed to break down an amino acid called phenylalanine. Many foods with proteins contain this amino acid. As a result, people who have PKU cannot eat certain protein-rich foods such as meats, eggs, cheese, and milk. If people with PKU do not watch their diet carefully, the amino acid may build up in the body and could eventually cause brain damage and mental disability.

◀ **Figure 3-32** People with PKU cannot eat certain foods such as fish, milk, and eggs.

3 **DESCRIBE:** What effect does the disease PKU have on the body?

**Tay-Sachs Disease** Tay-Sachs is a disease that affects mainly Jewish children with Eastern European ancestry. An abnormal gene stops the child's body from producing an enzyme that breaks down fat. As a result, the fat gathers in the brain cells. This can cause brain damage and death. Most children with Tay-Sachs disease die before their fourth birthday.

The gene for Tay-Sachs disease also is recessive. A person who inherits two recessive genes (tt) for this trait will have the disease. A person who inherits one recessive gene and one dominant gene (Tt) is a carrier.

4 **RELATE:** What body function does the recessive gene for Tay-Sachs disease affect?

**Huntington's Disease** Unlike many inherited diseases, Huntington's disease is caused by a dominant gene. People who carry the gene will have the disease. The gene prevents the brain cells from functioning properly. The symptoms of Huntington's disease include loss of muscle control, mental illness, and death at an earlier age than average. Unfortunately, most people with the disease do not know they have it until they have already passed the gene on to their offspring.

5 **CONTRAST:** How is Huntington's disease different from other genetic diseases?

## CHECKING CONCEPTS

1. What causes inherited diseases?
2. How do sickle cells differ from normal red blood cells?
3. Which disease leads to the blockage of blood vessels?
4. What is the percentage chance that the offspring of two parents who are both carriers of the Tay-Sachs gene will have the disease?
5. Huntington's disease is carried by which type of gene?

## THINKING CRITICALLY

6. **COMPARE:** How are the effects of PKU and Tay-Sachs disease similar?
7. **HYPOTHESIZE:** Are the offspring of parents who are both homozygous dominant for normal red blood cells in danger of getting sickle-cell anemia? Why?

## *People in Science*

### GENETIC COUNSELOR

Genetic counselors study family histories and interpret test results in order to predict the possible traits of offspring. Genetic counselors provide pregnant women with information about their risk of having a baby with a genetic disorder. They also counsel children and adults about their own chances of developing a genetic disease.

Sumedha Ghate, a genetic counselor, first became interested in the field when she took a genetics course in college. She also wanted to work with people. Sumedha now counsels approximately 200 patients each year. Her job is to provide the information and support people need to make their own choices.

▲ **Figure 3-33** Genetic counselors help potential parents learn about traits that may be passed to their children.

Genetic counselors take a two-year master's degree program of study after earning a college degree. They can major in various subjects in college, such as biology, chemistry, nursing, psychology, or social work. Most genetic counselors work directly with clients, but some act as educators for other health-care professionals, for companies, and for the general public. Some do research in medical genetics.

**Thinking Critically** How could a genetic counselor help a family that has a history of sickle-cell anemia?

# 3-11 How does the environment affect inherited traits?

*Objective*

Explain how the living conditions of an organism affect the way it develops.

*Key Term*

**mutation** (myoo-TAY-shuhn)**:** change in a gene

**Conditions in the Environment** Genes control many of your traits. This is true for all living things. Your hair color is determined by genes. The size and color of flowers also are determined by genes. However, other factors can affect traits. The environment affects the traits of living things in many ways. All organisms need certain things to survive. Green plants need sunlight to develop and grow properly. Plants that do not get enough sunlight will be smaller and weaker than normal.

1 **LIST:** What are two factors that can affect traits?

**Environment and Traits** The divi-divi tree in Figure 3-34 grows sideways. At first glance, it may appear to have a genetic trait that causes this unusual growth pattern. However, the reason the trees grow sideways is because of the strong winds on the island of Aruba.

▲ **Figure 3-34** This divi-divi tree lives in a windy environment.

2 **EXPLAIN:** What causes divi-divi trees to grow sideways?

**Environment and Genes** Plants that are grown in poor soil are small in size. They produce only a few fruits. Adding nutrients to the soil changes the environment. The plants grow larger and produce more fruit. The size of a plant and the amount of fruit it produces are traits. The genes for these traits are not affected by the environment. The genetic information is not changed. Only the development or expression of the trait is affected by the environment.

3 **INFER:** Would poor nutrition affect the traits or the genes of an organism?

**Genetic Mutations** A **mutation** is a change in the genetic material of an organism. A mutation can be harmful if it decreases the organism's ability to function properly. If the mutation occurs in the gametes of an organism, it can be passed on to the offspring. If the mutation only affects the body cells, then the mutation is usually not passed on. Mutations can occur in a single gene or to a whole chromosome.

4 **DEFINE:** What is a mutation?

**Causes of Mutations** Mutations occur randomly in nature but can also be increased by factors in the environment. Factors that increase mutations are called **mutagens**.

▲ **Figure 3-35** Frogs with genetic mutations have been found where mutagens are in the environment.

Some examples of mutagens are ultraviolet light and certain chemicals. Radiation from X-rays or nuclear power facilities have been identified as possible mutagens. The chemicals found in cigarettes also cause genetic mutations. Some of these mutagens have been known to cause cancer. These substances are called **carcinogens**. Scientists are studying these substances to determine how they affect the human body.

5 **LIST:** What are three types of mutagens?

## CHECKING CONCEPTS

1. Many of the traits of all living things are controlled by ___________.
2. A ___________ is a change in genetic material.
3. The environment affects the development of ___________.
4. Living things develop normally when conditions in the ___________ are normal.
5. A mutation can be passed on to offspring if it occurs in the ___________.
6. Factors that increase the amount of mutations are called ___________.

## THINKING CRITICALLY

7. **INFER:** A green plant was stored in a school closet during the summer vacation. When students returned to the school in the fall, they found the plant had died. What probably caused the plant to die?
8. **HYPOTHESIZE:** Sunlight helps the body to synthesize vitamin D. What would happen to a person who was never exposed to sunlight?
9. **PREDICT:** Suppose a divi-divi tree was planted in a location with very little wind. What do you think it would look like?

## DESIGNING AN EXPERIMENT

*Design an experiment to solve the following problem. Include a hypothesis, variables, a procedure, and the type of data to collect and study.*

PROBLEM: Kathy and Ann both received the same type of hydrangea plant as gifts. After planting the hydrangea in each of their yards, they discovered that one had blue flowers and the other had pink flowers. What do you think caused the difference in flower color?

## *Integrating Earth Science*

**TOPICS: soil, minerals, humus**

### PLANT NEEDS

▲ **Figure 3-36** Planes are used to spray fertilizer on crops.

Plants make their own food during photosynthesis. However, they need nutrients from the soil to carry on photosynthesis. Plants need important minerals such as phosphorus, potassium, nitrogen, and magnesium. Sometimes soil does not have enough of these substances. Plant "food,"or fertilizer, needs to be added to the soil. Fertilizers may come from natural sources but may also be a mixture of chemicals produced in a factory.

The type of soil plants are grown in also has an effect on the health of the plants. Soils are made mostly of sand, silt, and clay. Usually, soils that contain a balanced amount of these three materials are the best for growing plants. Organic material called humus is also important for healthy plants. Humus is formed from the decomposition of dead plants and animals. It provides important nutrients needed by the plant. Balanced soil is also important because it can hold more water when water is scarce and allows water to drain when there is too much of it.

**Thinking Critically** Why do you think farmers are interested in the science of soil?

# 3-12 How is genetics used to improve living things?

## *Objective*

Explain the different methods of controlled breeding.

## *Key Terms*

**controlled breeding:** mating organisms to produce offspring with certain traits

**mass selection:** crossing plants with desirable traits

**hybridization** (hy-brihd-ih-ZAY-shuhn)**:** mating two different kinds of organisms

**inbreeding:** mating closely-related organisms

**Controlled Breeding** People have raised animals and planted crops for thousands of years. Over time, they learned that some plants produced better crops than others. They saw that some animals had more desirable traits than others. People learned to mate animals with desirable traits. Mating organisms to produce offspring with certain traits is called **controlled breeding**. The offspring produced usually have the same desirable traits as their parents.

1 DEFINE: What is controlled breeding?

**Mass Selection** Plant growers use a process called **mass selection** to produce plants with certain traits. For example, mass selection is used to grow larger strawberries.

▲ **Figure 3-37** The larger strawberry in this picture was created by mass selection.

In mass selection, plants with desirable traits are crossed. Seeds produced by these plants are collected and planted. New plants develop from these seeds. If the new plants have the same desirable traits, their seeds are collected and planted. The process goes on for many generations of the plants. The result of mass selection is a new kind of plant with certain desirable traits.

2 DESCRIBE: What is the purpose of mass selection?

**Hybridization** Sometimes two organisms with different kinds of genes are crossed. The offspring show traits of both parents. The mating of two different kinds of organisms is called **hybridization**. A mule is the result of hybridization. Its father is a donkey and its mother is a horse.

▲ **Figure 3-38** Mules are sterile, which means they cannot produce offspring.

When two different organisms are crossed, the offspring will often show more desirable traits than those of both parent organisms. For example, when a rye plant and a wheat plant are crossed, they produce triticale (triht-ih-KAY-lee). Triticale is more nutritious than either wheat or rye.

3 EXPLAIN: How is a mule produced?

**Inbreeding** Another way of producing organisms with favorable traits is by **inbreeding**. Inbreeding is the mating of closely related organisms. Offspring produced by inbreeding have genes that are very similar to their parents' genes.

For example, inbreeding is used to breed racehorses, whose desirable trait is speed. Inbreeding is done only with animals with desirable traits.

4 **COMPARE:** How do the genes of offspring produced by inbreeding compare with their parents' genes?

## CHECKING CONCEPTS

1. What is the purpose of controlled breeding?
2. How are new plants with desirable traits sometimes produced?
3. What is the mating of closely-related organisms called?
4. What is hybridization?
5. Why is mass selection considered a form of controlled breeding?

## THINKING CRITICALLY

6. **COMPARE:** How are mass selection, inbreeding, and hybridization alike?
7. **RELATE:** Could inbreeding and hybridization be considered opposite processes? Why?
8. **INFER:** Why is inbreeding dangerous to the organism?
9. **INFER:** Would you rather have an inbred dog as a pet or a hybrid dog as a pet? Explain your answer.

### Web InfoSearch

**Problems with Inbreeding** When inbreeding is allowed to continue for a number of generations, undesirable traits may begin to show. Hereditary diseases in animals usually are very rare. However, inbreeding of animals may cause these diseases to appear much more often.

**SEARCH:** Use the Internet to find out more about inbreeding in plants and animals. List the organisms and explain what problems have developed as a result of inbreeding. Start your search at www.conceptsandchallenges.com. Some key search words are **inbreeding** and **genetic disorders.**

## *People in Science*

### ANIMAL BREEDER

Animal breeders study the genes that control certain traits in animals. They use this information to breed animals and produce offspring with desirable traits. For example, a thoroughbred racehorse is bred for speed. A workhorse is bred for strength. Horses that compete in shows are bred for their ability to jump.

▲ **Figure 3-39** A horse breeder with a mare and a foal

Pat Limage is a horse breeder. Her job includes a lot of hands-on activities, such as taking care of young horses, called foals. She grew up loving horses and now owns her own farm. According to Pat, a knowledge of biology, math, and computer skills is important for a successful career in horse breeding.

In order to become an animal breeder, you need a high school diploma. You should take courses in agriculture and biology. A four-year degree in animal science often is necessary. You should also enjoy working with animals and being outdoors. To find out more about horse breeding, contact your county or state department of agriculture.

**Thinking Critically** What traits do you think an animal breeder would try to breed for in cows? What about in dogs?

*Integrating Mathematics*

# THE Big IDEA

## How do you use mathematics in dog breeding?

Probability is a branch of mathematics that describes the pattern of outcomes that occur by chance. It measures, for example, how likely it is that a coin will land heads up. Probability deals with predictable patterns that occur over time. It does not guarantee individual outcomes.

To measure the probability of an event, you divide the number of ways an event can occur by the total number of possible outcomes. For example, to measure the probability of rolling a 2 on a single die, you divide 1 (the number of ways to roll a 2) by 6 (the total number of sides). The probability of rolling 2 is 1/6.

Breeders use probability to predict the traits of offspring. Dog breeders use the information they know about parent dogs to determine the possible traits of the offspring. Some traits a breeder might be interested in are coat color and length. To predict the coat color and length in puppies, the breeder must know more than just the appearance of the parents. The breeder must also know the gene combinations each parent has for those particular traits.

Look at the pictures and Punnett square that appear on this page and the next. They point out the gene combinations and traits of the adult dogs and their offspring. Follow the directions in the science log to learn more about "the big idea."✦

### Gene Combinations of Parents

Both parent dogs have the gene combination BbLl. This means they are both heterozygous for each trait shown in the key. Because the parents have a dominant gene for each trait, they both have long, black fur.

| KEY |
|---|
| B = black fur |
| L = long fur |
| b = brown fur |
| l = short fur |

**Mother (BbLl)**

**Father (BbLl)**

▲ **Figure 3-40** Both of these dachshunds have long, black fur.

### Reading a Punnett Square

One way a breeder can determine the possible traits of offspring is by making a Punnett square. The following Punnett square is used to predict two traits at the same time—coat color and coat length. It has more boxes than the Punnett squares you have studied before because it is based on two traits instead of one.

| Mother (BbLl) \ Father (BbLl) | BL | Bl | bL | bl |
|---|---|---|---|---|
| BL | BBLL | BBLl | BbLL | BbLl |
| Bl | BBLl | BBll | BbLl | Bbll |
| bL | BbLL | BbLl | bbLL | bbLl |
| bl | BbLl | Bbll | bbLl | bbll |

▲ **Figure 3-41** This Punnett square shows the possible gene combinations for two traits.

## Gene Combinations of Offspring

When two heterozygous parents are bred, there are four trait combinations possible in the offspring. You can see three of them: short, black coat; long, brown coat; and short, brown coat. What is the missing trait?

Look at Figure 3-42. Then, follow the steps below to determine the probability of each combination occurring. Which trait combination has the least probability of occurring?

**WRITING ACTIVITY**

**Science Log**

In your science log, write about other traits that breeders are interested in. Choose two traits and create a Punnett square to determine the probability for these traits. You can make up the gene combination of the parents. For more information on breeding and probability, go to www.conceptsandchallenges.com.

| | | | |
|---|---|---|---|
| What will this dog look like? |  |  |  |
| **STEP 1** Count the yellow boxes and put that number above the total number of boxes. $\frac{9}{16}$ | **STEP 1** Count the tan boxes and put that number above the total number of boxes. ——— | **STEP 1** Count the green boxes and put that number above the total number of boxes. ——— | **STEP 1** Count the purple boxes and put that number above the total number of boxes. ——— |
| **STEP 2** Divide the numerator by the denominator. $16\overline{)9.00}$ = 0.5625 | **STEP 2** Divide the numerator by the denominator. $16\overline{)?}$ | **STEP 2** Divide the numerator by the denominator. $16\overline{)?}$ | **STEP 2** Divide the numerator by the denominator. $16\overline{)?}$ |
| **STEP 3** Round to the nearest hundredths place. 0.5625 rounds to 0.56 | **STEP 3** Round to the nearest hundredths place. ? rounds to ? | **STEP 3** Round to the nearest hundredths place. ? rounds to ? | **STEP 3** Round to the nearest hundredths place. ? rounds to ? |
| **STEP 4** Change the decimal to a percent. 0.56 = 56% | **STEP 4** Change the decimal to a percent. ? = ?% | **STEP 4** Change the decimal to a percent. ? = ?% | **STEP 4** Change the decimal to a percent. ? = ?% |
| There is a 56% chance the offspring will have a ______, ______ coat. | There is a ?% chance the offspring will have a short, black coat. | There is a ?% chance the offspring will have a long, brown coat. | There is a ?% chance the offspring will have a short, brown coat. |

▲ **Figure 3-42** Each puppy's appearance has a specific probability of occurring.

# 3-13 What is genetic engineering?

## *Objective*

Describe one method used to produce new DNA.

## *Key Terms*

**genetic engineering:** methods used to produce new forms of DNA

**gene splicing** (SPLYS-ing)**:** moving a section of DNA from the genes of one organism to the genes of another organism

**Changing DNA** Until recently, new forms of life could only be invented in books and movies. Today, however, advances in modern genetics have made it possible for new forms of bacteria and other simple organisms to be made in the laboratory. This is the result of **genetic engineering**. Genetic engineering is a process by which new forms of DNA are produced.

1 **DEFINE:** What is genetic engineering?

**Gene Splicing** One method of genetic engineering is called **gene splicing**. Gene splicing is a process in which a section of DNA from one organism is transferred to the DNA of another organism. Figure 3-43 shows the three steps in gene splicing. First, a DNA ring is temporarily opened. This is done with certain enzymes. New genes from another organism are then added, or spliced, into the DNA. Finally, the DNA ring is closed.

2 **DESCRIBE:** What occurs during gene splicing?

**Benefits** Genetic engineering has many benefits. New genes have been added to the DNA of certain bacteria. These bacteria can then produce substances that otherwise could only be made by the human body. Human insulin needed by diabetics is an example of such a substance. Bacteria can produce insulin after human genes are spliced into the DNA of bacteria. Scientists hope that someday genetic engineering can be used to correct genetic disorders. This may involve adding normal genes to cells that are missing these genes or have abnormal genes.

Another use of genetic engineering could be to improve certain traits in plants and animals used for food. Many farmers are now raising genetically engineered plants and animals. One problem food growers have is that food ripened on the vine becomes too soft to ship. For example, tomatoes are often picked green and then refrigerated while they are shipped. When they reach their destination, the tomatoes are sprayed with ethylene gas to make them turn red. These tomatoes usually do not have a good flavor. Through genetic engineering, scientists have produced a tomato that can ripen on the vine without becoming soft. Food stores get a better-tasting tomato.

3 **EXPLAIN:** How does genetic engineering benefit humans?

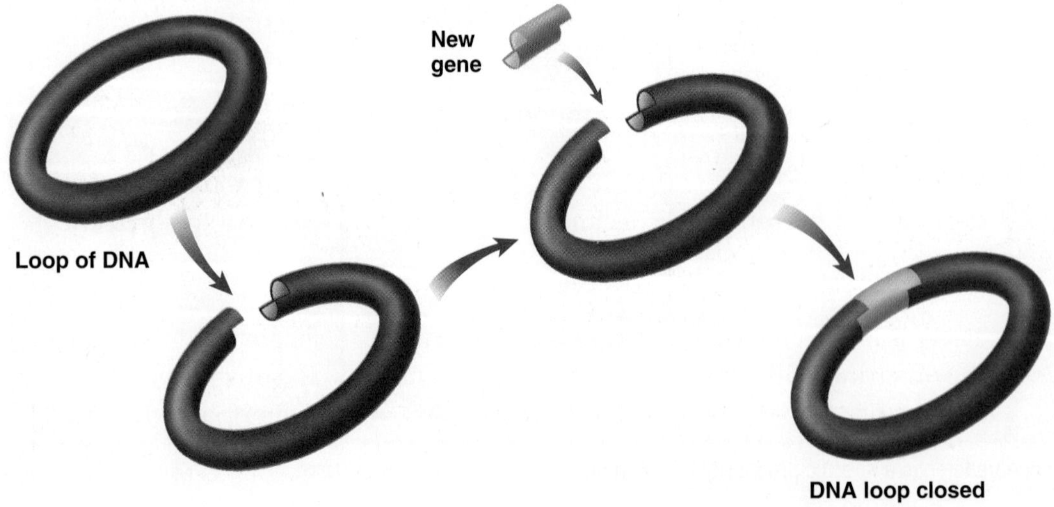


**Figure 3-43** DNA can be cut and "spliced" with the help of special enzymes.

**Disadvantages** Some scientists are concerned about possible dangers in working with new forms of DNA. There is some concern that experiments with the DNA of bacteria might produce an organism that causes a disease for which there is no cure. To help prevent this from happening, the federal government has set up special rules that must be followed in experiments using genetic engineering.

4 **IDENTIFY:** What is a possible danger in working with new forms of DNA?

## CHECKING CONCEPTS

1. Methods used to produce new forms of DNA are called ___________.
2. A process in which DNA from one organism is added to the DNA of another organism is called ___________.
3. Certain kinds of genetically engineered bacteria can produce ___________, which is needed by diabetics.
4. Scientists hope that someday genetic engineering can be used to correct ___________.
5. A danger with genetic engineering is the possibility of producing a ___________ organism for which there is no known cure.

## THINKING CRITICALLY

6. **RELATE:** PKU is a genetic disorder that causes the lack of a certain enzyme. How might genetic engineering someday be used to correct this disorder?
7. **INFER:** Through genetic engineering, scientists have been able to place a gene from a firefly into the DNA of a plant. What effect do you suppose this gene has on the plant?

## *Science and Technology*

### CLONING

▲ **Figure 3-44** Dolly

Cloning is the production of cells or organisms with identical traits. One way of cloning animals is by taking the nucleus out of a cell from a donor animal. This nucleus is placed into an egg cell whose own nucleus has been removed. Then the egg cell is placed into the uterus of an adult animal and allowed to develop. When the baby animal is born, it is identical to the donor animal. In 1997, Dolly, the first sheep cloned from an adult body cell, was born.

People can benefit from the cloning of large numbers of organisms that make desired products. For example, scientists often clone bacteria to make drugs. One type of bacteria is cloned because it makes insulin. Insulin is a drug used by people with diabetes. Cloning might be a way to produce animals with desired traits, such as cows that produce more milk or chickens that resist disease.

Scientists also clone organisms to study diseases. Mice that are likely to get cancer can be cloned. Scientists use these mice to study the causes and treatment of this disease.

**Thinking Critically** What do you think are possible disadvantages to cloning?

# Chapter 3 Challenges

## Chapter Summary

### Lesson 3-1

- **Traits** are the characteristics of an organism.The passing of traits from parents to offspring is called **heredity.**

### Lesson 3-2

- Reproductive cells called **gametes** contain half the number of chromosomes of a body cell.

### Lesson 3-3

- Chromosomes are made up of **DNA,** which contains sugars, phosphates, and four nitrogen bases.

### Lessons 3-4 and 3-5

- **Genes** control inherited traits. A **dominant gene** always shows itself over a **recessive gene.**
- **Homozygous** organisms have two of the same genes; **heterozygous** organisms have two different genes for the same trait.

### Lessons 3-6 and 3-7

- A **Punnett square** shows possible gene combinations.
- **Incomplete dominance** occurs when traits are blended. **Codominance** occurs when both alleles are expressed.

### Lessons 3-8 and 3-9

- Male sex chromosomes determine the **gender** of offspring.
- Traits that are inherited with the gender chromosomes are called **sex-linked traits.**

### Lesson 3-10

- An **inherited disease** is caused by an inherited abnormal gene.

### Lesson 3-11

- The environment can change the way a trait is expressed. The environment can also cause **mutations** in genes.

### Lesson 3-12

- Mating organisms to produce offspring with certain traits is called **controlled breeding.**

### Lesson 3-13

- **Genetic engineering** is a process used to produce new forms of DNA.

## Key Term Challenges

allele (p. 70)
carrier (p. 82)
centromere (p. 70)
codominance (p. 78)
controlled breeding (p. 88)
DNA (p. 68)
dominant gene (p. 72)
egg cell (p. 66)
gamete (p. 66)
gender (p. 80)
gene splicing (p. 92)
genes (p. 70)
genetic engineering (p. 92)
genetics (p. 64)
heredity (p. 64)
heterozygous (p. 72)
homozygous (p. 72)
hybridization (p. 88)
inbreeding (p. 88)
incomplete dominance (p. 78)
inherited disease (p. 84)
inherited trait (p. 64)
karyotype (p. 70)
mass selection (p. 88)
meiosis (p. 66)
mutation (p. 86)
pedigree (p. 82)
protein synthesis (p. 68)
Punnett square (p. 74)
recessive gene (p. 72)
replication (p. 68)
RNA (p. 68)
sex-linked traits (p. 82)
sperm cell (p. 66)
trait (p. 64)

**MATCHING Write the Key Term from above that best matches each description.**

1. moving a section of DNA from the genes of one organism to the genes of another organism
2. the field of biology that studies heredity
3. the mating of closely-related organisms
4. traits that are passed from parents to their offspring
5. mating organisms to produce offspring with certain traits

**FILL IN Write the Key Term from above that best completes each statement.**

6. The characteristics of an organism are called ___________.
7. The process by which DNA is duplicated is called ___________.
8. An organism is ___________ if it has two like genes for a given trait.
9. A disease caused by an inherited abnormal gene is called a(n) ___________.
10. Organisms that have two unlike genes for a trait are ___________ for that trait.

## *Content Challenges* TEST PREP

**MULTIPLE CHOICE Write the letter of the term or phrase that best completes each statement.**

**1.** Mendel found that when he crossed homozygous tall pea plants with homozygous short pea plants, the offspring were all
- **a.** short.
- **b.** tall.
- **c.** medium height.
- **d.** both tall and short.

**2.** Male organisms have
- **a.** two X chromosomes.
- **b.** two Y chromosomes.
- **c.** three Y chromosomes.
- **d.** one X and one Y chromosome.

**3.** The nitrogen base adenine always pairs with the nitrogen base
- **a.** cytosine.
- **b.** guanine.
- **c.** thymine.
- **d.** chromosomes.

**4.** Two sex-linked traits that are carried on the X chromosome are
- **a.** hemophilia and eye color.
- **b.** hemophilia and color blindness.
- **c.** color blindness and sickle-cell anemia.
- **d.** sickle-cell anemia and PKU.

**5.** Humans have
- **a.** 46 pairs of chromosomes.
- **b.** 23 chromosomes.
- **c.** 21 chromosomes.
- **d.** 23 pairs of chromosomes.

**6.** Genes that are not expressed in the presence of a dominant gene are called
- **a.** hybrid.
- **b.** recessive.
- **c.** allele.
- **d.** heterozygous.

**7.** The field of biology that studies the inheritance of traits is
- **a.** heredity.
- **b.** embryology.
- **c.** genetics.
- **d.** ecology.

**8.** When Mendel crossed homozygous short plants with homozygous tall plants, the result was tall plants. He concluded that the tall trait is
- **a.** dominant.
- **b.** homozygous.
- **c.** hidden.
- **d.** recessive.

**9.** A special diet can be prescribed for a child with
- **a.** hemophilia.
- **b.** Down syndrome.
- **c.** sickle-cell anemia.
- **d.** PKU.

**10.** The sides of a DNA ladder are made up of
- **a.** nitrogen bases.
- **b.** sugars and phosphates.
- **c.** proteins.
- **d.** melanin.

**TRUE/FALSE Write *true* if the statement is true. If the statement is false, change the underlined term to make the statement true.**

**11.** Hybridization is the crossing of organisms that are closely related.

**12.** Protein synthesis occurs in the nucleus of a cell.

**13.** The parent who determines the sex of human offspring is the female.

**14.** A change in a gene or chromosome is called a mutation.

**15.** A karyotype is an organized display of the chromosomes of an organism.

## Concept Challenges TEST PREP

WRITTEN RESPONSE **Answer each of the following questions in complete sentences.**

1. INFER: Why do you think some people are against genetic engineering?
2. INFER: If a genetic disorder were present in your family, would you go to a genetic counselor before having children? Why or why not?
3. EXPLAIN: How does the genetic code control an organism's traits?
4. EXPLAIN: How do Punnett squares help in the prediction of the inheritance of traits?

INTERPRETING A DIAGRAM **Use the diagram in Figure 3-45 to answer the following questions.**

5. What does the letter A stand for?
6. What does the letter C stand for?
7. What does the letter T stand for?
8. What does the letter G stand for?
9. What process is shown in the diagram?
10. Explain how this process is important to an organism.

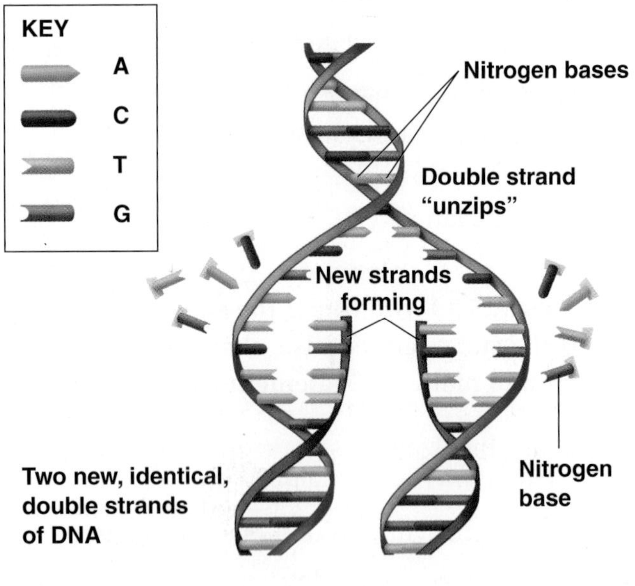


▲ **Figure 3-45** Use this diagram to answer the questions above.

# Chapter 4 Life Changes Over Time

▲ **Figure 4-1** The tortoises on the Galápagos Islands have different shells from island to island.

In 1835, a young man named Charles Darwin visited the Galápagos Islands, off the coast of South America. Darwin was interested in the different organisms he saw there, including the Galápagos tortoise. Every island had tortoises. However, no two islands had the same type of tortoise. Darwin spent the next 20 years developing a theory about why the Galápagos tortoises are different.

▶Why do you think the Galápagos tortoises vary from island to island?

## Contents

# 4-1 What is evolution?

*Objectives*

Define evolution. Explain how organisms change because of adaptations and mutations.

*Key Terms*

**species:** group of organisms that look alike and can reproduce among themselves

**evolution** (ev-uh-LOO-shuhn)**:** process by which species change over time

**adaptation** (ad-uhp-TAY-shuhn)**:** trait that helps an organism survive in its environment

**mutation** (myoo-TAY-shuhn)**:** change in a gene

**Evolution** Evidence shows that the earliest living things on Earth were very simple organisms. In the billions of years that have passed, organisms have become more and more complex. Many **species** have become extinct and other species have taken their place. A species is a group of organisms that look alike and can reproduce among themselves. Most scientists believe that new species develop from older species as a result of gradual change, or **evolution.** Evolution is the process by which living things change over time.

1 **DEFINE:** What is evolution?

**Adaptations** Living things can be found everywhere on Earth, from the highest mountaintops to the deepest oceans, and from hot, dry deserts to polar ice caps. Some bacteria live in rocks 1,609 meters deep in Earth's crust. How do different organisms survive such a wide variety of conditions?

All organisms have **adaptations.** An adaptation is a feature, or trait, that helps an organism to live in a certain environment. Look closely at Figure 4-2. The yellow spider blends into the background of the flower. This is an adaptation. Birds and other predators will have difficulty seeing the spider because it blends with its environment.

2 **HYPOTHESIZE:** What adaptations help birds to live in trees?

▲ **Figure 4-2** This spider blends into its environment.

**Mutations** Species evolve over time. Generally, a change in a species is caused by genetics. With each new generation, there is a new combination of genes. In time, new species can develop that will be different from their ancestors. Such changes take place over a very long period of time. These changes are needed to adapt to new environments.

Sometimes, however, something may cause a gene to change suddenly. A sudden change in a gene is called a **mutation.** If the mutation is helpful to the organism, it may be kept and passed on to future generations. Eventually, the species changes. This may result in the evolution of a new species. If the mutation is harmful, the individual will probably die without passing the trait on.

The white python in Figure 4-3 is an albino. Albino organisms do not have any pigments in their skin. It is a harmful mutation.

▲ **Figure 4-3** Albinism is a harmful mutation.

3 **INFER:** Why do you think albinism is a harmful mutation?

## CHECKING CONCEPTS

1. Most scientists believe that new species evolve from __________.
2. Organisms change over time by the process of __________.
3. A feature or trait that helps an organism live in a certain environment is an __________.
4. A sudden change in a gene is a __________.

## THINKING CRITICALLY

5. **APPLY:** What adaptations have chameleons developed to protect them from predators?
6. **EXPLAIN:** How do genetics play a role in evolution?
7. **ANALYZE:** Not all mutations are passed on to offspring. Explain.

## DESIGNING AN EXPERIMENT

*Design an experiment to solve the following problem. Include a hypothesis, variables, a procedure, and the type of data to study.*

PROBLEM: Desert plants, such as the cactus, have certain adaptations that help them to survive in a hot, dry environment. What would happen to a cactus if its environment suddenly changed to a cool, wet environment?

▲ **Figure 4-4** Desert plants are adapted to specific conditions.

## *Integrating Earth Science*

**TOPIC: continental drift**

### EARTH'S EVOLUTION

Fossil evidence shows that while life on Earth has been evolving, Earth itself has been changing too. Fossils are the remains of once-living organisms. Fossils of tropical plants, which can grow only in hot climates, have been found near the South Pole, where it is very cold.

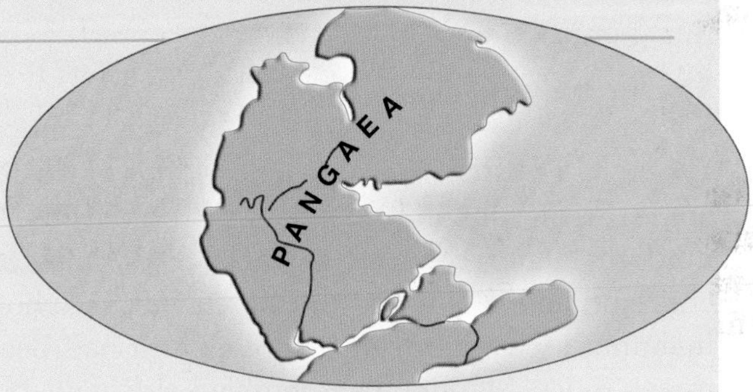


▲ **Figure 4-5** Pangaea

Meanwhile, fossils found in South America and in Africa are very similar, even though the Atlantic Ocean separates these continents. Some living animals and plants in South America, including turtles, snakes, monkeys, and ferns, also seem to be close relatives of those in Africa. How could their ancestors have crossed all that water?

These puzzling findings are explained by continental drift, the theory that Earth's continents have not always been where they are now. Earth scientists believe that about 220 million years ago all the modern-day continents of Earth were gathered into one big supercontinent, called Pangaea. Gradually, Pangaea split up into a number of large pieces, which slowly drifted apart. The northern continents of today were once near the equator, and the parts of Pangaea that formed today's southern continents were close to the South Pole.

**Thinking Critically** The Atlantic coastlines of South America and Africa look like pieces of a jigsaw puzzle that snap together. How does this support the continental drift theory?

# 4-2 What are fossils?

## *Objective*

Explain how different kinds of fossils are formed.

## *Key Terms*

**extinct** (ehk-STINKT)**:** no longer found as a living species

**fossil** (FAHS-uhl)**:** remains or traces of a once-living organism

**amber:** hardened tree sap

**Fossils** At the scene of a crime, detectives look for fingerprints. The criminals are gone, but they may have left behind clues. Many kinds of organisms are now **extinct,** or no longer found as a living species. However, some of these organisms left behind clues that they existed. These clues are **fossils.** Fossils are the remains or traces of once-living organisms.

1 **DEFINE:** What are fossils?

**Types of Fossils** There are many kinds of fossils. Some fossils are imprints left by organisms in mud that later changed to rock. Sometimes an entire organism is found. In March 1990, a whole mammoth was discovered in Siberia. It had been frozen in ice. Mammoths resembled elephants but were covered in thick fur. Mammoths became extinct about 10,000 years ago.

▼ **Figure 4-6** This mammoth is being defrosted by scientists.

Insects have been trapped and preserved in **amber.** Amber is hardened tree sap that has been preserved in the earth for millions of years. Most fossils, however, are the remains of hard parts of organisms, such as bones, teeth, and shells.

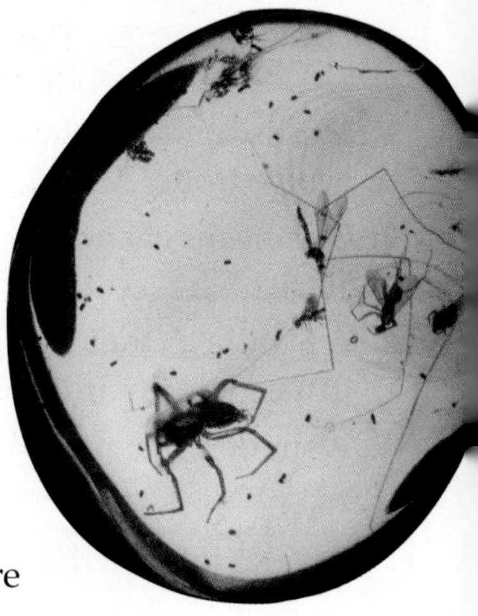

▲ **Figure 4-7** Ancient insects preserved in amber

2 **HYPOTHESIZE:** Which would be most likely to leave fossil remains: a worm, a rabbit, or a butterfly?

**Fossils in Rocks** Most fossils are found in sedimentary rocks. Sedimentary rock is made up of layers of sediments. Sediments are bits of clay, soil, sand, and other earth materials.

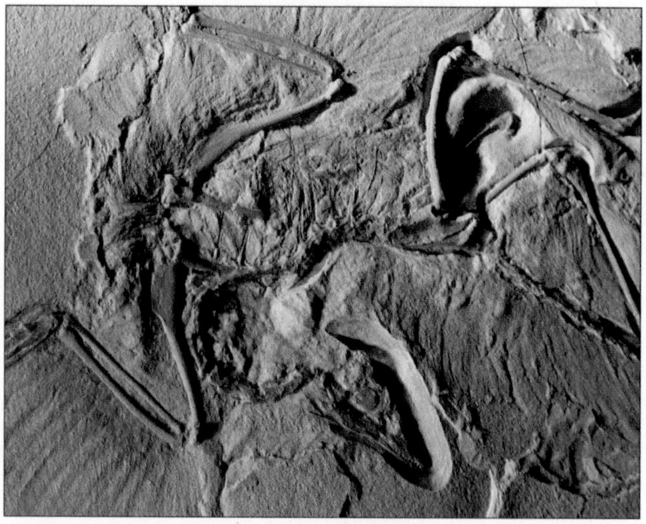

▲ **Figure 4-8** This fossil shows the skeleton and feather impressions of the first bird, an *Archaeopteryx.*

Sedimentary rocks usually form in water. When an animal living in the water dies, its body may sink to the bottom. The soft parts decay quickly. The bones or shells may remain and become covered by sediments. The sediments build up, layer by layer. Great pressure presses the sediments together. Slowly, through chemical processes, the sediments and bones or shells change into rock. The shape of fossil bones or shells are preserved in the rock.

Two types of fossils found in rocks are molds and casts. Molds are formed when an organism is buried by sediments and the sediments change into rock. The organism decays and leaves a cavity, or opening, in the rock. The cavity is a mold. Sometimes, a mold fills with sand or mud. The sand or mud hardens and a cast is formed.

3 **NAME:** In what kind of rock are most fossils found?

## CHECKING CONCEPTS

1. A mammoth is an example of an __________ species.
2. Insect fossils often are found preserved in __________.
3. Sand and mud that are carried and deposited by a river are __________.
4. Most fossils form in __________.

## THINKING CRITICALLY

5. **EXPLAIN:** Why can most fossils in sedimentary rock not be seen unless the rock has been cut from top to bottom?
6. **ANALYZE:** Why do you think there are more fossils of water organisms than of land organisms?

## Web InfoSearch

**Petrified Wood** The remains of an organism may decay very slowly. Minerals dissolved in water take the place of the original materials. The minerals form an exact stone copy of the remains. The fossil that forms is called petrified. Many trees are petrified. You can see petrified trees in the Petrified Forest of Arizona.

**SEARCH:** Use the Internet to find out more about petrified trees. Write a report on them. Start your search at www.conceptsandchallenges.com. Some key search words are **fossils, petrified wood**, and **tree fossils**.

## *Hands-On Activity*

### MAKING FOSSILS

*You will need two large paper cups, clay, and a small object such as a shell, a key, or a coin, plaster of Paris, petroleum jelly, and safety goggles.*

1. Put on the goggles. Press some clay into each of two paper cups so that the clay is 2 to 3 cm high in each cup.
2. Push a small object down into the clay of one cup. Then, carefully remove the object.
3. Coat the object with petroleum jelly. Very lightly press the object into the clay of the second cup and leave it there.
4. Prepare the plaster of Paris according to the directions.
5. Pour some of the plaster into each cup. Let the cups stand overnight. After the plaster hardens, tear away the cups. Remove the clay from the plaster.

▲ **STEP 3** Very lightly press the object into the clay.

Go Online
*active art*
**For:** Fossil Formation activity
**Visit:** PHSchool.com
**Web Code:** cep-3053

### Practicing Your Skills

6. **COMPARE AND CONTRAST:** How are the two fossils similar? How are they different?
7. **ANALYZE:** Which fossil is the mold and which is the cast?

# 4-3 What evidence supports evolution?

*Objective*

Describe the evidence that is used to support the theory of evolution.

*Key Terms*

**homologous** (hoh-MAHL-uh-guhs) **structures:** body parts that have the same basic structure

**vestigial** (vehs-TIHJ-ee-uhl) **structures:** body parts that seem to have no function

**The Fossil Record** The fossil record clearly shows that changes have taken place throughout Earth's history. There is evidence that Earth's climate has changed many times. Fossils of ferns have been found on Antarctica, indicating that the now frozen continent once had warmer temperatures. There are also fossils of many extinct organisms. Perhaps the best-known group of extinct organisms is the dinosaurs. Fossils of more than 400 different species of dinosaurs have been found.

1 **DESCRIBE:** What does the fossil record show?

**The Changing Horse** Fossils also provide scientists with clues about how species have evolved. The most complete fossil record of evolutionary change is that of the horse. Through fossils, scientists have traced animals related to the modern horse as far back as 60 million years ago. Figure 4-9 shows how the horse has evolved.

2 **OBSERVE:** How has the horse evolved?

**Similar Body Structures** Scientists also study living animals for clues about evolution. Look at Figure 4-10. The lion's foreleg, the bat's wing, and the dolphin's flipper are similar in bone structure. Body parts that are similar in structure are called **homologous structures**. Homologous structures in different organisms are clues that these organisms may have evolved from the same ancestor.

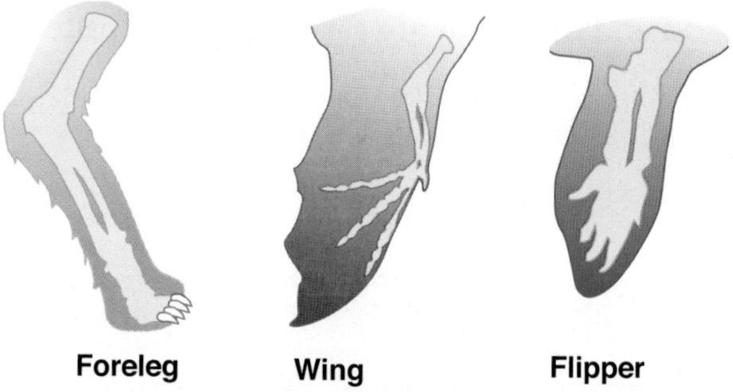


▲ **Figure 4-10** Homologous structures are clues that some organisms might have evolved from the same ancestor.

Body structures that seem to have no function are called **vestigial structures**. Your appendix is an example of a vestigial structure. It has no known

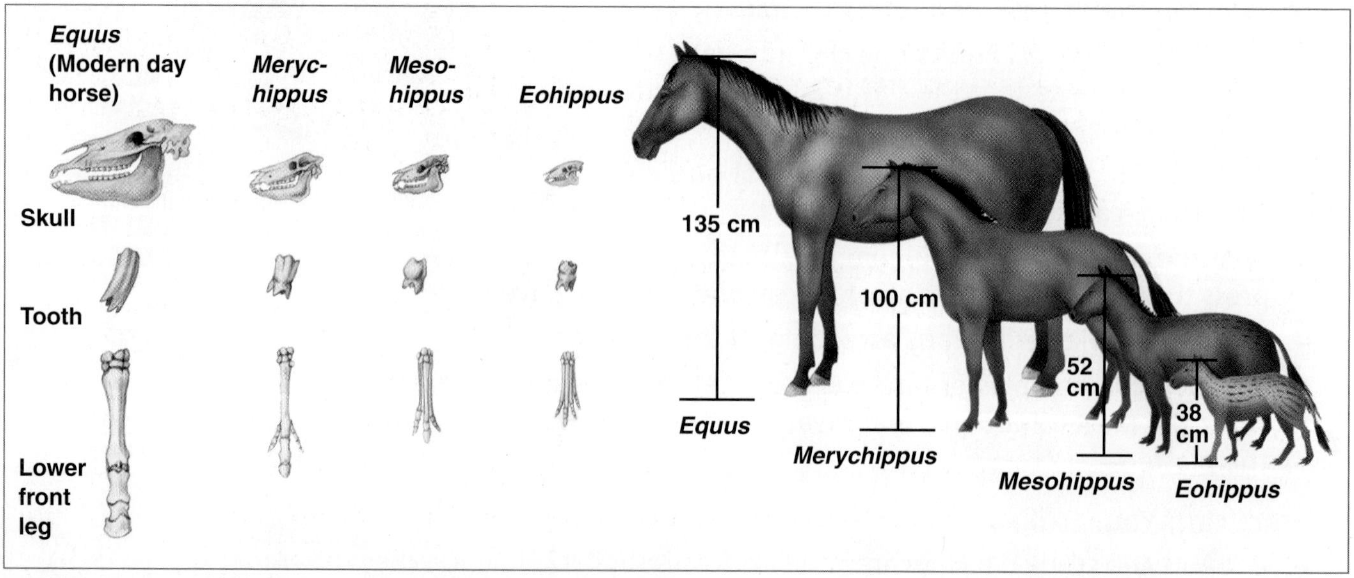


▲ **Figure 4-9** The horse has changed over millions of years.

function in modern humans. If vestigial structures have no function, then why do they exist? Scientists believe that at one time vestigial structures did have a function in the ancestors of the organisms that now have them.

3 **INFER:** What other different organisms may have similar body structures?

**DNA Evidence** Scientists also study an organism's DNA to learn more about evolution. For example, scientists have learned that dogs and bears have very similar DNA. This means dogs and bears are closely related and could have evolved from a common ancestor.

Scientists have also developed a way to remove DNA from fossils. By using DNA from some fossils, scientists can find out more about evolution.

4 **EXPLAIN:** How has DNA helped scientists learn more about evolution?

## ✓ CHECKING CONCEPTS

1. What does the fossil record show?
2. Why is the horse used to support the theory of evolution?
3. How can living things provide clues to support the theory of evolution?

## THINKING CRITICALLY

4. **INFER:** How does the fossil record show changes in climate?

## INTERPRETING VISUALS

*Use Figure 4-9 to answer the following questions.*

5. **CALCULATE:** How much bigger is the *Equus* than the *Merychippus*?
6. **OBSERVE:** How has the size of the horse's jaw changed through time?
7. **OBSERVE:** How has the horse's toes changed through time?

## *Science and Technology*

### RADIOACTIVE DATING

▲ **Figure 4-11** Scientists use radioactive materials to test the age of fossils.

Scientists can measure the actual age of a fossil or a rock by a method called radioactive dating. Radioactive dating involves the use of radioactive elements found in a sample. The atoms of radioactive elements decay, or break down, into atoms of other elements. The unit used to measure the rate of decay of a radioactive element is called a half-life. A half-life is the time it takes for one-half of the atoms in a sample of a radioactive element to decay. Some radioactive materials used in dating methods are uranium and argon 40, the radioactive form of argon.

Carbon-14, or C-14, is the radioactive form of carbon. The half-life of C-14 is 5,370 years. If you had a 10-g sample of C-14 today, in 5,370 years, only half of the C-14 atoms, or 5 g, would remain. The other 5 g would have broken down into nitrogen.

C-14 is present in all living things. When an organism dies, the C-14 continues to decay. By measuring the amount of C-14 and other radioactive materials in a fossil, a scientist can tell how old the fossil is.

**Thinking Critically** If you had a 32-g sample of C-14 today, how much would remain in 10,740 years?

# 4-4 What is natural selection?

## INVESTIGATE

### *Modeling Bird Beaks*

**HANDS-ON ACTIVITY**

**1.** Scatter a teaspoon of bird seed and a tablespoon of raisins on a plate. The raisins represent insects.

**2.** Using tweezers, see how many seeds you can pick up. Then, see how many raisins you can pick up. The tweezers represent a bird's beak. Which was easier to pick up, the seeds or the raisins?

**3.** Using a hairpin as a bird's beak, see how many seeds you can pick up. Then see how many raisins you can pick up. Which was easier to pick up?

**THINK ABOUT IT:** How might having differently shaped beaks help birds obtain food?

### *Objective*

Explain Darwin's theory of natural selection.

### *Key Terms*

**natural selection:** survival of offspring that have favorable traits

**variation** (ver-ee-AY-shuhn)**:** differences in traits among individuals of a species

**Explaining Evolution** The fossil record shows that living things have evolved throughout Earth's history. However, knowing this fact does not explain how the changes happened. Offspring are supposed to be the same species as their parents. So how can a new species develop from an old one?

1 **STATE:** What evidence shows that organisms have changed throughout Earth's history?

**Lamarck's Theory** Jean Baptiste de Lamarck was one of the first scientists to develop a theory of evolution. According to Lamarck, all organisms developed new characteristics to help them adapt to their surroundings. Then, they passed on those adapted traits to their offspring. Lamarck used a giraffe as a model for his theory.

Lamarck hypothesized that the first giraffes had short necks and ate grass. As time went on, the grass died and the giraffes had to find a new food source. The new food source was tree leaves. In order to reach the leaves, however, the giraffes needed to stretch their necks. This made their necks longer. Parent giraffes then passed on this new trait to their offspring. Lamarck did not have much evidence to support his hypothesis. Eventually, it was proven wrong.

2 **EXPLAIN:** Why do you think Lamarck's hypothesis was proven wrong?

**The Voyage of the *Beagle*** Over 150 years ago, the English naturalist Charles Darwin suggested a theory of evolution that is accepted by most scientists today.

In 1831, Darwin set sail on the HMS *Beagle*. The trip was a five-year expedition to the South Pacific and South America. The purpose was to make maps and to observe and collect specimens of various plants and animals.

▲ **Figure 4-12** Charles Darwin

▲ **Figure 4-13** The tortoises are different on each of the Galápagos Islands.

One of the places the *Beagle* visited was the Galápagos Islands. There, Darwin saw the Galápagos tortoises. Every island had a different species of tortoise. Some of the tortoises had dome-shaped shells, whereas others had saddle-shaped shells.

Darwin also discovered 13 different species of finches. Darwin observed that each species of finch had a differently shaped beak. Each beak was adapted for eating a certain type of food. Most of the finches' other traits were similar. Darwin inferred that all the finches had evolved from a common ancestor. Darwin used his observation of the finches and the tortoises as the basis for his ideas about **natural selection**.

▲ **Figure 4-14** Darwin drew this picture of the finches on the Galápagos Islands.

3 **EXPLAIN:** Explain why Darwin thought the finches may have had a common ancestor.

**Natural Selection** Darwin used the term natural selection to describe his theory of evolution. Nature favors the survival of organisms that are best suited for their environment. The theory of natural selection includes the following ideas:

- **Overproduction** Each species produces more offspring than can survive. Not all can survive because there is not enough food or living space for all.
- **Struggle for Existence** The offspring of each generation compete for things that they need to survive. Only a few will live long enough to reproduce. The others will die.
- **Variation** The offspring of each generation are not exactly alike. For example, some organisms are faster or stronger than others. Differences in traits among individuals of a species are called **variations**.
- **Survival of the Fittest** Some variations make organisms better suited for survival in their environments. These organisms are more likely to survive and reproduce than are others.
- **Evolution of New Species** Individuals with favorable variations survive and reproduce. They pass their favorable traits to their offspring. Therefore, their offspring are more likely to survive and reproduce in the next generation. Unfavorable variations eventually disappear. In this way, favorable variations remain in the species. Over many generations, these changes can result in the appearance of a new species.

4 **LIST:** List the main ideas of the theory of natural selection.

## ✓ CHECKING CONCEPTS

1. Natural selection is a theory of ___________.
2. The idea which states that a species produces more offspring than can survive is called ___________.
3. Individuals with ___________ variations survive and reproduce.

## THINKING CRITICALLY

4. **CONTRAST:** How is Lamarck's theory of evolution different from Darwin's theory of evolution?
5. **INFER:** How would Darwin explain why giraffes have long necks?

### Web InfoSearch

**Isolation and Evolution** Finches on the Galápagos Islands were similar to finches in South America. Darwin inferred that Galápagos finches had a common ancestor, one related to the South American finch. As individual groups of finches were isolated from one another, they evolved different traits to help them adapt to their new surroundings.

**SEARCH:** Use the Internet to find out more about finches and write a report. Start your search at www.conceptsandchallenges.com. Some key search words are **finches, Darwin**, and **Galapagos Islands**.

# LAB ACTIVITY
# Modeling Natural Selection

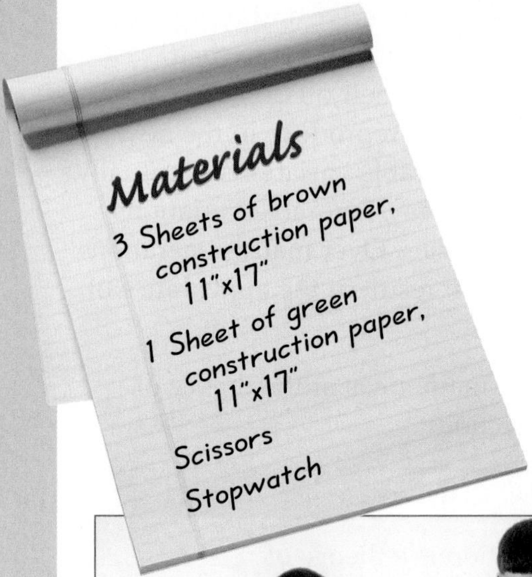

▲ **STEP 1** Cut 15 brown squares and 15 green squares.

▲ **STEP 3** Scatter the pieces of paper.

### *BACKGROUND*

Natural selection is the survival of offspring that have favorable traits. One favorable trait for many animals is having a color that blends into their environment.

### *PURPOSE*

In this activity, you will model how a favorable trait can be passed on because of natural selection.

### *PROCEDURE*

1. Copy the chart in Figure 4-15 onto your own paper. Label the chart. Then take one sheet of brown construction paper and one sheet of green construction paper and cut out 15 brown squares and 15 green squares. Make sure the squares are the same size. The squares represent insects. ⚠ CAUTION: Be careful when using scissors.

2. Place the other sheets of brown construction paper on the floor. The paper represents the environment.

3. Cover your eyes while your partner scatters the squares on the construction paper.

4. While your partner times you for 30 seconds, pick up as many squares as you can.

5. Count the number of squares remaining on the paper. Record the numbers in row 1 of your chart. They represent the brown and green insects that have survived and can now reproduce.

6. Now, double the number of each color by scattering more squares on the paper. For example, if there are 5 brown squares and 10 green squares still remaining on the paper, add 5 more brown squares and 10 more green squares. You may need to make more squares.

7. Have your partner count the number of brown squares and green squares now on the paper. Enter these numbers in row 2 of your chart.

8. Double the number of each color by scattering more squares on the paper. You may need to make more squares. Then have your partner count the number of brown squares and green squares now on the paper. Record the number of insects in this third generation in row 3 on your chart.

▲ **STEP 4** Use a stopwatch to time your partner.

▲ **STEP 5** Record the numbers in row 1.

| Trial | Number of Insects | |
|---|---|---|
| | Brown | Green |
| 1. | | |
| 2. | | |
| 3. | | |
| Total | | |

▲ **Figure 4-15** Copy this chart. Leave enough room to write in each row.

### *CONCLUSIONS*

1. **ANALYZE:** Which color insect is most visible in a brown environment?
2. **EXPLAIN:** How does this experiment show that natural selection helps pass along certain traits?
3. **HYPOTHESIZE:** Which insects would more likely be picked from a green leaf by a bird? Why?

# 4-5 How does the environment affect natural selection?

*Objective*

Describe the ways in which the environment affects natural selection.

*Key Term*

**extinction:** disappearance of all members of a species

**Factors in Living Space** All organisms must have a living space that provides food, water, and shelter. Often, members of a species must compete for resources in their living space. As a result, many of an organism's offspring do not survive and reproduce. One reason is because there is not enough food and living space for all of them.

For example, in some parts of Asia, tigers and deer share a living space. Tigers prey on deer. The tigers in that living space are competing with each other for food. Tigers that are stronger and faster are more likely to catch deer and survive. Tigers that are slower and weaker are less likely to catch deer. Without food, it is unlikely that the weaker tiger will survive and reproduce.

1 **APPLY:** How do the tigers show survival of the fittest?

**Human Activities** Human activities can produce great changes in the living spaces of other organisms. Some species have become extinct because people have hunted them or built roads and buildings that took away their living space.

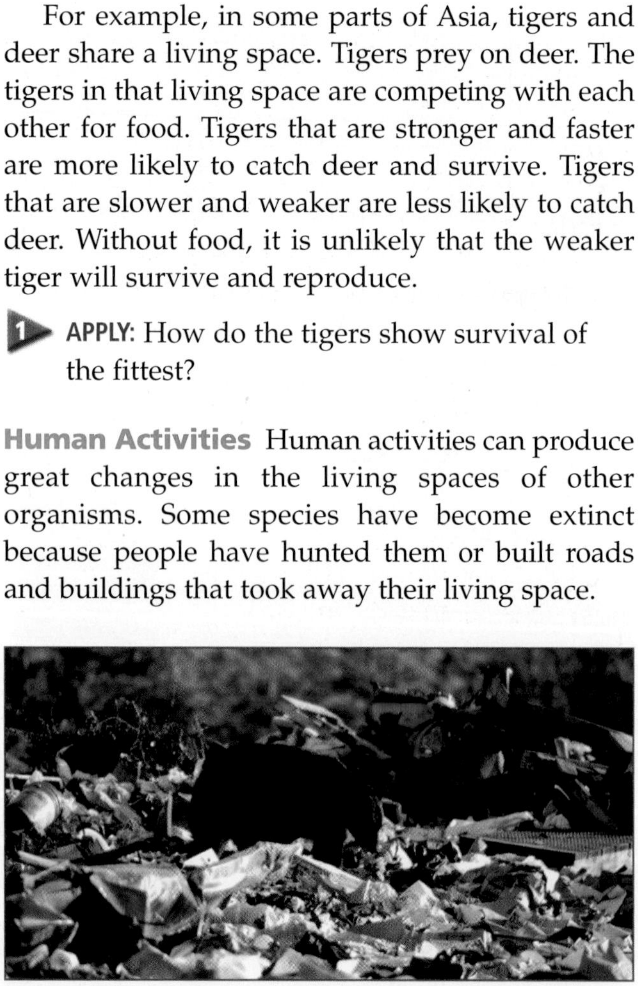

▲ **Figure 4-16** This black bear looks for food in garbage dumps.

Black bears are one species that has been affected by human activities. Humans have created garbage dumps in places where black bears live. Many times, they find food in the garbage humans have thrown away. The bears have become accustomed to this easy source of food and may lose the ability and desire to find their usual food.

2 **LIST:** How do human activities affect other organisms?

**Pollution** Pollution is another example of how human activities affect other organisms. Harmful materials from factories and cars pollute the air, water, and land.

In the early 1800s, most of the peppered moths in England were light gray in color. Very few of the moths were black. The trunks of the trees the moths lived on were the same color as the light gray moths. Birds could not see the gray moths against the tree trunk. Birds could, however, see black moths. As a result, many of the black moths were eaten by the birds. Few survived to reproduce.

During the Industrial Revolution, many large coal-burning factories were built near where the moths lived. The soot given off by these factories soon changed the color of the tree trunks to black. The black moths blended into the environment and were difficult to see. The birds began to eat more of the gray moths. After a short period of time, most of the British peppered moths were black.

Since the 1970s, when laws were passed in England to reduce air pollution, the number of gray peppered moths has risen, while the number of black peppered moths has fallen.

3 **EXPLAIN:** Why is it helpful for the moths to be the same color as the tree trunks?

**Extinction** **Extinction** is the disappearance of all members of a species. As organisms are unable to adapt to changes in their environment, they become extinct. Thousands of organisms have become extinct.

Most of these extinctions occurred because of a slow change in the environment, such as climate or lack of available food. Dinosaurs became extinct because of natural occurrences. Human activities can also cause extinction. For example, the dodo bird was hunted to extinction.

▲ **Figure 4-17** A model of a dodo bird

In recent years, more and more animal species have faced the danger of extinction. The giant panda and the grizzly bear are both examples of endangered species. There are now laws in place to protect endangered species.

4 **PREDICT:** What could happen to an endangered species if there were no laws to protect it?

## CHECKING CONCEPTS

1. What is one reason that many offspring may not survive?
2. How can human activities affect other organisms?
3. What is pollution?
4. What is extinction?
5. What are some reasons organisms become extinct? Why?

## THINKING CRITICALLY

6. **PREDICT:** What might happen to a young black bear that had eaten from a garbage dump its entire life and was then relocated to a forest?
7. **DISCUSS:** Do you think it is a good idea to have laws to protect endangered species? Explain.
8. **ANALYZE:** How do the British peppered moths support the theory of natural selection?

## *Real-Life Science*

### OVERFISHING

Many species have become extinct as a result of human activity. Other species are endangered. Laws can help some of these species make a comeback. The swordfish is an example of an animal that was hunted almost to extinction.

▲ **Figure 4-18** New laws protect animals, such as the swordfish.

Some experts believe the cause of the problem is the way the fish are caught. Many years ago, swordfish were caught with harpoons. Then, the fishing industry began to use "longlines," fishing lines that are 30 to 40 miles long and hold hundreds of baited hooks. Many young swordfish would bite the bait and get hooked. Because these fish were being killed before they had a chance to breed, the size of the population decreased dramatically.

In 1999, the United States government proposed new fishing rules to protect the swordfish. At certain times of the year, the places where swordfish breed are closed to longline fishing. With this new protection, the North Atlantic swordfish population is already starting to grow again. Scientists believe the swordfish population can recover fully by 2010.

**Thinking Critically** Do you think the government was right to impose rules to protect the swordfish? Explain.

# 4-6 How have humans changed over time?

### *Objective*

Describe some of the ways that humans have changed over time.

### *Key Term*

**anthropology** (an-throh-PAHL-uh-jee): science that deals with the study of human beings

**Early Humanlike Species** The fossil record of human evolution is not complete. It is still being pieced together by scientists who work in the field of anthropology. **Anthropology** is the study of human beings.

In 1974, Donald Johanson, an American anthropologist, discovered one of the oldest fossils of humanlike ancestors. The shape of the pelvis indicated that the fossil came from a female. Johanson named her Lucy. Lucy is about 3.5 million years old. Her skeleton indicates that she was a little more than 1 m tall and walked upright.

Later fossils of different species of humans also have been found. The ages of these fossils range from about 500,000 to 6 million years. Fossils of each species show more humanlike traits and behaviors than the species that lived before them. These changes include increased body size and larger skulls. Evidence also indicates that some of the later species lived in caves, used fire, and made tools.

**1 INTERPRET:** What does fossil evidence show about the evolution of humanlike species?

**Modern Humans** All modern humans belong to the species *Homo sapiens* (SAY-pee-ehnz), which means "wise human." Fossils of two early types of *Homo sapiens* have been found. The two types are Neanderthals (nee-AN-duhr-thawlz) and Cro-Magnons (kroh-MAG-nuhnz). Neanderthals, *Homo sapiens neanderthalensis*, lived from 130,000 to 35,000 years ago. They were shorter than modern humans. However, they had much larger skulls than earlier humanlike species did. The skulls had sloping foreheads and heavy brow ridges. Cro-Magnons, *Homo sapiens sapiens*, looked like modern humans.

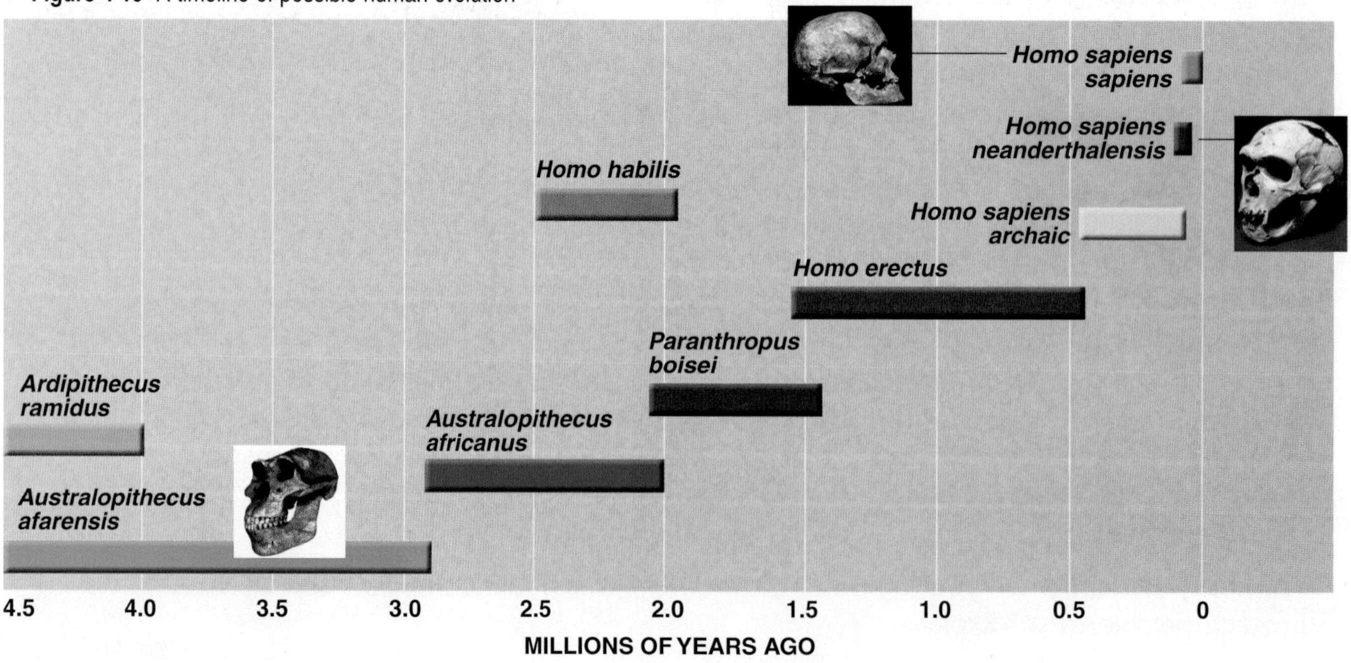


▼ **Figure 4-19** A timeline of possible human evolution

They lived from 35,000 to 10,000 years ago. They were tall and had large brain cases and rounded skulls. Fossil evidence shows that Cro-Magnons lived together in large groups. They were skilled hunters and toolmakers.

**2** **CONTRAST:** How are the fossils of Neanderthals different from the fossils of earlier humanlike species?

## CHECKING CONCEPTS

1. What is the science that deals with the study of human beings?
2. How old is the oldest humanlike fossil ever discovered?
3. Which humanlike fossil most resembles modern humans?
4. What evidence tells anthropologists about early human activities?
5. Which *Homo sapiens* skulls had sloped foreheads and heavy brow ridges?

## THINKING CRITICALLY

6. **INFER:** Why do you think modern humans were named *Homo sapiens*?
7. **HYPOTHESIZE:** A fossil skeleton is found in a layer of sedimentary rock. The skull has a sloped forehead and heavy brow ridges. Several years earlier, a Cro-Magnon skeleton was found several layers deeper in the same sedimentary rock. What might an anthropologist infer by the arrangement of the two fossil skeletons?

## BUILDING READING SKILLS

***Analyzing Vocabulary*** Anthropology is the science that deals with the study of human beings. Find out where the word *anthropology* comes from. In the dictionary, look up the prefix *anthrop-* and the suffix *-logy*. Write the meanings on a sheet of paper together with their origins.

## *People in Science*

### THE LEAKEYS

▲ **Figure 4-20** The Leakeys made many contributions to anthropology.

In the field of anthropology, no name is more familiar than that of the Leakey family. For more than 50 years, Mary and Louis Leakey searched for and studied the fossil remains of early ancestors of humans. Like most anthropologists, their goal was to trace the evolutionary development of humans.

In 1959, Mary Leakey found a humanlike skull that was more than 1.75 million years old. It was called "Nutcracker Man" because of its large jaws and teeth. Its scientific name was *Paranthropus boisei*. In 1972, Richard Leakey, Mary and Louis's son, discovered the skull of another early human ancestor. This second skull was determined to be about 2 million years old. Simple stone tools found with the fossil led Richard to call his discovery "Handyman." The scientific name is *Homo habilis*.

In 1984, Richard Leakey and his coworkers made a very significant discovery in Kenya, Africa. They found an almost complete skeleton of a 12-year-old male. The skeleton, which was about 1 million years old, was of a species known as "Upright Human." The scientific name is *Homo erectus*. This species is the closest known ancestor to modern humans. It is one of the most complete specimens discovered to date.

**Thinking Critically** Why is an almost complete skeleton a significant discovery?

*Integrating Earth Science*

# THE Big IDEA

## What is geologic time?

There are three types of rocks that make up Earth's crust: sedimentary rocks, igneous rocks, and metamorphic rocks. Sedimentary rocks are made up of compressed layers of sediments. Igneous rocks are formed when molten rock, such as lava, cools and hardens. Metamorphic rocks are rocks that have been changed by heat and pressure. Rocks can change from one kind to another. The series of natural processes by which rocks slowly change from one kind to another is called the rock cycle.

Most fossils are found in sedimentary rocks. By comparing the positions of the layers of sedimentary rocks in which fossils are found, scientists can find the relative ages of different fossils. Usually, fossils found in a lower layer of rock are older than fossils found in a higher layer.

Scientists have studied fossils from rocks all over the world. They have arranged the fossils in order, from oldest to youngest. They have used this information to construct a geologic time scale, or a record of Earth's history based on the types of organisms that lived at different times. The **geologic time scale** is divided into **eras.** Eras are divided into periods. Periods are divided into epochs.

The timeline on these two pages offers information about the periods in the geologic time scale. Follow the directions in the Science Log to learn more about "the big idea."✦

### GEOLOGIC TIME SCALE

| Era | PRECAMBRIAN | PALEOZOIC | |
|---|---|---|---|
| Period | | Cambrian | Ordovic |
| Approx. Start Date (millions of years ago) | 4,600 | 600 | 480 |
| Major Events | Life on Earth began about 3 billion years ago.<br><br>Earliest life forms were blue-green bacteria and other bacteria-like organisms.<br><br>Mountain building began. | Earliest signs of diverse marine life, including trilobites and brachiopods appeared.<br><br>This period was called the Cambrian Explosion.<br><br>This period ended with mass extinction. | Many ne marine invertebra appeared<br><br>The first vertebra appeared<br><br>The first plants ma have develope<br><br>At the en of this period, more tha half of th marine organism became extinct. |

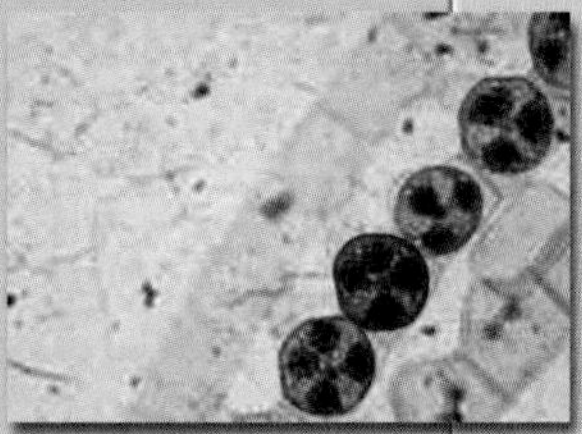

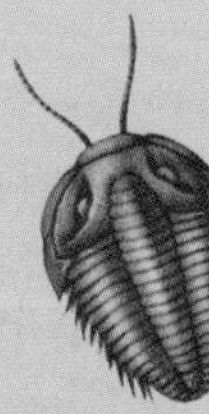

**WRITING ACTIVITY**

**Science Log**

Look at the timeline on these two pages. Which period would you like to visit? In your science log, research and write about what Earth was like in the period you chose and why you would like to visit that period. Write about the organisms you would see. Start your search at www.conceptsandchallenges.com.

| | | | | | | | | |
|---|---|---|---|---|---|---|---|---|
| | | | | MESOZOIC | | | CENOZOIC | |
| urian | Devonian | Carboniferous | Permian | Triassic | Jurassic | Cretaceous | Tertiary | Quaternary |
| 5 | 405 | 345 | 275 | 225 | 180 | 130 | 65 | 1.75 |
| ral reefs t peared.<br><br>less fish ead idly.<br><br>first fish h jaws eloped.<br><br>nitive d anisms eloped. | Amphibians were the first vertebrates to live on land.<br><br>First insects and arachnids became widespread.<br><br>Many new fish appeared in the oceans.<br><br>Ferns and seed plants also appeared, producing the first trees and forests. | Swamp forests were filled with seedless plants. The decaying plants formed coal in many parts of the world.<br><br>The evolution of the egg led to more four-legged vertebrates. It protected their embryos, so they could reproduce on land.<br><br>Ice covered much of Earth. | Land plants continued to evolve.<br><br>Several important reptiles appeared.<br><br>The period ended with the largest extinction yet recorded. | Vertebrates survived the Permian mass extinction better than inverte-brates did. The remaining species spread, and new ones evolved.<br><br>Primitive dinosaurs and the first true mammals appeared.<br><br>Modern conifers filled Triassic forests. | Dinosaurs dominated the land. They included giant sauropods and plated stegosaurs.<br><br>The first birds evolved at this time.<br><br>Forests consisted of ferns, conifers, cycads, and ginkgoes.<br><br>Mammals at the time looked like the shrew. | Tyrannosaurus and other dinosaurs roamed the land. Birdlike dinosaurs flew overhead.<br><br>Fossils show the first examples of flowering plants and the earliest bees and butterflies.<br><br>Pouched mammals and placental mammals evolved.<br><br>At the end of this period, all dinosaurs and many forms of marine reptiles became extinct. | Most of today's major mountain ranges formed during this period.<br><br>As grasses evolved, some mammals began to graze.<br><br>The first apes, horses, and elephants with trunks evolved.<br><br>Flowering plants thrived.<br><br>New insect species developed. | This is the period we are in today.<br><br>Humans evolved early in the Quaternary and spread rapidly.<br><br>Other mammals with larger brains also evolved.<br><br>Extreme climate changes may have led to rapid rates of evolution and extinction. |

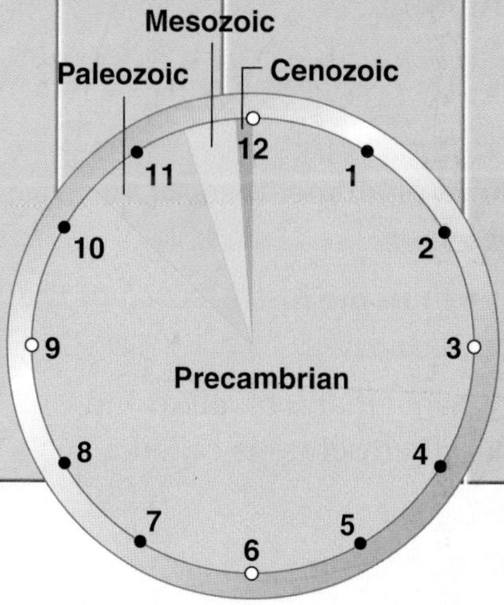


▲ **Figure 4-21** The geologic time scale

# Chapter 4 Challenges

## Chapter Summary

### Lesson 4-1

- **Evolution** is the process by which organisms change over time.
- **Adaptations** are special traits that help organisms to survive in their environments.
- **Mutations** can produce a change in an organism that can be passed on to future generations and may eventually result in a new species.

### Lesson 4-2

- Most **fossils** are the remains of hard parts of organisms, such as bones, teeth, and shells.
- Most fossils are formed in sedimentary rock. Fossils form when organisms are buried quickly beneath layers of sediment.

### Lesson 4-3

- The fossil record clearly shows that living things have changed throughout Earth's history.
- Similar body structure and DNA show that many animals are closely related and may have evolved from a common ancestor.

### Lesson 4-4

- A new species can develop from an old one by the process of evolution. Darwin's theory of **natural selection** describes how evolution may occur.

### Lesson 4-5

- Organisms must compete for resources in their living space. Weaker members of the species may not survive to reproduce.
- Human activities play a role in the survival or possible extinction of other animals.

### Lesson 4-6

- Fossils show that humans have evolved physically over time. Other evidence shows that as humans evolved they began to use more complex tools.

## Key Term Challenges

adaptation (p. 98)
amber (p. 100)
anthropology (p. 110)
evolution (p. 98)
extinct (p. 100)
extinction (p. 108)
fossil (p. 100)
homologous structures (p. 102)
mutation (p. 98)
natural selection (p. 104)
species (p. 98)
variation (p. 104)
vestigial structures (p. 102)

MATCHING **Write the Key Term from above that best matches each description.**

1. similar body structures
2. a change in organisms over time
3. the sudden change in a gene
4. the remains of a once-living organism
5. the survival of offspring that have favorable traits
6. differences in traits among individuals of a species
7. no longer found as a living species
8. hardened tree sap
9. the science that deals with the study of human beings
10. a special trait that helps an organism survive in its environment

FILL IN **Write the Key Term from above that best completes each statement.**

11. Body structures that seem to have no function are ___________.
12. The disappearance of all members of a species is called ___________.
13. The changes shown in the fossil record of the horse illustrate ___________.
14. A group of organisms that look alike and can reproduce among themselves is called a ___________.

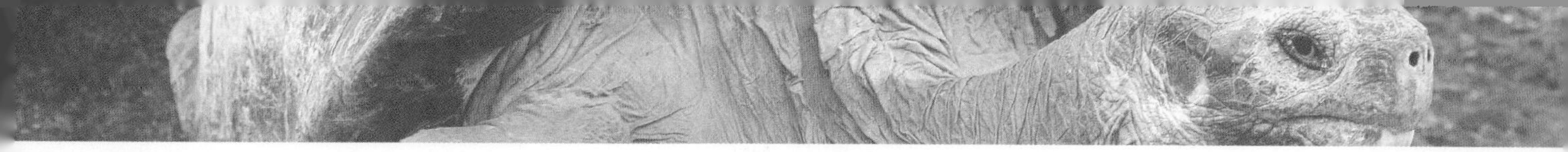

## *Content Challenges* TEST PREP

**MULTIPLE CHOICE Write the letter of the term or phrase that best completes each statement.**

**1.** An insect in amber is an example of
- **a.** a mutation.
- **b.** a fossil.
- **c.** variation.
- **d.** evolution.

**2.** Organisms that are no longer found as living species are
- **a.** mammals.
- **b.** fossils.
- **c.** extinct.
- **d.** endangered.

**3.** A fossil that forms when an organism decays and leaves an opening in the rock is called
- **a.** an amber.
- **b.** a mold.
- **c.** a cast.
- **d.** a sediment.

**4.** A sudden change in a gene is called
- **a.** an adaptation.
- **b.** a variation.
- **c.** evolution.
- **d.** a mutation.

**5.** Most fossils are found
- **a.** in metamorphic rock.
- **b.** in soil.
- **c.** in sedimentary rock.
- **d.** in tar.

**6.** The long neck of a giraffe is an example of
- **a.** an adaptation.
- **b.** a mutation.
- **c.** a variation.
- **d.** extinction.

**7.** The animal with the most complete fossil record is the
- **a.** elephant.
- **b.** finch.
- **c.** human.
- **d.** horse.

**8.** Neanderthals are a type of
- **a.** *Homo sapiens.*
- **b.** *Homo erectus.*
- **c.** *Paranthropus boisei.*
- **d.** *Homo habilis.*

**9.** The science that deals with the study of humans is
- **a.** geology.
- **b.** genetics.
- **c.** anthropology.
- **d.** biology.

**10.** Of the organisms listed, the one least likely to be found as a fossil is a
- **a.** dinosaur.
- **b.** horse.
- **c.** jellyfish.
- **d.** finch.

**TRUE/FALSE Write *true* if the statement is true. If the statement is false, change the underlined term to make the statement true.**

**11.** Sedimentary rocks usually form in <u>water</u>.

**12.** <u>Lamarck</u> developed the theory of natural selection.

**13.** The change in a species over time is called <u>variation</u>.

**14.** <u>Survival of the fittest</u> is also known as natural selection.

**15.** All modern humans belong to the species <u>*Homo sapiens*</u>.

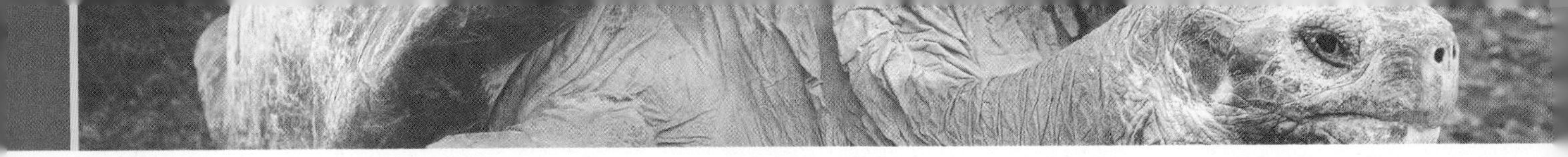

## *Concept Challenges* TEST PREP

**WRITTEN RESPONSE** **Answer each of the following questions in complete sentences.**

1. **EXPLAIN:** How might homologous structures help prove that certain organisms evolved from a common ancestor?
2. **HYPOTHESIZE:** How might the story of the British peppered moths have been different if the factories burned natural gas?
3. **APPLY:** What role does extinction play in evolution?
4. **EXPLAIN:** How do the Galápagos finches support Darwin's theory of natural selection?
5. **ANALYZE:** What role do changes in an organism's living space have on natural selection?

**INTERPRETING A TIMELINE** **Use the timeline in Figure 4-22 to answer the following questions.**

6. **IDENTIFY:** How old is the earliest known humanlike fossil?
7. **ANALYZE:** How many years does this timeline cover?
8. **IDENTIFY:** Which early humans lived approximately 1.5 million years ago?
9. **IDENTIFY:** Which appeared first, *Australopithecus africanus* or *Homo erectus*?
10. **CALCULATE:** How many years after the *Ardipithecus ramidus* period ended did the *Homo habilis* develop?

▼ **Figure 4-22** A timeline of possible human evolution

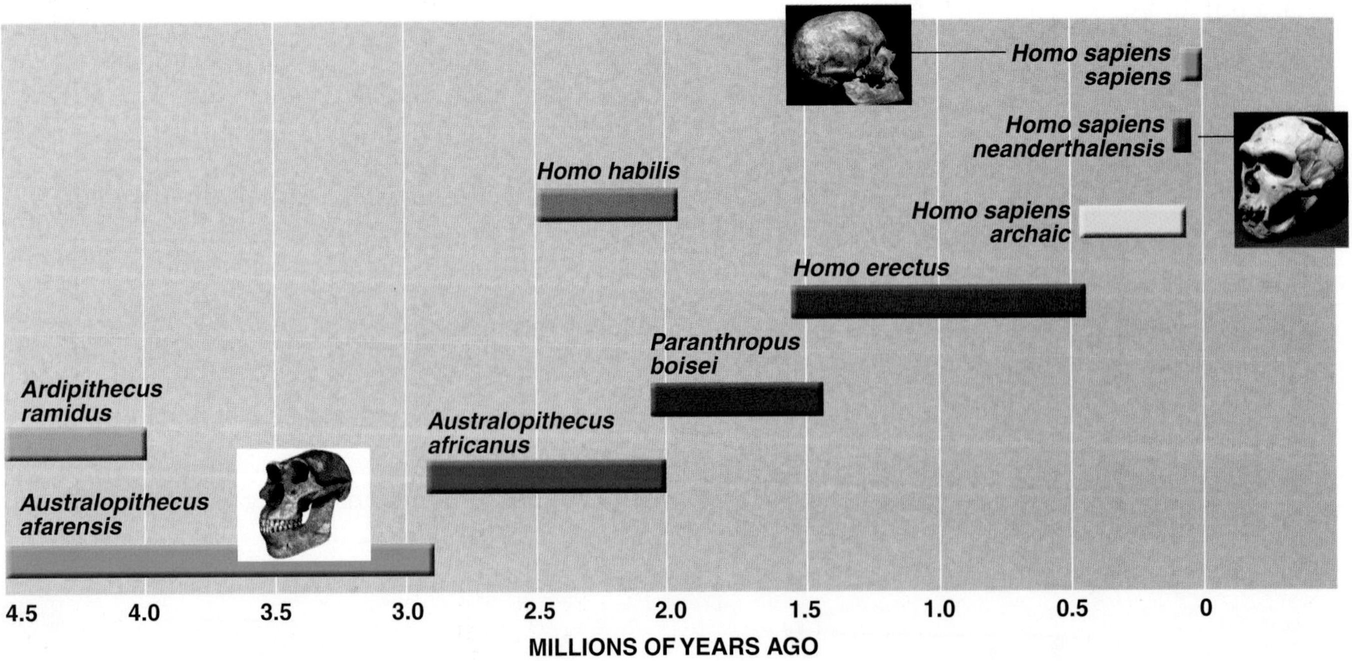

# Chapter 5 Classification

▲ **Figure 5-1** This insect collection has been classified by a person who studies insects, called an entomologist.

Scientists have identified at least 2.5 million different kinds of organisms so far. Every year, many more new species are discovered. It is important for scientists to keep information about the different species organized. To do this, many scientists use a classification system based on six kingdoms.

►How would you classify living things?

## Contents

# 5-1 What is classification?

### *Objective*

Explain why it is necessary to classify things.

### *Key Terms*

**classification** (klas-uh-fih-KAY-shuhn): grouping things according to similarities

**taxonomy** (tak-SAHN-uh-mee): science of classifying living things

**Classification** You are in a library, looking for a mystery novel. You look at the signs above each group of books. Each sign tells you what types of books are in each area. In no time at all, you find your book and are on your way. In a library, you are able to find books quickly because they are classified, or grouped, by subject. Grouping things according to similarities, or how they are alike, is called **classification.**

1 CLASSIFY: Name one other way you could classify books.

▲ **Figure 5-2** Like books in a library, insects can be classified according to similarities.

**Taxonomy** About 2.5 million different kinds of organisms have been discovered so far. Each year the list of living things grows longer. How do scientists keep track of so many organisms? Scientists use a system of classification. The science of classifying living things is called **taxonomy.** Scientists who classify living things are taxonomists.

Why do scientists classify living things? Classification is a way of organizing information about different kinds of living things. Classification also makes it easier for scientists to identify a newly discovered organism.

2 NAME: What is the science of classifying living things called?

**Classifying Living Things** Organisms are classified based on how they are alike. Taxonomists do not group organisms together simply because they look alike. Taxonomists use many characteristics to classify organisms. For example, taxonomists study the cells of an organism and the organelles that make up the cell. They study the way the organism grows and develops before it is born. They also study the blood of animals. Sometimes they study an organism's DNA. Taxonomists also study how an organism gets its energy.

3 STATE: What are two ways scientists classify organisms?

**Early Classification Systems** One of the first known systems used to classify living things was developed more than 2,000 years ago by the Greek philosopher Aristotle (AR-ihs-taht-ul). Aristotle classified organisms as either plants or animals. Animals were classified into smaller groups based upon where they lived. Aristotle's classification system had three groups of animals: land, water, and air.

One of Aristotle's students, Theophrastus (thee-uh-FRAS-tuhs) classified plants according to their sizes and kind of stem. Small plants with soft stems were called herbs. Medium-sized plants with many woody stems were called shrubs. Large plants with one woody stem were called trees.

In the 18th century, a Swedish botanist named Carolus Linnaeus (li-NEE-uhs) developed a new way to classify organisms. Linnaeus classified organisms according to their physical characteristics. Organisms that looked alike were grouped together. Linnaeus is known as the father of modern taxonomy.

▲ **Figure 5-3** In Aristotle's classification systems, walruses could have been classified as water animals.

4 LIST: What are the three groups of animals in Aristotle's classification system?

## CHECKING CONCEPTS

1. When you classify, you put things into __________ according to similarities.
2. The science of classifying living things is __________.
3. Taxonomists study the way organisms grow and develop before they are __________.
4. About __________ million different kinds of organisms have been discovered so far.

## THINKING CRITICALLY

5. INFER: Why is taxonomy an ongoing science?
6. APPLY: Food is classified in a supermarket. Books are classified in a library. Name two other classification systems that are used in daily life.
7. ANALYZE: Why do you think taxonomists do not use appearance alone to classify organisms?

## BUILDING SCIENCE SKILLS

***Comparing*** When you compare things, you look at how the things are alike and how they are different. Libraries classify books using either the Dewey Decimal System or the Library of Congress classification system. Find out how these two classification systems compare. What are some similarities and differences between the two systems?

## *Hands-On Activity*

## CLASSIFYING BUTTONS

*You will need a sheet of paper, a pencil, and an assortment of buttons.*

1. Carefully examine the buttons.
2. On a sheet of paper, list as many characteristics of the buttons as you can.
3. Classify the buttons according to one of their characteristics.
4. Repeat Step 3 two more times. Each time, use a different characteristic.

▲ **Figure 5-4** Classify an assortment of buttons.

### Practicing Your Skills

5. EXPLAIN: What characteristics did you use to classify the buttons?
6. ANALYZE: Which classification system had the most groups?
7. ANALYZE: Which classification system had the fewest groups?

# 5-2 How are living things classified?

### *Objective*

Explain the different levels of classification.

### *Key Terms*

**kingdom:** classification group made up of related phyla

**phylum** (FY-luhm), *pl.* **phyla:** classification group made up of related classes

**species:** group of organisms that look alike and can reproduce among themselves

**genus:** classification group made up of related species

**domain:** very broad classification group

**Classification Levels** Organisms that are classified in the same group are alike in some ways. The more alike organisms are, the more classification groups they share.

Altogether, there are seven major classification levels. The number of different kinds of organisms in each level decreases as you move from the kingdom level to each of the next smaller levels. From largest to smallest, the classification groups are kingdom, phylum, class, order, family, genus, and species.

1 **SEQUENCE:** List the seven classification levels from largest to smallest.

**Comparing the Levels** The largest classification group is a **kingdom.** Organisms in the same kingdom have similar cell structure and functions. In Figure 5-5, all of the organisms in Kingdom Animalia are multicellular and get energy from food. Each kingdom is divided into levels called **phyla.** The organisms in a phylum have similar body plans or structures. Each phylum is divided into still smaller levels. These levels are called classes. The organisms in a class have more details of structure and function in common. Classes are further divided into orders. Orders are divided into families. Families are divided into genuses.

A **species** is the smallest classification group. A species is a group of organisms that have similar characteristics and can reproduce among themselves. For example, all dogs belong to the same species. A **genus** is made up of two or more species that are very much alike. For example, dogs and wolves belong to different species, but they belong to the same genus.

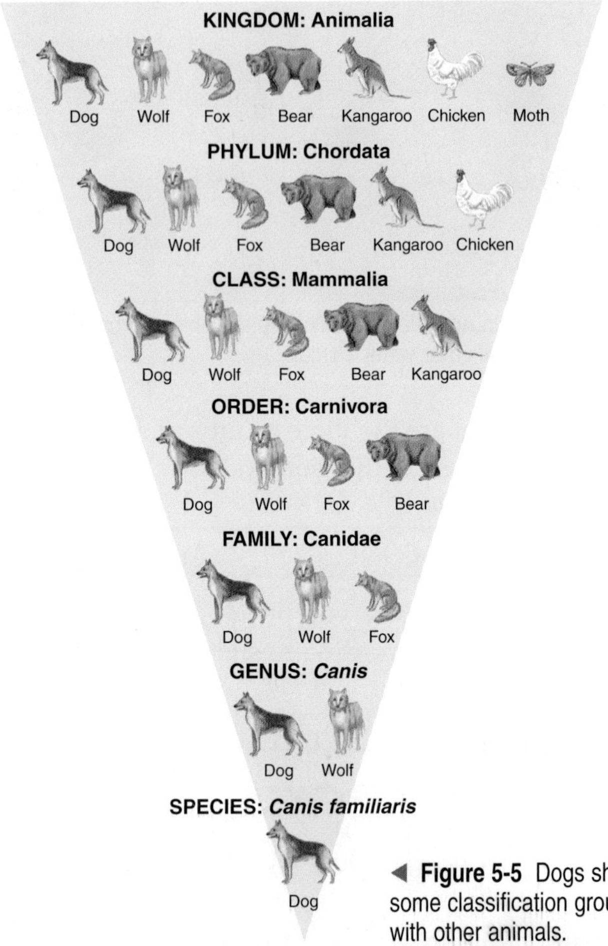


◀ **Figure 5-5** Dogs share some classification groups with other animals.

All organisms are classified using this system. For example, humans are members of Kingdom Animalia. They belong to the Phylum Chordata. They are members of the Class Mammalia. The order humans belong to is Primate and the family is Hominid. Humans are members of genus *Homo* and species *Homo sapiens*.

2 **RELATE:** Name an animal that belongs to the same phylum as humans.

**Naming Organisms** In Carolus Linnaeus's classification system, each kind of organism is identified by a two-part scientific name. A scientific name is made up of the genus and species names of an organism. For example, the scientific name for humans is *Homo sapiens*. When writing scientific names, always capitalize the genus name.

**3** **NAME:** What are the two parts of a scientific name?

**The Three-Domain System** Scientists also classify organisms into groups based on how they have evolved, or changed, over time. **Domains** are very broad classification categories. There are three domains: Bacteria, Archae, and Eukarya. The six kingdoms correspond to these domains. Kingdom Eubacteria is in the domain Bacteria. Kingdom Archaebacteria is part of domain Archaea. The other four kingdoms, Protista, Fungi, Plantae, and Animalia, make up the domain Eukarya.

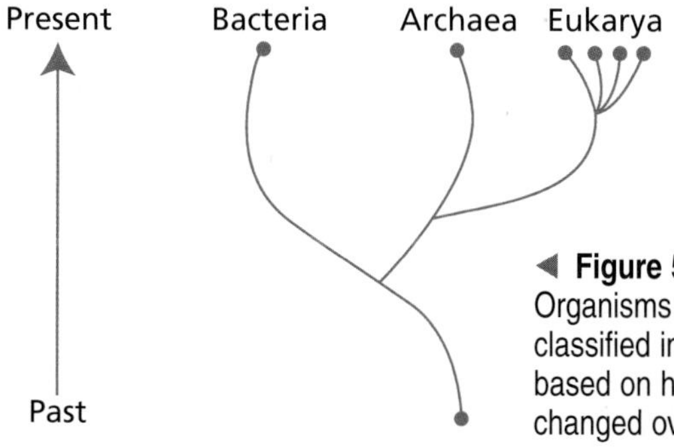


◀ **Figure 5-6** Organisms are classified into domains based on how they changed over time.

**4** **ANALYZE:** Which domain has the most kingdoms in it?

## ✓ CHECKING CONCEPTS

1. The largest classification group is the __________.
2. The classification group that is made up of related species is the __________.
3. A group of organisms that look alike and can reproduce among themselves is a __________.
4. The organisms in a phyla have similar body __________.

## THINKING CRITICALLY

*Use Figure 5-5 to answer the following questions.*

5. **INTERPRET:** How many classification groups do dogs and bears have in common?
6. **APPLY:** What is the scientific name for a pet dog?
7. **ANALYZE:** Which two animals are the most closely related?

## *Science and Technology*

### USING DNA TO CLASSIFY ORGANISMS

In addition to looking at an organism's physical traits, scientists are now using DNA to classify organisms. By testing an organism's DNA, scientists also can identify related organisms. In the late 1990s, scientists studied the DNA of whales and hippopotamuses. Both species have similar mutations in their DNA that are not found in other animals. This means that whales and hippopotamuses may have had a common ancestor.

DNA studies can also help scientists identify new species. In 2000, scientists studied DNA samples from living right whales in the Atlantic and Pacific Oceans and from museum specimens as much as 100 years old. They found that the right whales of the North Pacific show definite DNA differences from the two species of right whales that live in the Atlantic Ocean. These differences are large enough to classify the North Pacific right whales as a separate species.

▲ **Figure 5-6** Right whales of the North Pacific

**Thinking Critically** Why do you think scientists use DNA to classify organisms?

# LAB ACTIVITY
# Classifying Shells

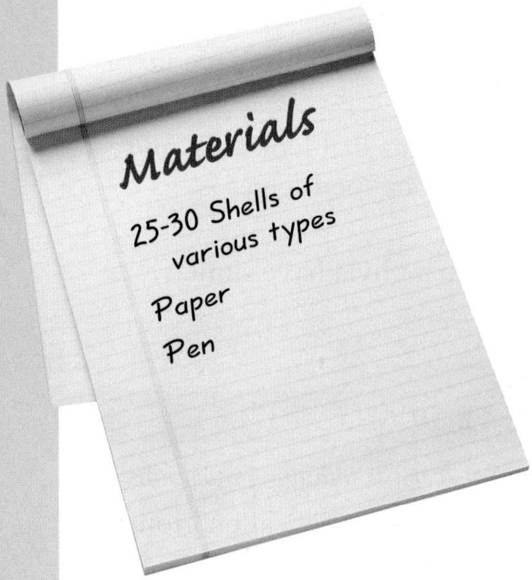


### *BACKGROUND*

Scientists need a system to keep track of the millions of living things discovered. A classification system groups things according to similarities. Such a system helps scientists organize information as well as identify newly discovered organisms.

### *PURPOSE*

In this activity, you will classify shells based on similar characteristics.

### *PROCEDURE*

1. Copy the chart in Figure 5-7 onto a sheet of paper.

2. Take several minutes to examine each of your seashells. Pay close attention to any similarities and differences among the shells.

3. With a partner, discuss how the shells should be classified. Some ways to classify shells are by color, by texture, and by shape.

4. Determine a classification system with at least three levels of classification. Divide the shells accordingly. Label each level. Then, draw and describe the shells that fit into each level.

▲ **STEP 3** Discuss how the shells should be classified.

▲ **STEP 4** Divide the shells.

5. Pick one of the levels of shells. Classify the shells in that level into three smaller groups.

6. Count the number of shells in each smaller level and complete the chart. Compare your chart with the charts of your classmates.

▲ **STEP 5** Classify the shells into three smaller groups.

*Classifying Shells*

| *Group Name* | *Group Features* | *Number of Shells* |
|---|---|---|
| | | |
| | | |
| | | |
| | | |

▲ **Figure 5-7** Copy this chart onto a sheet of paper.

## *CONCLUSIONS*

1. **EXPLAIN:** What characteristics helped you determine each level?

2. **ANALYZE:** How did the number of shells in each level change as the levels became more specific?

3. **COMPARE:** How did your classification system compare with those of your classmates?

4. **DISCUSS:** What is the importance of a classification system?

5. **APPLY:** Have your partner describe a new shell. Decide into which classification group it should be placed.

# 5-3 What are the kingdoms?

## *Objective*
Name and describe the kingdoms of living organisms.

## *Key Terms*
**fungus** (FUHN-guhs), *pl.* **fungi:** plantlike organism that lacks chlorophyll

**protist** (PROHT-ihst)**:** simple organism that has cells with nuclei

**Naming the Kingdoms** In Carolus Linnaeus's classification system, he classified all organisms as either plants or animals. With the invention of the microscope, scientists discovered new organisms. They placed these organisms into a third kingdom.

▲ **Figure 5-8** Carolus Linnaeusr

As more powerful microscopes were developed, scientists found that microscopic organisms are not all alike. Some microscopic organisms lack nuclei or various organelles. Scientists placed these organisms into kingdoms of their own. Studies also showed that a **fungus** and a plant were not as closely related as previously thought. Fungi are plantlike organisms that do not have chloroplasts in their cells. Scientists placed fungi in a kingdom of their own.

Today, most scientists use a six-kingdom classification system. Organisms are classified according to cell structure, whether they are unicellular or multicellular, and how they obtain food. Figure 5-9 shows the six kingdoms.

1 **HYPOTHESIZE:** Could the six-kingdom classification system change over time?

**Kingdom Archaebacteria** Members of the kingdom Archaebacteria are unicellular organisms. They do not have a true nucleus. Instead, their genetic material is coiled and located in one region. Archaebacteria also lack many of the organelles found in other kinds of cells.

Archaebacteria live in extreme environments. These include hot springs, very salty or acidic conditions, and the bottom of the ocean. The term archaebacteria means "ancient bacteria." Members of the kingdom Archaebacteria were on Earth billions of years before the dinosaurs.

2 **DEFINE:** What does the term *archaebacteria* mean?

**Kingdom Eubacteria** Like archaebacteria, members of the kingdom Eubacteria are unicellular organisms without a true nucleus. They are in their own kingdom, however, because they have different types of cell walls and cell membranes. Eubacteria live in more moderate conditions than archaebacteria. They live in soil, water, and even on your body. E. Coli is a eubacteria found in human intestines. *Streptococci* is a eubacteria that causes strep throat.

3 **COMPARE:** How are eubacteria and archaebacteria similar?

**Kingdom Protista** Most **protists** are unicellular organisms, such as parameciums. Others, such as algae, form colonies and are multicellular. Unlike bacteria, protists have a nucleus surrounded by a membrane. Protists also have a variety of organelles. The protist kingdom includes both plant-like and animal-like organisms. Some protists can make their own food, while others cannot. An amoeba is an example of a protist that cannot make its own food. A euglena is a protist that has a chloroplast and can make its own food.

4 **CONTRAST:** How do protists differ from bacteria?

**Kingdom Fungi** Most fungi are made up of many cells. Mushrooms are multicellular fungi. Some fungi, such as yeast, are unicellular. Like plants, the cells of most fungi have a cell wall. However, fungi do not have chlorophyll. Fungi do not make their own food. They absorb food from their environment. Most fungi feed on dead organisms.

5 **ANALYZE:** Why is "nature's recycler" a good nickname for fungi?

| THE SIX-KINGDOM CLASSIFICATION SYSTEM | | | |
|---|---|---|---|
| **Archaebacteria**  | • Archaebacteria are simple, unicellular organisms.<br>• An archaebacteria cell does not have a true nucleus.<br>• Archaebacteria live in extremely harsh environments. | **Fungi**  | • Fungi are unicellular or multicellular plant-like organisms.<br>• Fungi get the food they need from dead organisms.<br>• Yeasts and mushrooms are fungi. |
| **Eubacteria** 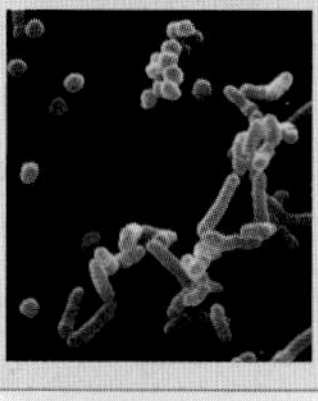 | • Eubacteria are simple, unicellular organisms.<br>• A eubacteria cell does not have a true nucleus.<br>• Eubacteria live in soil, water, and even in humans. | **Plantae**  | • Plants are multicellular organisms.<br>• Plants use chlorophyll to make their own food.<br>• Trees and flowers are plants. |
| **Protista** 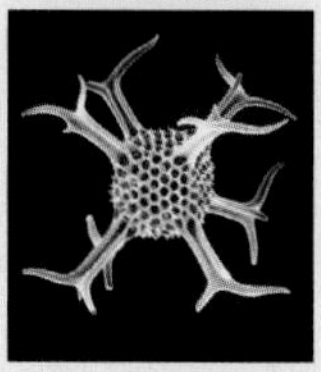 | • Protists are simple, unicellular or multicellular organisms.<br>• A protist cell does have a true nucleus.<br>• Amoebas and diatoms are protists. | **Animalia**  | • Animals are multicellular organisms.<br>• Animals get their food by eating other organisms.<br>• Birds, reptiles, fish, and mammals are animals. |

▲ **Figure 5-9** This table shows the characteristics of organisms in each kingdom.

**Kingdom Plantae** Plants are multicellular organisms. Plant cells have a cell wall made up of cellulose. Plant cells also have chloroplasts. Plants use chlorophyll contained in chloroplasts to make their own food. Members of the plant kingdom usually do not move on their own. Trees, grasses, and flowering plants are all members of the plant kingdom.

6 **INFER:** Why do you think the movement of plants is limited?

**Kingdom Animalia** Animals are made up of many cells. Most animals have organs that form organ systems. Animal cells do not have a cell wall or chlorophyll. Animals obtain food by eating plants and other animals. Unlike most members of other kingdoms, animals are able to move great distances on their own. Mammals, insects, and birds are all examples of animals.

7 **APPLY:** Why can't animals make their own food?

## CHECKING CONCEPTS

1. At one time, scientists classified all organisms as either plants or ___________.
2. Today, we use a ___________-kingdom classification system.
3. Members of the kingdom ___________ live in extreme environments.
4. Amoebas are members of the ___________ kingdom.
5. Mammals, fish, and reptiles all belong to the kingdom ___________.
6. The yeasts belong to the ___________ kingdom.

## THINKING CRITICALLY

7. **ANALYZE:** Why are archaebacteria and eubacteria placed in separate kingdoms?
8. **ANALYZE:** Why are fungi and plants placed in separate kingdoms?
9. **PREDICT:** How might new technologies affect the current classification system?

## INTERPRETING VISUALS

*Use Figure 5-9 to answer the following questions.*

10. **INTERPRET:** What kingdom do trees belong to?
11. **ANALYZE:** How many kingdoms contain unicellular organisms?
12. **INFER:** What types of organisms belong to the animal kingdom?

Integrating Language Arts

# THE Big IDEA

## How are organisms named?

In the Middle Ages, Latin and Greek were the languages used in universities and literature. They were also used in government and law. Scientists wrote in Latin and Greek.

Many terms in science come from Latin and Greek words. The names of the five kingdoms are examples of terms that come from Latin and Greek words. Plantae, for example, comes from the Latin *planta*, or "plant." Archaea is Latin that comes from the Greek *archaios*, which means "ancient." The word *genus* is a Latin term that means "type."

Both green and red algae are plant-like protists. The scientific term for green algae is Chlorophyta. The term *chloro* means "green." Red algae are called Rhodophyta. The term *rhodo* means "red." The term *phyta* means "plant."

A prefix is a word part that is added to the beginning of a root word. A suffix is a word part that is added to the end of a root word. These additions change the meaning of a word. In science, many prefixes and suffixes come from the Greek and Latin languages.

The table on page 127 lists some common Latin and Greek word parts used in science. You can use this table to identify some of the organisms in Figure 5-10. Then, follow the directions in the science log to learn more about "the big idea."✦

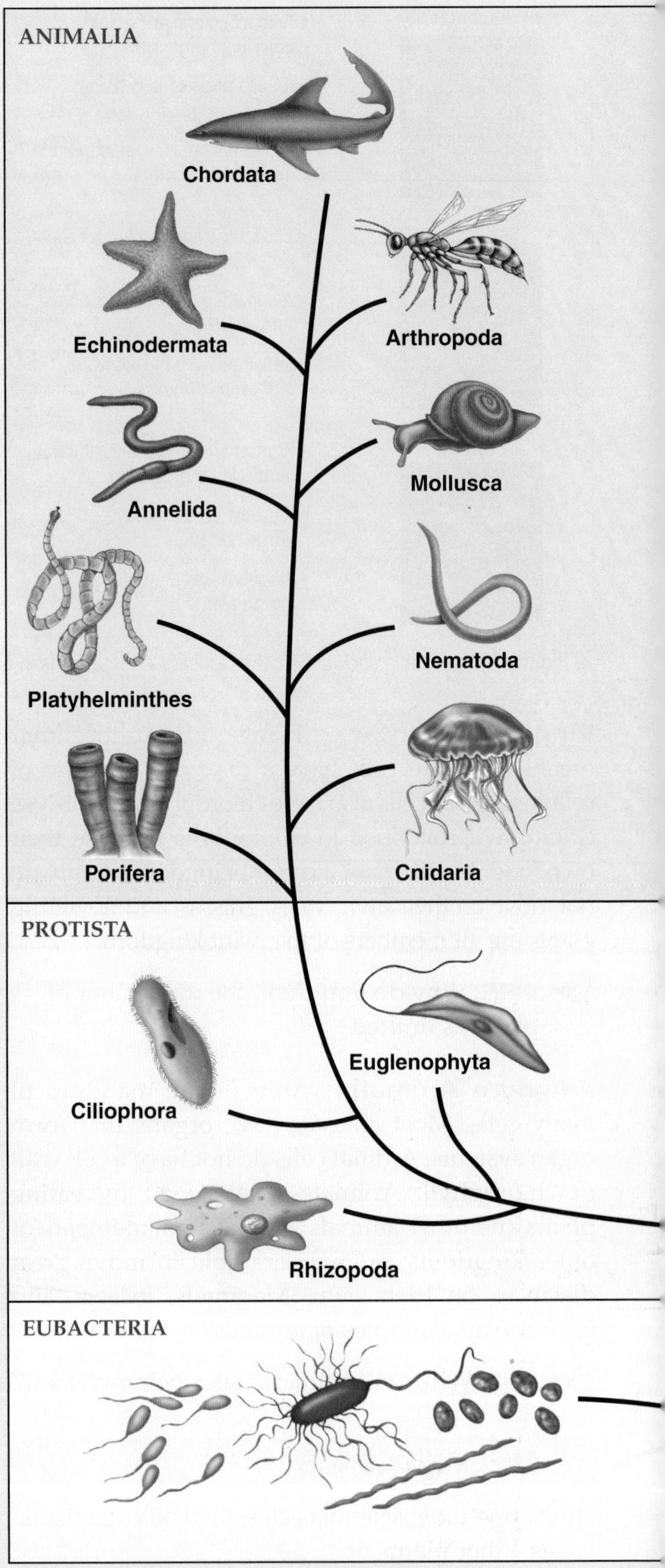


▲ **Figure 5-10** Many of the Latin and Greek word parts used in science describe an organism's characteristics.

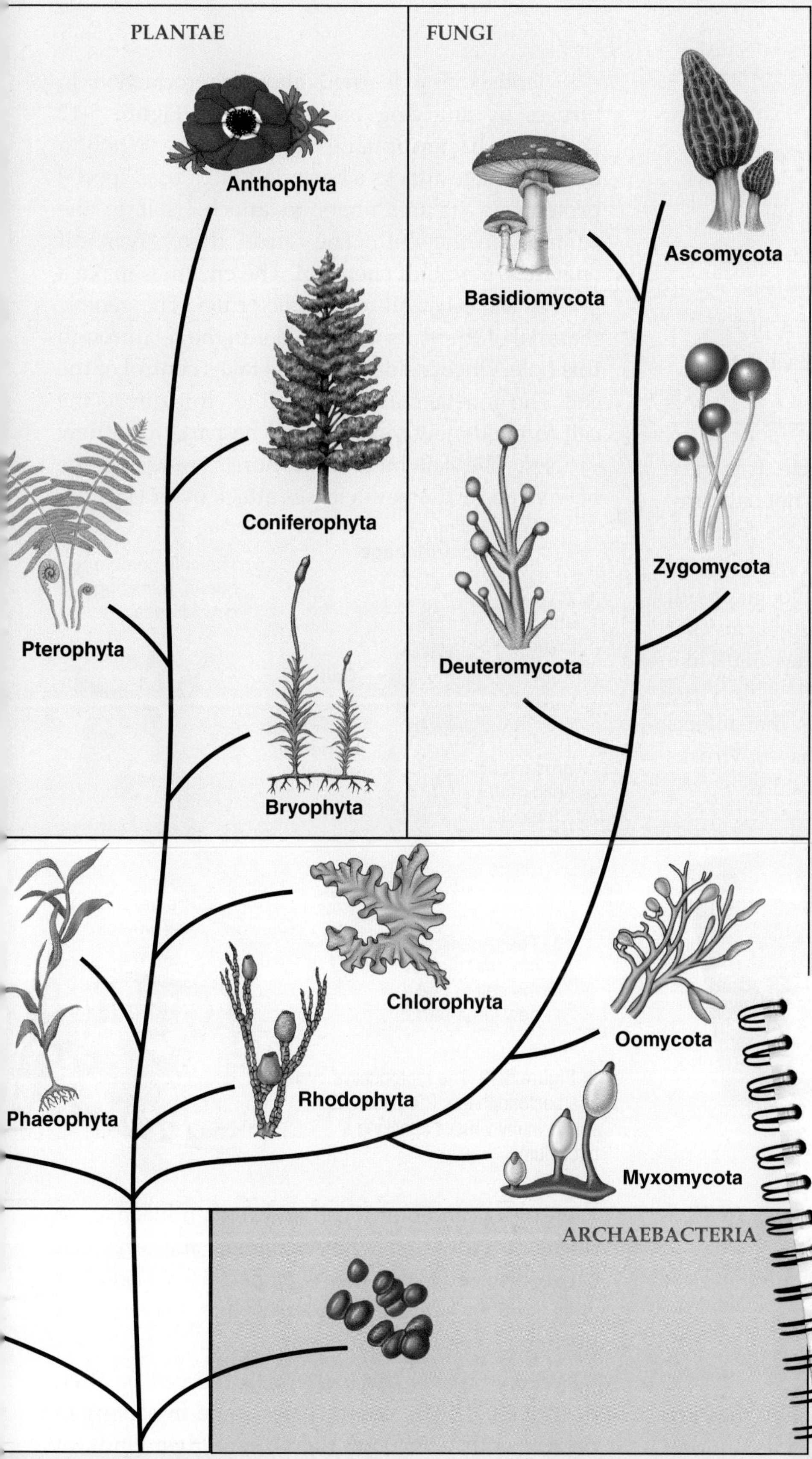


| UNDERSTANDING ORGAMISM NAMES | |
|---|---|
| **Word Part** | **Meaning** |
| Archae– | Ancient |
| Arthr– | Joint |
| Chlor– | Green |
| Cili– | Small hair |
| Con– | Cone |
| Derm– | Skin |
| Eu– | True |
| Myc– | Fungus |
| Oo– | Egg |
| –phyt | Plant |
| Platy– | Flat |
| –pod | Foot |
| Por– | Pore |
| Rhod– | Red |

WRITING ACTIVITY

### Science Log

Look at the tree of life on these two pages. Which group of organisms would you like to learn more about? In your science log, research and write about one of the phyla shown or one species in that group. Include information about the Greek or Latin meaning of its name. Write about why it interested you. Start your search at www.conceptsandchallenges.com.

# 5-4 What are viruses?

## *Objective*

Describe the structure of a virus.

## *Key Terms*

**virus** (VY-ruhs)**:** nonliving particle made up of a piece of nucleic acid covered with a protein

**capsid** (KAP-sihd)**:** protein covering of a virus

**bacteriophage** (bak-TIHR-ee-uh-fayj)**:** virus that infects bacteria

**Viruses** A **virus** is a nonliving particle. It is very different from a living cell. A virus does not have any organelles. Viruses do not grow, take in food, or make waste. A virus is just a piece of nucleic acid covered with an outer coat of protein called a **capsid.** The capsid makes up most of the virus and gives it its shape. Some viruses are round. Others look like long rods, like the one in Figure 5-11. This virus attacks and destroys bacteria. A virus that infects bacterial cells is called a **bacteriophage.** Viruses depend on living cells in order to reproduce.

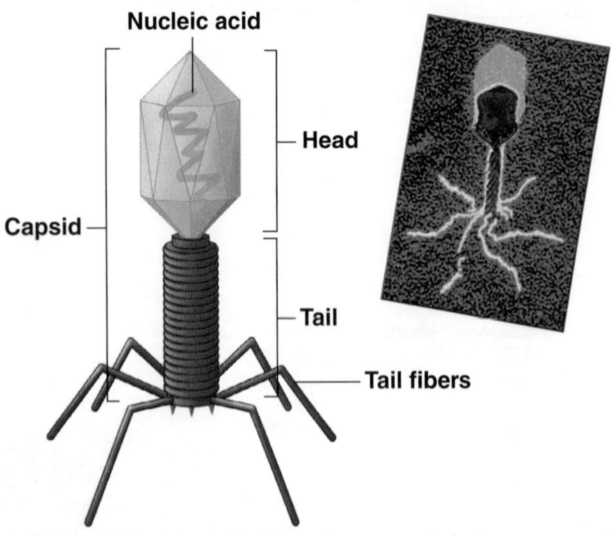


▲ **Figure 5-11** A bacteriophage diagram and photo

**1 DEFINE:** What is a capsid?

**Reproduction in Viruses** Even though they are not living, viruses are like living cells in one important way. They are able to reproduce more viruses. However, viruses can reproduce more viruses only inside a living cell.

Scientists first learned about reproduction in viruses by studying bacteriophages. Figure 5-12 shows a bacteriophage reproducing. When a bacteriophage attacks a bacterial cell, it uses special proteins in its tail fibers to attach itself to the surface of the cell. The virus then gives off enzymes, a type of chemical. The enzymes make a hole in the cell wall of the bacterium. The genetic material of the virus is injected into the cell through this hole. Once inside, the virus takes control of the cell. The genetic material from the virus directs the cell to make new virus parts. The parts form new viruses. The cell membrane bursts, releasing the new viruses. The new viruses attack other cells.

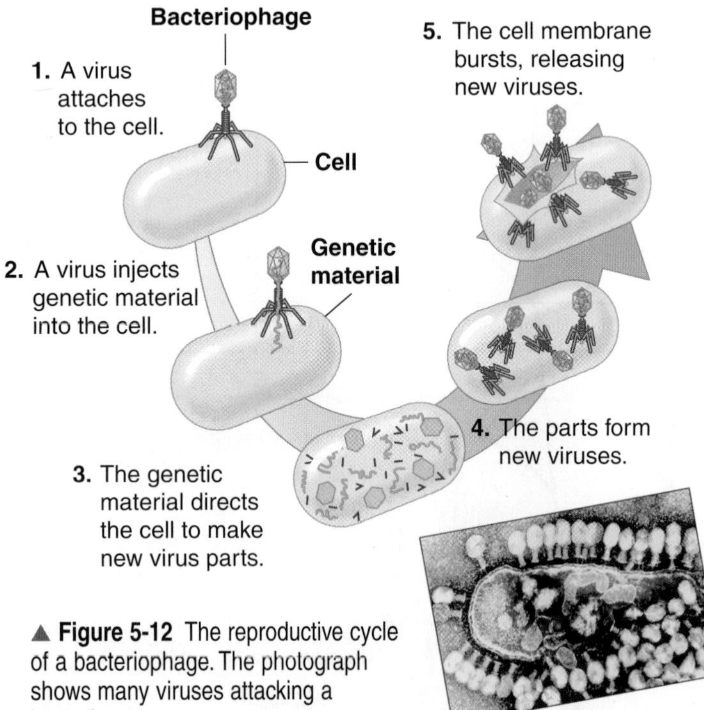


▲ **Figure 5-12** The reproductive cycle of a bacteriophage. The photograph shows many viruses attacking a bacterium.

A virus can enter a cell and remain inactive, or dormant. However, when activated, the virus can cause disease. Have you ever had a cold sore? A cold sore is caused by a virus that may remain dormant in your cells for years.

When viruses leave the cell, the cell is often destroyed. This is what causes some infections in people with a cold or flu virus. Other kinds of viruses reproduce differently. For example, when the HIV virus takes over a cell, it can force the cell to release new viruses gradually by budding, without causing the cell to burst.

**2** **SEQUENCE:** What happens once a virus enters a living cell?

**Classifying Viruses** Because viruses do not have all the characteristics of living things, they are not classified in the six-kingdom system. Scientists used to classify viruses based on which type of organism they infected. For example, there were plant viruses, animal viruses, and viruses that infect bacteria. Today scientists classify these viruses based on their shape and structure. There are three basic characteristics used to classify viruses. One is the structure of their capsid. Another characteristic is the type of nucleic acid they contain. Viruses can be DNA viruses or RNA viruses. The last characteristic is the way in which the virus reproduces.

Sometimes the common name of a virus is based on the disease that it causes. For example, the virus that causes the plant disease *tobacco mosaic disease* is called the tobacco mosaic virus. The common name for the virus that causes rabies is the rabies virus.

**3** **EXPLAIN:** How do scientists classify viruses?

## CHECKING CONCEPTS

1. A virus is a piece of __________ covered with a protein coat.
2. Scientists classify viruses based on their shape and __________.
3. A virus that infects a bacterial cell is called a __________.
4. Viruses can reproduce more viruses only inside __________ cells.
5. Scientists first learned about reproduction in viruses by studying __________.

## THINKING CRITICALLY

6. **CONTRAST:** How does a virus differ from a living cell?
7. **HYPOTHESIZE:** Why is it difficult to classify viruses?
8. **SEQUENCE:** List the steps of viral reproduction.

## HEALTH AND SAFETY TIP

Viruses can be contagious. This means they can be spread from one organism to another. The common cold is caused by a virus. One way to keep from spreading it is to wash your hands often.

## *Hands-On Activity*

### MODELING A VIRUS

*You will need a 5-inch dowel screw, one acorn nut that fits the screw, pliers, three pieces of metal wire, and a pipe cleaner.*

1. Screw the acorn nut onto the top of the screw.
2. Wrap the pipe cleaner around the middle of the screw.
3. Twist the three pieces of metal wire around the opposite end of the screw. Use the pliers to bend the ends of the wires down.

▲ **STEP 3** Twist metal wire around the end of the screw.

**Practicing Your Skills**

4. **IDENTIFY:** What type of virus does the model represent?
5. **IDENTIFY:** What kinds of organisms can be infected by the virus represented by the model?
6. **APPLY:** In which part of your model would the substance that enters living cells be contained?

# Chapter 5 Challenges

## Chapter Summary

### Lesson 5-1

- Grouping things according to how they are alike is called **classification.**
- **Taxonomy** is the science of classifying living things.
- Classification is a way of organizing information about living things.
- Taxonomists use many features to classify living things.

### Lesson 5-2

- Organisms are classified into a series of groups or levels.
- The seven classification levels from largest to smallest are **kingdom, phylum,** class, order, family, **genus,** and **species.**
- A species is a group of organisms that look alike and can reproduce among themselves.
- The two parts of a scientific name include the genus and species names of an organism.

### Lesson 5-3

- Most scientists follow the six-kingdom classification system.
- As new information becomes available, the six-kingdom classification system may change.
- Organisms can be classified as either archaebacteria, eubacteria, **protists, fungi,** plants, or animals.

### Lesson 5-4

- **Viruses** are made up of a strand of nucleic acid covered by a protein coat.
- **Capsids** give viruses their shape.
- Viruses can reproduce only inside a living cell.
- Once inside a living cell, the virus's genetic material takes control of the cell.
- Viruses are classified according to their shape and structure.

## Key Term Challenges

bacteriophage (p. 128)
capsid (p. 128)
classification (p. 118)
domain (p. 120)
fungus (p. 124)
genus (p. 120)
kingdom (p. 120)
phylum (p. 120)
protist (p. 124)
species (p. 120)
taxonomy (p. 118)
virus (p. 128)

MATCHING **Write the Key Term from above that best matches each description.**

1. plantlike organisms that lack chlorophyll
2. virus that infects bacteria
3. way of grouping things together based on how they are similar
4. very broad classification categories; includes Bacteria, Archae, and Eukarya
5. protein covering of a virus
6. science of classifying things
7. classification group made up of related phyla
8. simple organism that has cells with true nuclei; includes diatoms and amoebas

IDENTIFYING WORD RELATIONSHIPS **Explain how the words in each pair are related. Write your answers in complete sentences.**

9. genus, species
10. classification, taxonomy
11. capsid, virus
12. kingdom, phylum

## Content Challenges TEST PREP

**MULTIPLE CHOICE Write the letter of the term or phrase that best completes each sentence.**

1. Grouping things according to how they are alike is
   - **a.** taxonomy.
   - **b.** classification.
   - **c.** photosynthesis.
   - **d.** organization.
2. Scientists first learned about viral reproduction by studying
   - **a.** fungi.
   - **b.** algae.
   - **c.** bacteriophages.
   - **d.** bacteria.
3. The largest classification group is the
   - **a.** order.
   - **b.** class.
   - **c.** phylum.
   - **d.** kingdom.
4. Today, most scientists accept a classification system with
   - **a.** two kingdoms.
   - **b.** three kingdoms.
   - **c.** four kingdoms.
   - **d.** six kingdoms.
5. Organisms that look alike and can reproduce among themselves make up a
   - **a.** species.
   - **b.** genus.
   - **c.** family.
   - **d.** kingdom.
6. The kingdom made up of mostly single-celled organisms that have real nuclei is the
   - **a.** plant kingdom.
   - **b.** animal kingdom.
   - **c.** fungi kingdom.
   - **d.** protist kingdom.
7. The smallest classification group or level is a
   - **a.** genus.
   - **b.** species.
   - **c.** class.
   - **d.** kingdom.
8. Two groups of viruses are DNA viruses and
   - **a.** capsid viruses.
   - **b.** protist viruses.
   - **c.** RNA viruses.
   - **d.** yeast viruses.
9. Mushrooms are
   - **a.** bacteria.
   - **b.** protists.
   - **c.** fungi.
   - **d.** animals.
10. The two parts of a scientific name include the
    - **a.** family and order names.
    - **b.** genus and species names.
    - **c.** kingdom and phylum names.
    - **d.** class and order names.

**TRUE/FALSE Write *true* if the statement is true. If the statement is false, change the underlined term to make the statement true.**

11. The two kingdoms of bacteria are Archaebacteria and Potista.
12. Taxonomy is the study of living things.
13. There are ten major classification groups for living things.
14. Dogs and wolves belong to the same genus.
15. Scientists who classify living things are botanists.
16. The protein covering of a virus is called a capsid.

## Concept Challenges TEST PREP

**WRITTEN RESPONSE** **Answer each of the following questions in complete sentences.**

1. **ANALYZE:** If you were to discover a new species, how would you determine its classification?
2. **EXPLAIN:** Why is taxonomy a complex subject?
3. **HYPOTHESIZE:** Why is it difficult to treat an infection caused by a virus?
4. **LIST:** What do scientists use to classify an organism?
5. **ANALYZE:** Fungi were once called the nongreen plants. Why do you think fungi were described in this way?

**INTERPRETING A DIAGRAM** **Use Figure 5-13 to answer the following questions.**

6. **IDENTIFY:** What is shown in the diagram?
7. **IDENTIFY:** What is the structure labeled *A* called?
8. **IDENTIFY:** What is the structure labeled *B* called?
9. **OBSERVE:** What is happening in Step 2?
10. **OBSERVE:** What is happening in Step 5?

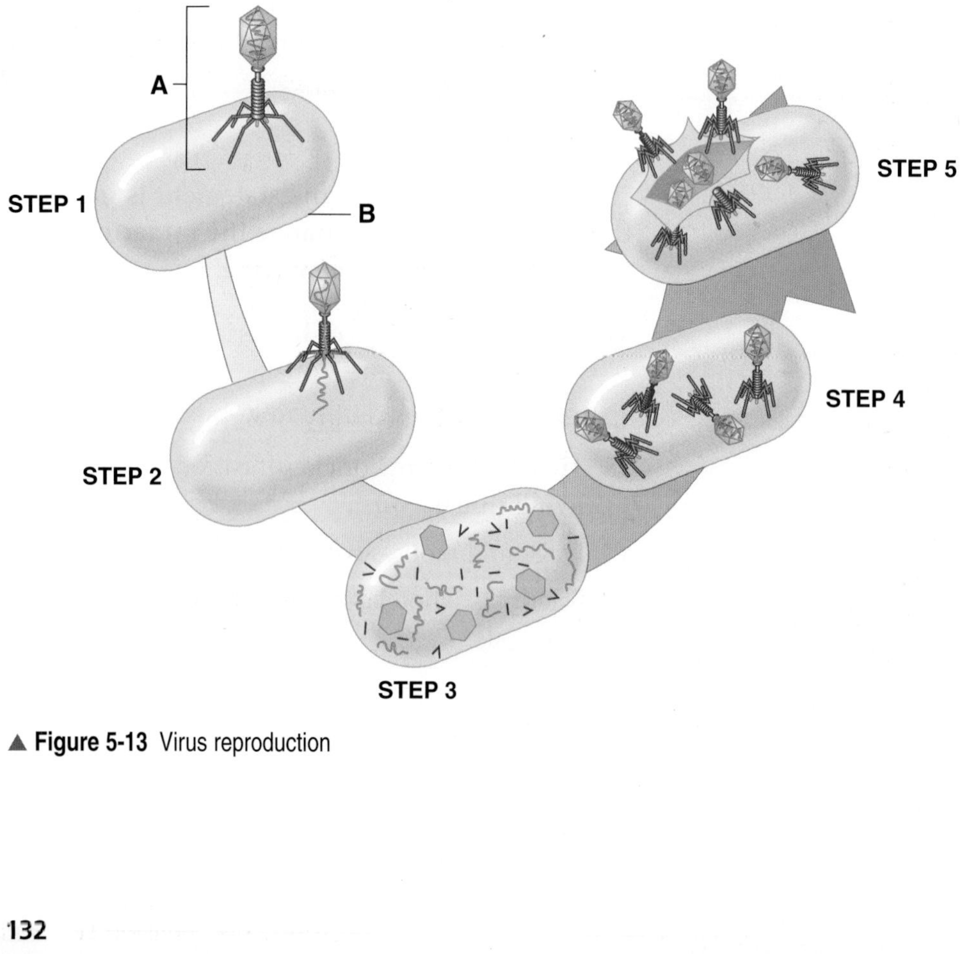


▲ **Figure 5-13** Virus reproduction

# Chapter 6 Simple Organisms

▲ **Figure 6-1** Diatoms come in many interesting shapes and patterns.

Diatoms are microscopic organisms that live in water. These organisms are capable of making their own food through photosynthesis. Diatoms have shells made of silica, a component of glass. When diatoms die, their shells fall to the bottom of the ocean and form layers of material called diatomaceous earth, or DE. This material is a rough powder because of the silica shells. DE is mined for use in many products, such as cleaning products, filters, and even toothpaste!

▶Why do you think DE would be used in toothpaste?

## Contents

# 6-1 What is the Kingdom Archaebacteria?

## *Objectives*

Explain why there are two kingdoms of bacteria. Identify traits of Archaebacteria.

## *Key Terms*

**Archaebacteria** (ar-KEE-back-teer-eeya)**:** the most ancient type of simple, single-celled organisms on Earth

**Extremophile** (ex-TREEM-uh-file)**:** an organism that lives under extreme environmental conditions

**Chemosynthetic** (keemo-syn-THEH-tic)**:** an ability of some organisms to use sulfur as a source of energy

**Flagellum** (FLAH-jel-umm)**:** a whip-like structure used for movement

**Kingdom Archaebacteria** **Archaebacteria**, also called Archaea (ar-KEE-uh), are simple, single-celled organisms. They are the most ancient type of living things on Earth. They live in harsh, extreme conditions that existed even when Earth was young. Scientists believe Archaea make up the largest portion of all living things on Earth.

1 **IDENTIFY:** What are Archaebacteria?

**Characteristics of Archaebacteria** Archaea once shared a kingdom with Eubacteria. They both appear to be alike under the microscope. However, their many differences led scientists to split them into separate kingdoms. Figure 6-3 shows some of their differences and similarities.

▲ **Figure 6-2** Archaebacteria exist in environments that are deadly to most living things.

| Traits | Archaea | Eubacteria |
|---|---|---|
| Single-celled | X | X |
| No nucleus | X | X |
| Require sunlight | | X |
| Require oxygen | | X |
| Live in extreme environments | X | |
| Asexual reproduction (binary fission) | X | X |
| Form spore | | X |
| Can cause dieases | | X |

▲ **Figure 6-3**

2 **EXPLAIN:** Why did scientists make Archaebacteria its own kingdom?

**Extremophiles** Many of the Archaeobacteria are **extremophiles.** This means they live in extreme conditions of temperature, pressure, acidity, alkalinity, or the lack of oxygen. The Archaea are classified into three types of extremophiles.

- The **Methanogens** are anaerobic. That means the oxygen in normal air is poisonous to them. They convert hydrogen ($H_2$) and carbon dioxide ($CO_2$) to methane gas ($CH_4$). Methanogens are found in bogs, sewage treatment plants, and the intestinal tracts of cattle, termites, and humans. Ancient Methanogens are the source of our deposits of natural gas ($CH_4$).
- The **Thermoacidophiles** are composed of Thermophiles and Acidophiles. Both of these groups are **chemosynthetic.** That means they use sulfur or other elements as a source of energy. Thermophiles can withstand extreme heat, often over the boiling point of water (100° C). They are found near hydrothermal vents, which are cracks on the ocean floor that spew out lava and scalding water. They are also found in hot springs, geysers, and petroleum deposits. Acidophiles can live in highly acidic environments. They are used in industry to extract metals, such as gold, cobalt, and copper from rocks.

- The Halophiles live in highly saline environments, such as salt lakes, pools of sea water, and the intestines of sea animals. One type can use sunlight as a source of energy even though it does not contain chlorophyll.

3 **IDENTIFY:** What is an extremophile?

▲ **Figure 6-4** Halophiles (above) live in salty conditions.

**Movement** Some Archaea have the ability to move with the help of a **flagellum.** A flagellum is a whip-like structure. By moving the flagellum back and forth, bacteria can move through liquids. Some have multiple flagella. Others have few or no flagella. Most Archaea are found in places where movement is not necessary.

4 **DESCRIBE:** How do some Archaea move?

## CHECKING CONCEPTS

1. Archaea are simple, __________ organisms.
2. Archaebacteria used to share a kingdom with __________, because of their similarities.
3. An Archaea cell does not contain a __________.
4. An __________ is able to live in extreme environmental conditions.
5. A __________ is a whip-like structure used for movement.

## THINKING CRITICALLY

6. **INFER:** A single-celled organism with no nucleus is found near a vent on the ocean floor. Is this most likely Archaebacteria or Eubacteria?
7. **PREDICT:** The Dead Sea is one of the saltiest bodies of water on Earth. What type of bacteria would be found there?

## BUILDING LANGUAGE ARTS SKILLS

***Using Word Parts*** Look up the prefixes *thermo-*, *chemo-*, and *archae-* in the dictionary. Then use the prefixes to define the following terms: *thermophiles*, *chemosynthetic*, and *archaebacteria*.

## Real-Life Science

### DEEP-SEA VENT COMMUNITIES

Archaeobacteria have been found in the boiling waters around deep-sea vents on the ocean floor. These vents are underwater volcanoes that produce magma and superheated water. Most are thousands of feet beneath the surface of the oceans, where sunlight cannot reach. Dissolved metals in these superheated waters form chimneys called black smokers and white smokers. Diverse communities live around these chimneys. They include tube worms, blind crabs and shrimp, giant clams, mussels, sponges, and a variety of vent fish that live without sunlight.

When scientists first discovered these communities, they wondered how these creatures could live without sunlight. They found that the base of the food chains in these communities were Archaea. The Archaea oxidize sulfides as a source of energy.

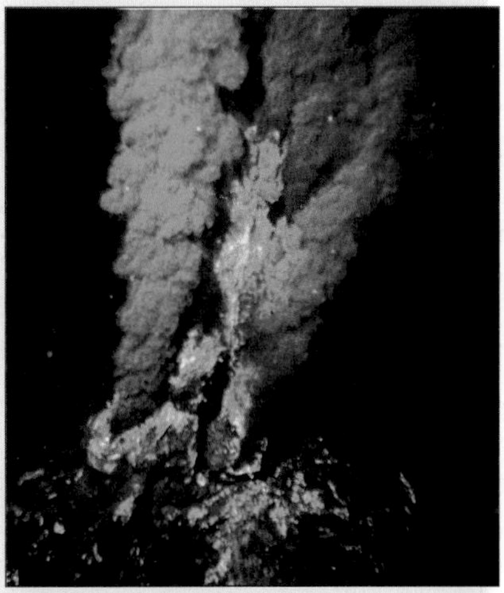

▲ **Figure 6-5** Black smoker community

**Thinking Critically** Why do you think darkness and heat are not a problem for Archaea?

# 6-2 What is the Kingdom Eubacteria?

## *Objective*

Describe a Eubacterium. Classify bacteria by shape.

## *Key Terms*

**Eubacteria** (YOO-back-teer-eeya)**:** simple, single-celled organisms that live nearly everywhere in the world

**coccus** (KAHK-uhs), *pl.* **cocci:** spherical-shaped bacterium

**spirillum** (spy-RIHL-uhm), *pl.* **spirilla:** spiral-shaped bacterium

**bacillus** (buh-SIHL-uhs), *pl.* **bacilli:** rod-shaped bacterium

**endospore** (en-DOH-spor)**:** inactive bacterium surrounded by a thick wall

**Eubacteria** Generally, when people talk about bacteria, they are talking about Eubacteria. Eubacteria are single-celled organisms that live nearly everywhere in the world. Like Archaebacteria, they are simple, single-celled organisms. Their many differences, however, placed them in a separate kingdom.

**Three Groups of Eubacteria** The Eubacteria are grouped by their shapes. Some are round, or spherical, and are called **cocci.** Cocci can grow in pairs, grape-like clusters, and chains like beads on a string. Chains of cocci are called streptococci. This type of bacteria is responsible for the disease "strep throat." Other Eubacteria have a curved or spiral shape and are called **spirilla.** One type of spirilla causes syphilis. The most common types of Eubacteria are rod shaped, and are called **bacilli.** Bacilli are responsible for tuberculosis and anthrax.

1 **DESCRIBE:** What are the three basic shapes of Eubacteria?

**Needs of Eubacteria** Many of the Eubacteria need water and a moderate temperature. Many are aerobic and need oxygen, while others are anaerobic and do not require oxygen. Some thrive on nutrients inside living plants and animals. Others break down and absorb nutrients from the remains of dead plants and animals. Many thrive in darkness, while others are photosynthetic and produce their own food in sunlight. Some of these Eubacteria are known as cyanobacteria. Like green plants, they contain chlorophyll. They were once known as blue-green algae. Scientists now know they are Eubacteria because they lack the nucleus and chloroplasts present in algae.

2 **EXPLAIN:** What are the needs of aerobic Eubacteria?

**Bacterial Reproduction** The Eubacteria reproduce by binary fission. Each cell can split into two daughter cells, which are identical to the parent cell. In pathogenic (disease-causing) Eubacteria, small numbers of cells can multiply many times in a short period of time. This leads to harmful infections that can overwhelm the host organism's defenses.

▲ **Figure 6-6** Cocci bacteria

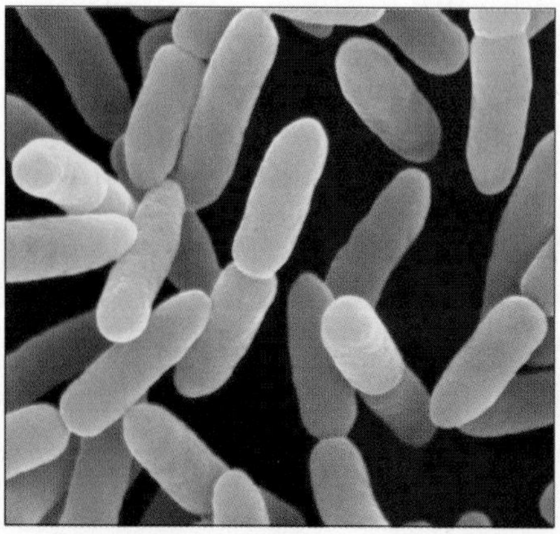

▲ **Figure 6-7** Bacilli bacteria

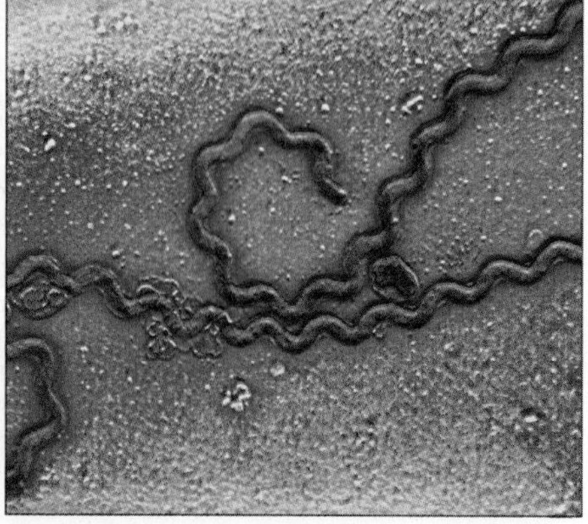

▲ **Figure 6-8** Spirilla bacteria

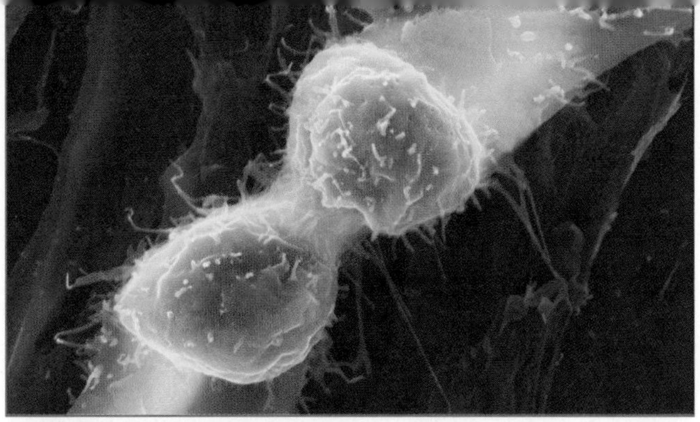

▲ **Figure 6-9** Binary fission in Eubacteria.

**Endospores** Some Eubacteria can live through periods of extreme heat or cold. When conditions in their environment are not ideal, each bacteria cell can form a protective wall around itself. Eubacteria that have these protective walls are called **endospores.** The endospores may be resistant to drying, heat and cold, chemical disinfectants, and even radiation. This allows them to survive for long periods in soil, air, or water. When conditions become favorable, they will return to their active state.

3 **EXPLAIN:** What do endospores do?

▲ **Figure 6-10** Eubacteria decompose dead materials.

**Useful Eubacteria** Eubacteria enrich soil through the process of decomposition. They break down dead organic materials such as leaves and animal wastes. This material is turned into useful organic compounds. These compounds return important nutrients to the soil. Eubacteria in the soil change nitrogen to compounds plants can use to make proteins. These Eubacteria are known as **nitrogen-fixing bacteria.**

Eubacteria also play an important role in the digestion of food. Your digestive tract naturally contains billions of Eubacteria. They help digest nutrients and form the essential vitamins K and B-12. Humans also use other Eubacteria to make buttermilk, yogurt, cheese, sauerkraut, and antibiotics.

4 **DESCRIBE:** What are some of the foods that Eubacteria help to produce?

**Eubacteria and Food Decay** Some Eubacteria can cause foods to spoil or decay. Some produce poisons while they are acting on food. Cooking foods thoroughly at high temperatures kills many harmful bacteria. Canning, pickling, and freezing food are other ways of preventing or slowing down the action of harmful bacteria.

Sometimes, heating and canning are not enough. The bacteria that causes botulism can withstand the canning process by forming endospores. One sign of this harmful bacterium is bulging or exploded cans. Eating foods that contain harmful bacteria can make you very sick.

5 **INFER:** Why are many foods refrigerated?

## CHECKING CONCEPTS

1. Eubacteria are grouped by their __________.
2. Eubacteria with a protective wall are known as __________.
3. Nitrogen-fixing bacteria change __________ in the soil to a form useful to plants.
4. Cooking, canning, and freezing food __________ the action of harmful bacteria.

## THINKING CRITICALLY

5. **EXPLAIN:** Foods that are canned are cooked at high temperatures and pressures, and then placed in airtight containers. What effect do these actions have on food?
6. **APPLY:** Identify three ways that Eubacteria affect your life.

## INTERPRETING VISUALS

*Use Figures 6-6 to 6-8 to answer the question.*

7. **INFER:** How can health professionals use a microscope to study disease?

# 6-3 What is the Kingdom Protista?

## *Objective*

Identify some common protists and how they move.

## *Key Terms*

**protozoan** (proht-uh-ZOH-uhn)**:** one-celled, animal-like protist

**pseudopod** (SOO-doh-pahd)**:** fingerlike extension of cytoplasm

**cilium** (SIHL-ee-uhm), *pl.* **cilia:** tiny, hairlike structures

**Kingdom Protista** Kingdom Protista, or the protist kingdom, is made up of very simple organisms. Most protists are unicellular. A few kinds are multicellular. A protist cell has a nucleus surrounded by a membrane. The protist kingdom is divided into three large groups. The three groups are the protozoans, the algae, and the slime molds. These groups are made up of many different phyla of organisms.

1 DESCRIBE: What are two characteristics of protists?

**Animal-like Protists** **Protozoans** are one-celled, or unicellular, organisms. They often are called the animal-like protists because they cannot make their own food. They need to get food by eating other organisms. Most protozoans can move about on their own. Amoebas, paramecia, and trypanosomes are all examples of animal-like protists.

2 LIST: Name three animal-like protists.

**Amoeba** An amoeba is a protozoan. Most amoebas live in fresh water. They have fingerlike projections of cytoplasm called **pseudopods.** The cell membrane of an amoeba is very flexible, so the pseudopods can stretch and shrink. An amoeba uses its pseudopods to move through water and to trap and take in food. When the amoeba approaches a food particle, its pseudopods surround the particle and form a food vacuole around it.

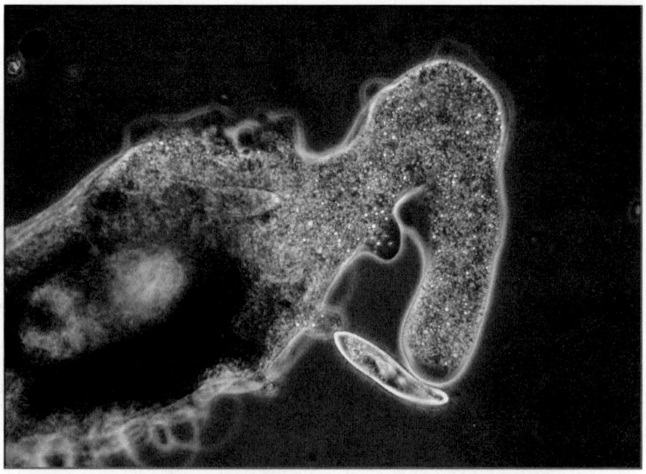

▲ **Figure 6-11** This amoeba is about to eat a paramecium.

3 EXPLAIN: How are pseudopods beneficial to the amoeba?

**Paramecium** A paramecium is a slipper-shaped protozoan. Like an amoeba, a paramecium lives in fresh water. It is part of a phylum of protozoa that use **cilia** for movement. Cilia are tiny, hairlike structures that move. They are found around the edge of the paramecium. The cilia move back and forth like tiny oars. The beating of cilia moves a paramecium through water.

The cilia also help the paramecium get food. When the paramecium finds food, the moving cilia create a current in the water. This current moves the food particles down into a mouthlike structure called an oral groove.

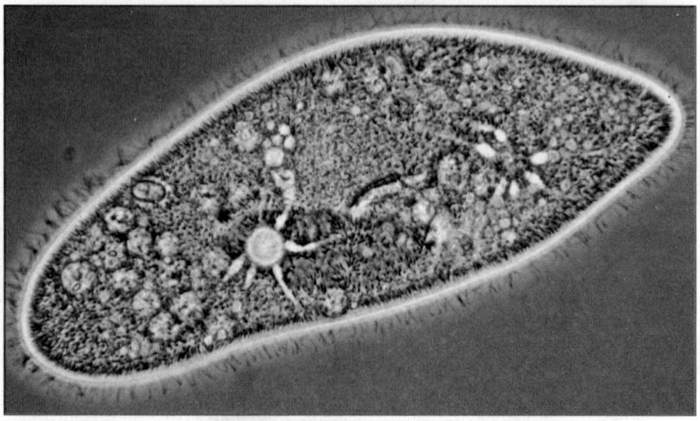

▲ **Figure 6-12** A paramecium uses cilia for movement and for capturing food.

4 IDENTIFY: What structures does a paramecium use to move?

**Trypanosomes** A trypanosome is a disease-causing protozoan. In humans, it causes a disease called African sleeping sickness. Trypanosomes also cause diseases in horses and cattle. Trypanosomes are part of a group of protozoa with flagella. The common name for this group is the flagellates. Some flagellates have one flagellum. Others have two or more flagella.

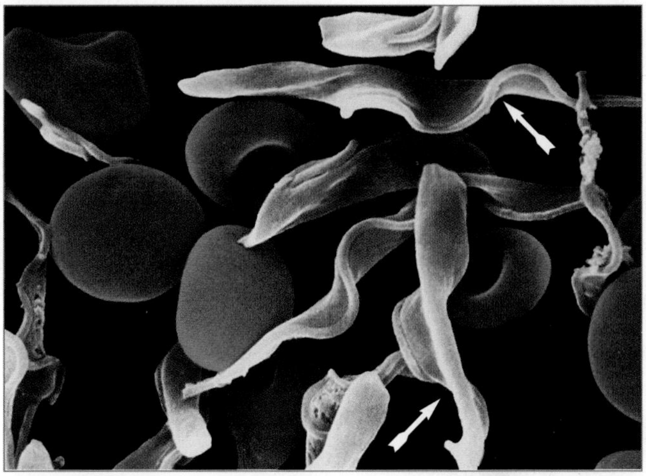

▲ **Figure 6-13** Trypanosomes (shown with arrows) are protozoans that cause African sleeping sickness.

5 NAME: How do flagellates move?

## CHECKING CONCEPTS

1. Protozoans, algae, and slime molds are all classified in the __________ kingdom.
2. Amoebas move by extending their __________.
3. A paramecium moves by beating the __________ that extend from its surface.
4. Protozoa with flagella are called __________.
5. Sleeping sickness is caused by a __________.

## THINKING CRITICALLY

6. **ANALYZE:** Why is it important that protozoans have structures that help them move?
7. **COMPARE:** How are flagella and cilia alike?

## BUILDING SCIENCE SKILLS

***Modeling*** Make a model of one of the three protozoans described in this lesson. Make sure your model shows the structures that the organism uses for movement and capturing food. Present your model to the class.

## *Integrating Earth Science*

TOPICS: sediments

### WHITE CLIFFS OF DOVER

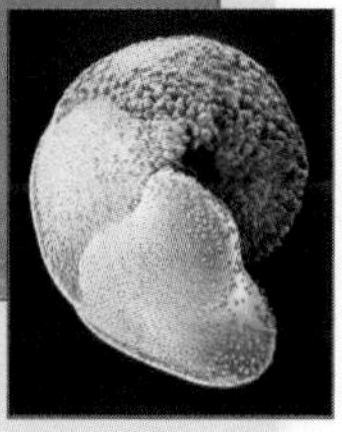

▲ **Figure 6-14** The White Cliffs of Dover, in the larger picture, are made from the shells of the foraminifera, shown in the smaller picture.

The Strait of Dover is a narrow body of water that connects the English Channel with the North Sea. Both English and French shores of the strait are formed mainly by chalk cliffs. The most famous of these cliffs may be the White Cliffs of Dover in southeast England.

The chalk cliffs were formed during the Cretaceous Period, about 100 million years ago. At that time, Earth's climate was warmer and sea levels were much higher. Warm seas covered most of Europe, providing an ideal place for protozoans to live. Protozoa that still flourish there are called foraminifera. Some of these protists have tiny shells made of calcium carbonate ($CaCO_3$). When these protists die, their shells sink to the ocean bottom as fine sediment. Gradually, this sediment builds up to become hundreds of meters thick. The thick sediment eventually is compressed to form solid white rock cliffs.

**Thinking Critically** Why do you think the cliffs of Dover are white?

# LAB ACTIVITY
# Examining Life in Pond Water

### BACKGROUND

A sample of water taken from a stream, pond, or lake may contain hundreds of living organisms. Many of the organisms belong to the Kingdom Protista. Most protists are too small to see with your eyes alone. You can use a microscope to observe these organisms.

### PURPOSE

In this activity you will observe the structure and behavior of several organisms found in pond water by using a microscope.

### PROCEDURE

1. Put on goggles. Using an eyedropper or pipette, place 1 to 2 drops of pond water onto a clean slide. ⚠ CAUTION: Be careful when handling the slide.

2. Add a drop of methyl cellulose to the sample. Use a toothpick to carefully mix the methyl cellulose with the pond water. This substance forms a thick mixture with water and slows down the movement of organisms swimming in it.

3. Gently place a cover slip on top of your slide. Try not to get any air bubbles under the cover slip.

4. Place the slide onto the stage of your microscope. Secure the slide with the stage clips. Make sure to use the lowest power objective lens.

5. Focus the microscope using the coarse and fine adjustment knobs. Do you see any living things? How do you know they are alive? Copy the chart in Figure 6-14 onto a sheet of paper. Record your observations in this chart.

6. Try to identify each of the organisms in your sample. Base your decision on shape, structure, and movement. Record whether they are plantlike or animal-like protists in your chart. Use your science book or other references if you need to.

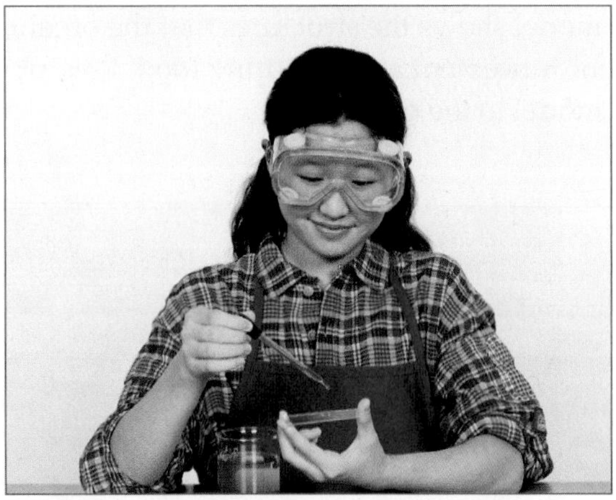

▲ **STEP 1** Place a drop of pond water on a slide.

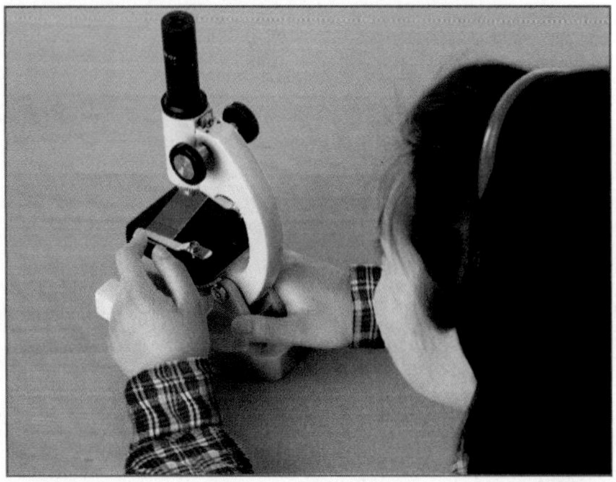

▲ **STEP 4** Place the slide onto the stage.

7. Move the high power objective lens into place. ⚠ CAUTION: Be sure the objective does not touch the slide. Focus the microscope using the fine adjustment knob only. For a review of microscope use, see Appendix B.

8. Observe the pond water sample under high power. What can you see now that you could not see before? Record your observations in your chart.

9. Draw several of the organisms in your pond water sample. Make sure your drawing shows the correct shape, structure, and color of each organism.

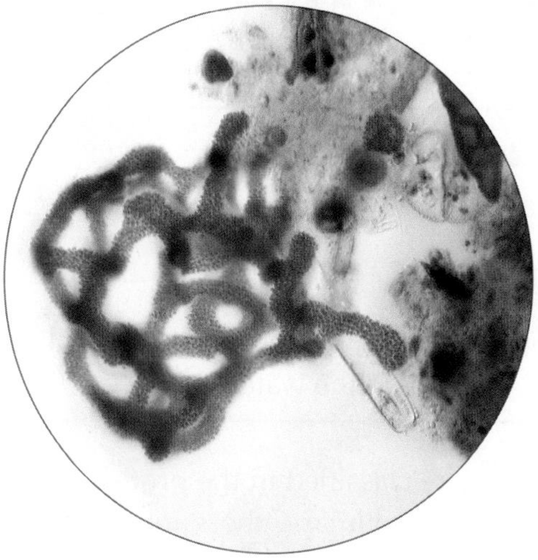

▲ **STEP 8** Observe the pond water under high power.

| Magnification | General Observations | Plantlike Organisms | Animal-like Organisms |
|---|---|---|---|
| Low power | | | |
| High power | | | |

▲ **Figure 6-15** Copy this chart onto a sheet of paper.

## *CONCLUSIONS*

1. **OBSERVE:** How many different types of organisms did you observe?

2. **COMPARE:** How were the organisms you observed alike? How were they different?

3. **CLASSIFY:** List the types of organisms you observed. Provide reasons for placing organisms in certain groups.

4. **CALCULATE:** Include the power of magnification next to each of your drawings. To calculate the power of magnification, multiply the magnification of the eyepiece by the magnification of the objective lens the organism was viewed under. The formula is eyepiece × objective = total power of magnification.

# 6-4 What are algae and slime molds?

*Objective*

Identify and describe different kinds of algae.

*Key Term*

**plankton** (PLANK-tuhn)**:** microscopic organisms that float on or near the water's surface

**Algae** Algae are classified in the protist kingdom. Some algae are unicellular. Others are multicellular. All algae contain chlorophyll. Because they have chlorophyll, algae can make their own food through photosynthesis. For this reason, algae are sometimes called plantlike protists.

1 COMPARE: How are algae and plants alike?

**Unicellular Algae** Some kinds of algae are made up of only one cell. Most unicellular algae live in a watery environment. They float on the surface of the water. Some of these unicellular algae are part of plankton. **Plankton** is any collection of microscopic organisms that float on or near the surface of the oceans. Diatoms are a type of unicellular algae that make up a large percent of the world's plankton. Diatoms have an unusual geometric shape.

Although all algae have chlorophyll, not all kinds of algae are green. Fire algae are unicellular algae that are red in color. Golden-brown algae can have a color ranging from yellowish-green to golden-brown. These differences in color are due to the pigments, or colorings, in the algae.

2 IDENTIFY: What is plankton?

**Euglena** The euglena is a unicellular algae. It is both plantlike and animal-like. The euglena is so unique that it has its own phylum within the protist kingdom. Like all algae, the euglena contains chlorophyll. It uses the chlorophyll to carry out photosynthesis. A structure in the euglena called the eyespot can detect light. The euglena uses its eyespot to find light in the water. The euglena then moves to the light by beating the flagellum that extends from its body. When light is not available, the euglena can also take in food. The euglena also has a flexible outer covering. This allows it to change shape.

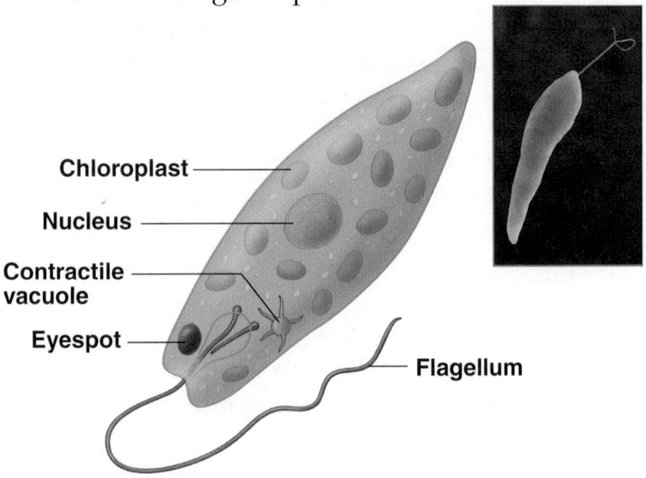


▲ **Figure 6-16** The euglena, shown in the photograph, contains chloroplasts used during photosynthesis.

3 EXPLAIN: How is the euglena animal-like?

**Multicellular Algae** Some kinds of algae are made up of many cells. These are the multicellular algae. Pigments in multicellular algae may give them a green, red, or brown coloring. Many green algae live in fresh water.

Red and brown algae live in the ocean. Brown algae often are called seaweed or kelp. Brown algae grow to be the largest of all algae. If you have visited a beach, you may have seen brown algae washed up along the shoreline.

▲ **Figure 6-17** Kelp can grow to heights of more than 65 meters.

4 INFER: Why are some types of algae a color other than green?

**Slime Molds** The protist kingdom also contains several funguslike organisms. These protists are multicellular. Two examples of funguslike protists are the slime molds and the water molds. Slime molds can be found living in moist soil or on rotting logs. Some slime molds are bright yellow or red in color. Water molds can be found in lakes and ponds. They can also be found on diseased aquarium fish. Many water molds are parasites, or live off other organisms.

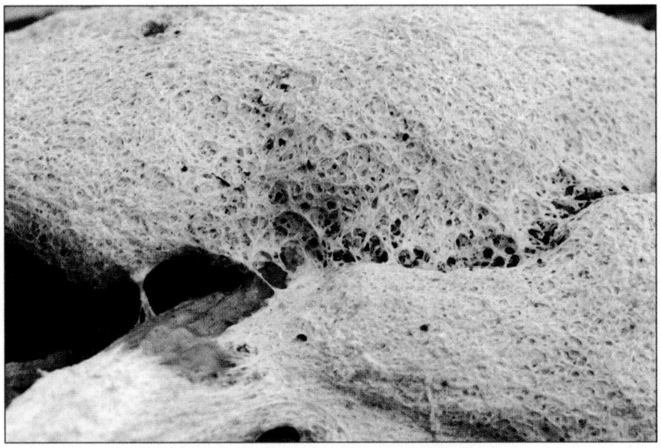

▲ **Figure 6-18** Slime molds grow in moist areas.

5 **CONTRAST:** How are slime molds and water molds different?

## CHECKING CONCEPTS

1. Algae make their own food through __________.
2. Plants and algae both contain the green pigment __________.
3. A euglena uses its __________ to detect light.
4. The largest kind of algae is __________.

## THINKING CRITICALLY

5. **COMPARE:** How is a euglena similar to a trypanosome?
6. **HYPOTHESIZE:** Where would you go to collect a water sample that contained both algae and protozoans? Explain.

## DESIGNING AN EXPERIMENT

*Design an experiment to solve the following problem. Include a hypothesis, variables, a procedure, and the type of data to be collected.*

PROBLEM: Autotrophs are organisms that can make their own food during photosynthesis. Heterotrophs must take in food. How can you prove that the euglena can be considered both an autotroph and a heterotroph?

## *Integrating Earth Science*

**TOPIC: pollution**

### ALGAL BLOOMS

Algae make their own food by photosynthesis. For photosynthesis to occur, chlorophyll, sunlight, and carbon dioxide must be present. Algae also need water and other nutrients, such as nitrogen, to carry out their life processes. When all of these elements are present, algae can reproduce quickly and in large numbers. A sudden large growth of algae is called an algal bloom.

▲ **Figure 6-19** Algal blooms can be caused by green algae such as the spirogyra shown in the circle.

Algal blooms often occur when wastes such as fertilizers and detergents are dumped into ponds or lakes. These products contain the nutrients that allow the algae to reproduce quickly. Algal blooms can be very harmful to the organisms that live in the lake or pond. Bacteria use oxygen in the water to help them break down dead algae. If the bacteria use too much oxygen, other organisms in the water do not have enough oxygen to survive. As a result, these organisms die.

**Thinking Critically** How do you think unwanted algal blooms could be prevented?

# 6-5 What is the Kingdom Fungi?

INVESTIGATE

### *Observing the Structure of Mushrooms*
HANDS-ON ACTIVITY

1. Examine the structure of three to six different kinds of mushrooms, such as white button, shiitake, and portobello.
2. Record your observations in your notebook.
3. Use a hand lens to examine the underside of the top cap of each mushroom.
4. Describe the appearance. Draw and label each mushroom in your notebook.

**THINK ABOUT IT:** How are mushrooms similar to plants? How are they different from plants?

### *Objective*
Describe the different kinds of fungi.

### *Key Terms*
**stalk:** stemlike part of a mushroom

**cap:** umbrella-shaped top of a mushroom

**hypha** (HY-fuh), *pl.* **hyphae** (HY-fee)**:** threadlike structure that makes up the body of molds and mushrooms

**gills:** structures in a mushroom that produce spores

**spore:** reproductive structure in fungi

**fermentation:** process by which a cell releases energy from food without using oxygen

**Kingdom Fungi** Fungi are like plants in some ways. The cells of fungi have cell walls. Many fungi also are multicellular, or many-celled, organisms. Like most plants, fungi grow well in soil. For these reasons, scientists once classified fungi in the plant kingdom.

Later, scientists discovered that fungi and plants are not really very much alike. The cells of fungi do not have chloroplasts or chlorophyll. Therefore, fungi cannot make their own food as plants do. Fungi usually get the food they need from dead and decaying organisms. They grow well in dark, warm, and wet places. Today, scientists classify fungi in a kingdom of their own. The fungi kingdom includes yeasts, molds, and mushrooms.

1 **DESCRIBE:** Where do fungi usually grow?

**Mushrooms** You probably know a mushroom when you see one because of its shape. The stemlike part of a mushroom is called the **stalk.** At the top of the stalk is an umbrella-shaped top, or **cap.** The body of a mushroom is made up of threadlike structures called **hyphae.** The underside of the cap is lined with **gills.** The gills are made of many hyphae tightly packed together. The gills produce **spores.** Spores are the reproductive structures of mushrooms. They are lightweight and easily carried by wind and water or on the bodies of insects.

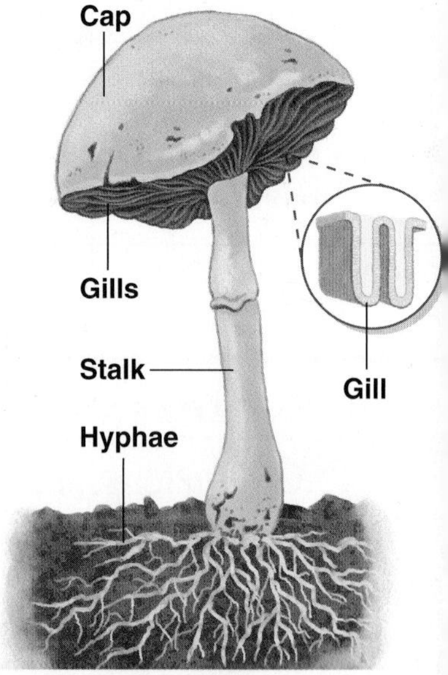


▲ **Figure 6-20** A mushroom

2 **INFER:** What is the job of the stalk of a mushroom?

**Molds** Molds are a common kind of fungi. They grow on bread, fruits, vegetables, and even leather. Most molds look like a mass of threads. These threads are the hyphae. The hyphae in molds are not as closely packed together as in mushrooms. If you look closely at a bread mold, you will see hyphae growing along the surface of the bread. The hyphae in bread mold are not divided into separate cells. Instead, each strand has many nuclei.

3 **COMPARE:** How are molds different from mushrooms?

**Yeasts** Yeasts are colorless, unicellular fungi. Yeast cells are surrounded by a cell membrane and a cell wall. The cell contains cytoplasm and a nucleus. Yeasts grow well where sugar is present. They use the sugar for food. Yeasts are used to make bread rise. As yeast cells break down sugar, bubbles of carbon dioxide gas form. This causes the dough to rise. This process is called **fermentation.** Fermentation is a type of cellular respiration that takes place without oxygen.

4 **DESCRIBE:** What structures are found in a yeast cell?

## CHECKING CONCEPTS

1. What are three kinds of fungi?
2. Why is it that fungi cannot make their own food?
3. Which fungi are colorless and unicellular?
4. Where are the gills of a mushroom located?
5. What are the reproductive structures of a mushroom?
6. Where are spores produced in mushrooms?

## THINKING CRITICALLY

7. **INFER:** A mushroom may develop hundreds of kilometers away from the parent mushroom. How might this happen?
8. **HYPOTHESIZE:** Mushrooms produce a large number of spores. Why is the ground not covered with mushrooms?

## HEALTH AND SAFETY TIP

Never eat mushrooms that you find growing outdoors. Many mushrooms are poisonous and can be deadly if consumed. The Amanita mushroom can destroy the human liver in one week. Poisonous mushrooms and edible mushrooms look very similar. Use library references to find out the names of three kinds of poisonous mushrooms. Then draw a picture of each type. Identify any unique trait for each poisonous mushroom you choose.

## *Real-Life Science*

### FUNGAL INFECTIONS

Some fungi can cause infections and diseases in people, animals, and plants. Chemical preparations called fungicides are used to prevent or cure diseases caused by fungi. Athlete's foot is a common infection caused by fungi. Fungal diseases are a concern for humans not only because they attack us, but because they attack our food crops as well.

▲ **Figure 6-21** Corn smut

Many types of fungi are plant pathogens, which means they attack and destroy plants. Wheat can suffer from a fungal infection called wheat rust. Corn plants can become infected with a fungus that causes corn smut. This fungus attacks the corn kernels, causing them to expand and burst. Other fungi destroy important food crops such as peaches, onions, squash, and tomatoes. These fungal infections can spread very quickly and cause substantial damage to crops. Scientists are researching ways to prevent or slow down these infections.

**Thinking Critically** What are some ways to reduce possible fungal infections without using fungicides?

Integrating Health

# THE Big IDEA

## What simple organisms exist in our daily lives?

From the time we are very young, we learn about safety in the kitchen, such as being careful with knives or staying away from hot ovens. Harmful microorganisms pose a different danger in the kitchen. You can become very sick if you eat food that harbors certain types of bacteria or protozoans.

Whereas some bacteria and fungi play a helpful role in producing or flavoring foods like cheese and yogurt, others can cause foods to spoil or decay. Some bacteria produce toxins while they are acting on food. They can be present in raw eggs, meat, and shellfish. Eating them can cause digestive problems. Some people can get very sick or die.

Protozoans have also been known to cause disease in humans. Parasitic protozoans can be spread to humans through contaminated water or foods. Many times these harmful protozoans are found on vegetables or fruits that have been fertilized with manure or washed with contaminated water.

Most illnesses caused by microorganisms in foods can be prevented. The key is to kill or slow the action of the bacteria. You can do this by following basic rules for food safety.

Look at the text and photos that appear on this page and the next. They point out helpful and harmful simple organisms. Follow the directions in the science log to learn more about "the big idea." ✦

**Mold in Cheese**

Bacteria and molds are used to ripen cheeses. *Penicillium roqueforti* is a mold like the one shown here. It causes the blue veins in Roquefort cheese. Bacteria are responsible for the holes in Swiss cheese. The bacteria give off gases that produce the holes.

**Bacteria in Yogurt**

Two types of bacteria are needed to convert milk into yogurt. One is called *Streptococcus thermophilus*. The other is *Lactobacillus bulgaricus* (shown below). Evidence suggests that live bacteria in yogurt aid digestion. Researchers are still studying other possible health benefits.

Basic Rules for Food Safety

1. Wash foods thoroughly.
2. Keep cold foods cold and hot foods hot.
3. Cook foods to the proper temperature.
4. Clean hands and surfaces with hot soapy water.
5. Keep raw meat, eggs, and seafood away from foods that are ready to eat.

### Protozoa In Water

The protozoan *Giardia lamblia*, shown here, is found in some streams, lakes, and reservoirs. Drinking water contaminated with this organism can lead to intestinal problems. Water treatment facilities destroy harmful organisms, providing safe drinking water. It can be dangerous to drink water that hasn't been treated.

### Red Algae in Ice Cream

Many desserts such as ice cream and frozen yogurt contain an ingredient called carageenan. Carageenan is a sticky substance that coats the cells of some types of red algae like the *Euchema* algae shown below. Carageenan gives ice cream a smooth, creamy texture.

**WRITING ACTIVITY**

**Science Log**

If you owned a restaurant or food store, how would you make sure your customers were safe from harmful microorganisms? Research safety precautions used in the food industry. Write a plan for your business that maintains high safety standards. Start your search at www.conceptsandchallenges.com.

# 6-6 How do yeasts and molds reproduce?

## *Objective*

Compare and contrast reproduction of yeasts and molds.

## *Key Terms*

**budding:** kind of asexual reproduction in which a new organism forms from a bud on a parent

**spore case:** structure that contains spores

**sporulation** (spawr-yoo-LAY-shuhn)**:** kind of asexual reproduction in which a new organism forms from spores released from a parent

**Budding** One kind of asexual reproduction is **budding**. In budding, a new cell is formed from a tiny bud on a parent cell. Most yeasts reproduce by budding. During budding, the cell wall of the parent cell pushes outwards. This is the beginning of the bud. The cell nucleus moves toward the bud. The nucleus divides. One nucleus moves into the bud. The other nucleus stays in the parent cell. The bud remains attached to the parent cell and grows larger. In time, a cell wall forms between the parent cell and the bud. The bud breaks away from the parent cell and develops into a mature yeast cell.

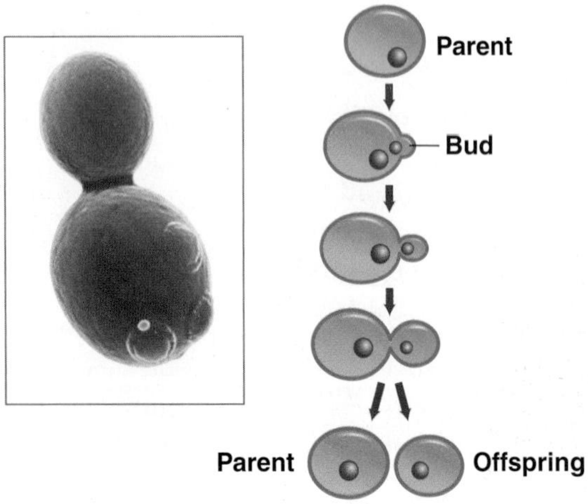


▲ **Figure 6-22** Budding in yeast

**1** CLASSIFY: By what kind of asexual reproduction do yeast cells reproduce?

**Sporulation** Have you ever seen mold growing on bread? It looks like tangled cotton. Many parts of it are black or gray. Under the low power of a microscope, bread mold looks like many tiny threads. On the top of some of the threads you will see a ball. This is the **spore case.** Each spore case holds thousands of spores.

When a spore case breaks, thousands of microscopic spores are released. Each spore can eventually grow into a new mold offspring if it lands in a warm and moist environment. This kind of reproduction is called **sporulation.** Sporulation is another kind of asexual reproduction. It produces many more offspring than budding does.

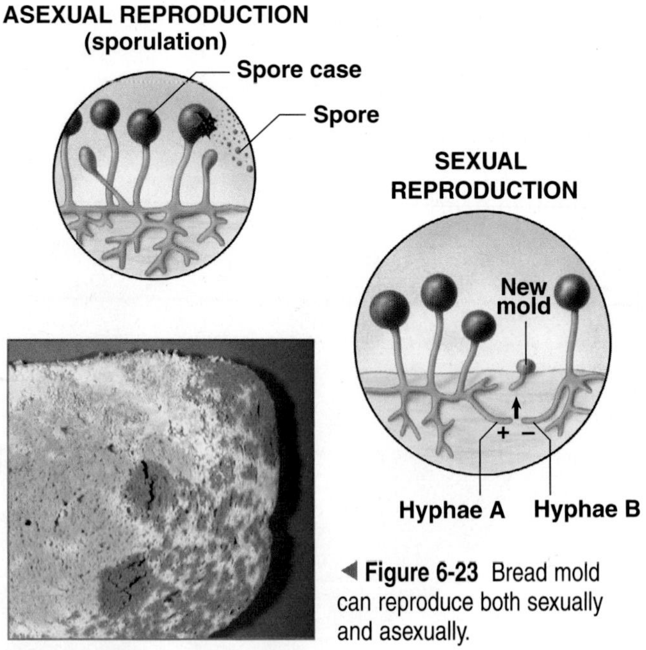


◄ **Figure 6-23** Bread mold can reproduce both sexually and asexually.

**2** CLASSIFY: What kind of reproduction is sporulation?

**Sexual Reproduction in Fungi** Fungi do not always reproduce asexually. Sometimes molds and mushrooms can reproduce sexually. This type of reproduction occurs when the hyphae of two different molds come into contact with each other as shown in Figure 6-23.

Mushrooms can also reproduce sexually. When the underground hyphae of one mushroom comes into contact with the hyphae of another mushroom, the nucleus of one hypha can combine with the nucleus of another hypha. This produces a new cell with genetic information from both mushrooms. This cell can eventually grow into a new mushroom.

3 **COMPARE:** Compare the two types of reproduction in fungi.

**Mold and Penicillin** In 1928, a scientist named Alexander Fleming accidentally discovered a mold that could destroy many different kinds of bacteria. Fleming had set aside a dish containing bacteria and forgot to throw it away. A mold called penicillium grew in the dish. Surprisingly, no bacteria were found growing near the mold. Penicillium reproduces asexually by producing spores. As the mold grows, it produces a chemical that kills bacteria. This is why there were no bacteria growing near the mold. The chemical produced by penicillium is used to make the antibiotic penicillin. Penicillin is one of the most common medicines used today.

4 **EXPLAIN:** Why do you think Fleming's discovery was important?

## ✓ CHECKING CONCEPTS

1. What are two ways that fungi can reproduce?
2. What fungus reproduces by budding?
3. How many spores are inside a spore case?
4. What is budding?
5. Which type of reproduction is sporulation?

## THINKING CRITICALLY

6. **COMPARE:** How is the reproduction of mushrooms similar to that of mold?
7. **HYPOTHESIZE:** Why do you think molds are not growing all over everything around you?
8. **EXPLAIN:** How do mushrooms reproduce?
9. **INFER:** Why do you think sporulation produces more offspring than budding?

## INTERPRETING VISUALS

*Use Figure 6-23 to answer the following question.*

10. **INFER:** Why does sporulation produce more offspring than sexual reproduction?

## *Hands-On Activity*

### GROWING MOLD

*You will need three plastic containers with covers, damp paper towels, a hand lens, a slice of bread made without preservatives, an orange rind, and a slice of potato.*

1. Line the bottom of each container with damp paper towels. Place the bread in one container, the orange rind in another container, and the potato slice in the third container.
2. Store the containers in a dark place for a few days.
3. Use a hand lens to observe the changes in each food sample. Draw a diagram to show the structures you see.

▲ **STEP 1** Place the orange in the container.

### Practicing Your Skills

4. **IDENTIFY:** On which food samples did mold grow?
5. **OBSERVE:** Are the molds all the same color? Describe the color of each mold.
6. **INFER:** What do the differences in color tell you about the molds?
7. **INFER:** What conditions were needed to grow molds?
8. **HYPOTHESIZE:** How could the food samples have been protected from mold growth?

# Chapter 6 Challenges

## Chapter Summary

### Lesson 6-1

- All bacteria are classified in the Kingdoms **Archaebacteria** and **Eubacteria.**
- Archaea tend to live in extreme conditions of temperature, pressure, and acidity.

### Lesson 6-2

- An **endospore** is a bacterium covered by a protective outer wall.
- Examples of ways Eubacteria are helpful include making many foods, decomposing dead matter, and adding nitrogen to the soil. Examples of ways Eubacteria are harmful include causing diseases and causing food to spoil.

### Lesson 6-3

- The protist kingdom includes very simple organisms such as **protozoans**, algae, and slime molds.
- Protozoans are animal-like protists that move freely. Algae are plantlike protists that can make their own food. Slime molds are funguslike protists.

### Lesson 6-4

- All algae contain chlorophyll and make their own food by photosynthesis.
- Some kinds of algae are unicellular. The euglena is a unicellular algae that is both plantlike and animal-like. Some algae are multicellular. Red and brown algae are multicellular algae.

### Lesson 6-5

- The fungi kingdom includes organisms with cell walls that live in warm, moist conditions. Fungi can be unicellular or multicellular. Fungi cannot make their own food, cannot move freely, and have large cells with many nuclei.
- Yeast are one-celled fungi. Molds are common fungi that are made up of many threads, or **hyphae.** Mushrooms have a **stalk, cap,** and **gills.**

### Lesson 6-6

- Yeast can reproduce asexually by **budding**.
- Molds and mushrooms can reproduce both asexually and sexually. Molds and mushrooms have **spore cases** that contain thousands of spores. **Sporulation** is a kind of asexual reproduction.

## Key Term Challenges

Archaebacteria (p. 134)
bacillus (p. 134)
budding (p. 148)
cap (p. 144)
chemosynthetic (p. 134)
cilium (p. 138)
coccus (p. 136)
endospore (p. 136)
Eubacteria (p. 136)
extremophile (p. 134)
fermentation (p. 144)
flagellum (p. 134)
gills (p. 144)
hypha (p. 144)
plankton (p. 142)
protozoan (p. 138)
pseudopod (p. 138)
spirillum (p. 136)
spore (p. 144)
spore case (p. 148)
sporulation (p. 148)
stalk (p. 144)

MATCHING **Write the Key Term from above that best matches each description.**

1. curved or spiral-shaped bacterium
2. one-celled, animal-like protists
3. threadlike structure that makes up the body of molds and mushrooms
4. inactive bacterium surrounded by a thick wall
5. fingerlike projection of cytoplasm, used for movement and food-getting
6. spherical bacterium
7. microscopic organisms that float on or near the ocean's surface

IDENTIFYING WORD RELATIONSHIPS **Explain how the words in each pair are related. Write your answers in complete sentences.**

8. spore cases, sporulation
9. Archaea, extremophile
10. cilia, flagella
11. cap, gills
12. asexual reproduction, budding
13. chlorophyll, algae
14. pseudopod, protozoan

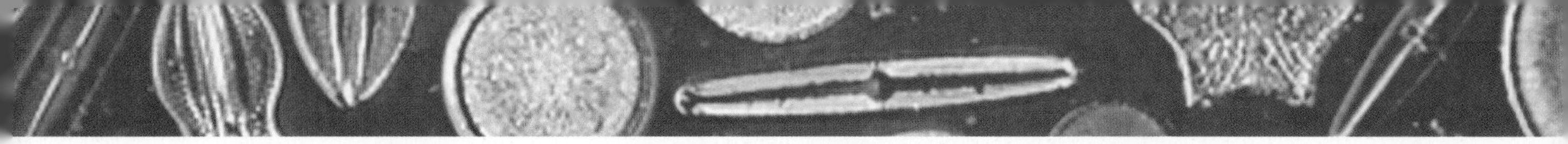

## Content Challenges TEST PREP

**MULTIPLE CHOICE Write the letter of the term or phrase that best completes each statement.**

1. Fire algae are
   a. white.
   b. red.
   c. green.
   d. brown.
2. The fungi kingdom includes yeasts, molds, and
   a. slime molds.
   b. algae.
   c. mushrooms.
   d. protists.
3. Strep throat is caused by
   a. Eubacteria.
   b. fungi.
   c. trypanosomes.
   d. protists.
4. A paramecium moves by means of
   a. pseudopods.
   b. flagella.
   c. eyespots.
   d. cilia.
5. Yeasts can reproduce asexually by
   a. budding.
   b. sporulation.
   c. photosynthesis.
   d. pasteurization.
6. Bacteria with a round shape are called
   a. cocci.
   b. spirilla.
   c. bacilli.
   d. flagella.
7. African sleeping sickness is caused by
   a. a paramecium.
   b. a slime mold.
   c. an amoeba.
   d. a trypanosome.
8. The reproductive cells of fungi are called
   a. rhizoids.
   b. gills.
   c. spores.
   d. threads.
9. The algae that grow to be the largest are the
   a. red algae.
   b. brown algae.
   c. green algae.
   d. golden-brown algae.
10. Nitrogen is changed into compounds that plants can use by
    a. fungi.
    b. bacteria.
    c. algae.
    d. protists.

**TRUE/FALSE Write *true* if the statement is true. If the statement is false, change the underlined term to make the statement true.**

11. Most amoeba live in salt water.
12. The stemlike part of a mushroom is called the cap.
13. All algae contain chlorophyll.
14. Green algae often are called seaweed.
15. Eubacteria are grouped according to their colors.
16. Most protists are many-celled organisms.
17. A bread mold reproduces by budding.
18. The paramecium is a slipper-shaped bacteria.
19. The Kingdom Protista includes all mushroons.
20. Sporulation produces fewer offspring than budding does.
21. The most common bacteria have a spiral shape.
22. Protozoans often are called plantlike protists.

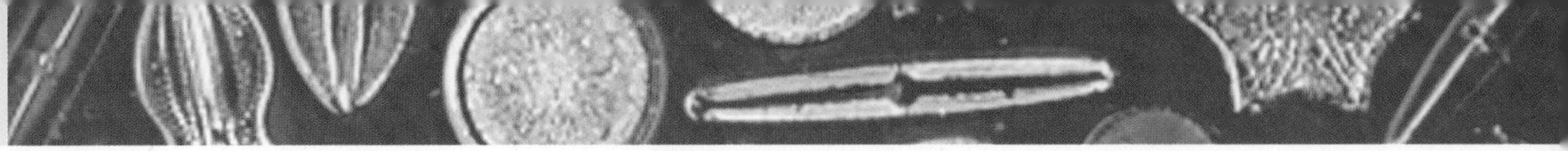

## *Concept Challenges* TEST PREP

WRITTEN RESPONSE **Answer each of the following questions in complete sentences.**

1. EXPLAIN: How do canning, pickling, and freezing foods prevent the growth of bacteria?
2. ANALYZE: Why do you think algae were originally classified as plants?
3. COMPARE: How are fungi similar to plants? How are they different?
4. HYPOTHESIZE: If you wanted to find fungi where you live, where would you look? Explain your answer.
5. INFER: Almost all living things depend on energy from the Sun. How can archaebacteria live deep in the ocean where there is no sunlight?

INTERPRETING A DIAGRAM **Use Figure 6-24 to answer the following questions.**

6. What is the part labeled *A* called?
7. What are the parts labeled *B* called?
8. What is the function of the parts labeled *B*?
9. What is the part labeled C called?
10. What is the body of the mushroom made up of?

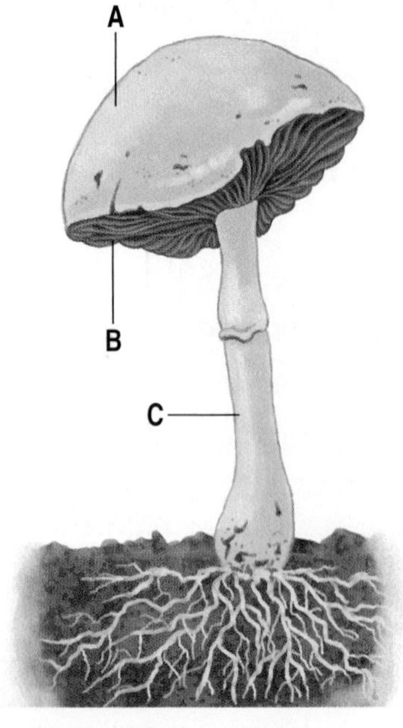


▲ **Figure 6-24** A mushroom

# Chapter 7 Types of Plants

▲ **Figure 7-1** Tropical rain forests are home to tens of thousands of different plant species.

## Contents



Tropical rain forests are found in warm regions near the equator. A tropical rain forest is filled with plant life of all shapes and sizes. Large amounts of rainfall, moderate temperatures, and year-round sunlight lead to the high growth rate in a rain forest. The trees in a rain forest can grow to great heights. Many other plants such as vines, mosses, and orchids grow on the trees themselves.

▶ Strangely, the floor of a tropical rain forest has only a small amount of plant life. Why do you think most of the plants in a rain forest live near the treetops?

# 7-1 How are plants classified?

## INVESTIGATE

### *Classifying Plants*

**HANDS-ON ACTIVITY**

1. Examine the leaves, stems, and flowers of several different plants.
2. Record your observations of each plant. Include characteristics such as size, shape, texture, and color.
3. Based on your observations, classify the plants into different categories. Make sure you give evidence or reasons for putting plants in certain categories.
4. Make a classification chart based on your conclusions.

**THINK ABOUT IT:** How did the similarities and differences of the plant parts help you classify the plants?

### *Objective*

Identify the characteristics of plants.

### *Key Terms*

**tracheophytes** (TRAY-kee-uh-fyts): group of plants that have transport tubes

**vascular plant:** plant that contains transport tubes

**bryophytes** (BRY-oh-fyts): group of plants that do not have transport tubes

**nonvascular plant:** plant that does not have transport tubes

**Characteristics of Plants** Some organisms, such as algae, look like plants. How do scientists classify organisms as plants? Plants are multicellular. These cells also have cell walls and contain chloroplasts.

Plants use chlorophyll in the chloroplasts to absorb the energy in sunlight. Plants use the Sun's energy to combine carbon dioxide and water to make food in the form of sugar. The food-making process is called photosynthesis. Photosynthesis provides plants with the food they need for growth and development.

$$\text{Water} + \text{Carbon dioxide} \xrightarrow{\text{Light energy}} \text{Sugar} + \text{Oxygen}$$

▲ **Figure 7-2** In photosynthesis, plants use light energy to make food.

Plant cells are organized into tissues and organs. Tissues are groups of cells that look alike and work together. Tissues are often named for the job they do. Organs are a group of tissues that work together to do a special job. Some organs in plants are the roots, stem, and leaves. In flowering plants, the flower is also an organ.

**1 STATE:** What are three plant characteristics?

**Plant Divisions** Botanists have classified more than 250,000 organisms in the plant kingdom. They have divided the plant kingdom into two large groups. The groups are based on how water and dissolved nutrients are moved throughout the plant. The two groups are the tracheophytes and the bryophytes.

| Tracheophytes | Bryophytes |
|---|---|
| • Vascular, grow larger, have well-developed root system<br>• Examples are ferns, pine trees, roses<br>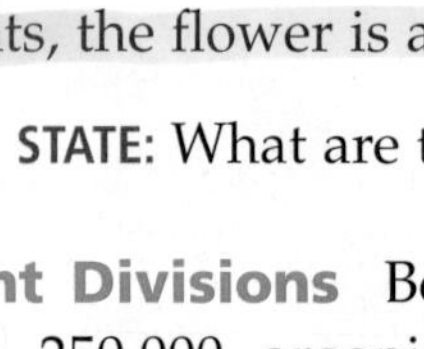 | • Nonvascular, small, live in damp areas<br>• Examples are mosses, liverworts, hornworts<br>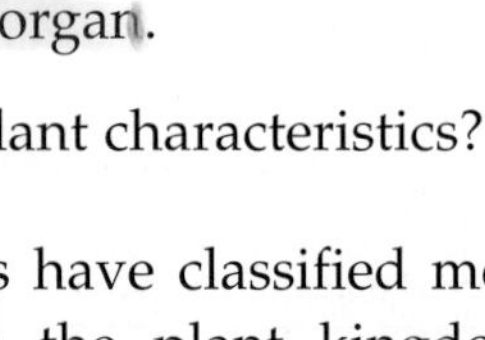 |

▲ **Figure 7-3** Characteristics of tracheophytes and bryophytes

**2 IDENTIFY:** What are the two large groups of the plant kingdom?

**Tracheophytes** Most of the plants you are familiar with are probably tracheophytes. Ferns, pine trees, rose bushes, and cherry trees are all examples of tracheophytes. **Tracheophytes** are a group of plants that have transport tissue. This means that water and nutrients move through special tubelike cells to all parts of the plant. These tubelike cells make up the transport tissue of the plant. Tracheophytes are considered **vascular plants** because they have this transport tissue.

Plant tissue in tracheophytes is organized into roots, stems, and leaves. The roots of a tracheophyte anchor the plant in the soil. The vascular tissue takes in water and dissolved nutrients from the soil. Stems help to support a plant. The vascular tissue found in stems transfers water and nutrients throughout the plant. The presence of this tissue also gives strength to the plant, allowing some tracheophytes to grow very tall.

▲ **Figure 7-4** A cherry tree is a tracheophyte.

**3** **DESCRIBE:** What are two jobs of vascular tissue?

**Bryophytes** If you have seen moss growing on the side of a tree, then you have seen a **bryophyte.** Bryophytes are a group of plants that do not have transport tissue. In bryophytes, water and nutrients seep from one cell to another. Because bryophytes do not have transport tissue, they are called **nonvascular plants.** Bryophytes do not have true roots, stems, or leaves. They have rootlike and leaflike structures. Bryophytes are small plants. They usually grow to be only a few centimeters in height.

Bryophytes are land plants. However, they need water to reproduce. For this reason, botanists believe that bryophytes may have evolved from a water plant.

▲ **Figure 7-5** The moss on these trees is a bryophyte.

**4** **INFER:** Why do you think that bryophytes cannot grow to great heights?

## CHECKING CONCEPTS

1. The two large plant groups are the tracheophytes and the __________.
2. Tubelike cells make up the __________ tissue of tracheophytes.
3. Among tracheophytes, plant tissues are organized into roots, stems, and __________.
4. Bryophytes need __________ to reproduce.

## THINKING CRITICALLY

5. **CONTRAST:** How do bryophytes differ from tracheophytes?
6. **HYPOTHESIZE:** Why do you think tracheophytes are successful land plants?

### Web InfoSearch

**Local Plant Life** The types of plants that are able to grow in a specific area depend on many factors, such as soil, climate, and altitude.

**SEARCH:** Use the Internet to research plants in your area. Make a poster showing examples of local plant life. Begin your search at www.conceptsandchallenges.com. Some key words are **plants** and **flora.**

# 7-2 How do bryophytes reproduce?

## *Objective*

Describe how bryophytes reproduce.

## *Key Terms*

**spore:** reproductive cell in some plants

**rhizoid** (RY-zoid)**:** fine, hairlike structure that acts as a root

**Bryophytes** The most primitive plants on Earth are the bryophytes. Mosses are classified in the phylum Bryophyta (BRY-oh-fy-tuh). Mosses can be found growing on the sides of trees or on the forest floor. Two other kinds of plants classified as bryophytes are shown in Figures 7-6 and 7-7. They are liverwort and hornwort. Even though they live on land, bryophytes can live only where there is a good supply of water. Because they are nonvascular plants, they do not have transport tubes to carry water throughout the plant. They also need water for reproduction. Bryophytes are spore plants, which means that they produce spores instead of seeds. A **spore** is a reproductive cell in some plants.

▲ **Figure 7-6** Liverwort

▲ **Figure 7-7** Hornwort

**1** EXPLAIN: Why do mosses have to grow in moist areas?

**Structure of Bryophytes** Bryophytes are small plants that differ from most other plants. Unlike most plants, bryophytes do not have true roots, stems, or leaves. Instead of roots, they have fine hairlike structures called **rhizoids.** Rhizoids anchor the plant in the soil. They also take in water and dissolved minerals.

**2** IDENTIFY: What are two characteristics of bryophytes?

**Mosses** If you look closely at a moss plant, you will see thin stalks with tiny leaflike parts. The leaflike parts and green stems make food for the plants. Rhizoids anchor the mosses. You also may see taller stalks. At the top of these stalks, there are spore cases. The spore cases are filled with spores.

▲ **Figure 7-8** Moss grows in moist areas.

**3** NAME: What structure of a moss holds the spores?

**Life Cycle of Bryophytes** Bryophytes have a life cycle that consists of two phases. The plant looks very different during each of the two phases. The first phase is the gamete-producing phase. During this phase, sperm and egg cells are produced. The gamete-producing phase of the plant is the larger green part of the plant shown in Figure 7-9.

Once fertilization occurs, the fertilized egg grows into a new plant. This is called the spore-producing phase. In Figure 7-9, the spore-producing plant has a tall, thin stalk and a round spore case at the top. During this phase, the plant forms spores and then releases them into the air. The spores can develop into another gamete-producing plant. Then the cycle starts all over again.

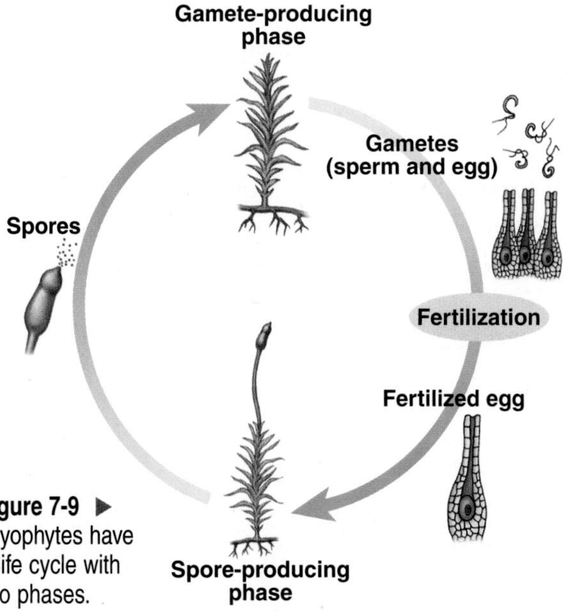


**Figure 7-9** ▶ Bryophytes have a life cycle with two phases.

**4** ▶ **DESCRIBE:** Describe the two phases in the bryophyte life cycle.

**Pioneer Plants** Bryophytes are sometimes called pioneer plants. Pioneer plants are the first plants to grow in bare or rocky places. Their rhizoids help break down rocks to form soil. As the plants die and decay, they add nutrients to the soil. As the soil layer builds up, other plants may grow.

**5** ▶ **DEFINE:** What are pioneer plants?

## ✓ CHECKING CONCEPTS

1. What are the reproductive cells of bryophytes called?
2. Name three kinds of bryophytes.
3. What are the rootlike structures of bryophytes called?
4. In what structure are the spores of mosses produced?

## THINKING CRITICALLY

5. **INFER:** In what ways are bryophytes less suited to life on land than other plants?
6. **COMPARE:** In what ways are rhizoids like roots?

## BUILDING LANGUAGE ARTS SKILLS

***Building Vocabulary*** *Bryophyte* is made up of the word parts *bryo* and *phyt*. Look up the word parts in a dictionary or Appendix D. Find two other life science words that contain the word part *phyt*. Define the two words. To what kind of living things do the word parts relate?

## *Science and Technology*

### USE OF PEAT AS A FUEL

Sphagnum (SFAG-nuhm) moss can grow under very wet conditions. The plants that die decompose very slowly, forming a bog of wet, spongy soil. The partly decayed plant matter that builds up over thousands of years is called peat. Today, peat bogs cover about 4 million square kilometers of North America, northern Europe, and Asia.

▲ **Figure 7-10** Peat moss grows in bogs around the world. Here the peat is being harvested.

Peat is an important energy source for many countries. About 1,400 square kilometers are harvested each year. This peat moss is converted into about 70 million cubic meters of "energy peat." The peat is burned, producing an energy source. This energy is then used for heating homes and for cooking.

Peat is a renewable resource. Peat bogs can be restored to thriving wetlands within 5 to 20 years after the peat is harvested. New peat forms at a rate of 1 to 2 millimeters a year.

**Thinking Critically** Do you think it is more important to use the peat as fuel or to protect the bogs for wildlife? Explain.

# 7-3 What are ferns?

## *Objective*

Name and describe the structure of a fern.

## *Key Terms*

**frond:** leaf of a fern

**rhizome** (RY-zohm)**:** horizontal underground stem

**Ferns** Ferns are one of the oldest groups of tracheophytes. They have a system of transport tubes that carry water and nutrients throughout the plant. Ferns are spore plants. They are considered seedless tracheophytes. They grow in great numbers in warm, moist areas, but they also live in cooler, drier areas. Most ferns can be recognized by their featherlike leaves. Ferns vary greatly in size and shape. Most ferns are about a half meter tall. Some ferns are only 3 centimeters tall. Other ferns, however, are giants. For example, fern trees of the South Pacific can grow to be more than 10 meters tall.

▲ **Figure 7-11** Ferns are spore plants.

**1 DESCRIBE:** What are two characteristics of ferns?

**Structure of a Fern** Ferns have true roots, stems, and leaves. The leaves are called **fronds.** The fronds are the part of the fern that can be seen above ground. In many ferns, the fronds are divided into smaller leaf-like parts called **leaflets.** Fern stems usually grow underground. The underground stems are called **rhizomes.** They grow parallel to the surface. Roots grow downward from the rhizome, while the fronds grow upward.

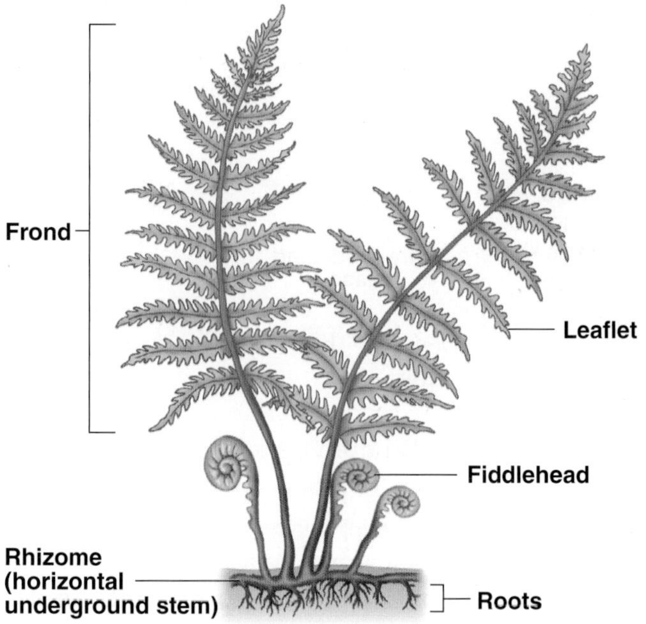


▲ **Figure 7-12** The structure of a fern

Ferns reproduce by spores. If you look at the underside of some kinds of fern fronds, you will see tiny brown spots. These are spore cases. Each case is filled with hundreds of spores. Ferns also have structures called fiddleheads. These structures resemble the end of a violin. They are young fronds that are tightly coiled.

**2 IDENTIFY:** What is the underground stem of a fern called?

▲ **Figure 7-13** Spores can be found on the underside of a frond.

**Fern Life Cycle** Like bryophytes, ferns have a two-phase life cycle. Ferns look different in each of the two phases. In ferns, the spore-producing plant is the larger plant. The ferns you usually see are in the spore-producing phase. Most of a fern's life is spent in the spore-producing phase. The gamete-producing plant is small and heart-shaped. The gamete-producing phase does not last very long.

3 **IDENTIFY:** Which is the shorter phase in the life cycle of a fern?

## CHECKING CONCEPTS

1. The featherlike leaves of ferns are the ___________.
2. The rhizome of a fern is an underground ___________.
3. Ferns have true roots, ___________, and leaves.
4. In most ferns, spore cases form on the underside of the ___________.
5. The ___________ is a tightly coiled young frond.
6. The ___________ phase is the longer of the two phases in ferns.

## THINKING CRITICALLY

7. **MODEL:** Draw a diagram of a fern. Label the frond, leaflets, rhizome, and roots.
8. **INFER:** What part of a fern makes food for the fern? How do you know?
9. **MODEL:** Draw a diagram that shows the life cycle of a fern. Include the phases, gametes, and ferns.

## DESIGNING AN EXPERIMENT

*Design an experiment to solve the following problem. Make sure you include materials to be used, a procedure, variables, and possible data to be collected.*

Megan wants to grow her own ferns at home. She has several spores but does not know what to do with them. She needs to find out what conditions are best for growing ferns.

▲ **Figure 7-14** Ferns were one of the dominant plants during the Carboniferous Period.

## *Integrating Earth Science*

TOPIC: geologic time

### PREHISTORIC FERNS

About 300 million years ago, giant tree ferns were the most common kind of land plant. This time in Earth's history is often called the Carboniferous Period. During this time, fern forests covered much of Earth. Most of the giant tree ferns died out about 225 million years ago.

The giant tree ferns usually grew in swamps. As the ferns died, their remains fell into the water and stayed there. They were covered by mud, water, and other sediments. The remains of these and other plants eventually became buried under thick layers of earth. Heat, pressure, and the actions of certain bacteria slowly caused chemical changes to take place. After millions of years, most of the compounds in the plants changed so that only carbon was left. This condensed form of carbon became coal. Coal is a fossil fuel. It has been used as a fuel since the 1800s. Coal is burned to produce electricity. This electricity is then transferred to homes, businesses, and schools.

**Thinking Critically** Why do you think coal is referred to as a "fossil fuel"?

# LAB ACTIVITY
# Examining the Structure of a Fern Frond

▲ **STEP 2** Sketch the entire frond on a sheet of paper.

▲ **STEP 4** Using a hand lens, observe the spore cases on the underside of the frond.

### *BACKGROUND*

Ferns are spore plants that grow in fields, forests, and wetlands. The stem of a fern, or rhizome, is underground. The leaves of a fern are called fronds. Each frond is made up of leaflets. On the underside of the leaflets, spore cases develop. If the environmental conditions are right, each spore can grow into a new fern plant.

### *PURPOSE*

In this activity, you will examine the structure of a fern frond.

### *PROCEDURE*

1. Obtain one fern frond.

2. Observe the fern frond. Sketch the entire frond on a sheet of paper. Label the main stalk and the leaflets.

3. Copy the chart in Figure 7-15 onto your own paper. Using a hand lens, examine the upper and lower sides of the frond. Draw what you see on your paper.

4. Using a hand lens, observe the spore cases on the underside of the frond. Draw what you see.

5. Estimate the number of spore cases on one fern frond. Record your estimate in your chart.

6. Using tweezers, scrape a few of the spore cases off the frond onto a clean white sheet of paper. Gently crush the spore cases by rolling a pencil over the cases.

7. Using a hand lens, examine the spores. Estimate the number of spores in one spore case. Record your estimate.

8. Use your estimates from Steps 5 and 7 to determine an estimated number of spores on an entire fern frond. Record this estimate in your chart.

9. Fill a small paper cup three-quarters of the way with moist soil. Now sprinkle several of the spores from the opened spore cases onto the soil. Cover the cup with clear plastic wrap. Place your cup in a warm area with indirect light.

10. After 2 weeks have passed, observe your paper cup. Do you see any growth?

▲ **STEP 6**
Scrape a few of the spore cases off the frond.

| Item | Estimated Number |
|---|---|
| Spore cases on entire frond | |
| Spores in one spore case | |
| Spores on entire frond | |

▲ **Figure 7-15** Copy this chart onto a sheet of paper.

## *CONCLUSIONS*

1. **OBSERVE:** Does the fern frond have veins or tubes to transport water?

2. **INFER:** Is the fern a vascular or nonvascular plant?

3. **INFER:** Is the fern frond the spore-producing phase or the gamete-producing phase of the plant? How can you tell?

4. **CALCULATE:** Suppose a fern plant has 10 fronds on it. Use your estimate from step 8 to determine the approximate number of spores on the entire fern.

5. **OBSERVE:** Did your fern produce a new plant? What stage was this new plant in?

6. **HYPOTHESIZE:** If a fern plant produces so many spores, why isn't Earth covered in ferns?

# 7-4 What are gymnosperms?

*Objectives*

Name and describe three kinds of gymnosperms.

*Key Terms*

**gymnosperm** (JIHM-noh-spuhrm)**:** type of land plant that has uncovered seeds

**seed:** structure that contains a tiny living plant and food for its growth; a reproductive cell

**conifer** (KAHN-uh-fuhr)**:** tree that produces cones and has needlelike leaves

**Gymnosperms** Millions of years after the appearance of ferns, a group of woody land plants arose. These plants were gymnosperms. The **gymnosperms** are a large group of vascular land plants that have uncovered, exposed seeds. A **seed** is a reproductive structure of a plant. The seeds of many vascular plants are enclosed in a fruit. The seeds of gymnosperms, however, are not. Gymnosperms have true roots, stems, and leaves. They have stiff, woody stems. They have a system of tubes for carrying water and dissolved materials.

▲ **Figure 7-16** Gymnosperms such as spruce and pine trees keep their leaves year-round.

**1** DEFINE: What is a gymnosperm?

**Conifers** The most common and best known of the gymnosperms are the **conifers.** Conifers are plants that produce cones. The seeds are in the cones. Many conifers have special leaves called needles. The needles of most conifers stay green throughout the year. For this reason, many conifers are called "evergreens." Pines, cedars, spruces, and hemlocks are examples of evergreen conifers.

Conifers grow in many different climates and soil types. Many conifers grow in the forests of northern Europe and North America. The giant redwood trees, or sequoias (si-KWOI-uhz), of California also are conifers. Some of these trees are more than 100 meters tall and 9 meters in diameter.

▲ **Figure 7-17** Pine cones contain seeds.

**2** INFER: Why are some conifers also called evergreens?

**Importance of Conifers** The conifers are an important group of plants. They are widely used as a source of lumber and fuel. They also are used in the production of paper, turpentine, charcoal, and tar. In some northern areas, spruces and firs are planted along the edges of fields. This wall of trees slows down the wind, keeping soil from blowing away.

**3** LIST: What are three uses of gymnosperms?

**Ginkgos and Cycads** Two other kinds of gymnosperms are ginkgos (GIN-kohs) and cycads (SY-kadz). Ginkgos have fan-shaped leaves. Unlike the evergreens, ginkgos shed their leaves in the fall. Ginkgos often are grown along city streets because they grow well even in polluted air.

Cycads grow mainly in tropical areas. Most look like small palm trees. They have large, feathery, fernlike leaves. Many plant species, such as cycads, have separate male and female plants. Female cycads produce seeds. The male plant produces pollen. Cycads often have very large cones.

▲ **Figure 7-18** Cycads grow in warm, tropical regions.

**4** **NAME:** What are two other groups of gymnosperms?

## ☑ CHECKING CONCEPTS

1. The most common gymnosperms are __________.
2. A pine tree is an example of a __________.
3. Conifers produce __________ in cones.
4. Conifers have special leaves called __________.
5. Gymnosperms have transport tubes so they are called __________ plants.
6. In autumn, __________ shed their leaves.

## THINKING CRITICALLY

7. **MODEL:** A giant redwood tree has a diameter of 9 m. Use the scale 1 mm equals 50 cm. Draw a circle to represent the 9 m diameter of the redwood tree's trunk. Draw a second circle inside the first showing the trunk of an oak tree that is 2 m in diameter.
8. **INFER:** What characteristics of a giant sequoia allow it to grow so tall?

## HEALTH AND SAFETY TIP

***Dietary Supplements*** Many plants are used as dietary supplements. A Chinese root called ginseng has been used to build up the body's resistance to disease. *Ginkgo biloba* has been used to increase memory. The benefits of herbal supplements are highly controversial. Because herbs are not yet required to undergo safety tests, it is difficult to be sure any are completely safe. Never take any dietary supplements without talking to a doctor first.

## *Hands-On Activity*

### OBSERVING PINE CONES

*You will need several different conifer cones, a hand lens, a field guide to trees, and a metric ruler.*

1. Gather cones from three different conifers.
2. Use the field guide to help you identify which kind of tree each cone comes from. Label the cones.
3. Use a hand lens to look at the cones. Each scale of the cone can hold a seed. Count the number of scales in one cone. Record the number of seeds possible in that cone.
4. Remove a few seeds from one cone. Examine the seeds and draw a diagram of one.

▲ **STEP 3** Count the number of scales in each cone.

### Practicing Your Skills

5. **COMPARE AND CONTRAST:** How are the cones from the same tree alike? How are they different?
6. **HYPOTHESIZE:** Why do you not find a seed behind every scale?
7. **INFER:** Why are there seeds in some cones but not others?

# 7-5 What are angiosperms?

## *Objective*

Identify monocots and dicots as two kinds of angiosperms.

## *Key Terms*

**angiosperm** (AN-jee-oh-spuhrm)**:** type of vascular, flowering plant

**cotyledon** (kaht-uh-LEED-uhn)**:** leaflike structure inside a seed that contains food for the developing plant

**monocot:** flowering plant with one cotyledon, or seed leaf, in its seeds

**dicot:** flowering plant with two cotyledons, or seed leaves, in its seeds

**Angiosperms** **Angiosperms** are flowering plants. Scientists estimate that angiosperms first appeared about 150 million years ago. They gradually replaced the gymnosperms as the major land plants. Today, scientists have classified about 250,000 kinds of angiosperms. They are the largest plant group.

1 **IDENTIFY:** What are angiosperms?

**Characteristics of Angiosperms** Most of the plants you see every day are angiosperms. Angiosperms are tracheophytes. Like gymnosperms, angiosperms have true roots, stems, and leaves. They also have a highly developed vascular system of transport tubes.

All angiosperms have flowers. No other plant group has flowers. In some angiosperms, the flowers are not very noticeable. You probably have never seen the flowers of grasses, oak trees, or corn. They have very small flowers. Other angiosperms, such as tulips, sunflowers, and lilies, have large, colorful flowers.

2 **NAME:** What is the main characteristic of angiosperms?

**Seeds and Fruits** Like gymnosperms, angiosperms are seed plants. The flowers of angiosperms produce seeds and fruits. The seeds of angiosperms are inside the fruit, which covers and protects them. The next time you eat a piece of fruit look for the seeds. You will see one seed or many seeds. Peaches have one seed, whereas apples have many. Most angiosperms produce a lot of seeds.

3 **NAME:** What do the flowers of angiosperms produce?

**Monocots and Dicots** Angiosperms are classified into two groups based on their seed structure. Within the seeds of angiosperms are leaflike structures that contain food for the developing plant. These structures are called **cotyledons.** The seeds of one group of angiosperms contain a single cotyledon. Plants of this group are **monocots.** Corn and wheat are examples of monocots. In the second group, the seeds have two cotyledons. These plants are **dicots.** Greenbeans and roses are examples of dicots.

4 **IDENTIFY:** What is a cotyledon?

▲ **Figure 7-19** These sunflowers produce thousands of seeds.

**Identifying Monocots and Dicots** You can tell if a plant is a monocot or a dicot by looking at its seeds, flowers, and leaves. Monocots have flowers with petals arranged in groups of three. Petals are the colorful parts of the flower. The veins in the leaves of monocots are parallel. Dicots have flowers with petals arranged in groups of four or five. The veins in the leaves of dicots are branched.

| | Monocot | Dicot |
|---|---|---|
| Seed | 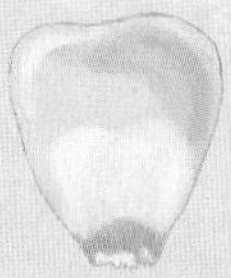 Single cotyledon | 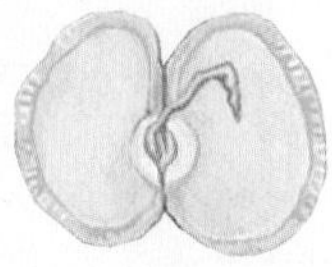 Pair of cotyledons |
| Leaf | 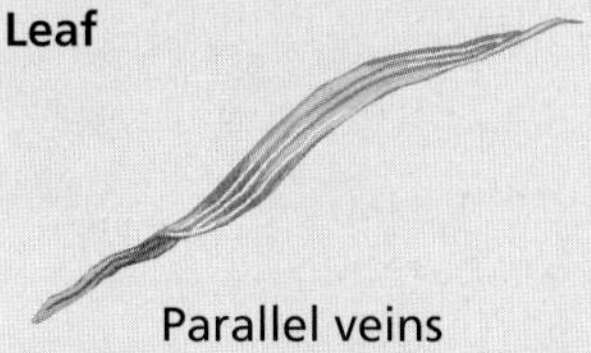 Parallel veins |  Branched veins |
| Flower |  Petals in groups of 3 |  Petals in groups of 4 or 5 |

▲ **Figure 7-20** Characteristics of monocots and dicots

5 CONTRAST: In what way are monocot flowers and dicot flowers different?

## CHECKING CONCEPTS

1. Monocots have leaves with __________ veins.
2. The seeds of angiosperms are enclosed in __________.
3. Angiosperms are also called the __________ plants.
4. Fruits are produced by the plant parts called __________.
5. The number of cotyledons in a dicot seed is __________.

## THINKING CRITICALLY

6. HYPOTHESIZE: What may have caused the angiosperms to become more common than the gymnosperms?
7. MODEL: Draw a model of a monocot plant and a dicot plant. Label the number of petals and the pattern of leaf veins in each.

## BUILDING LANGUAGE ARTS SKILLS

***Using Prefixes*** Monocots are also called monocotyledons. Dicots are called dicotyledons. What do the prefixes *mono-* and *di-* tell you about the difference between monocots and dicots? Use the meaning of the prefixes *mono-* and *di-* to define the words *monorail, monosyllable,* and *disaccharide.*

## *Hands-On Activity*

### CLASSIFYING MONOCOTS AND DICOTS

*You will need five different leaves, flowers, and seeds.*

1. Observe the seeds. Record your observations in a table.
2. Observe the flowers. Count the number of petals on each flower. Record your observations in your table.
3. Draw the vein patterns in each leaf.

### Practicing Your Skills

4. ANALYZE: **a.** Which parts came from monocots? **b.** Which came from dicots?

▲ **Figure 7-21** In Step 3, you will draw the veins of each leaf.

Integrating Social Studies

# THE Big IDEA

## How do plants affect the economy of the United States?

Economics is a branch of social studies. It looks at how goods and services are made, distributed, and used. The United States has the largest economy in the world. There are several ways to measure the economy. One way is to add up the value of everything produced in the United States. That figure is called the gross domestic product, or GDP. The GDP for the United States is about $10 trillion. Two percent of that comes from agriculture, or farming. That is almost $200 billion.

About 100 different plants are grown as major food crops. Trees are used for building materials and for making paper. Some plants are used to make medicines. The oils for perfume come from flowers and other plant parts. Plants are also used to make rubber, cloth, paints, plastics, and film. Plants are bought and sold for landscaping and decorating.

The economy of a state or region may depend a lot on certain plants. In Idaho, for example, potatoes are a very important crop. They make up about 15 percent of Idaho's economy. Plant crops also provide jobs. More than 100,000 people work in Florida's citrus fruit industry.

Look at the map that appears on this page and the next. It points out plants that are important in certain states or regions. Follow the directions in the Science Log to learn more about "the big idea." ✦

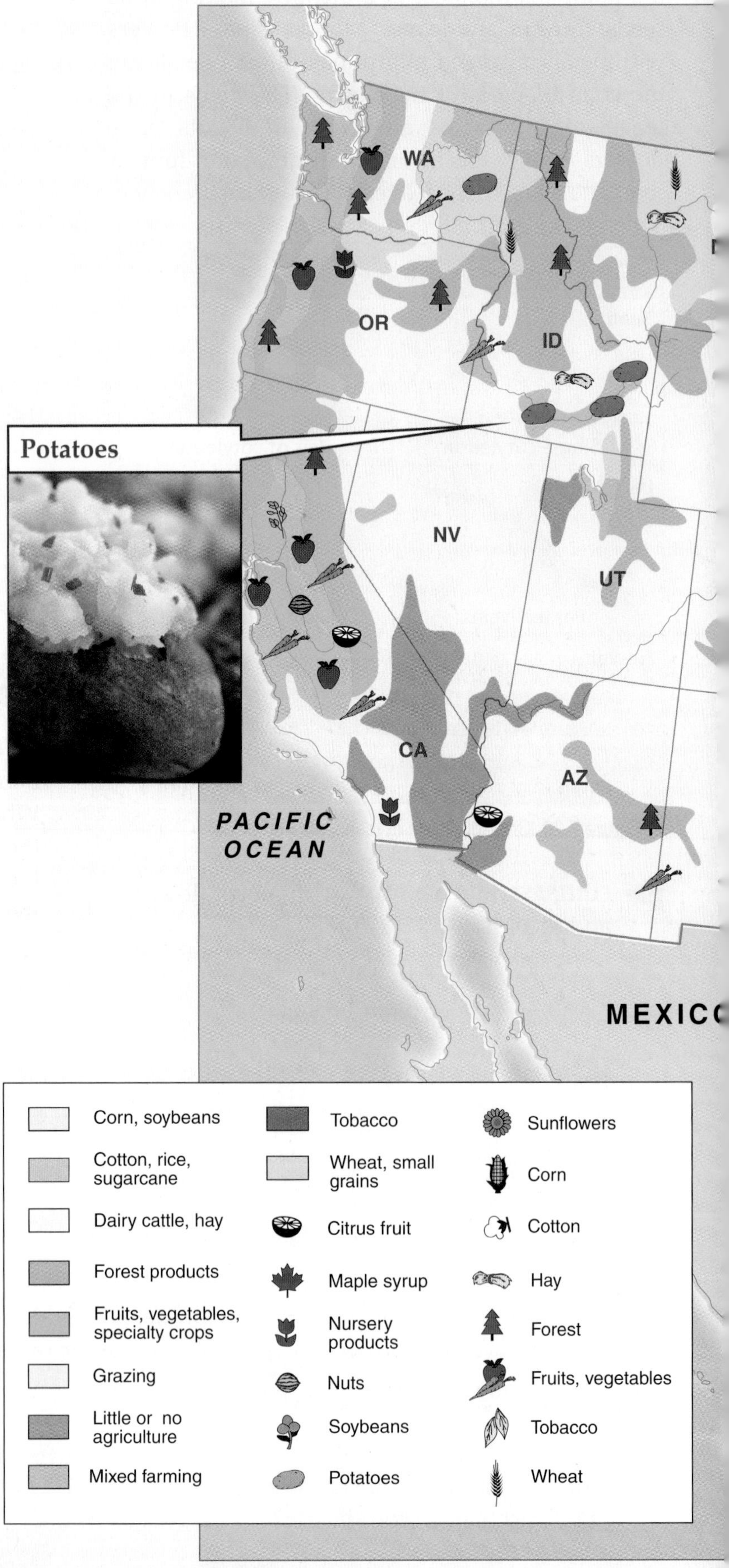


Potatoes

▲ **Figure 7-22** An agricultural economic map of the United States

WRITING ACTIVITY

## Science Log

Which kind of plant might you like to produce? Research this plant and write about it in your science log. Describe some products that come from this plant. Start your search at www.conceptsandchallenges.com.

# Chapter 7 Challenges

## Chapter Summary

### Lesson 7-1

- The plant kingdom is divided into two large groups: **bryophytes** and **tracheophytes.**
- Bryophytes are small plants that lack transport tissues. Bryophytes do not have true roots, stems, or leaves.
- Tracheophytes have tubelike cells used to transport materials to all plant parts. They are **vascular plants.** Tracheophytes have true roots, stems, and leaves.

### Lesson 7-2

- The phylum Bryophyta includes mosses, liverworts, and hornworts.
- Bryophytes are **spore** plants. Bryophytes have a life cycle that includes two phases.
- Pioneer plants are the first plants to grow in bare or rocky places.

### Lesson 7-3

- Ferns are seedless tracheophytes that have spores.
- Ferns have true roots, stems, and leaves. The leaves of a fern are called **fronds.**

### Lesson 7-4

- **Gymnosperms** are woody land plants that have uncovered seeds and true roots, stems, and leaves. Gymnosperms are vascular plants.
- **Conifers** are a group of gymnosperms that produce **seeds** in cones and have needles. Seeds are reproductive cells.
- Conifers are used as a source for many different products such as lumber and fuel.
- Cycads and ginkgos are two other groups of gymnosperms.

### Lesson 7-5

- **Angiosperms** are the flowering plants. Angiosperms have true leaves, roots, and stems. They are vascular plants. The flowers of angiosperms produce seeds inside fruits.
- Angiosperms are classified as **monocots** and **dicots** based upon the number of **cotyledons** in their seeds.
- Monocots and dicots can be identified by examining their seeds, leaf vein patterns, and the number of petals that make up the flowers.

## Key Term Challenges

angiosperm (p. 164)
bryophytes (p. 154)
conifer (p. 162)
cotyledon (p. 164)
dicot (p. 164)
frond (p. 158)
gymnosperm (p. 162)
monocot (p. 164)
nonvascular plant (p. 154)
rhizoid (p. 156)
rhizome (p. 158)
seed (p. 162)
spore (p. 156)
tracheophytes (p. 154)
vascular plant (p. 154)

MATCHING **Write the Key Term from above that best matches each description.**

1. fine, hairlike structure that acts as a root
2. tree with cones and needlelike leaves
3. flowering plant
4. group of flowering plants with parallel leaf veins
5. reproductive cell of bryophytes and ferns
6. seed plant with two cotyledons
7. group of plants without transport tissues

IDENTIFYING WORD RELATIONSHIPS **Explain how the words in each pair are related. Write your answers in complete sentences.**

8. seed, angiosperm
9. bryophyte, spore
10. conifers, gymnosperms
11. stem, rhizome
12. cotyledons, monocots
13. root, rhizoid
14 frond, leaf
15. conifer, evergreen

## Content Challenges TEST PREP

**MULTIPLE CHOICE Write the letter of the term or phrase that best completes each sentence.**

1. A group of gymnosperms that loses its leaves in the fall is the
   - **a.** conifers.
   - **b.** cycads.
   - **c.** ginkgos.
   - **d.** ferns.
2. The leaves of a fern are called
   - **a.** fronds.
   - **b.** blades.
   - **c.** fiddleheads.
   - **d.** spores.
3. The underground stem of a fern is a
   - **a.** root.
   - **b.** rhizome.
   - **c.** frond.
   - **d.** rhizoid.
4. The leaves of conifers are called
   - **a.** needles.
   - **b.** fronds.
   - **c.** cones.
   - **d.** blades.
5. Plant structures common to all angiosperms are
   - **a.** spore cases.
   - **b.** flowers.
   - **c.** rhizomes.
   - **d.** monocots.
6. The number of cotyledons in a dicot is
   - **a.** one.
   - **b.** two.
   - **c.** three.
   - **d.** four.
7. The seeds of a conifer can be found in the
   - **a.** flower.
   - **b.** cone.
   - **c.** needle.
   - **d.** spore.
8. Pioneer plants are usually
   - **a.** angiosperms.
   - **b.** gymnosperms.
   - **c.** bryophytes.
   - **d.** tracheophytes.
9. Pines, cedars, spruces, and hemlocks are
   - **a.** cycads.
   - **b.** ginkgos.
   - **c.** angiosperms.
   - **d.** conifers.
10. The largest plant group is made up of
    - **a.** gymnosperms.
    - **b.** angiosperms.
    - **c.** bryophytes.
    - **d.** rhizoids.

**TRUE/FALSE Write *true* if the statement is true. If the statement is false, change the underlined term to make the statement true.**

11. Conifers are used to make many things such as lumber, turpentine, and charcoal.
12. Monocots have leaves with branched veins.
13. Mosses have a life cycle with three phases.
14. Three plants classified as bryophytes are mosses, liverworts, and hornworts.
15. Spore plants produce flowers instead of seeds.

## *Concept Challenges* TEST PREP

**WRITTEN RESPONSE** **Answer each of the following questions in complete sentences.**

1. **CONTRAST:** How do bryophytes differ from other groups of plants?
2. **COMPARE:** In what way are ferns similar to bryophytes?
3. **IDENTIFY:** What is the reproductive structure of a gymnosperm?
4. **CONTRAST:** How does a monocot differ from a dicot?
5. **PREDICT:** How would the world be different if there were no plants?

**INTERPRETING A DIAGRAM** **Use Figure 7-23 to answer the following questions.**

6. Both corn and beans are members of a group of plants called angiosperms. What features of the plants identify them as angiosperms?
7. Which seed is a monocot? How do you know?
8. Which seed is a dicot? How do you know?
9. How are the leaf veins in monocots and dicots different?
10. How does the flower in plant *A* differ from the flower in plant *B*?

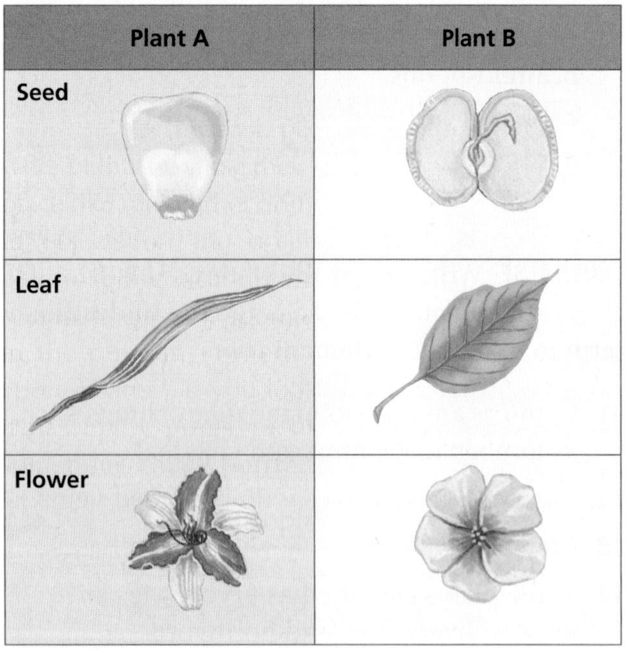


▲ **Figure 7-23**

# Chapter 8 Plant Structure and Function

▲ **Figure 8-1** Hummingbirds help some flowers reproduce.

There are many different species of plants. Some are trees and some are ferns. Others are flowering plants. People admire the beauty and color of the flowers on these plants. Many birds and insects are also attracted to the bright colors of flowers. Flowers are necessary for some plants to reproduce. Birds and insects play an important role in plant reproduction.

▶How do you think the hummingbird in Figure 8-1 helps the plant to reproduce?

## Contents

# 8-1 What are roots?

## *Objective*

Describe the structure and the functions of roots.

## *Key Terms*

**fibrous** (FY-bruhs) **root system:** root system made up of many thin, branched roots

**taproot system:** root system made up of one large root and many small, thin roots

**root hair:** thin, hairlike structure on the outer layer of the root tip

**root cap:** cup-shaped mass of cells that covers and protects a root tip

**Functions of Roots** Most roots grow underground. However, some plant roots grow in water, on rocks, and even in the open air. Roots have many important functions. They anchor, or hold, a plant firmly in the soil. Roots take in water and dissolved minerals from the soil. In some plants, food is stored in the roots.

1 **LIST:** What are some functions of roots?

**Kinds of Roots** The two main kinds of root systems are fibrous root systems and taproot systems. **Fibrous root systems** are made up of many thin, branched roots. Grass, wheat, and barley have fibrous roots. A **taproot system** has one large root. Many small, thin roots grow from the large root. Some taproots can store food. Carrots, radishes, and dandelions have taproots.

▲ **Figure 8-2** A fibrous root

▲ **Figure 8-3** A taproot

2 **NAME:** What are two kinds of root systems?

**Parts of a Root** Roots are tubelike structures made up of three layers. The outer part of the root is made up of one layer of cells called the epidermis. Many tiny, hairlike structures called **root hairs** extend from the outer layer. Root hairs increase the surface area of the root, allowing the root to absorb more water and minerals. The second root layer, called the cortex, has soft, loose tissue. Food for the root can be stored here.

The inner part of a root contains transport tubes that are part of the vascular system. These tubes extend up through the root and into the stems and leaves. Some tubes carry water and dissolved minerals upward. Others carry food made in the leaves to all parts of the plant.

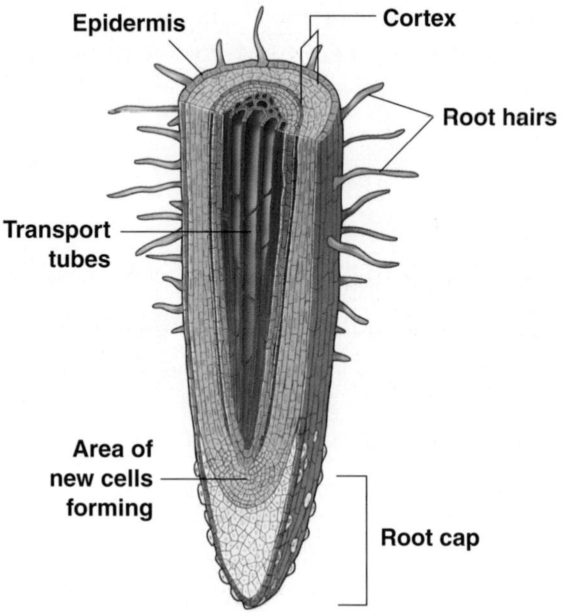


▲ **Figure 8-4** The parts of a root

3 **OBSERVE:** Look at Figure 8-4. What is the outer layer of the root called?

**The Root Tip** Roots grow from the tip. The tip of a root is covered by a root cap. The **root cap** is a cup-shaped mass of cells. It protects the root tip from damage as the root grows into the soil. As root cap cells are worn off, new cells are produced to take their place. Behind the root cap is an area where new root cells are formed. These new cells gradually change into the different kinds of cells that make up the root.

4 **ANALYZE:** Why is the root cap at the end of the root?

## CHECKING CONCEPTS

1. Roots take in water and __________ from soil.
2. A taproot system has __________ large root.
3. Structures that increase the surface area of roots are the __________.
4. The __________ part of the root contains transport tubes.
5. A root cap serves to __________ a root tip.

## THINKING CRITICALLY

6. **INFER:** Would a plant with a fibrous root system be easy or difficult to pull out of the ground? Explain.
7. **CLASSIFY:** Look at Figure 8-5. Which plants have a taproot? Which have fibrous roots?

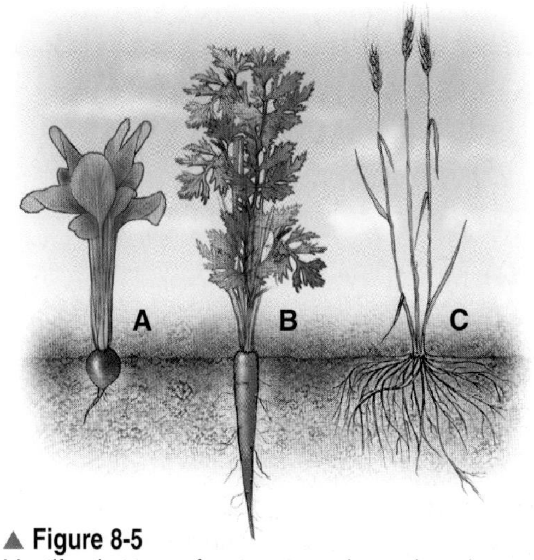


▲ **Figure 8-5**
Identify what type of root systems these plants have.

## BUILDING SCIENCE SKILLS

***Organizing Information*** Make a table with the following headings: Name of Plant, Type of Root System, and Depth of Roots. Use library references to find this information for the following plants: beet, oak tree, alfalfa, turnip, and corn.

## *Integrating Earth Science*

TOPIC: soil

### CROP ROTATION

In the one-crop system, farmers plant the same crop in the same field every year. In the crop rotation system, however, farmers plant a different crop in the same field every year. Crop rotation is a proven method for conserving soil nutrients.

▲ **Figure 8-6** Farmers alternate the crops they plant in a crop rotation system.

When planted in the same field every year, certain crops—such as corn and cotton—deplete the soil of nutrients, especially nitrogen. Using a crop rotation system, farmers plant fields with nutrient-depleting crops the first year. The next year, they plant crops that add nutrients to the soil. Plants in the legume family—such as alfalfa, peas, and beans—add nutrients to the soil. These plants have root nodules that are home to special "nitrogen-fixing" bacteria. These bacteria convert nitrogen from the air into a form that is useable by the plants.

Crop rotation also lowers the amount of pests and diseases in the soil. This reduces the amount of chemical fertilizers and pesticides that farmers sometimes use.

**Thinking Critically** A farmer rotates crops each year. If the farmer plants corn one year, what crop should the farmer plant on that same field the next year? Explain.

# 8-2 What are stems?

## *Objectives*

Distinguish between herbaceous and woody stems. Explain the jobs of stems.

## *Key Terms*

**herbaceous** (huhr-BAY-shuhs) **stem:** stem that is soft and green

**woody stem:** stem that contains wood and is thick and hard

**xylem** (ZY-luhm)**:** tissue that carries water and dissolved minerals upward from the roots

**phloem** (FLOH-em)**:** tissue that carries food from the leaves to other parts of the plant

**Kinds of Stems** Two types of plant stems are herbaceous stems and woody stems. **Herbaceous stems** are soft, smooth, and green. Usually, plants with herbaceous stems do not grow taller than 2 meters. Plants with these stems grow one season and then die. Tomato plants and bean plants have herbaceous stems. Some herbaceous plants have underground roots that survive the winter. These plants will grow new stems the next growing season.

▲ **Figure 8-7** Tomato plants have herbaceous stems.

**Woody stems** are thick, hard, and rough. The rough outer layer of the stem is the bark. Woody stems are not usually green. Plants with woody stems may live for many growing seasons. They grow taller and wider each year. All trees have woody stems. Rose bushes also have woody stems. Plants with woody stems can grow to be over 100 meters tall. Most woody plants are gymnosperms or dicots.

**1** **NAME:** What are two kinds of plant stems?

**Functions of Stems** Most stems grow aboveground. The main job of stems is to support the leaves. Stems also are organs of transport. The vascular tubes within the stems carry materials between the roots and the leaves. In some plants, stems also store food. For example, the stems of sugar cane store large amounts of sugar. Potatoes are actually underground storage stems.

A tree trunk is a woody stem that has an outer layer of bark. The outer layer of bark is made of dead cells. A trunk supports very large trees and is a source of lumber.

**2** **LIST:** What are some functions of plant stems?

**Stem Structure** Both woody and herbaceous stems have similar tissues. However, the arrangement of the tissues is different in the two types of stems. Stems of both types contain tubes that carry water and dissolved minerals up from the roots. These tubes are made of tissue called **xylem**. Xylem carries water to the leaves. Extra water evaporates into the air through the leaves. Tissue that carries dissolved food, made in the leaves, downward to other parts of the plant is called **phloem**. Xylem and phloem make up the transport or vascular system of the plant.

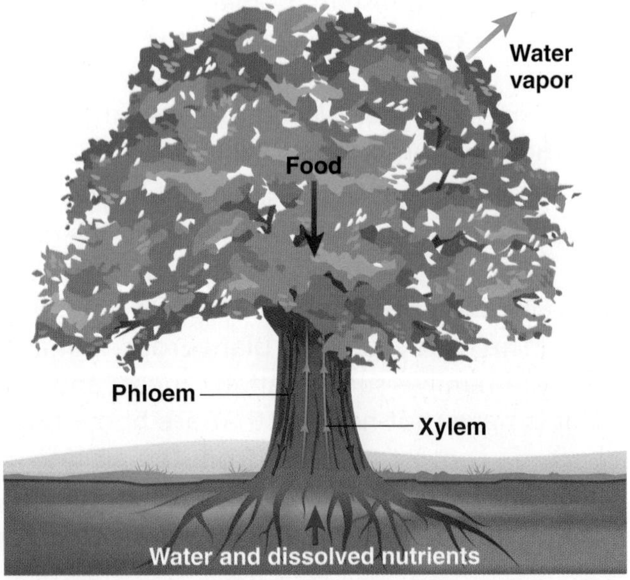


▲ **Figure 8-8** Transport tubes carry nutrients throughout a plant.

In different plants, xylem and phloem are arranged differently. In monocots, the xylem and phloem are in bundles throughout the stem. In dicots and gymnosperms, the phloem form an outer ring around an inner ring of xylem. As woody stems get thicker each year, the inner layer of xylem gets thicker. The phloem always stay in the outer layer.

3 **ANALYZE:** Why does a plant need xylem and phloem?

## CHECKING CONCEPTS

1. __________ stems are usually soft, smooth, and green.
2. Plants with __________ stems live for many growing seasons.
3. Roots and leaves are connected by __________.
4. Oak trees have __________ stems.
5. In monocots, xylem and phloem are found in __________.

## THINKING CRITICALLY

6. **SEQUENCE:** Make a flowchart that shows the paths of water and food in a plant.
7. **CLASSIFY:** Which plants listed have herbaceous stems? Which plants have woody stems?

| | |
|---|---|
| **a.** tulip | **d.** apple tree |
| **b.** oak tree | **e.** sunflower |
| **c.** daisy | **f.** willow |

## Web InfoSearch

**Tree Rings** The xylem of a tree goes through two growth periods a year. These periods form bands called annual rings. You can determine a tree's age by counting the rings.

**SEARCH:** Use the Internet to find out more about tree rings. Then, put your findings into a report. Start your search at www.conceptsandchallenges.com. Some key search words are **annual growth rings** and **tree rings**.

## *Hands-On Activity*

### TRANSPORT IN PLANTS

*You will need a beaker, water, red or blue food coloring, a leafy celery stalk, and a knife.*

1. Put water in the beaker. Add 10–15 drops of food coloring.
2. Use a knife to cut a slice on an angle off the bottom of the celery stalk. Discard the slice. ⚠ CAUTION: Be careful when using a knife. Always cut away from yourself.
3. Put the cut end of the stalk into the water.
4. **OBSERVE:** Record your observations of the celery after 5, 10, 15, and 30 minutes.
5. **PREDICT:** What do you think will happen to the food coloring in the celery after 24 hours?
6. Keep the celery in the food coloring for 24 hours. Observe the location of the food coloring.

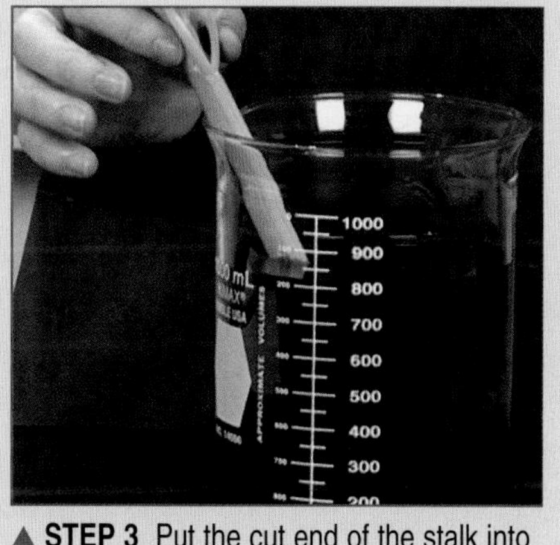


▲ **STEP 3** Put the cut end of the stalk into the colored water.

### Practicing Your Skills

7. **DESCRIBE:** What happened to the food coloring in the celery?
8. **EVALUATE:** Was your prediction correct? Explain.
9. **INFER:** What life processes of a plant does this activity show?

# 8-3 What are leaves?

## INVESTIGATE

### *Classifying Leaves*
HANDS-ON ACTIVITY

1. Collect a sample of several different leaves.
2. On a sheet of paper, trace the outline of each leaf. Draw in the vein pattern for each leaf.
3. Use a field guide to identify each leaf.

**THINK ABOUT IT:** How many basic leaf shapes can you identify?

### *Objectives*
Describe the structure of leaves. Classify leaves as simple or compound.

### *Key Terms*
**blade:** wide, flat part of a leaf

**vein** (VAYN)**:** bundle of tubes that contain the xylem and phloem in a leaf

**epidermis** (ehp-uh-DUR-mihs)**:** outer, protective layer of the leaf

**stoma** (STOH-muh), *pl.* **stomata** (STOH-muh-tuh)**:** tiny opening in the upper or lower surface of a leaf

**mesophyll** (MEHS-uh-fihl)**:** middle layer of leaf tissue in which photosynthesis occurs

**Leaf Structure** Most leaves have a stalk and a wide, flat part called the **blade**. The blade is the most important part of the leaf. Food-making takes place in the blade. The stalk supports the blade and attaches it to the stem of the plant. Throughout the leaf, there is a system of tubes called **veins** as shown in Figure 8-9. They are made up of xylem and phloem. They connect to the xylem and phloem in the stem. The xylem carries water and dissolved minerals into the leaf and the phloem carries food out of the leaf. Veins and stalks also support the leaf blade.

**1 IDENTIFY:** What are the main parts of a leaf?

**Kinds of Leaves** In some plants, the leaf blades are in one piece. This kind of leaf is called a simple leaf. Maple, oak, and elm trees have simple leaves.

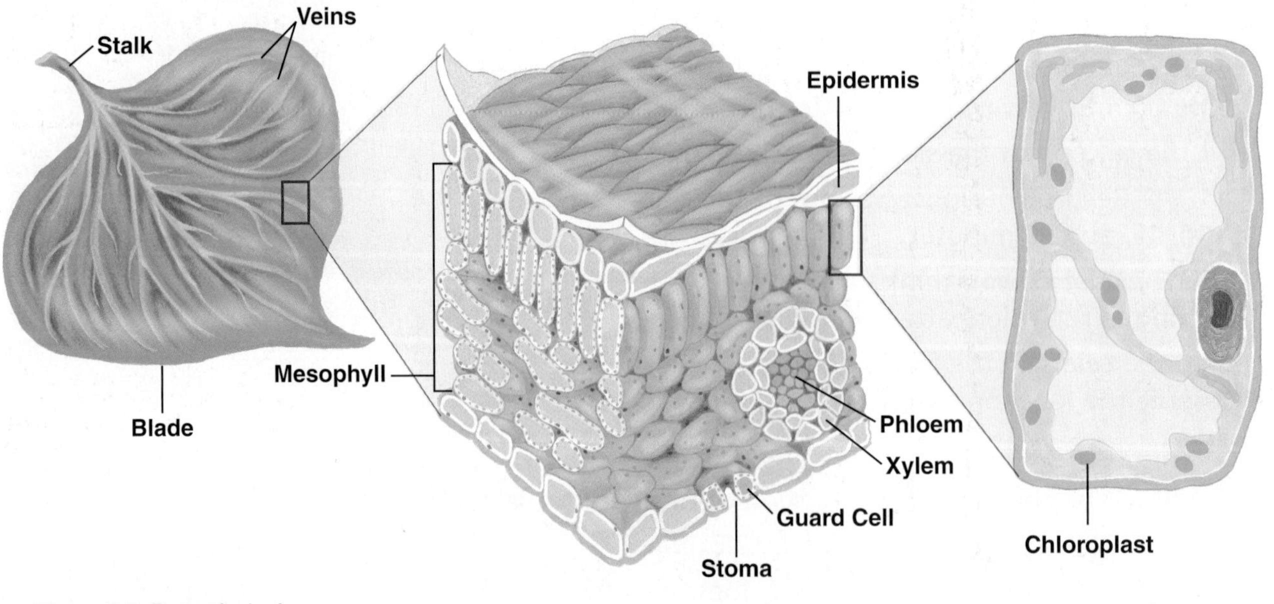


▲ **Figure 8-9** Parts of a leaf

In other plants, leaf blades are divided into pieces. This kind of leaf is called a compound leaf. The pieces that make up a compound leaf are called leaflets. Each leaflet looks like a small leaf. Poison ivy and roses have compound leaves.

**2** **OBSERVE:** What kind of leaf is shown in Figure 8-9?

**Leaf Tissues** Leaves are covered by a protective layer called the **epidermis** as shown in Figure 8-9. This layer prevents excess loss of water from the leaf. Scattered throughout the upper and lower epidermis are many tiny openings called **stomata**. Two guard cells control the size of each stoma. They open and close the stoma, controlling water loss. They also control the exchange of water vapor, oxygen, and carbon dioxide between the inner tissues of the leaf and the surrounding air. There are usually more stomata on the underside of a leaf than on the top.

Beneath the epidermis is a layer of tissue called the **mesophyll**. The cells in the mesophyll contain chloroplasts. Most of the food-making in the plant occurs in these cells. Veins extend throughout the mesophyll.

**3** **IDENTIFY:** In what tissue layer does most food-making take place in a leaf?

## ✓ CHECKING CONCEPTS

1. The flat part of a leaf is called a __________.
2. Leaves that are made up of leaflets are __________.
3. The outer, protective layer of a leaf is the __________.
4. Water and gases pass into and out of leaves through tiny holes called __________.

## THINKING CRITICALLY

5. **APPLY:** How is the function of a leaf's epidermis similar to the function of your skin?
6. **HYPOTHESIZE:** Would stomata be opened or closed on a very dry day? Explain.
7. **INFER:** Why is air in a forest usually humid?

## HEALTH AND SAFETY TIP

Some plants are poisonous to the touch. They contain chemicals that can irritate the skin. Poison ivy, poison oak, and poison sumac are three common examples. Avoid touching any part of these plants. Find pictures of poison ivy, oak, and sumac. How can you identify these plants? Do they have simple or compound leaves?

## *Integrating Physical Science*

**TOPIC: chemistry**

### THE CHEMISTRY OF CHANGING LEAVES

During the spring and summer months, the leaves on most deciduous trees appear green. That is because leaves contain chlorophyll, a pigment that reflects green light. Carotene, xanthophyll, and anthocyanin are other pigments also found in some trees. They reflect yellow and red light. The green chlorophyll masks the other pigments found in the leaves.

Sunlight causes chlorophyll to decompose. Plants constantly remake chlorophyll. To produce chlorophyll, plants need a lot of light and warm temperatures. When the temperatures get colder and the days become shorter, the trees begin to break down chlorophyll and store it for the next season. The absence of chlorophyll means the other pigments can be seen as reds, yellows, and oranges. Eventually, the leaves die and fall off the tree.

**Thinking Critically** Why do you think the trees store chlorophyll for the next season?

▲ **Figure 8-10** In autumn, the leaves of some trees change to bright reds, oranges, and yellows.

# 8-4 What is photosynthesis?

## *Objective*

Explain the importance of photosynthesis.

## *Key Terms*

**autotroph:** organism that can make its own food

**photosynthesis** (foht-oh-SIHN-thuh-sihs)**:** food-making process in plants that uses sunlight

**chlorophyll** (KLAWR-uh-fihl)**:** green material that is needed by plants for photosynthesis

**chloroplast:** organelle in plant cells that contains chlorophyll

**heterotroph:** organism that cannot make its own food

**Food Factories** Green plants are **autotrophs**. They can make their own food in their leaves. The leaves are like "food factories." Some green stems also can make food. Food-making in plants is called **photosynthesis**. The food that plants make is a sugar called sucrose. You may know sucrose as the sugar you put on cereal. Plants change this sugar into starch, fats, and proteins. These nutrients are stored in the plants. They can be used at a later time.

1 NAME: What food do green plants make?

**Photosynthesis** In photosynthesis, water and carbon dioxide are used to make simple sugars, such as glucose. These simple sugars are eventually made into sucrose, a more complex sugar. Roots absorb the needed water from the soil. Xylem carry the water up into the leaves. Carbon dioxide enters the plant through the stomata. Sunlight supplies the energy the plant needs to make the sugar. During photosynthesis, oxygen and water are given off as byproducts. The equation for photosynthesis is shown in Figure 8-11.

2 OBSERVE: On which side of the equation are the products shown?

**Chlorophyll** Photosynthesis cannot occur without **chlorophyll**. Chlorophyll is a chemical pigment, or coloring, needed for photosynthesis. Other pigments in leaves are masked by chlorophyll. You see the colors of these pigments during the fall. Leaves change color. The different colors are caused by the other pigments.

Wherever there is chlorophyll in a plant, photosynthesis can occur. The chlorophyll is inside special organelles of plant cells. The organelles that contain chlorophyll are called **chloroplasts**. Leaf mesophyll cells contain many chloroplasts. Most photosynthesis takes place in the mesophyll layer.

3 NAME: What organelle contains chlorophyll?

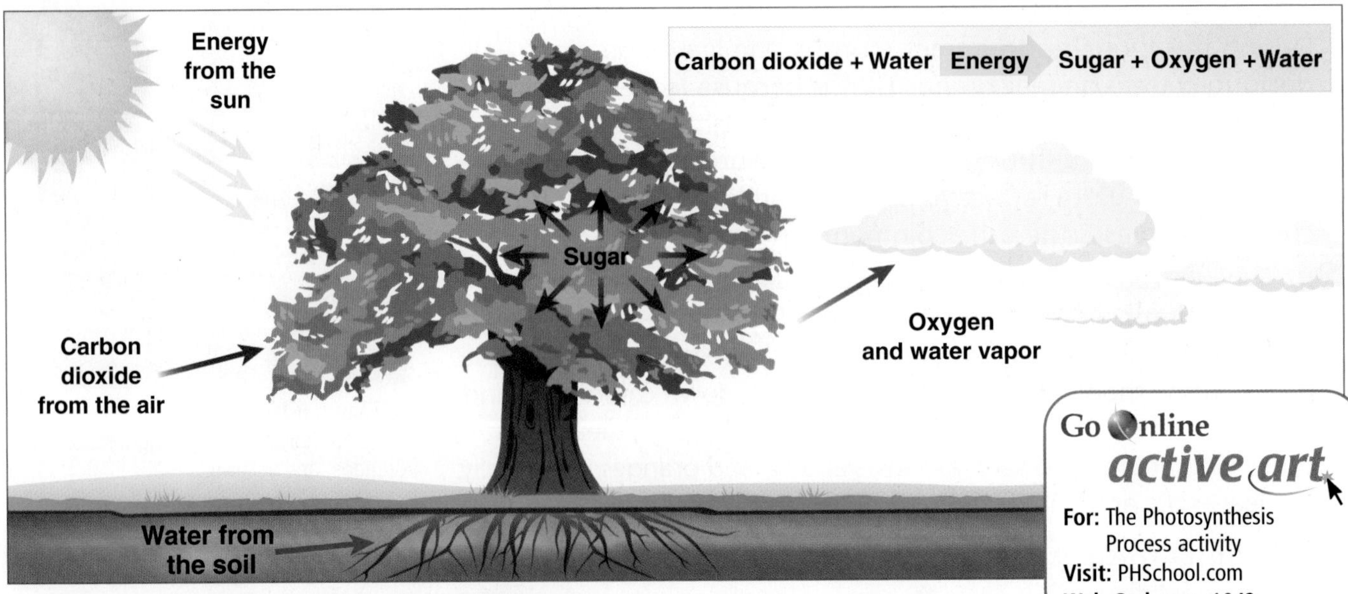


▲ **Figure 8-11** Plants make food during photosynthesis.

Go Online
*active art*

**For:** The Photosynthesis Process activity
**Visit:** PHSchool.com
**Web Code:** cep-1042

**Plants and Animals** Animals cannot make their own food. They are **heterotrophs**. Instead, they get their energy by eating plants or by eating other animals that have eaten plants. Almost all living things, either directly or indirectly, get energy from the food made during photosynthesis.

In addition, most organisms get the oxygen they need from plants. About 21 percent of Earth's atmosphere is made up of oxygen. Living things need this oxygen to survive. Plants produce most of this oxygen during photosynthesis.

4 EXPLAIN: How are plants important to people?

## CHECKING CONCEPTS

1. The food plants make is __________.
2. Chloroplasts contain the green material __________.
3. The materials a plant uses to make sugar are __________.
4. Water enters the plant through the __________.

## THINKING CRITICALLY

5. EXPLAIN: What happens to the oxygen produced during photosynthesis?
6. APPLY: What are two ways plants are important to you?

## INTERPRETING VISUALS

*Use Figure 8-12 to answer the following questions.*

7. IDENTIFY: In which layer does photosynthesis occur?
8. IDENTIFY: Through which structure does water for photosynthesis enter the leaf?
9. INFER: Which structure allows oxygen and carbon dioxide to enter and leave the leaf?

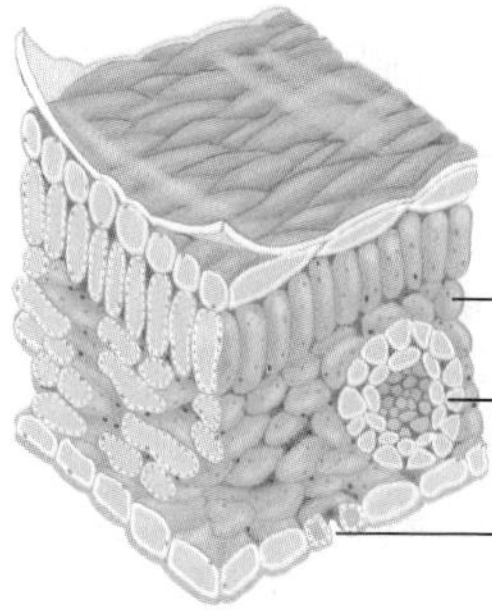


◀ Figure 8-12

## *Hands-On Activity*

### SEPARATING PIGMENTS

*You will need goggles; a paper towel; scissors; a metric ruler; a timer; red, blue, and black nonpermanent felt pens; isopropyl alcohol; and a small bowl.*

1. Cut a strip of paper towel 3 cm wide and 12 cm long.
2. Use the red, blue, and black felt pens to make one dot about 5 cm from the bottom of the strip. Make only one dot on the paper towel.
3. Pour 1 cm of alcohol into the glass. ⚠ CAUTION: Do not breathe the fumes. Stand the strip of paper towel in the glass. One end of the paper towel should be over the rim.
4. PREDICT: What will happen to the dot on the strip?
5. OBSERVE: After 5 minutes, look at the strip. What happened to the dot after 5 minutes?

▲ **STEP 3** Stand the strip of paper towel in the glass.

### Practicing Your Skills

6. INFER: What would happen if plant pigment were used instead of ink in this experiment?
7. HYPOTHESIZE: If you made a dark pigment from a plant that was green and red, what colors might you see in a separation?

# THE Big IDEA

## What are the physics of a tree?

Physics is the study of force and energy. Both energy and force play an important role in the life of plants.

Chloroplasts absorb sunlight, a form of light energy. That energy helps change carbon dioxide and water into sugars and oxygen. Sugar contains chemical energy and is transferred to the fruit and leaves. Later, the energy is transferred again to birds, insects, or humans who eat the plant.

The amount of force acting on a surface is called pressure. Pressure helps explain how water travels from a plant's roots to its highest leaves. Molecules move from areas of high pressure to areas of low pressure. As leaf cells lose water through evaporation, they also lose pressure. A low-pressure cell quickly draws water from a high-pressure cell. This chain continues, pulling water from the base to the top.

Many other physical science principles are at work in the life of a tree. Look at the boxes of text that appear on this page and the next. They point out some of these processes. Follow the directions in the Science Log to learn more about "the big idea." ✦

**WRITING ACTIVITY**

### Science Log

Look at the tree on these two pages. Which part of the tree do you think uses the most energy to do its job? In your science log, research and write about the physical science processes at work in this part of the tree. Start your search at www.conceptsandchallenges.com.

### Root

Typically, molecules move from more crowded areas to less crowded areas. That is how root hairs absorb water from soil. The process is called **osmosis**. The opposite happens when roots absorb minerals. Energy is used to pump the minerals from a less crowded area to a more crowded area. This process is called **active transport**.

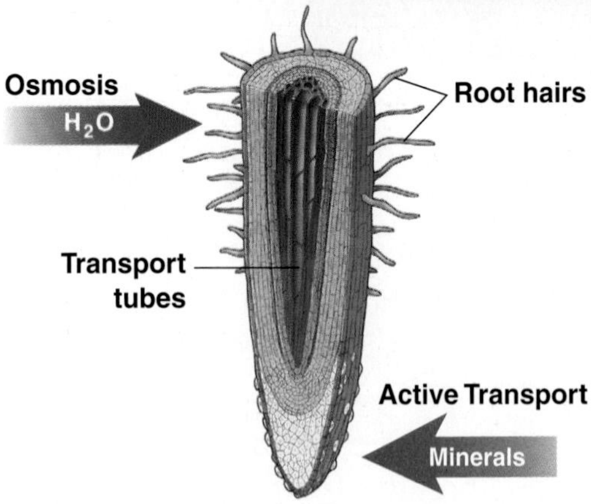


**Figure 8-13** ▶ Energy and force play an important role in the life of a tree.

## Stomata

Water evaporates into the air in a process called **transpiration**. During transpiration, water molecules escape from the leaf through the stomata. This action causes more water molecules to be drawn up the trunk and into the leaves.

## Trunk

Inside of tree trunk

One of the main reasons water moves up a tree is because it is pulled upward. As water evaporates, a force called **transpiration pull** draws water up through the trunk of the tree. The water flows upward through the xylem. The strong attraction of water molecules to each other, called **cohesion**, also helps to pull water upward. Transpiration pull and cohesion are strong enough to raise water more than 300 feet.

# 8-5 What are flowers?

## *Objectives*

Identify the flower as the reproductive organ of a plant. Describe the parts of a flower.

## *Key Terms*

**sepal** (SEE-puhl)**:** special kind of leaf that protects the flower bud

**petal:** white or brightly colored structure above the sepal of a flower

**pistil:** female reproductive organ in a flower

**stamen** (STAY-muhn)**:** male reproductive organ in a flower

**perfect flower:** flower with both female and male reproductive organs

**imperfect flower:** flower with either male or female reproductive organs, but not both

**Flowers** Not all plants have flowers. However, in plants with flowers, the flower is the organ of sexual reproduction. Flowers contain the male and female reproductive parts of a flowering plant, or an angiosperm.

**1** DEFINE: What are flowers?

**Parts of a Flower** A flower is made up of several parts. The bottom of a flower is surrounded by **sepals.** Sepals are a special kind of leaf. They protect the flower bud. In some flowers, the sepals look like small green leaves. In others, they are large and brightly colored. In Figure 8-14, the sepals look similar to the petals.

The **petals** of a flower are just inside the sepals. After the sepals fold back, the petals of the flower can be seen. The petals are another kind of leaf. They may be white or brightly colored. Some flowers, such as roses and lilies, are sweet-smelling and have large, colorful petals. Unlike roses and lilies, the flowers of grass plants have very small petals that are not colorful or sweet-smelling. Petals protect the reproductive organs of the plant and attract insects and other pollinators. Inside the petals are the reproductive organs for the plant.

**2** IDENTIFY: What are two special kinds of leaves in a flower?

**Reproductive Organs** The reproductive organs in a flower are the pistil and the stamen. The **pistil** is the female reproductive organ. The **stamen** is the male reproductive organ. A flower usually has one pistil with several stamens around it. These organs are located inside the circle of petals.

▲ **Figure 8-14** The parts of a perfect flower

Some flowers have both male and female reproductive organs. These flowers are called **perfect flowers**. The lily in Figure 8-14 is an example of a perfect flower. Other flowers may have only male or only female reproductive organs. These flowers are called **imperfect flowers**. Male flowers only have stamens. Female flowers only have pistils. Look at Figure 8-15 on the next page. It shows an imperfect flower.

▲ **Figure 8-15** The holly tree has imperfect flowers. The male flower is shown on the left and the female on the right.

**3** CLASSIFY: The pistil and the stamen are parts of what plant system?

## ✓ CHECKING CONCEPTS

1. The organs of sexual reproduction in plants are the __________.
2. Sepals and petals are special kinds of __________.
3. The __________ is the female reproductive organ in a flower.
4. The __________ is the male reproductive organ in a flower.

## THINKING CRITICALLY

5. **MODEL:** Draw a model of a flower. Label the petals, sepals, stamen, and pistil.
6. **HYPOTHESIZE:** Why is it important for insects to be attracted to flowers?

## BUILDING SCIENCE SKILLS

***Researching*** Use a dictionary or library references to find out the meaning of the terms *pistillate* and *staminate*. Research five different types of imperfect flowers. Then classify each imperfect flower as pistillate or staminate.

## Real-Life Science
### BOTANICAL GARDENS

▲ **Figure 8-16** The Missouri Botanical Garden

A wide variety of plants are on public display at botanical gardens. Visitors to the Missouri Botanical Garden, for example, can explore theme gardens, educational greenhouses, and hundreds of acres of nature preserve. There is even a miniature rain forest housed in a building called the Climatron.

Botanical gardens are necessary because many plants are becoming rare. Plant habitats often are destroyed when people develop land. Introducing new plants to an area when people travel or relocate also can endanger plants. In botanical gardens, plants are protected and displayed for people's enjoyment.

People who work in botanical gardens realize the importance of plants. Plants are an important source of food and oxygen. The chemistry of plants can help to control pests. Also, certain plants may hold the key that unlocks the cure of a fatal disease, such as cancer.

**Thinking Critically** Why are botanical gardens important to the community?

Go Online
*active art*
**For:** The Structure of a Flower activity
**Visit:** PHSchool.com
**Web Code:** cep-1053

# 8-6 How do flowering plants reproduce?

*Objective*

Describe how flowering plants reproduce.

*Key Terms*

**filament:** stalk of the stamen

**anther:** part of the stamen that produces pollen

**pollen grain:** male reproductive cell of a plant

**fertilization** (fuhrt-uhl-ih-ZAY-shuhn)**:** joining of the nuclei of the male and female reproductive cells

**pollination** (pahl-uh-NAY-shuhn)**:** movement of pollen from a stamen to a pistil

**Stamens and Pollen** Stamens have two main parts. These parts are the filament and the anther. The **filament** is the thin stalk that holds up the anther. The **anther** is the part that produces pollen grains. **Pollen grains** are the male reproductive structures that contain sperm. Pollen is released when an anther bursts open.

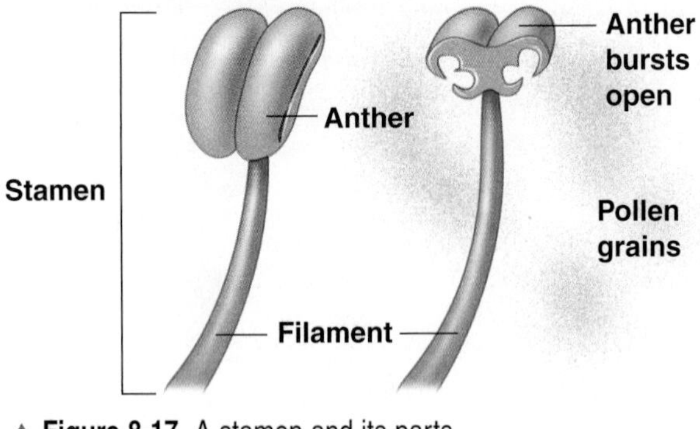


▲ **Figure 8-17** A stamen and its parts

**1** **DEFINE:** What is pollen?

**Fertilization** In sexual reproduction, reproductive cells from the male and female must meet. The joining of the nuclei of male and female reproductive cells is called **fertilization**. In flowering plants, fertilization takes place inside the pistil.

**2** **DEFINE:** What is fertilization?

▲ **Figure 8-18** Bees carry pollen from plant to plant.

**Pollination**
For fertilization to take place, pollen grains must first move from a stamen to a pistil. This is called **pollination**. Pollen often is moved by wind, insects, birds, and even bats. Sometimes, pollen is carried by water.

**3** **CLASSIFY:** What activity of a plant is pollination a part of?

**Self-Pollination** In many flowers, the stamens are taller than the pistil. Pollen can fall off the anther on top of a stamen and land on the pistil in the same flower. This kind of pollination is called self-pollination. Self-pollination also occurs when pollen from one flower is carried to the pistil of another flower on the same plant.

▲ **Figure 8-19** Self-pollination

**4** **EXPLAIN:** In what two ways may self-pollination occur?

**Cross-Pollination** Sometimes pollen is carried from the stamen of a flower on one plant to the pistil of a flower on another similar plant. This is called cross-pollination. Some plants have separate male and female flowers. Sometimes the male and female flowers are on different plants. This means they are male and female plants. These plants must cross-pollinate. Cross-pollination also can occur between two different plants that have perfect flowers.

▲ **Figure 8-20** Cross-pollination can occur between different plants with perfect flowers.

5 **NAME:** What kind of pollination occurs between flowers on different plants?

## CHECKING CONCEPTS

1. The nuclei of male and female reproductive cells join in the process of __________.
2. Male reproductive cells are the __________.
3. Movement of pollen from a stamen to a pistil is __________.
4. Pollination between flowers on different plants is called __________.
5. Pollination between flowers on the same plant is called __________.

## THINKING CRITICALLY

6. **INFER:** Would flowers that depend on wind for pollination probably have flat, open flowers or tall, closed flowers? Explain.
7. **ANALYZE:** How might an insect move pollen from one flower to another?

## HEALTH AND SAFETY TIP

Hay fever is an allergic reaction to the pollen of certain plants. Large amounts of pollen in the air cause people with hay fever to sneeze. Their eyes may become red and watery. Prepare a poster that shows which plants cause hay fever, the times of the year that people suffer from hay fever, and how it can be treated.

## *People in Science*

### PLANT GENETICIST

Plant geneticists are scientists who work on ways to improve plant varieties. They study how to make plants and crops more suited to people's needs. Plant geneticists breed plants with desirable traits. They want to find out if the new breeds are more resistant to disease, more nutritious, and easier to grow.

Surinder K. Vasal, a plant geneticist from India, developed a new variety of corn. In many countries, people rely on corn as their basic food. Although corn is a good food, it is not rich in nutritionally balanced protein. Poor children who cannot get quality protein from other sources often become malnourished. Working with Evangelina Villegas, a Mexican scientist, Vasal perfected a protein-rich variety of corn called quality protein maize (QPM). This corn looks and tastes like regular corn, but it has twice as much protein and produces a larger crop. Now, QPM is grown in parts of Africa, China, Mexico, and Central America. There has been a big improvement in nutrition levels in those areas. In 2000, Vasal and Villegas received the $250,000 Millennium World Food Prize for their work on QPM.

**Thinking Critically** What are some desirable traits of a plant that a plant geneticist may be interested in reproducing?

# 8-7 What are seeds and fruits?

## *Objectives*

Identify the parts of the pistil. Explain how seeds and fruits form.

## *Key Terms*

**stigma** (STIHG-muh)**:** top part of the pistil
**style:** stalk of the pistil of a flower
**ovary** (OH-vuh-ree)**:** bottom part of the pistil
**ovule** (AHV-yool)**:** part of the ovary that develops into a seed after fertilization
**embryo:** undeveloped plant or animal
**fruit:** mature ovary and its seeds

**Parts of a Pistil** A pistil is made up of three parts. The top part is the **stigma**. Below the stigma is a tube called the **style**. The style connects the stigma to the bottom of the pistil. The bottom of the pistil is called the **ovary**. Inside the ovary are the **ovules**. The ovule is the part of the ovary that develops into a seed after fertilization. It contains the female reproductive cell, or egg.

1 IDENTIFY: What are the parts of a pistil?

**Forming a Seed** After a pollen grain lands on the stigma, it begins to change. The pollen cell grows a tube. This tube is called a pollen tube. The pollen tube grows down into the stigma. It continues to grow down through the style and the ovary. Finally, the tip of the pollen tube enters the ovule.

After the pollen tube enters the ovule, the tip of the tube dissolves. The sperm in the pollen grain move into the ovule. The nucleus of the pollen cell joins with the nucleus of the egg in the ovule. The joining of the two nuclei is called fertilization. After fertilization, the ovule develops into a seed. A new plant can grow from a seed.

2 ANALYZE: Why does the pollen grain grow a tube after it lands on the stigma?

**Fruits** Ovules are found inside an ovary. An ovary may have only one ovule or it may have more than one ovule. When the ovules are fertilized, they develop into seeds. Each seed contains a very young, or undeveloped, plant. Scientists call an undeveloped plant or animal an **embryo**. A seed contains a plant embryo.

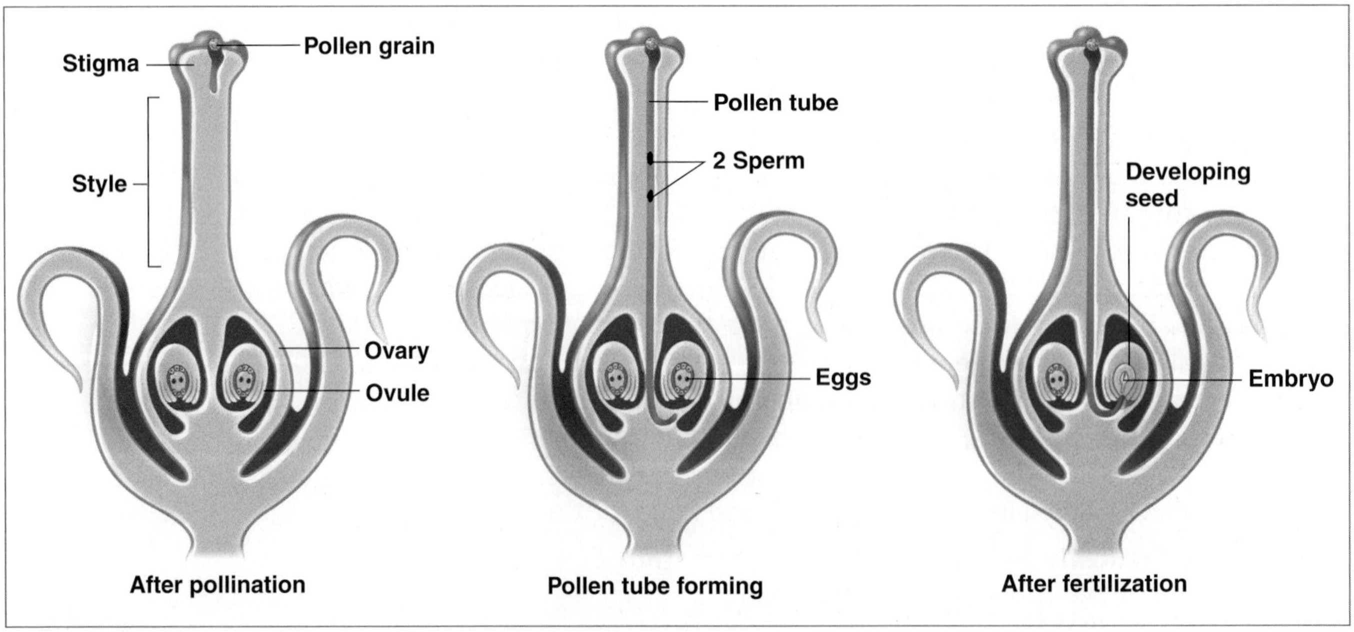


▲ **Figure 8-21** Pollination leads to fertilization and the formation of a seed.

While the seeds are forming, the ovary is changing. The ovary becomes very large. It surrounds and protects the seeds and the embryos inside the seeds. A mature ovary and its seeds are called a **fruit**. Plums and tomatoes are examples of fruits.

▲ **Figure 8-22** Apples have seeds.

**DISTINGUISH:** What is the relationship between the ovary and the seed?

## CHECKING CONCEPTS

1. The female reproductive cells are in the __________.
2. A seed is formed after __________.
3. The undeveloped plant inside a seed is called an __________.
4. A pollen grain that lands on a stigma grows a __________.

## THINKING CRITICALLY

5. **MODEL:** Draw and label the parts of a pistil.
6. **INFER:** The top of a stigma is usually sticky. What might be an advantage of this stickiness?

## BUILDING SCIENCE SKILLS

***Classifying*** Scientists classify any plant part with seeds as fruit. Vegetables are the leaves, stems, or roots of plants. People classify fruits and vegetables differently. Classify each of the plant parts listed as if you were a scientist and then as you would every day.

**a.** tomato
**b.** beets
**c.** cucumber
**d.** carrot
**e.** peach
**f.** celery
**g.** lettuce
**h.** papaya
**i.** green pepper

## *Real-Life Science*

### SEED PLANTS YOU EAT

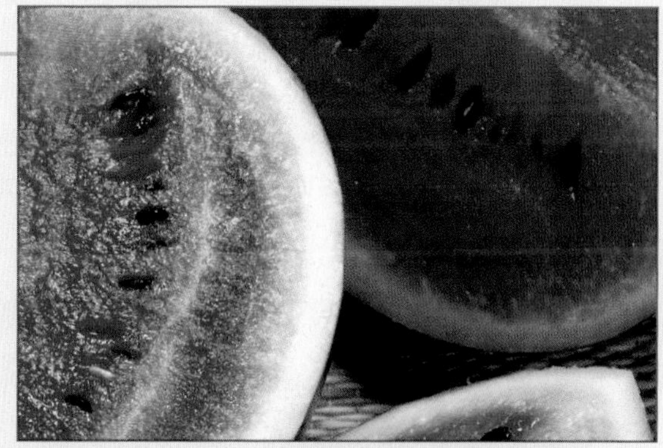

▲ **Figure 8-23** Watermelons are fruits with seeds.

You may have eaten popcorn the last time you went to the movies. Popcorn comes from a seed plant. Have you ever had a peanut butter sandwich? Peanuts also come from a seed plant. So does the wheat used to make bread. Many of the foods we eat come from seed plants.

Apples, watermelons, and oranges are the fruits of a seed plant. The fruit of a seed plant is really a fleshy, juicy container for the seed. The fruit protects the seed. For example, inside a watermelon, there are a lot of black seeds. All the rest of the melon is protecting those seeds from water loss, disease, and insects.

Many of the foods we call vegetables and grains are really fruits of a seed plant. Anything that has seeds in it but is not a cone is a fruit. This includes tomatoes, beans, oats, and wheat. All these fruits have seeds.

**Thinking Critically** How many other fruits can you name?

# LAB ACTIVITY
# Identifying the Parts of a Flower

**Materials**

Sheet of white paper
Dissecting needle
Tulip, daffodil, lily, or gladiolus flower
Hand lens

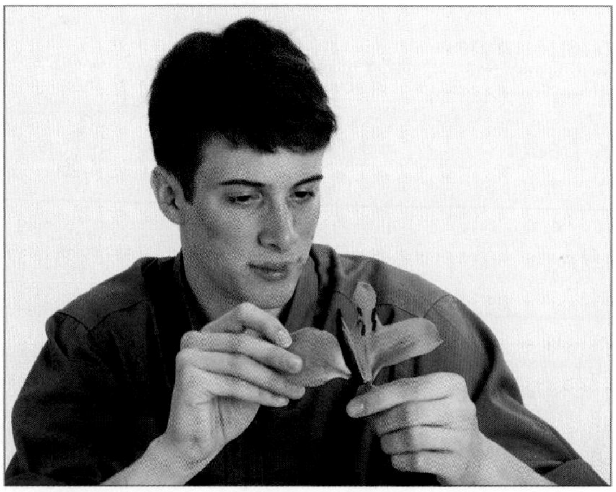

▲ **STEP 3** Carefully remove the petals from a flower.

▲ **STEP 4** Examine the stamens.

### *BACKGROUND*

Most flowers contain a pistil, stamens, sepals, and petals. The pistil and stamens are the reproductive organs. The sepals and petals are specialized kinds of leaves. The ovary is the place that seeds will be formed.

### *PURPOSE*

In this activity, you will dissect a flower and study its parts.

### *PROCEDURE*

1. Copy the chart in Figure 8-24 onto a sheet of paper. Label the chart.

2. Carefully remove the sepals from a flower. How many sepals does your flower have? What color are they? Record your observations in your chart.

3. Remove the petals from your flower. How many petals does your flower have? What color are they? Record your observations in your chart.

4. Look at one of the stamens through a hand lens. Identify the anther and the filament.

5. Use a dissecting needle to release the pollen grains from the anther onto a sheet of white paper. Examine the pollen grains with a hand lens. Draw the pollen grains below your chart.

6. Remove the pistil from your flower. Examine it through the hand lens. Identify the stigma, the style, and the ovary. How many pistils does your flower have? Record your observations in your chart.

▲ **STEP 5** Remove the pollen from the anther.

▲ **STEP 7** Slice the pistil down the middle.

7. Using the dissecting needle, slice the pistil down the middle. Examine the inside of the ovary with the hand lens. ⚠ **CAUTION:** Be extremely careful when using dissecting needles.

8. Remove an ovule from the ovary and study it with the hand lens. Draw an ovule below your chart.

| Part | Number | Color |
|---|---|---|
| Sepals | | |
| Petals | | |
| Stamens | | |
| Pistil | | |

▲ **Figure 8-24** Copy this chart onto a sheet of paper.

## *CONCLUSIONS*

1. **IDENTIFY:** How are the parts of a flower arranged?
2. **OBSERVE:** Is there a pattern to the number of sepals and petals in your flower?
3. **EXPLAIN:** How do you think your flower is pollinated?
4. **APPLY:** How many seeds could have developed in the ovary?

# 8-8 What are the parts of a seed?

### *Objective*

Identify the parts of a seed.

### *Key Terms*

**germinate** (JUR-muh-nayt)**:** to grow from a seed into an embryo plant

**seed coat:** outside covering of a seed

**hilum** (HY-luhm)**:** mark on the seed coat where the seed was attached to the ovary

**Inside a Seed** Food is stored in the seed. The developing embryo uses the food as it grows. Figure 8-25 shows the inside of a green bean seed that has two large leaves, called cotyledons. In dicots, cotyledons are large and store food as starch. Monocots only have one small cotyledon. In monocots, food is stored in a special tissue called the endosperm. This food is absorbed through the cotyledon. The corn in Figure 8-25 is a monocot.

The embryo is attached to one of the seed halves. The embryo has a tiny root, a stem, and one or two cotyledons. If you plant the seed in good soil and water it, the embryo will begin to grow, or **germinate**. For some plants, as the seed germinates, the cotyledons are pushed above ground. When the first true leaves unfold and begin photosynthesis, the cotyledons wither and die. In time, the embryo will develop into an adult plant.

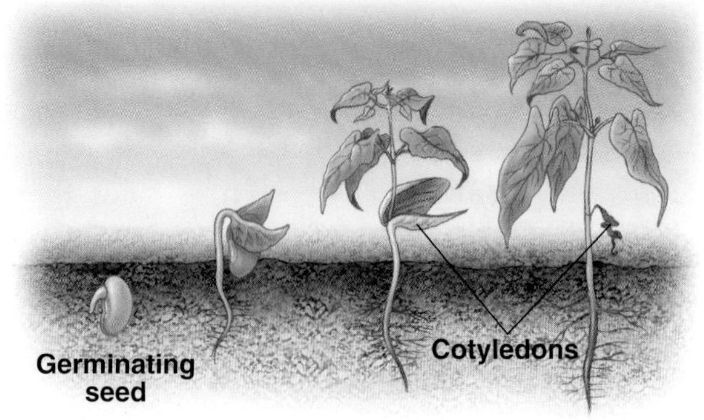


▲ **Figure 8-26** Germination

**1** **INFER:** Why would the cotyledons no longer be needed once photosynthesis begins?

**Seed Coat** All seeds have an outside covering. This outer covering is called the **seed coat**. Most seed coats are hard. The hard coat protects the embryo. Some seeds are protected so well that they can be kept for many years. They will still grow when they are planted.

**2** **NAME:** What is the outside covering of a seed called?

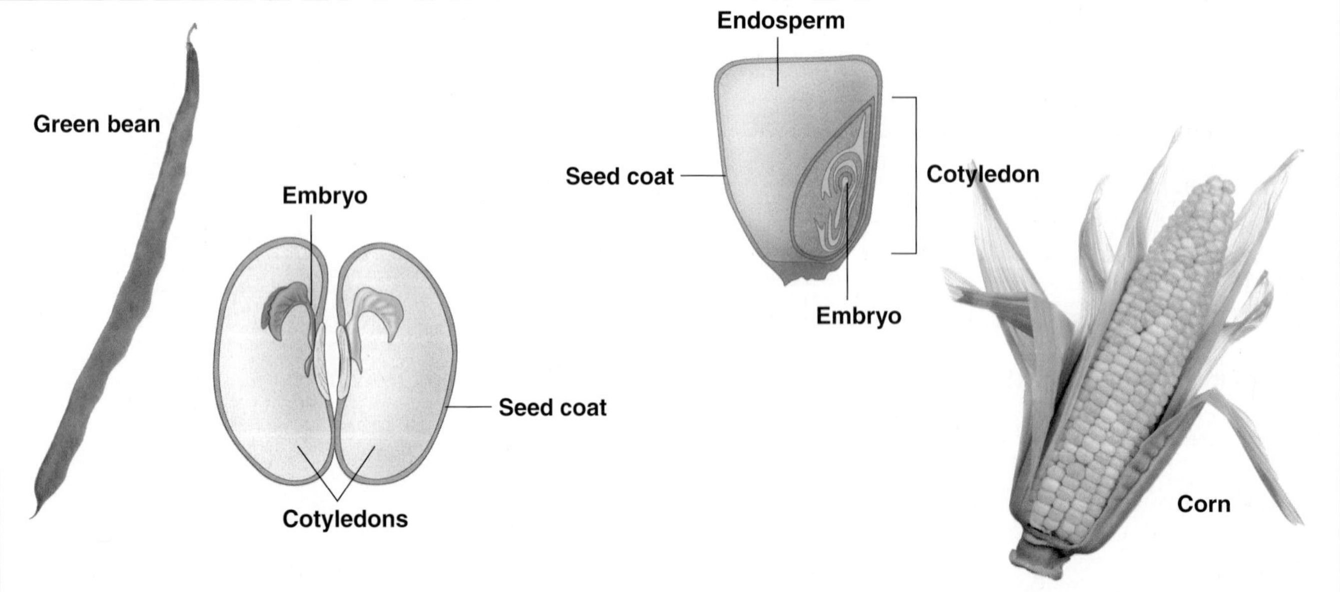


▲ **Figure 8-25** Inside a dicot and monocot seed

**Hilum** The **hilum** is a small mark, or scar, on the seed. The hilum is where the seed was attached to the ovary. Near the hilum, there is a small opening. The opening is where the pollen tube entered the ovule.

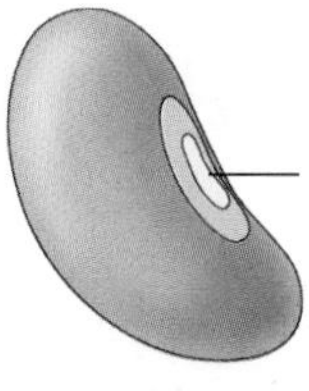

▲ **Figure 8-27** A seed showing a hilum

**3** DESCRIBE: What is the hilum?

**Seed Dispersal** Some seeds, such as dandelion seeds, are scattered, or dispersed, by the wind. Other seeds are dispersed by water. The fruit of a coconut plant can carry its seed thousands of kilometers on ocean currents.

Animals also help disperse seeds. For example, many animals eat berries and then eliminate the seeds in their waste. Some seeds have hooklike structures that stick to a mammal's fur. As the animal moves from place to place, so do the seeds. If a seed lands in a place with enough light, water, and nutrients, it will begin to germinate.

**4** LIST: What are three ways seeds can be dispersed?

## CHECKING CONCEPTS

1. What is the outside of a seed called?
2. What part of a seed develops into an adult plant?
3. In what form is food stored in a seed?
4. What are the three parts of all seeds?
5. What is germination?

## THINKING CRITICALLY

6. INFER: All plants need water, sunlight, and nutrients to grow. Which of these does a seed not need to germinate?
7. MODEL: Draw a diagram showing three types of seeds that are dispersed by the following methods.
   a. water
   b. wind
   c. animal fur

## *Hands-On Activity*

### GROWING SEEDS

*In this activity, you will need eight pinto beans, paper towels, potting soil, and two glasses.*

1. Fold a sheet of paper towel in half. Line one glass with the paper towel. Stuff a wad of paper towel into the bottom of the glass.
2. Place four pinto beans between the paper towel lining and the glass. Make sure the beans are placed an equal distance from each other.
3. Dampen the paper towels with water. Do not drench the paper towels. They should be damp to the touch.
4. Observe the glass for a week. Make sure that the paper towels are always damp. Record your observations.
5. Fill the second glass with soil. Place four pinto beans in the soil. Water the soil.

▲ **STEP 2** Make sure the beans are spaced apart equally.

### Practicing Your Skills

6. OBSERVE: At the end of the week, which seeds had the most growth?
7. INFER: What can you tell about the best conditions to germinate seeds from this experiment?

# 8-9 How do plants reproduce asexually?

### *Objective*
Identify ways that plants reproduce asexually.

### *Key Terms*
**asexual reproduction:** reproduction needing only one parent

**vegetative propagation** (VEHJ-uh-tayt-ihv prahp-uh-GAY-shuhn)**:** kind of asexual reproduction that uses parts of plants to grow new plants

**tuber:** underground stem

**bulb:** underground stem covered with fleshy leaves

▲ **Figure 8-28** Potatoes are tubers.

**Reproduction Without Seeds** Some plants can reproduce without male and female cells joining to form seeds. This method of reproduction is called **asexual reproduction**. One type of asexual reproduction in plants is called **vegetative propagation,** or vegetative reproduction. During vegetative propagation, the growing parts of plants develop into new plants. The growing parts are roots, stems, or leaves. In vegetative propagation, the new plants that develop are genetically identical to the parent plant.

1 **DEFINE:** What is vegetative propagation?

**Tubers** Some plants, such as white potatoes, have underground stems. An underground stem is called a **tuber**. A white potato may have many small white buds growing on its skin. These buds are called eyes. The eyes of the potato are the organs of vegetative reproduction. When planted in soil, each eye may grow into a new potato plant. Each new plant is genetically identical to the parent plant.

When farmers plant tuber crops, they must be careful to dig them all up at the end of the growing season. If parts of the tubers are left in the ground, they will begin growing the next season and may interfere with other crops.

2 **DEFINE:** What is a tuber?

**Bulbs** A **bulb** is an organ of vegetative reproduction in some plants. A bulb is an underground stem. It differs from the underground stem called a tuber. A bulb is covered with thick leaves. An onion is an example of a bulb. When planted, each bulb may grow into a new onion plant. Other plants that grow from bulbs are daffodils, lilies, and tulips.

3 **NAME:** What are two plants that grow from bulbs?

**Cuttings** Some plants can grow new plants from pieces of themselves. These plant pieces are called cuttings. Roots make good cuttings. For example, the roots of asparagus are organs of vegetative reproduction. If fleshy roots are divided and planted, they will begin to grow new roots. In time, a new asparagus plant will grow. The new plant will be genetically identical to the parent.

New plants may also grow from some leaf and stem cuttings. A leaf is cut off of the plant. The leaf stalk is placed in water. Roots will grow from the stalk, and a new plant will grow. The same thing can be done with the stems of some plants.

◀ **Figure 8-29** These houseplants are growing from cuttings.

4 ▶ **CLASSIFY:** What type of reproduction are cuttings?

## CHECKING CONCEPTS

1. What kind of reproduction is vegetative propagation?
2. What are the growing parts of a plant?
3. What are the organs of vegetative propagation in a potato?
4. What kind of organ of reproduction is an onion?

## THINKING CRITICALLY

5. **EXPLAIN:** How can a houseplant be grown asexually?
6. **INFER:** What are the advantages of using asexual reproduction in farming?

### Web InfoSearch

**Grafting** Grafting is a kind of vegetative propagation. It is used to produce new kinds of plants. Twigs from one tree are attached to another. For example, seedless oranges cannot reproduce themselves. They can only reproduce by grafting. Twigs from a branch with seedless oranges are grafted onto a regular orange tree. Seedless oranges grow on the grafted branch.

**SEARCH:** Use the Internet to find out more about grafting. Then, write your findings in a report. Start your search at www.conceptsandchallenges.com. Some key search words are **grafting** and **seedless oranges**.

## *Hands-On Activity*

### GROWING PLANTS ASEXUALLY

*You will need safety goggles, gloves, two plastic cups, soil, water, four toothpicks, an onion, a potato with eyes, and a knife.*

1. Put on safety goggles and gloves. Half-fill one cup with water. Half-fill the other with soil.
2. Equally space four toothpicks around the "equator" of the onion. Set the onion, root end down into the cup of water. The toothpicks should sit on the rim of the cup so the onion is touching the water, but not the bottom of the cup.
3. Cut a piece of potato that has an eye. Put it in the cup with soil. Add some more soil. Water the soil.
   ⚠ CAUTION: Be careful when using a knife.
4. Place the plants out of direct sunlight. Check your plants every day. Keep the bulb bottom wet and the soil moist.

▲ **STEP 2** Push toothpicks into the onion.

### Practicing Your Skills

5. **IDENTIFY:** Which plant grew roots first?
6. **COMPARE:** How is the reproduction of the onion and the potato similar?

# 8-10 What are tropisms?

## INVESTIGATE

### Observing Tropisms
HANDS-ON ACTIVITY

1. Get a sample of a mimosa plant.
2. Use a hand lens to carefully observe the leaves of the plant. Draw a model of the leaves in your notebook.
3. Touch the leaves of the plant. What happens? Draw a picture or diagram of the leaves in your notebook.

**THINK ABOUT IT:** Touching the mimosa plant was a stimulus. How did the plant respond?

### Objective
Relate different stimuli to the tropisms they cause.

### Key Terms
**stimulus:** change that causes a response

**tropism** (TROH-pihz-uhm)**:** a change in a plant's growth in response to a stimulus

**phototropism:** plant's response to light

**gravitropism:** plant's response to gravity

**hydrotropism:** plant's response to water

**thigmotropism:** plant's response to touch

**Plant Responses** All plants respond to changes in their environment. They may respond to light, gravity, water, or touch. Each response is caused by a stimulus. A **stimulus** is a change that causes a response. The reaction of a plant to a stimulus that causes a change in growth is called a **tropism**. Usually, a plant responds to each stimulus by growing in a certain direction. Because most tropisms happen very slowly, you may not notice them.

**1 HYPOTHESIZE:** What stimulus do you think would make a plant grow upward?

**Light** Green plants respond to the stimulus of light. This is called **phototropism**. Most stems and leaves grow toward light. A plant left near a sunny window will bend toward the light.

Some stems even change their response to light. The flower stem of a peanut plant grows toward sunlight. After pollination, the flower stem grows away from light. It grows down into the soil, where the peanuts can develop in the dark.

▲ **Figure 8-30** This plant's response is an example of phototropism.

**2 EXPLAIN:** How do most plant stems respond to light?

**Gravity** Plants respond to the stimulus of gravity. This is called **gravitropism**. Gravity is the force of attraction that exists between all objects in the universe. Roots grow down in response to gravity. If a plant in a flowerpot is tilted on its side, its roots will bend and grow down. If that plant is turned upright, its roots will bend again and grow down.

Most stems grow away from the pull of gravity. If a plant in a flowerpot is tilted on its side, its stem will respond by bending and growing up again. Rhizomes, the underground stems of some plants, grow sideways in response to gravity. They grow horizontally just under the surface of the soil.

▲ **Figure 8-31** This tree is responding to gravity.

**3 DESCRIBE:** How does a plant root respond to gravity?

**Water** Plants respond to the stimulus of water. This is called **hydrotropism**. Roots grow toward water. In most plants, this tropism is not very strong. It occurs only when water touches the roots. In some plants, this tropism is very strong. For example, the roots of a willow tree will grow into and clog sewer and water pipes.

**4 EXPLAIN:** How do roots respond to water?

**Touch** Plants respond to the stimulus of touch. When a vine touches a fence, it grows around it. A plant's response to touch is called **thigmotropism**.

Some plants respond immediately to stimuli. Since growth is not involved, it is not a tropism. The Venus flytrap is a plant that responds quickly to touch. Each leaf of the Venus flytrap is hinged so that it can close like a book. Each leaf has stiff spines on its edges. The inner surface of each leaf has six stiff hairs. When an insect walks across a leaf, it may touch the hairs. Touching only one hair causes no reaction. Touching two hairs or jiggling one hair twice makes the leaf snap shut in one second or less. The spines interlock to form a cage. The insect is trapped inside the closed leaf. The leaf stays closed as the insect is digested.

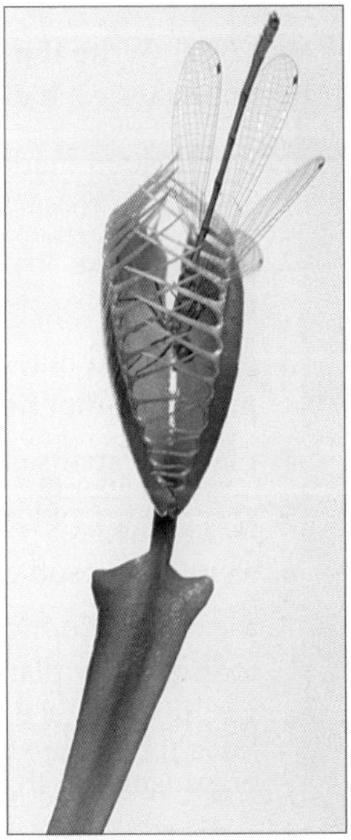

▲ **Figure 8-32** A Venus flytrap responds to touch.

**5 DEFINE:** What is thigmotropism?

## ✓ CHECKING CONCEPTS

1. Something in the environment that causes a reaction to occur is a __________.
2. A change in a plant's growth in response to stimuli is a __________.
3. Green plants grow toward the stimulus of __________.
4. Roots grow down in response to __________.
5. In hydrotropism, roots grow toward __________.
6. A Venus flytrap responds quickly to __________.
7. Plants bending toward a window is evidence of __________.

## THINKING CRITICALLY

8. **ANALYZE:** In what direction would plant stems grow in the dark? Explain your answer.
9. **HYPOTHESIZE:** What would happen to a plant's roots if you turned the plant upside down?
10. **INFER:** A drain pipe from a house seems to be clogged. A willow tree has been growing near the house for many years. What is one possible reason for the clogged drain?

## DESIGNING AN EXPERIMENT

*Design an experiment to solve the following problem. Include a hypothesis, variables, a procedure, and a type of data to study.*

PROBLEM: Luis wants to know how his houseplant will respond to stimuli, such as light, gravity, water, and touch. Pick one of these stimuli. Design an experiment that will help Luis learn how his plant will respond to this stimulus.

# Chapter 8 Challenges

## Chapter Summary

### Lessons 8-1 and 8-2

- Roots hold plants in the soil, absorb water and minerals, and some store food.
- Stems support leaves and transport materials between the roots and the leaves.

### Lesson 8-3

- Most leaves have a **blade**, a stalk, and **veins**.
- The **epidermis** and the **mesophyll** are layers of leaf tissues.

### Lesson 8-4

- In **photosynthesis**, sunlight provides energy for carbon dioxide and water to form sugar. Oxygen and water are given off as byproducts.

### Lesson 8-5

- Flowers are organs of sexual reproduction.
- The reproductive organs in a flower are the **stamens** and **pistil**.

### Lesson 8-6

- **Fertilization** occurs when the nuclei of a male and a female reproductive cell join.
- **Pollination** is the movement of pollen from a stamen to a pistil. Self-pollination is pollination of flowers on the same plant. Cross-pollination is pollination between flowers on different plants.

### Lesson 8-7

- A **pollen grain** that lands on a **stigma** forms a pollen tube that grows down into the **ovary**.
- A fertilized **ovule** becomes a seed that contains an **embryo**. The ovary surrounds and protects the seeds and becomes a **fruit**.

### Lesson 8-8

- Seeds contain food that the embryo uses as it grows. The **embryo** in a seed is a tiny plant that has a tiny root, a stem, and leaves.

### Lesson 8-9

- Plants can reproduce asexually by **vegetative propagation**. **Tubers** and **bulbs** are organs of vegetative propagation.

### Lesson 8-10

- **Tropisms** are a change in a plant's growth in response to **stimuli**.

## Key Term Challenges

anther (p. 184)
asexual reproduction (p. 192)
autotroph (p. 178)
blade (p. 176)
bulb (p. 192)
chlorophyll (p. 178)
chloroplast (p. 178)
embryo (p. 186)
epidermis (p. 176)
fertilization (p. 184)
fibrous root system (p. 172)
filament (p. 184)
fruit (p. 186)
germinate (p. 190)
gravitropism (p. 194)
herbaceous stem (p. 174)
heterotroph (p. 178)
hilum (p. 190)
hydrotropism (p. 194)
imperfect flower (p. 182)
mesophyll (p. 176)
ovary (p. 186)
ovule (p. 186)
perfect flower (p. 182)
petal (p. 182)
phloem (p. 174)
photosynthesis (p. 178)
phototropism (p. 194)
pistil (p. 182)
pollen grain (p. 184)
pollination (p. 184)
root cap (p. 172)
root hair (p. 172)
seed coat (p. 190)
sepal (p. 182)
stamen (p. 182)
stigma (p. 186)
stimulus (p. 194)
stoma (p. 176)
style (p. 186)
taproot system (p. 172)
thigmotropism (p. 194)
tropism (p. 194)
tuber (p. 192)
vegetative propagation (p. 192)
vein (p. 176)
woody stem (p. 174)
xylem (p. 174)

MATCHING **Write the Key Term from above that best matches each description.**

1. root system made up of large root and many small thin roots
2. thin, hairlike structure on the outer layer of the root tip
3. cup-shaped mass of cells that covers and protects a root tip
4. plant's response to gravity
5. special kind of leaf that protects the flower bud
6. stem that is soft and green
7. asexual reproduction that uses parts of plants to grow new plants
8. plant's response to touch
9. organism that makes its own food
10. outside covering of a seed

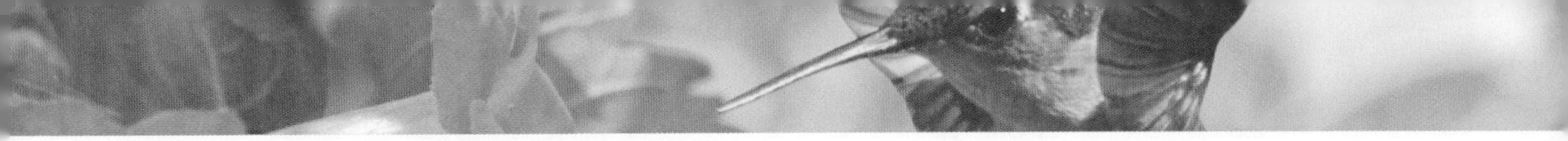

## Content Challenges TEST PREP

**MULTIPLE CHOICE Write the letter of the term or phrase that best completes each sentence.**

**1.** In flowering plants, fertilization takes place inside the
- **a.** stamen.
- **b.** pistil.
- **c.** anther.
- **d.** sepal.

**2.** Most of the photosynthesis in a plant occurs in the
- **a.** epidermis.
- **b.** mesophyll.
- **c.** stomata.
- **d.** guard cells.

**3.** Perfect flowers have
- **a.** only male reproductive organs.
- **b.** only female reproductive organs.
- **c.** both male and female reproductive organs.
- **d.** neither male nor female reproductive organs.

**4.** The rough outer layer of a woody stem is the
- **a.** root cap.
- **b.** xylem.
- **c.** mesophyll.
- **d.** bark.

**5.** During photosynthesis, the food that plants make is a
- **a.** starch.
- **b.** protein.
- **c.** sugar.
- **d.** fat.

**6.** Fibrous root systems are found in
- **a.** grass.
- **b.** carrots.
- **c.** radishes.
- **d.** dandelions.

**7.** Chloroplasts contain the green material
- **a.** chlorophyll.
- **b.** mesophyll.
- **c.** xylem.
- **d.** phloem.

**8.** The small white buds growing on a potato are called
- **a.** bulbs.
- **b.** eyes.
- **c.** tubers.
- **d.** cuttings.

**9.** A large ovary and its seeds are called
- **a.** an embryo.
- **b.** an ovule.
- **c.** a fruit.
- **d.** a seed coat.

**TRUE/FALSE Write *true* if the statement is true. If the statement is false, change the underlined term to make the statement true.**

**10.** The two main parts of a pistil are the filament and anther.

**11.** Asexual reproduction in plants is called vegetative pollination.

**12.** Most seed coats are soft.

**13.** Tropisms usually happen very quickly.

**14.** In some plants, food can be stored in the roots.

**15.** Roots grow from the tip.

**16.** An onion is an example of a bulb.

**17.** Petals are a kind of stem.

**18.** The pieces that make up a simple leaf are called leaflets.

# Concept Challenges TEST PREP

WRITTEN RESPONSE **Answer each of the following questions in complete sentences.**

1. APPLY: What would happen to the stem of a potted plant if you placed the plant on its side?
2. HYPOTHESIZE: What do you think might happen if an herbaceous plant grew taller than 2 m?
3. CONTRAST: What is the difference between pollination and fertilization?
4. ANALYZE: Fruit does not usually ripen until a seed is mature. Why is this important for the survival of the plant?
5. EXPLAIN: A slimy substance is produced by the root cap. How do you think this substance helps a plant grow?

INTERPRETING A DIAGRAM **Use Figure 8-33 to answer the following questions.**

6. Which structure is the male reproductive organ?
7. Which structure is the female reproductive organ?
8. Which structures protect the reproductive organs of a plant?
9. Which structures protect the flower bud?
10. Is the flower a perfect flower or an imperfect flower? Explain.
11. Which structure produces pollen grains?
12. Which structure contains female reproductive cells?

▲ **Figure 8-33** A lily

# Chapter 9 Animals Without Backbones

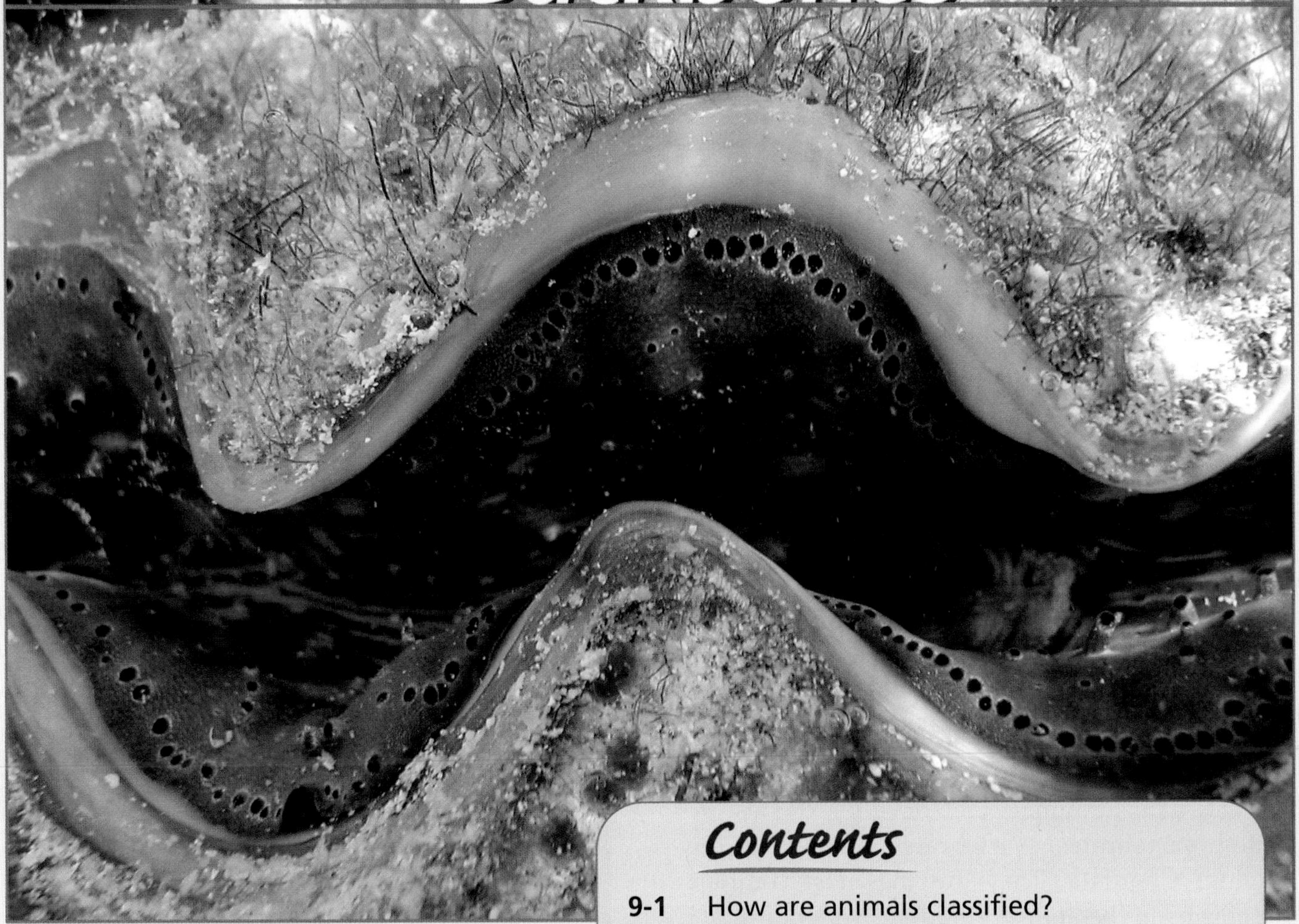

▲ **Figure 9-1** The giant clam has an outer shell but no backbone.

Giant clams live in the ocean. They usually stay in one place or move very little throughout their lives. They can grow to be 1 m in length and weigh 200 kg. They feed by taking ocean water in through a special tube and trapping tiny organisms found in the water. After a clam has absorbed the food, it releases the water. This process is called filter feeding because the clam filters food out of the water.

▶Why do you think clams only live in water?

## Contents

# 9-1 How are animals classified?

## *Objective*

Identify characteristics used to classify animals.

## *Key Terms*

**vertebrate** (VER-tuh-briht)**:** animal with a backbone

**endoskeleton** (en-doh-SKEL-uh-tuhn)**:** skeleton inside the body

**invertebrate** (ihn-VER-tuh-brih)**:** animal without a backbone

**exoskeleton** (eks-oh-SKEHL-uh-tuhn)**:** skeleton on the outside of the body

**Two Large Groups** The animal kingdom is made up of more species than the other four kingdoms combined. Scientists classify animals into two large groups. One group is made up of animals with backbones. The other group is made up of animals without backbones.

1 **NAME:** What are the two groups into which the animal kingdom is divided?

**Vertebrates** Animals that have backbones are called **vertebrates.** Vertebrates belong to the phylum Chordata. They are the most complex organisms in the animal kingdom. Vertebrates are also the most widely recognized and familiar of all animals. Vertebrates include fish, frogs, snakes, birds, cats, and many other animals. Humans are vertebrates as well.

Look at Figure 9-2. It shows killer whales. Whales are among the largest animals found on Earth. The largest animals on Earth are vertebrates. Vertebrates may grow very large because they have an **endoskeleton,** or a skeleton inside their bodies. The endoskeleton surrounds and protects soft body parts. It also helps to give shape and support to an organism. The endoskeleton is a framework that is strong enough to support large, heavy bodies. Because the endoskeleton does not limit the growth and size of an animal, vertebrates are usually larger than other kinds of animals.

▲ **Figure 9-2** Killer whales are animals with an endoskeleton.

2 **DEFINE:** What is an endoskeleton?

**Invertebrates** Animals without backbones are called **invertebrates.** Most animals are invertebrates. In fact, more than 90 percent of all animals are invertebrates. There are many different phyla of invertebrate animals. Sponges and jellyfish are invertebrates. Other invertebrates include snails, clams, sea stars, spiders, and insects.

▲ **Figure 9-3** This nudibranch is an invertebrate that has no skeleton.

Some invertebrates, such as worms, do not have any skeleton at all. They are soft-bodied animals. Other invertebrates have an **exoskeleton.** An exoskeleton is a skeleton on the outside of the body. It is made up of a hard, waterproof substance. The exoskeleton protects and supports the body. Spiders, lobsters, and insects, such as the walking stick in Figure 9-4, have an exoskeleton.

▲ **Figure 9-4** Insects, such as this walking stick, have an exoskeleton.

3 **LIST:** What are three kinds of animals that are invertebrates?

## CHECKING CONCEPTS

1. Animals with backbones are classified as __________.
2. An endoskeleton is a skeleton found __________ the body.
3. More than 90 percent of animals are __________.
4. Invertebrates are animals without __________.
5. A skeleton on the outside of the body is called an __________.

## THINKING CRITICALLY

6. **CLASSIFY:** Classify each of the following organisms as a vertebrate or an invertebrate.
   **a.** worm
   **b.** housefly
   **c.** robin
   **d.** squirrel
   **e.** sea star
   **f.** clam

## BUILDING LANGUAGE ARTS SKILLS

***Building Vocabulary*** Look up the prefixes *endo-* and *exo-* in a dictionary, and write their meanings. In your own words, list and define five words that begin with the prefix *endo-* and five words that begin with the prefix *exo-*. Circle the part of each definition that relates to the meaning of the prefix.

## *People in Science*

### TAXONOMIST

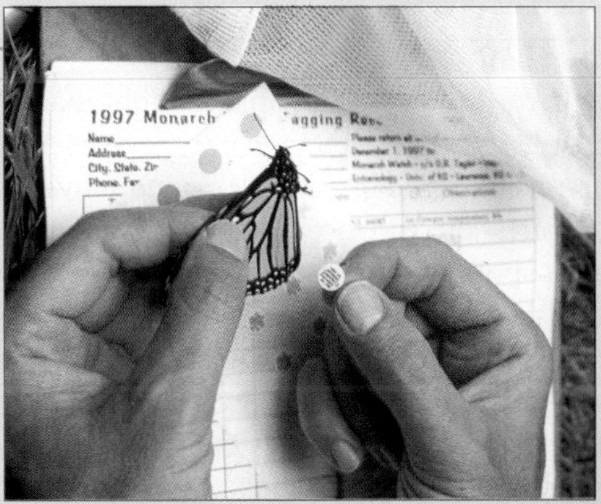


▲ **Figure 9-5** Taxonomists classify organisms.

Taxonomists are scientists who classify organisms. Many taxonomists only study animals. To classify animals, taxonomists compare the physical appearances of different animals. However, classification is not based on physical traits alone.

Taxonomists also compare the chromosomes and blood proteins of different kinds of animals. Taxonomists have discovered that the chromosomes and proteins in the blood of certain animals are quite similar. If the chromosomes and blood proteins are similar, taxonomists infer that the organisms are related.

Taxonomists often study embryology. Embryology is the study of organisms in the early stages of development. Embryology helps taxonomists determine how closely some animals are related. Scientists have found that certain animals show similarities as embryos. If the embryos develop in the same way, taxonomists infer that the animals are related to each other.

**Thinking Critically** Why do you think taxonomists use several different characteristics to determine how animals are related?

# 9-2 What are sponges?

## INVESTIGATE

### Examining Sponges
HANDS-ON ACTIVITY

1. Examine a natural sponge. Look at the shape, color, and texture of it. Then, use a hand lens to observe the surface and the holes in the sponge more closely.
2. Record your observations, and make a drawing of the sponge.
3. Repeat Steps 1 and 2 with an artificial sponge.

**THINK ABOUT IT:** Compare the two type of sponges. What do you think is the function of the holes?

### Objective
Describe the structure of a sponge.

### Key Terms
**pores:** tiny openings

**poriferan** (poh-RIHF-uhr-ran)**:** invertebrate animal with pores

**spicule** (SPIHK-yool)**:** small, hard, needlelike structure of a sponge

**Porifera** In the past, people thought that sponges were plants because they do not move from place to place like most other animals. Sponges live attached to objects on the ocean floor. However, unlike plants, sponges cannot make their own food. Today, scientists classify sponges in the animal kingdom in the phylum Porifera. The word *porifera* means "pore-bearer." If you look at a sponge, you will see it has many **pores,** or tiny openings. Sponges are sometimes called **poriferans.**

1 **IDENTIFY:** In what phylum are sponges classified?

**Structure of a Sponge** Sponges are very simple animals. You can compare the body of a sponge to an empty sack. The sponge is closed at the bottom, and has a large opening at the top. The center of the sponge is hollow. The body of a sponge is made up of only two layers of cells. The outer layer is made up of thin, flat cells. The inner layer is made up of special cells called collar cells. The collar cells line the hollow center of the sponge. Each collar cell has a flagellum. A jellylike substance fills the space between the two cell layers. In the jellylike substance, there are special cells called amoebocytes. These cells carry food to other cells. They also help a sponge to reproduce.

Small, needlelike structures called **spicules** are in the jellylike layer. They link together to form a simple skeleton. Spicules support the sponge. Some spicules are made up of a rubbery, flexible material called spongin (SPUHN-jin). Spongin skeletons are dried and sold in stores as natural sponges. Most sponges you use are not natural sponges. They are factory produced.

2 **DESCRIBE:** What is the shape of a sponge?

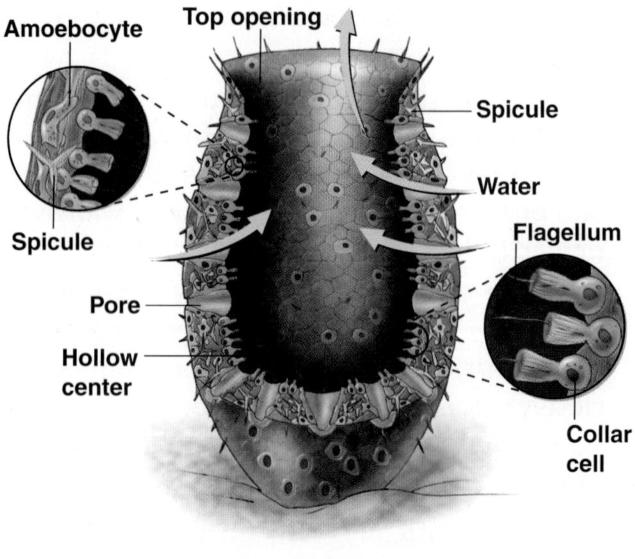


▲ **Figure 9-6** Sponges take in water through their pores.

**Life Functions** Sponges eat by filter feeding. They eat tiny organisms and bits of material in water that passes through their bodies. Water flows through the pores into a hollow center. Water flows out through a large opening at the top of a sponge. The constant beating of each flagellum keeps water moving into and out of a sponge. As water flows by, tiny bits of food are trapped by collar cells. These cells also absorb oxygen from water. Amoebocytes carry food to all cells.

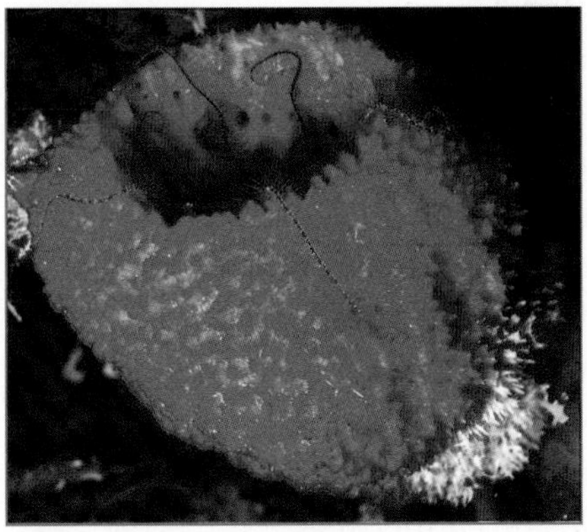

◀ **Figure 9-7** Sponges can vary greatly in color, size, and shape.

3 **OBSERVE:** In how many directions does water move in a sponge?

## ✓ CHECKING CONCEPTS

1. Sponges have __________ cell layers.
2. __________ help move water through a sponge.
3. Water enters a sponge through its __________.
4. Sponges are classified in the phylum __________.
5. The rubbery material that makes up some spicules is called __________.

## THINKING CRITICALLY

6. **EXPLAIN:** Think about the structure of a sponge. Why is Porifera a good name for this phylum?
7. **HYPOTHESIZE:** Suppose each flagellum was removed from the collar cells of a sponge. What effect might this loss have on the sponge's ability to feed?

## *Real-Life Science*

### SNORKELING

Have you ever wondered what kinds of plants and animals live in the ocean? Snorkeling is a good way to find out how fish and other water animals live together.

You only need a few pieces of equipment to go snorkeling: fins, a face mask, and a snorkel. Fins help you move quickly and easily through the water. A face mask gives you a clear view through the water. A snorkel is a breathing tube that allows you to swim along the surface of the water without raising your head to breathe.

▲ **Figure 9-8** You can see a variety of sponges while snorkeling.

Many people like to go snorkeling in areas with coral reefs. The reefs are home to many different types of fish and sponges. The coral provides a protective habitat for these organisms. It is illegal to remove coral from reefs in the United States. Some environmental groups want to stop snorkeling near coral reefs altogether because many reefs are very fragile. If you go snorkeling, look but do not touch any part of them.

**Thinking Critically** Do you think snorkeling near coral reefs should be prohibited?

# 9-3 What are cnidarians?

## Objectives

Identify and describe the body forms of cnidarians.

## Key Terms

**cnidarian** (nih-DER-ee-uhn)**:** invertebrate animal with stinging cells and a hollow central cavity

**polyp** (PAHL-ihp)**:** cuplike form of a cnidarian

**medusa** (muh-DOO-suh)**:** umbrella-like form of a cnidarian

**Cnidarians** If you have ever seen a jellyfish, you have seen a cnidarian. **Cnidarians** are invertebrate animals with stinging cells and a hollow body cavity. Jellyfish are classified in the phylum Cnidaria. All cnidarians have tentacles, or long, armlike structures, that have special stinging cells. All cnidarians live in water. Most cnidarians, such as corals and jellyfish, live in the ocean. Other cnidarians, such as hydra, live in lakes, ponds, and streams.

1 CLASSIFY: Name three cnidarians.

**Body Forms** Cnidarians have two body forms, or shapes. Some cnidarians have a tube-shaped body called a **polyp.** A hydra is an example of a polyp. A polyp does not usually move from place to place. It lives attached to a surface in the water. The mouth is at the top of the polyp and is surrounded by tentacles.

Other cnidarians, such as jellyfish, have an umbrella-shaped body called a **medusa.** Tentacles hang down from the edge of the umbrella. The mouth is in the center of the bottom surface of the medusa. A medusa can float on the surface of water or swim through water. Cnidarians may alternate between the two body forms in their lifetime. Many cnidarians begin life as a medusa and develop into a polyp. Others start life as a polyp and develop into a medusa.

2 CLASSIFY: Is a jellyfish a medusa or a polyp?

**Structure of Cnidarians** Like sponges, cnidarians have two layers of cells. There is a jellylike layer in between the two layers of cells. In cnidarians, however, the cells are organized into tissues. Cnidarians have digestive, muscle, nerve, and sensory tissues. The tissues surround a central

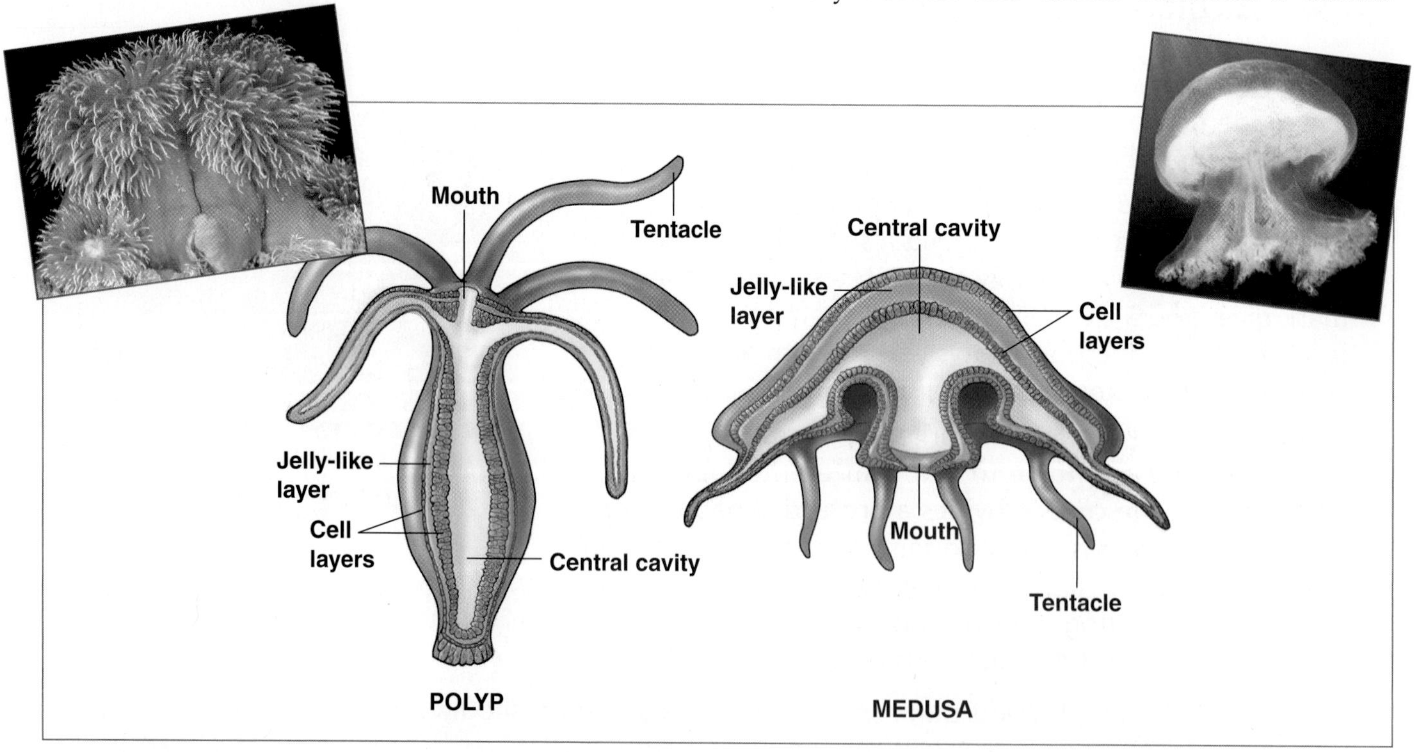


▲ **Figure 9-9** Cnidarians have two body forms, polyp and medusa.

cavity, or hollow space. A mouth opens into the cavity. The mouth is the only body opening.

**3 INFER:** Why are cnidarians considered more complex than sponges?

**Getting Food** Cnidarians use their tentacles to catch food. The cells on the tentacles have stingers that contain poison. When the tentacles touch an organism, stingers shoot out very quickly, and the poison stuns or kills the organism. The tentacles wrap around the animal and pull it into the mouth and body cavity. There the food is broken down and digested.

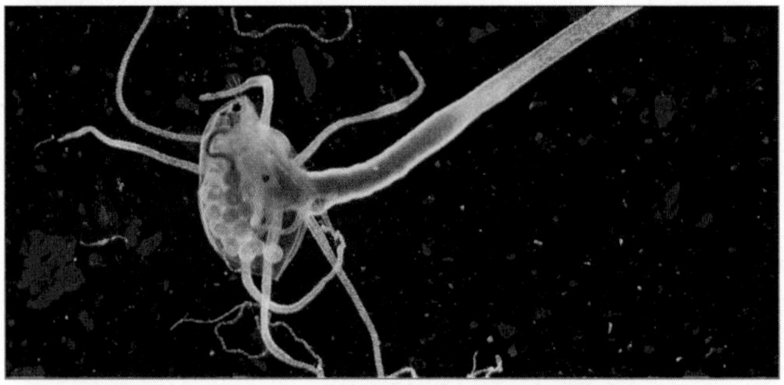

▲ **Figure 9-10** A hydra uses its tentacles to catch food.

**4 EXPLAIN:** How do cnidarians get food?

## CHECKING CONCEPTS

1. Where do cnidarians live?
2. What is the umbrella-shaped body form of a cnidarian called?
3. What types of tissue are found in cnidarians?
4. How does a cnidarian capture prey?

## THINKING CRITICALLY

*Use Figure 9-9 to answer the following questions.*

5. **ANALYZE:** Which has a larger layer of jellylike material—a polyp or a medusa?
6. **COMPARE:** How are the two body shapes of cnidarians alike?

## HEALTH AND SAFETY TIP

Many jellyfish have poison in their stingers that is dangerous to humans. Never touch a jellyfish, even if it looks dead. It may still be able to sting you. If you are stung by a jellyfish, get first aid as soon as you can. Use a first-aid manual or other reference to find out how to treat a jellyfish sting.

## *Hands-On Activity*

### OBSERVING A HYDRA

*For this activity, you will need a sample of live hydra, a sample of live daphnia, a dropper, two depression slides, two cover slips, and a microscope.*

1. Use a dropper to remove a hydra from the sample. Place the hydra in the well of the depression slide.
2. Place the cover slip carefully on the slide. Then, place the slide on the stage of the microscope.
3. Use the lowest power objective of the microscope to observe the hydra. Locate the hydra's mouth and tentacles.
4. On another depression slide, place a sample of hydra and a sample of daphnia. Place the cover slip carefully on the slide. Then use the microscope to examine the behavior of the hydra and daphnia.

▲ **STEP 1** Place the hydra on a slide.

**Practicing Your Skills**

5. **MODELING:** Draw and label the hydra on your paper.
6. **OBSERVING:** How did the hydra respond to the daphnia?
7. **PREDICT:** What are some other factors the hydra might respond to?

# 9-4 What are worms?

## *Objective*

Compare the different phyla of worms.

## *Key Terms*

**platyhelminth** (plat-uh-HEHL-mihnth)**:** type of worm with a flattened body

**parasite** (PAR-uh-syt)**:** organism that gets its food by living on or in the body of another organism.

**nematode** (NEHM-uh-tohd)**:** type of worm with a round body

**annelid** (AN-uh-lihd)**:** type of worm with a segmented body

**setae** (SEET-ee)**:** tiny, hairlike bristles

**closed circulatory system:** organ system in which blood moves through vessels

**Classification of Worms** When you think of worms, you probably think of earthworms. However, there are many different kinds of worms. They are so different from each other that they are classified into several different phyla. Three of these phyla are flatworms, roundworms, and segmented worms.

1 **IDENTIFY:** What are the three phyla of worms?

**Flatworms** The simplest types of worms are flatworms. They are classified in the phylum Platyhelminthes. Flatworms, or **platyhelminthes,** have flattened, ribbonlike bodies. A common flatworm is the planarian (pluh-NER-ee-uhn). Planaria are small flatworms that live in freshwater ponds and streams. They can be microscopic or as long as 25 mm. They have two small eyespots that can sense light.

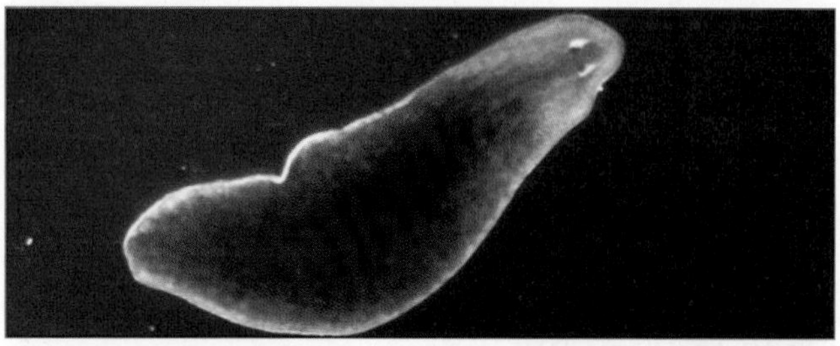

▲ **Figure 9-11** Planaria live in ponds and streams.

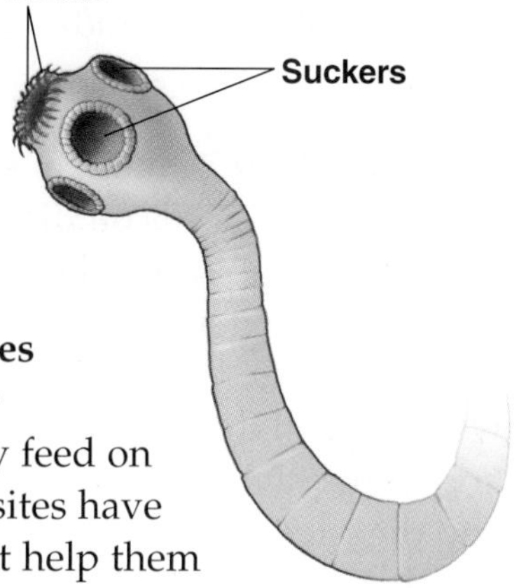


▲ **Figure 9-12** Tapeworms are parasitic flatworms.

The other two groups of flatworms are called flukes and tapeworms. They are both parasites. **Parasites** live inside or on other organisms, which they feed on and harm. Some parasites have special body parts that help them live inside other organisms. They have hooks and suckers that hold them in place. In the intestines, they absorb, or take in, food as it is digested. For example, tapeworms live in the intestines of many kinds of animals, including humans. Tapeworms can grow to several meters in length.

2 **CLASSIFY:** Name three examples of flatworms.

**Roundworms** Roundworms make up the phylum Nematoda. They are sometimes called **nematodes.** Roundworms can live almost anywhere. They can live in soil or in water. Some are parasites of plants or animals. Hookworms, pinworms, and *Ascaris* worms are roundworms that live in the intestines of humans and animals. Roundworms have a threadlike body with one pointed end. They are one of the simplest animals that have a complete digestive system. Roundworms also have simple excretory and nervous systems. They do not have a circulatory or a respiratory system.

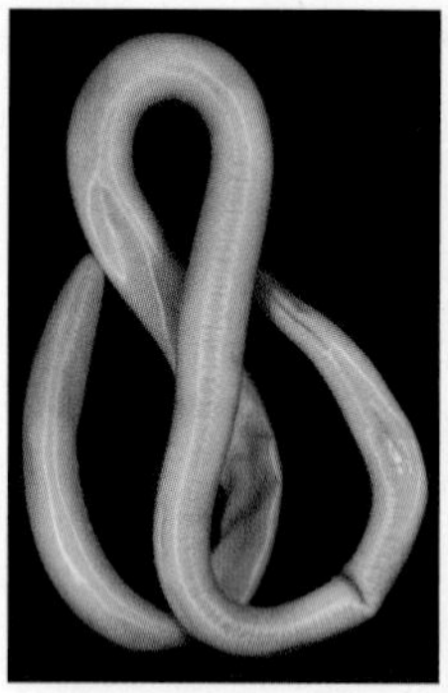

▲ **Figure 9-13** *Ascaris* worms live in the intestines of humans and animals.

3 **CONTRAST:** How are roundworms different from flatworms?

**Segmented Worms** The most complex worms are the segmented worms. They are classified in the phylum Annelida. Segmented worms are sometimes called **annelids.** The word *annelid* means "little rings." If you look at the body of a segmented worm, you will see that it is made up of

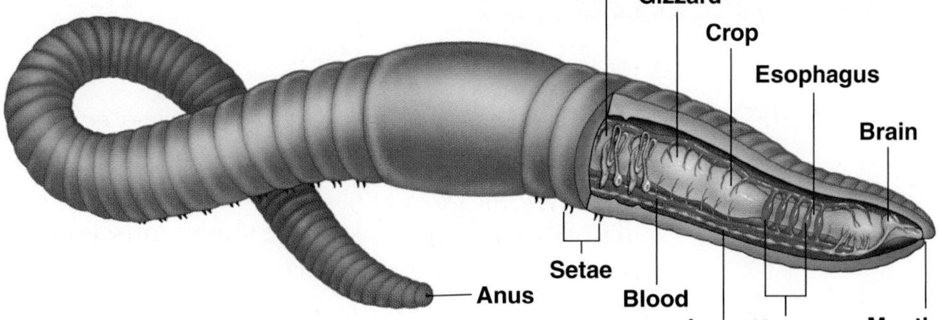

▲ **Figure 9-14** The structure of an earthworm

many ringlike sections, or segments. There are more than 9,000 species of segmented worms. Most live in the ocean. Others live in fresh water. The best-known segmented worm is the earthworm. It lives in the soil.

**4** NAME: Where do most segmented worms live?

**Earthworms** Earthworms are the most complex worms. Look at Figure 9-14 as you read about earthworms. Like all worms, they have a head end and a tail end. Each segment except the first and last has four pairs of small bristles called **setae.** Earthworms use their setae and sets of tiny muscles to move. A list of other earthworm features follows.

- Earthworms have a complex digestive system. Food passes into the crop and gizzard where it is stored and then ground up. Food is digested and absorbed in the intestine.
- Earthworms have a **closed circulatory system.** In a closed circulatory system, blood moves through vessels, or tubes, in the body. In the head end, two large vessels meet and form five pairs of hearts, which pump blood through the vessels.
- Earthworms have a nervous system. Nerves run along the body and connect to a simple brain.
- Earthworms have male and female sex organs. A single worm, however, does not mate with itself. Earthworms reproduce sexually.
- Earthworms do not have a respiratory system. Gases pass into and out of the earthworm through its moist skin.

**5** OBSERVE: What are the two organs that store and grind up food called?

## CHECKING CONCEPTS

1. The simplest types of worms are ___________.
2. Planaria are a type of ___________.
3. Special body parts, such as hooks and ___________, help some parasites live inside other organisms.
4. Segmented worms live in the ___________, fresh water, and soil.
5. The earthworm uses small bristles called ___________ for movement.

## THINKING CRITICALLY

6. **COMPARE/CONTRAST:** How are the three phyla of worms alike? How are they different? Make a chart that summarizes the similarities and differences among the three phyla of worms.
7. **HYPOTHESIZE:** A parasite often causes the organism it lives in to lose weight. Why?

### Web InfoSearch

**Leeches** Leeches are parasitic segmented worms. Many years ago, leeches were used to suck "bad blood" out of sick people. Today, doctors are using leeches again but in different ways.

**SEARCH:** Find out more about the uses of leeches in medicine. Start your search at www.conceptsandchallenges.com. Some key search terms are **leech**, **medicine**, and **annelid**.

# 9-5 What are mollusks?

## *Objectives*

Describe the features of mollusks. Give examples of different classes of mollusks.

## *Key Terms*

**mollusk** (MAHL-uhsk)**:** soft-bodied organism

**mantle:** thin membrane that covers a mollusk's organs

**radula** (RAJ-oo-luh)**:** rough, tonguelike organ of a snail

**Mollusks** **Mollusks** are soft-bodied animals. They are classified in the phylum Mollusca. The mollusk phylum is divided into eight classes. The three most common of these are described below. Most mollusks are covered by hard shells. Mollusks have a head, a foot, and a mass of tissue that contains a number of well-developed organ systems. These systems include excretory organs, reproductive organs, and a heart. A thin membrane covers the soft fleshy body of a mollusk. The membrane is the **mantle.** In some mollusks, the mantle forms the shell. Mollusks live in salt and fresh water and on land.

1 **DEFINE:** What is the mantle?

**Snails and Slugs** The most common type of mollusk has a single shell or no shell at all. Mollusks that are like this belong to the class Gastropoda. This class includes snails, slugs, and sea slugs. In gastropods, the foot is used for movement. Many of these mollusks, such as snails, have a **radula**. The radula is a tonguelike organ. It is covered with toothlike structures. The radula is used to scrape food from plants and rocks.

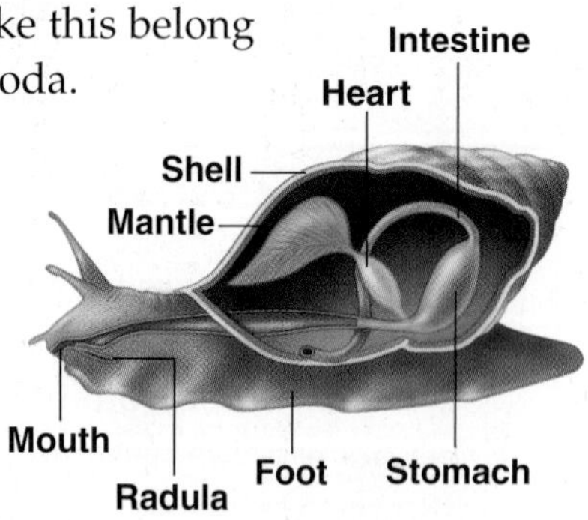


▲ **Figure 9-15** The basic structure of a snail

2 **DEFINE:** What is a radula?

**Two-Shelled Mollusks** A second class consists of mollusks made up of two-part shells. This class is called Bivalvia. Clams, oysters, and mussels are all bivalves. The bivalves have strong muscles that are used to hold their shells closed. Bivalves feed by taking in water into their bodies through a special tube. As the water comes in, the microscopic organisms in the water are trapped. The water is then released, and the organisms are digested. This method of feeding is called filter feeding.

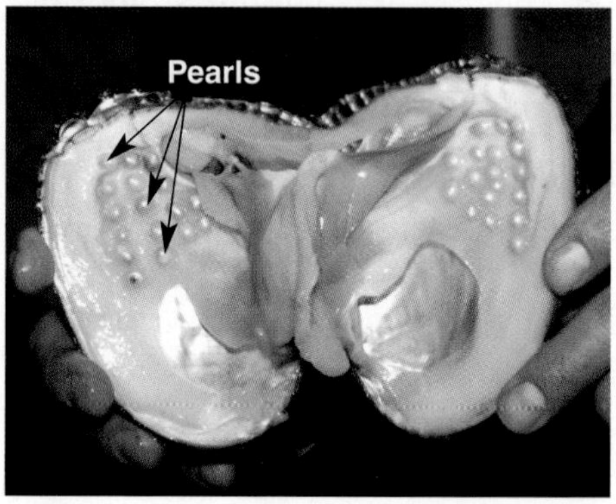


◀ **Figure 9-16** When sand grains are caught inside the oyster, its mantle coats the sand with a shiny substance, producing pearls.

3 **DESCRIBE:** What are the steps of filter feeding?

**Mollusks with Tentacles** A third class of mollusks contains animals that have tentacles. This class is called Cephalopoda. Squids and octopuses are included in this class. They have very complex brains and excellent eyesight. All cephalopods have tentacles which are used for movement and feeding. Each tentacle has many suction cups, used for capturing prey.

▲ **Figure 9-17** This octopus has eight tentacles.

Mollusks with tentacles can slowly crawl around rocks and through small spaces. However, they can also swim freely. Squids and octopuses swim by jet propulsion. They take in water and squirt the water back out. The force of the water squirted out pushes the animal forward. Using jet propulsion, cephalopods can quickly travel great distances.

**4** **EXPLAIN:** Why are cephalopods considered the most advanced mollusks?

## CHECKING CONCEPTS

1. A __________ covers the internal organs of a mollusk.
2. A __________ is the tonguelike organ found in snails.
3. Snails and slugs belong to the class __________.
4. Squids and octopuses use __________ for feeding and movement.
5. Bivalves take in water through a __________.

## THINKING CRITICALLY

6. **INFER:** Newton's Third Law of Motion states that for every action there is an equal and opposite reaction. How does this law relate to jet propulsion by squids and octopuses?
7. **CONTRAST:** How are the feeding methods of the three types of mollusks different?

## BUILDING SCIENCE SKILLS

***Researching*** The world's largest known invertebrate is the giant squid. The giant squid reaches lengths of up to 18 meters, or 60 feet. Scientists have been unable to photograph or capture a live specimen, but they are still searching. Use library references and scientific journals to find out more about the search for the giant squid. Write a report about your findings.

## *Hands-On Activity*

### MODELING SQUID JET PROPULSION

*You will need a plastic straw, scissors, a fishing line, cellophane tape, an elongated balloon, and 2 desk chairs.*

1. Use the scissors to cut a 10-cm long piece of straw. ⚠ CAUTION: Be careful when using scissors.
2. Place the two chairs back to back about 2 m apart.
3. Tie one end of the line to the back of one of the chairs. Thread the line through the piece of straw. Tie the other end of the line to the other chair. Make sure the line is pulled tight between the two chairs.
4. Blow up the balloon, but do not tie a knot. Tape the balloon to the piece of straw on the fishing line while still holding the balloon closed. Let go of the balloon. Observe the direction in which it moves.

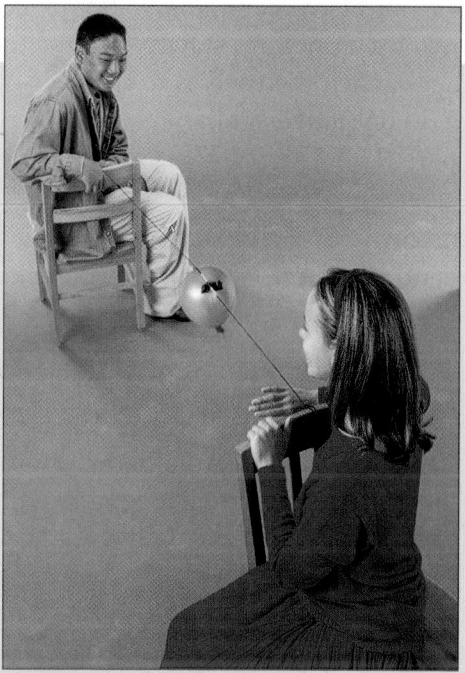

▲ **STEP 4** Tape the balloon to the straw on the fishing line. Then, let go.

### Practicing Your Skills

5. **IDENTIFY:** In which direction did the balloon move?
6. **COMPARE:** How does the movement of the balloon compare to the movement of the squid?
7. **ANALYZE:** Do you think the amount of water taken in by the squid affects its movement? Explain.

# 9-6 What are echinoderms?

## *Objectives*

List the common characteristics of echinoderms. Name some echinoderms.

## *Key Terms*

**echinoderm** (ee-KY-noh-duhrm)**:** spiny-skinned animal

**water-vascular system:** system of tubes used to transport water

**tube feet:** small structures of echinoderms used for movement and feeding

**Echinoderms** **Echinoderms** are spiny-skinned animals classified in the phylum Echinodermata. Sea stars are the best-known echinoderms. Other echinoderms are sea urchins, sand dollars, brittle stars, and sea cucumbers. Some echinoderms move by crawling slowly on the ocean floor. Others attach themselves to rocks or other objects and do not move at all.

1 LIST: Name three echinoderms.

**Anatomy of Echinoderms** Echinoderms have an endoskeleton, or an internal skeleton. The endoskeleton is made up of spines. The most noticeable thing about echinoderms is their spiny skin. In fact, the name *echinoderm* means "spiny skin." In some echinoderms, such as the sea stars, the spines are hard, rounded lumps. In the sea urchins, the spines are like long needles. The skin of the sea cucumber is soft and leathery.

▲ **Figure 9-18** This sea urchin has long needlelike spines for protection.

Echinoderms do not have a left side or a right side. Most have rays, or arms, around a central point. Their body structures are arranged like the spokes of a wheel around a central body point. Echinoderms do not have circulatory, excretory, or respiratory systems. They have a nervous system, but echinoderms do not have a brain. Echinoderms also have a system called the **water-vascular system.** This system controls movement and respiration. The water-vascular system is a network of tubes that moves water throughout the body of the echinoderm. Water enters the echinoderm through an opening on the upper surface.

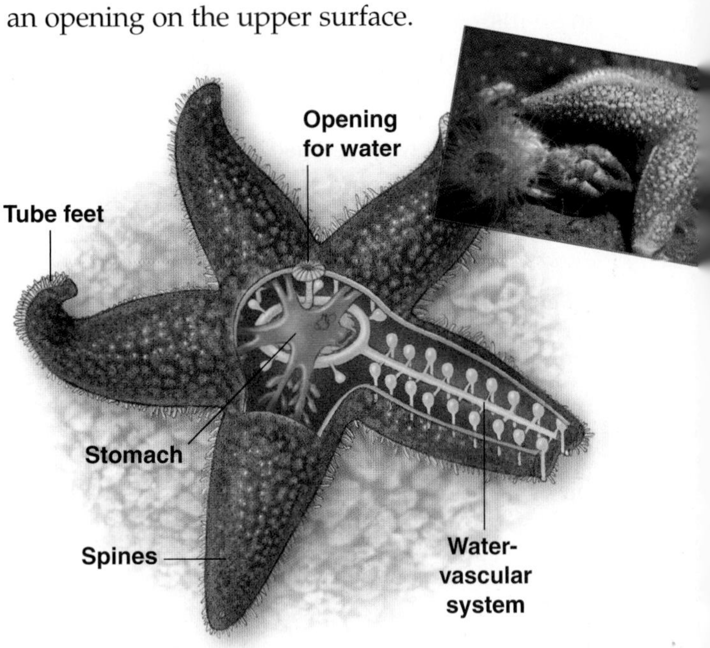


▲ **Figure 9-19** The anatomy of a sea star

2 OBSERVE: What is the most noticeable thing about the echinoderm in Figure 9-18?

**Tube Feet** Sea stars move using hundreds of small structures called **tube feet.** Tube feet are part of the water-vascular system that works to pull a sea star forward. Each tube foot is like a suction cup. Using its tube feet, a sea star can move slowly across the ocean floor.

Tube feet are also used to get food. Sea stars usually eat mollusks. They use their tube feet to pull open shells of mollusks, such as clams. The clam uses its muscles to keep its shell closed. Eventually, the clam's muscles will tire, and the shell will open a bit. The sea star will then push its stomach out of its mouth and into the clam. When the clam is digested, the sea star will pull its stomach back inside its body.

3 **NAME:** For what two purposes does a sea star use its tube feet?

## CHECKING CONCEPTS

1. Name four echinoderms.
2. What kind of skeleton do echinoderms have?
3. Which echinoderm has long needlelike spines?
4. What are tube feet?
5. What type of organisms do sea stars usually eat?
6. To what phylum do sea stars belong?

## THINKING CRITICALLY

7. **INFER:** Why do you think a sea star would have trouble moving over sand or mud?
8. **INFER:** If all the sea stars in a clam bed were destroyed, what would happen?

## BUILDING MATH SKILLS

***Understanding Symmetry*** Animals have different kinds of symmetry. For example, sea stars have radial symmetry. Some animals have no symmetry at all. Use a dictionary or science references to define bilateral symmetry and radial symmetry. Then, trace the outlines of the animals shown below. What kind of symmetry does each animal have?

▲ **Figure 9-20** Different animals have different kinds of symmetry.

Go Online
active art
**For:** Water Vascular System activity
**Visit:** PHSchool.com
**Web Code:** cep-2025

## *Integrating Physical Science*

**TOPICS: hydraulics, force, pressure**

### HYDRAULIC SYSTEMS IN SEA STARS

A sea star's tube feet are connected to its water-vascular system. Water enters the system through a small round opening on the upper surface. This opening leads to a ring-shaped tube with branches leading out into the sea star's arms. Along the underside of each arm are two rows of tube feet. Muscles push water into the tube feet, making them longer. When the muscles relax, the water is released, and the tube feet get shorter. This action allows the sea star to move.

A sea star's water-vascular system works very much like the hydraulic brake system in a car. Hydraulic machines, such as brakes, use liquid to function. When a force exerts pressure on one part of the system, the pressure is transmitted through the liquid in the tubes. In a car's brakes, the driver's foot on the brake pedal creates pressure that travels through the hydraulic brake system to the wheels. The pressure then makes pistons press on brake pads to stop the wheels from turning.

▲ **Figure 9-21** The tube feet of a sea star are part of its water-vascular system.

**Thinking Critically** Explain how the water-vascular system of a sea star is similar to the braking system of a car.

# 9-7 What is regeneration?

*Objective*

Explain how some organisms can regrow lost parts.

*Key Term*

**regeneration** (rih-jehn-uh-RAY-shuhn): ability to regrow lost parts

**Regeneration** New plants can grow from a part of a plant by vegetative propagation. Does this kind of asexual reproduction also take place in animals? Some animals have the ability to regrow lost parts. This ability is called **regeneration.** Some animals can develop a whole new animal from just a part of the original animal's body. If an entire new animal develops from a part, regeneration is considered a kind of asexual reproduction.

1 **DEFINE:** What is regeneration?

**Regeneration of Body Parts** Not all animals have the same ability to regenerate, or regrow, lost body parts. A few kinds of animals can regenerate a large body part. Most animals, however, can regrow only a small part. Lobsters and crabs, for example, can regenerate claws that have broken off.

Most sea stars have five arms, or rays. If a ray is cut off, a new ray grows back. Sea stars can even regenerate all five rays as long as the central body region is still intact.

▲ **Figure 9-22** Crabs can regenerate lost claws.

Many animals use their ability to regenerate lost parts as a defense against predators. When an animal is being threatened or attacked, it can shed a body part without causing harm to itself. This ability allows it to escape while the predator is feeding on the lost body part. For example, the glass lizard can regenerate its tail. If the lizard is attacked and grabbed by its tail, its tail breaks off. The lizard escapes, and gradually, its tail grows back.

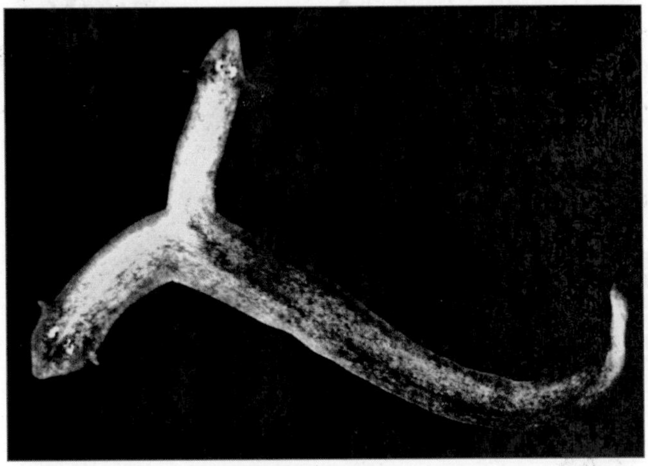

▲ **Figure 9-23** Under laboratory conditions, the flatworm planarian can even regenerate a second head!

2 **EXPLAIN:** How is the ability to regenerate helpful to an organism?

**Asexual Reproduction** Some animals can reproduce asexually by regeneration. The flatworm planarian is one example of an organism that can reproduce through regeneration under natural conditions. The planarian attaches to a stick or rock and then begins stretching its head region forward. It continues stretching until it splits in two. Then, the two parts develop into new organisms. Because each part of the planarian keeps its original genetic material, the two new organisms are genetically identical.

Sponges can also reproduce by regeneration. If a sponge is cut into pieces, each piece can develop into a new sponge. The process is slow, and it takes many months for the new sponge to grow as large as the parent sponge.

3 **NAME:** What are two organisms that can reproduce by regeneration?

## ✓ CHECKING CONCEPTS

1. What are some animals that can regenerate lost body parts?
2. How does regeneration help the glass lizard?
3. What type of reproduction is regeneration?
4. How does a planarian reproduce through regeneration?
5. What body parts can crabs and lobsters regenerate?

## THINKING CRITICALLY

6. **RELATE:** How are vegetative propagation and regeneration similar?
7. **INFER:** Why is regeneration of a lobster's claw not a kind of asexual reproduction?
8. **CONTRAST:** How is regeneration in a lobster different from regeneration in a sponge?

### Web InfoSearch

**Regeneration of Human Tissue** Humans do not have the same ability as some invertebrates to regenerate. We cannot regrow lost limbs. However, some of our tissues do have the ability to regenerate.

**SEARCH:** Use the Internet to find out which tissues in humans can regenerate. Write a report about your findings. Explain how the ability to regenerate tissue plays a role in medicine. Start your search at www.conceptsandchallenges.com. Some key search words are **tissue regeneration** and **skin regeneration.**

## *Real-Life Science*

### REGENERATION IN SEA STARS

Sea stars feed on mollusks, such as clams, mussels, and oysters. The more of these mollusks that are eaten by the sea stars, the fewer there are for humans to harvest. This feeding pattern was a problem for people who made their living catching and selling mollusks. In the 19th century, these people thought they had a solution. Whenever they caught a sea star, they chopped it in half and threw the "dead" pieces back into the sea. What they did not realize was that they were helping the sea stars to multiply!

▲ **Figure 9-24** This sea star is in the process of regenerating three of its arms.

Sea stars have the ability to regenerate. If a sea star is cut into two pieces, each piece can regenerate the missing half to create two sea stars out of one. This process usually takes about a year. When a sea star regenerates from a single arm, the new rays are much smaller. This kind of sea star is called a comet. People who caught sea stars that were regenerating lost parts finally figured out what the oyster harvesters were doing wrong.

**Thinking Critically** Why do invertebrates, such as sea stars, regenerate more easily than vertebrates?

# LAB ACTIVITY
# Determining the Age of a Clam

**Materials**

4 Different size clam shells of the same species
Masking tape
Hand lens
Metric ruler

▲ **STEP 1** Obtain four clam shells of different sizes.

▲ **STEP 3** Measure the width of five bands.

### *BACKGROUND*

Mollusks, such as clams and oysters, have hard protective shells. Clams grow in size each year. However, they do not shed their shells every year. Their shells have to grow with them. A new layer is added to the shell of a clam every year as it grows. This growth can be seen on the outside of the shell in the form of large ridges, or bands, that form at the end of each year's growth spurt. These ridges can help determine a clam's age.

### *PURPOSE*

In this activity, you will examine the shells of clams to determine their ages.

### *PROCEDURE*

1. Obtain four clam shells of different sizes, but of the same species. Arrange the shells on your desk in order from largest to smallest.

2. Use the masking tape to make four labels for the shells. Label the shells *A*, *B*, *C*, and *D*. Label your largest shell *A* and your smallest shell *D*.

3. Copy the chart in Figure 9-25 onto your paper. Look at the outside of the shell for ridges and bands. On shell *A*, use a ruler to measure the width of five different bands in millimeters. The bands are formed by groups of smaller ridges. Record your measurements on your chart.

4. Find the average width of the five bands by adding the measurements together and dividing by five. Record the average value on your chart.

5. Repeat Steps 3 and 4 for shells *B*, *C*, and *D*.

6. Use the hand lens to look at the bands more closely. Count the number of bands on each shell starting at the crown of the shell. Record the number of bands on each shell on your chart.

7. The number of bands on the shell represents the approximate age of the clam. Record the approximate age of each clam on your chart.

▲ **STEP 6** Use a hand lens to examine the bands.

**Structure of Clam Shells**

| Shell | Width of Five Bands | Average Number of Bands | Total Number of Bands | Age |
|---|---|---|---|---|
| A | | | | |
| B | | | | |
| C | | | | |
| D | | | | |

▲ **Figure 9-25** Copy this chart onto a sheet of paper.

### CONCLUSIONS

1. **OBSERVE:** Which shells had the wider bands?

2. **OBSERVE:** Which shells had the most bands?

3. **CALCULATE:** Which clam was the oldest? How can you tell?

4. **HYPOTHESIZE:** Why do you think some bands are wider than others on the same shell? What might the width of one particular band tell you about that year in the clam's life?

# 9-8 What are arthropods?

## *Objectives*

List the main features of arthropods and give examples of some arthropods.

## *Key Terms*

**arthropod** (AHR-throh-pahd)**:** animal with an exoskeleton and jointed legs

**chitin** (KY-tin)**:** hard material that makes up the exoskeleton of arthropods

**open circulatory system:** circulatory system in which blood does not flow constantly through tubes

**molting:** process by which an animal sheds its outer covering

**Classifying Arthropods** **Arthropods** are animals that have jointed legs and an exoskeleton. They are classified in the phylum Arthropoda. Arthropods make up the largest phylum of animals. Scientists think that there are more than one million species of organisms in the phylum Arthropoda.

Arthropods are divided into several groups shown in Figure 9-26. The three largest groups are the crustaceans (kruhs-TAY-shuhnz), arachnids (uh-RAK-nidz) and insects. Crustaceans include lobsters, crabs, and shrimp. Arachnids include spiders, ticks, mites, and scorpions. Insects include flies, butterflies, moths, ants, bees, mosquitoes, and cockroaches. There are two other groups of arthropods which together are called myriapods (MYR-ee-uh-pahdz). Myriapods include centipedes and millipedes.

**1** **IDENTIFY:** Name the three largest groups of arthropods.

**Arthropod Characteristics** All arthropods have an exoskeleton and a segmented body. The exoskeleton protects and supports the soft, inner body parts. The exoskeleton is made of a material called **chitin.** Chitin is tough, but light in weight. Arthropods have jointed legs that are made of several sections. The sections are connected by joints that can bend and are moved by muscles attached to the exoskeleton. Arthropods have an **open circulatory system.** Blood moves through open spaces in their bodies. It does not flow through vessels, or tubes.

**2** **IDENTIFY:** Of what material is the exoskeleton of an arthropod made?

**Molting** When you grow, your bones grow. Your skeleton grows along with the rest of your body. An exoskeleton, however, cannot grow. It is not made of living material. As an arthropod grows, it becomes too big for its exoskeleton and must shed it. This process is called **molting.** The exoskeleton

### THE MAJOR GROUPS OF ARTHROPODS

**Crustaceans**
- Crustaceans usually have two body parts and five pairs of legs.
- Most crustaceans live in water.
- Some examples are lobsters, crayfish, crabs, and shrimp.

**Insects**
- Insects have three body parts and three pairs of legs.
- There are more species of insects than of any other animal.
- Some examples are bees, ants, houseflies, beetles, and grasshoppers.

**Arachnids**
- Most arachnids have two body parts and four pairs of legs.
- Most arachnids live on land.
- Some examples are spiders, ticks, mites, and scorpions.

**Myriapods**
- Centipedes have one pair of legs per body segment. Some centipedes are poisonous.
- Millipedes have two pairs of legs per body segment.

▲ Figure 9-26

splits open, and the animal works its way out. Gradually, a new, larger exoskeleton forms and hardens.

**3** **DEFINE:** What is molting?

**Special Body Parts** Depending on where they live, what they eat, and how they move, arthropods have different body parts. Insects have special mouth parts that help them get food. These mouth parts may be used for biting, chewing, or sucking, based on how the insect feeds. Most insects also have wings. Some crustaceans, such as lobsters and crabs, have large front claws. They use the claws to get food and to protect themselves. Spiders have silk glands that make silk for their webs.

**4** **LIST:** What are some special body parts of arthropods?

## ✓ CHECKING CONCEPTS

1. What is an exoskeleton made of?
2. Describe the characteristics of arthropods.
3. What is the name of the largest animal phylum?
4. What is molting?
5. How are large claws helpful for a crustacean?

## THINKING CRITICALLY

6. **ANALYZE:** Can you tell which of the arthropods in Figure 9-26 can fly? How?
7. **INFER:** How are the grasshopper's large back legs suited to how it moves?

## HEALTH AND SAFETY TIP

***Arthropods and Disease*** Some arthropods have been known to carry diseases. Deer ticks may carry the bacteria that causes Lyme disease. Mosquitoes have been known to carry several diseases, including malaria and the West Nile virus. To protect yourself from these diseases, it is a good idea to wear insect repellent anytime you plan to be outside in the summer. It is also helpful to wear long pants when hiking or camping.

## *Science and Technology*

### USES OF CHITIN

▲ **Figure 9-27** Chitin is a material that can be found in the shells of crabs.

What do crab shells, some contact lenses, and certain types of varnish have in common? They are all made of chitin. Scientists are finding new uses for the tough, protective chitin.

Chitin is especially good as a material for medical uses because it does not cause allergic reactions in most people. For this reason, chitin is used to make some kinds of contact lenses. Chitin is also used to make artificial skin that can be used to protect badly burned parts of the human body until new skin can form. A type of thread made from chitin is used for sewing wounds or incisions. This type of thread dissolves in the body and does not need to be removed.

Researchers have found many other uses for chitin. Varnish made of chitin makes an excellent finish for some musical instruments. Seeds coated with chitin are protected from infection. Chitin has also been used in filters to clean water in swimming pools. Research on the uses of chitin continues. Chitin is now being tested as a coating for fabrics and paper. Who knows? Some day you may be wearing chitin-treated T-shirts and reading books printed on chitin-coated paper!

**Thinking Critically** Why is chitin a good material to use in surgery?

Integrating Environmental Science

# THE Big IDEA

## Why should coral reefs be protected?

Environmental science is the study of how humans interact with their surroundings. It looks at how we use and conserve natural resources. The protection of ecosystems is also a major concern of environmental scientists.

Many environmental scientists are concerned about coral reefs, which are home to one-fourth of all marine plants and animals, including sponges, worms, mollusks, crustaceans, and fish.

Many countries depend on coral reefs for economic reasons. The reefs provide fishing grounds for food and produce income from tourism and recreation. Reefs also shield about one-sixth of the world's coasts from storm damage.

Coral reefs around the world are in danger. Human activities and natural factors are damaging them. There are many diseases that kill coral. Some are related to water quality.

In some places, poor fishing practices threaten reefs. Many reef organisms depend on each other for food or protection. Removing one species from the ecosystem affects the other species living there. Pollution, coral mining, and careless divers or boaters also damage reefs. Many efforts are now under way to protect coral reefs, and several programs have been developed to map and monitor reefs. Countries are now working together to promote good fishing practices. Some reefs have become preserves.

Look at the boxes of text that appear on these two pages. They point out some reef invertebrates and their relationship to humans. Follow the directions in the Science Log to learn more about "the big idea."✦

**Queen Conch**

The queen conch is a mollusk. A large, spiral shell protects its soft body. Many people collect conch shells because of their beauty. The shells also are used to make jewelry and lamps. Conch is a popular food in Florida and islands in the Caribbean. There is concern that strong demand may lead to the extinction of the conch.

**Sponge**

For hundreds of years, people have used sponges for bathing, painting, and mopping. They also provide hiding places for small reef creatures, such as shrimp. Scientists are now studying the use of certain sponges in medicine. They have found that one sponge species produces a chemical that kills cancer cells.

▲ **Figure 9-28** Coral reefs are home to hundreds of different animal species.

### Sea Urchins

Sea urchins play an important role in many coral reefs. By eating algae, they prevent it from smothering the coral. Many people eat sea urchins and their eggs.

### Spiny Lobster

Spiny lobsters are a valuable seafood export for many countries. These crustaceans are also known as rock lobsters. During the spiny lobster's first year, it hides in reef crevices to avoid predators.

### Coral

Some corals look like plants, but they are animals. They are classified as cnidarians. As each coral polyp grows, it forms a hard external skeleton. Billions of skeletons covered by a layer of living coral make up a coral reef.

**WRITING ACTIVITY**

*Science Log*

Which kind of organism from the coral reef would you like to see up close? Research and write about one of the invertebrates in the reef community. Explain why they should be protected. Start your search at www.conceptsandchallenges.com.

# 9-9 What are insects?

## *Objective*

Describe the features of insects.

## *Key Terms*

**antenna** (an-TEHN-uh), *pl.* **antennae:** structure used for touch, taste, and smell

**thorax** (THAWR-aks)**:** middle section of an insect's body

**abdomen** (AB-duh-muhn)**:** third section of an insect's body

**spiracle** (SPIR-uh-kuhl)**:** opening to an air tube of a grasshopper

**tympanum** (TIHM-puh-nuhm)**:** hearing organ in a grasshopper

**Insects** Insects are the largest class of arthropods. There are more different kinds of insects than of any other kind of animals. In fact, more than one million insects have been identified. Insects live almost everywhere, except in the oceans. They live in the air, the soil, on plants, and even in the walls of buildings. Beetles, fleas, termites, moths, and ants are all insects.

1 CLASSIFY: What is the largest class of arthropods?

**The Grasshopper** The grasshopper is a good model to use when you study insects. Like all arthropods, a grasshopper has jointed legs, a segmented body, and an exoskeleton.

▲ **Figure 9-29** Grasshoppers use their hind legs to jump.

A grasshopper has three pairs of legs and one pair of **antennae.** Antennae are sensory structures that detect touch, taste, and smell. All insects have three body segments—the head, the thorax, and the abdomen. The **thorax** is the middle section of an insect's body. The three pairs of legs are attached to the thorax. The **abdomen** is the third section of an insect's body. Like most insects, the adult grasshopper also has wings.

Look at the grasshopper in Figure 9-30. Find the **spiracles.** The spiracles are openings to air tubes inside the grasshopper. The grasshopper breathes by moving air in and out through the spiracles. Find the **tympanum.** It is used for hearing.

2 STATE: What are three features of all insects?

**Social Insects** Some insects live together in colonies. Insects that live in colonies are called social insects. Ants and honeybees are social insects. In a honeybee hive, there are three kinds of honeybees.

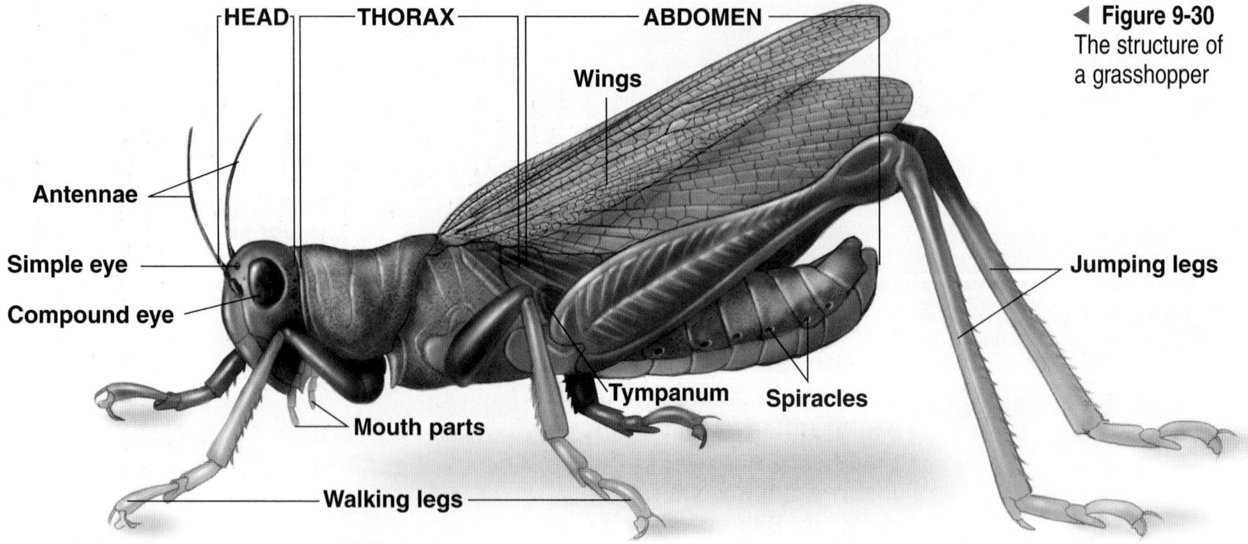


◀ **Figure 9-30** The structure of a grasshopper

They are the queen, the drones, and the workers. Each one has its own job in the beehive. The queen bee lays eggs. The drones fertilize the eggs. The workers take care of the eggs and feed the queen and the drones. Workers also gather nectar and pollen and build and protect the hive.

▲ **Figure 9-31** Bees are social insects.

**3 NAME:** Name the three kinds of honeybees.

## ✓ CHECKING CONCEPTS

1. What are three body parts of an insect?
2. How many legs do insects have?
3. What are the openings to air tubes on a grasshopper called?
4. What do grasshoppers use for hearing?
5. What are insects that live in colonies called?

## THINKING CRITICALLY

6. **INFER:** Why do you think insects are the most common kind of animal?
7. **COMPARE:** Explain the difference between breathing in earthworms and breathing in insects.
8. **PREDICT:** What might happen to a colony of bees if all the worker bees were removed?
9. **MODEL:** Draw and label a diagram of an insect.

## INTERPRETING VISUALS

*Look at the diagram in Figure 9-30. Determine whether the parts listed below are used for moving, feeding, breathing, or sensing the environment.*

**a.** simple eye
**b.** mouth parts
**c.** walking legs
**d.** antennae
**e.** spiracles
**f.** wings
**g.** tympanum
**h.** jumping legs

## *How Do They Know That?*

### SOCIAL INSECTS FORM A SOCIETY

▲ **Figure 9-32** Each kind of ant in a colony has its own job to do.

In 1975, American sociobiologist Edward Osborne Wilson proposed an interesting hypothesis. Wilson believed that insects, like humans, behaved in certain ways because of genetics.

Wilson developed the theory that social insects live in groups divided by class. These insects displayed three major characteristics. First, the mother, along with other individuals, took care of the young together. Second, some individuals in the group were born to work, rather than to reproduce. Lastly, there was the presence of overlapping generations in which the younger generation took care of the older one. These social systems have been proven to exist among many types of insects including ants, bees, wasps, and termites.

Today, researchers continue to study the behavior of social insects. For example, a recent study found that honeybees could understand abstract thoughts, such as "sameness" and "difference." Scientists may now take this information and apply it to the study of humans.

**Thinking Critically** How is human behavior similar to that of social insects?

# 9-10 How do insects develop?

## *Objective*

Identify and describe the stages of metamorphosis.

## *Key Terms*

**metamorphosis** (meht-uh-MAWR-fuh-sihs): series of developmental changes of an organism

**larva** (LAHR-vuh), *pl.* **larvae:** immature stage of many animals that usually looks different from the adult form

**pupa** (PYOO-puh): resting stage during complete metamorphosis

**cocoon** (kuh-KOON): protective covering around the pupa

**nymph** (NIHMF): young insect that looks like the adult

**Metamorphosis** All insects lay eggs. The developing insect, or embryo, feeds on yolk stored in the egg. The eggs are laid on or near a food supply. After the eggs hatch, the young insects use this food.

When an insect hatches from its egg, it may not look at all like the adult insect. For example, a small butterfly does not hatch from a butterfly egg. After the insect hatches from the egg, it goes through changes in form and size. The series of developmental changes is called **metamorphosis.**

1 DEFINE: What is metamorphosis?

**Complete Metamorphosis** Some insects, such as butterflies, moths, and houseflies, undergo complete metamorphosis. Complete metamorphosis has four stages. There is a change in body form in each stage of development.

The egg hatches into a **larva.** The larva is a newly hatched organism that usually looks very different from the adult form. Larvae eat a lot of food and grow very quickly. After a time, the larva goes into a resting stage called the **pupa.** During this stage, many insects spin a covering called a **cocoon** around themselves. In the pupa stage, the insect does not eat. Many body changes take place inside the cocoon. The structures of the adult, including the wings, form. When the adult is formed, it comes out of its cocoon. Look at the left side of Figure 9-33 to learn about the stages of complete metamorphosis.

2 SEQUENCE: Name the stages of complete metamorphosis in the correct order.

**Incomplete Metamorphosis** Some insects, such as grasshoppers, crickets, and termites, undergo incomplete metamorphosis. In incomplete metamorphosis, an insect hatches from an egg and gradually develops into an adult. There are three basic stages—egg, **nymph,** and adult. First, the eggs hatch into nymphs. Nymphs look very much like a small adult. However, nymphs do not have working wings and have no reproductive organs.

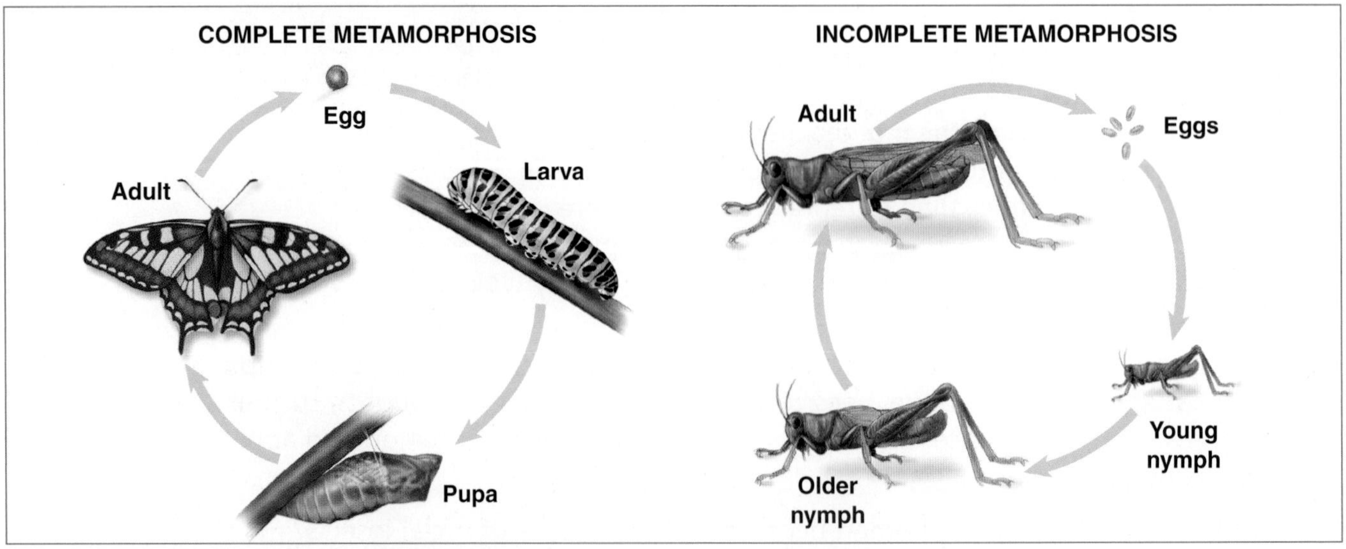


▲ **Figure 9-33** There are two types of metamorphosis.

Then, nymphs gradually change and grow into adult insects. They do so by molting several times. Nymphs eventually reach adult size and develop wings. Look at the right side of Figure 9-33 to learn about the stages of incomplete metamorphosis.

3 **LIST:** What are the three stages of incomplete metamorphosis?

## CHECKING CONCEPTS

1. In insects, the third stage in complete metamorphosis is the __________.
2. In insects, the first stage of metamorphosis is always an __________.
3. A caterpillar is the __________ stage of a butterfly.
4. Nymphs develop into adults by __________.
5. The stage of incomplete metamorphosis in which some insects look like a small adult is the __________.

## THINKING CRITICALLY

6. **INFER:** Why is the pupa called the resting stage?
7. **COMPARE:** Explain the differences between incomplete and complete metamorphosis.

## INTERPRETING VISUALS

*Look at Figure 9-34 to answer the question.*

8. Place the stages in the development of the housefly in the correct order. Then, write a paragraph explaining what is happening at each stage.

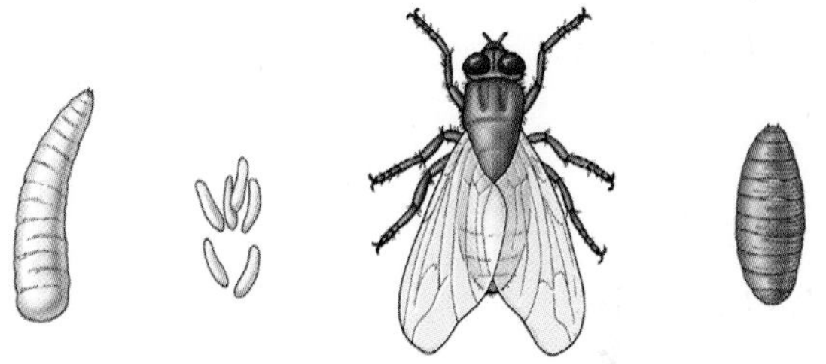


▲ **Figure 9-34**

## *Hands-On Activity*

### OBSERVING METAMORPHOSIS

*You will need a butterfly-raising kit from your teacher.*

1. Set up the kit according to your teacher's instructions.
2. Create a science journal to record your observations. Draw the eggs in your science journal.
3. After 2–3 days, observe the eggs hatching into larvae. Draw the larvae and record the date in your science journal.
4. Place several leaves in the container for the larvae to eat.
5. After several more days, the larvae will begin to form pupas. Observe the pupas. Record the date and your observations in your science journal.

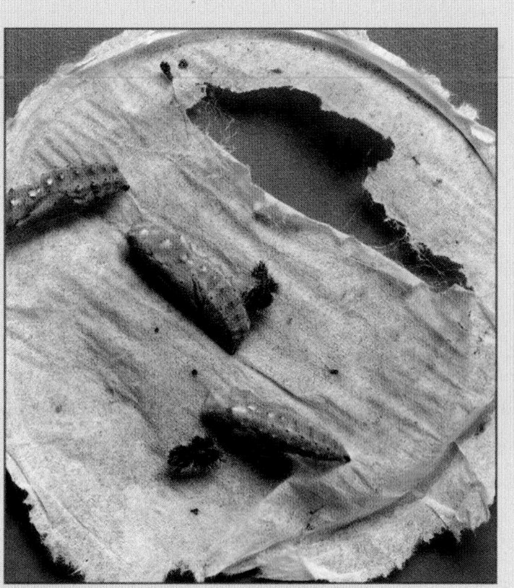

▲ **STEP 5** Observe the pupas.

6. After another day, young butterflies will emerge from the cocoons. Observe the butterflies. Record the date and your observations in your science journal.

**Practicing Your Skills**

7. **OBSERVE:** Explain the developmental changes that took place during the life cycle of the butterfly.
8. **CALCULATE:** Based on the dates you recorded in your science journal, approximately how long does the complete metamorphosis of a butterfly take?

# Chapter 9 Challenges

## Chapter Summary

### Lesson 9-1

- **Vertebrates** are animals with backbones. **Invertebrates** are animals without backbones. Some invertebrates are soft-bodied; others have an **exoskeleton**.

### Lesson 9-2

- Sponges are classified in the phylum *Porifera*. **Poriferans** have many **pores. Spicules** form a simple skeleton and support the sponge.

### Lesson 9-3

- All **cnidarians** have tentacles and live in water. The two body forms of cnidarians are **polyps** and **medusas.**

### Lesson 9-4

- Worms are classified into several different phyla, including flatworms, roundworms, and segmented worms. The earthworm is typical of segmented worms. Earthworms have a **closed circulatory system** and a complex digestive system.

### Lesson 9-5

- **Mollusks** are soft-bodied animals with a head, a foot, and a **mantle.** Many mollusks have a **radula** used for getting food.

### Lessons 9-6 and 9-7

- **Echinoderms** are spiny-skinned animals. Echinoderms have **tube feet** that are part of a **water-vascular system** used to move and to get food. The ability of an animal to regrow lost parts is called **regeneration.**

### Lessons 9-8, 9-9, and 9-10

- **Arthropods** are animals with jointed legs and an exoskeleton. The three largest arthropod groups are the insects, crustaceans, and arachnids.
- Insects are the most common type of animal on Earth. All insects have three pairs of legs, three body segments, and two antennae.
- The series of developmental changes of an insect is called **metamorphosis.** The three stages of incomplete metamorphosis in insects are egg, **nymph,** and adult. The four stages of complete metamorphosis in insects are egg, **larva, pupa,** and adult.

## Key Term Challenges

abdomen (p. 220)
annelid (p. 206)
antenna (p. 220)
arthropod (p. 216)
chitin (p. 216)
closed circulatory system (p. 206)
cnidarian (p. 204)
cocoon (p. 222)
echinoderm (p. 210)
endoskeleton (p. 200)
exoskeleton (p. 200)
invertebrate (p. 200)
larva (p. 222)
mantle (p. 208)
medusa (p. 204)
metamorphosis (p. 222)
mollusk (p. 208)
molting (p. 216)
nematode (p. 206)
nymph (p. 222)
open circulatory system (p. 216)
parasite (p. 206)
platyhelminth (p. 206)
polyp (p. 204)
pores (p. 202)
poriferan (p. 202)
pupa (p. 222)
radula (p. 208)
regeneration (p. 212)
setae (p. 206)
spicule (p. 202)
spiracle (p. 220)
thorax (p. 220)
tube feet (p. 210)
tympanum (p. 220)
vertebrate (p. 200)
water-vascular system (p. 210)

MATCHING **Write the Key Term from above that best matches each description.**

1. tiny openings
2. small, hard needlelike structures of a sponge
3. animal without a backbone
4. thin membrane that covers the mollusk's body
5. tough, lightweight material that makes up an arthropod's exoskeleton
6. structures on an echinoderm used for movement and feeding

FILL IN **Write the Key Term from above that best completes each statement.**

7. The protective covering of a pupa is called a ____________.
8. A ____________ is a soft-bodied organism.
9. The two forms of a cnidarian are the ____________ and the medusa.
10. The ability to regrow body parts is called ____________.

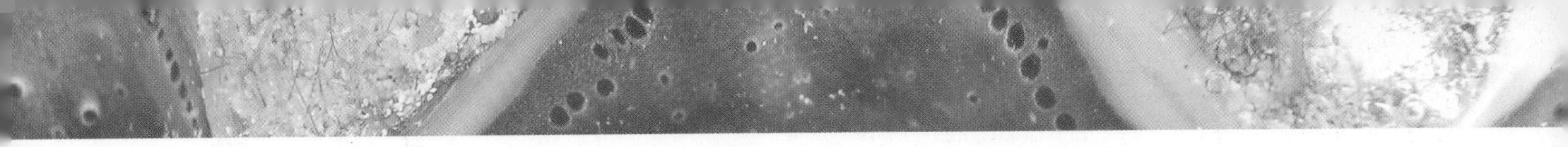

## *Content Challenges* TEST PREP

**MULTIPLE CHOICE Write the letter of the term or phrase that best completes each statement.**

1. Spicules are found in a sponge's
   **a.** jellylike substance.
   **b.** hollow center.
   **c.** endoskeleton.
   **d.** cell layer.

2. All porifera and cnidarians have
   **a.** four cell layers.
   **b.** three cell layers.
   **c.** two cell layers.
   **d.** one cell layer.

3. The simplest worms are the
   **a.** segmented worm.
   **b.** roundworms.
   **c.** flatworms.
   **d.** earthworms.

4. Roundworms belong to the phylum
   **a.** Platyhelminthes.
   **b.** Porifera.
   **c.** Nematoda.
   **d.** Annelida.

5. Sea stars and sea urchins belong to the phylum
   **a.** Porifera.
   **b.** Echinodermata.
   **c.** Annelida.
   **d.** Mollusca.

6. All insects have
   **a.** two body parts.
   **b.** four pairs of legs.
   **c.** an exoskeleton.
   **d.** wings.

7. Clams and oysters belong to the class of mollusks that have
   **a.** no shell.
   **b.** a one-part shell.
   **c.** a two-part shell.
   **d.** a three-part shell.

8. Complete metamorphosis has
   **a.** two stages.
   **b.** three stages.
   **c.** four stages.
   **d.** five stages.

9. The largest group of arthropods is the
   **a.** insects.
   **b.** crustaceans.
   **c.** arachnids.
   **d.** myriapods.

**TRUE/FALSE Write *true* if the statement is true. If the statement is false, change the underlined term to make the statement true.**

10. The organ used by a grasshopper for hearing is the tympanum.
11. Both hydra and sponges have tentacles.
12. The umbrella-like form of a cnidarian is called a polyp.
13. An earthworm uses its setae and muscles to move.
14. Sponges take in water through their pores.
15. All arthropods have an endoskeleton.
16. Insects develop through a series of stages of development called mimicry.

## Concept Challenges TEST PREP

**WRITTEN RESPONSE** **Answer each of the following questions in complete sentences.**

1. **INFER:** Until the mid-nineteenth century, most scientists thought that sponges were plants. Why might scientists have considered sponges to be part of the plant kingdom?
2. **INFER:** Why do you think earthworms avoid sunlight?
3. **RELATE:** How is the ability to regenerate related to an animal's ability to survive?
4. **INFER:** Why do you think insects are able to survive in so many different types of habitats?
5. **CONTRAST:** What are the differences between an open circulatory system and a closed circulatory system?

**INTERPRETING A DIAGRAM** **Use Figure 9-35 to answer the following questions.**

6. Identify each of the parts labeled below.
7. What letter represents a grasshopper's hearing organ?
8. Which letter represents the openings to air tubes?
9. Which letter represents the segment to which a grasshopper's legs attach?
10. Which part is not fully developed in a nymph?

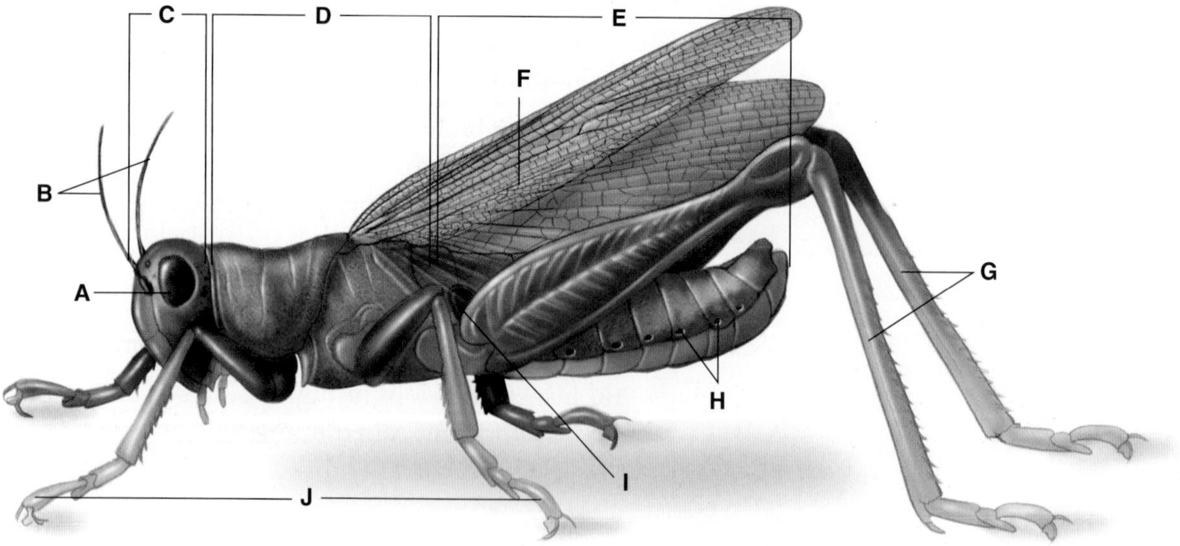


▲ **Figure 9-35** A grasshopper

# Chapter 10 Animals With Backbones

▲ **Figure 10-1** Some animals, such as this spotted owl, have a backbone.

What do a fish, an owl, and a giraffe have in common? They all have endoskeletons with backbones. The skeleton gives a body its shape and protects organs. Some bones in the skeleton help animals move. Other bones limit an animal's movement. An owl's eyes are held in place by bony structures in its skull. That means an owl cannot move its eyes. Flexible joints in its neck allow the owl to turn its head almost three-quarters of the way around so it can see behind itself.

►What part of an owl's skeleton helps the owl see behind itself?

## Contents

# 10-1 What are chordates?

## *Objective*

Identify the structure of chordates.

## *Key Terms*

**notochord** (NOHT-uh-kawrd)**:** strong, rodlike structure in chordates that can bend

**chordate** (kawr-DAYT)**:** animal with a notochord at some time during its development

**vertebrate** (VER-tuh-briht)**:** animal with a backbone

**Phylum Chordata** Fish, frogs, snakes, birds, cats, and many other animals all have something in common. They have a notochord at some time during their development. A **notochord** is a strong, rodlike structure that can bend. It is used for support. The notochord is located just below the nerve cord that runs down the back of the animal. An animal with a notochord is called a **chordate**. They are classified in the phylum Chordata, some of which are shown in Figure 10-2.

**1 DEFINE:** What is a chordate?

**Other Chordate Features** Besides a notochord, chordates have a hollow nerve cord. It runs down the back of the animal. The nerve cord carries messages between all the nerves in the body and the brain. Chordates also have paired gill slits at some time during their development. In fish, the gill slits become gills. Gills are used to take in oxygen dissolved in water. In most other chordates, the gill slits are on an embryo but disappear as the embryo develops.

**2 NAME:** What are two chordate features besides a notochord?

**Body Plan of Chordates** Chordates have a bilateral symmetry. An animal with bilateral symmetry can be divided into similar halves at only one place. Each half is a mirror image of the other. Chordates also have a tail at some point in their development. In humans, the tail is reduced to the tailbone.

Chordates have many organ systems. One of these organ systems is a closed circulatory system. It is made up of a heart and many blood vessels. Chordates also have the most highly developed nervous systems of all animals.

**3 INFER:** Based upon the body plan of chordates, why are you classified as a chordate?

**TYPES OF CHORDATES**

**Lancelets**

Lancelets are a simple chordate with no backbone. These fishlike animals keep their notochords throughout their lifetime.

**Fish**

Fish are simple vertebrates. They have a closed circulatory system with a two-chambered heart. Sharks, tuna, and trout are examples of fish.

**Amphibians**

Amphibians are vertebrates that live part of their lives in water and part on land. They have a closed circulatory system with a three-chambered heart. Frogs, toads, and salamanders are examples of amphibians.

**Reptiles**

Reptiles are land vertebrates. They have a closed circulatory system with a three- or four-chambered heart. Snakes, turtles, and alligators are examples of reptiles.

**Birds**

Birds are the only animals with feathers. They have a closed circulatory system with a four-chambered heart. Eagles, hawks, and parrots are examples of birds.

**Mammals**

Mammals are vertebrates with body hair. They have a closed circulatory system with a four-chambered heart. Opossums, elephants, and humans are examples of mammals.

▲ **Figure 10-2**

**Lancelets** In most adult chordates, the notochord is replaced by the backbone. Only a few kinds of simple chordates, such as lancelets, do not have a backbone. Lancelets are small, fishlike animals. A lancelet keeps its notochord throughout its life. It is never replaced by a backbone.

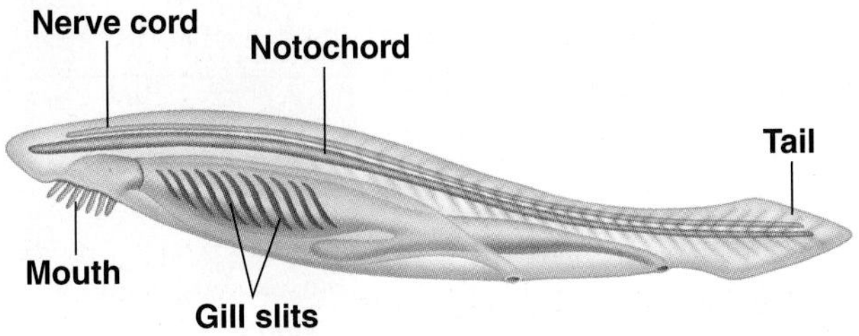


▲ **Figure 10-3** A lancelet keeps its notochord throughout its life.

**4** **ANALYZE:** Look at the lancelet in Figure 10-3. Why is it classified as a chordate?

**Vertebrates** Animals that have a backbone are called **vertebrates.** There are five major groups of vertebrates: fish, amphibians, reptiles, birds, and mammals. Vertebrates also have an endoskeleton, or a skeleton inside the body. The endoskeleton protects the organs and gives the body its shape and support.

**5** **DEFINE:** What are vertebrates?

## ✓ CHECKING CONCEPTS

1. A notochord is a strong, flexible __________ structure.
2. The nerve cord of a chordate runs down the __________ of the animal.
3. Animals with backbones are called __________.
4. An endoskeleton protects organs and gives the body __________.
5. Chordates have a __________ circulatory system.

## THINKING CRITICALLY

6. **INFER:** What structure do you think replaces the notochord in vertebrates?
7. **CONTRAST:** Identify two features of vertebrates that invertebrates do not have.

## INTERPRETING VISUALS

*Use Figure 10-2 to answer the question.*

8. **INFER:** What makes all of these animals chordates?

## *People in Science*

### VETERINARIAN

▲ **Figure 10-4** Zoo veterinarians work with many wild animals.

Treating an elephant's foot infection, cleaning and polishing a bear's teeth, and checking bison for complications after surgery are all in a day's work for a zoo veterinarian. Veterinarians are doctors who treat animals. They may treat household pets or farm animals. Zoo veterinarians specialize in the treatment of wildlife species that live in zoos.

A large part of a zoo veterinarian's job is knowing how to restrain and soothe wild animals such as tigers and gorillas. They give routine exams to healthy animals and they treat and perform surgery on animals with health problems. Also, zoo veterinarians help animals—especially endangered species—give birth and raise their young.

In order to become a veterinarian, students must first attend college and earn a bachelor's degree. Many students hoping to become veterinarians take courses in biology, chemistry, and mathematics. After college, students must attend a veterinary medial school for approximately four years.

**Thinking Critically** Would you enjoy a career as a veterinarian? Why or why not?

# 10-2 What are fish?

## *Objective*

Give examples of the different types of fish.

## *Key Terms*

**ectotherm:** animal whose body temperature changes with its environment; cold-blooded animal

**gill:** organ that absorbs dissolved oxygen from water

**cartilage** (KAHRT-uhl-ihj)**:** tough, flexible connective tissue

**swim bladder:** organ of a fish that allows the fish to remain at a specific depth in the water

**Fish** Fish are the oldest group of vertebrates. Fish first appeared more than 450 million years ago. Today, fish live in most of Earth's waters.

Fish are **ectotherms,** or cold-blooded animals. The body temperature of an ectothermic animal changes with the temperature of its surroundings. When the water temperature drops, the body temperature of a fish also drops.

1 **PREDICT:** How would the body temperature of a fish change if the water temperature rose?

**Gills** Fish breathe through organs called **gills.** Gills are protected by a hard covering called a gill cover. Fish take water in through their mouths and get rid of it through their gills. Dissolved oxygen in the water is absorbed by the gills. The oxygen passes into the blood through the walls of the gills. Blood carries the oxygen to all the cells in the fish's body. Carbon dioxide passes out of the blood in the gills, and then into the water. Look at Figure 10-5 to learn about the parts of a fish.

▲ **Figure 10-6** Like all fish, a seahorse has gills.

2 **IDENTIFY:** What organs do fish use to breathe?

**Four Classes** Fish are the largest group of vertebrates. They have a two-chambered heart. The top chamber is the atrium, and the bottom chamber is the ventricle. Fish are grouped into four classes: lampreys, hagfish, cartilaginous fish, and bony fish.

Lampreys and hagfish are both jawless fish. They look very different from most fish. These fish are long and snakelike. They do not have scales.

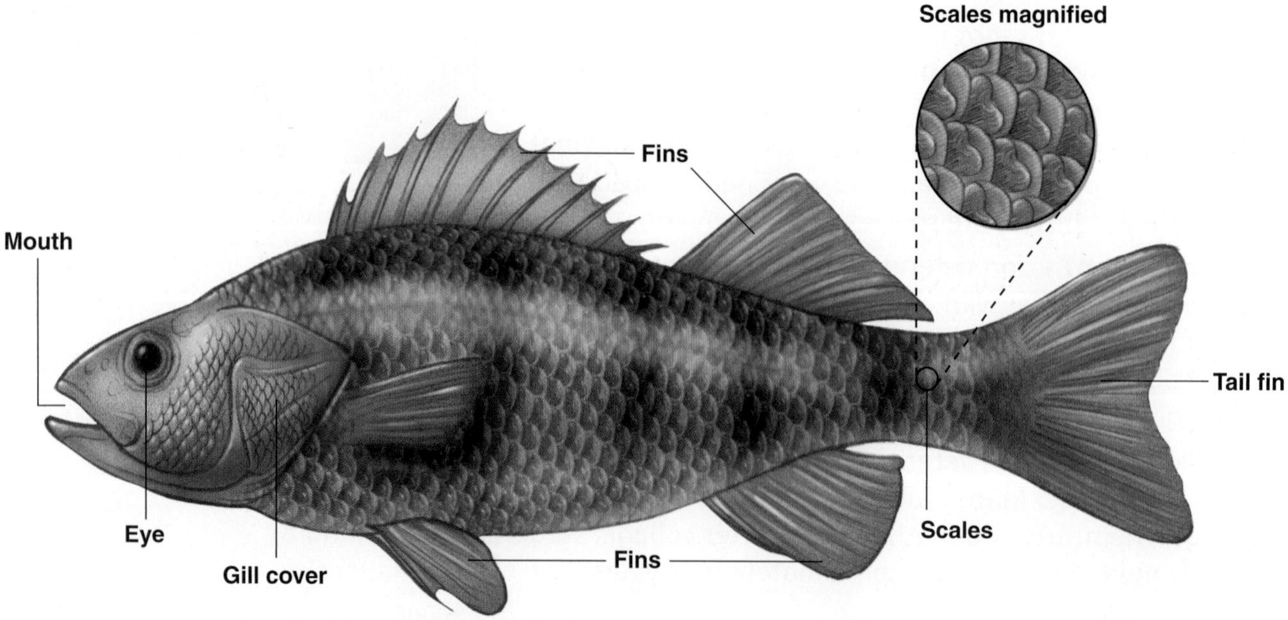


▲ **Figure 10-5** The basic anatomy of a fish

The cartilaginous fish include sharks, rays, and skates. These fish have skeletons made of cartilage. **Cartilage** is a strong, flexible tissue. The tip of your nose and your ears are made of cartilage. Cartilaginous fish also have specialized fins for steering and balance.

▲ **Figure 10-7** A hammerhead shark is a cartilaginous fish.

Bony fish have skeletons made of bone. Tuna, salmon, bass, and flounder are all examples of bony fish. Bony fish are suited to many different environments. Most have streamlined bodies for easy movement through the water. They also have different kinds of fins that are used for steering and balance. Their bodies are covered with tough, overlapping scales that protect their skin.

Bony fish also have a **swim bladder**. The swim bladder adjusts the average density of the fish. The fish can control the amount of gas in the swim bladder to equal the pressure of the water. As a result, the fish can remain at any depth in the water.

3 CLASSIFY: What are the four classes of fish?

## CHECKING CONCEPTS

1. What is an ectothermic animal?
2. How do fish breathe?
3. How many chambers does a fish's heart have?
4. What are the only two kinds of jawless fish?
5. What is the main characteristic of a cartilaginous fish?

## THINKING CRITICALLY

6. CLASSIFY: Place each of the following fish into its correct class:
   - a. tuna
   - b. bass
   - c. sea skate
   - d. hammerhead shark
   - e. salmon
   - f. whale shark

## BUILDING SCIENCE SKILLS

***Inferring*** When you infer, you form a conclusion based on facts. Both of a flounder's eyes are on one side of its head. A flounder is also the color of sand or mud. Both of these features are adaptations. How do you think a sandy color and eyes on one side of its head make a flounder suited to life on the ocean floor?

## *Hands-On Activity*

### MODELING A SWIM BLADDER

*You will need safety goggles, two balloons, a large bowl filled with water, and extra water.*

1. Inflate a balloon with air. Then place it in a bowl of water.
2. Fill the second balloon half-way with water. Then, blow air into it until it is approximately the same size as the first balloon.
3. Place the second balloon in the bowl of water.

▲ **STEP 3** Place the second balloon in a bowl of water.

### Practicing Your Skills

4. IDENTIFY: Which balloon is floating on the surface of the water? Which is floating below the surface of the water?
5. APPLY: How do the balloons model a swim bladder?

# 10-3 What are amphibians?

## *Objective*

Identify the characteristics of amphibians.

## *Key Term*

**amphibian** (am-FIHB-ee-uhn)**:** animal that lives part of its life in water and part on land

**Amphibians** An **amphibian** is an animal that lives part of its life in water and part on land. In fact, the word *amphibian* comes from a Greek word meaning "double life." The young of most amphibians live in water. As they grow, they undergo changes. Adult amphibians usually live on land and only return to the water to lay eggs. Scientists think that the first amphibians developed from fish that could stay out of water for long periods of time. These fish had lungs and could breathe air.

Amphibians are ectothermic. Look at Figures 10-8 and 10-9. Except for toads, amphibians, such as the leopard frog, have smooth, moist skin. Toads have bumpy skin. Most amphibians also have webbed feet. Because they live part of their life in water and part on land, they use gills, lungs, and their skin to exchange oxygen and carbon dioxide. Amphibian eggs do not have shells and are usually laid in water.

▲ **Figure 10-8** A leopard frog

▲ **Figure 10-9** A toad

1 **PREDICT:** As the temperature of the mud that a toad is in drops, what will happen to its body temperature?

**Classify Amphibians** Scientists have classified more than 4,000 different species of amphibians. Scientists classify amphibians into three orders based on their body structures. The best-known amphibians are frogs and toads. They are the order of tailless amphibians. Salamanders and newts belong to the order of amphibians with tails. The third order of amphibians is the caecilians (see-SIL-ee-uhns), which do not have legs. Caecilians are wormlike animals that live mainly in the forests of South America.

▲ **Figure 10-10** Salamanders are amphibians with tails.

2 **LIST:** What are the three orders of amphibians?

**More About Amphibians** Amphibians have a three-chambered heart that is part of a closed circulatory system. The heart has two atria and one ventricle.

Almost all amphibians have gills during the early stages of development. As adults, they have lungs. Some water salamanders have gills throughout their lives. Many amphibians also breathe through their skin. Their skin must stay moist so that oxygen and carbon dioxide can be exchanged through it.

3 **INFER:** If a type of amphibian needed to keep its skin moist, in what kind of environment would it live?

Go Online
*active art*
**For:** Respiration and Circulation activity
**Visit:** PHSchool.com
**Web Code:** cep-2032

## ✓ CHECKING CONCEPTS

1. What does the word *amphibian* mean?
2. From what animals do most scientists think amphibians developed?
3. What kind of skin do toads have?
4. What kind of amphibians are frogs and toads?
5. Why must amphibians keep their skin moist?

## THINKING CRITICALLY

6. **CONTRAST:** How does the body structure of a frog differ from that of a salamander?
7. **INFER:** Why do you think most amphibians have webbed feet?
8. **IDENTIFY:** List four characteristics of amphibians.

## Web InfoSearch

**Caecilians** Caecilians are amphibians without legs. Caecilians look like long, colorful earthworms. Like earthworms, caecilians live in soil. Some caecilians have very small eyes. Most caecilians, however, are considered blind.

▲ **Figure 10-11**
A caecilian

**SEARCH:** Use the Internet to find out more about caecilians. Use your findings to make a model of a caecilian and its environment. Start your search at www.conceptsandchallenges.com. Some key search words are **amphibian** and **caecilian.**

## *Science and Technology*

### COMPUTER DISSECTIONS

Computers have become useful tools in science. They can be used to store data, make calculations, add color to photographs, and help keep track of research. Computers can also be used to run simulations, or moving models.

In many schools, animal dissections are no longer done on preserved animals. Instead, computers are used to run a dissection simulation. A special computer program may be on a CD-ROM, a DVD, or even the Internet. For example, you can dissect a frog by using a dissection simulation program. On the computer screen, you use laboratory equipment to open the frog and explore the different organ systems.

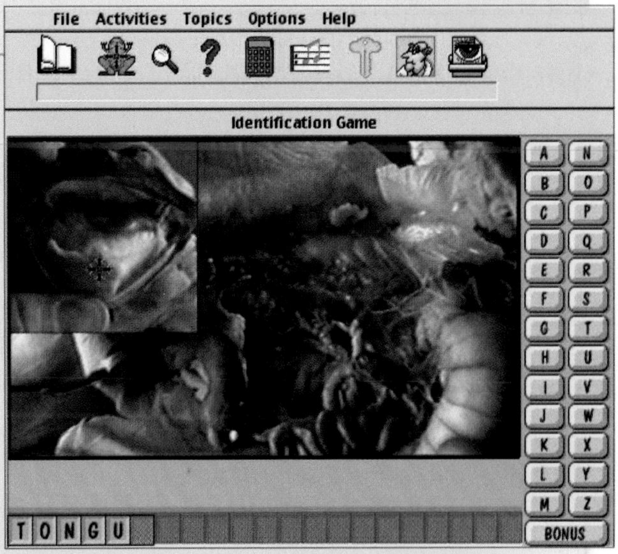


▲ **Figure 10-12** Some schools use dissection simulation programs instead of dissecting preserved animals.

Many people prefer using computer dissection. They do not think animals should be killed for dissections. Other people think that dissection on preserved specimens is important to the study of life science. Medical students still practice surgery on preserved animals, however. What do you think?

**Thinking Critically** What are some benefits of using a computer dissection program?

# 10-4 How do amphibians develop?

*Objective*

Explain metamorphosis in frogs.

*Key Terms*

**larva** (LAHR-vuh)**:** immature stage of many animals that usually looks different than the adult form

**tadpole:** larval stage of a frog

**Metamorphosis** The series of developmental changes of an organism is called metamorphosis. Like some insects, the appearance of amphibians changes dramatically during their life cycles. During the early stages, amphibians can live only in water. They breathe through gills. As adults, most amphibians live on land. They use their lungs to breathe. When under water, adult amphibians absorb oxygen through their moist skin because most of them no longer have gills.

1 **NAME:** What are two groups of animals that change during their life cycle?

**Amphibian Eggs** All amphibians lay eggs. Amphibian eggs do not have a shell. Instead, they are covered with a clear, jellylike substance that protects the embryo. This substance also helps the eggs cling to each other or to water plants. Amphibians usually lay their eggs in water. For example, frogs and toads lay their eggs in freshwater lakes, ponds, and other bodies of water. They lay their eggs in the spring. Toads lay long strings of eggs. Frogs lay clumps of eggs.

2 **IDENTIFY:** Do frogs lay many eggs, a few eggs, or one egg?

**Larva** Usually in about 12 days, amphibian eggs hatch into larvae. A **larva** is a newly hatched organism that usually looks very different from the adult form. Frog eggs hatch into tadpoles. **Tadpoles** are the larval stage of a frog. Tadpoles do not look like adult frogs at all. They look like very small fish. Their bodies are streamlined, they have a thin tail, and they breathe with gills.

Unlike tadpoles, most salamander larvae do not look very different from adult salamanders. Salamander larvae have small legs and a tail. The big difference between salamander larvae and adult salamanders is that the larvae have external gills.

3 **NAME:** What is the early stage of a frog called?

**Larva to Adult** As a tadpole grows, its body changes. Legs begin to develop. As the tadpole begins to develop into a young frog, its tail shrinks and gradually disappears. Lungs develop and the gills disappear. At this point, the young frog leaves the water. It is adapted, or suited, to a life on land.

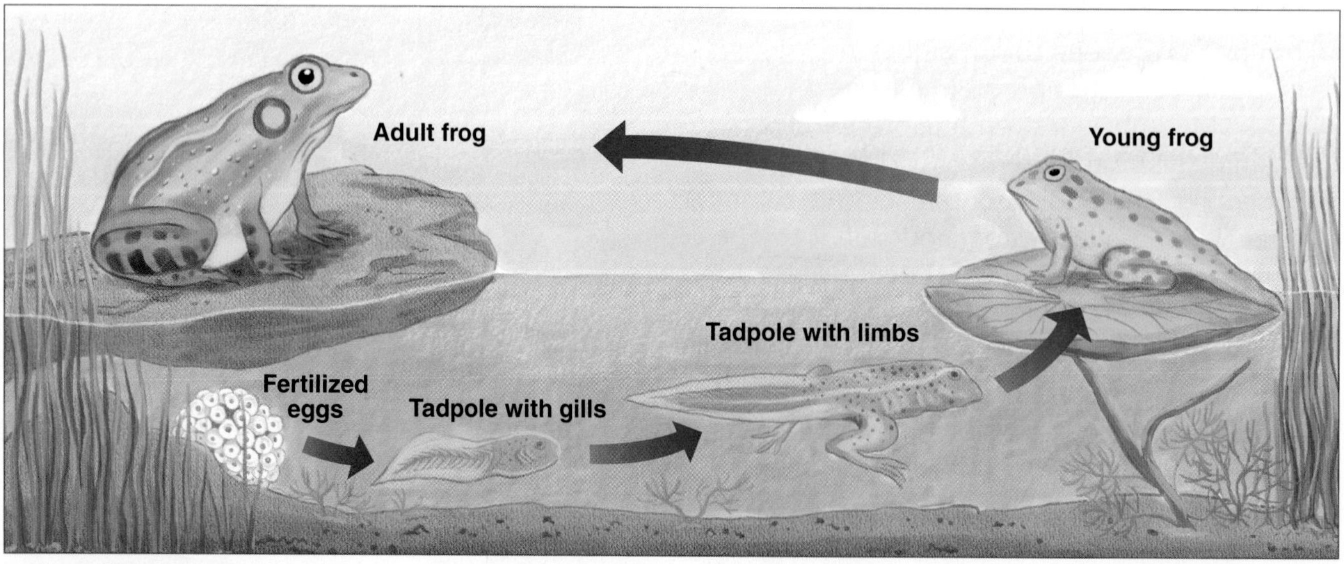


▲ **Figure 10-13** Life cycle of a frog

For salamander larvae, the change is not as dramatic. When a salamander larva metamorphoses, it loses its gills. The lungs develop and the salamander is adapted to life on land.

4 **INFER:** What adaptation does a young amphibian have for breathing air?

## CHECKING CONCEPTS

1. During the early stages in their development, amphibians breathe with ____________.
2. Amphibians and insects undergo ____________.
3. Most amphibians lay their eggs in ____________.
4. The larval stage in the development of a frog is a ____________.
5. Frog eggs hatch into tadpoles in about 12 ____________.
6. The eggs of frogs are surrounded by a ____________.

## THINKING CRITICALLY

7. **MODEL:** Make a flowchart that shows the stages in frog development.
8. **INFER:** Why do you think frogs lay so many eggs at one time?
9. **HYPOTHESIZE:** Why do you think amphibians lay their eggs in water?

## BUILDING SCIENCE SKILLS

***Comparing and Contrasting*** When you compare and contrast things, you look at how they are alike and how they are different. Use library resources to find out more about the metamorphosis of insects and amphibians. How do they compare? What are the similarities? What are the differences?

## *Integrating Earth Science*

**TOPICS: storm water, water pollution**

### POLLUTANTS AND FROG DEVELOPMENT

Water pollution is the release of harmful substances into Earth's waters. One way that pollutants get in the water is through storm water, or water than runs off our houses and streets when it rains. This water is caught in gutters, drains, creeks, and rivers and eventually makes its way to the sea. Pollutants, such as litter, fertilizers, and chemicals used to wash cars, get picked up by storm water.

▲ **Figure 10-14** Pollutants in water may have led to mutations in this frog.

Environmental scientists believe that pollutants in the water affect the development of frogs. In 1995, science students on a field trip in Minnesota discovered more than two dozen frogs with severe mutations, including extra limbs and eye mutations. To find the cause of the mutations, scientists conducted an experiment. A group of 40 tadpoles were placed in either water from water sources in Minnesota or purified water. More than half of the frogs that developed in the water from Minnesota had mutations. As a result, the Minnesota water was analyzed. A chemical called methoprene was found. Methoprene is a pesticide used to kill mosquitoes. Scientists believe that this chemical, when heated by the sun, caused mutations in the frog-egg genes.

**Thinking Critically** How could humans help to decrease mutations found in frogs?

# 10-5 What are reptiles?

## *Objectives*

Explain how reptiles are adapted to life on land.
Describe the four orders of reptiles.

**Life on Land** Reptiles were the first true land animals. Unlike amphibians, most reptiles do not need water for reproduction. They lay their eggs on land. Most reptile eggs are covered with a leathery shell. The shell keeps the eggs from drying out. Young reptiles develop in the eggs.

Reptiles have lungs throughout their lives. They have hard, dry skin covered with scales. The skin is waterproof. The waterproof skin reduces water loss from the body.

▲ **Figure 10-15** A komodo dragon is a reptile.

**1 EXPLAIN:** How are reptiles adapted for life on land?

**Reptiles** Reptiles are ectothermic. They have a three-chambered or four-chambered heart. Most reptiles also have two pairs of legs and clawed feet.

More than 100 million years ago, reptiles were the major group of animals on Earth. By about 65 million years ago, most of those reptiles had died out. Today, there are almost 8,000 different species of reptiles.

**2 NAME:** What are some of the characteristics of reptiles?

**Orders of Reptiles** The smallest order of reptiles includes the tuataras (too-uh-TAH-ruhz). In fact, this order is so small it has only two species—both types of tuataras. They are sometimes called living fossils because they have many features of ancient reptiles. These animals have changed very little since they first appeared about 200 million years ago. Tuataras look like lizards, but have spikes on their backs.

The largest order of reptiles includes snakes and lizards. When snakes and lizards grow, they shed their skins. Most snakes and lizards live in warm areas. The main difference between snakes and lizards is that snakes do not have legs. There are more than 4,500 different kinds of snakes and lizards.

◀ **Figure 10-16** This viper is well suited for life in the trees.

Turtles and tortoises make up another order of reptiles. This group of animals has shells. Instead of teeth, most reptiles in this order have beaks. Turtles live mostly in water. Tortoises live mostly on land. Turtles have flat, streamlined shells. Tortoises have high, domed shells.

▲ **Figure 10-17** How has this green sea turtle adapted to life under water?

The fourth order of reptiles includes crocodiles and alligators. These animals spend much of their time in water. You can tell the difference between them by looking at their heads. Alligators have broad, rounded heads. Crocodiles have more triangular heads.

▲ **Figure 10-18** A crocodile

▲ **Figure 10-19** An alligator

3 ▶ **INFER:** Why do you think a flat, streamlined shell is helpful to a turtle in water?

## ✓ CHECKING CONCEPTS

1. Where do young reptiles develop?
2. Why are tuataras called living fossils?
3. Which animals are members of the largest order of reptiles?
4. Where do most tortoises live?
5. How can you tell an alligator from a crocodile?

## THINKING CRITICALLY

6. **CONTRAST:** How do snakes differ from all other reptiles?

### Web InfoSearch

**Whiptail Lizards** Most animals reproduce sexually. One animal that reproduces asexually is the whiptail lizard. Whiptail lizards reproduce by parthenogenesis, or the production of offspring from unfertilized eggs. All whiptail lizards are female.

**SEARCH:** Use the Internet to find out more about whiptail lizards. Write your findings in a report. You can start your search at www.conceptsandchallenges.com. Some key search words are **whiptail lizards** and **parthenogenesis.**

## *Real-Life Science*

### HELPFUL SNAKES

Most people do not want to get too close to a venomous snake. Some scientists, however, have been researching possible medical uses of snake venom. Snake venom may contain many helpful chemicals and proteins.

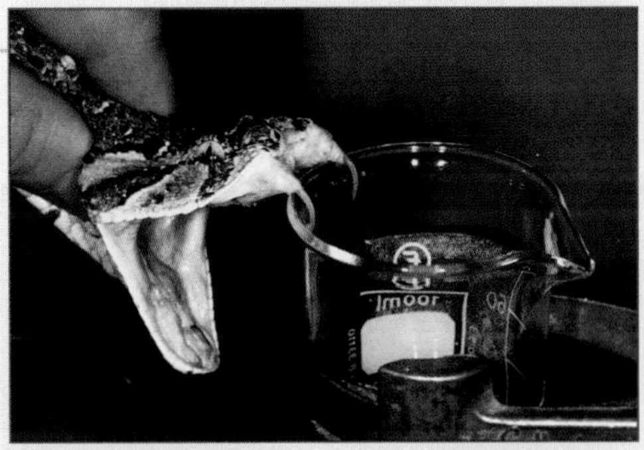

▲ **Figure 10-20** Snake venom is collected by a process called milking.

For example, stroke victims usually have problems with their circulatory system. Venom from the Malayan pit viper has been used in new drugs that thin the blood and prevent blood clots from forming. Because cobra venom contains an enzyme that breaks down virus cell walls, scientists have been researching possible medical uses for it. Snake venom also greatly affects the nervous system. As a result, medical researchers are studying snake venom to find medications for people who have Alzheimer's disease or epilepsy.

To study venom, first scientists must remove it from the snake. This process is known as milking the snake. When working with venomous snakes, scientists must be careful. Snake venom can be fatal to humans.

**Thinking Critically** Should snake venom be used in medical research? Explain.

# 10-6 What are birds?

## *Objectives*

Describe the characteristics of birds. Classify different kinds of birds.

## *Key Term*

**endotherm:** vertebrate whose body temperature remains about the same; a warm-blooded animal

**Features of Birds** Unlike fish, amphibians, and reptiles, birds are **endotherms,** or warm-blooded. The body temperature of an endothermic animal remains about the same. It does not change when the temperature of the animal's surroundings changes. Birds maintain their body temperatures by using heat produced by the breakdown of food.

Birds are very easy to recognize. They are the only animals with feathers. Birds also have other characteristics.

- Birds have two wings and two legs.
- Birds have lightweight bones.
- Birds have a beak without teeth.
- Birds lay hard-shelled eggs.

Birds have well-developed organ systems. Their respiratory system, in particular, works very well. It supplies the wing muscles with large amounts of oxygen during flight. Birds also have a four-chambered heart. The two upper chambers are the atria. The two lower chambers are the ventricles.

1 **COMPARE:** What is the difference between ectothermic and endothermic animals?

**Five Groups** All birds are classified in the class Aves (AH-vays). They can be further classified by comparing their beaks and feet. Figure 10-21 shows some characteristics that different birds share. All swimming birds, such as ducks, have webbed feet for paddling through water. Hawks and other meat-eating birds, or birds of prey, have long, sharp claws to capture animals. Wading birds have long legs.

Look at the structure of the bill, or beak, in each group. The beak varies with eating habits. Birds that feed on seeds have short, strong beaks. Hunting birds, such as hawks, owls, and eagles, have curved beaks for tearing meat. Wading birds have long beaks.

2 **INFER:** Why do you think wading birds need long beaks?

**Feathers** Birds have different types of feathers. Different feathers have different functions. Down feathers insulate, or keep warm, a bird's body. They are soft and fluffy. Contour feathers streamline a bird's body and help it fly. Contour

| TYPES OF BIRDS | | | | |
|---|---|---|---|---|
| **Birds of Prey** | **Perching Birds** | **Nonperching Birds** | **Swimming Birds** | **Wading Birds** |
|  |  |  |  |  |
| **Body features:**<br>Sharp, curved claws<br>Strong, sharp beak<br>**Examples:**<br>Hawks, owls, eagles, falcons | **Body features:**<br>Curved toes<br>Small beaks<br>**Examples:**<br>Cardinals, sparrows, crows, lorikeets | **Body feature:**<br>Long, clinging toes<br>**Examples:**<br>Turkeys, hummingbirds, grouse, chickens | **Body feature:**<br>Webbed feet<br>**Examples:**<br>Ducks, geese, swans, loons, gulls | **Body features:**<br>Long legs<br>Long, sharp beaks<br>**Examples:**<br>Herons, flamingoes, sandpipers, cranes |

▲ **Figure 10-21**

feathers are made up of a shaft and many branches called barbs.

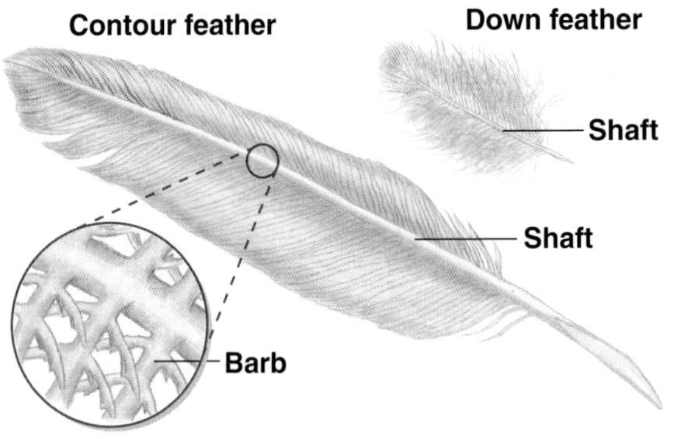


▲ **Figure 10-22** Each type of feather has a specific function.

**3 STATE:** What is the purpose of down feathers?

## ✓ CHECKING CONCEPTS

1. Unlike reptiles and fish, birds are __________ animals.
2. Birds are the only animals with __________.
3. Perching birds have __________ toes.
4. Birds have __________ feathers to help insulate them.

## THINKING CRITICALLY

5. **CLASSIFY:** *Use Figure 10-21 to classify each of the birds listed.*
   **a.** hawk
   **b.** duck
   **c.** cardinal
   **d.** heron
   **e.** eagle
6. **APPLY:** Sea gulls live near oceans. Describe what kind of feet and beaks you think sea gulls have.
7. **INFER:** People, like birds, have four-chambered hearts. What do you think the upper and lower chambers of the human heart are called?
8. **APPLY:** What characteristic can you use to classify an animal as a bird?

## HEALTH AND SAFETY TIP

The meat and eggs of poultry might contain bacteria called *Salmonella. Salmonella* causes food poisoning. Use library references to find out what the symptoms of *Salmonella* poisoning are. Also find out two ways to help reduce your risk of poisoning from this bacteria.

## *Integrating Physical Science*

**TOPICS: gravity, force, air pressure**

### THE MECHANICS OF BIRD FLIGHT

Four different forces act on a flying bird. One is weight, the force of gravity that pulls an object downward. A bird's weight is opposed by a force called lift, which is produced when a bird flaps its wings. As the wings move downward, the pressure from air above the wings decreases, while the pressure from air below them increases. A bird's forward motion adds to this pressure difference. The higher air pressure below a flying bird pushes it up. As the bird flaps its wings, it tilts its main flight feathers so that the lower air pressure is toward the front. This movement produces a force called thrust, which propels the bird forward. Thrust is opposed by drag from the air through which the bird is moving.

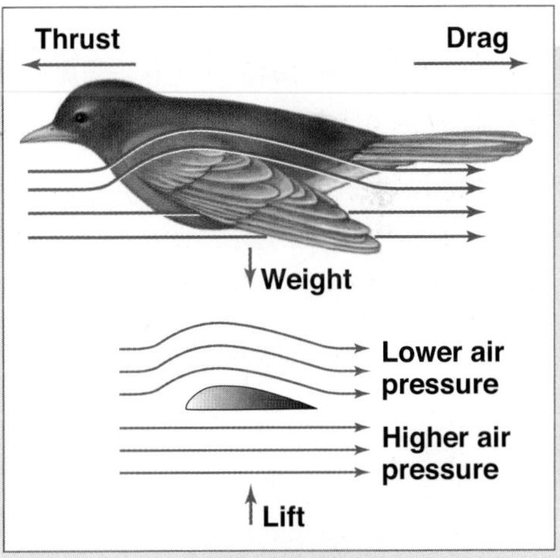


▲ **Figure 10-23** A bird's body is built for flight.

Very strong chest muscles power the wings, and feathers can be turned to different angles to help a bird steer. A bird's body has a streamlined shape. Air flows around it smoothly, reducing drag. A bird uses drag to slow down and land by spreading its tail and lowering its feet.

**Thinking Critically** Do you think an animal without feathers could fly? Explain.

LAB ACTIVITY

# Investigating an Owl Pellet

**Materials**
- Safety goggles
- Gloves
- Owl pellet
- Ruler
- Hand lens
- Forceps
- Tweezers
- Dissecting needle

### *BACKGROUND*

Owls are carnivores. Carnivores feed on other animals. Because birds do not have teeth, their food remains partially intact before it is digested. An owl pellet is the undigested materials an owl coughs up after it eats.

### *PURPOSE*

In this activity, you will learn about an owl's diet by examining an owl pellet.

### *PROCEDURE*

1. Observe the outside of an owl pellet with a hand lens. Record your observations.
2. Using the forceps, hold the owl pellet in place. Hold the forceps with one hand.
3. Use the dissecting needle to separate the owl pellet. ⚠ CAUTION: Be very careful when using dissecting needles.
4. Remove the bones from the owl pellet. If there is any fur attached to the bones, remove it with tweezers.
5. Group the bones together based on similarities. Observe the bones with a hand lens.
6. Record the number of skulls you find. Observe the skulls with a hand lens. Record the shape of the skulls and the number of teeth each skull has.

▲ **STEP 1** Observe the outside of a pellet with a hand lens.

▲ **STEP 3** Use the dissecting needle to separate the owl pellet.

▲ **STEP 4** Remove any bones from the pellet.

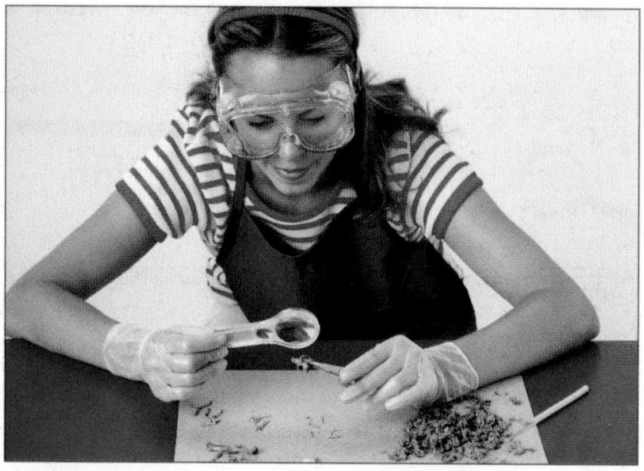

▲ **STEP 6** Observe the skulls with a hand lens.

7. Measure the skulls with a ruler. Record the measurement of each skull.

8. Use Figure 10-24 to identify the types of skulls you found. Record this information.

9. Use the bones and skulls you have found to reconstruct a skeleton of one of the organisms eaten by the owl.

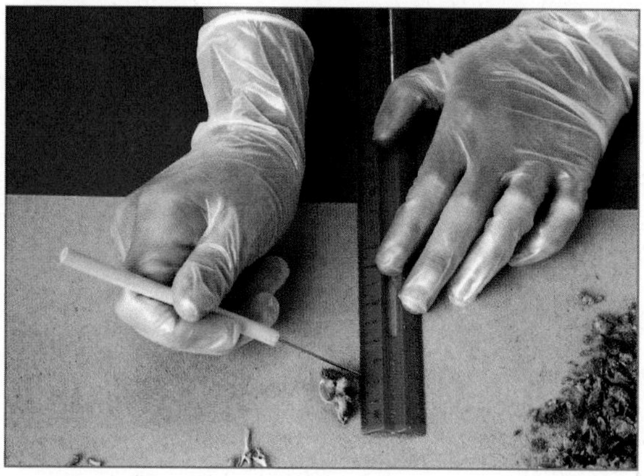

▲ **STEP 7** Measure the skulls.

| IDENTIFYING FEATURES OF OWL PELLET REMAINS | | | | |
|---|---|---|---|---|
| **Shrew** | **Mouse** | **Vole** | **Mole** | **Rat** |
|  |  |  |  |  |
| Upper jaw has at least 18 teeth. | Upper jaw has two biting teeth and extends over lower jaw. | Upper jaw has two biting teeth and does not extend over lower jaw. | Upper jaw has at least 18 teeth. | Upper jaw has two biting teeth and extends over lower jaw. |
| Skull is less than 23 mm long. | Skull is less than 22 mm long. | Skull is more than 23 mm long. | Skull is more than 23 mm long. | Skull is more than 22 mm long. |

▲ **Figure 10-24** Use this chart to determine what an owl eats.

## *CONCLUSIONS*

1. IDENTIFY: How many animal remains did you find in the owl pellet?

2. CALCULATE: If owls cough up approximately two pellets a day, about how many animals might an owl eat in a week?

3. INFER: Compare your results with the results of two classmates. Based on your combined data, what animal do owls eat most frequently? Are they also vertebrates? How do you know?

# 10-7 What are mammals?

## INVESTIGATE

### *Modeling Insulation*
HANDS-ON ACTIVITY

1. Put on a pair of rubber gloves.
2. Spread a thick coat of shortening over one glove. Do not coat the other glove.
3. Remove the glove you used to spread the shortening over the first glove. Put on a clean glove. One glove should have shortening on it, the other glove should be clean.
4. Place both hands in a bowl of cold water for three minutes.

**THINK ABOUT IT:** Which hand got colder faster? Explain.

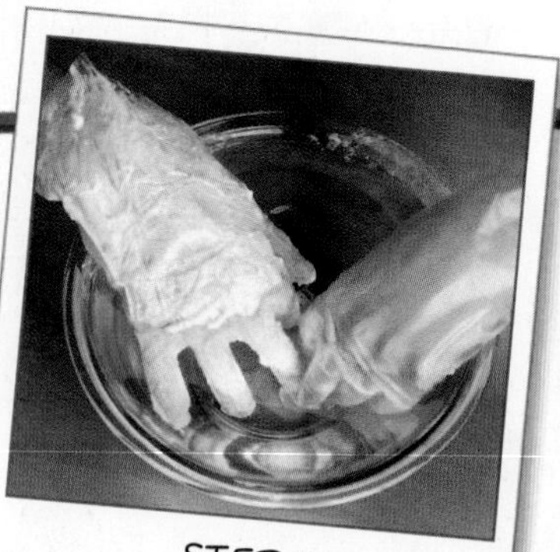
STEP 4

### *Objective*
Describe the characteristics of mammals.

### *Key Terms*
**mammary** (MAM-uh-ree) **gland:** gland that produces milk in female mammals

**monotreme:** mammal that lays eggs

**marsupial:** mammal whose young develops in pouches

**placenta** (pluh-SEN-tuh)**:** structure through which materials are exchanged between the mother and the developing embryo

**Conquerors of the Earth** More than 250 million years ago, animals called therapsids (thuh-RAP-sihdz) roamed the Earth. Fossils show this animal had characteristics of reptiles and mammals. Some biologists infer that all modern mammals came from the therapsids. When the dinosaurs became extinct, early mammals no longer had to compete with them for food and living space. The mammals adapted to the new environment and reproduced. Today, mammals are one of the most successful groups of animals on Earth.

1 ANALYZE: Why did mammals survive after the dinosaurs died out?

**Characteristics of Mammals** Mammals are a class of vertebrates that include humans and most of the best-known large animals. Mammals are endothermic. Because they are warm-blooded, mammals can live almost everywhere. They live on the plains, in forests, in deserts, and in swamps. Some live in oceans and a few can even fly.

Besides being endothermic, mammals have the following characteristics.

- Mammals have body hair. Body hair provides insulation that helps keep body heat from escaping.
- Mammals have a four-chambered heart.
- Mammals have specialized teeth to help them chew their food. Most mammals have four different types of teeth.

▲ **Figure 10-25** Mammals have specialized teeth.

- Most mammals have a highly developed brain and nervous system.
- Female mammals nurse their young with milk. The milk is produced by **mammary glands**.

2 LIST: What are the characteristics of mammals?

**Kinds of Mammals** There are over 4,000 species of mammals. They are sometimes grouped according to how they give birth to their young. There are three basic mammal groups. One group is made up of egg-laying mammals, or **monotremes.** There are only three kinds of animals in this group. These are the duckbill platypus (PLAT-uh-puhs) and two types of spiny anteater. In these animals, the young develop in an egg surrounded by a shell.

▲ **Figure 10-26** Monotremes, such as this duckbill platypus, are mammals that lay eggs.

The second mammal group is the pouched mammals, or **marsupials**. In marsupials, the young are born at a very early stage of development. They then crawl into a pouch, or pocket, on the belly of the mother. They remain in the pouch until they are big enough to survive on their own. Kangaroos, opossums, and koalas are pouched mammals.

◀ **Figure 10-27** Koalas carry their young in pouches.

The third and largest group of mammals is the placental mammals. In these animals, a special structure called the **placenta** develops in the female during pregnancy. The placenta is a structure through which materials are exchanged between the mother and the developing embryo. Dogs, cats, cattle, seals, whales, bats, apes, and humans are placental mammals.

▲ **Figure 10-28** White-tailed deer are placental mammals.

3 **LIST:** What are the three groups of mammals?

## CHECKING CONCEPTS

1. Mammals have __________ on their bodies.
2. Female mammals produce milk in __________ glands.
3. Materials are exchanged between a mother and an embryo through a __________.
4. The young of spiny anteaters develop inside an __________.
5. Kangaroos are __________ mammals.

## THINKING CRITICALLY

6. **CONTRAST:** How do spiny anteaters and duckbill platypuses differ from reptiles?
7. **COMPARE:** What characteristics are used to classify mammals into each of their groups?

### Web InfoSearch

**Marine Mammals** Dolphins and whales are marine mammals. Marine mammals live in water but come to the surface for oxygen.

**SEARCH:** Use the Internet to find out more about marine mammals. Then, write your findings in a report. Start your search at www.conceptsandchallenges.com. Some key search words are **marine mammals, dolphins,** and **whales.**

Integrating Physical Science

# THE Big IDEA

## How are the skeletons of vertebrates like levers?

Physical science involves the study of machines and the study of motion. Did you know the bones in your neck, arms, and legs are like machines?

A machine makes it easier to do work. A lever is a simple machine. A lever is a bar that turns on a fixed point called the fulcrum. See Figure 10-29. Something pushes or pulls the lever to lift a weight. The weight is called the load. The push or pull is the effort force. Many bones and muscles work as levers to move your body.

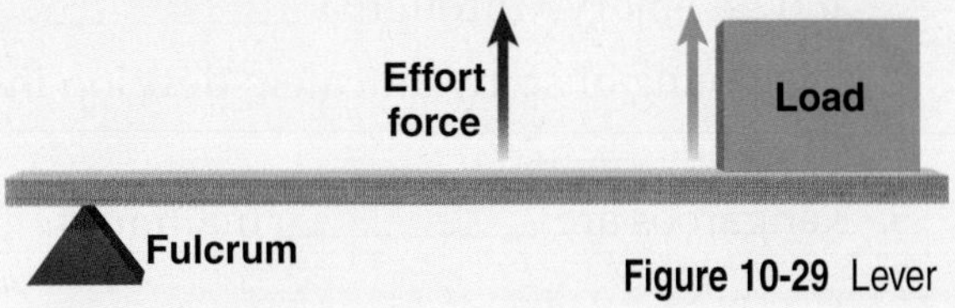


**Figure 10-29** Lever

Your forearm is a lever. Your elbow joint is the fulcrum, and the weight of your wrist and hand is the load. When your bicep muscle applies the effort force on your forearm, your wrist and hand are lifted up.

Bones and joints have different shapes, depending on their purpose. Knee and elbow joints are hinges. Shoulder and hip joints are a ball and socket. Joints are coated with a slippery fluid and smooth tissue to reduce friction. This makes movement easier.

The skeleton of each animal affects how it moves. Look at the images that appear on this page and the next. They show how the skeletons of some vertebrates allow them to move in special ways. Follow the directions in the Science Log to learn more about "the big idea." ✦

**Bird**

A bird is designed for flight. Its short backbone makes its body compact and stiff. This provides strength and stability as the bird flies. Its neck, however, is flexible. This allows the bird to reach for food and twist to preen its feathers. Powerful flight muscles are anchored to a large breastbone. The flight muscles power a bird's wings.

**Cheetah**

The cheetah is the fastest land animal. Its leg bones are long and thin, and its backbone is flexible. When the cheetah's strong muscles pull on these bones, its backbone arches and springs back like a bow. The vertebrae in its backbone and the bones in its legs act as levers.

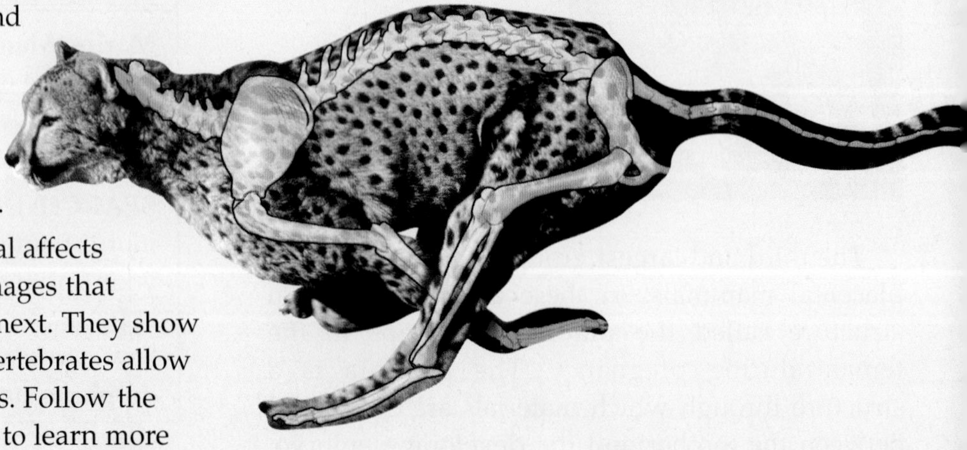

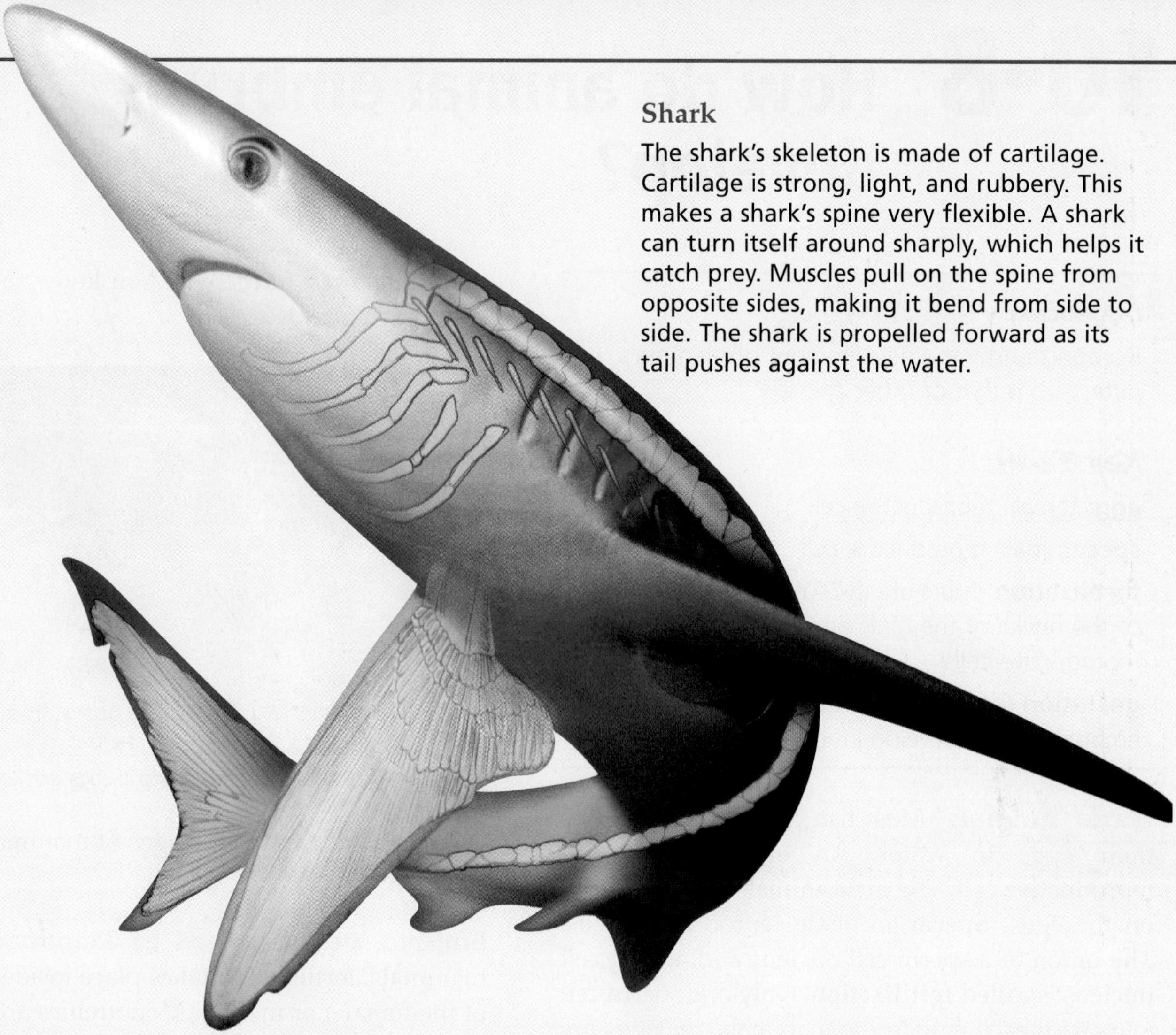

**Shark**

The shark's skeleton is made of cartilage. Cartilage is strong, light, and rubbery. This makes a shark's spine very flexible. A shark can turn itself around sharply, which helps it catch prey. Muscles pull on the spine from opposite sides, making it bend from side to side. The shark is propelled forward as its tail pushes against the water.

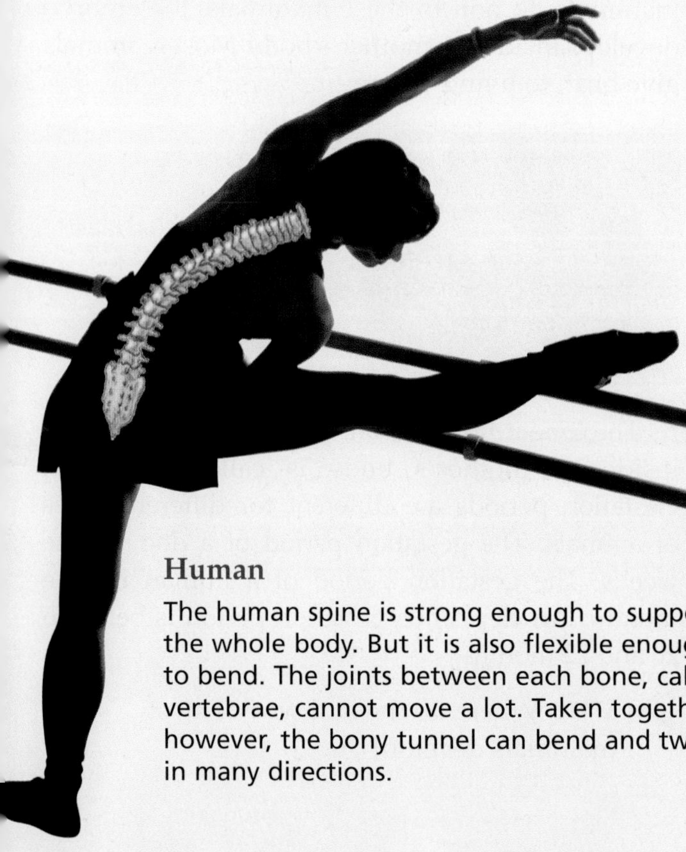

**Human**

The human spine is strong enough to support the whole body. But it is also flexible enough to bend. The joints between each bone, called vertebrae, cannot move a lot. Taken together, however, the bony tunnel can bend and twist in many directions.

**WRITING ACTIVITY**

*Science Log*

Which animal's movements do you think are the most interesting? In your science log, research and write about how this animal moves. Then, describe how the structure of its body helps it move. Start your search at www.conceptsandchallenges.com.

# 10-8 How do animal embryos develop?

## *Objective*

Recognize how the development of mammals differs from that of other animals.

## *Key Terms*

**egg:** female reproductive cell

**sperm:** male reproductive cell

**fertilization** (fuhrt-uhl-ih-ZAY-shuhn)**:** joining of the nuclei of the male and female reproductive cells

**gestation** (jehs-TAY-shuhn)**:** time it takes an embryo to fully develop inside its mother's body

**Water Animals** Most fish and amphibians lay their eggs in water. An **egg** is a female reproductive cell. The male animal deposits sperm on the eggs. **Sperm** are male reproductive cells. The union of a sperm cell nucleus and an egg cell nucleus is called **fertilization.** Only one sperm cell joins with each egg. In these animals, the eggs are fertilized outside the female's body. After fertilization, the embryo begins to develop inside the egg. Remember, the egg is outside the female's body. The embryo uses food stored in the egg.

◀ **Figure 10-30** Salmon eggs are laid in water.

**1** INFER: Where do the embryos of frogs develop?

**Land Animals** The eggs of reptiles, birds, and mammals are fertilized inside the body of the female. In some animals, such as snakes and birds, the eggs develop a shell after fertilization and are then laid. The embryos develop in the eggs outside the body of the female. The embryo uses the food stored in the egg. You know the food as the yolk.

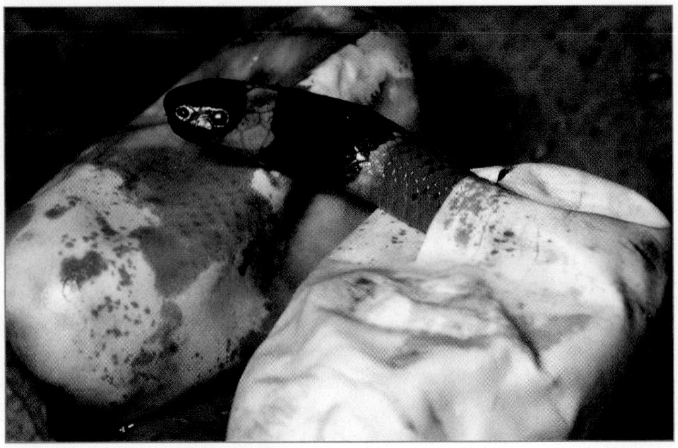

▲ **Figure 10-31** Young snakes develop in eggs with leathery shells.

**2** STATE: Where are the eggs of mammals fertilized?

**Embryo Development in Mammals** In all mammals, fertilization takes place inside the body of the female, or mother. Monotremes are the only mammals that lay eggs. Marsupials and placental mammals do not. In these mammals, the embryo develops inside the mother's body. Most mammals give birth to living young.

◀ **Figure 10-32** A kangaroo embryo develops in its mother's pouch.

The time it takes for an embryo to fully develop inside its mother's body is called **gestation**. Gestation periods are different for different types of animals. The gestation period of a dog is nine weeks. The gestation period of a human is nine months. An elephant's gestation period is between 20 and 22 months.

**3** STATE: Where do the embryos of most mammals develop?

**Embryo Nutrition** The embryos of placental mammals get their food from the mother through the placenta. Digested food and oxygen from the mother's blood pass into the bloodstream of the embryo. The embryo uses this food and oxygen for growth and development. Waste substances produced by the embryo pass into the mother's blood. These wastes are then excreted from the mother's body together with her own waste products.

4 STATE: Where do mammal embryos get their food supply?

## CHECKING CONCEPTS

1. What is an egg?
2. What are sperm?
3. What is fertilization?
4. What is an embryo?
5. Where does an embryo that develops inside an egg get its food?
6. Where do the embryos of placental mammals get their food?
7. Where do the embryos of most mammals develop?

## THINKING CRITICALLY

8. CONTRAST: How is the development of the embryos of most animals different from the development of a mammal embryo?

## BUILDING SCIENCE SKILLS

***Researching*** When you do research, you gather information about a topic. Use library references to find out the gestation periods for the following mammals: whale, mouse, dog, cat, human, horse, and cow. Present your findings in a graph.

## *Hands-On Activity*

### OBSERVING A BIRD EGG

*You will need a chicken egg, a hand lens, and a small dish.*

1. Obtain a raw chicken egg.
2. Use the hand lens to observe the shell of the chicken egg. Describe the shell of the chicken egg.
3. Crack open the egg into the dish.
4. Look at the inside of the shell. Find the shell membrane and the air space. Draw a model of the inside of the eggshell. Label the parts.
5. Look at the egg in the dish. Draw a model of the inside of the egg. Label the yolk and the egg white.

▲ **STEP 2** Examine the shell of the egg.

### Practicing Your Skills

6. OBSERVE: What color is the eggshell? Is the shell smooth or slightly bumpy?
7. IDENTIFY: What part of the egg is the embryo?
8. IDENTIFY: What two parts make up most of the bird egg?
9. INFER: What is the function of the shell? The egg white?
10. HYPOTHESIZE: Why do you think birds make nests for their eggs?

# 10-9 What are innate and learned behaviors?

## INVESTIGATE

### Observing Learning
HANDS-ON ACTIVITY

1. Stand with your back to a partner, who will stand on a chair.
2. Your partner will drop a meter stick in front of you. Try to catch the meter stick.
3. Repeat Step 2 several times. How high was the meter stick when you caught it?

**THINK ABOUT IT:** Were you able to catch the meter stick the first time? How did your reaction change each time?

### Objective
Describe innate and learned behaviors.

### Key Terms
**innate behavior:** behavior an animal is born with

**instinct:** innate behavior that animals perform correctly the first time

**learned behavior:** behavior an animal practices and learns

**Innate Behavior** The way an animal reacts to its environment is called behavior. One type of behavior is **innate behavior,** or behavior an animal is born with. Reflexes are innate behaviors and do not involve any learning or thought and cannot be controlled. Swallowing is a reflex. Another innate behavior is an **instinct.** Animals perform instinctive behaviors correctly the first time. A spider spinning a web is an example of an instinctive behavior.

1 IDENTIFY: What kind of behavior is a reflex?

**Learned Behavior** Behavior that is not innate must be learned. These behaviors are called **learned behaviors.** Learned behaviors are not present at birth. They may not be performed correctly the first time. Learned behaviors usually need to be practiced. Throwing a ball and birds flying are examples of learned behaviors.

2 DESCRIBE: What are learned behaviors?

**Imprinting** Imprinting is another way some animals learn behaviors. Imprinting is a permanent behavior that comes from observations made by an animal during the early stages of development. For example, a newborn animal forms an attachment to the first animal it sees, usually its mother. The newborn then imitates this animal. By imitation, the newborn learns how to find food. Scientists have also learned that imprinting is the means by which an animal recognizes members of its species.

◀ **Figure 10-33** In imprinting, newborns develop an attachment to the first thing they see. These geese imprinted on a human.

3 DEFINE: What is imprinting?

**Trial and Error** Animals also learn behaviors through trial and error. Have you ever tried a new recipe? Each time you make the recipe, you experiment with the ingredients until the finished dish tastes exactly like you want it. This is learning through trial and error. When animals learn behaviors through trial and error, they learn from repeated practice and from their errors until they can perform their new skill perfectly.

**4 DESCRIBE:** What is trial and error?

**Conditioning** Conditioning is one way some animals learn behaviors. In conditioning, behaviors are changed so that a response associated with one stimulus becomes associated with a new stimulus. The response to the new stimulus is a conditioned response. Ivan Pavlov performed an experiment about stimulus and response in dogs. Figure 10-34 shows his experiment.

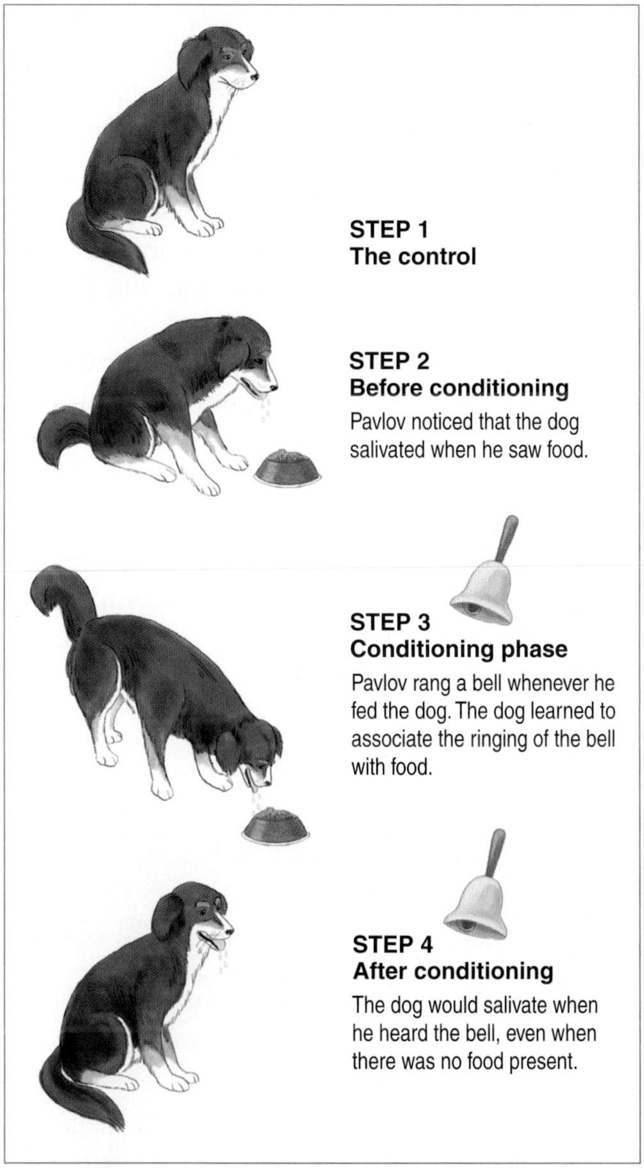


▲ **Figure 10-34** Pavlov experimented with conditioning.

**5 EXPLAIN:** What is conditioning?

**Rewards and Punishment** Rewards can help animals learn new behaviors. B. F. Skinner performed an experiment. He placed a rat in a box with a lever. Behind the lever was food. When the rat accidentally touched the lever, food dropped into the box. The rat learned that pressing the lever caused a reward, the food, to appear.

Punishments can help stop bad behaviors. For example, if your parents punish you for ignoring your chores, you will learn not to ignore your chores again.

**6 IDENTIFY:** Who was B. F. Skinner?

**Insight** Animals also use insight to learn new behaviors. With insight, animals use what they have already learned about a similar problem to solve a new problem. In insight learning, animals perform a task by using what they already know without a period of trial and error.

**7 APPLY:** What is insight?

## ✓ CHECKING CONCEPTS

1. What are the main types of behavior?
2. What is conditioning?
3. How do rewards help animals learn new behaviors?
4. What is a conditioned response?

## THINKING CRITICALLY

5. **ANALYZE:** When have you used insight to solve a problem?
6. **PREDICT:** How would students learn to behave if each time they were late, the teacher awarded the students an A for the day?

## DESIGNING AN EXPERIMENT

*Design an experiment to solve the following problem. Include a hypothesis, variables, a procedure, and a type of data to study.*

PROBLEM: Lara wants her dog to roll over. She gives the dog a command to roll over, but the dog does not respond. How can Lara teach her dog to roll over?

# 10-10 What are social behaviors?

*Objective*

Describe social behaviors.

**Social Behaviors** Animals interact with other animals. These interactions and reactions to other animals are called social behaviors. Most social behaviors are innate behaviors.

Communication is a very important part of social behaviors. Communication is the process of sharing information. Animals communicate in many different ways. Some communicate with sound. A wolf may growl or howl to let other wolves know its position in the pack. Other animals use movement to communicate. When a bee has found food, it returns to the hive and performs a "dance." This allows other bees to know that food has been found and where it is.

1 **IDENTIFY:** What forms of communication have you used today?

**Courtship and Parenting** Before animals of the same species mate, they engage in courtship behaviors. Courtship behaviors allow males and females to recognize each other. Courtship behaviors also signal that both animals are ready to mate and reproduce.

One way animals communicate that they are ready to mate is visually. When a male peacock is seeking a mate, he spreads out the colorful feathers on his lower back.

▲ **Figure 10-35** Male peacocks display their colorful feathers when they are ready to mate.

Animals mate to reproduce. Many fish, amphibians, and reptiles do not care for their young. The young are on their own once they are born. Other animals, such as birds and mammals, care for their offspring. They feed and protect them. In addition, they teach them how to survive on their own.

2 **EXPLAIN:** What are courtship behaviors?

**Territory** All animals need space in which to live, reproduce, and find food. This space is called an animal's territory. Many animals claim a territory as their own. They defend their territories from other members of the same species.

Many animals make substances in special scent glands. Some mammals rub against trees and bushes to spread their scent and mark their territory. Scent-marking is a form of communication. By scent-marking its territory, an animal warns others in its species to keep away.

3 **DEFINE:** What is a territory?

**Aggression** Animals often compete for territory and other limited resources, such as food, water, and mates. Sometimes when animals compete, they display aggressive behaviors. Aggressive behaviors are threatening behaviors. Animals use aggressive behaviors to intimidate and control other animals. Some aggressive behaviors are visual. The skin around an Australian frill lizard's neck fans out when it is faced with danger. Some animals use sound. When faced with a threat, a dog may growl.

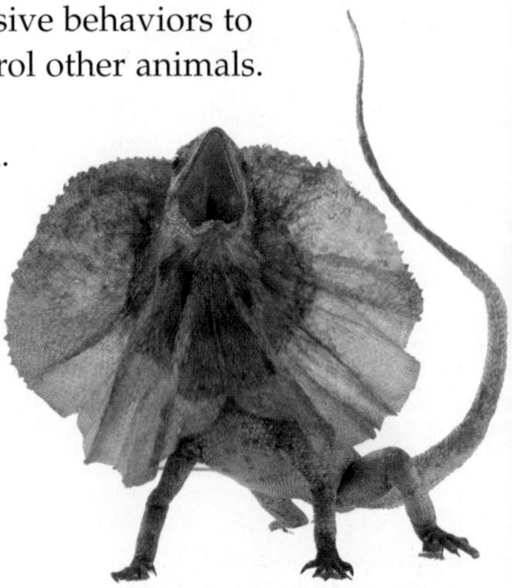

▲ **Figure 10-36** This lizard expands its frills when it is threatened.

4 **EXPLAIN:** How do animals use aggressive behaviors?

**Societies** Animals often live in groups with other members of their species. These groups are called societies. In societies, animals work together for the benefit of the whole society. Each member of the society has a specific job. For example, in a honeybee society, the job of the drone is to mate with the queen bee. Most societies have leaders. In a society of gorillas, the strongest male is usually the leader.

▲ **Figure 10-37** The silverback is often the head of a gorilla society.

5 **APPLY:** How is a sports team like a society?

## CHECKING CONCEPTS

1. What is communication?
2. How do bees communicate with each other?
3. How do peacocks display courtship behaviors?
4. What is scent-marking?
5. What is a society?

## THINKING CRITICALLY

6. **EXPLAIN:** Why is communication an important part of social behaviors?
7. **APPLY:** What are some benefits to living in a society?
8. **IDENTIFY:** What are some social behaviors humans engage in?
9. **INFER:** Look at the photos of animals on these two pages. What adaptations have they evolved to help their social behaviors?

## *Integrating Physical Science*

**TOPIC: chemistry**

### PHEROMONES

Scent is another way animals in the same species communicate. Pheromones are chemical scents that are made by one animal and influence the behavior of other animals in the same species. Pheromones are unique. Pheromones are made up of long chains of atoms. Each pheromone has a different set of atoms and a unique chemical structure when the atoms combine. This means that no two species have the same pheromone. In fact, some species have several pheromones that identify members of different societies.

▲ **Figure 10-38** The sensors on the antennae of this male Atlas silkworm can pick up the scent of a female Atlas silkworm's pheromones.

Animals use pheromones to establish their territories, find mates, and identify members of their society. When scent-marking a territory, dogs use pheromones. The female Atlas silkworm uses pheromones to let males know she is ready to mate. If an ant wanders into a different colony, its pheromone alerts the members of the colony to its presence. The members of the colony then attack the stranger.

Go Online
*active art*
**For:** Pheromones activity
**Visit:** PHSchool.com
**Web Code:** cep-2052

**Thinking Critically** How could pheromones be used to help control insects at a picnic?

# Chapter 10 Challenges

## Chapter Summary

**Lesson 10-1**

- Chordates are animals that have a **notochord** at some time during their development. Animals with a backbone are **vertebrates.**

**Lesson 10-2**

- Fish are **ectothermic** marine animals that breathe through **gills.** Some types of fish are jawless fish, cartilaginous fish, and bony fish.

**Lessons 10-3 and 10-4**

- **Amphibians** are ectothermic animals that live part of their lives in water and part on land. They usually have smooth skin and webbed feet.
- Amphibians lay eggs without shells in water. As a **larva** develops into an adult, it develops legs, loses its tail, develops lungs, and loses its gills.

**Lesson 10-5**

- Reptiles are ectothermic land animals that lay eggs. They have lungs and scaly, waterproof skin.
- Reptiles are classified into four orders: tuataras, snakes and lizards, turtles and tortoises, and alligators and crocodiles.

**Lesson 10-6**

- Birds are **endotherms.** They are the only animals with feathers.
- Birds can be classified by comparing the shapes of their beaks and feet.

**Lesson 10-7**

- Mammals are endotherms that have body hair, a four-chambered heart, and a highly developed nervous system. They nurse their young with milk produced in **mammary glands.**

**Lesson 10-8**

- The **eggs** of land and sea mammals are fertilized inside the body of the mother. In most mammals, the embryo develops inside the mother's body.

**Lessons 10-9 and 10-10**

- A reflex is an **innate behavior. Learned behavior** must be practiced.
- Social behaviors, such as courtship, are how animals interact with other animals.

## Key Term Challenges

amphibian (p. 232)
cartilage (p. 230)
chordate (p. 228)
ectotherm (p. 230)
egg (p. 246)
endotherm (p. 238)
fertilization (p. 246)
gestation (p. 246)
gill (p. 230)
innate behavior (p. 248)
instinct (p. 248)
larva (p. 234)
learned behavior (p. 248)
mammary gland (p. 242)
marsupial (p. 242)
monotreme (p. 242)
notochord (p. 228)
placenta (p. 242)
sperm (p. 246)
swim bladder (p. 230)
tadpole (p. 234)
vertebrate (p. 228)

MATCHING **Write the Key Term from above that best matches each description.**

1. union of a sperm cell nucleus and an egg cell nucleus
2. organ used for obtaining oxygen dissolved in water
3. animal with a backbone
4. organ in female mammals that produces milk
5. organ through which materials are exchanged between the mother and the developing embryo
6. organ that allows a fish to remain at any depth in the water

APPLYING DEFINITIONS **Explain the difference between the terms in each pair. Write your answers in complete sentences.**

7. sperm, egg
8. ectotherm, endotherm
9. amphibians, reptiles
10. cartilage, bone
11. marsupials, monotremes
12. notochord, nerve cord
13. gills, lungs
14. larva, tadpole
15. innate behavior, learned behavior

## *Content Challenges* TEST PREP

MULTIPLE CHOICE **Write the letter of the term or phrase that best completes each statement.**

1. The three features common to all chordates are a hollow nerve cord, gill slits at some time during their development, and
   **a.** cartilage.
   **b.** a notochord.
   **c.** an endoskeleton.
   **d.** a placenta.

2. In most adult chordates, the notochord is replaced by
   **a.** gills slits.
   **b.** lungs.
   **c.** a backbone.
   **d.** an endoskeleton.

3. Fish are classified as either hagfish, lampreys, cartilaginous fish, or
   **a.** bony fish.
   **b.** tailless fish.
   **c.** tailed fish.
   **d.** venomous fish.

4. Fish, amphibians, and reptiles all
   **a.** are ectotherms.
   **b.** are endotherms.
   **c.** have a three-chambered heart.
   **d.** have smooth, moist skin.

5. Amphibians are classified into three orders based on their
   **a.** heart chambers.
   **b.** lungs.
   **c.** body structures.
   **d.** skin.

6. In the larval stage, a frog is called
   **a.** a toad.
   **b.** an egg.
   **c.** an adult.
   **d.** a tadpole.

7. The largest order of reptiles is made up of
   **a.** tuataras.
   **b.** snakes and lizards.
   **c.** turtles and tortoises.
   **d.** alligators and crocodiles.

8. Both birds and mammals
   **a.** have lightweight bones.
   **b.** have mammary glands.
   **c.** are endotherms.
   **d.** are ectotherms.

9. The duckbill platypus is
   **a.** a placental mammal.
   **b.** a pouched mammal.
   **c.** an egg-laying mammal.
   **d.** a marine mammal.

10. Biologists believe mammals come from a group of animals called
    **a.** dinosaurs.
    **b.** therapsids.
    **c.** carnivores.
    **d.** marsupials.

11. Blinking is
    **a.** a learned behavior.
    **b.** a conditioned response.
    **c.** an innate behavior.
    **d.** a stimulus.

TRUE/FALSE **Write *true* if the statement is true. If the statement is false, change the underlined term to make the statement true.**

12. Fish, amphibians, reptiles, birds, and mammals are invertebrates.
13. When you use what you already know to solve a problem, you are using trial and error.
14. Animals are born with learned behaviors.
15. Communication is a very important part of social behaviors.

## *Concept Challenges* TEST PREP

WRITTEN RESPONSE **Answer each of the following questions in complete sentences.**

1. DISCUSS: How do ectothermic animals differ from endothermic animals? Are humans ectotherms or endotherms? Explain.
2. DESCRIBE: What are the major characteristics of an amphibian? Explain the characteristics that help it survive in its environment.
3. CONTRAST: What are three differences between amphibians and reptiles?
4. INFER: Why do you think birds that feed on seeds have short, strong beaks?
5. COMPARE: In what two ways are birds and mammals alike?
6. CONTRAST: How is insight different from trial-and-error learning?

INTERPRETING A DIAGRAM **Use Figure 10-39 to answer the following questions.**

7. What is the part of the fish labeled *B*?
8. What is the part of the fish labeled *C*?
9. What does the part labeled *C* protect?
10. Which parts help the fish swim through the water?
11. What is the part of the fish labeled *E*?
12. What is the function of the part labeled *E*?

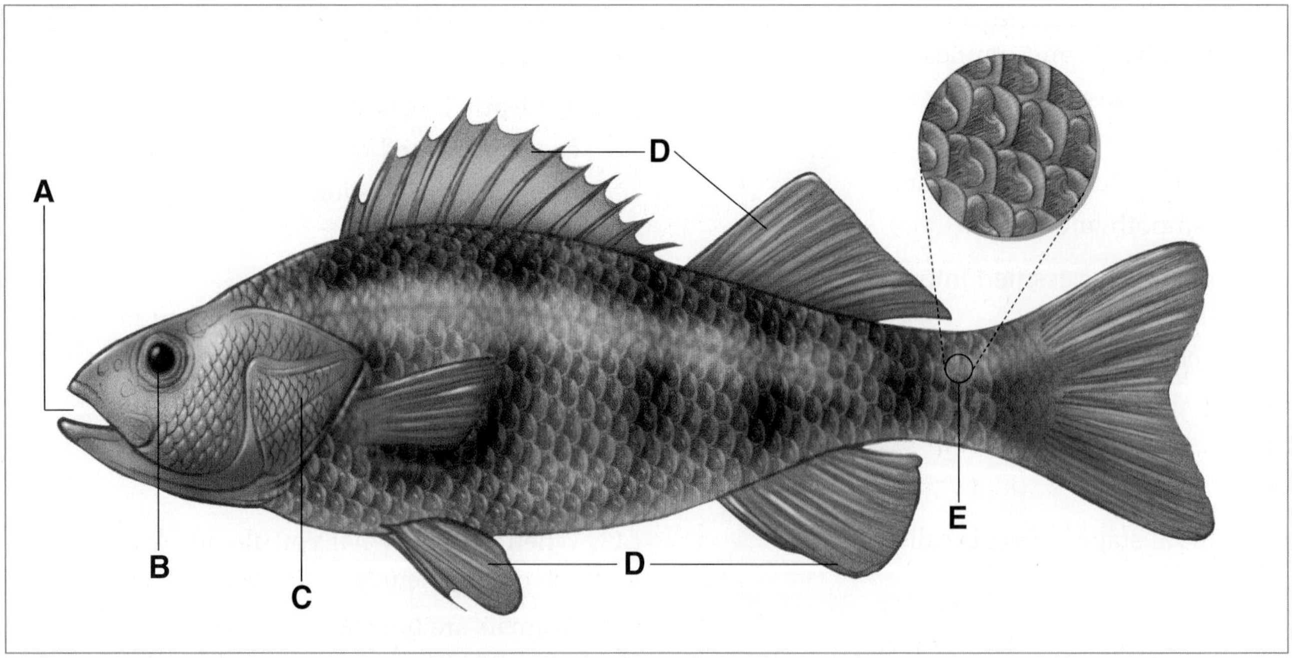


▲ **Figure 10-39** A fish

# Chapter 11 Living Things and the Environment

▲ **Figure 11-1** The Sonoran desert is the environment of the cactus.

## Contents



It may seem impossible that a living thing could survive in the dry environment of a desert. However, there are many species of plants and animals that live in deserts. All of the organisms that live in this kind of environment must be able to endure long periods of drought.

▶What features of the cacti shown in Figure 11-1 might allow them to survive in the desert? What do you think might happen if desert organisms were moved to an area that received a large amount of rainfall?

# 11-1 What is ecology?

## *Objective*

Describe how organisms interact with their environments.

## *Key Terms*

**environment** (ehn-VY-ruhn-muhnt)**:** everything that surrounds an organism and acts upon it

**ecology** (ee-KAHL-uh-jee)**:** study of the relationship between living things and their environments

**interact:** process of organisms acting upon one another or on the nonliving parts of their environment

**Ecology** Everything that surrounds a living thing makes up its **environment.** Living things are affected by their environments. Living things also have an effect on their environments.

The study of the relationship between living things and their environments is called **ecology.** Scientists who study ecology are ecologists. Ecologists study how living things are adapted, or suited, to their environments.

**1 DEFINE:** What is ecology?

**Importance of the Environment** All living things need materials to carry out their life processes. Organisms get all the materials they need from their environments. Some materials, called nutrients, are used by living things for growth and energy. Green plants get nutrients and water from soil. They take carbon dioxide from the air. They use sunlight, water, minerals, and carbon dioxide to grow and to make food for energy. Plants also take in oxygen from the air and use it for cellular respiration.

Many animals get nutrients and energy by eating plants. Other animals get nutrients and energy by eating animals. Most animals get oxygen from the air. Fish get their oxygen from the dissolved oxygen in water.

**2 LIST:** What are some materials that organisms get from their environment?

**Interactions** Look at Figure 11-2. It shows a marsh environment. Many different kinds of organisms live in marshes. The organisms living here **interact,** or act on each other. The organisms also interact with the nonliving parts of the environment, such as the water and the soil. For example, snails such as the periwinkle feed on grasses and algae living in the marsh. The wastes produced by the snail enrich

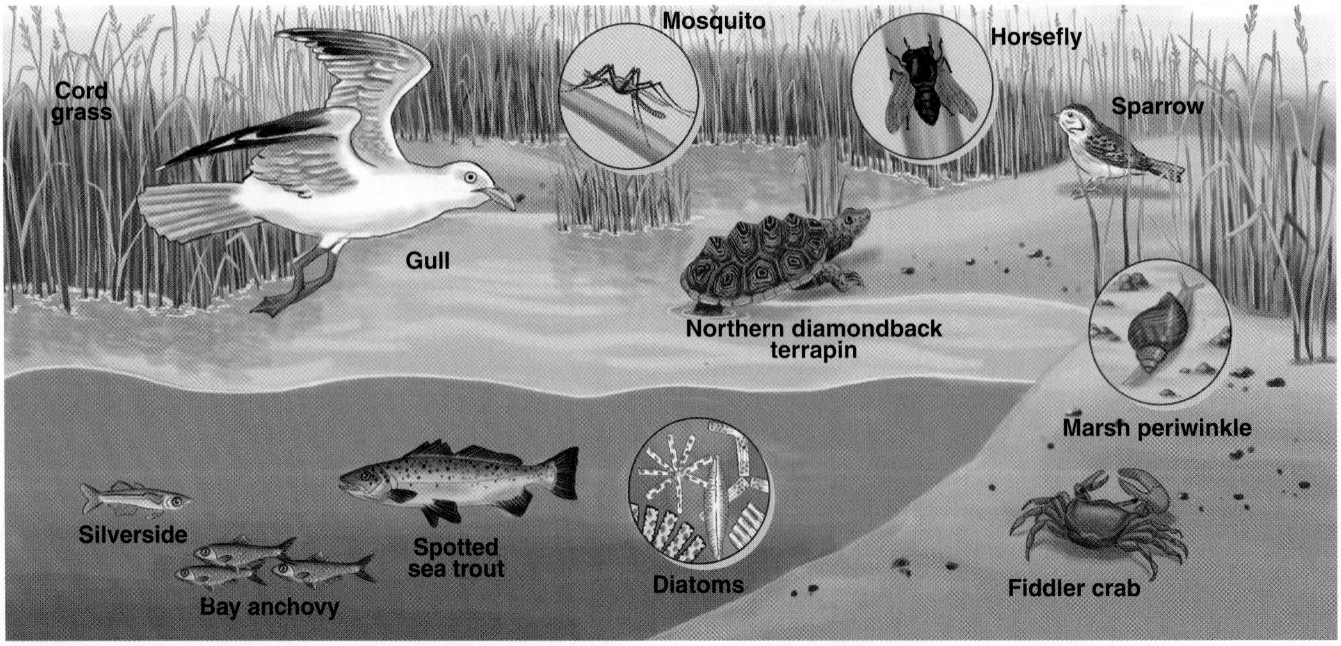


▲ **Figure 11-2** Many species live and interact in a marsh.

the soil. The enriched soil makes the grasses grow better. The grasses, soil, and snail each have an effect on the others. An interaction also takes place between birds and snails. Some birds, such as gulls, eat snails. If there are many birds hunting snails, the number of snails will decrease. With fewer snails, some birds will have to find other food. Some will die from a lack of food. As a result, the number of birds will decrease.

3 **INFER:** What will happen to the number of snails if the number of birds decreases?

## CHECKING CONCEPTS

1. All of the things that surround an organism makes up its __________.
2. __________ study the relationship between living things and their environments.
3. Plants use sunlight, water, minerals, and __________ to grow and to make food.
4. The organisms in an environment __________ with each other.

## THINKING CRITICALLY

5. **INFER:** Suppose a green plant was placed in a dark basement. How would this environment affect the plant?
6. **RELATE:** How is your living space an environment? What materials do you get from your environment?

### Web InfoSearch

**The Everglades** The Everglades is a large region in Florida made up of several different kinds of living spaces, such as rivers, lakes, marshes, and forests of mangrove trees.

**SEARCH:** Use the Internet to find out more about the Everglades. Pick one type of environment found in the Everglades and describe that environment in a report. Start your search at www.conceptsandchallenges.com. Some key search words are **Everglades** and **Florida.**

## *People in Science*

### FIELD BIOLOGIST

Ecologists can be involved in different aspects of ecology. Many ecologists are field biologists. They work outdoors, collecting data from plant surveys, bird counts, and similar activities. Many ecologists use mathematics and computer models and develop field and laboratory experiments to create possible explanations for the data that have been collected. Still other ecologists work on conservation and education. They design nature preserves, study ways to protect fragile environments, and help prevent the extinction of species.

▲ **Figure 11-3** Ecologists like Dirzo study organisms and their environments.

Rodolfo Dirzo is a field biologist who is interested in the loss of animals in tropical areas. Among other things, he analyzes the ecology of tropical environments, mostly in Mexico. Dirzo wants to know how the loss of animals in Mexico may affect plant life in the area. To become a field biologist, Dirzo got advanced degrees in science.

**Thinking Critically** Rodolfo Dirzo believes that education about ecology is important. Do you agree? Explain.

# 11-2 What is an ecosystem?

*Objective*

Describe the parts of an ecosystem.

*Key Terms*

**population:** group of the same kind of organisms living in a certain place

**community:** all the populations that live in a certain place and can interact with one another

**ecosystem** (EE-koh-sihs-tuhm)**:** group of communities interacting with each other and the nonliving parts of their environment

**Populations** A **population** is all of the same species of organisms living in a certain place. Different populations may live in the same environment. Look at the first photograph in Figure 11-4. There is a herd of zebras. These zebras make up one population of the grassland.

1 INFER: Can a lion and a gazelle be part of the same population?

**Communities** Look at the second photograph in Figure 11-4. This shows a herd of zebras together with a population of wildebeest. The grasses are another population. All the different populations living in a certain place make up a **community.** This community is made up of the three populations you see in the second photograph in Figure 11-4, along with others that are not shown, such as ants and termites.

2 DEFINE: What is a community?

**Ecosystem** Several communities together make up an ecosystem. An **ecosystem** is a group of communities interacting with each other and the nonliving parts of their environment. Nonliving parts of an environment include water, air, and soil.

There are many kinds of ecosystems. An ecosystem can be as large as a desert or as small as a rotting log. Ecosystems can be rivers, lakes, or ponds. Even a puddle of water can be an ecosystem. In Figure 11-4, the ecosystem is a grassland in Africa.

3 LIST: List three living and three nonliving parts of an ecosystem.

**A Self-Supporting Unit** An ecosystem is a self-supporting unit. Four processes occur in an ecosystem to make it self-supporting.

- **Production of Energy** The Sun is the source of energy in most ecosystems.
- **Transfer of Energy** Energy is transferred from the Sun to plants that make their own food. The stored energy in plants is transferred to animals that eat the plants. Energy is transferred to other animals when they eat the plant-eating animals.

| POPULATION | COMMUNITY IN AN ECOSYSTEM |
|---|---|
|  |  |

▲ **Figure 11-4** Zebras are one population in this grassland community.

- **Breakdown of Materials** When organisms die, their bodies decompose, or break down. The chemicals are reused by other living things.
- **Recycling** The materials needed by organisms in an ecosystem are recycled, or used over and over.

4 LIST: What are the four processes that make an ecosystem self-supporting?

## CHECKING CONCEPTS

1. All the different kinds of organisms that live in a pond make up a __________.
2. All the living and nonliving things in an environment together with their interactions make up __________.
3. When organisms die, their bodies __________.
4. When animals eat green plants, the stored __________ in the plants is transferred.

## THINKING CRITICALLY

5. **CONTRAST:** What is the difference between a population and a community?
6. **PREDICT:** What might happen to the populations shown in Figure 11-4 if there was a severe drought?

## INTERPRETING VISUALS

*Use Figure 11-5 to answer the following questions.*

7. **OBSERVE:** How many different populations live in the pond?
8. **OBSERVE:** What is the size of the turtle population of the pond?
9. **EXPLAIN:** Why is the pond considered an ecosystem?

▲ **Figure 11-5** A pond ecosystem

## *Integrating Earth Science*

**TOPICS: water cycle, salinity**

### THE GAIA HYPOTHESIS

The amount of salt in a given amount of water is called salinity. The salinity of Earth's oceans is about 3.5%. Rainwater seeps into the ground and also collects in rivers and lakes. Then, running water picks up salt from the rocks and soil it passes over and carries it to the oceans. This cycle has been going on for millions of years. Yet, the salinity of the oceans does not increase.

▲ **Figure 11-6** Earth seen from space

James Lovelock and Lynn Margulis proposed a hypothesis that may help explain how Earth's salinity has remained the same over millions of years. The hypothesis is called the Gaia Hypothesis. According to this hypothesis, Earth acts as a living organism. The parts of Earth work together just as the parts of a body work together. The living components of Earth, such as plants and animals, have a direct effect on the different cycles of Earth. In other words, the living things control the nonliving things. Lovelock and Margulis proposed that over time this has helped maintain balance in Earth's cycles.

**Thinking Critically** Compare the Gaia Hypothesis to homeostasis.

# 11-3 What are habitats and niches?

### *Objective*

Explain how organisms may have the same habitat but not the same niche.

### *Key Terms*

**habitat** (HAB-ih-tat)**:** place where an organism lives

**niche** (NIHCH)**:** organism's role, or job, in its habitat

**Habitat** The place where an organism lives is its **habitat.** The habitat of an organism has the food and water the organism needs to live. An organism's habitat also provides shelter and a place to reproduce.

There are many different kinds of habitats. Habitats can be very large or very small. There are land habitats and water habitats. An ocean is the habitat of a whale. The habitat of a woodpecker can be a forest. An anthill is a habitat.

▲ **Figure 11-7** This cave is a habitat for thousands of ghost bats.

**1** **INFER:** What is your habitat?

**Niche** What is your role, or job, in life? Did you answer that you are a student? Being a student is the role that you carry out where you live. Organisms also have roles in their communities. The role of each organism is its **niche.** It includes everything an organism does and everything it needs.

**2** **IDENTIFY:** What is a niche?

**Different Niches** Many kinds of organisms share the same habitat. Polar bears and seals both swim in the icy waters of the Arctic Ocean. They have different needs and roles in the habitat. Polar bears hunt seals and other animals. Seals feed on fish. Polar bears have one kind of shelter. Seals have another. They live in the same habitat, but they do not have the same niche.

▲ **Figure 11-8** Polar bears, fish, and seals live in the same habitat but have different niches.

Two populations cannot have the same niche for very long. For example, one animal may be able to hunt better and also find shelter better than another animal. The animals that hunt better or are better able to find shelter are more likely to survive and reproduce. Eventually, members of other populations may be crowded out. The niches of both populations may also change so that both populations can adapt to one another.

**3** **INFER:** Can a seal and a fish share the same habitat? The same niche?

## CHECKING CONCEPTS

1. A forest can be the __________ of woodpeckers.
2. An organism's habitat has the food and __________ the organism needs to live.
3. The role of an organism in its habitat is its __________.
4. An anthill is an example of a __________.
5. If two populations have the same niche, the population best-suited to the niche will __________.

## THINKING CRITICALLY

6. **PREDICT:** Two populations of moths live in the same habitat. They will share the same niche. What will happen to these populations?
7. **INFER:** The habitat of a rattlesnake is the hot, dry desert. Could this organism live in an arctic habitat? Explain.
8. **CLASSIFY:** In which kinds of habitats do each of the following organisms live—water, air, or land?
   - **a.** blue jay
   - **b.** garter snake
   - **c.** seaweed
   - **d.** shark
   - **e.** water lily
   - **f.** bat

## BUILDING SCIENCE SKILLS

***Researching*** Many species of plants and animals have become endangered or extinct because of a loss of habitat. When people build new roads, houses, and offices, the natural habitat for wildlife is lost. Research endangered plants and animals. Make a list that includes the species, their habitats, and the possible causes of their decline.

## *Real-Life Science*

### NONNATIVE SPECIES

Species that are taken from one environment and put into a new environment are called nonnative species. These organisms are usually introduced to the new location accidentally. When there are no native species to compete with, the nonnative species become very successful in their new surroundings. However, nonnative species can be a threat to organisms already living in the environment.

▲ **Figure 11-9** These zebra mussels have clogged this pipe.

The zebra mussel is an example of a nonnative species that is a threat to native species. In 1988, this mollusk was accidentally brought to the Great Lakes. The zebra mussel quickly spread to many other parts of the country by attaching to the sides of boats. Today, these mollusks can be found in at least 20 states. Most ecologists feel the zebra mussels are a nuisance because they clog water pipes and disturb the food webs of the ecosystem. However, some scientists feel zebra mussels have improved the water quality of the Great Lakes by filter feeding algae and other microscopic organisms.

**Thinking Critically** Do you think the zebra mussels should be controlled by humans or left alone?

# 11-4 What are limiting factors?

***Objective***

Explain what affects population size.

***Key Terms***

**limiting factor:** condition in the environment that puts limits on the size a population can grow to

**carrying capacity:** largest population size that can be supported by the available resources of an area

**range** (RAYNJ): area where a type of animal or plant population is found

**Limiting Factors** Certain conditions in the environment limit how much a population can grow. These conditions are called **limiting factors.** Suppose a type of plant needs a lot of water to survive. In an area with little rainfall, only a few of these plants might be able to survive. The amount of water is a limiting factor for the plant. Other limiting factors of plants are the amount of sunlight and the type of soil. Animals also are limited by conditions in the environment. Limiting factors of animals include temperature, water, food supply, and shelter.

▲ **Figure 11-10** This black-footed ferret lives in a burrow. What do you think are some of this ferret's limiting factors?

**1** **LIST:** What are three limiting factors of plants?

**Plants as Limiting Factors** The number of green plants in a community is a limiting factor of the animals in the community. Suppose many green plants in a meadow died. Some of the mice that eat the plants would starve. With fewer mice to eat, some of the owls also would starve. Even though owls do not eat plants, the number of owls is affected by the number of plants. The sizes of animal populations are limited by the sizes of plant populations.

**2** **PREDICT:** How would the number of mice and owls change if more plants grew than usual?

**Carrying Capacity** The largest population that can be supported by an area is the area's **carrying capacity.** An area has different carrying capacities for different populations. When a population becomes too large, some of its members must move or they will die from lack of resources. The spread of organisms from one area to another is called dispersal (dih-SPUR-suhl). Look at the graph in Figure 11-11. It shows the growth of a population as it approaches the carrying capacity. The actual growth pattern of a population may not always follow this model. In nature, growth rates and carrying capacity change as the environment changes.

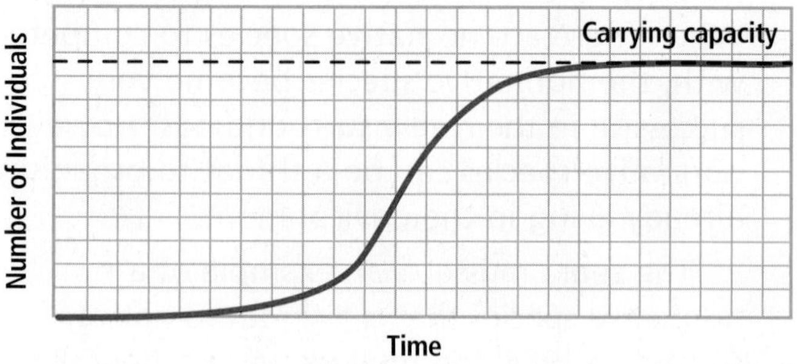


▲ **Figure 11-11** This graph can be used to show carrying capacity.

**3** **DEFINE:** What is carrying capacity?

**Range** The area where a kind of population lives is called its **range.** The size of an organism's range is determined by its limiting factors. For example, American black bears can eat a large variety of foods, including berries, nuts, and small mammals. As a result, their range is large.

American black bears can be found across much of the United States. Giant pandas eat only bamboo. The range for the giant panda is very small. Pandas are only found in forested areas of China.

4 **RELATE:** What is the relationship between an organism's diet and its range?

## CHECKING CONCEPTS

1. A limiting factor of plants is the amount of __________.
2. The sizes of animal populations are limited by the __________ populations.
3. Carrying capacity is the __________ size of a population that can be supported by an area.
4. The area where a type of plant or animal population is found is its __________.
5. The __________ of a range is determined by an organism's limiting factors.

## THINKING CRITICALLY

6. **INFER:** Why are humans able to live in a variety of places on Earth?
7. **RELATE:** Do changes in the size of plant populations have an effect on humans?

### Web InfoSearch

**Human Population Growth** The current population of Earth is over 6 billion people. As this number increases, there may be less food, land, and other resources for each person.

**SEARCH:** Use the Internet to find out more about human population growth. Make a line graph showing the increase in population from the year 1800 to the present. Start your search at www.conceptsandchallenges.com. Some key search words are **world population growth** and **demography.**

## *Hands-On Activity*

### GRAPHING POPULATION GROWTH

*You will need graph paper, a regular pencil, two different colored pencils, and a ruler.*

1. Draw a horizontal line across the bottom of the graph paper. Label this line the *x*-axis. Draw a vertical line up the left side of the paper from where the first line begins. Label this line the *y*-axis.
2. Label the *x*-axis "Year." Just below the *x*-axis, write the years from the data in Figure 11-12.
3. Label the *y*-axis "Population Size." Going up the *y*-axis, number from 0 to 500 in intervals of 25. Start with zero at the point where the *x*- and *y*-axes meet.
4. Use the data in Figure 11-12 to make a line graph for the deer population. Use the same color for each year. Then, connect all of the dots using a ruler.
5. Using a different colored pencil, repeat Step 4 for the wolf population.

| POPULATION DATA TABLE | | |
|---|---|---|
| Year | White-tailed Deer | Gray Wolves |
| 1986 | 285 | 85 |
| 1988 | 140 | 110 |
| 1990 | 75 | 140 |
| 1992 | 145 | 55 |
| 1994 | 300 | 10 |
| 1996 | 455 | 40 |
| 1998 | 305 | 80 |
| 2000 | 180 | 120 |

▲ **Figure 11-12** Use the data in this table to create your graph.

Go Online
*active art*
**For:** Changes in Population activity
**Visit:** PHSchool.com
**Web Code:** cep-5012

### Practicing Your Skills

6. **HYPOTHESIZE:** What do you think are the limiting factors of the deer? The wolf?
7. **INFER:** Based on the graph, what affect do you think the wolf population has on the deer population?

# 11-5 What are biomes?

*Objective*

Describe different biomes.

*Key Terms*

**climate:** average weather of an area over a long period of time

**biome** (BY-ohm)**:** large region with a characteristic climate and plant and animal communities

**Biomes** The average weather of an area over a long period of time is the area's **climate.** Climate helps determine the kinds of plants and animals that live in an area. A **biome** is a large region that has similar types of plants and animals regardless of where on Earth it is located. Each biome has a particular climate and type of soil.

1 **DEFINE:** What is a biome?

**Seven Major Land Biomes** Particular kinds of organisms live in different biomes. Biomes often are named for their most common plants. Earth's land areas can be divided into seven major biomes.

- The **tundra** is found in the far north. The ground is permanently frozen. Mosses, lichens, grasses, small flowers, and shrubs are the only plants that can survive in the tundra. Animals that live in the tundra include birds, wolves, foxes, and reindeer.

▲ **Figure 11-13** Only small plants grow in the tundra.

- South of the tundra is an area with a cold climate called the **taiga**. The taiga receives enough rainfall for trees to grow. Coniferous (koh-NIHF-uhr-uhs) forests made up of evergreens cover the area. Many animals, such as moose, squirrels, rabbits, and beavers, live in the coniferous forest biome.
- South of the taiga is a region with a moderate climate. This biome, called the **temperate deciduous forest**, has a long growing season followed by a cold winter. Deciduous trees, such as oak, maple, and birch, grow well here. Unlike the needles of evergreens, the leaves of deciduous trees fall off in autumn. Many kinds of birds and animals live in the deciduous forest biome.
- Some areas have a moderate climate but not enough rain for tall trees to grow. These areas are grasslands. There are two biomes that can be considered grasslands—the temperate grasslands and the savannas. **Temperate grasslands** can be found in the interior of continents. Because of their rich soils, much of the temperate grasslands have been used for farming. **Savannas** are similar to temperate grasslands but are found closer to the equator. Large herds of animals feed on the many kinds of grasses that grow in this biome. Savannas also have some scattered trees and shrubs.
- **Tropical rain forests** occur in areas near the equator. These regions receive large amounts of rainfall and are hot all year. Tall trees and many kinds of plants grow well in tropical rain forests. Many different animals also live in this biome.
- **Deserts** form where temperatures are moderate or hot, and where there is very little rain. Very few plants can grow in desert biomes. The plants that do grow in this biome, such as cacti, must be well suited for hot, dry conditions. Many kinds of animals, such as birds, lizards, and scorpions, live in the desert.

2 **ANALYZE:** Look at Figure 11-14. In which biome do you live?

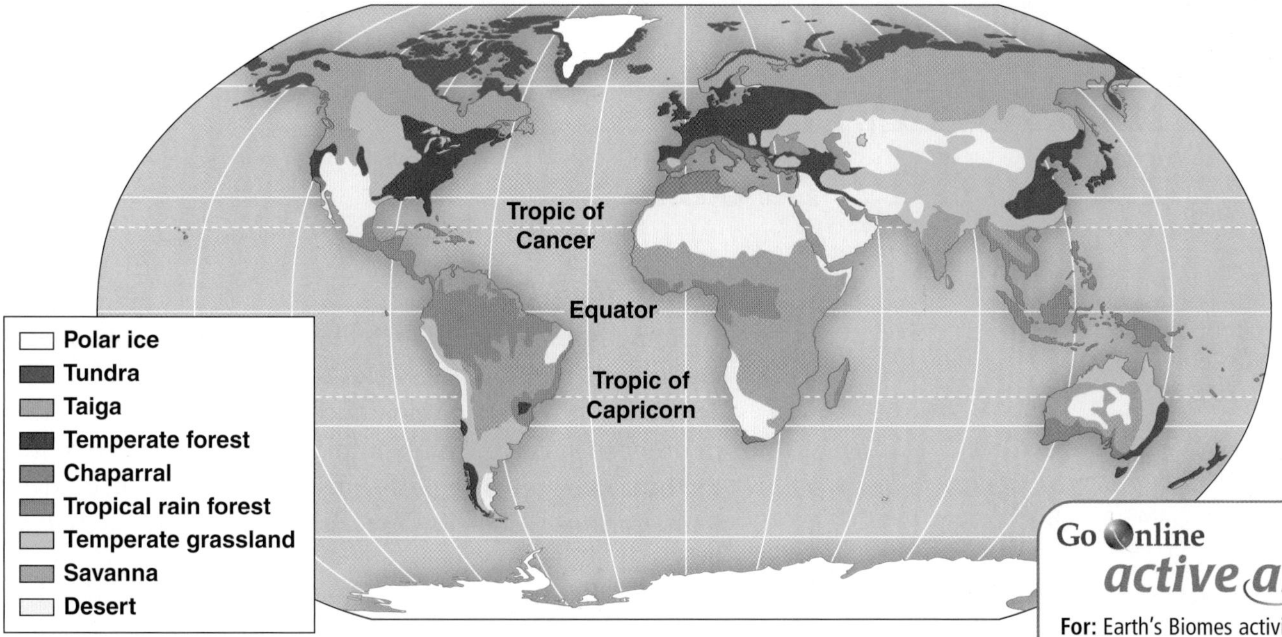


▲ **Figure 11-14** Earth can be divided into many different biomes.

**Go Online** *active art*
**For:** Earth's Biomes activity
**Visit:** PHSchool.com
**Web Code:** cep-5024

**Other Biomes** In addition to the major land biomes, there are other minor biomes. These include the polar ice biome and the chaparral zones. The **polar ice biome** surrounds the North and South Poles and has extremely cold temperatures. This biome is composed of thick sheets of ice and may appear lifeless. However, large populations of penguins live in the polar regions near the South Pole.

▲ **Figure 11-15** Penguins live in a polar ice biome.

The **chaparral** is found in coastal areas that have mild and rainy winters and long, dry summers. Some of the plants in this biome have adaptations that help them regrow after frequent fires. These fires usually occur during lightning storms in the dry summer months. Some examples of chaparral are along the coasts of California and the Mediterranean.

3 **CONTRAST:** How are polar ice zones and chaparral different?

## ✓ CHECKING CONCEPTS

1. The coldest biome is the ___________.
2. The biome that is hot and wet is the ___________.
3. The biome that occurs in coastal areas with mild, rainy winters is the ___________.

## THINKING CRITICALLY

4. **INFER:** Why do more kinds of animals live in the deciduous forest than in the tundra?
5. **CONTRAST:** How are deserts and tropical rain forests different?

## Web InfoSearch

**Aquatic Life Zones** There are also different aquatic, or water, life zones. These can either be freshwater or saltwater life zones. Examples of freshwater ecosystems are rivers and lakes. Oceans also have different life zones.

**SEARCH:** Use the Internet to find out more about an aquatic life zone in your area. Make a poster depicting the life zone. Start your search at www.conceptsandchallenges.com. Some key search words are **ocean zones, aquatic life zone,** and **freshwater ecosystem.**

# LAB ACTIVITY
# Exploring Biomes

## Materials
- Safety goggles
- Plastic containers with lids
- 3 Thermometers
- Piece of foam rubber
- Scissors
- Tape
- Article of warm clothing such as a sock or mitten
- 3 Colored pencils
- Water

▲ **STEP 1** Label the small containers.

▲ **STEP 3** Insert a thermometer into the hole in each lid.

### *BACKGROUND*

A biome is a region of Earth that has characteristic plant and animal communities. These organisms must be adapted to the environmental conditions of that biome in order to survive. For example, organisms that live in the tundra or polar regions must be able to withstand temperatures well below freezing. Many animals that live in these biomes have a layer of fat or thick fur to insulate themselves from the cold.

### *PURPOSE*

In this activity, you will explore how insulation helps organisms handle long periods of very cold temperatures.

### *PROCEDURE*

1. Put on the goggles. Label the small containers *A*, *B*, and *C*. These will represent three animals.

2. Measure an equal amount of hot tap water into each of the three small containers.
⚠ CAUTION: Be careful when handling hot water.

3. Use the scissors to make a hole in the middle of each lid. Make sure the hole is only large enough for a thermometer to fit through. Put the lids on the containers. Insert a thermometer into each lid.
⚠ CAUTION: Be careful when using scissors.

4. Leave container *A* as it is. This will represent an animal with no insulation.

5. Place the article of warm clothing on container *B*. This will represent an animal with some fur.

6. Wrap the piece of foam rubber around container *C*. Make sure the foam rubber completely covers all sides of the container. Secure the foam rubber with tape. This will represent an animal with a thick coat of fur.

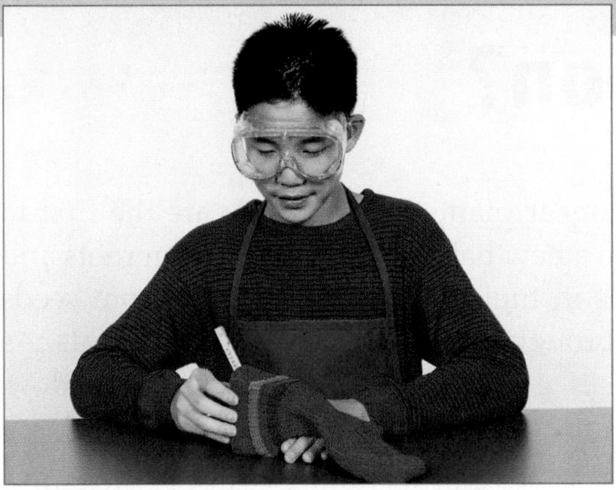


▲ **STEP 5** Place an article of warm clothing on container *B*.

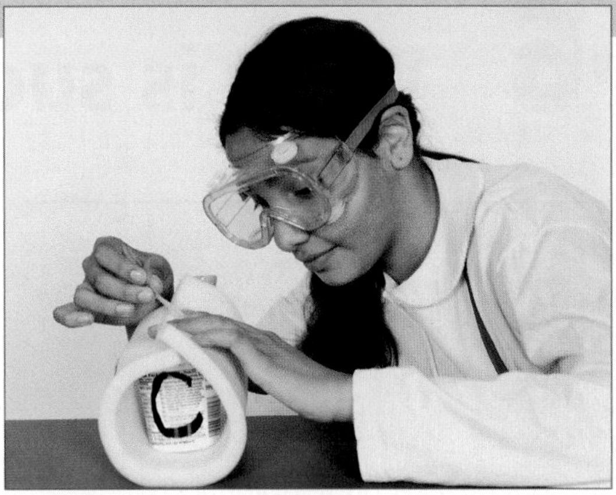


▲ **STEP 6** Wrap a piece of foam rubber around container *C*.

7. Copy the chart in Figure 11-16 onto a sheet of paper. Record the temperature of each container under the heading "0 min."

8. Wait 5 minutes. Record the temperature of the water in each container again under the appropriate heading on your chart.

9. Repeat Step 8 after 10 minutes have passed and again after 15 minutes have passed.

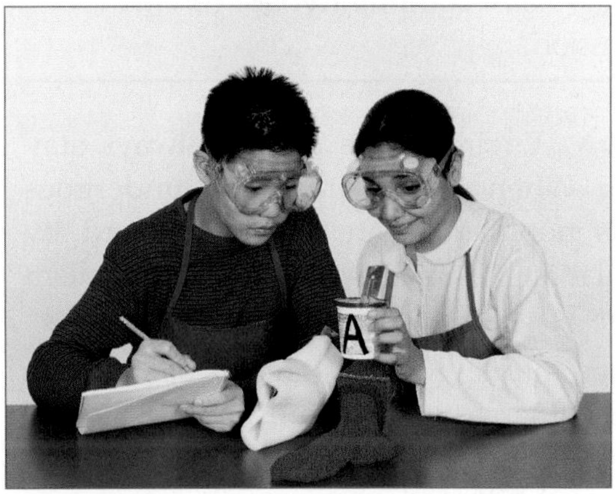


▲ **STEP 8** Record the temperature of the water in each container.

| Animal | Temperature | | | |
|---|---|---|---|---|
| | 0 min. | 5 min. | 10 min. | 15 min. |
| A | | | | |
| B | | | | |
| C | | | | |

▲ **Figure 11-16** Copy this chart onto a sheet of paper.

## CONCLUSIONS

1. **OBSERVE:** Which "animal" had the smallest decrease in temperature?
2. **OBSERVE:** Which "animal" had the largest decrease in temperature?
3. **INFER:** What effect does the amount of insulation have on the temperature of warm-blooded animals?
4. **GRAPHING:** Use the results of your experiment to create a line graph. Use a different colored pencil to represent each "animal." Make sure you include a title, labels, and units in your graph.

# 11-6 What is succession?

### *Objective*

Describe how communities of organisms develop.

### *Key Terms*

**succession** (suhk-SEHSH-uhn)**:** gradual change in populations of organisms that occurs when the environment changes

**climax** (KLY-maks) **community:** last community in a succession

**Succession** Environments do not always stay the same. When an environment undergoes change, its populations are slowly replaced by new populations. This slow change in organism populations is called **succession.**

A change in one group of organisms causes a change in another group of organisms. Usually, the first populations to change are the plant populations. As the plant populations change, different animal populations move in.

1 **IDENTIFY:** What is succession?

**Open Field to Forest** Suppose a fire burns a forest to the ground. This disaster causes succession to occur in several stages.

**Open Field** The first organisms to grow in the burnt area are grasses and weeds. These plants are called pioneer plants because they are the first to appear in a new habitat. They grow from roots and seeds left in the soil. They also grow from seeds that are brought in by wind, water, or animals. As the grasses grow into a thick field, or meadow, small animals move into the area.

**Shrub Land** Shrubs and trees begin to grow. Because they shade the grasses, some of the original grasses die. More shrubs grow and different kinds of animals move in. A new community replaces the community that lived in the grassy field.

**Pine Forest** Pine trees begin to grow in the area. Because the pine trees shade parts of the area, some of the shrubs die. Eventually, a pine forest develops. The community that lives in the pine forest is different from that of the shrub land.

**Hardwood Forest** Eventually, hardwood trees, such as oak and maple, may begin to grow in the area. They grow taller than the pine trees, so the pine trees do not get as much sunlight. Many pine trees die, and the forest becomes a hardwood forest. A different animal community develops.

Once the hardwood forest has formed, succession stops. The hardwood forest is a **climax community,** or the final community in a succession. It will remain in the area until another disaster disturbs the environment.

2 **DEFINE:** What is a climax community?

▲ **Figure 11-17** Succession occurs in stages and may take hundreds of years to complete.

**Succession in Water** A lake or pond can develop into a hardwood forest. As small organisms in the water die, their bodies fall to the bottom. The decomposed bodies build up slowly, making the lake shallow. Large plants begin to grow in the pond. When they die, they fall to the bottom and make the pond even more shallow. In time, the pond will develop into a marsh. Eventually the marsh may dry up and allow grasses and shrubs to fill in.

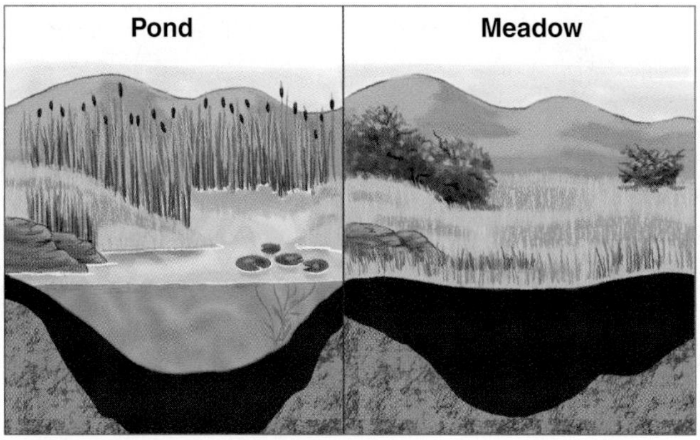


▲ **Figure 11-18** Succession of a pond

**3** **LIST:** List the steps in the succession of a lake.

## ✓ CHECKING CONCEPTS

1. What are the first populations to change in a succession on land?
2. What might cause succession to occur?
3. What happens in the shrub land stage of succession?
4. What is a climax community?
5. How is lake succession different from the succession of an open field?

## THINKING CRITICALLY

6. **RELATE:** Is the climax community the same everywhere?
7. **INFER:** Suppose a maple-beech forest burns. Why is it that maples and beeches are not the first community in the succession?
8. **PREDICT:** Besides a fire, what other events might cause succession to begin?

*Real-Life Science*

### SUCCESSION AT MOUNT SAINT HELENS

Mount Saint Helens, a volcano in Washington State, erupted on May 18, 1980, producing devastating damage to more than 500 square kilometers of forest. The force of the blast blew away huge trees and stripped away the soil on the ridges closest to the volcano, leaving bare rock. Hot gases and mudflows killed much of the wildlife. However, life soon began to return to the slopes and the valleys.

In 1981, a single wildflower, the lupine plant, was found growing in an area covered by pumice, a volcanic rock. Soon, other plants began to grow there. Elk and other grazing animals came to feed on the new vegetation. Meanwhile, winds blew seeds of evergreen trees to other damaged areas. Fast-growing species, such as lodgepole pine and red alder, which can grow in nutrient-poor soil, spread quickly. In the 1990s, seedlings of willow and Douglas fir trees appeared. Scientists expect that it will take about 100 to 200 more years for mature hardwood forests to grow and cover most of the devastated area.

▲ **Figure 11-19** The top photograph shows Mount Saint Helens after the eruption in 1980. The bottom photograph was taken in 2004.

**Thinking Critically** What characteristics of the lupine plant might have allowed it to be the first to grow in this environment?

# 11-7 What are natural resources?

*Objective*

Distinguish between renewable and nonrenewable natural resources.

*Key Terms*

**natural resource** (REE-sawrs)**:** material found in nature that is used by living things

**renewable resource:** natural resource that can be reused or replaced

**nonrenewable resource:** natural resource that cannot be reused or replaced

**conservation** (kahn-suhr-VAY-shuhn)**:** wise use of natural resources

**Natural Resources** Living things use materials found in nature to survive. These materials are called **natural resources.** Air and water are natural resources needed by almost all organisms. People use other natural resources such as oil, coal, and gas as fuels.

▲ **Figure 11-20** Water is an important natural resource.

1 CLASSIFY: What other natural resources can you name?

**Renewable Resources** Some natural resources can be reused or replaced. These resources are called **renewable resources.** Water, soil, and lumber are examples of renewable resources. Water is replaced naturally through a process called the water cycle. Forests can be replanted. However, these processes take many years to complete.

▲ **Figure 11-21** Trees are harvested for use in lumber, paper, and other materials. Trees are renewable resources.

2 DEFINE: What is a renewable resource?

**Nonrenewable Resources** Some natural resources cannot be reused or replaced. These resources are called **nonrenewable resources.** Oil, coal, natural gas, and minerals are examples of nonrenewable resources. Nonrenewable resources need millions of years to form. Once existing supplies of these resources are used up, they cannot be replaced.

▲ **Figure 11-22** Oil can be found in the ocean floor by huge drills.

3 CONTRAST: What is the difference between renewable and nonrenewable resources?

**Conservation** The wise use of natural resources is called **conservation.** Conservation of all natural resources, including renewable resources, is important. Although renewable resources are replaced by the environment, the supply of these resources is limited. People must be careful not to use renewable resources faster than they can be replaced.

Because nonrenewable resources such as coal and oil cannot be replaced, it is especially important to use them wisely. One way of conserving nonrenewable resources is by buying products such as cars, air conditioners, and light bulbs that are more energy efficient. Other ways of conserving nonrenewable resources are by carpooling and using solar power.

4 **IDENTIFY:** Why is it necessary to conserve renewable resources?

## CHECKING CONCEPTS

1. Nonrenewable resources __________ be replaced.
2. All organisms use __________ in order to survive.
3. Oil and natural gas are examples of __________ resources.
4. Using natural resources wisely is called __________.

## THINKING CRITICALLY

5. **RELATE:** What are five more ways in which you can conserve natural resources?
6. **INFER:** Why are coal and oil considered nonrenewable resources?

## BUILDING WRITING SKILLS

***Writing to Persuade*** The Arctic National Wildlife Refuge is a protected preserve in Alaska that is home to polar bears, caribou, and other animals. Some people want to drill for oil in the preserve. Should oil companies be allowed to drill there, despite the possible effects on the environment and wildlife living there? Write a letter to your congressional representative describing your beliefs. Make sure you support your opinion with evidence and examples.

## *Science and Technology*

### NUCLEAR ENERGY

As the world's population continues to increase dramatically, so does its demand for energy. How will this energy be supplied? This has become a critical issue because of increasing energy prices. Coal, oil, and natural gas have long been the primary energy sources. Recently, however, nuclear energy has gotten renewed attention from policy makers and energy companies.

▲ **Figure 11-23** Nuclear energy has many advantages and disadvantages.

Nuclear energy is the energy released when atoms, such as uranium or plutonium atoms, are split. This splitting, or fission, of atoms causes a release of heat energy. When this heat energy is produced in a nuclear power plant, it in turn is used to produce steam, which turns a large turbine. The turbine produces electricity.

Many people have been reluctant to support the use of nuclear energy. People fear the effects of a possible accident at a nuclear power plant. Such an accident could spread harmful radiation over a large area. Another problem is the storage of nuclear wastes. These wastes remain radioactive for many years and therefore must be stored safely. On the other hand, nuclear power has many advantages over the use of coal or oil. Nuclear power does not produce air pollution. It can also be produced where it is needed; it does not have to be transported over great distances.

Go Online
*active art*
**For:** Nuclear Power Plant activity
**Visit:** PHSchool.com
**Web Code:** cep-5053

**Thinking Critically** Compare the positive and negative aspects of nuclear energy.

*Integrating Environmental Science*

# THE Big IDEA

## What are the effects of deforestation?

Tropical rain forests are a very important ecosystem. They cover just 2 percent of Earth's surface, yet they are home to half of all species. Tropical rain forests are disappearing very quickly. Almost 34 million acres, an area the size of Arkansas, are lost each year. Forests are cleared for farming, firewood, logging, and mining. The removal of large numbers of trees from a forest is called deforestation.

This destruction has many tragic effects. It can change the levels of oxygen and carbon dioxide in the air, and thus cause global warming. On cleared land, storms are more likely to wash away soil and much of the plant life. Many of the plant species found in the rain forest contain chemicals that could be used in medicine. Scientists and doctors are very interested in saving these plants.

One of the worst effects is the loss of biodiversity. Biodiversity is the variety of living things in a particular area. The rain forest has an incredible variety of life. For example, in 4 square miles of one area, you might find 125 kinds of mammals and 400 kinds of birds. In another area, there might be 100 kinds of reptiles, 60 kinds of amphibians, and 150 kinds of butterflies. Deforestation destroys habitats. Living things become extinct when their habitats are destroyed. Many people are trying to save the rain forests. Studying its plant and animal species may unlock secrets that can help us in the future.

Look at the boxes of text that appear on this page and the next. They point out what may be affected when a rain forest is destroyed. Follow the directions in the Science Log to learn more about "the big idea." ✦

**Erosion**

Tropical rains can be heavy and long lasting. The rains wash away the soil and its nutrients. Heavy rains can produce floods and landslides. Left intact, the tall, dense forest reduces the impact of the storms. The root system holds the thin soil in place.

Go Online
active art
**For:** Logging Methods activity
**Visit:** PHSchool.com
**Web Code:** cep-5032

**Interdependence**

Animals and plants in the rain forest depend on each other for survival. If the habitat for one is destroyed, the other is threatened, too. The Brazil nut tree protects its seeds in rock-hard cases. The agouti is one of the few animals that can crack it. Without the agouti, the Brazil nut tree could not reproduce.

## Medicines

Rain forest plants are a source of lifesaving drugs. For example, quinine comes from the cinchona (sihn-KOH-nuh) tree in South America. It is used to treat malaria. Scientists have already found 2,000 tropical plants that fight cancer.

## Local Climate

Tropical rain forests act like an air conditioner. Rain forest plants release huge quantities of water into the atmosphere. Clouds and rain cool the tropical air. Cleared forests produce less rain. This affects the water supply and local agriculture.

**WRITING ACTIVITY**

### Science Log

Which effects of deforestation concern you? In your science log, research and write about one effect of deforestation. Explain why people should be concerned about it. Start your search at www.conceptsandchallenges.com.

▲ **Figure 11-24** Much of the Brazilian rain forest has been cut down for farming.

# Chapter 11 Challenges

## Chapter Summary

### Lesson 11-1

- Everything that surrounds a living thing makes up its **environment.**
- **Ecology** is the study of the relationships between living things and their environments.
- Organisms **interact** with each other and with the nonliving parts of their environment.

### Lessons 11-2 and 11-3

- A **population** is made up of all organisms of the same kind that live in a certain place.
- All the populations that live in a certain place make up a **community.**
- An **ecosystem** is a group of communities interacting with each other and the nonliving parts of their environment.
- The place where an organism lives is its **habitat.** An organism's **niche** is its role, or job.

### Lesson 11-4

- All organisms are limited by conditions in the environment called **limiting factors.**
- The largest amount of a population that can be supported by an area is the area's **carrying capacity.**
- The **range** of a population is determined by its limiting factors.

### Lesson 11-5

- The earth can be divided into seven major land **biomes:** tundra, taiga, deciduous forest, tropical rain forest, two types of grassland, and desert. Different biomes have different **climates,** vegetation, and wildlife.

### Lesson 11-6

- Changes in an environment are called **succession.** As the environment in an area changes, the populations of organisms also change. Populations change in a series of stages, ending with a **climax community.**

### Lesson 11-7

- **Renewable resources** can be reused or replaced. **Nonrenewable resources** cannot be reused or replaced. All **natural resources** should be conserved.

## Key Term Challenges

biome (p. 264)
carrying capacity (p. 262)
climate (p. 264)
climax community (p. 268)
community (p. 258)
conservation (p. 270)
ecology (p. 256)
ecosystem (p. 258)
environment (p. 256)
habitat (p. 260)
interact (p. 256)
limiting factor (p. 262)
natural resource (p. 270)
niche (p. 260)
nonrenewable resources (p. 270)
population (p. 258)
range (p. 262)
renewable resource (p. 270)
succession (p. 268)

MATCHING **Write the Key Term from above that best matches each description.**

1. living and nonliving parts of an environment together with their interactions
2. average weather in an area
3. area where a certain population is found
4. to act on each other
5. everything that surrounds an organism
6. large region with a characteristic climate
7. materials found in nature that are used by living things
8. last community in a succession

APPLYING DEFINITIONS **Explain the difference between the words in each pair. Write your answer in complete sentences.**

9. community, population
10. habitat, niche
11. limiting factors, carrying capacity
12. environment, ecology
13. renewable resources, nonrenewable resources
14. range, biome

## Content Challenges TEST PREP

**MULTIPLE CHOICE Write the letter of the term or phrase that best completes each sentence.**

**1.** Oil and coal are examples of
- **a.** nonrenewable resources.
- **b.** pollutants.
- **c.** scavengers.
- **d.** bacteria.

**2.** Materials used by living things for growth and energy are
- **a.** nutrients.
- **b.** pollutants.
- **c.** scavengers.
- **d.** bacteria.

**3.** The major source of energy for most ecosystems is
- **a.** plants.
- **b.** algae.
- **c.** uranium.
- **d.** the Sun.

**4.** An anthill is an example of a
- **a.** biome.
- **b.** habitat.
- **c.** niche.
- **d.** succession.

**5.** The spread of organisms from one area to another is called
- **a.** succession.
- **b.** climate.
- **c.** carrying capacity.
- **d.** dispersal.

**6.** Coniferous forests are found in the
- **a.** desert.
- **b.** taiga.
- **c.** tundra.
- **d.** tropics.

**7.** The tundra and deciduous forest are
- **a.** biomes.
- **b.** climax communities.
- **c.** climates.
- **d.** niches.

**8.** The first organisms to grow in a burnt area are
- **a.** shrubs.
- **b.** trees.
- **c.** grasses.
- **d.** animals.

**9.** The biome that is hot and dry is the
- **a.** desert.
- **b.** taiga.
- **c.** tundra.
- **d.** grassland.

**TRUE/FALSE Write *true* if the statement is true. If the statement is false, change the underlined term to make the statement true.**

**10.** Tropical rain forests are located near the equator.

**11.** Oil and coal are renewable resources.

**12.** The climate of the tundra is cold.

**13.** The climate of the tropical rain forest is warm and dry.

**14.** Two populations can have the same niche for a long time.

**15.** Green plants get nutrients from soil.

**16.** The largest population that can be supported by an area is the area's range.

## Concept Challenges TEST PREP

WRITTEN RESPONSE **Answer each of the following questions in complete sentences.**

1. EXPLAIN: What are the stages of succession? Describe how each stage occurs.
2. CONTRAST: What is the difference between habitat and niche? Give an example to help explain your response.
3. CLASSIFY: Make a list of natural resources. Classify each as renewable or nonrenewable. Explain each classification.
4. RELATE: What is the relationship between populations, communities, and ecosystems? Give an example of each.
5. PREDICT: What might happen if a population size grew beyond an area's carrying capacity?

INTERPRETING VISUALS **Use Figure 11-25 to answer the following questions.**

6. What type of map is shown in Figure 11-25?
7. Which biomes are found near the equator?
8. Which biomes are found near the North and South Poles?
9. Which biome covers most of the eastern United States?
10. Which biome covers most of the central United States?
11. What are the biomes of the western United States?
12. Which continent has the largest number of different types of biomes?

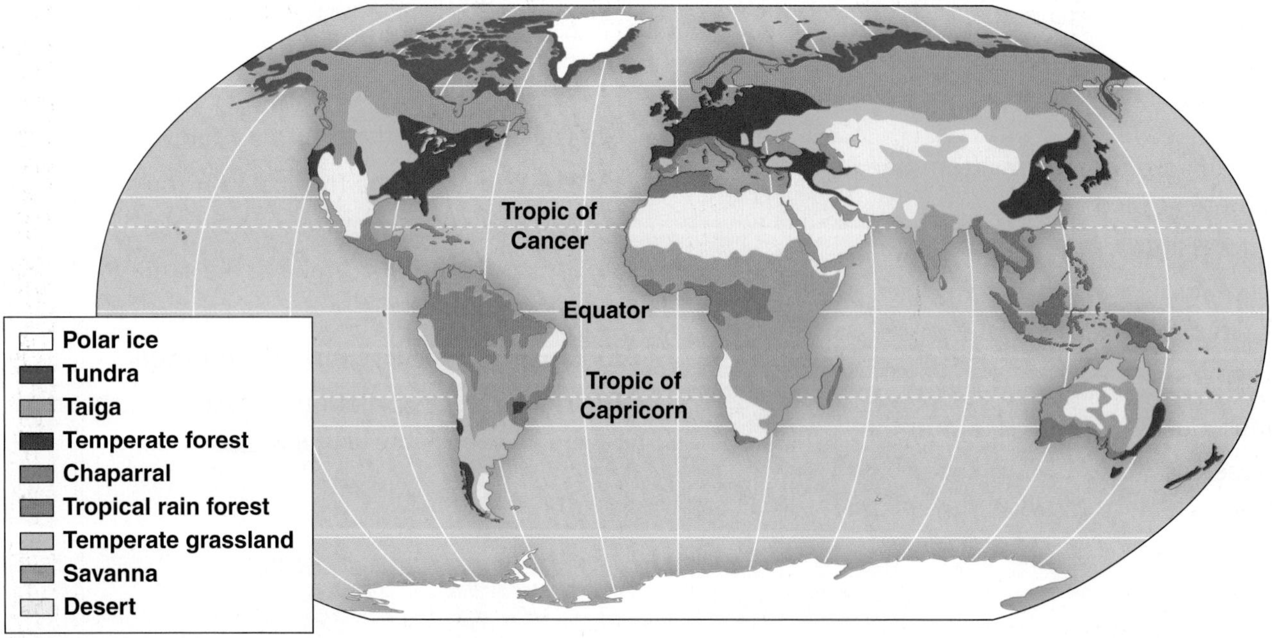


▲ **Figure 11-25** Some of Earth's biomes

# Chapter 12 Interactions Among Living Things

▲ **Figure 12-1** This sea anemone is poisonous to many organisms, but not to this clown fish.

## Contents



Most types of living things are not self-sufficient. They rely on different species of organisms for survival. Most of the relationships between organisms involve the transfer of energy through feeding. Some relationships between organisms involve living space and protection from predators. Sometimes species benefit from the relationship. At other times, only one species benefits from the relationship.

▶How do you think the organisms in Figure 12-1 are interacting?

# 12-1 What are producers and consumers?

### *Objective*

Identify producers and different feeding levels of consumers in an ecosystem.

### *Key Terms*

**producer** (pruh-DOOS-uhr)**:** organism that makes its own food

**consumer:** organism that obtains food by eating other organisms

**herbivore:** consumer that only eats plants

**carnivore:** consumer that only eats animals

**omnivore:** consumer that eats both plants and animals

**scavenger** (SKAV-ihn-juhr)**:** animal that only eats dead organisms

**decomposer:** organism that breaks down the wastes or remains of other organisms

**Producers** Almost all energy that is used by living things comes from the Sun. Organisms that use the Sun's energy to make their own food are called **producers.** On land, the main producers are plants. The main producers in lakes and oceans are algae and phytoplankton.

1 **OBSERVE:** Name all the producers shown in Figure 12-2.

**Consumers** Most types of organisms cannot make their own food. Instead, they get energy by eating other organisms. An organism that eats other organisms is a **consumer.** Some consumers eat only plants. They are called **herbivores.** Rabbits are herbivores. They eat grass and other plants. Some consumers only eat animals. They are called **carnivores.** Lions are carnivores because they eat other animals. Other consumers are omnivores. **Omnivores** eat both plants and animals. Humans are omnivores because we eat plants and animals.

2 **IDENTIFY:** Why is a human considered an omnivore?

**Levels of Consumers** A primary consumer is an organism that eats producers. Most herbivores are primary consumers. Caterpillars eat leaves and other plants. They are primary consumers. Organisms that eat primary consumers are secondary consumers. Tree frogs eat small plant-eating animals, such as caterpillars and butterflies. Tree frogs are secondary consumers. Consumers that eat secondary consumers are called tertiary consumers. Toucans are birds that eat small meat-eating animals, such as tree frogs and snakes. Toucans are tertiary consumers.

▲ **Figure 12-2** A rain forest ecosystem

Some animals, such as toucans, are both secondary and tertiary consumers. Most humans are primary, secondary, and tertiary consumers.

3 CLASSIFY: Squirrels eat seeds and small insects or animals. Are squirrels primary, secondary, or tertiary consumers?

**Scavengers and Decomposers** Some animals feed on dead animals. These animals are **scavengers.** Scavengers eat animals that have died or been killed by other animals. Vultures, hyenas, and certain ants, beetles, and worms are scavengers. Scavengers can be both secondary and tertiary consumers. Organisms that break down the wastes or remains of organisms are **decomposers.** Decomposers return materials from dead organisms to the soil, air, and water. Most bacteria and fungi are decomposers.

4 LIST: List three organisms that are scavengers.

## CHECKING CONCEPTS

1. Producers use energy from the __________ to make their own food.
2. Some producers in lakes are __________.
3. Organisms that eat the remains of dead animals are __________.
4. Organisms that eat only producers are __________ consumers.
5. Secondary consumers are eaten by __________.

## THINKING CRITICALLY

6. ANALYZE: What is one way in which organisms in an ecosystem depend on each other?
7. EXPLAIN: Give examples of when humans are primary, secondary, and tertiary consumers.

## BUILDING SCIENCE SKILLS

***Classifying*** Classify the following organisms as herbivore, carnivore, or omnivore.

a. black bear
b. wolf
c. horse
d. hawk
e. human
f. giraffe
g. cat
h. cow

## *Science and Technology*

### HYDROPONICS

Plants use energy from the Sun to make food. They also use minerals such as nitrogen, potassium, and phosphorus. These minerals are passed on to consumers when the plants are eaten. Most plants get these minerals from soil.

A method of growing plants without soil has been developed. This method is called hydroponics (hy-droh-PAHN-ihks). The roots of plants are placed in a special liquid. Minerals the plants need are dissolved in the liquid. Most plants grown this way develop as well as plants grown in soil. Plants can also be grown hydroponically in sand, gravel, or peat.

▲ **Figure 12-3** Some plants are grown hydroponically.

Plants grown by hydroponics can be protected from harsh weather and from insect and animal pests. The plants can be checked and cared for more easily than if they were outdoors. In addition, the amounts of minerals provided for the plants can be carefully controlled. Hydroponics is a way of growing crops in areas with poor soil. As people look for new and better ways of growing crops, hydroponics is sure to attract more interest.

**Thinking Critically** What do you think are the benefits of hydroponics?

# 12-2 What are food chains and food webs?

### *Objectives*

Explain and construct food chains and webs to show how organisms are related by how they get their food.

### *Key Terms*

**food chain:** way of showing how the energy from food moves through populations of organisms in a community

**food web:** way of showing how food chains are related

**Food Chains** Organisms in a community are related by how they get their food. A **food chain** is a way of showing how the energy from food moves through populations of organisms. Every organism is part of a food chain.

Figure 12-4 shows a food chain. The arrows in the food chain show the direction that food and energy move along the chain. A producer, or part of a producer, is always the first link of a food chain. This food chain starts with a phytoplankton.

▲ **Figure 12-4** A food chain: phytoplankton to mussels to herring gull

Most food chains have no more than five links. There is less energy available at the last link than at the first. That is because every time the energy passes from one organism to another, a portion of the energy is lost. Each consumer loses energy through activities, such as searching for food or escaping from predators.

1 **OBSERVE:** In Figure 12-4, which organism is eaten by the mussel?

**Food Webs** Do you eat the same food at every meal every day? Neither do most organisms. Most producers and consumers are part of several food chains. A **food web** shows how several food chains are related. Figure 12-5 shows a food web. Notice

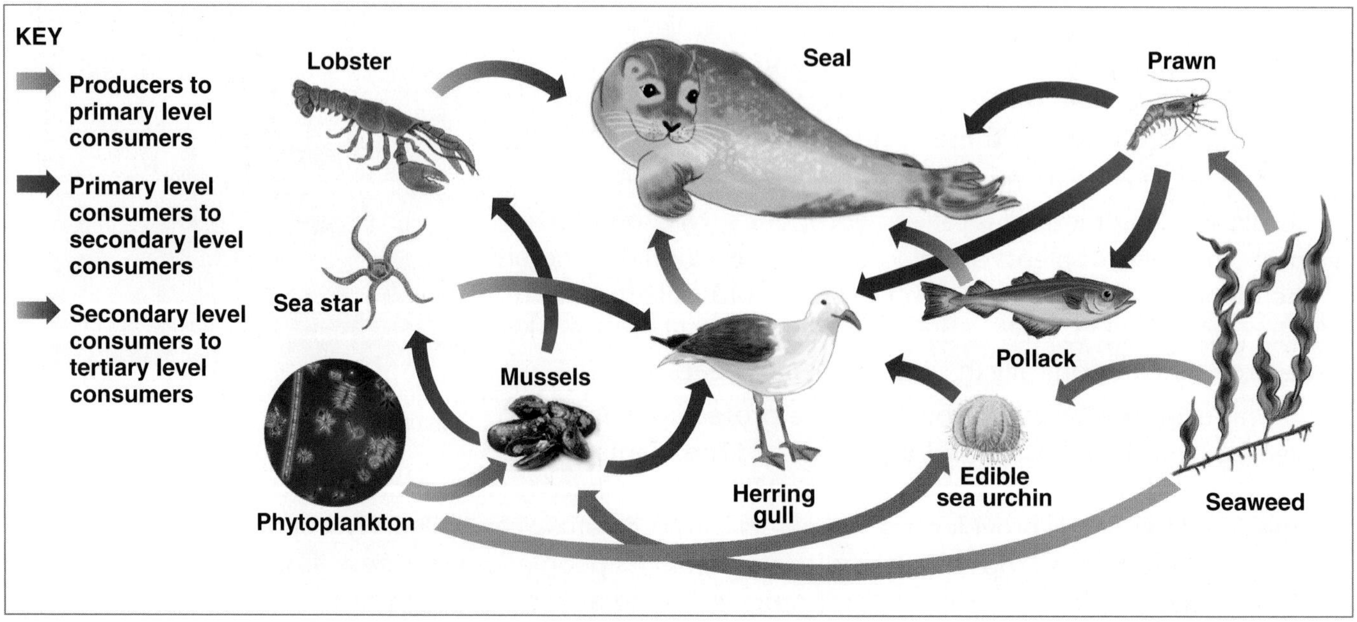


▲ **Figure 12-5** A food web

that the mussel can eat either the phytoplankton or the seaweed. Likewise, the herring gull can eat the mussel, the sea urchin, the sea star, or the prawn. Most organisms in a food chain eat more than one type of food. Many organisms also are a food source to more than one organism. The phytoplankton can be food for the mussel or the sea urchin. The mussel can be food for the herring gull, the lobster, or the sea star.

**2** **OBSERVE:** In Figure 12-5, which organisms eat prawn?

## CHECKING CONCEPTS

1. What type of organism is always the first link in a food chain?
2. What do arrows show in a food chain?
3. Why is there less energy at the end of a food chain?
4. What is a food web?

## THINKING CRITICALLY

5. **INFER:** Minnows are small fish that eat plant materials. Bass are large fish that feed on minnows. Would you expect to find more minnows or more bass in a pond? Why?

## INTERPRETING VISUALS

*Use Figure 12-5 to answer the following questions.*

6. What organisms eat seaweed?
7. How many primary consumers are in this food web?
8. Does a seal eat a lobster or a mussel?
9. Is a pollack a producer or a consumer?
10. Which organisms are tertiary consumers?

## *Hands-On Activity*

### MODELING FOOD CHAINS

*You will need 12 index cards, a pen, red yarn, yellow yarn, and blue yarn.*

▲ **Figure 12-6** Use as many cards as possible to make a food chain and a food web.

1. Write the name of the following organisms on 12 index cards: *Tree, Grass, Rabbit, Mouse, Snake, Owl, Shrub, Elk, Cricket, Mountain Lion, Hawk,* and *Frog.* Write each name on its own index card.
2. Mix up the cards. Choose six cards.
3. Using as many of the six cards as possible, arrange the cards into a food chain. Use yarn to show the flow of energy through the chain. Use yellow yarn to show energy from producers, blue yarn to show energy from primary consumers, and red yarn to show energy from secondary consumers. Then, record the food chain.
4. Return the cards to the pile. Shuffle the cards.
5. Using all the cards, arrange the cards into a food web. Use the yarn to show the flow of energy in the web. Record the food web.

### Practicing Your Skills

6. **IDENTIFY:** How many organisms were in your food chain?
7. **CLASSIFY:** Which organisms on your cards are producers? Which organisms on your cards are consumers?

# 12-3 What are energy pyramids?

### *Objective*

Explain and construct an energy pyramid to show how organisms are related by how they get their food.

### *Key Term*

**energy pyramid:** way of showing how energy moves through a food chain

**Energy Levels** In each link of a food chain, approximately 10 percent of the energy in the food chain is transferred to the next level. What happens to the other 90 percent?

At each link in a food chain, energy is lost. All life processes require energy. Organisms use energy when they grow, search for food, and reproduce. So organisms store some of the energy from their food in their bodies. However, a large amount of energy in a food chain is lost into the atmosphere as heat. Once energy is lost, it can never be replaced. An **energy pyramid** shows how energy moves through a food chain. Figure 12-7 shows an energy pyramid.

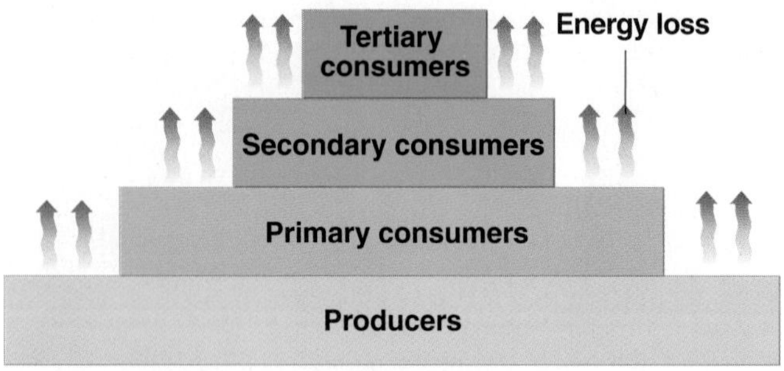


▲ **Figure 12-7** The loss of energy in a food chain is shown in this energy pyramid.

**1 EXPLAIN:** What happens to most of the energy in a food chain?

**Energy Pyramids** Look at the energy pyramid in Figure 12-8. At the bottom level is grass. Grass is a producer. It uses the energy from the Sun to make its own food. The Sun is the source of energy for the entire pyramid. Because there is the most energy at this level of the pyramid, it is the widest part of the pyramid. The producer layer always has the most energy in the pyramid. As you move up the pyramid, the amount of energy decreases. Less energy means fewer organisms can be supported at each level. The tertiary consumers, such as hawks and falcons, are always at the top of an energy pyramid. They gain the least amount of energy from the food chain.

▲ **Figure 12-8** An energy pyramid

Just because an organism is at the top of the energy pyramid does not mean that it requires less energy than the organisms at the bottom of the pyramid. Instead, the loss of energy limits the number of consumers in a food chain. That is why there are far more producers in an ecosystem than there are consumers. There are more primary consumers than there are secondary consumers. There are even fewer numbers of the tertiary consumers.

**ANALYZE:** Which consumers require more food and energy, primary or secondary consumers?

## CHECKING CONCEPTS

1. What is an energy pyramid?
2. Approximately what percentage of energy is transferred to each level in an energy pyramid?
3. Which level of an energy pyramid has the most energy?
4. Which level of consumers is on the top of the energy pyramid?
5. Where does all the energy in an energy pyramid come from?

## THINKING CRITICALLY

6. **COMPARE:** How are a food chain and an energy pyramid related?
7. **EXPLAIN:** Why do you think most energy pyramids have less than five levels?

## BUILDING SCIENCE SKILLS

***Modeling*** Draw an energy pyramid on a sheet of paper. Decide which of the following organisms belongs at each level:

- mouse
- grass
- snake
- fox

Label each level of the pyramid with the correct organism.

## *Integrating Physical Science*

**TOPICS: energy, chemistry**

### CHEMOSYNTHESIS

While exploring the Pacific Ocean, scientists studied large communities of life living around vents, or openings, on the ocean floor. They found giant tube worms that were up to 3 meters long. The tube worms have no mouths or digestive systems. Other creatures in this community include giant white spider crabs, huge yellow mussels, and pink fish. Deep in the ocean, no sunlight reaches the ocean floor. Yet, there are organisms living on the ocean floor. Where does the energy in their food chain come from?

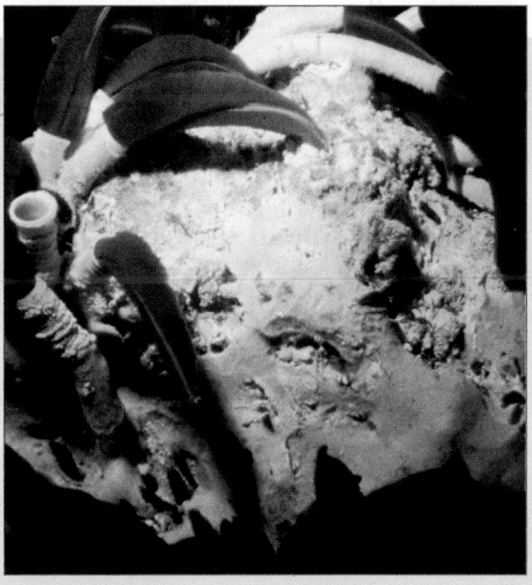

▲ **Figure 12-9** Tube worms feed on deep-sea bacteria.

Since there is no sunlight in this ecosystem, organisms that live on the ocean floor have another way of making their own food. Bacteria living inside the tube worms help them get food. These bacteria live near the vents. Sulfur compounds shoot out of the vents. The bacteria change the chemical energy in the sulfur compounds into food. The process of making food from chemicals is called chemosynthesis.

The temperature near the ocean vents is so great that most organisms could not survive. However, tube worms, giant clams, and giant white spider crabs live near the vents. They feed on the deep-sea bacteria. Because the bacteria are able to use chemicals to produce food, a chain of unusual life-forms exists.

**Thinking Critically** What organisms are producers in the deep-sea food chain?

# 12-4 How do living things interact?

## *Objective*

Explain how interactions between living things help maintain balance in an ecosystem.

## *Key Terms*

**competition:** struggle among organisms for resources in an ecosystem

**predation:** relationship in which an organism kills and eats another organism

**predator:** organism that kills and eats another organism

**prey:** organism that is killed and eaten by another organism

**symbiosis** (sihm-by-OH-sihs)**:** relationship between different species living in close association with one another

**Competition** Resources in an ecosystem are limited. Animals sharing a habitat struggle for resources, such as food, water, shelter, territory, and mates. **Competition** is the struggle among organisms for resources in an ecosystem. Animals can compete with members of the same species or members of a different species. In competition, animals that are better adapted to conditions in the habitat are more likely to survive and reproduce.

▲ **Figure 12-10** These rams are in competition for a mate.

Plants also compete for resources. Competition among plants is less active than competition among animals. Plants compete for sunlight, water, and growing space. Some plants release poisonous chemicals into the ground around them to prevent grass and weeds from crowding their growing space and using their resources.

1 ANALYZE: A wolf and a bear share a habitat. What might they compete for?

**Predation** All animals get energy from the foods they eat. Some animals eat plants, whereas other animals eat animals. A relationship in which an organism kills and eats another organism is called **predation.** An organism that kills and eats another organism is called a **predator.** An organism that is killed and eaten by another organism is called **prey.** Look at Figure 12-11. The spider is the predator. It is about to eat an insect, its prey. Predators obviously benefit from predation because they eat the prey. However, the prey species can also benefit from predation.

▲ **Figure 12-11** This spider is about to kill its prey.

Predators are more likely to catch, kill, and eat weak or unhealthy animals than strong, healthy ones. This means that the strongest members of the prey population are left to reproduce and pass on their traits to their offspring.

2 INFER: Why might predators be more likely to catch and kill weaker members of the prey population?

**Symbiosis** In an ecosystem, there are many relationships between species. **Symbiosis** is a close relationship between two organisms from different species that may help or harm the organism.

3 INFER: Can two deer have a symbiotic relationship?

## ✓ CHECKING CONCEPTS

1. What is competition?
2. For what do animals compete?
3. For what do plants compete?
4. What is predation?
5. What is symbiosis?

## THINKING CRITICALLY

6. HYPOTHESIZE: If predators kill more members of a prey population than are born in one season, how will this affect the population?
7. INFER: What role does predation play in natural selection?

### Web InfoSearch

**Predator Adaptations** Predators have certain adaptations that help them catch and kill prey. Tigers and cougars have sharp teeth and claws. Jellyfish have a poisonous substance in their tentacles that allows them to paralyze their prey.

**SEARCH:** Use the Internet to find out more about predator adaptations. Then, write a report about how predators use their adaptations to catch and kill their prey. Start your search at www.conceptsandchallenges.com. Some key search words are **adaptations, catch,** and **kill prey.**

## *How Do They Know That?*

### KEYSTONE SPECIES

In 1966, ecologist Robert Paine realized that a single species can make a big difference. In the rocky tide pools he was observing off the coast of Washington State, the species that made a big difference was a sea star, which ate mussels. Many kinds of water animals lived in the tidal pools. When Paine took all the sea stars away, the mussels multiplied wildly. Most of the other animals in the tidal pool disappeared. Paine called the sea star a keystone species. This name comes from the stone in the center of an arch. If the keystone of an arch is removed, the arch falls apart. A keystone species has a big effect on the life around it.

▲ **Figure 12-12** Elephants are a keystone species.

Elephants in Africa are another example of a keystone species. They pull down trees, break up bushes, make trails, and dig waterholes. Their activities open up the forest for other animals and help keep grasslands from turning into forests. Elephant droppings help to fertilize the soil. They contain many undigested seeds and nuts, which are eaten by birds and baboons. Elephants also spread plants to new areas. In fact, some seeds cannot sprout until they have passed through an elephant's digestive system.

**Thinking Critically** Can humans be a keystone species? Why or why not?

# LAB ACTIVITY
# Observing Decomposers in Soil

**Materials**
- Safety goggles
- 3 Plastic containers
- Marking pen
- Newspaper
- Soil
- Water
- Ruler
- Earthworms

### *BACKGROUND*

The last major feeding group in an ecosystem is the decomposers. Decomposers break down waste products and dead organisms and return them to the soil as nutrients. Earthworms are an important decomposer.

### *PURPOSE*

In this lab activity, you will be observing how decomposers in soil break down waste products and dead organisms. The newspaper you will be using was made from plant materials.

⚠ CAUTION! The earthworms you will use in this experiment are alive. They should be kept in moist soil and cared for properly.

### *PROCEDURE*

1. Put on the goggles. Label the three containers—*Dry Soil, Damp Soil, Damp Soil With Earthworms.*
2. Tear three strips of newspaper approximately 4-cm wide and 12-cm long.
3. Lay a strip of newspaper in each container with one end of the strip hanging over the edge.
4. Fill the three containers with soil. Remember to leave the strips of newspaper hanging over the edge.
5. Add a little water to the container marked *Damp Soil.*
6. Add water to the container marked *Damp Soil With Earthworms.*

▲ **STEP 4** Fill each container with soil.

▲ **STEP 6** Add water to the container marked *Damp Soil With Earthworms.*

▲ **STEP 7** Carefully add earthworms to the container.

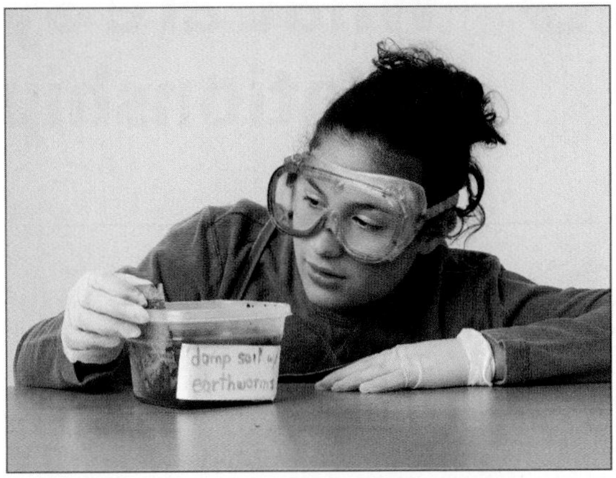


▲ **STEP 9** Observe the containers for a month.

7. Add earthworms to the container marked *Damp Soil With Earthworms*. Wash your hands with soap and water after handling the earthworms.

8. Add water to both of the Damp containers every day.

9. Copy the data chart in Figure 12-13. Observe the condition of the strips of newspaper in all three containers every week for a month. Record your observations on your data chart.

| Container | Observations |
|---|---|
| Dry Soil | |
| Damp Soil | |
| Damp Soil With Earthworms | |

▲ **Figure 12-13** Copy this chart onto a sheet of paper.

### *CONCLUSIONS*

1. **OBSERVE:** In which container did the strip of newspaper decompose the most? Why do you think this happened?

2. **OBSERVE:** What happened to the strip of newspaper in the container that was kept dry? Why do you think this happened?

3. **COMPARE:** Is there a difference in decomposition in the container with the damp soil with nothing in it and the damp soil with the earthworms? Why do you think this happened?

4. **APPLY:** How do decomposers help the environment?

# 12-5 What are symbiotic relationships?

*Objective*

Describe the three types of symbiotic relationships.

*Key Terms*

**mutualism:** relationship between two different kinds of organisms that benefits both of them

**commensalism:** relationship between two different kinds of organisms in which one benefits and the other is unaffected

**parasitism:** relationship between two different kinds of organisms in which one organism lives on or in another organism and causes it harm

**host:** organism a parasite feeds on

**Symbiotic Relationships** Symbiosis is a close relationship between two organisms that may help or harm them. There are three types of symbiotic relationships. They are mutualism, commensalism, and parasitism.

1 LIST: What are the three types of symbiotic relationships?

**Mutualism** Some relationships between organisms make survival easier. For example, the desert yucca plant depends on the yucca moth to pollinate its flowers. The yucca moth depends on the yucca plant to provide protection and food for its larvae. This is an example of **mutualism,** or a relationship between two different kinds of organisms that benefits them both.

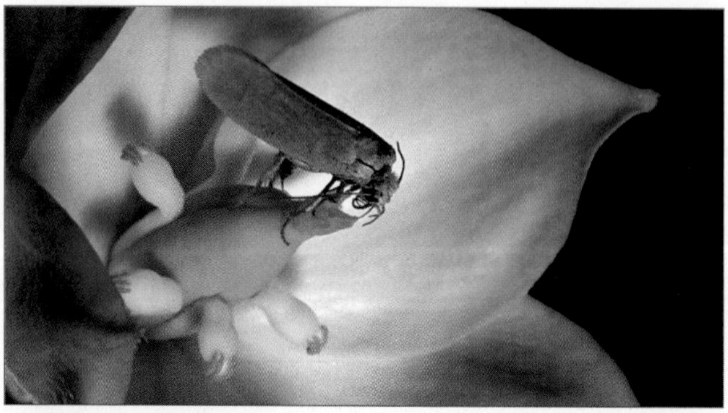

▲ **Figure 12-14** The desert yucca plant and the yucca moth have a relationship that benefits them both.

A lichen is another example of mutualism. A lichen is really two organisms living together. The two organisms that make up a lichen are a fungus and an alga. The alga provides the fungus with nutrients. The fungus provides the alga with the water and carbon dioxide needed for photosynthesis. Together, they can live where neither organism could survive alone.

2 DEFINE: What is mutualism?

**Commensalism** Look at Figure 12-15. The organisms on the whale are barnacles. Barnacles are arthropods that cannot move from one place to another to look for food. By attaching themselves to the body of a whale, barnacles can feed while moving through nutrient-rich water. The whale is not harmed by the barnacles. This is an example of commensalism. **Commensalism** is a relationship between two different kinds of organisms in which one benefits and the other is unaffected.

▲ **Figure 12-15** The relationship between whales and barnacles is an example of commensalism.

3 CONTRAST: How is commensalism different from mutualism?

**Parasitism** **Parasitism** is a relationship between two different kinds of organisms in which one lives in or on the other and causes it harm. A parasite is an organism that lives in or on another living organism and feeds on it. The organism that the parasite feeds on is called a **host.** Ticks, fleas, and leeches are examples of parasites. They feed on the blood of their hosts. Some worms, fungi, and microorganisms are parasites that live inside their hosts.

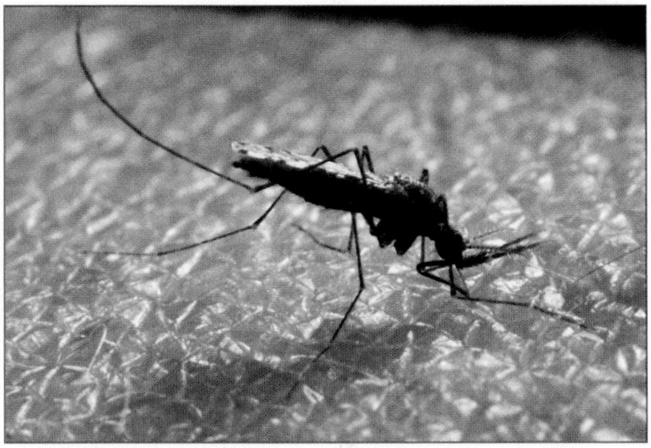

▲ **Figure 12-16** Mosquitoes feed on the blood of their hosts.

Parasitism is different from predation. Predators capture and kill their prey before eating it. Although parasites may eventually weaken or kill their hosts, it is in the parasites' best interest to keep their hosts alive so they can continue to live off them.

4 **LIST:** Name three organisms that are parasites.

## ✓ CHECKING CONCEPTS

1. What are the three types of symbiotic relationships?
2. What is a lichen?
3. What is commensalism?
4. What is parasitism?

## THINKING CRITICALLY

5. **CLASSIFY:** Some bacteria live in the intestines of cows. The bacteria help the cows digest their food. The cows provide the bacteria food and shelter. What type of symbiotic relationship exists between the bacteria and the cows?
6. **COMPARE:** How are predation and parasitism similar?

## HEALTH AND SAFETY TIP

Cooking pork at high temperatures kills the trichina (trih-KY-nuh) worm, which is a parasite of pigs. Eating undercooked pork can cause a life-threatening disease called trichinosis. Find out the temperature at which pork must be cooked to kill the trichina worm.

## *People in Science*

### ECOLOGIST

▲ **Figure 12-17** Ecologists study the relationships between organisms.

Ecologists are interested in symbiotic relationships. They want to find out how organisms that live closely together affect one another. They want to learn how different kinds of symbiotic relationships affect an environment.

Caroline Bledsoe studies organisms that live in soil to find out how these living things depend on each other. Bledsoe and a team of ecologists studied oak trees and fungi. They hypothesized that networks of fungi might connect the roots of oak trees underground. The oaks might use the network to pass nutrients from tree to tree. The trees would be providing nourishment for the fungi, but the fungi would be helping the trees, too.

In college, Bledsoe was a math and botany student. She also earned advanced degrees in plant physiology and biochemistry. She won a five-year grant from the National Science Foundation to study the relationship between oak trees and fungi.

**Thinking Critically** What type of symbiotic relationship is Bledsoe studying?

# 12-6 What are adaptations?

## INVESTIGATE

### *Modeling Adaptations*
HANDS-ON ACTIVITY

1. Which hand do you write with? Tape your thumb to the palm of that hand.
2. Use the taped hand to try to write your name on a sheet of paper. What happens?
3. Use your other hand to try to write your name on a sheet of paper. What happens?

**THINK ABOUT IT:** Which hand was it easier to write with? Explain.

### *Objective*
Identify and describe some adaptations of organisms.

### *Key Term*
**adaptation** (ad-uhp-TAY-shuhn)**:** trait that helps an organism survive in its environment

**Adaptations** Any trait of an organism that helps the organism live in its environment is called an **adaptation.** Adaptations also allow one kind of organism to live where other kinds of organisms cannot live.

▲ **Figure 12-18** Whales are adapted to life in cold water.

Some living things are adapted to cold environments. Whales that live in very cold environments have a thick layer of fat called blubber. The blubber helps keep the whales warm. Organisms adapted to cold environments would not be able to survive in a hot climate.

A cactus has adaptations that allow it to live in a desert environment. A cactus has a thick, leathery stem that stores water. It also has spines. Spines are special leaves that keep a cactus from losing too much water.

Your thumb is an example of an adaptation. Your thumb can touch all of your other fingers. It is called an opposable thumb. Opposable thumbs allow you to use your hands to do many things. You can write, build things, draw, and so on.

1 **INFER:** How do you think fish are adapted to their environments?

**Adaptations Against Predators** Some adaptations protect organisms against predators. These adaptations are part of an evolution. Species develop helpful adaptations over time and pass them on to following generations.

- **Camouflage** is one adaptation that protects an organism against predators. The more an organism looks like its environment, the less likely a predator is to notice it. Camouflage also helps a predator hide as it waits for its prey.

▲ **Figure 12-19** The coloration of this cheetah cub matches its surroundings.

- Some organisms have a **protective covering** that guards them against predators. Look at the prickly pear cactus in Figure 12-20. Its sharp needles keep herbivores away. Porcupines have a similar protective covering.

▲ **Figure 12-20** The prickly pear's sharp needles keep predators at a distance.

- Have you ever seen a yellow jacket wasp? Its bright yellow and black stripes are an adaptation called **warning coloration.** Animals that use warning coloration are usually poisonous. They use bright colors to warn other animals not to eat them.

▲ **Figure 12-21** Many animals, such as this blue poison dart frog, use bright colors to warn predators of the poison they contain.

- Another adaptation that organisms use to protect themselves is **mimicry.** In mimicry, a species has evolved to look like another type of organism. For example, a monarch butterfly has a warning coloration that keeps other animals away because it is poisonous to eat.

The wings of a viceroy butterfly have a very similar pattern to that of the monarch butterfly. By mimicking the monarch butterfly, the viceroy butterfly keeps predators away.

2 **LIST:** What are four types of adaptations that protect organisms from predators?

## CHECKING CONCEPTS

1. What is an adaptation?
2. To what kind of environment is a cactus adapted?
3. Why is your thumb an adaptation?
4. What is protective covering?
5. How do animals use warning coloration?

## THINKING CRITICALLY

6. **COMPARE:** How are camouflage and mimicry similar? How are they different?

*Match each organism with the environment to which it is most suited.*

| | |
|---|---|
| **7.** a snowy climate | **a.** frog |
| **8.** a desert | **b.** octopus |
| **9.** an ocean | **c.** polar bear |
| **10.** a pond | **d.** cactus |
| **11.** a forest | **e.** raccoon |

### Web InfoSearch

**Mimicking Behaviors** Some organisms mimic the behaviors of their predators. One example is the snowberry fly. When a snowberry fly sees its predator, the territorial jumping spider, it starts to "dance." This dance mimics the movements of the jumping spider as it defends it territory. The spider flees, leaving the fly unharmed.

**SEARCH:** Use the Internet to find out more about mimicking behaviors. Then, write your findings in a report. Start your search at www.conceptsandchallenges.com. Some key search words are **mimicry** and **animal behaviors.**

# 12-7 What is the water cycle?

### *Objective*

Explain the water cycle.

### *Key Terms*

**water cycle:** repeated movement of water between Earth's surface and the atmosphere

**evaporation:** changing of a liquid to a gas

**transpiration:** process by which plants lose water through the stomata in their leaves

**condensation:** changing of a gas to a liquid

**precipitation:** water that falls to Earth from the atmosphere

**The Water Cycle** Without water, there would be no life on Earth. All living things need water to survive. A cycle is something that happens over and over in the same way. The **water cycle** is the repeated movement of water between Earth's surface and the atmosphere. It is the process by which Earth's water is recycled. Evaporation, condensation, transpiration, and precipitation make up the water cycle.

**1** IDENTIFY: What is the water cycle?

**Evaporation** The changing of a liquid to a gas is **evaporation.** The major sources of water on Earth are the oceans. The oceans cover almost three-fourths of Earth's surface and contain more than 97 percent of Earth's water. When liquid water from oceans, lakes, and other bodies of water absorbs heat energy from the Sun, it changes to a gas. This gas is called water vapor. The water vapor formed by evaporation rises into the air. Air always contains some water vapor.

Some water is absorbed into the soil and is used by plants. Plants lose water through the stomata in their leaves. This process is called **transpiration.** Water released from the plant then evaporates and becomes water vapor.

Animals use water during cellular respiration. They release it when they breathe, sweat, or excrete. The water given off by animals enters the air as water vapor.

**2** IDENTIFY: What are the major sources of water on Earth?

**Condensation** The changing of a gas to a liquid is called **condensation.** When air containing water vapor rises, it cools. The water vapor loses heat. If

Go Online
active art
**For:** Water Cycle activity
**Visit:** PHSchool.com
**Web Code:** cfp-4024

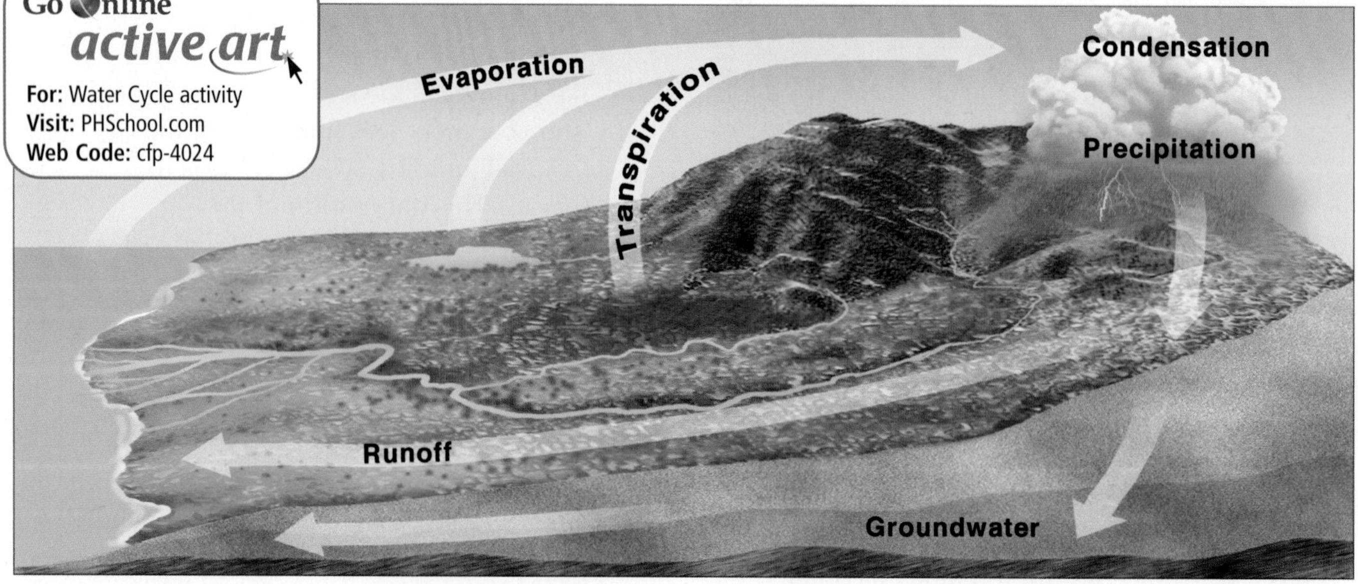


▲ **Figure 12-22** Water on Earth is recycled through the water cycle.

the water vapor loses enough heat, it changes back to a liquid. The water vapor condenses into tiny water droplets. These droplets form clouds. A cloud is a collection of water droplets or ice.

3 **EXPLAIN:** What can happen when water vapor loses heat?

**Precipitation** Water that falls to Earth from the atmosphere is called **precipitation.** Rain and snow are the two main forms of precipitation. As the water droplets in a cloud get bigger, they become too heavy to stay in the air. Gravity pulls the water droplets to Earth.

4 **LIST:** What are the two main forms of precipitation?

## CHECKING CONCEPTS

1. The process by which plants lose water is __________.
2. Water condenses into tiny water __________.
3. A collection of water droplets is called a __________.
4. Water that falls to Earth from the atmosphere is called __________.

## THINKING CRITICALLY

5. **HYPOTHESIZE:** Suppose dust in the air blocks out sunlight from Earth's surface. What effect might this have on the water cycle?
6. **EXPLAIN:** How are plants and animals part of the water cycle?

## DESIGNING AN EXPERIMENT

*Design an experiment to solve the following problem. Include a hypothesis, variables, a procedure, and a type of data to study.*

PROBLEM: Thomas does not believe that plants give off water. Design an experiment to prove to Thomas that plants do give off water.

## Science and Technology

### IRRIGATION

Water is needed by all living things. Water is provided to land through the water cycle. Humans interact with the water cycle when they withdraw water from streams, lakes, and underground sources. They do so because often water from the water cycle is not immediately available for use.

Irrigation is an artificial way to supply water to land. There are several types of irrigation systems. Most irrigation systems rely on gravity to send water from a main source downhill through ditches. Another major irrigation system is drip irrigation. In drip irrigation, pipes deliver water directly to an individual plant's roots. A third system is called center-pivot. In this system, water is pumped and sprayed through sprinklers.

▲ **Figure 12-23** The green farmland in this desert area uses irrigation.

Irrigation can provide water to areas without a nearby water source or to areas with little rainfall. Irrigation systems also provide a constant supply of water for agriculture.

**Thinking Critically** Where are some places that irrigation would be common?

# 12-8 What is the carbon cycle?

*Objective*

Explain the carbon cycle.

*Key Terms*

**carbon cycle:** repeated movement of carbon between Earth's atmosphere and organisms

**fossil fuel:** nonrenewable energy source formed from the remains of plants and animals that lived and died long ago

**deforestation:** excessive cutting of forests

**Carbon Cycle** Living things are made up of organic compounds. Organic compounds contain carbon. Carbon is found in the atmosphere in the form of carbon dioxide, or $CO_2$. The process by which carbon is recycled is called the **carbon cycle.** It is the repeated movement of carbon between Earth's atmosphere and living things. Photosynthesis and cellular respiration are the main parts of the carbon cycle. Producers use carbon dioxide to make food in photosynthesis. Some of this carbon dioxide is returned to the atmosphere when this food is used for energy during cellular respiration. The rest is stored in the producer's body as sugar. It becomes available to consumers for energy. Primary consumers eat producers. They release some carbon dioxide through cellular respiration. This transfer of carbon continues throughout the food chain.

All organisms eventually die. Their bodies are broken down by decomposers. Decomposers release carbon dioxide into the atmosphere through cellular respiration.

1 **DEFINE:** What is the carbon cycle?

**Fossil Fuels** **Fossil fuels** are a nonrenewable energy source formed from the remains of plants and animals that lived and died long ago. They are a major source of carbon. Oil, coal, and natural gas are three types of fossil fuels. The carbon found in ancient organisms has been transformed into oil, coal, and natural gas by high temperatures and pressure. This process took millions of years.

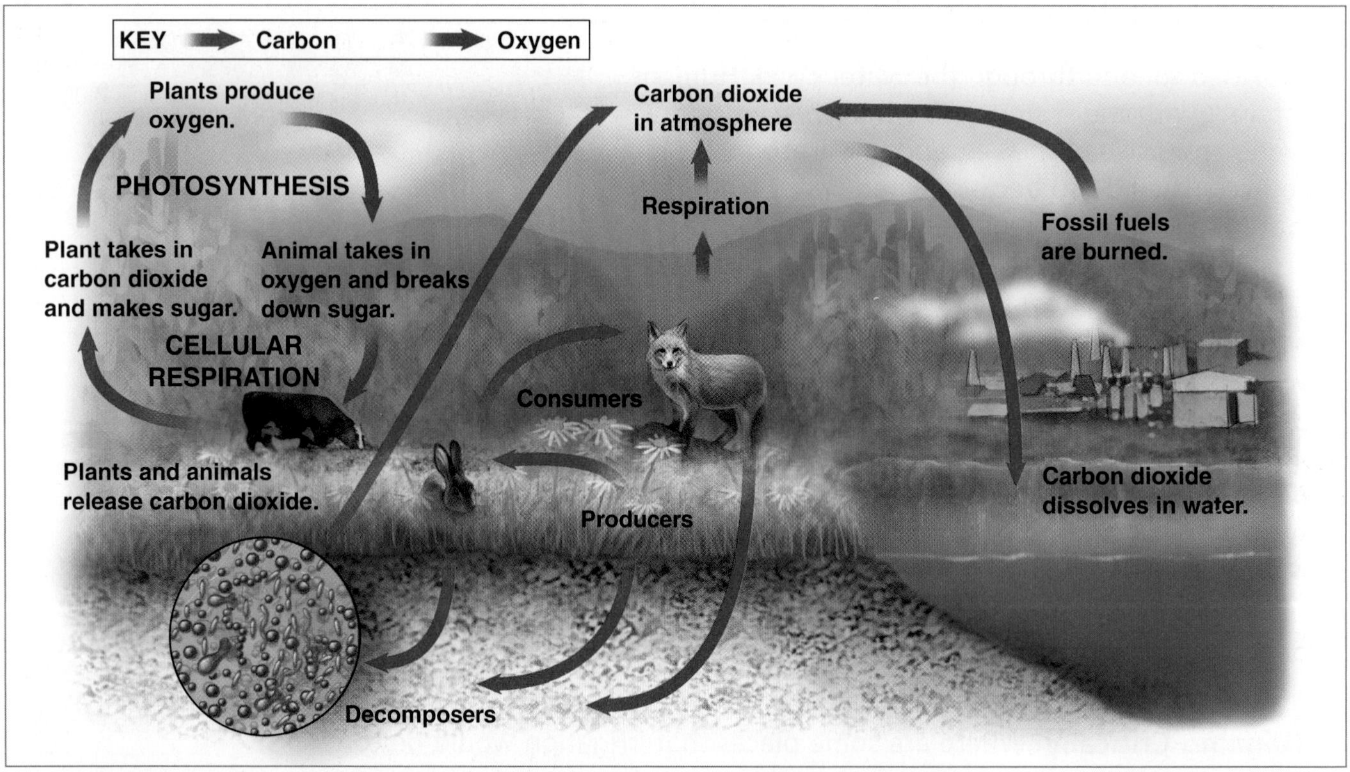


▲ **Figure 12-24** The repeated movement of carbon between Earth's atmosphere and organisms is called the carbon cycle.

When fossil fuels are burned to release energy, carbon dioxide is released into the atmosphere.

**2** LIST: What are three types of fossil fuels?

**Human Activities and the Carbon Cycle** In the late 1800s, people started making more goods in factories. This required more energy. Humans began using more fossil fuels as an energy source. This led to an increase in the amount of carbon dioxide released into the atmosphere.

Another factor that contributed to the release of more carbon dioxide into the atmosphere is **deforestation.** Deforestation is the excessive removal of forests. Tens of millions of acres of forests are cut down each year. In many cases, deforestation occurs because people need the land. In these cases, the trees are usually burned. The carbon stored in trees is released into the atmosphere through burning. The burning of fossil fuels and deforestation has added to the amount of carbon dioxide in the atmosphere. It has increased by almost 28 percent since 1850.

**3** IDENTIFY: What human activities affect the carbon cycle?

## CHECKING CONCEPTS

1. During which life process do producers use carbon dioxide?
2. What role do decomposers play in the carbon cycle?
3. What are fossil fuels?
4. Why has the amount of carbon dioxide increased in the atmosphere since 1850?
5. What is deforestation?

## THINKING CRITICALLY

6. **HYPOTHESIZE:** If all the green plants on Earth died, what would happen to the carbon content of air?
7. **RELATE:** What role do food chains play in the carbon cycle?
8. **MODEL:** Draw the possible path of carbon from a producer to the atmosphere and back again.

## *Integrating Earth Science*

**TOPICS: greenhouse effect, atmosphere**

### GLOBAL WARMING

Some of the gases in Earth's atmosphere absorb heat from sunlight and trap it close to Earth's surface. This is known as the greenhouse effect. It is a natural occurrence. Without the greenhouse effect, the average temperature of our planet would be colder than it is now by about 17°C. Recently, however, the Earth has been gradually getting warmer.

▲ **Figure 12-25** A blanket of carbon dioxide traps heat in Earth's atmosphere.

The main "greenhouse gas" is carbon dioxide. Carbon dioxide traps heat. Carbon dioxide occurs naturally in the atmosphere, but during the last 200 years human activities, such as burning fossil fuels and deforestation, have added a lot more carbon dioxide to the atmosphere. Thus, more heat is trapped in the atmosphere. This is called global warming.

There can be serious consequences of global warming. Even a small increase in temperature can have global effects on weather, agriculture, and sea levels. Many countries are working together to find ways to reduce the risk of global warming.

**Thinking Critically** How can you help reduce global warming?

# 12-9 What is the nitrogen cycle?

## *Objective*

Explain the nitrogen cycle.

## *Key Terms*

**nitrogen fixation:** process of combining nitrogen with other elements to make usable compounds

**nitrogen cycle:** repeated movement of nitrogen compounds between the atmosphere, the soil, and living organisms

**Nitrogen in the Air** Nitrogen is one of the elements that organisms need to make proteins. About 78 percent of the atmosphere is made up of nitrogen gas. However, most organisms cannot use the nitrogen found in air. It needs to be combined with other elements before most organisms can use it. The process of combining nitrogen with other elements in order to make usable compounds is called **nitrogen fixation.**

Most nitrogen is transformed into usable nitrogen compounds by nitrogen-fixing bacteria. Some nitrogen-fixing bacteria live in water and soil. Other nitrogen-fixing bacteria live in special swellings on the roots of legume plants. Legumes include beans, peas, and peanuts. The nitrogen-fixing bacteria change the nitrogen gas into a usable compound called ammonia. Other bacteria change ammonia into nitrates. These are two different processes. Lightning is another way nitrogen gas is transformed into nitrogen compounds.

1 **IDENTIFY:** Why do organisms need nitrogen?

**The Nitrogen Cycle** Once the nitrogen gas has been transformed into nitrogen compounds, plants and animals can use it to build proteins and other complex substances. Plants get nitrogen from the soil. Animals get nitrogen by eating plants and by eating other animals that have eaten plants. Decomposers break down animal wastes and the

▲ **Figure 12-26** The using and reusing of nitrogen in an ecosystem is called the nitrogen cycle.

remains of dead organisms into ammonia. This ammonia can be turned into nitrates again by other bacteria. This means the nitrogen is back in the soil for other plants to use.

Other kinds of bacteria break down nitrates and release nitrogen gas. The nitrogen gas is then returned to the air and the nitrogen cycle continues. The **nitrogen cycle** is the using and reusing of nitrogen in an ecosystem.

2 DEFINE: What is the nitrogen cycle?

## CHECKING CONCEPTS

1. The process of combining nitrogen with other elements to make usable compounds is called __________.
2. Most nitrogen is transformed into usable forms of compounds by nitrogen-fixing __________.
3. Some nitrogen-fixing bacteria live in special swellings on the roots of __________.
4. Plants and animals need nitrogen to make __________.

## THINKING CRITICALLY

5. RELATE: How are animals dependent on plants?
6. EXPLAIN: Why might some farmers plant legumes to enrich their soil?

### Web InfoSearch

**Composition of the Atmosphere** The atmosphere is a mixture of gases. Gases in the atmosphere include nitrogen, oxygen, and carbon dioxide. Nitrogen makes up about 78 percent of the atmosphere. Oxygen makes up about 21 percent of the air.

**SEARCH:** Use the Internet to find out if the percentages of gases in the atmosphere have always been the same. Then, write your findings in a report. Start your search at www.conceptsandchallenges.com. Some key search words are **atmosphere** and **nitrogen.**

## *Hands-On Activity*

### EXAMINING ROOT NODULES

*You will need the roots of a legume plant, the roots of a nonlegume plant, and a hand lens.*

1. Carefully wash the roots of the legume plant and the nonlegume plant.
2. Examine the roots of both plants with a hand lens.

### Practicing Your Skills

3. OBSERVE: Are there any differences in how the roots look? Explain.
4. INFER: How do the nodules help the plant?
5. EXPLAIN: What kind of relationship exists between the legume and the nitrogen-fixing bacteria?

▲ **STEP 2** Examine the roots with a hand lens.

# 12-10 What is balance in an ecosystem?

## INVESTIGATE

### *Making a Terrarium*
HANDS-ON ACTIVITY

1. Work with a group of classmates. Organize your materials.
2. Add a layer of rocks or pebbles to the bottom of an empty fish bowl or tank. Then, layer gravel or sand on top of the rocks or pebbles.
3. Add a layer of soil to the terrarium.
4. Add plants to your terrarium. Then, add small animals, such as worms and insects to your terrarium.

**THINK ABOUT IT:** Do you think your terrarium has everything needed to support the different organisms for a long period of time? Explain.

### *Objective*
Recognize that in an ecosystem, every organism is part of an ever-changing environment.

### *Key Term*
**endangered species:** species of living organisms in danger of becoming extinct

**Balance** An ecosystem is constantly changing. Sometimes the changes work together to keep the ecosystem stable. Then, the ecosystem is balanced. In a balanced ecosystem, the size of a population may go up and then go down. However, the average size of the population remains the same over time. Sometimes the balance in an ecosystem is upset. A change in the balance of just one species can be harmful to the other organisms in the ecosystem.

1 **DEFINE:** What is the balance of nature?

**Natural Disturbances** Natural causes such as a volcano, flood, or an earthquake can upset the balance of an ecosystem. These disturbances destroy organisms and their habitats. There is a great loss of wildlife. It may take many years for the ecosystem to return to its original condition.

2 **INFER:** What other natural disturbances can upset the balance of nature?

▲ **Figure 12-27** A volcanic eruption destroyed the balance of this Hawaiian town.

**The Role of People** People also can upset the balance of an ecosystem. Often the actions of people destroy the habitats of other organisms. People cut down forests to create farms and towns. They build dams and dig mines. Unfortunately, the disturbances caused by people are often permanent. The ecosystem cannot return to normal.

People also damage the ecosystem by releasing harmful substances, or pollutants, into the environment. Harmful gases from cars, power plants, and factories pollute the air. Wastes and chemicals pollute the water. Improper disposal of waste materials pollutes the land. All of these acts upset the balance of nature.

3 **EXPLAIN:** How can people upset the balance of an ecosystem?

▲ **Figure 12-28** Pollution caused this bird's beak to become deformed.

**Endangered Species** Upsetting the balance of an ecosystem has made it hard for many species to survive. Species in danger of becoming extinct are called **endangered species.** The whooping crane, giant panda, elephant, and humpback whale are all endangered species.

4 **PREDICT:** What will happen to the number of endangered species if people continue to pollute the environment?

## ✓ CHECKING CONCEPTS

1. Changes in the balance of an environment can be __________ to organisms that live there.
2. A volcano is an example of a __________ disturbance.
3. A species that is in danger of dying out is said to be __________.
4. Disturbances caused by __________ may be permanent.
5. The addition of harmful substances to the environment results in __________.

## THINKING CRITICALLY

6. **SEQUENCE:** Put the following events in the order in which they most likely would occur.
   - **a.** species becomes endangered
   - **b.** volcano erupts
   - **c.** species becomes extinct
   - **d.** environment is in balance
7. **RELATE:** Some states have laws that require deposits on beverage containers. How do these laws help reduce land pollution?

## *How Do They Know That?*

### DANGERS OF PESTICIDES

Rachel Carson (1907–1964) was a biologist who worked for many years for the U.S. Fish and Wildlife Service. She used her spare time to write about science. In 1952, Carson received the National Book Award for nonfiction. Her book, *The Sea Around Us,* became an international best seller.

Carson wrote many other books. She is best remembered for her book *Silent Spring,* published in 1962. In the book, she made people realize that chemical poisons in insect sprays could harm other living things. She made people aware that these poisons could find their way into the plants and animals that people eat.

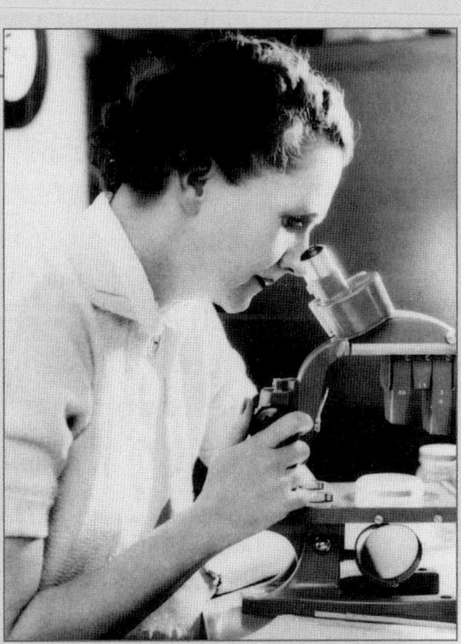

▲ **Figure 12-29** Rachel Carson

Carson was the first person to point out the danger of using pesticides. Pesticides are used to kill unwanted organisms. As a result of Carson's book *Silent Spring*, chemical pesticides are used more carefully.

**Thinking Critically** Why was Rachel Carson's book *Silent Spring* important?

*Integrating Earth Science*

# THE Big IDEA

## How does Earth support life?

Earth scientists study the major components that make up the planet Earth: the land, the water, and the air. These parts of Earth are closely related to each other and they exist in a delicate balance with living things.

Water, carbon dioxide, and nitrogen move through cycles in nature. For example, respiration and photosynthesis recycle oxygen and carbon dioxide in an ecosystem. Bacteria in soil change nitrogen from the air into forms that plants and animals can use. When living things die, bacteria break down the compounds and nitrogen is released back into the air.

In the 1960s, the scientist James Lovelock expressed the idea that Earth is a living, self-regulating superorganism. He called it the Gaia hypothesis. He observed that like living things, the planet regulates itself. In the process of regulation, living and nonliving things work together. Living things have an active role in how the planet works.

For example, the atmosphere is a product of the biosphere. It is also maintained by the biosphere. Early microorganisms first released oxygen into the air through photosynthesis. The amount of oxygen in the present-day atmosphere is controlled by plants and other organisms that use photosynthesis.

In addition, much of the lithosphere comes from the biosphere. Sedimentary rocks make up part of the lithosphere. Some sedimentary rocks are the remains of dead organisms from the biosphere.

Look at the illustration on these pages. It points out the parts of Earth and how they sustain life. Follow the directions in the Science Log to learn more about "the big idea." ✦

**WRITING ACTIVITY**

*Science Log*

Look at the illustration on these two pages. Choose one of Earth's spheres. In your science log, research and write about your sphere. What is it made of? How do its components work together to sustain life? Start your search at www.conceptsandchallenges.com.

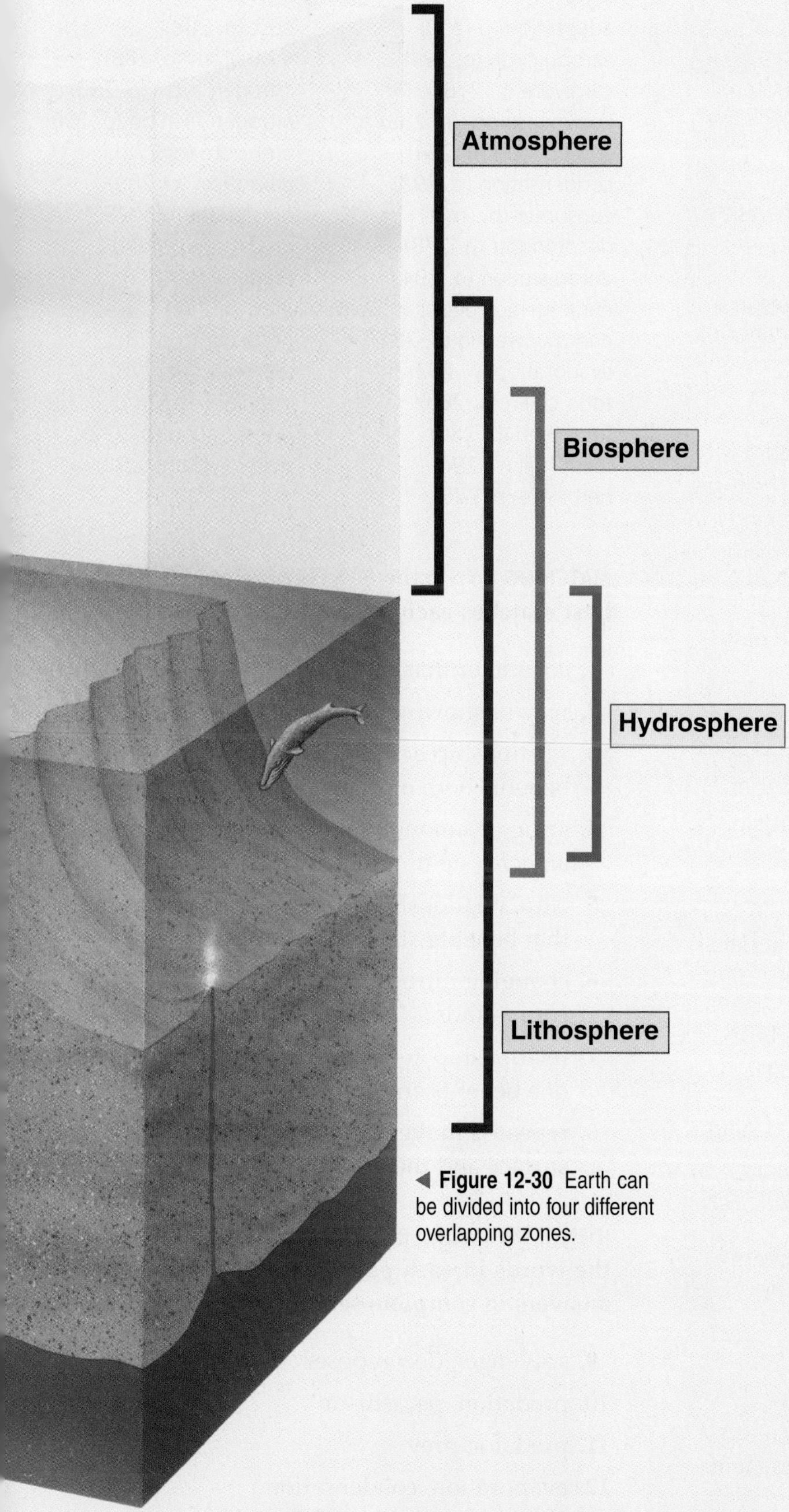


◀ **Figure 12-30** Earth can be divided into four different overlapping zones.

**Atmosphere**

The atmosphere is a blanket of gases that surrounds Earth. It provides the air we breathe. About 78 percent of air is nitrogen, and about 21 percent is oxygen. Nitrogen is an important nutrient for living things. Living things also need oxygen to produce energy. The atmosphere recycles water and protects us from the harmful rays of the Sun.

**Biosphere**

The biosphere is the part of Earth that supports living things. This includes several kilometers of both the atmosphere and hydrosphere, as well as a small part of the lithosphere. All ecosystems taken together make up Earth's biosphere.

**Hydrosphere**

The oceans and other water on Earth make up the hydrosphere. The hydrosphere nourishes life on Earth. Plants and animals need water to live. They also give off water during cellular respiration. The water evaporates into the air.

**Lithosphere**

The lithosphere consists of Earth's crust and the uppermost layer of mantle just beneath it. It is the land beneath our feet, the ocean floor, and the soil in which plants grow. It is mountains, and it is rocks. Rocks are made of minerals. Minerals are important nutrients. Some rocks, like limestone and coal, are the products of living organisms.

# Chapter 12 Challenges

## Chapter Summary

### Lesson 12-1

- **Producers** are organisms that make their own food. **Consumers** get food by eating other organisms.
- **Scavengers** and **decomposers** eat or break down the remains and wastes of other organisms.

### Lesson 12-2

- Every organism is linked to other organisms in a **food chain. Food webs** show how a number of food chains are related.

### Lesson 12-3

- An **energy pyramid** shows that the amount of energy decreases at each level of a food chain.

### Lesson 12-4

- Organisms in an environment interact. They compete for resources.
- **Predation** is when one organism kills and eats another organism.

### Lesson 12-5

- A symbiotic relationship is a close relationship between two organisms from different species.
- **Mutualism, commensalism,** and **parasitism** are all symbiotic relationships.

### Lesson 12-6

- **Adaptations** are traits of living things that help them survive in their environment.

### Lessons 12-7, 12-8, and 12-9

- Oxygen, carbon dioxide, water, and nitrogen cycle through the environment.
- Water is cycled through the environment, falling as a liquid and then evaporating as a gas.
- Carbon dioxide is cycled through photosynthesis and cellular respiration.
- Nitrogen is cycled from gas in the atmosphere into other forms in soil that can be used by plants and animals.

### Lesson 12-10

- Changes in an ecosystem work to keep it balanced. Natural disturbances and human activities can upset the balance of an ecosystem.

## Key Term Challenges

adaptation (p. 290)
carbon cycle (p. 294)
carnivore (p. 278)
commensalism (p. 288)
competition (p. 284)
condensation (p. 292)
consumer (p. 278)
decomposer (p. 278)
deforestation (p. 294)
endangered species (p. 298)
energy pyramid (p. 282)
evaporation (p. 292)
food chain (p. 280)
food web (p. 280)
fossil fuel (p. 294)
herbivore (p. 278)
host (p. 288)
mutualism (p. 288)
nitrogen cycle (p. 296)
nitrogen fixation (p. 296)
omnivore (p. 278)
parasitism (p. 288)
precipitation (p. 292)
predation (p. 284)
predator (p. 284)
prey (p. 284)
producer (p. 278)
scavenger (p. 278)
symbiosis (p. 284)
transpiration (p. 292)
water cycle (p. 292)

MATCHING **Write the Key Term from above that best matches each description.**

1. consumer that eats both plants and animals
2. way of showing how food chains are related
3. relationship between two organisms that benefits both of them
4. struggle among organisms for resources in an ecosystem
5. close relationship between two organisms that benefits at least one of them
6. changing nitrogen gas into nitrogen compounds
7. relationship between two organisms in which one benefits and the other is unaffected
8. repeated movement of water between Earth's surface and the atmosphere

IDENTIFYING WORD RELATIONSHIPS **Explain how the words in each pair are related. Write your answers in complete sentences.**

9. scavenger, decomposer
10. predation, parasitism
11. predator, prey
12. evaporation, condensation

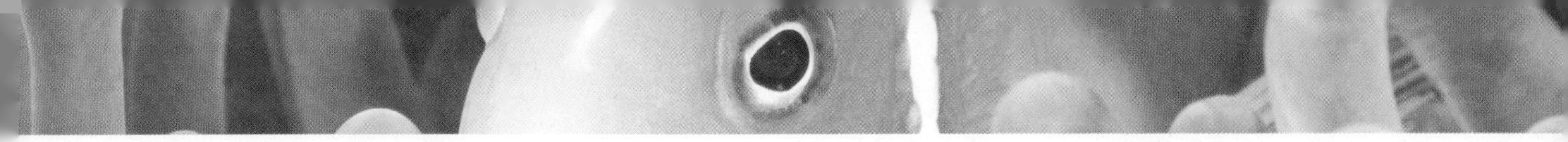

## Content Challenges TEST PREP

**MULTIPLE CHOICE Write the letter of the term or phrase that best completes each statement.**

1. In a food chain, plants are classified as
   **a.** scavengers.
   **b.** producers.
   **c.** consumers.
   **d.** decomposers.
2. Organisms at the top of an energy pyramid are
   **a.** producers.
   **b.** primary consumers.
   **c.** scavengers.
   **d.** tertiary consumers.
3. Oil and coal are examples of
   **a.** producers.
   **b.** nitrogen.
   **c.** fossil fuels.
   **d.** decomposers.
4. The major energy source for most organisms is
   **a.** plants.
   **b.** algae.
   **c.** coal.
   **d.** the Sun.
5. The relationship between bees and flowers is
   **a.** commensalism.
   **b.** mutualism.
   **c.** predation.
   **d.** competition.
6. When water evaporates, it changes to
   **a.** a liquid.
   **b.** a solid.
   **c.** a gas.
   **d.** rain.
7. Consumers that eat primary consumers are
   **a.** producers.
   **b.** tertiary consumers.
   **c.** omnivores.
   **d.** secondary consumers.
8. Plants compete for sunlight, water, and
   **a.** growing space.
   **b.** mates.
   **c.** food.
   **d.** animals.
9. An opposable thumb is an example of
   **a.** camouflage.
   **b.** mimicry.
   **c.** an adaptation.
   **d.** protective covering.
10. People can damage an environment by causing
    **a.** fossil fuels.
    **b.** pollution.
    **c.** balance.
    **d.** natural disturbances.

**TRUE/FALSE Write *true* if the statement is true. If the statement is false, change the underlined term to make the statement true.**

11. An organism that eats grass is a <u>tertiary consumer</u>.
12. Ammonia is part of the <u>nitrogen</u> cycle.
13. The organisms at the bottom of a food chain are <u>secondary consumers</u>.
14. The <u>greatest</u> amount of energy is at the top of an energy pyramid.
15. Resources in an environment are <u>unlimited</u>.
16. A lichen is an example of <u>parasitism</u>.
17. The viceroy butterfly uses <u>mimicry</u> to keep predators away.
18. <u>Transpiration</u> is water that falls to Earth from the atmosphere.
19. Producers use <u>nitrogen</u> to make food during photosynthesis.
20. Most organisms <u>can</u> use the nitrogen gas found in the atmosphere.

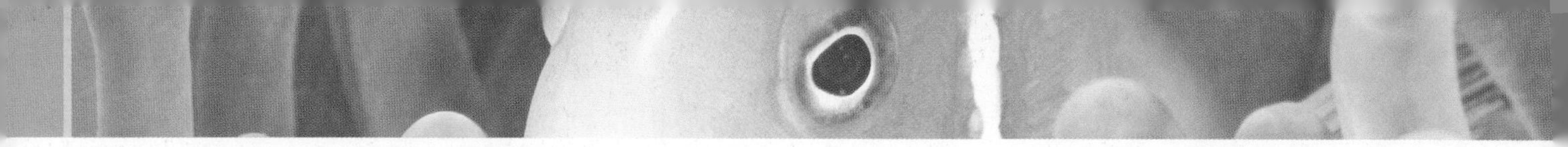

## *Content Challenges* TEST PREP

WRITTEN RESPONSE **Answer each of the following questions in complete sentences.**

1. CLASSIFY: Some bacteria can make their own food by chemosynthesis. Are these organisms producers?
2. COMPARE: Explain the three types of symbiotic relationships.
3. INFER: Barnacles cannot move from one place to another to search for food. How does attaching to a whale help a barnacle?
4. PREDICT: What would happen if sunlight could not get to an ecosystem?
5. PREDICT: What would happen if decomposers did not break down the remains of dead organisms?

INTERPRETING A DIAGRAM **Use Figure 12-31 to answer the following questions.**

6. What is shown in the diagram?
7. Which organisms in the diagram are producers?
8. Which organisms in the diagram are primary consumers?
9. Which organisms in the diagram are secondary consumers?
10. Which organisms in the diagram are tertiary consumers?
11. Draw and label one of the food chains shown in the diagram.
12. Name an organism that could replace one of the producers shown in the diagram.

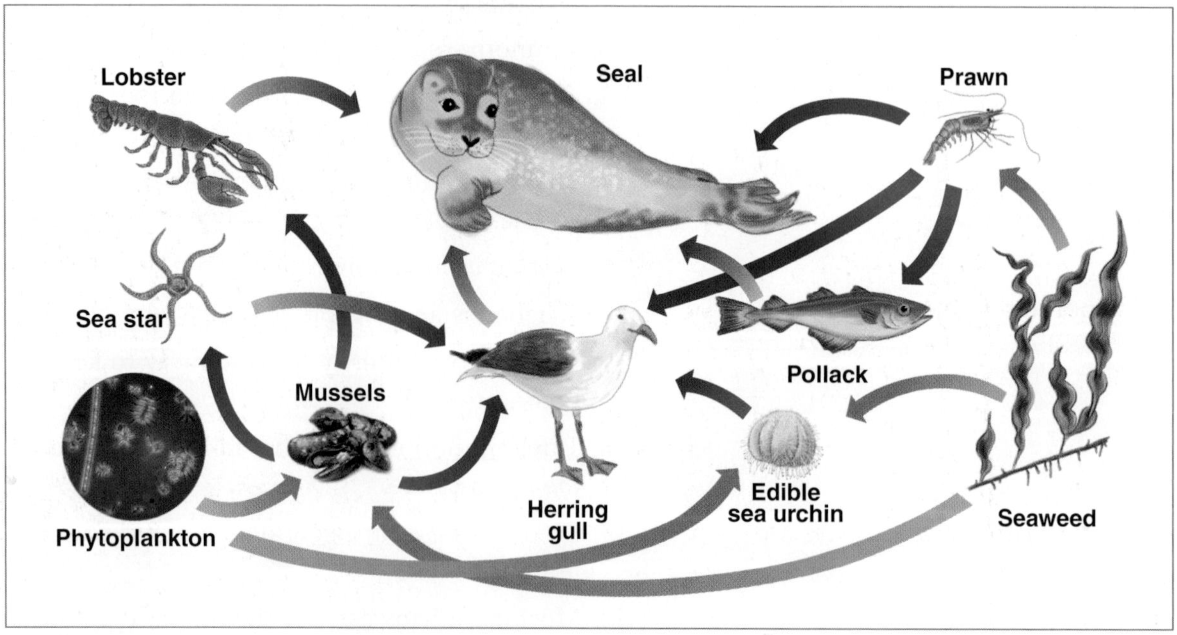


▲ **Figure 12-31**

# Chapter 13 Support and Movement

▲ **Figure 13-1** Physical activities, such as martial arts, require strength and flexibility.

Humans have an internal skeleton made of bone and cartilage. This skeleton acts as a flexible framework that supports the body and allows for a variety of movements. Joints and the muscles attached to the bones allow different types of movements, such as stretching, twisting, and turning.

▶Why do you think strong bones and muscles are important to the athletes in Figure 13-1?

## Contents

# 13-1 What are tissues?

## *Objective*

Describe the four main kinds of tissues.

## *Key Terms*

**tissue:** group of cells that look alike and work together

**epithelial** (ehp-ih-THEE-lee-uhl) **tissue:** tissue that covers and protects parts of the body

**connective tissue:** tissue that holds parts of the body together

**ligament:** type of tissue that connects bones

**tendon:** type of tissue that connects muscle to bone

**Tissues** On a baseball team, the players work together. They wear uniforms that make them look alike. In multicellular organisms, cells work as teams. A group of cells that look alike and work together make up a **tissue.** Tissues are named for the jobs they do. There are four main kinds of tissue.

**1** DEFINE: What is a tissue?

**Muscle Tissue** Muscle tissue makes up muscles. Muscle tissue is made up of cells that can become shorter. There are different kinds of muscle tissue. One kind is attached to bones. When these muscles shorten, they pull on bones and make the bones move.

**2** RELATE: How do some muscles and bones work together?

**Covering Tissue** The skin that covers your body is made of **epithelial tissue.** Epithelial tissue is made up of cells that join tightly together. Epithelial tissue also covers many parts inside your body. It protects your body by keeping harmful microscopic organisms out of your body.

**3** NAME: What type of tissue is skin?

**Connective Tissue** Tissue that holds some parts of the body together is called **connective tissue.** Connective tissue also supports and protects the body. Bone is a connective tissue. Other kinds of connective tissue are ligaments and tendons. **Ligaments** connect bones to one another. **Tendons** connect muscles to bones.

Blood is a liquid connective tissue. It has blood cells that float in a yellow liquid. Blood carries food, gases, and other important substances to and from all the cells in the body.

**4** LIST: What are four kinds of connective tissue?

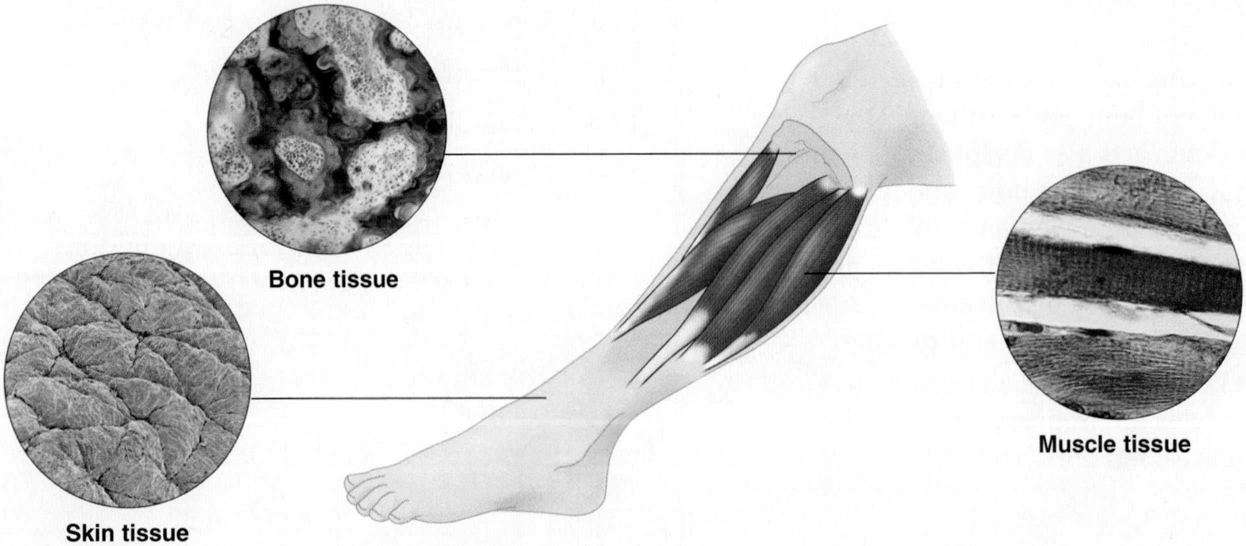


▲ **Figure 13-2** The human body is made of many different kinds of tissue.

**Nerve Tissue** Nerve tissue is made up of nerve cells, or neurons. Nerve tissue carries messages. It causes muscles to act. It controls breathing, digestion, and heartbeat. Your brain and spinal cord are made mostly of nerve tissue.

5 **INFER:** What is the function of the brain?

## CHECKING CONCEPTS

1. What are the four main types of tissue?
2. What is one function of muscle tissue?
3. Where could you find epithelial tissue?
4. What type of tissue makes up the brain?
5. What type of tissue connects muscles to bones?

## THINKING CRITICALLY

6. **CONTRAST:** What are the functions of muscle, connective, and nerve tissues?
7. **INFER:** Why do you think blood is classified as connective tissue?

## HEALTH AND SAFETY TIP

The ligaments in the knee connect the upper and lower leg bones. This area gets injured very easily. The knee carries a large portion of the body's weight. The knee also contains many ligaments that can be strained or even torn. One way to prevent this type of injury is by stretching before and after exercising and by not pushing yourself too far.

## *Science and Technology*

### TESTING MUMMY DNA

Three thousand years ago, the ancient Egyptians carefully wrapped, dried, and preserved the bodies of people who died, producing mummies. Although these mummies are very fragile today, some of their tissues have been so well preserved that they still contain fragments of DNA. Recently, scientists have been carefully removing small tissue samples from mummies and studying them.

The teeth are tissues that have most of their DNA still intact. The scientists test the DNA samples from the teeth by comparing them to DNA strands of closely related modern-day people.

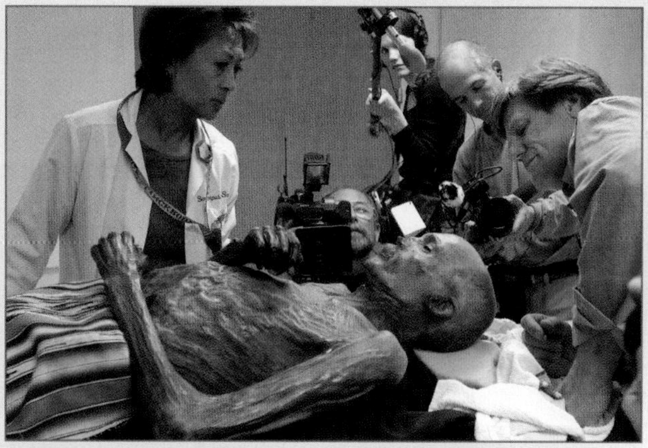

▲ **Figure 13-3** Mummy tissues still contain DNA.

By testing mummy tissue, scientists can learn specific information about the health and family relationships of the person who was preserved. Scientists use the information they discover from mummy tissue to learn about ancient people and cultures. They work together with historians to piece together clues about a mummy's life story.

**Thinking Critically** Why do you think mummy tissue must be handled carefully?

# 13-2 What are organs and organ systems?

### *Objective*

Describe organs and organ systems.

### *Key Terms*

**organ:** group of tissues that work together to do a special job

**organ system:** group of organs that work together

**gland:** organ or group of cells that produces and secretes substances used by the body

**endocrine** (EHN-doh-krihn) **system:** organ system that includes all of the glands of the body

**Organs** Groups of cells that work together form tissues. Different tissues work together, too. A group of tissues that works together to do a special job is called an **organ.**

Your body has many different organs. Each organ has a special shape and job. Your heart is an organ. It is made of several different tissues. A special type of muscle tissue makes up most of the heart. It pumps blood into the blood vessels. Nerve tissue carries impulses to the heart and controls the heartbeat. Blood vessels surround the heart, supplying its cells with oxygen and nutrients.

1 **DEFINE:** What is an organ?

**Organ Systems** Organs do not work alone. Groups of organs work together. These groups of organs form **organ systems.** All the organs in an organ system work together to carry out certain life processes. For example, your heart works together with the blood vessels in your body to make up the circulatory system. This system moves blood throughout the body. All the organ systems of a living thing work together to keep the organism alive. Each organ system carries out a different life process. Some of the major organ systems are listed in Figure 13-4.

2 **ANALYZE:** What is the job of the circulatory system?

| SUMMARY OF ORGAN SYSTEMS | | |
|---|---|---|
| **System** | **Major Structures** | **Function** |
| Skeletal | Bones | Provides structure; supports and protects internal organs |
| Muscular | Muscles (skeletal, cardiac, and smooth) | Provides structure; supports and moves trunk and limbs |
| Circulatory | Heart, blood vessels, blood | Transports nutrients and wastes to and from all body tissues |
| Respiratory | Air passages, lungs | Carries air into and out of lungs, where gases (oxygen and carbon dioxide) are exchanged |
| Immune | Lymph nodes and vessels, white blood cells | Provides protection against infection and disease |
| Digestive | Mouth, esophagus, stomach, liver, pancreas, small and large intestines | Stores and digests food; absorbs nutrients; eliminates wastes |
| Excretory | Kidneys, ureters, bladder, urethra, skin, lungs | Eliminates waste; maintains water and chemical balance |
| Nervous | Brain, spinal cord, nerves, sense organs, receptors | Controls and coordinates body movements and senses; controls consciousness and creativity; helps monitor and maintain other body systems |
| Endocrine | Glands (such as adrenal, thyroid, and pancreas), hypothalamus | Maintains homeostasis; regulates metabolism, water and mineral balance, growth and sexual development, and reproduction |
| Reproductive | Ovaries, uterus, mammary glands (in females), testes (in males) | Produces offspring |

▲ **Figure 13-4**

**Glands** Some organs and groups of cells make and give off substances used by the body. These special organs and groups of cells are called **glands.** Some glands produce chemicals that act as messengers. The blood carries these "messengers" to organs. The glands that produce chemical messengers make up an organ system called the **endocrine system.** Many of the chemical messengers made by glands control the activities of other tissues and organs.

3 **DEFINE:** What is a gland?

## ✓ CHECKING CONCEPTS

1. A group of tissues that works together is called an __________.
2. Groups of organs form __________.
3. Each organ system carries out a life __________.
4. Your heart and blood vessels make up the __________ system.
5. Glands make and give off __________ messengers.

## THINKING CRITICALLY

6. **RELATE:** How is your body similar to a machine with many parts?
7. **SEQUENCE:** Place the levels of organization in an organism from smallest to largest. **a.** organism **b.** cells **c.** organ **d.** tissues **e.** organ systems
8. **APPLY:** What organ systems do you think work together to move your leg?

## Web InfoSearch

**Plant Organs** Plant tissues have organs with special jobs. The roots, stems, leaves, and flowers of a plant are all organs.

**SEARCH:** Use the Internet to find out more about plant organs. Make a chart explaining each organ, its function, and which organ from the human body it is most similar to. Start your search at www.conceptsandchallenges.com. Some key search words are **plant, plant anatomy,** and **botany.**

## *Real-Life Science*

## ORGAN TRANSPLANTS

When any of its organs fail to do its job, an organism becomes ill and may die. In an organ transplant, a failing organ is replaced with a healthy organ from a donor. Once a new organ is surgically transplanted, the body may accept the organ as its own and function regularly again.

Medical advances in organ transplant surgery have increased the success rate for patients. However, the demand for organs is so great that many people wait years for an organ. Each day, about 60 people in the United States receive an organ transplant, but another 15 people die waiting for one. As a result, the U.S. government passed an act that set up a waiting system for people in need of organ donations.

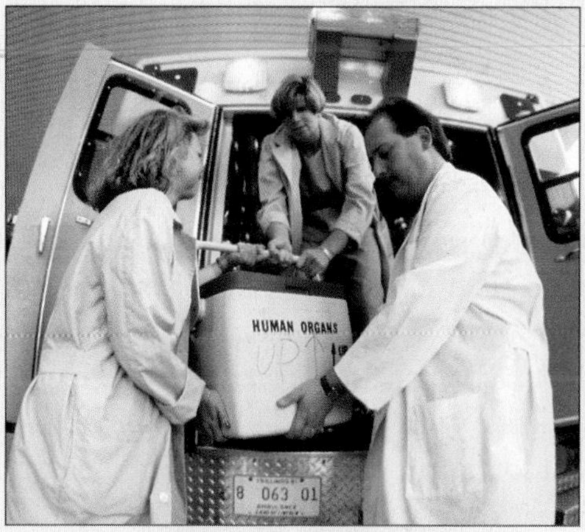


▲ **Figure 13-5** Donated organs must be kept cool until they are transplanted.

Scientists are also looking for ways to help people. Doctors have conducted transplant experiments involving artificial organs. They have also transplanted organs from animals, such as baboons and pigs, into patients waiting for organ transplants.

**Thinking Critically** Why is it important that individuals fill out donor cards or make their wishes about organ donation known in some other way?

# 13-3 What is the skeletal system?

## INVESTIGATE

### *Examining Bone Structure and Function*

HANDS-ON ACTIVITY

1. Observe a model or poster of the human skeletal system.
2. Create a chart on a separate sheet of paper. In your chart, list at least 10 different bones.
3. Describe the structure or shape of each bone in your chart.
4. Try to guess the function or job of each bone in your chart. Include this in your chart as well.

**THINK ABOUT IT:** How is the structure of each bone related to its function?

### *Objective*

Describe the functions of the skeletal system and its parts.

### *Key Terms*

**skeletal system:** system of bones and cartilage that helps to support and protect the body

**vertebra,** *pl.* **vertebrae:** bone that makes up the backbone

**cartilage** (KAHRT-uhl-ihj)**:** tough, flexible connective tissue

**The Skeletal System** Have you ever seen a house being built? If you have, you have probably seen the wooden framework that makes up a house. The framework of a house is important. It gives a house its shape. The framework also supports a house. You also have a frame that supports your body. This frame is your skeleton. Most of your **skeletal system** is made of bone. Bone is a very hard tissue.

1 **COMPARE:** How is a skeleton similar to the frame of a house?

**Kinds of Skeletons** Some living things do not have a skeleton. Their bodies are entirely soft. Other organisms, such as lobsters and insects, have an exoskeleton, or a skeleton outside their bodies. An exoskeleton is tough and hard. It protects the animal. Humans and many other animals have an endoskeleton, or a skeleton inside their bodies.

2 **INFER:** List three organisms with an exoskeleton and three with an endoskeleton.

**Jobs of the Skeleton** A major job of the skeletal system is to support the body. The spine, or backbone, supports the body and also allows for a variety of movements. The backbone is made up of separate bones called **vertebrae.** These bones resemble a stack of hollow rings. Because they are separate bones, the backbone can bend and twist.

Besides giving support and shape to your body, your skeletal system has many other important jobs. One of these jobs is to work together with muscles to move the body. Another job of the skeleton is to protect important organs. For example, the skull protects the brain. The backbone protects the spinal cord. Blood cells are made inside some bones. Bones also store minerals, such as calcium, that are required by the body. When the body needs these minerals, the bone releases them into the blood so they can be used.

| JOBS OF THE SKELETON | | |
|---|---|---|
| **Bone** | **Common Name** | **Job** |
| Clavicle | collar bone | supports the shoulder and arm bones |
| Sternum | breast bone | protects the heart; supports the rib cage |
| Cranium | skull | protects the brain |
| Vertebrae | backbones | supports the body; protects the spinal cord |

▲ **Figure 13-6**

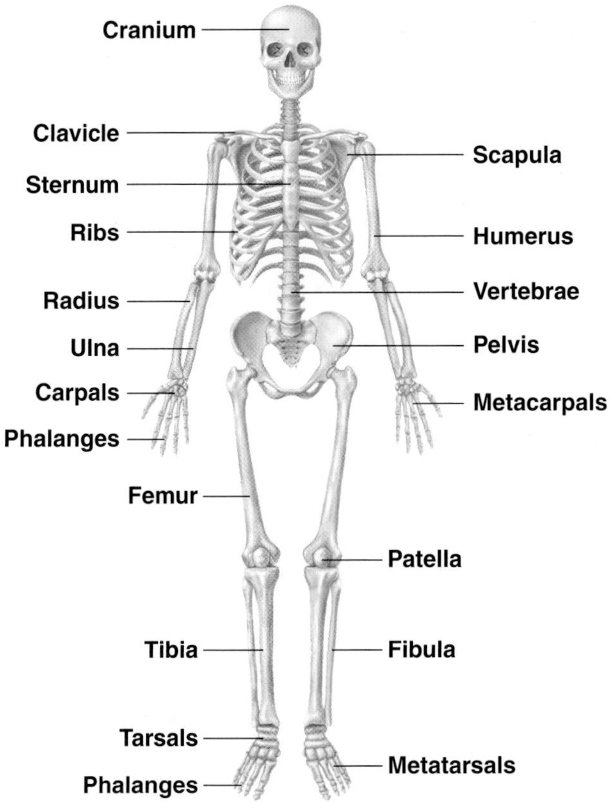


▲ **Figure 13-7** The human skeletal system

**3 INFER:** What do you think the rib cage protects?

**Cartilage** Feel your knee. The bones of your knee are very hard. Some parts of your skeleton are not as hard. Move the tip of your nose. Bend one of your ears with your hand. These two parts of your body are not made of bone. They are made of cartilage. **Cartilage** is a tough, but flexible, connective tissue. Before you were born, your skeleton was made of cartilage. However, during the second and third months of embryonic development, bone slowly replaced most of the cartilage in your skeleton.

**4 DEFINE:** What is cartilage?

**Bone Formation** Over time, the cartilage in most bones is replaced by hard, living bone tissue. This process is carried out by several specialized cells. One type of cell produces the calcium-enriched material that makes up most bones. Another cell breaks down bone tissue during the growth and remodeling of bones. It may seem strange to have a cell that destroys bone tissue. However, this process is very important because the size and shape of bones change as a person matures.

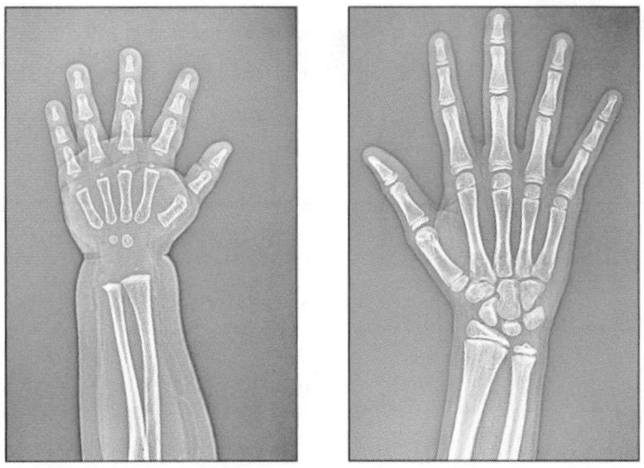

▲ **Figure 13-8** X-rays of infants (left) show that they have fewer bones than older children (right).

**5 EXPLAIN:** How does cartilage become bone?

## CHECKING CONCEPTS

1. A very hard tissue that makes up the skeletal system is __________ tissue.
2. An internal skeleton is called an __________.
3. The backbone is made up of __________.
4. The skeletal system works with __________ to move the body.
5. Before a baby is born, most of its skeleton is made up of __________.

## THINKING CRITICALLY

6. **RELATE:** How is the structure of the ribs related to their function?
7. **PREDICT:** The backbone is made of 33 separate vertebrae. What might happen if several of those vertebrae were fused together?

## INTERPRETING VISUALS

*Use Figure 13-7 to answer the following questions.*

8. **ANALYZE:** How many bones make up the lower arm?
9. **ANALYZE:** What is another name for the breastbone?

# 13-4 What are bones?

*Objective*

Describe the parts of a bone.

*Key Terms*

**periosteum** (per-ee-AHS-tee-uhm)**:** thin membrane that covers a bone

**compact bone:** mostly solid, dense part of a bone

**spongy bone:** part of a bone with many small pores or spaces

**marrow:** soft tissue inside bones that produces blood cells

**fracture:** crack or break in a bone

**Bones** The adult human skeleton is made up of 206 bones. Bones come in all shapes and sizes. Some bones are very small. There are three small bones in your ear that help you hear. Other bones are quite large. The bone in your thigh is the longest bone in the body. Some bones are tubelike. Others are flat. Although bones are different in size and shape, they all have similar structures.

**1** **INFER:** Name some places in your body where there are small bones.

**Structure of Bones** Bones are made up of both living and nonliving material. Each bone is covered by the **periosteum.** It is a thin membrane. The periosteum has many blood vessels in it that carry food molecules and oxygen to living bone cells.

The hardest part of a bone is called **compact bone.** Compact bone is made up of living bone cells, protein fibers, and nonliving minerals. The mineral calcium makes compact bone hard. Calcium in your diet helps keep your bones hard and strong. Dairy products are rich in calcium.

Bones are not entirely hard, however. The ends of bones are soft and spongy. The soft part of bones is called **spongy bone.** Spongy bone looks like a sponge. It has many holes in it. Spongy bone is lightweight and gives the bone its strength.

**2** **DESCRIBE:** What is the function of the periosteum?

**Marrow** The spaces in spongy bone are filled with bone marrow. Bone **marrow** is a soft connective tissue. It is red or yellow in color. Spongy bone contains red bone marrow. New red blood cells are made in the red bone marrow. When you were younger most of your bones contained red marrow. Adults only have red marrow in certain bones such as the femur and hips. Long bones contain yellow marrow. Yellow marrow contains mostly fat.

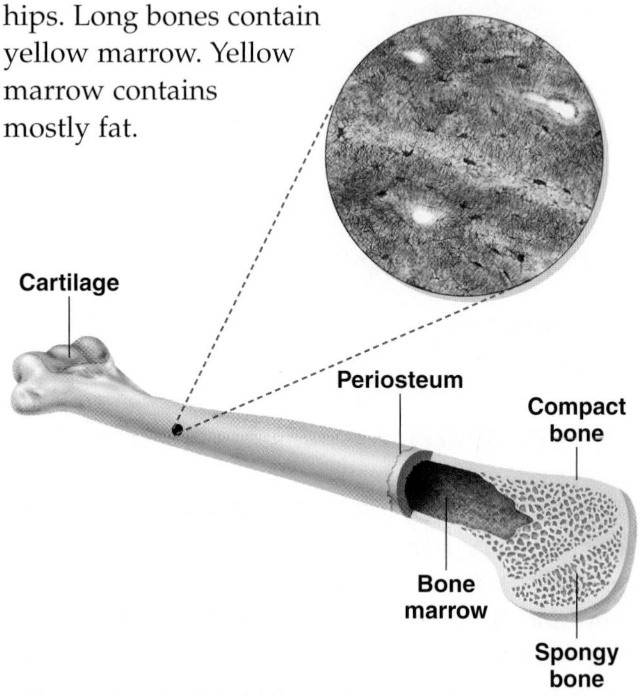


▲ **Figure 13-9** Bone is made up of several layers of living and nonliving material.

**3** **NAME:** In which kind of bone marrow are red blood cells made?

**Fractures** Injuries to bones are quite common. A **fracture** is a crack or break in a bone. Some fractures can be more severe than others. In open fractures, the bone breaks through the skin. Closed fractures do not break the skin. Another fracture called a hairline fracture is a very thin crack in the bone. Doctors use X-rays to determine the severity and the exact location of the fracture. Many times patients must wear a cast to prevent the injured bone from moving while it heals.

**4** **INFER:** Why do you think it is important that a bone with a fracture should not move?

## ✓ CHECKING CONCEPTS

1. New blood cells are made in __________ bone.
2. The membrane that covers bone is called the __________.
3. The mineral __________ keeps bones strong.
4. Blood vessels in spongy bone supply the bones with food and __________.
5. Red blood cells are made in the __________.
6. A break or crack in a bone is called a __________.

## THINKING CRITICALLY

7. **INFER:** Is the periosteum living or nonliving?
8. **PREDICT:** What might happen if the blood vessels in the periosteum were blocked?
9. **RELATE:** Why is living bone tissue important for growth?

## DESIGNING AN EXPERIMENT

*Design an experiment to solve the following problem. Include a list of materials, variables, a procedure, and a type of data to study.*

PROBLEM: Calcium and other minerals give bones their strength and firmness. These minerals can be dissolved by vinegar. Design an experiment that proves that calcium and other minerals are contained in bone.

## *Science and Technology*

### BONE MARROW TRANSPLANTS

Bone marrow transplants are used to treat many different blood disorders, such as leukemia and certain kinds of anemia. The marrow in many bones produces new blood cells. A bone marrow transplant is needed when a person's bone marrow produces abnormal blood cells instead of normal blood cells.

A healthy donor is needed for a bone marrow transplant. Radiation treatments are given to the person with the abnormal bone marrow cells. The radiation kills the marrow cells in the body. Healthy bone marrow is then taken from the donor and inserted into the patient's bloodstream.

One factor in the success of a bone marrow transplant is whether the patient's body accepts or rejects the new bone marrow. One of the major drawbacks of transplants is that the body may reject the new bone marrow. Another drawback is the possibility of infection.

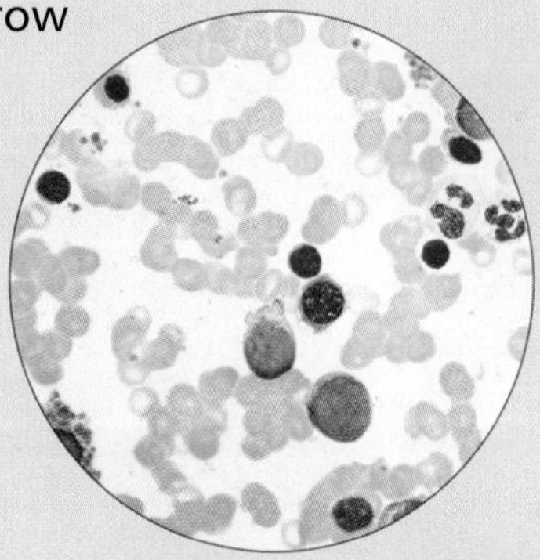

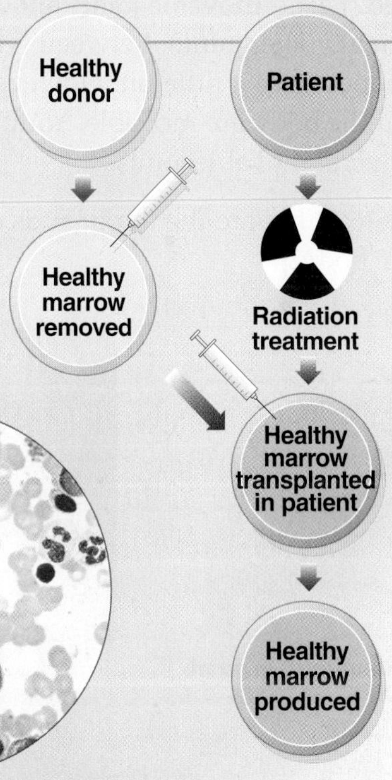


▲ **Figure 13-10** The flowchart above shows the process of a bone marrow transplant. The photo on the left shows new blood cells forming in marrow.

**Thinking Critically** Why are patients treated with radiation before a bone marrow transplant?

# 13-5 How do joints work?

***Objective***

Identify the motions and locations of the four kinds of movable joints.

***Key Term***

**joint:** place where two or more bones meet

**Joints** The place where two bones or more meet is called a **joint.** Some bones are connected directly to other bones at the joint. However, most bones are held together at joints by ligaments.

**1** **DEFINE:** What is a joint?

**Kinds of Joints** There are three main kinds of joints in the body. They are fixed joints, partly movable joints, and movable joints. Fixed joints do not allow any movement. The joints in your skull are fixed. Partly movable joints allow a little bit of movement. The joints between your ribs and breastbone move a little bit. However, most of the joints in the body are movable. Your arms and legs have several movable joints.

**2** **STATE:** What are the three kinds of joints in the body?

**Movable Joints** There are four major kinds of movable joints. These joints are ball-and-socket joints, gliding joints, hinge joints, and pivotal joints.

- **Ball-and-Socket Joints** Ball-and-socket joints allow bones to move in most directions. The joint between your upper arm and shoulder is a ball-and-socket joint. Your arm can move up and down, side to side, front to back, and around in a circle.
- **Gliding Joints** Gliding joints allow some movement in all directions. In a gliding joint, the bones slide along each other. Your wrist has gliding joints.
- **Hinge Joints** Hinge joints allow bones to move forward and backward in only one direction. This movement is similar to a door opening and closing. Hinge joints are located in your elbows and knees.
- **Pivotal Joints** Pivotal joints allow bones to move side to side and up and down. The joint between your skull and neck is a pivotal joint.

**3** **LIST:** List the four major kinds of movable joints and give examples of where they are found in the body.

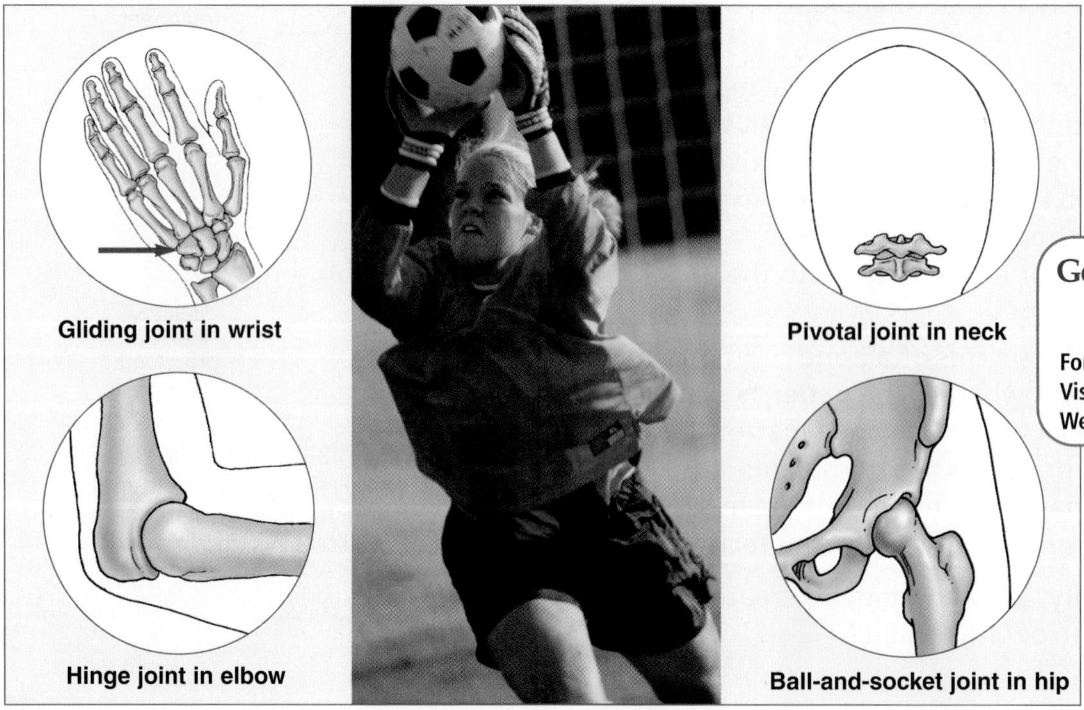


◀ **Figure 13-11** The joints inside this soccer goalie allow her to move in many different ways.

**Go Online**
***active art***
**For:** Movable Joints activity
**Visit:** PHSchool.com
**Web Code:** cep-4012

**Cartilage and Bones** Cartilage is found in the joints of many bones. Movable joints such as the knee, shoulder, and hip all have cartilage between the bones. This layer of cartilage cushions the bones and prevents them from rubbing against each other. Cartilage is smoother than bone so it causes less friction when rubbed together. This allows for easier movement of the bones. Cartilage is also found between the bones of the spinal column. The cartilage there acts as shock-absorbing padding for the vertebrae.

4 **INFER:** Would you expect to find more cartilage between your arm and shoulder bones or between the bones of the skull?

## CHECKING CONCEPTS

1. Joints can be either fixed, partly movable, or __________.
2. The joints between your breastbone and ribs are __________.
3. Most bones are held together at joints by __________.
4. The joint in your elbow is a __________ joint.

## THINKING CRITICALLY

5. **HYPOTHESIZE:** What would happen if the joint between your arm and shoulder was not a ball-and-socket joint?
6. **INFER:** Why do you think the joints between your rib cage and breastbone are partly movable?

### Web InfoSearch

**Arthritis** Do you know anyone who has arthritis? Arthritis affects people who are both young and old. Arthritis is a term that describes many different joint problems. The most common form of arthritis occurs when the cartilage between the bones is replaced with bone deposits. Movement in these joints is limited and can be very painful.

**SEARCH:** Use the Internet to find out more about arthritis. Write a report about the different types of arthritis and possible treatments. Start your search at www.conceptsandchallenges.com. Some key search words are **arthritis** and **joint pain.**

## *Hands-On Activity*

### OBSERVING JOINT MOVEMENTS

*You will need a sheet of paper and a pencil.*

1. Move your ankle in as many different ways as possible. Write down all the movements your ankle can make.
2. Move your fingers in as many different ways as possible. ⚠ CAUTION: Do not force movements at the joint. Write down all the movements your fingers can make.
3. Move your head in as many different ways as possible. Write down all the movements your head can make.
4. Move your leg and hip joints in as many different ways as possible. Write down all the movements your leg can make at the hip.

▲ **STEP 1** Observe the movements of your ankle.

**Practicing Your Skills**

5. **INFER:** What kind of joint was used in each step? How can you tell?
6. **OBSERVE:** Based on the movements in your fingers, how many joints do you think are in your fingers?

# 13-6 What is the muscular system?

*Objective*

Describe how muscles work.

*Key Terms*

**flexor:** muscle that bends a joint

**extensor:** muscle that straightens a joint

**Muscles** More than 600 muscles make up the muscular system. Muscles are tissues that can shorten along their length. Without muscles, the bones of the skeletal system could not move the body. Muscles are attached to bones by tendons. A tendon is a strong elastic band of tissue. Tendons make movement possible. When a muscle contracts, or shortens, it pulls on the tendon, which makes the bone move.

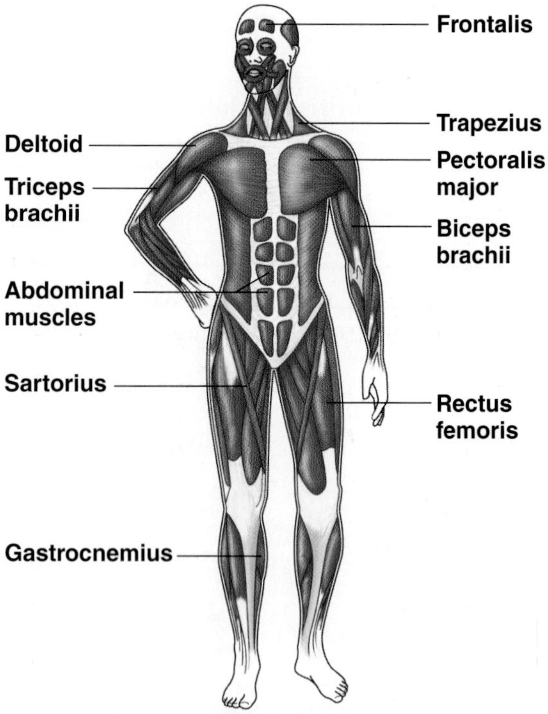


▲ **Figure 13-12** The muscular system

**1** CONTRAST: What is the difference between a tendon and a ligament?

**Muscle Actions** Muscles only move bones when the muscles contract. For this reason, muscles can only pull bones. They cannot push bones. For example, there are muscles that bend, or flex, your knee joint. These muscles are called **flexors.** There are other muscles that straighten, or extend, your knee joint. These muscles are **extensors.**

**2** DEFINE: What does a flexor muscle do?

**Teamwork** Most muscles must work in teams of two. The muscles that bend and straighten the arm are examples of muscles working together. These muscles are called biceps and triceps. Biceps are flexors. They bend the arm at the elbow. Triceps are extensors. They straighten the arm at the elbow. As you bend your arm, the biceps contract, and the triceps relax. As you straighten your arm, the biceps relax while the triceps contract and pull the arm straight.

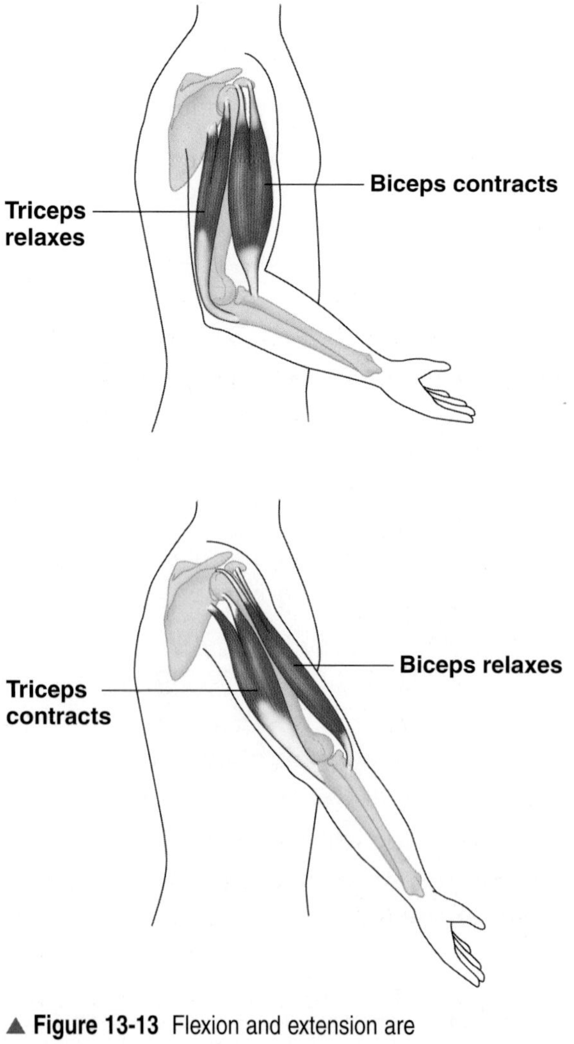


▲ **Figure 13-13** Flexion and extension are

**3** STATE: Name a muscle in the arm that is a flexor.

## ✓ CHECKING CONCEPTS

1. What is a tendon?
2. Are muscles relaxed or contracted when they move bones?
3. What is the main function of the muscular system?
4. What do extensor muscles do?
5. Why must muscles work together?

## THINKING CRITICALLY

6. **HYPOTHESIZE:** If your biceps muscle was injured, which motion would you be unable to do?
7. **INFER:** When exercising, why do you think it is important to use both muscles in a pair?

### Web InfoSearch

**Anabolic Steroids** Anabolic steroids are drugs that duplicate the male hormone testosterone. Some people take this drug illegally to increase muscle mass. However, these drugs affect many parts of the body, not just the muscles. The steroids have harmful side effects and can even be life threatening.

**SEARCH:** Use the Internet to research the effects of anabolic steroids. Present your findings to the class in a report or health brochure. Start your search at www.conceptsandchallenges.com. Some key search words are **steroid** and **anabolic steroid.**

## *Real-Life Science*

### EXERCISE AND MUSCLES

Keeping the muscles in your body healthy is very important to your overall well-being. The muscles in your body will be stronger and more flexible if you exercise regularly. Exercise will build endurance, or allow your muscles to withstand more activity. Having well-conditioned muscles can also prevent injuries. Examples of exercises that strengthen and condition your muscles are weight training and hiking.

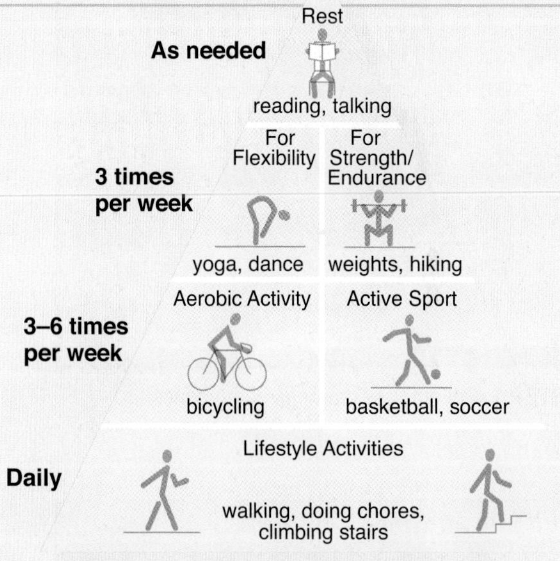

▲ **Figure 13-14** The exercise pyramid

Exercise is also important to your heart. Your heart is made of muscle and requires conditioning. Aerobic activities are those that force the heart to pump blood to the muscles continuously. Examples of aerobic activities include running, bicycling, and swimming. Playing sports such as basketball and soccer also improve the condition of your heart.

Many people do not exercise regularly. It may help if you make an exercise program or schedule and include it in your daily routine. You may also be more likely to exercise if you choose activities that you enjoy or exercise with a friend. Talk with your doctor before starting any exercise program.

**Thinking Critically** What are some ways that you exercise already? What are some other ways you could include exercise in your life?

# LAB ACTIVITY
# Modeling Muscle Movement

### BACKGROUND

Bones are connected to each other at the joints. They cannot move by themselves. Muscles make bones move. Muscles are attached to bones. When muscles contract, they cause bones to move.

### PURPOSE

In this activity you will construct a model of an arm to show how muscles and bones work together to cause movement.

### PROCEDURE

1. Trace and cut out the drawings of bones in Figure 13-15. Glue the paper cutouts to a sheet of cardboard. Let the glue dry. Then, cut the shapes out of the cardboard. ⚠ CAUTION: Be careful when using scissors.

▲ **STEP 1** Cut out your drawings of the bones.

2. Use the hole punch to make holes in the cardboard bones where the small circles are.

3. Push a paper fastener through the hole marked *elbow joint* in the humerus bone, then through the hole marked *elbow joint* in the forearm bone.

4. Fasten the cardboard bones together. Test the bones to make sure they can move freely.

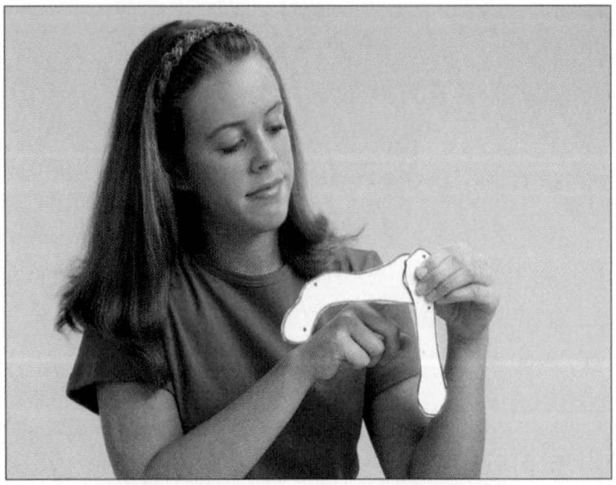

▲ **STEP 4** Fasten the cardboard bones together.

5. Thread a piece of elastic cord through the *biceps muscle* hole in the forearm bone. Tie a knot behind the bone so that the cord cannot slip through.

6. Pull the cord through the *biceps muscle* hole in the humerus. Pull the cord so that it pulls the two bones nearly together. Then, knot the cord behind the humerus bone.

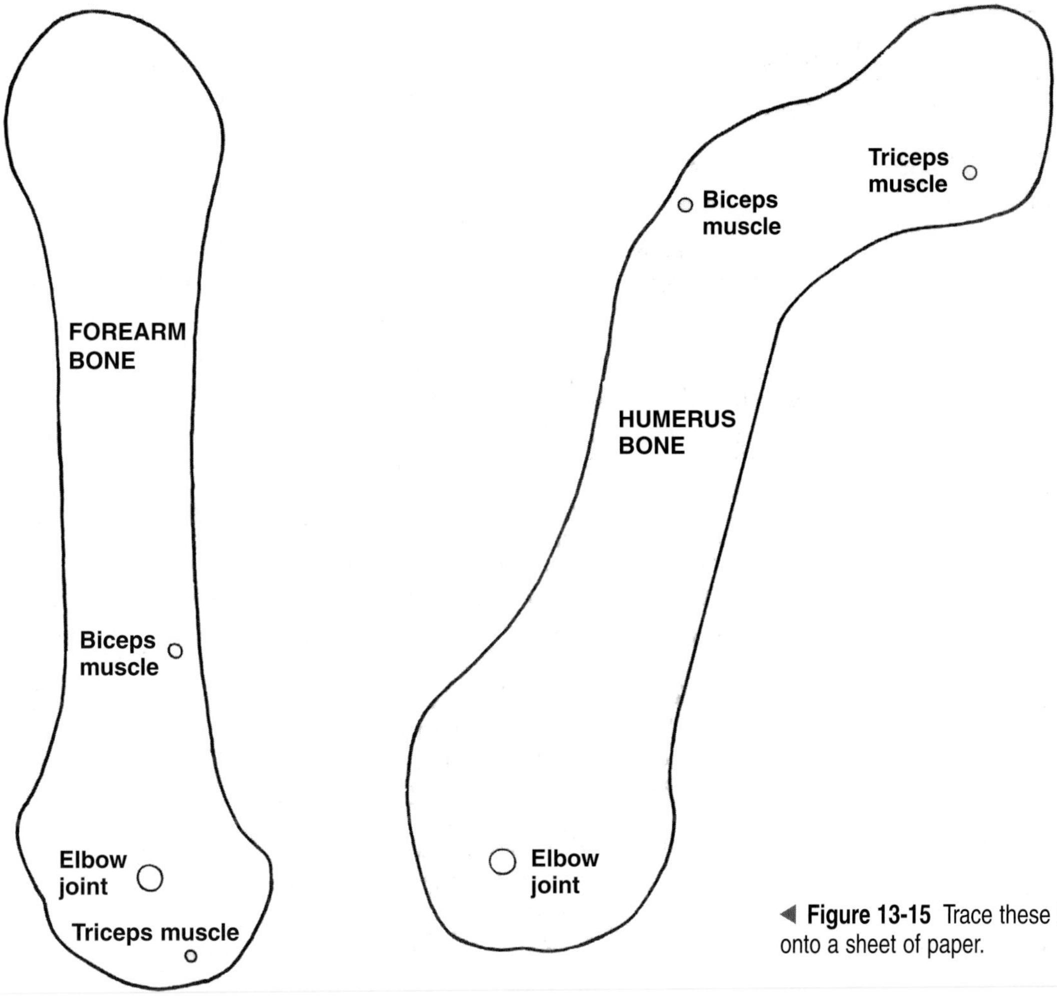


◀ **Figure 13-15** Trace these figures onto a sheet of paper.

7. Use another piece of elastic cord to attach the *triceps muscle* holes of the humerus and forearm bones. Follow Steps 5 and 6. This cord should be tight enough so that it is stretched somewhat between the two holes.

8. Bend your model arm back and forth at the elbow. Watch the elastic cords as you do this.

## CONCLUSIONS

1. **OBSERVE:** Which muscle pulls on the model arm to bend it? Which muscle pulls on the model arm to straighten it?
2. **ANALYZE:** What does the fastener represent?
3. **ANALYZE:** Which bones of the arm do the cardboard pieces represent? What muscles do the elastic cords represent?
4. **INFER:** Why do muscles have to work in pairs?

# 13-7 What are the kinds of muscles?

## *Objectives*

Name three kinds of muscle and identify where they are located in the body.

## *Key Terms*

**striated** (STRY-ayt-uhd) **muscle:** muscle tissue with stripes, or dark bands

**skeletal muscle:** muscle attached to the skeleton that makes movement possible

**smooth muscle:** muscle that causes movements which you cannot control

**cardiac** (KAHR-dee-ak) **muscle:** type of muscle found only in the heart and major blood vessels

**Skeletal Muscle** There are three different kinds of muscle tissue in the human body. Each kind of muscle tissue has a different job. Some kinds of muscle tissue are striated. **Striated muscles** have stripes or dark bands. If you look at Figure 13-16, you can see how striated muscle gets its name.

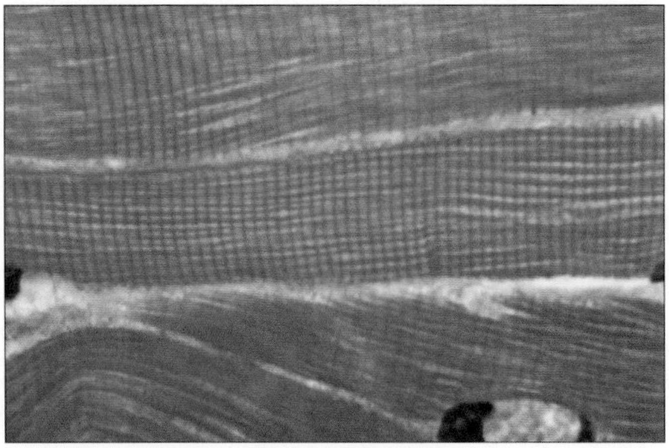

▲ **Figure 13-16** Striated muscle shown at 250 magnification

**Skeletal muscle** is a type of striated muscle. It is attached directly to the skeleton. Skeletal muscles make the body move. Move your foot. Open and close your fingers. These are movements you can control. Skeletal muscles are usually voluntary muscles. They are voluntary muscles because you can control their movements.

1 **NAME:** Name three places in your body where skeletal muscle is found.

**Smooth Muscle** Muscle tissue that is found in the walls of blood vessels, the stomach, and other internal organs is called smooth muscle. **Smooth muscle** causes movements that you cannot control. For this reason, smooth muscle is sometimes called involuntary muscle. For example, after you eat, you cannot stop the muscles lining your stomach from moving to help digest the food.

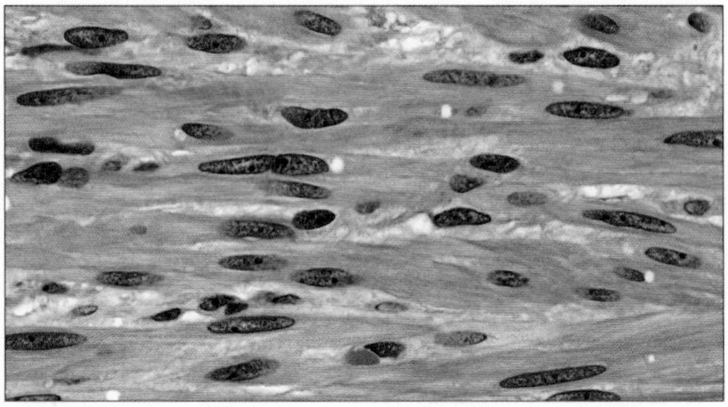

▲ **Figure 13-17** Smooth muscle shown at 160 magnification

2 **INFER:** Why do you think smooth muscle is often called involuntary muscle?

**Cardiac Muscle** The third kind of muscle is called cardiac muscle. The word *cardiac* means "heart." **Cardiac muscle** is found only in the heart and major blood vessels. Cardiac muscle is very strong. The heart must be strong to pump blood throughout the body. Cardiac muscle is striated. Unlike most striated muscle, cardiac muscle is involuntary. You have no control over your heart beating.

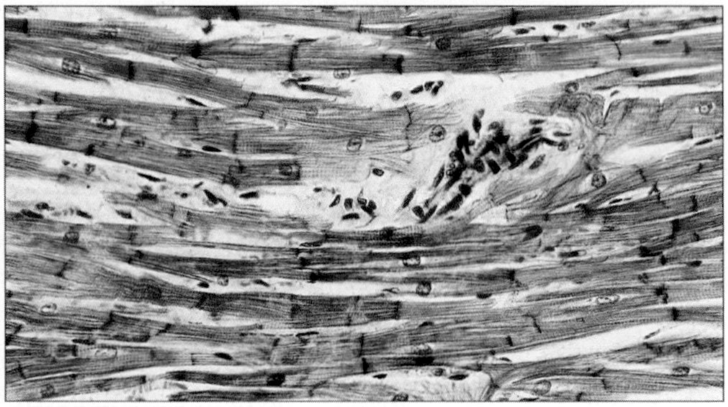

▲ **Figure 13-18** Cardiac muscle shown at 250 magnification

3 **IDENTIFY:** Where are the only places cardiac muscle is found?

## CHECKING CONCEPTS

1. The word *cardiac* means __________.
2. Smooth muscles are __________ muscles.
3. Blinking your eyes is usually caused by __________ muscles.
4. Striated muscle is usually __________ muscle.
5. The heart is made of __________ muscle.

## THINKING CRITICALLY

6. **COMPARE:** How are cardiac muscle and smooth muscle similar?
7. **INFER:** Why is the muscular system necessary for the circulatory and digestive systems to function?

## BUILDING SCIENCE SKILLS

***Classifying*** When you classify, you group things together based on similarities. Using reference materials, classify the following muscles as being voluntary or involuntary.

a. muscles in the eye that move your eye back and forth
b. cardiac muscle
c. muscles in your abdomen that you use to do sit-ups
d. muscles in the stomach that help digest your food
e. muscles in your blood vessels
f. muscles in your jaw
g. muscles in your legs

## *People in Science*

### PHYSICAL THERAPIST

▲ **Figure 13-19** Physical therapists help children improve their physical abilities.

Physical therapy is a medical specialty. Physical therapists help restore normal body functioning to patients who have some type of physical impairment. They often use exercise as a form of treatment. Many physical therapists work only with patients in a specific age group or with a specific disability. Physical therapists are employed by hospitals, clinics, and schools. Some work independently and are hired by the family of a disabled person.

Joelle Kelly is a physical therapist. She works only with children. Her day includes traveling to various schools and homes. Joelle treats children with a variety of conditions, such as Down syndrome and autism. She works with the children to improve their flexibility and muscle strength. These exercises help her patients carry out everyday activities such as walking to class and climbing stairs.

In order to become a physical therapist, you need a four-year college degree and a degree in physical therapy. Most physical therapists study biology, chemistry, and human anatomy. Students of physical therapy are often required to observe other physical therapists at work for many hours before they are allowed to treat their own patients.

**Thinking Critically** How could a physical therapist help a person who was injured in an accident?

Integrating Health

# THE Big IDEA

## How are sports injuries treated?

Sports and exercise can strengthen bones and muscles. They also can help make your joints more flexible. Flexibility allows your body to move easily. It also reduces strain on your back and other parts of your body. Sports and exercise are also good for your heart and your lungs.

Even though sports and exercise are good for you, they have risks. Sports injuries send 2.6 million children and young adults to hospitals each year. Some injuries are caused by overuse of a muscle. Other injuries are caused by trauma, such as a fall. Broken bones and sprained ankles are common injuries. Rest, ice, and special exercises heal many injuries.

Medical technology helps doctors examine and treat sports injuries. X-ray machines help doctors see bone injuries. Ultrasound imaging and magnetic resonance imaging are able to show soft tissue, such as ligaments.

An arthroscope helps doctors view joints inside the body. An arthroscope is a tiny video camera that is inserted through tiny cuts in the skin. By looking at a screen, doctors can examine a joint carefully. Doctors also perform surgery in this way with tiny instruments. Patients recover much faster from arthroscopic surgery than from open surgery.

Look at the pictures and text on these two pages. They point out technologies used to examine and treat bone and muscle injuries. Follow the directions in the Science Log to learn more about "the big idea." ✦

**Low-level Lasers**

Low-level lasers are pen-like devices that give off a concentrated amount of ultraviolet light. This device is not yet approved in the United States but has been used in many European countries for years. Low-level lasers are used to relieve pain related to sprains, muscle inflammation, and other sports injuries.

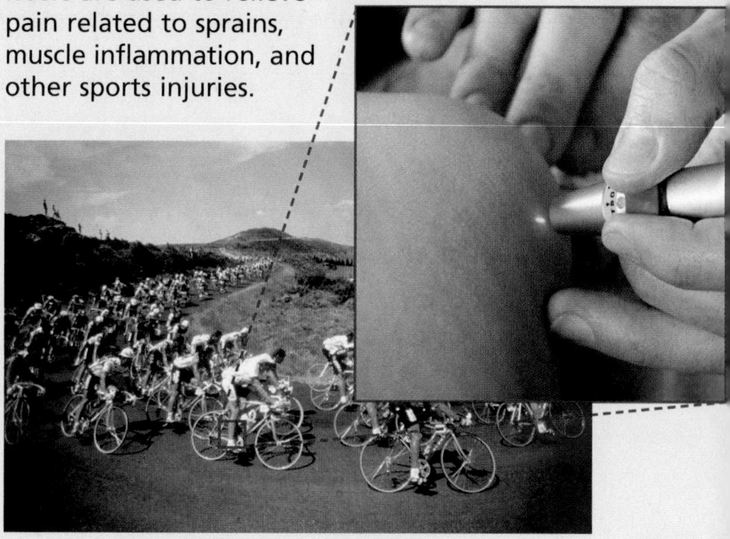

**Extracorporeal Shock Wave Therapy**

Tennis elbow gets its name because the backhand swing is a common cause of it. Tennis elbow is actually an irritated tendon in the forearm. It causes pain at the outside bump of the elbow. A technology used in Europe and Canada is being tested in the United States. It is called extracorporeal shock wave therapy. The machine uses low-energy shock waves to reduce pain.

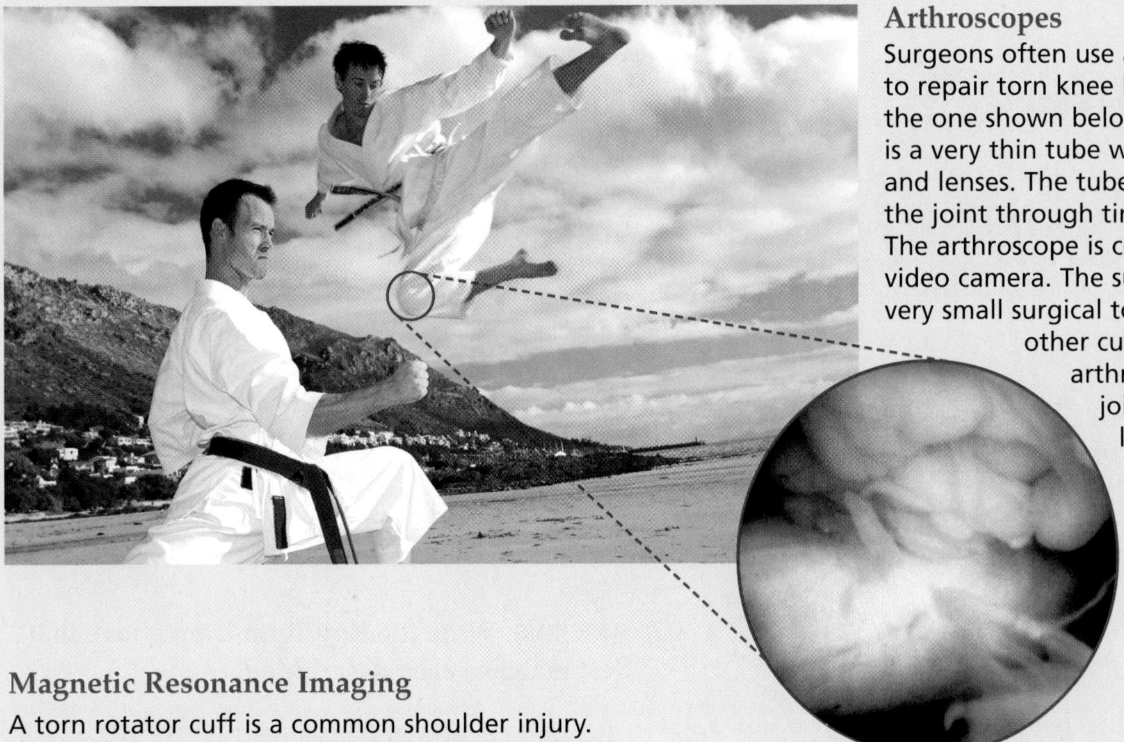

## Arthroscopes

Surgeons often use arthroscopes to repair torn knee ligaments like the one shown below. An arthroscope is a very thin tube with optical fibers and lenses. The tube is inserted into the joint through tiny cuts in the skin. The arthroscope is connected to a video camera. The surgeon inserts very small surgical tools through other cuts. The arthroscope makes the joint and the tools look large.

## Magnetic Resonance Imaging

A torn rotator cuff is a common shoulder injury. The rotator cuff is made up of four muscles that attach to the shoulder blade. The ends of the muscles are tendons that attach to the arm bone. MRI, or magnetic resonance imaging, is a medical tool that can be used to look at shoulder injuries. An MRI machine is a very strong magnet. It works with radio wave pulses of energy. Together they build a map of tissues. MRI can show the same tissue from different angles.

**WRITING ACTIVITY**

### Science Log

Look at the pictures on these two pages. Have you or anyone you know ever suffered a sports injury? In your science log, research and write about the technology that might be used to examine and treat this injury. Start your search at www.conceptsandchallenges.com.

# Chapter 13 Challenges

## Chapter Summary

### Lesson 13-1

- A group of cells that look alike and work together make up a **tissue.** Four types of tissues are muscle tissue, **epithelial tissue, connective tissue,** and nerve tissue.

### Lesson 13-2

- A group of tissues that work together to do a job is called an **organ.** A group of organs that works together is called an **organ system.**
- The **endocrine system** is made up of **glands** that make and give off substances used by the body.

### Lesson 13-3

- The skeleton supports and gives the body its shape. The bones of the **skeletal system** also protect organs and make red blood cells.
- **Cartilage** is a tough, flexible connective tissue that makes up parts of the skeletal system.

### Lesson 13-4

- The mostly solid part of a bone is called **compact bone.** The part of a bone with many spaces is called **spongy bone.** The spaces in spongy bone are filled with red bone **marrow.**

### Lesson 13-5

- A **joint** is where two bones meet. The three kinds of joints are fixed joints, partly movable joints, and movable joints.
- The four major kinds of movable joints are ball-and-socket joints, gliding joints, hinge joints, and pivotal joints.

### Lesson 13-6

- Muscles are tissues that can shorten along their length. Muscles usually work in pairs to move the body.
- **Flexors** are muscles that bend a joint. **Extensors** are muscles that straighten a joint.

### Lesson 13-7

- **Skeletal muscle** is muscle that you control for movement.
- **Smooth muscle** causes movements that you cannot control.
- **Cardiac muscle** is involuntary muscle found only in the heart and major blood vessels.

## Key Term Challenges

cardiac muscle (p. 320)
cartilage (p. 310)
compact bone (p. 312)
connective tissue (p. 306)
endocrine system (p. 308)
epithelial tissue (p. 306)
extensor (p. 316)
flexor (p. 316)
fracture (p. 312)
gland (p. 308)
joint (p. 314)
ligament (p. 306)
marrow (p. 312)
organ (p. 308)
organ system (p. 308)
periosteum (p. 312)
skeletal muscle (p. 320)
skeletal system (p. 310)
smooth muscle (p. 320)
spongy bone (p. 312)
striated muscle (p. 320)
tendon (p. 306)
tissue (p. 306)
vertebra (p. 310)

MATCHING **Write the Key Term from above that best matches each description.**

1. outer covering of a bone
2. striated, involuntary muscle found in the heart
3. place where two or more bones meet
4. connective tissue that connects bone to bone
5. bone made up of bone cells, protein fibers, and nonliving minerals
6. connective tissue that connects muscle to bone
7. strong, lightweight bone with many holes in it
8. organ that produces and secretes substances used by the body
9. involuntary muscle
10. group of organs that work together

IDENTIFYING WORD RELATIONSHIPS **Explain how the terms in each pair are related. Write your answers in complete sentences.**

11. extensor, flexor
12. bone, cartilage
13. skeletal muscle, cardiac muscle
14. tissues, organs
15. marrow, spongy bones

## Content Challenges TEST PREP

**MULTIPLE CHOICE** **Write the letter of the term or phrase that best completes each statement.**

1. The human skeletal system is made up of 206
   - **a.** bones.
   - **b.** muscles.
   - **c.** tendons.
   - **d.** ligaments.
2. Blood cells are made in the
   - **a.** periosteum.
   - **b.** compact bone.
   - **c.** striated muscle.
   - **d.** red bone marrow.
3. The kind of muscle found in the walls of blood vessels is
   - **a.** cardiac muscle.
   - **b.** skeletal muscle.
   - **c.** smooth muscle.
   - **d.** striated muscle.
4. Joints that allow movement in only one direction are
   - **a.** hinge joints.
   - **b.** ball-and-socket joints.
   - **c.** fixed joints.
   - **d.** gliding joints.
5. The joints that are found in the shoulder are
   - **a.** gliding joints.
   - **b.** pivotal joints.
   - **c.** hinge joints.
   - **d.** ball-and-socket joints.
6. As an embryo develops, the cartilage in the skeleton is replaced by
   - **a.** bone.
   - **b.** tendon.
   - **c.** ligaments.
   - **d.** muscle.
7. The connective tissue that connects a muscle to a bone is a
   - **a.** ligament.
   - **b.** tendon.
   - **c.** skeletal muscle.
   - **d.** bone marrow.
8. Skeletal muscle is
   - **a.** found in the heart.
   - **b.** found in the stomach.
   - **c.** involuntary.
   - **d.** voluntary.
9. Spongy bone is strong and
   - **a.** flexible.
   - **b.** lightweight.
   - **c.** fat.
   - **d.** heavy.
10. The backbone is made up of separate bones called
    - **a.** vertebrae.
    - **b.** cranium.
    - **c.** femurs.
    - **d.** tarsals.

**TRUE/FALSE** **Write *true* if the statement is true. If the statement is false, change the underlined term to make the statement true.**

11. The solid part of a bone is <u>compact</u> bone.
12. Fixed joints are found in the <u>neck</u>.
13. Muscles can only <u>push</u> bones.
14. Human beings have an <u>exoskeleton</u>.
15. Smooth muscle is <u>voluntary</u> muscle.

## *Concept Challenges* TEST PREP

**WRITTEN RESPONSE** **Answer each of the following questions in complete sentences.**

1. **EXPLAIN:** How do muscles work to move bones?
2. **INFER:** Discs of cartilage are found between the vertebrae. What function do you think these discs serve?
3. **INFER:** What happens to the cartilage between your ribs and breastbone when you breathe?
4. **PREDICT:** Calcium adds strength to bones. What might be the effect of a diet without enough calcium?
5. **LOCATE:** What are three parts of the human skeleton that contain cartilage?

**INTERPRETING A TABLE** **Use Figure 13-20 to answer the following questions.**

6. **OBSERVE:** How many organ systems does the human body have?
7. **NAME:** Which system includes the kidneys?
8. **IDENTIFY:** What is the function of the endocrine system?
9. **ANALYZE:** Which system is responsible for fighting disease?
10. **INFER:** Which body systems would be involved in an activity such as skate boarding? Explain your answer.

| SUMMARY OF ORGAN SYSTEMS | | |
|---|---|---|
| **System** | **Major Structures** | **Function** |
| Skeletal | Bones | Provides structure; supports and protects internal organs |
| Muscular | Muscles (skeletal, cardiac, and smooth) | Provides structure; supports and moves trunk and limbs |
| Circulatory | Heart, blood vessels, blood | Transports nutrients and wastes to and from all body tissues |
| Respiratory | Air passages, lungs | Carries air into and out of lungs, where gases (oxygen and carbon dioxide) are exchanged |
| Immune | Lymph nodes and vessels, white blood cells | Provides protection against infection and disease |
| Digestive | Mouth, esophagus, stomach, liver, pancreas, small and large intestines | Stores and digests food; absorbs nutrients; eliminates wastes |
| Excretory | Kidneys, ureters, bladder, urethra, skin, lungs | Eliminates waste; maintains water and chemical balance |
| Nervous | Brain, spinal cord, nerves, sense organs, receptors | Controls and coordinates body movements and senses; controls consciousness and creativity; helps monitor and maintain other body systems |
| Endocrine | Glands (such as adrenal, thyroid, and pancreas), hypothalamus | Maintains homeostasis; regulates metabolism, water and mineral balance, growth and sexual development, and reproduction |
| Reproductive | Ovaries, uterus, mammary glands (in females), testes (in males) | Produces offspring |

▲ **Figure 13-20**

# Chapter 14 Digestion and Nutrition

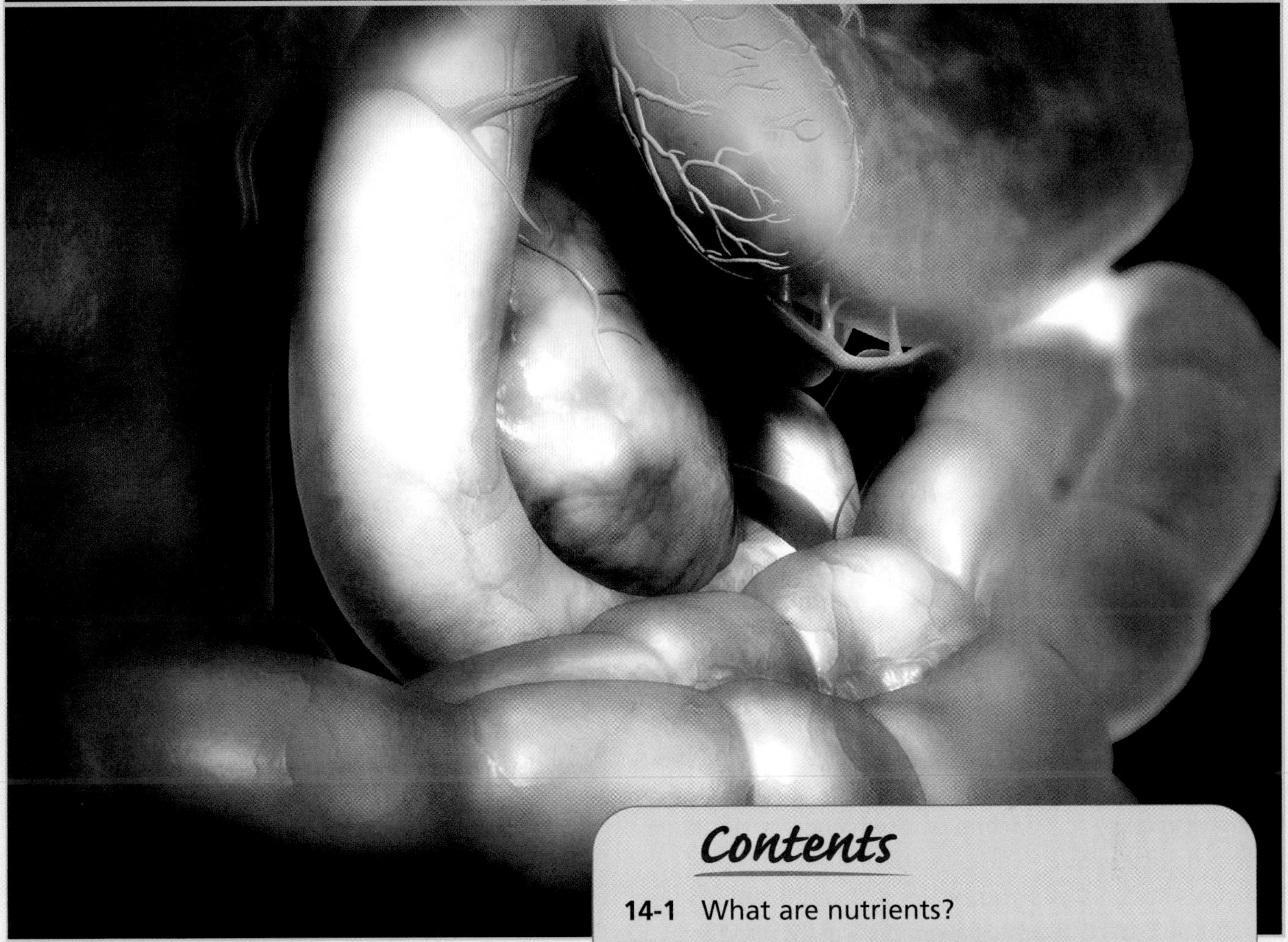

▲ **Figure 14-1** The digestive system

All of the nutrients your body needs come from food. However, the food you eat must be broken down into a form your body can use. This is done through digestion. Digested nutrients are absorbed into the bloodstream and carried to all of the cells in your body. Figure 14-1 shows an image of a healthy digestive system.

▶Why do you think digestive health is so important?

## Contents

# 14-1 What are nutrients?

***Objective***

Identify the nutrients used by the body.

***Key Terms***

**nutrient** (NOO-tree-uhnt): chemical substance that is needed to carry out life processes

**carbohydrate** (kahr-boh-HY-drayt): nutrient that supplies energy

**protein** (PROH-teen): nutrient needed to build and repair cells

**Nutrients** All foods contain nutrients. **Nutrients** are chemical substances in food that your body uses for growth and energy. Nutrients are also needed to carry out life processes. All of the cells of your body need nutrients in order to function. There are five main types of nutrients. They are carbohydrates, fats, proteins, vitamins, and minerals. There are not many foods that contain all five types of nutrients. This is why it is important to eat a variety of different foods.

1 **DEFINE:** What are nutrients?

**Carbohydrates** **Carbohydrates** are nutrients that supply your body with energy. Other nutrients such as fats and proteins provide energy as well but carbohydrates are more easily used by the body. They are your main source of energy.

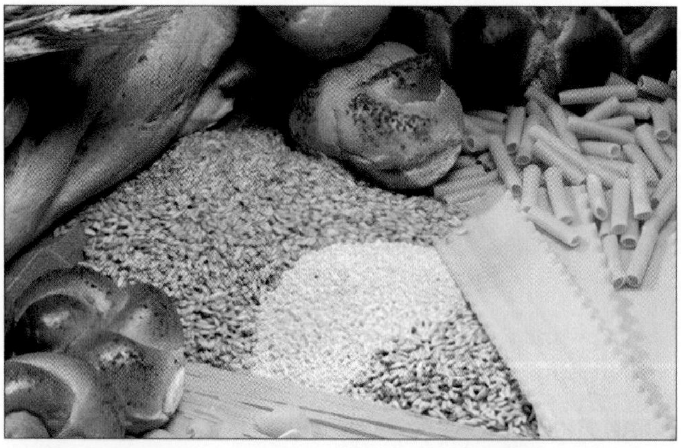

▲ **Figure 14-2** Common foods rich in carbohydrates

There are two kinds of carbohydrates, simple and complex. Sugars, such as sucrose and fructose, are simple carbohydrates. They give your body short, quick bursts of energy. Starches are complex carbohydrates. They give your body energy over a longer period of time. Breads, cereals, and pasta contain starch.

2 **NAME:** What are the two kinds of carbohydrates?

**Fats** Fats are the energy-storage nutrients. The stored energy in fats can be used if energy from carbohydrates is not available. Fat that is stored in the body is used for insulation (ihn-suh-LAY-shuhn). It keeps your body warm. Fat is also used to protect your body organs.

Fats can be either solids or liquids. Solid fats come mostly from animals. Butter and lard are solid fats. Liquid fats are called oils. They usually come from vegetables, such as corn or olives. Many oils are used in cooking.

▲ **Figure 14-3** Common foods rich in fats

3 **LIST:** Identify three ways the body uses fat.

**Proteins** Your body needs **proteins** for growth and repair. Proteins are also used to build tissues such as muscles. You get the building blocks for proteins from the foods you eat. Then, proteins are made in your body. When carbohydrates and fats have been used up, proteins can be used for energy. Milk, fish, meat, and cheese are good sources of protein. Peas, peanuts, and beans also contain protein.

▲ **Figure 14-4** Common foods rich in protein

**4** **EXPLAIN:** Why are proteins needed by the body?

**Essential Fluids** Although it is not a nutrient, your body needs a constant supply of water. More than two-thirds of your body is made up of water. Water is needed to carry out your life processes. Most of the chemical changes that take place in your body require water. Water also helps control your body temperature. You should try to drink at least six glasses of water each day.

**5** **INFER:** What might happen if you do not drink enough water?

## CHECKING CONCEPTS

1. Your body needs __________ for growth, for energy, and to perform life processes.
2. Simple carbohydrates give your body energy over a __________ period of time.
3. The energy-storage nutrients are __________.
4. Your body uses __________ to build and repair cells.
5. Breads and pastas are good sources of __________ carbohydrates.

## THINKING CRITICALLY

6. **HYPOTHESIZE:** Why is some fat a necessary part of your diet?
7. **INFER:** Why should you eat more complex carbohydrates than simple carbohydrates?
8. **EXPLAIN:** Why is water an important part of a diet?

## *Hands-On Activity*

### TESTING FOR STARCH

*You will need iodine, a medicine dropper, five different types of seeds, a small dish, water, and a knife.*

1. Soak the seeds in a dish of water overnight.
2. The next day, remove the seed coats from the seeds. Observe the seed coats.
3. Break apart the seeds. You may need to cut some of the seeds in half with the knife.
   ⚠ CAUTION: Be careful when cutting with a knife.
4. Place a drop of iodine on one side of each seed. Iodine changes color when starch is present.

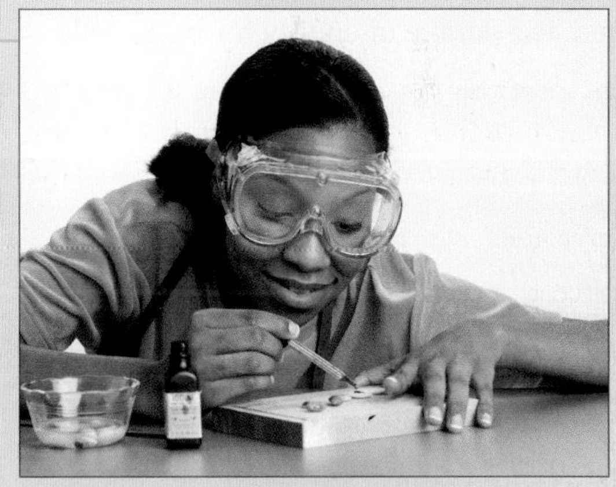

▲ **STEP 4** Place a drop of iodine on each seed.

**Practicing Your Skills**

5. **OBSERVE:** To what color did the iodine change when starch was present?
6. **APPLY:** Which of the seeds contained starch?
7. **INFER:** What do you think the starch in seeds is used for by plants?

# 14-2 Why are proteins important?

## *Objective*

List five ways the body uses proteins.

## *Key Terms*

**molecule:** smallest part of a substance that has all the properties of that substance

**amino acid:** building block of proteins

**Protein Molecules** A **molecule** is the smallest part of a substance that has all the properties of that substance. Proteins are giant molecules. In fact, proteins are one of the largest molecules in living things. All proteins contain atoms of carbon, hydrogen, oxygen, and nitrogen.

1 **NAME:** What atoms do protein molecules contain?

**Importance of Proteins** Proteins are the building blocks of living material. Your body uses proteins in several ways. One important use of proteins is to build new cells. Another use of proteins is to repair cells that are damaged. Proteins are also used to make enzymes. They can also be used as a source of energy for body cells.

2 **EXPLAIN:** How are proteins used by the body?

**Amino Acids** Proteins are formed when many smaller molecules join together. The smaller molecules that make up proteins are **amino acids.** There are about 20 different amino acids. Twelve of these amino acids are made in the body. The other eight amino acids must be taken into the body. The foods you eat contain different amino acids. The amino acids are put together in many different ways to form thousands of different proteins. This is like making thousands of words from the 26 letters of the alphabet.

3 **IDENTIFY:** What are the building blocks of proteins?

**Protein Synthesis** The body uses proteins in foods to make the special proteins it needs. When proteins in food are digested, the amino acids are separated from one another. Cells in your body make their own proteins by putting these amino acids together again in their own special way. This is called protein synthesis. Protein synthesis occurs in the endoplasmic reticulum and ribosomes of your cells. Your genes carry the genetic codes for protein synthesis.

4 **INFER:** Why do you think the body can make so many proteins?

| ESSENTIAL AMINO ACIDS | | |
|---|---|---|
| **Amino Acids** | **Use in Body** | **Food Sources** |
| Isoleucine | Works with leucine to promote alertness | Fish, meat, wheat germ, and most seeds and nuts |
| Lysine | Helps absorb calcium; helps hormones and enzymes | Wheat germ, dairy products, fish, meat, many fruits and vegetables |
| Valine | Helps in muscle coordination | Found in most foods |
| Threonine | Assists in digestive processes | Meat, dairy products, and eggs |
| Phenylalanine | Produces chemicals that transmit signals between nerve cells and the brain | Meat and dairy products |
| Leucine | Works with isoleucine to promote alertness | Meat, dairy products, wheat germ, and oats |
| Methionine | Helps reduce cholesterol; reduces liver fat; protects the kidneys; promotes healthy hair growth | Dairy products, eggs, and fish |
| Tryptophan | Relaxes; helps boost the immune system; helps to reduce cholesterol levels | Meat, eggs, dairy products, and most seeds and nuts |
| Histidine | Required by infants; helps promote healthy nerve tissue and hearing | Meat, eggs, cheese, lima beans, and peas |

▲ **Figure 14-5**

## ✓ CHECKING CONCEPTS

1. The smallest part of a substance that has all the properties of that substance is a __________.
2. All proteins contain atoms of carbon, oxygen, hydrogen, and __________.
3. Proteins are the __________ of living material.
4. Proteins are made of __________.
5. There are about __________ different amino acids.
6. Cells make proteins during a process called __________.

## THINKING CRITICALLY

7. **ANALYZE:** Why is a diet low in protein unhealthy?
8. **RELATE:** How are amino acids like letters of the alphabet?
9. **INTERPRET:** In which food sources can you find leucine?
10. **INTERPRET:** In which food sources can you find valine?

## INTERPRETING VISUALS

*Use Figure 14-5 and the list below to answer the following questions.*

| | | |
|---|---|---|
| **a.** spinach | **d.** meat | **g.** oatmeal |
| **b.** milk | **e.** eggs | **h.** wheat germ |
| **c.** beans | **f.** fish | **i.** peanut butter |

11. Many plant foods do not contain all of the essential amino acids. Which of the essential amino acids can be found in each of the foods listed above?
12. If you were a vegetarian, which foods could you eat in order to get all of the essential amino acids?

## *Integrating Physical Science*

**TOPIC: chemical bonds**

### PEPTIDE BONDS

Proteins are made up of building blocks called amino acids. Amino acids are made up of a molecule containing nitrogen and hydrogen and a molecule containing carbon, oxygen, and hydrogen. When a nitrogen molecule in one amino acid is joined with a carbon molecule from another amino acid, a peptide bond is formed and a molecule of water is given off as a byproduct. Small proteins are called peptides. More amino acids can be added until the peptide chain stretches out to dozens or even hundreds of amino-acid units. These very large peptides are proteins.

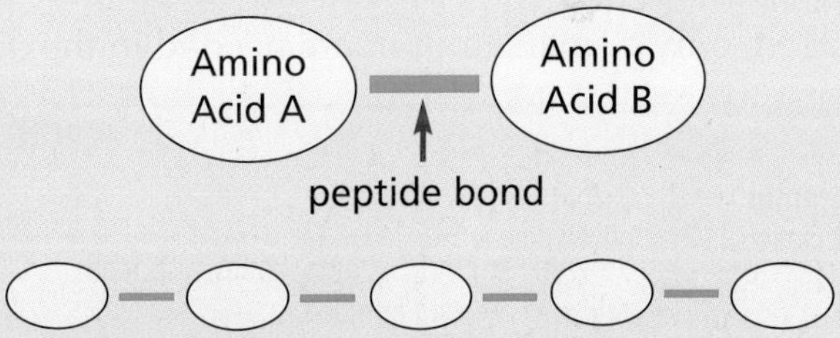


▲ **Figure 14-6** Peptide bonds form between two amino acids. Many amino acids form a chain.

The formation of a peptide bond does not happen by itself. Enzymes, or chemicals, bring the amino acids together and help them to react. Other enzymes help your body change the proteins you eat back into amino acids. To break a peptide bond and release the amino acids, a molecule of water must be added.

**Thinking Critically** Why is protein an important part of our diets?

# 14-3 Why are vitamins important?

*Objective*

Explain why vitamins are important.

*Key Terms*

**vitamin** (VYT-uh-mihn)**:** nutrient found in foods that is required by the body and is made by other organisms

**deficiency** (dee-FIHSH-uhn-see) **disease:** disease caused by the lack of a certain nutrient

**Vitamins** Your body needs small amounts of vitamins so it can function properly. **Vitamins** are nutrients that are made by living organisms. You get most of the vitamins you need from food. However, small amounts of vitamins D and K are made in your body. Figure 14-7 lists some vitamins humans need.

1 **DEFINE:** What are vitamins?

**Importance of Vitamins** Vitamins are important for proper growth. They are important for keeping bones, teeth, muscles, and nerves healthy. Vitamins also help control many of the chemical activities that take place in your body. Vitamins can be reused by the body. For this reason, only a small amount are needed in the diet.

Most vitamins work with other vitamins or nutrients. Some vitamins help to change carbohydrates and fats into energy. Unlike carbohydrates and fats, vitamins do not give off energy. Figure 14-7 lists some uses of vitamins in the body.

2 **EXPLAIN:** How are vitamins used in your body?

**Deficiency Disease** The tissues of your body need small amounts of vitamins every day. If your diet does not include enough of a certain vitamin, you may become sick. This kind of sickness is called a **deficiency disease.** Rickets is a deficiency disease that causes soft bones and teeth. Rickets is caused by a lack of vitamin D. Figure 14-7 lists some other deficiency diseases.

3 **DEFINE:** What is a deficiency disease?

**Classifying Vitamins** Vitamins are either fat soluble or water soluble. Fat soluble vitamins dissolve in fat. They are stored in fatty tissues. Some fat-soluble vitamins are vitamins A, D, E, and K. Water-soluble vitamins dissolve in water. They are not stored in the body. Vitamin C and all of the B vitamins are water-soluble vitamins.

4 **INFER:** Why is it very important to include water-soluble vitamins in your daily diet?

**IMPORTANCE OF VITAMINS**

| Vitamin | Use in Body | Sources | Deficiency Disease |
|---|---|---|---|
| A | Growth; healthy skin, eyes, bones, and teeth; ability to see well at night | Orange and dark green vegetables, eggs, fruits, liver, milk | Night blindness |
| $B_1$ (thiamine) | Growth; healthy nerves, muscles and heart; helps body get energy from carbohydrates | Pork, whole grain foods, soybeans | Beriberi |
| $B_2$ (riboflavin) | Growth; healthy skin and eyes; helps body get energy from carbohydrates, fats, and proteins | Green vegetables, milk, beef, chicken | Skin disorders |
| $B_2$ (folic acid) | Also called folate; healthy fetal development | Beans, leafy vegetables, peas, corn, beets, blackberries, strawberries | Birth defects |
| $B_3$ (niacin) | Growth; works with other B vitamins to get energy from nutrients in cells | Beans, chicken, eggs, tuna, potatoes | Pellagra |
| C | Healthy teeth, gums, and blood vessels | Citrus fruits, tomatoes, leafy vegetables | Scurvy |
| D | Healthy bones and teeth; helps body use calcium | Eggs, milk, made by skin in sunlight | Rickets |
| E | Healthy blood and muscles; normal reproduction | Leafy vegetables, vegetable oil, milk | Mild anemia |
| K | Healthy liver, normal blood clotting | Green vegetables, tomatoes | Poor blood clotting |

▲ **Figure 14-7**

## CHECKING CONCEPTS

1. Required nutrients in foods that are made by other living organisms are __________.
2. You get most of your vitamins from __________.
3. A __________ is caused by a diet that is missing a certain nutrient.
4. An example of a deficiency disease that causes soft bones is __________.

## THINKING CRITICALLY

5. **INFER:** How would eating a balanced diet help prevent a deficiency disease?
6. **HYPOTHESIZE:** Why do you think many foods you eat, such as bread and milk, are "fortified" with vitamins?
7. **INFER:** Why do you think many people take a vitamin supplement?

## INTERPRETING VISUALS

*Use Figure 14-7 to answer the following questions.*

8. **ANALYZE:** You have cut yourself and note that your blood is slow to clot. What vitamin might you be lacking in your diet? Explain.
9. **INTERPRET:** What vitamins help the body get energy from carbohydrates?
10. **ANALYZE:** If you have scurvy, what vitamin are you missing in your diet?
11. **INTERPRET:** What is another name for vitamin $B_1$?
12. **INTERPRET:** What is the deficiency disease for vitamin A?

## *How Do They Know That?*

### VITAMIN K AND BLOOD

▲ **Figure 14-8** Vitamin K is found in these foods.

Many biochemists study how vitamins behave in the body. They use that information to prevent or treat deficiency diseases. Biochemists conduct experiments to study the chemical nature of vitamins. One such study involved vitamin K. Vitamin K dissolves in fat. It is made in the body and is present in certain foods, such as leafy green vegetables.

Dr. Edward Doisy was an American biochemist. He studied vitamin K. In 1943, he shared a Nobel Prize in medicine with the Danish biochemist Dr. Henrik Dam for their research on vitamin K. Dr. Doisy determined the chemical structure of vitamin K. Dr. Doisy used this information to make a vitamin K pill. Dr. Dam's research team proved that vitamin K makes several proteins that are necessary to help blood to clot. If blood does not clot, a person could bleed to death.

Dr. Dam and Dr. Doisy's research led others to conclude that vitamin K could be used to cure diseases in which a person cannot stop bleeding.

**Thinking Critically** Why is the ability to reproduce vitamin K in a pill an important discovery?

# 14-4 Why are minerals important?

***Objective***

Explain why minerals are important.

***Key Term***

**mineral:** nutrient needed by the body to develop and function properly

**Minerals** Your body needs minerals as well as vitamins. **Minerals** are nutrients needed for the body to develop and function properly. You need small amounts of some minerals and large amounts of other minerals. For example, you need small amounts of iron, iodine, and zinc. You need larger amounts of calcium, phosphorus (FAHS-fuh-ruhs), and sodium.

1 **DEFINE:** What are minerals?

**Important Uses of Minerals** Each mineral has a different job. For example, iron is needed to form red blood cells. Calcium and phosphorus are needed to build strong teeth and bones. Bones contain calcium. It gives them strength. If calcium is removed from bones, they become soft and weak. Sodium is needed for healthy muscles and nerves. Chlorine is needed to make hydrochloric acid, a chemical used in digestion. Iodine controls body growth and the oxidation of food. Figure 14-9 lists some important minerals and their uses.

2 **EXPLAIN:** What happens when calcium is removed from bones?

**Deficiency Disease** A deficiency disease can be caused if certain minerals are missing from the diet. For example, if you take in too little iron, a deficiency disease called anemia can result. Anemia is sometimes called iron-poor blood. If you are deficient in iodine, a deficiency disease called goitre can result. Figure 14-9 lists some signs of mineral deficiency.

3 **IDENTIFY:** What deficiency disease is caused by too little iodine?

| IMPORTANCE OF MINERALS | | | |
|---|---|---|---|
| **Mineral** | **Use** | **Sources** | **Signs of Deficiency** |
| Calcium | Builds strong bones and teeth; healthy functioning of heart and muscles | Milk and milk products, fish, green leafy vegetables | Soft bones, poor teeth |
| Phosphorus | Builds strong bones and teeth; forms nucleic acids and energy molecules | Red meat, fish, milk products, poultry, whole grain cereal | Rickets, osteoperosis, muscle spasms in fingers and toes |
| Iron | Builds red blood cells | Red meat, whole grains, liver, egg yolks, nuts, green leafy vegetables | Paleness, weakness, tiredness, brittle fingernails |
| Sodium | Helps keep muscles and blood healthy; helps nerves function properly | Table salt, found naturally in many foods | None known |
| Iodine | Is used to make a chemical that controls oxidation | Seafood, iodized salt | Goitre, swelling of neck, difficulty swallowing |
| Potassium | Helps keep muscles and nerves healthy | Bananas, oranges, apricots, vegetables | Loss of water from cells, heart problems, high blood pressure |
| Magnesium | Builds strong bones and muscles, nerve action | Nuts, whole grains, green leafy vegetables | Kidney disease, weakness, dizziness, distention of abdomen, seizures |
| Zinc | Helps in the formation of enzymes | Milk, eggs, seafood, whole grains | Skin lesions, night blindness, hair loss |

▲ **Figure 14-9**

## ✓ CHECKING CONCEPTS

1. Your body needs __________ as well as vitamins.
2. The body needs large amounts of calcium, phosphorus, and __________.
3. Sodium is needed for healthy muscles and __________.
4. Bones are hard because they contain __________.

## THINKING CRITICALLY

5. INTERPRET: What foods contain iodine?
6. INTERPRET: Which minerals help build strong teeth and bones?
7. INTERPRET: What foods are good sources of potassium?
8. INFER: You are feeling tired and weak. What mineral might you be deficient in?

## Web InfoSearch

**Calcium** Ninety-nine percent of the calcium you need is in your teeth and bones. The other 1 percent is in body tissues such as blood and muscle. The only way that you get calcium is through your diet or from the calcium in your bones. If your body takes more calcium from your bones than it can replace, your bones become weak. This can lead to a disease called osteoporosis.

**SEARCH:** Use the Internet to find out more about calcium. Then, create a brochure encouraging people to make sure they have enough calcium in their diets. Start your search at www.conceptsandchallenges.com. Some key search words are **calcium** and **osteoporosis.**

## *Integrating Earth Science*

TOPICS: Earth's crust, rocks, minerals

### MINERALS FROM EARTH

The minerals that our bodies need are natural substances, but they are not produced by living things. Scientists call them inorganic compounds. Substances that are produced by living organisms are organic compounds. Minerals come from rocks in Earth's crust.

▲ **Figure 14-10** Minerals are found in rocks. Pyrite, shown above, contains the mineral iron.

Can you imagine eating rocks? Rocks are mixtures of minerals. Different processes on Earth change rock minerals into forms that we can use. Water flowing over a rock may dissolve small amounts of minerals and carry them into the soil and into rivers, streams, and oceans. Plants play an important role in supplying us with minerals we can use. They take up minerals through the film of moisture that surrounds their roots. They change these minerals into a form that can be digested. We take in minerals when we eat plants. We also get some minerals by eating animals that have eaten plants and by drinking water.

When nutritionists list minerals in foods, they use the names of the elements, such as sodium or calcium. Actually, minerals are often in the form of compounds, in which the elements are chemically bonded to other elements. Table salt, for example, is sodium chloride. Calcium can be obtained from the compound calcium carbonate.

**Thinking Critically** How do plants supply us with the minerals we need?

# LAB ACTIVITY
# Testing Foods for Nutrients

**Materials**

Safety goggles, apron, protective gloves, milk, beef broth, apple juice, orange juice, lemon juice, water, graduated cylinder, 12 test tubes with stoppers, Biuret solution, indophenol, test tube rack, dropper

### *BACKGROUND*

The useful parts of the food you eat are called nutrients. Carbohydrates, such as starches and sugars, are nutrients. Another important group of nutrients is proteins. Your body needs proteins to help build and repair its cells. Minerals and vitamins are also nutrients.

### *PURPOSE*

In this activity, you will learn how to test foods to see whether they contain proteins and vitamin C. Biuret solution will be used to test for proteins and indophenol will be used to test for vitamin C.

### *PROCEDURE*

1. Copy the data chart in Figure 14-11 onto a sheet of paper.

2. Make a hypothesis to predict which of the foods in the materials list will contain proteins and which will contain vitamin C. Put on your safety goggles, apron, and protective gloves.

3. Use a graduated cylinder to measure out 10 mL of milk into one of the test tubes.

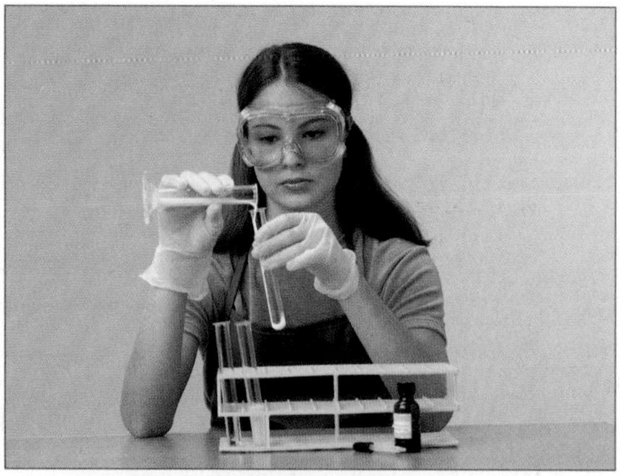

▲ **STEP 3** Measure 10 mL of milk into a test tube.

*Testing for Food Nutrients*

| Food | Test | Chemical | Observation | Nutrient |
|---|---|---|---|---|
| | | | | |

▲ **Figure 14-11** Copy this data chart onto a sheet of paper.

4. Add five drops of Biuret solution to the milk. Put a stopper in the test tube and shake it.

5. Compare the color of the tested milk to the color of the original milk. Record your observations.

6. Rinse out the dropper and the graduated cylinder. Measure out 10 mL of indophenol into a clean test tube.

7. Add milk drop by drop into the test tube of indophenol. Observe what happens to the color of the indophenol. Note how many drops were needed to cause a color change. Record your observations in your data chart.

8. Repeat Steps 3–7 for beef broth, apple juice, orange juice, lemon juice, and water. Make sure you rinse out the graduated cylinder and dropper after each food test.

9. In your data chart, underline the foods that turned color with the Biuret solution. Circle the foods that produced a color change with the indophenol most quickly.

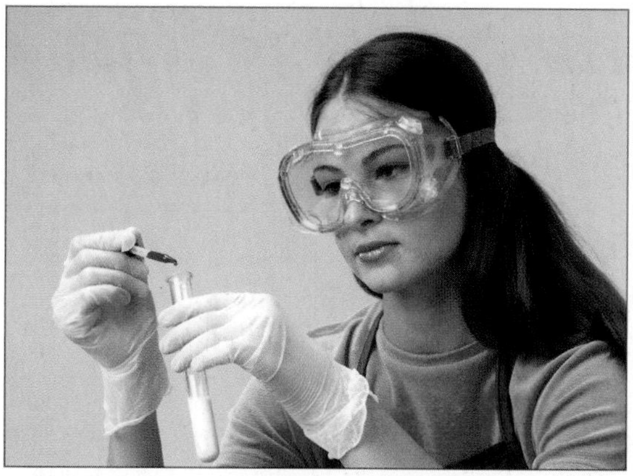

▲ **STEP 4** Add five drops of Biuret solution.

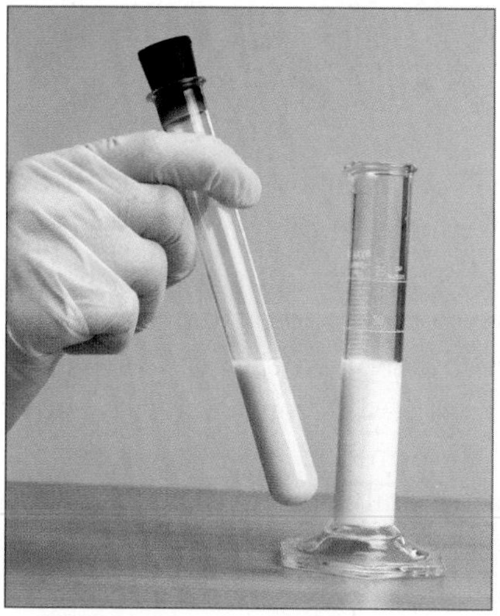

▲ **STEP 5** Record any changes in the milk in your data chart.

## *CONCLUSIONS*

1. **IDENTIFY:** Biuret solution turns purple in the presence of protein. Which of the foods tested contain protein? Was your hypothesis correct?

2. **APPLY:** The darker the purple color of the Biuret solution, the more protein is present. Which of the foods tested contain the greatest amount of protein?

3. **IDENTIFY:** Indophenol turns colorless when vitamin C is present. Which of the foods tested contain vitamin C? Was your hypothesis correct?

4. **APPLY:** The more vitamin C there is in a liquid, the less liquid it takes to turn indophenol colorless. Which of the liquids tested has the most vitamin C?

# 14-5 What is a balanced diet?

***Objective***

Describe how to use the Food Guide Pyramid to plan a balanced diet.

***Key Term***

**malnutrition** (mal-noo-TRISH-uhn)**:** poor nutrition caused by an unbalanced diet

**A Balanced Diet** Diets that contain the right amount of nutrients are called balanced diets. Eating a balanced diet will help you stay healthy. Many people think that eating a balanced diet is difficult. Eating a balanced diet is really quite simple.

**1 EXPLAIN:** Why is a balanced diet important?

**My Pyramid** The U.S. Department of Agriculture created the My Pyramid guide to help people balance their diets. The guide shows the types and amounts of foods a person should eat each day. Since all people are different, the USDA provides different pyramids to fit different dietary needs. These needs are determined by age, gender, weight, and amount of daily activity. The pyramid suggests eating a variety of foods to get the nutrients you need. You can find your pyramid at www.mypyramid.gov.

▲ **Figure 14-12** The My Pyramid guide

**2 STATE:** What is the My Pyramid guide?

**Reading Food Labels** The U.S. Food and Drug Administration requires that all processed foods have a food label. A food label lists the nutritional information of the food. It also lists all the ingredients in the food. Figure 14-13 is a food label.

**Nutrition Facts**

Serving Size: 1 cup
Servings Per Container: About 9

| | |
|---|---|
| **Calories** 100 | |
| Calories from fat 0 | |
| | % Daily Value |
| **Total fat** 0g | 0% |
| Saturated Fat 0g | 0% |
| **Cholesterol** 0mg | 0% |
| **Sodium** 10mg | 0% |
| **Total Carbohydrate** 31g | 10% |
| Dietary Fiber 2g | 9% |
| Sugars 29g | |

▲ **Figure 14-13** A food label

The first item listed on a food label is the serving size. This is the recommended amount you should eat. The rest of the information on the label is based on the serving size. If you eat twice the recommended serving size, you consume twice the number of nutrients and calories listed on the label. Next to each nutrient is the percent daily value. This tells you how the nutritional content of the food fits into your diet. The daily values are based on the diet of someone who consumes 2,000 calories a day.

**3 OBSERVE:** What is the percent daily value of sodium listed on the food label in Figure 14-13?

Go Online
*active art*

**For:** Reading a Food Pyramid activity
**Visit:** PHSchool.com
**Web Code:** cep-4022

**Planning a Balanced Diet** You can see in Figure 14-12 that foods are classified into six groups. The orange, blue, and green/red bands—grains, milk, and vegetables/fruits—should make up the largest part of your diet. The purple and yellow bands—meat/beans and oils—contain necessary nutrients, but your body needs smaller amounts per day.

You body needs a certain amount of calories each day. Calories can be divided into *essentials* and *extras.* If you eat all your essential calories, you may still have a small amount of calories left over for extras. These can be from the pyramid, or they can be foods with little or no nutritional value.

4 **EXPLAIN:** How can you use the My Pyramid guide to plan a balanced diet?

**Malnutrition** When your body is not properly nourished, it becomes weak. This disorder is called **malnutrition.** Many people think malnutrition occurs only from a lack of food. However, anyone can be malnourished. If you eat too many foods from one group and not enough foods from another group, you can become malnourished.

5 **STATE:** What might happen if you eat too much from one food group and not enough from another food group?

## CHECKING CONCEPTS

1. What is a balanced diet?
2. What is a food label?
3. Name two foods from each of the groups in the My Pyramid guide. Check your answers at www.Mypyramid.gov.

## THINKING CRITICALLY

4. **HYPOTHESIZE:** How can an overweight person be malnourished?
5. **EXPLAIN:** Is an all-protein diet healthy? Explain.

## HEALTH AND SAFETY TIP

***Eating Disorders*** Bulimia (byoo-LEE-mee-uh) and anorexia (an-uh-REHKS-ee-uh) are harmful eating disorders. Bulimia and anorexia threaten good health and even life. People with bulimia eat large amounts of food at one time. Then, they either throw up the food or use laxatives. People with anorexia are usually underweight. They refuse to eat food. There are many self-help groups that can help people with bulimia and people with anorexia. Create a prevention poster warning someone against eating disorders.

## Real-Life Science

### CHOLESTEROL

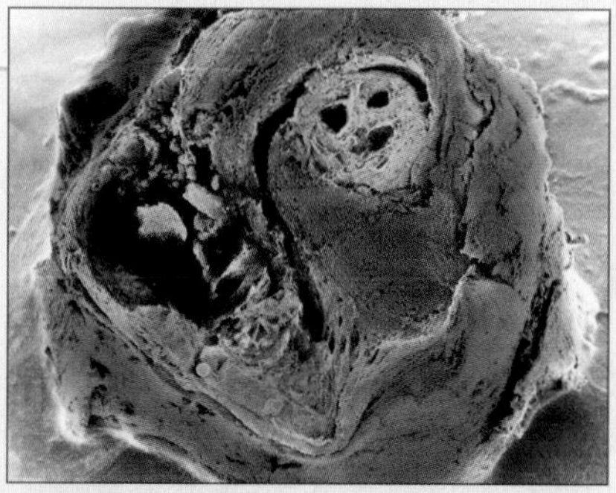

▲ **Figure 14-14** Thick plaque, shown in yellow, clogs arteries.

You have probably heard of people with high cholesterol watching what they eat. Cholesterol can form a yellow plaque on the inside of your arteries. The plaque can become thick enough to reduce the flow of blood to your heart. This may lead to a heart attack. This type of cholesterol is called low density lipoprotein, or LDL. This cholesterol is harmful to your body.

Not all cholesterol is bad. High density lipoprotein, or HDL, is good. Without HDL, the cell membranes of animals would have no support. HDL is also part of the chemical messengers that regulate many body functions.

The ratio of LDL to HDL in your blood can tell a physician if you are at risk for some types of heart disease. If you exercise regularly, the amount of HDL will increase and the amount of LDL may decrease. Once you are over the age of 20 years, you should have your cholesterol levels and ratios checked regularly.

**Thinking Critically** Fatty foods are usually high in LDL. Do you think someone with a high level of LDL should eat fatty foods?

# 14-6 What is the digestive system?

### *Objective*

Identify the organs in the human digestive system.

### *Key Terms*

**digestion** (dih-JEHS-chuhn): process of breaking down food so that it can be used by living things

**saliva:** liquid in the mouth that helps in digestion

**pharynx** (FAR-inks): tube connecting the mouth to the esophagus; throat

**epiglottis** (ehp-uh-GLAHT-ihs): flap of tissue that prevents food from entering the windpipe

**esophagus** (ih-SAHF-uh-guhs): tube that connects the mouth to the stomach

**peristalsis** (per-uh-STAL-sihs): wavelike movement that moves food through the digestive tract

**Digestion** Most of the foods that you eat are not in a form that your body can use. The foods you eat must be changed so that they can be used by the body. The process by which foods are changed into usable forms is called **digestion.** During digestion, larger pieces of food are broken down into smaller pieces. Complex molecules in food are changed into simpler ones.

1 **DEFINE:** What is digestion?

**The Digestive Tract** The foods that you eat move through a coiled tube inside the body. This tube is called the digestive tract. It is about 10 m long. Some parts are narrow. Other parts are wide. The digestive tract and all of the organs that help with digestion make up your digestive system. The digestive organs that help with digestion are the liver, the pancreas (PAN-kree-uhs), and the gallbladder. These organs are not part of the digestive tract. However, they play an important role in digestion.

2 **IDENTIFY:** What organs help with digestion but are not part of the digestive tract?

**Parts of the Digestive System** Figure 14-15 shows the digestive system. Food enters the digestive system through the mouth. In the mouth, food is chewed and mixes with a liquid called **saliva,** which is produced by the salivary glands.

Once food is swallowed, it enters the **pharynx,** or throat. The pharynx is a passageway for both food and air. Air moves from the pharynx to the windpipe. As you swallow, a thin flap of tissue keeps food from entering the windpipe. This flap of tissue is called the **epiglottis.** Food moves into a long tube called the **esophagus.** The esophagus connects the mouth to the stomach. From the stomach, food moves into another narrow tube called the small intestine. The small intestine leads into the large intestine. The end of the large intestine is called the rectum.

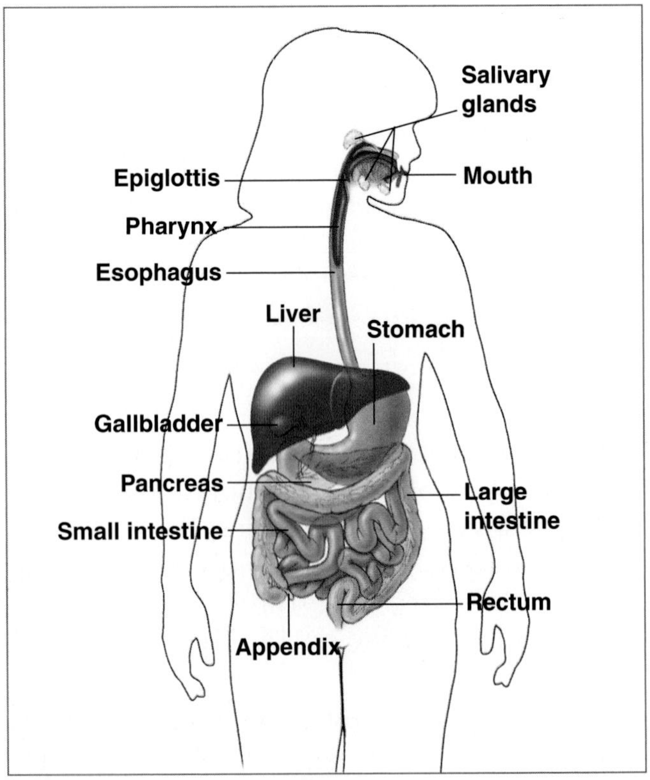


▲ **Figure 14-15** The digestive system

3 **NAME:** What are the organs of the digestive system?

**Peristalsis** Once food leaves the mouth, it enters the esophagus. The walls of the esophagus secrete mucus. The mucus helps the food move easily through the esophagus. Once food leaves the esophagus, it continues along the digestive tract. Food is moved through the digestive tract by wavelike movements of muscles. The wavelike movement that moves food through the digestive tract is called **peristalsis.**

4 DEFINE: What is peristalsis?

## CHECKING CONCEPTS

1. What is the process by which food is turned into usable forms?
2. What is the end of the large intestine called?
3. How does food move through the digestive tract?
4. What connects the mouth to the stomach?
5. What prevents food from entering the windpipe?

## THINKING CRITICALLY

6. **SEQUENCE:** Develop a flowchart to show the parts of the digestive tract through which food passes, in order, beginning with the mouth.
7. **INFER:** Why do you think food must be broken down into smaller pieces?

## HEALTH AND SAFETY TIP

Sometimes a piece of food accidentally enters the windpipe. When this happens, choking occurs. To help prevent choking, you should chew your food carefully, eat slowly, and avoid talking or running with food in your mouth. If you should choke on anything, give the universal sign of choking shown in Figure 14-16. Use library references to find out what to do if someone you are eating with begins to choke.

▲ **Figure 14-16** The universal sign of choking

## *Hands-On Activity*

### MODELING PERISTALSIS

*You will need a clear, flexible plastic straw and a small bead. The bead should fit snugly inside the straw.*

1. Insert the bead into the straw.
2. Pinch the straw directly above the bead so that the bead moves down the straw. Release the straw when the bead moves.
3. Continue to pinch and release the straw to move the bead until the bead exits the straw.

▲ **STEP 2** Pinch the straw above the bead.

**Practicing Your Skills**

4. **APPLY:** What does the bead represent?
5. **APPLY:** What does the plastic straw represent?
6. **EXPLAIN:** How does this activity model peristalsis?
7. **INFER:** What might happen if you try to swallow a large piece of food?

# 14-7 What is digestion?

## *Objectives*

Compare mechanical and chemical digestion.
Explain the function of enzymes.

## *Key Terms*

**mechanical digestion:** process by which large pieces of food are cut and crushed into smaller pieces

**enamel:** hard, outer coating of the tooth

**dentin:** spongy substance below the enamel of the tooth

**chemical digestion:** process by which large food molecules are broken down into smaller food molecules

**enzyme:** protein that controls chemical reactions in the body

**Digestion** Digestion is the process of changing foods into usable forms. Food is changed two ways, physically and chemically. Changes in shape and size are examples of physical changes. If you tear a sheet of paper, that is a physical change. A chemical change results in new substances. For example, a log burning is a chemical change. The wood is changed into ash and soot.

**1 IDENTIFY:** What are two ways food is changed?

**Mechanical Digestion** The physical change of food is called **mechanical digestion.** Mechanical digestion breaks large pieces of food into smaller pieces. In the mouth, teeth begin the mechanical digestion of food. You use your teeth to cut, tear, grind, and crush foods.

The part of the tooth that is visible is called the crown. The crown is covered with **enamel.** Enamel is the hardest substance in the human body. Underneath the enamel is a spongy substance called **dentin**. Dentin absorbs the shock of chewing. The roots secure the teeth in the jaw. The root canal is a space for nerves and blood vessels to get to the tooth. Look at Figure 14-17.

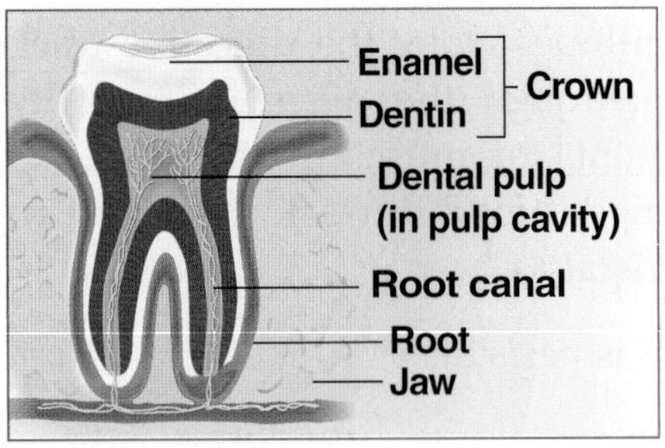


◀ **Figure 14-17** Parts of a tooth

Adults have 32 teeth. There are four different kinds of teeth. Incisors and canines cut and tear food. Bicuspids and molars grind and crush food. When food is crushed by the teeth, it is broken into small pieces. Your tongue moves the food around. This crushing of food is a physical change.

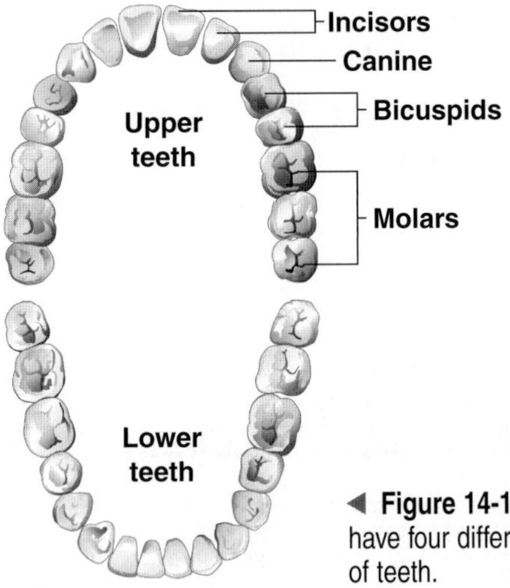


◀ **Figure 14-18** Humans have four different kinds of teeth.

**2 INTERPRET:** Look at Figure 14-18. How are the shapes of teeth adapted to their functions?

**Chemical Digestion** The process by which large food molecules are broken down into smaller food molecules is called **chemical digestion.** Chemical digestion begins in the mouth with saliva. Saliva mixes with foods and makes them soft and moist.

Saliva contains enzymes. **Enzymes** are proteins that control chemical reactions in the body. Enzymes help digest food. They break down the complex molecules in food into simpler molecules. Each enzyme can break down only one specific kind of food molecule. For example, one enzyme in saliva helps digest starch. It changes starch into sugar.

**3 DEFINE:** What is an enzyme?

**Process of Digestion** Enzymes act only on the outside surface of food particles. The mechanical breakdown of food provides a larger surface area for the enzymes to work on. The chemical digestion of food takes a number of steps. With each step, the food is broken down into smaller particles and then molecules. The body can use only the smallest, simplest molecules.

4 **INFER:** Why is the mechanical breakdown of food important?

## CHECKING CONCEPTS

1. Shape and size are __________ properties.
2. The crushing of food by the teeth is a __________ change.
3. The liquid found in the mouth is called __________.
4. Enzymes in saliva change __________ into sugars.
5. The breakdown of large food molecules into small food molecules is __________ digestion.

## THINKING CRITICALLY

6. **INFER:** Why do you think it is important to chew your food into small pieces?
7. **EXPLAIN:** What nutrient begins to be digested in the mouth?

## HEALTH AND SAFETY TIP

***Tooth Decay*** Tooth decay causes cavities. A cavity is a hole in the tooth. Saliva, food, and bacteria in the mouth mix to form a film called plaque (PLAK). Plaque breaks down the enamel of the tooth. If plaque is allowed to build up, it spreads to the soft parts of the tooth. Brushing and flossing your teeth daily can help prevent the buildup of plaque. Make a poster promoting good dental health. Include proper techniques for brushing and flossing. Present your poster to the class.

## *People in Science*

### DENTAL HYGIENIST

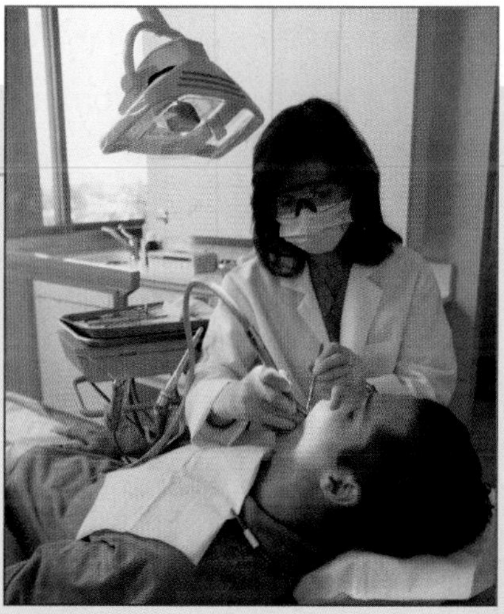

▲ **Figure 14-19** Dental hygienists examine teeth.

A trip to the dentist often includes a session with a dental hygienist. Dental hygienists help find, prevent, and treat mouth diseases. They examine teeth and gums, take X-rays, and clean and polish patients' teeth. They also remove plaque from under the gums. After oral surgery, dental hygienists may remove stitches or change dressings. Many dental hygienists work with dentists in private offices. Many work in other health-care facilities or in public health jobs. Often, dental hygienists specialize in education, teaching people how to take better care of their teeth and gums.

To be a dental hygienist, a person needs to complete a two-year course at a college or professional school. Some students take additional courses and training to earn a four-year college degree and sometimes even a graduate degree. Dental hygienists need to be skillful in working with their hands. They also need to be good at making worried patients feel comfortable.

**Thinking Critically** Why do you think it is important for people in all situations to take care of their teeth?

# 14-8 What happens to food in the stomach?

## INVESTIGATE

### Modeling Digestion
**HANDS-ON ACTIVITY**

1. Fill two glasses with water.
2. Place a mint in one of the glasses of water.
3. Break another mint into several small pieces. Put the pieces of mint in the second glass of water.
4. Observe which mint dissolves more quickly.

**THINK ABOUT IT:** Based on your observations, do you think food is digested more quickly when it is broken down into smaller pieces?

### *Objective*
Describe what happens to food once it enters the stomach.

### *Key Terms*
**gastric juice:** juice produced in the stomach that contains mucus, pepsin, and hydrochloric acid

**pepsin** (PEHP-sihn)**:** enzyme that digests proteins

**chyme** (KYM)**:** thick liquid form in which food leaves the stomach

**The Stomach** Once food leaves the esophagus, it enters the stomach. The stomach is a J-shaped, baglike organ that stores food. The stomach also breaks down food. In fact, mechanical digestion takes place in the stomach as well as in the mouth. The walls of the stomach are made up of layers of strong muscles. These muscles tighten and squeeze the food, changing it into smaller pieces.

1 **DESCRIBE:** How does the stomach aid in mechanical digestion?

**Gastric Juice** The small pieces of food in the stomach are mixed with stomach juice. This juice makes the food soft. The juice the stomach produces is called **gastric juice.** Gastric juice contains hydrochloric (hy-droh-KLAWR-ihk) acid, mucus, and pepsin.

2 **IDENTIFY:** What does gastric juice contain?

**Chemical Digestion in the Stomach** One of the enzymes in gastric juice is **pepsin.** Pepsin begins the digestion of proteins. Hydrochloric acid is a very strong acid. It is needed to make the stomach acidic. Pepsin can work only in an acidic environment. Hydrochloric acid kills bacteria in the stomach and helps to break down food. The mucus in gastric juice protects the stomach lining from the hydrochloric acid and pepsin.

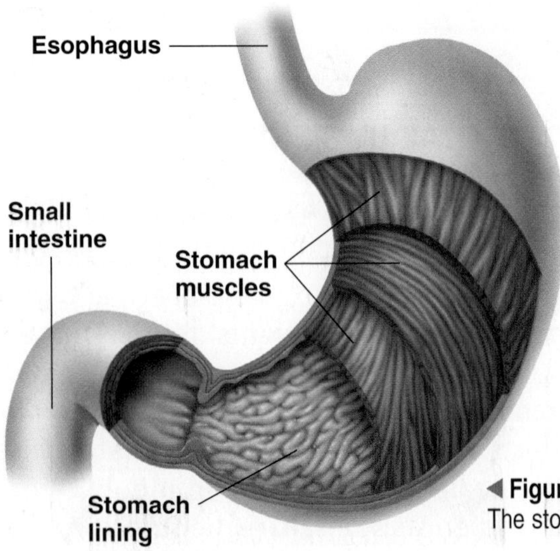


**Figure 14-20** The stomach

3 **DEFINE:** What is pepsin?

**Chyme** Once food has been crushed by the stomach and mixed with gastric juice, it is ready to leave the stomach. Food that leaves the stomach is in the form of a thick liquid. This liquid is called **chyme.** Chyme is released slowly from the stomach into the small intestine.

4 **DEFINE:** What is chyme?

## CHECKING CONCEPTS

1. What does mucus in the gastric juice do?
2. How is food mechanically digested in the stomach?
3. How is food chemically digested in the stomach?
4. What enzyme digests proteins?
5. In what form is food that leaves the stomach?
6. What does the stomach look like?

## THINKING CRITICALLY

7. **EXPLAIN:** Why is the stomach an important part of the digestive system?
8. **INFER:** What would happen if the stomach did not produce mucus?
9. **EXPLAIN:** Why is hydrochloric acid important to digestion?
10. **SEQUENCE:** Describe the change that food undergoes from the time it enters the mouth to the time it enters the small intestine. Put your answer in a flowchart.

## BUILDING SCIENCE SKILLS

***Researching*** A hole that occurs in the stomach lining is called an ulcer. A stomach ulcer is caused by bacteria. Ulcers can also occur in the small intestine. Use library references to find out the causes of ulcers, the signs and symptoms of ulcers, and the treatment of ulcers. Present your findings in a table.

## *How Do They Know That?*

### DR. WILLIAM BEAUMONT (1785–1853)

William Beaumont was an American army doctor in the early 1800s. On June 6, 1822, an 18-year-old named Alexis Saint Martin was accidentally shot in the stomach. Dr. Beaumont saved the young man's life. However, the wound never completely closed. For the rest of his life, Saint Martin had a two-and-a-half-inch opening in his left side.

▲ **Figure 14-21** Dr. Beaumont studied Saint Martin's stomach.

William Beaumont discovered that he could view the workings of the stomach through the opening. For the next eight years, with Saint Martin's cooperation, Dr. Beaumont studied the stomach. At that time, most information about human digestion was obtained by examining the remains of the deceased. The use of X-rays had not been discovered yet. Therefore, the ability to view a functioning body system was extraordinary. Dr. Beaumont published his findings in 1833, providing other doctors with valuable information about human digestion. Much of what people know today about the functions of the stomach is based on the observations of Dr. Beaumont.

**Thinking Critically** Why do you think the work of Beaumont was important?

# 14-9 What happens to food in the small intestine?

## INVESTIGATE

### *Modeling Fat Digestion*
HANDS-ON ACTIVITY

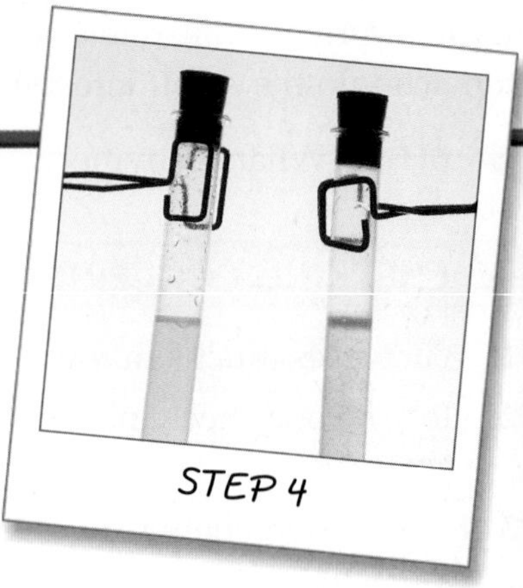


1. Half-fill two test tubes with water.
2. Using a medicine dropper, put four drops of cooking oil into each test tube.
3. Add 1/4 teaspoon of baking soda to one of the test tubes.
4. Put a stopper in each test tube and shake them well. Observe what happens.

**THINK ABOUT IT:** How did the baking soda affect the cooking oil? How might this effect speed the digestion of fats?

### *Objectives*

Describe what happens to food in the small intestine. Describe what happens to food after it leaves the small intestine.

### *Key Terms*

**lipase** (LY-pays)**:** enzyme that digests fats and oils

**bile:** green liquid that breaks down large droplets of fat into smaller droplets of fat

**emulsification** (ee-mul-suh-fih-KAY-shuhn)**:** process of breaking down large droplets of fat into smaller droplets of fat

**absorption** (ab-SAWRP-shuhn)**:** movement of food molecules from the digestive system to the blood

**villus,** *pl.* **villi:** fingerlike projection on the lining of the small intestine

**The Small Intestine** The small intestine is a long, coiled tube. It is about 6.5 m long and 2.5 cm wide. Like the stomach, the walls of the small intestine are muscular. Food moves through the small intestine by peristalsis. Most of the chemical digestion of food takes place in the small intestine. Look at the location of the small intestine in Figure 14-22 on the next page.

1 **EXPLAIN:** What happens in the small intestine?

**Digestion in the Small Intestine** Digestive juices in the small intestine contain many enzymes that complete digestion. One of these enzymes is **lipase.** Lipase digests fats and oils. Fats are digested only in the small intestine.

2 **DEFINE:** What is lipase?

**The Pancreas** The pancreas is a large gland that lies below the stomach (see Figure 14-22). When food first enters the small intestine, the pancreas releases digestive juices. These digestive juices travel to the small intestine through a small tube called the pancreatic duct. Pancreatic digestive juices contain enzymes. These enzymes change starches, proteins, and fats into simpler forms.

3 **IDENTIFY:** How does the pancreas aid in chemical digestion?

**The Liver** The liver is the largest organ in the human body. One job of the liver is to produce bile. **Bile** is a green liquid that breaks down large droplets of fat into smaller droplets of fat. The breaking down of large fat droplets into smaller fat droplets is called **emulsification.** The smaller droplets can then be used by the body.

Bile does not move directly from the liver to the small intestine. Bile is stored in a small sac under the liver. The sac is called the gallbladder. Bile moves from the gallbladder into the small intestine through a small tube.

4 **DEFINE:** What is emulsification?

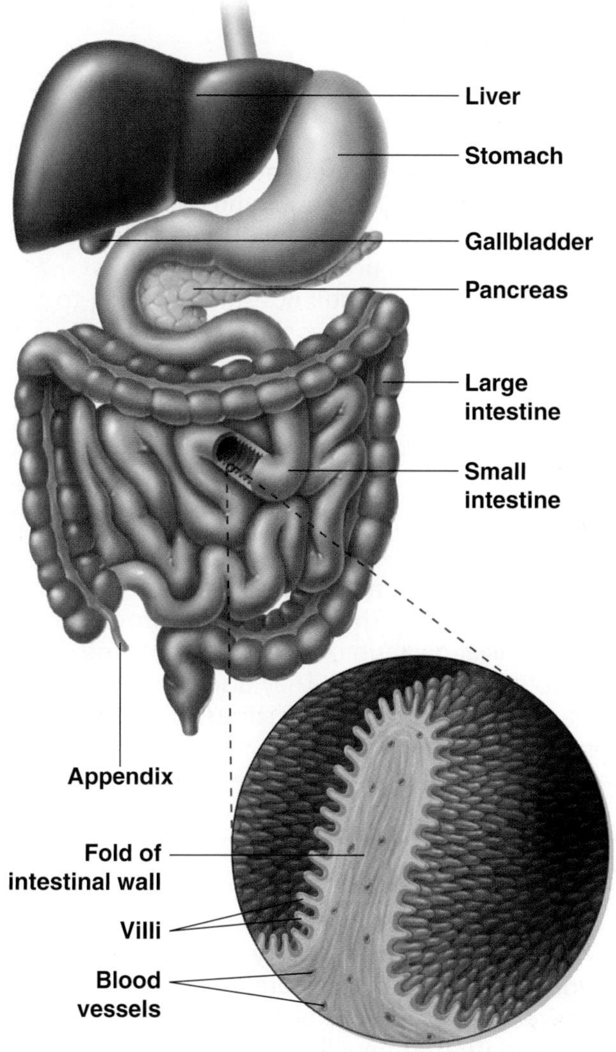


▲ **Figure 14-22** The small and large intestines

**Absorption in the Small Intestine** After food has been changed to usable molecules, it is ready to be absorbed. **Absorption** is the movement of food from the digestive system to the blood. Absorption of food molecules and water takes place through the walls of the small intestine. Once inside the blood, digested food is carried to all of the cells of your body.

The inner lining of the small intestine is folded. The folds have millions of tiny fingerlike projections called **villi.** The folds and villi make the surface area of the small intestine larger. Digested food passes through the layers of the villi and into the blood vessels.

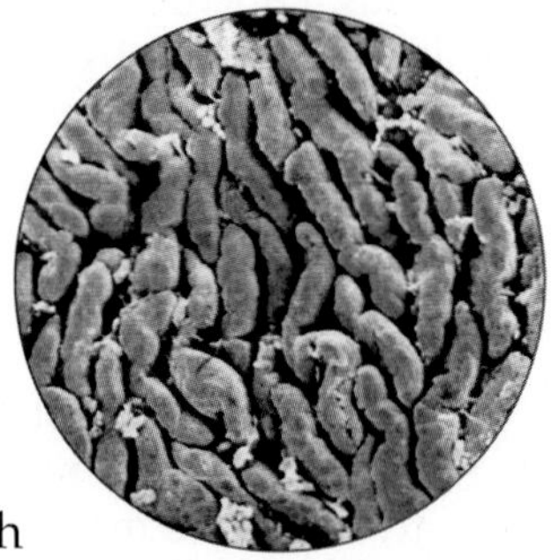

▲ **Figure 14-23** Villi

5 **EXPLAIN:** What is absorption?

**The Large Intestine** The large intestine is the last part of the digestive system. Some undigested food, minerals, and water are not absorbed in the small intestine. They form a watery mixture. This mixture enters the large intestine. Water and minerals are absorbed into the blood in the large intestine. The remaining solid wastes are stored temporarily in the rectum. Then, they are eliminated from the body.

6 **DESCRIBE:** What happens to food in the large intestine?

## CHECKING CONCEPTS

1. Most __________ digestion takes place in the small intestine.
2. Lipase is an enzyme that digests __________.
3. The gallbladder stores __________.
4. Bile is responsible for the __________ of fat.

## THINKING CRITICALLY

5. **INFER:** Why must food be absorbed?
6. **HYPOTHESIZE:** How do folds and villi increase the surface area of the small intestine?

### Web InfoSearch

**Appendix** The appendix is located where the small intestine and large intestine meet. It does not have a known use in humans. An infection of the appendix is called appendicitis. An infected appendix must be removed.

**SEARCH:** Use the Internet to find out more about the appendix. Write your findings in a report. Start your search at www.conceptsandchallenges.com. Some key search words are **appendix** and **appendicitis.**

*Integrating Chemistry*

# THE Big IDEA

## What chemical reactions take place during digestion?

Chemistry is a branch of physical science. It is the study of all forms of matter and changes in matter. Digestion changes food into usable forms. This involves chemistry.

Chemical digestion breaks large food molecules into smaller food molecules. For this to happen, a chemical change must take place in the food. The process by which a chemical change takes place is called a chemical reaction. In some chemical reactions, substances combine to form a more complex substance. This is called a synthesis reaction. In digestion, the opposite occurs. Complex substances are broken down into simpler substances. This is called a decomposition reaction. Enzymes are chemicals that speed up these reactions. Each enzyme works on only one type of food molecule.

The stomach secretes enzymes called pepsin. Pepsin enzymes start to digest protein. Proteins are giant molecules. Pepsin enzymes split proteins into small fragments. These fragments are still too big to be absorbed. In the small intestine, proteins break down further into substances that are called amino acids. Amino acids are the building blocks of protein. Amino acids pass easily through the lining of the small intestine.

In addition to protein, the digestive system breaks down carbohydrates and fats. Look at the boxes of text that appear on this page. They point out parts of the digestive tract where chemical reactions take place to digest food. Follow the directions in the Science Log to learn more about "the big idea." ✦

**Gastric Juices**

Gastric juices are released into the stomach. They contain mucus, pepsin, and hydrochloric acid. Hydrochloric acid breaks up particles of food. Pepsin splits proteins into fragments. These fragments are still not small enough to be absorbed. Food leaves the stomach as a thick liquid called chyme.

**Bile**

The liver secretes bile. Bile is stored in the gallbladder, which squirts it into the small intestine. Bile salts help in the digestion and absorption of fats. They coat the fat droplets. The chemical makeup of bile salts keeps the droplets from rejoining. They also combine with other substances to form particles that can dissolve in water.

**Bicarbonate**

The chyme moves to the small intestine. The chyme that enters is very acidic from the hydrochloric acid in the stomach. The pancreas secretes a chemical called bicarbonate that neutralizes the chyme.

**Pancreatic Enzymes**

Pancreatic juices enter the small intestine. These juices contain enzymes that change starches, proteins, and fats into simpler forms. Lipase splits fat molecules into more easily absorbed droplets. Enzymes in the wall of the small intestine break protein fragments into amino acids. Pancreatic amylase breaks down starch into simpler substances. Enzymes in the wall of the small intestine split these molecules further.

**Small Intestine**

Digestion is completed in the small intestine. Most nutrients move into the bloodstream through the intestinal lining by active transport. Energy pumps them from a less-crowded area to a more-crowded area. The other process, diffusion, does not require energy. Material moves from an area where molecules are crowded to an area where they are less crowded.

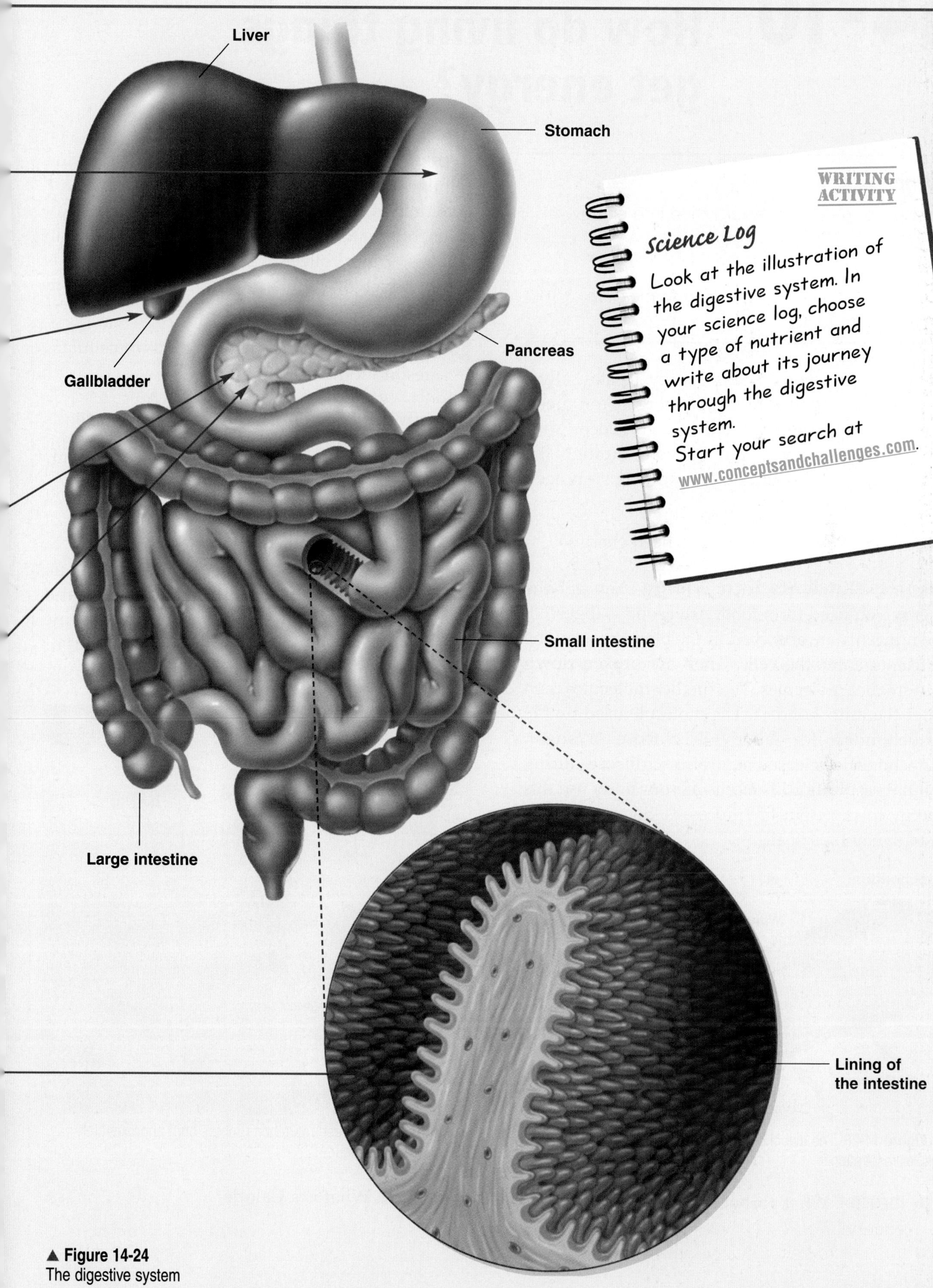


**WRITING ACTIVITY**

### Science Log

Look at the illustration of the digestive system. In your science log, choose a type of nutrient and write about its journey through the digestive system.
Start your search at www.conceptsandchallenges.com.

▲ **Figure 14-24**
The digestive system

# 14-10 How do living things get energy?

## *Objective*

Explain how organisms turn food into energy.

## *Key Term*

**Calorie** (KAL-uh-ree)**:** unit used to measure energy from foods

**Energy** Your body needs energy to stay alive. Everything you do requires energy. You need energy to walk, to run, and even to sleep. Your heart needs energy to pump blood through the body. Right now, your body is growing. You need energy to grow.

1 **STATE:** Why does your body need energy?

**Turning Nutrients into Energy** You get the energy you need from food. After food is digested, the nutrients are absorbed in the bloodstream. The nutrients enter the cells. They are broken down into smaller molecules. The smaller molecules then enter the mitochondria. The molecule used by the mitochondria for energy is glucose, a sugar. Mitochondria release energy from glucose during cellular respiration. The cells of your body use this energy to carry out life processes. Some energy is also given off as heat.

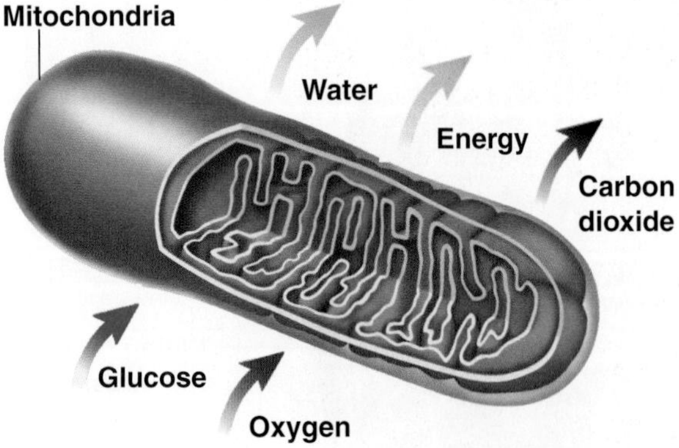


▲ **Figure 14-25** The mitochondria release energy during cellular respiration.

2 **IDENTIFY:** What part of the cell releases energy?

**Byproducts of Cellular Respiration** During cellular respiration, carbon dioxide and water are given off as byproducts. To show that your body gives off water, breathe on a mirror. What do you see? Water collects on the mirror. The water is a byproduct of cellular respiration going on in your body.

3 **IDENTIFY:** What are the byproducts of cellular respiration?

**Measuring Food Energy** Different foods contain different amounts of energy. The amount of energy contained in foods is measured in **Calories.** A Calorie is a unit used to measure food energy. Fat contains the most energy. Each gram of fat contains approximately 9 Calories of energy. No more than 30 percent of the Calories that you consume should be from fat. Proteins and carbohydrates each give off about the same amount of energy. Each gram of protein or carbohydrate gives off about 4 Calories of energy.

▲ **Figure 14-26** These marathon runners burn approximately 800 Calories per hour.

4 **DEFINE:** What is a Calorie?

## CHECKING CONCEPTS

1. What process produces the energy your body needs?
2. What are the byproducts of cellular respiration?
3. Do all foods give off the same amount of energy?
4. What unit is used to measure food energy?
5. Where do you get the energy you need?
6. What nutrient supplies the most energy?

## THINKING CRITICALLY

7. **CALCULATE:** If food contains 5 g of fat, how many Calories of fat are in the food?
8. **INFER:** Why do foods with high amounts of fat have more Calories than do foods that are high in carbohydrates?
9. **HYPOTHESIZE:** On average, boys ages 12 to 15 years need about 2,550 Calories each day. Girls the same age need about 2,150 Calories each day. What do you think would happen if you ate more Calories than what you needed?

## INTERPRETING VISUALS

*Use Figure 14-25 to answer the following questions.*

10. **SYNTHESIZE:** What is the chemical equation for cellular respiration?
11. **ANALYZE:** What are the byproducts?

## *Hands-On Activity*

### CALCULATING CALORIES

*You will need a sheet of paper and a pencil.*

1. To find the total number of Calories in food, multiply the total number of grams of fat the food contains by 9.5. Record the product.
2. Then, multiply the total number of grams of carbohydrates the food contains by 4. Record the product.
3. Multiply the total number of grams of protein the food contains by 4. Record the product.
4. Add the three products together to find out the total number of Calories in a serving of food.

Calories from fat =
$9.5 \times$ number of fat grams

Calories from carbohydrate =
$4 \times$ number of carbohydrate grams

Calories from protein =
$4 \times$ number of protein grams

▲ **Figure 14-27** Use these formulas to calculate the number of calories in food.

### Practicing Your Skills

*Find out the total number of Calories in each of the following examples.*

5. 8 g Protein, 11 g carbohydrates, 1 g fat
6. 4 g Protein, 10 g carbohydrates, 8 g fat
7. 0 g Protein, 1 g carbohydrates, 5 g fat
8. 14 g Protein, 4 g carbohydrates, 3 g fat
9. 5 g Protein, 7 g carbohydrates, 6 g fat
10. 7 g Protein, 4 g carbohydrates, 0 g fat

# Chapter 14 Challenges

## Chapter Summary

**Lesson 14-1**

- **Nutrients** are chemical substances in food that are needed by the body for growth, energy, and life processes.

**Lessons 14-2, 14-3, and 14-4**

- **Proteins** are used to build new cells, repair damaged cells, make enzymes, control chemical activities, and are a source of energy.
- **Vitamins** are important for growth and for proper body function. **Minerals** are nutrients needed by the body for it to develop and function properly.

**Lesson 14-5**

- Balanced diets contain the right amounts of nutrients to keep the body healthy.

**Lesson 14-6**

- **Digestion** is the process by which foods are changed so that they can be used by the body. The digestive tract and digestive organs make up your digestive system.

**Lesson 14-7**

- Large pieces of food are cut and crushed into smaller pieces of food during **mechanical digestion.**
- Large food molecules are broken down into smaller food molecules during **chemical digestion.**

**Lesson 14-8**

- The stomach is a baglike organ that stores food.
- **Gastric juice** contains mucus, **pepsin,** and hydrochloric acid and is produced by the stomach. **Chyme** is a thick liquid form of food that leaves the stomach.

**Lesson 14-9**

- The pancreas releases digestive juices into the small intestine to break up starch, protein, and fat. The liver produces **bile,** which emulsifies fats and oils. Bile is stored in the gallbladder.

**Lesson 14-10**

- Your body needs energy to stay alive. Cells produce energy during cellular respiration.
- The amount of energy food gives off is measured in **Calories.**

## Key Term Challenges

absorption (p. 346)
amino acid (p.330)
bile (p. 346)
Calorie (p. 350)
carbohydrate (p. 328)
chemical digestion (p. 342)
chyme (p. 344)
deficiency disease (p. 332)
dentin (p. 342)
digestion (p. 340)
emulsification (p. 346)
enamel (p. 342)
enzyme (p. 342)
epiglottis (p. 340)
esophagus (p. 340)
gastric juice (p. 344)
lipase (p. 346)
malnutrition (p. 338)
mechanical digestion (p. 342)
mineral (p. 334)
molecule (p. 330)
nutrient (p. 328)
pepsin (p. 344)
peristalsis (p. 340)
pharynx (p. 340)
protein (p. 328)
saliva (p. 340)
villus (p. 346)
vitamin (p. 332)

MATCHING **Write the Key Term from above that best matches each description.**

1. fingerlike projections on the lining of the small intestine
2. enzyme that begins the digestion of protein
3. breaking down of large food molecules into small food molecules
4. process by which foods are changed into forms the body can use
5. chemical substance in food needed by the body for growth, energy, and life processes
6. protein that controls chemical activity
7. nutrient needed by the body to develop properly
8. thick, liquidlike form of food

IDENTIFYING WORD RELATIONSHIPS **Explain how the words in each pair are related. Write your answers in complete sentences.**

9. lipase, emulsification
10. amino acid, protein
11. saliva, carbohydrate
12. bile, fat

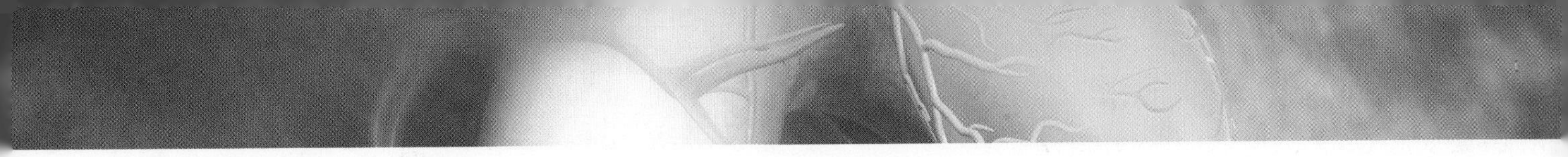

## Content Challenges TEST PREP

**MULTIPLE CHOICE Write the letter of the term or phrase that best completes each statement.**

1. The wavelike movement that moves through the digestive system is called
   **a.** chyme.
   **b.** mechanical digestion.
   **c.** peristalsis.
   **d.** chemical digestion.

2. The largest organ inside the body is the
   **a.** stomach.
   **b.** gallbladder.
   **c.** liver.
   **d.** pancreas.

3. Soft bones and teeth may be caused by a diet that lacks
   **a.** zinc.
   **b.** protein.
   **c.** calcium.
   **d.** vitamin A.

4. Starches are
   **a.** proteins.
   **b.** simple carbohydrates.
   **c.** fats.
   **d.** complex carbohydrates.

5. The largest amount of food energy comes from
   **a.** fats.
   **b.** carbohydrates.
   **c.** vitamins.
   **d.** proteins.

6. Mechanical digestion begins in the
   **a.** esophagus.
   **b.** pharynx.
   **c.** mouth.
   **d.** stomach.

7. Undigested food from the small intestine moves into the
   **a.** pancreas.
   **b.** appendix.
   **c.** stomach.
   **d.** large intestine.

8. Saliva begins the chemical digestion of
   **a.** proteins.
   **b.** starches.
   **c.** fats.
   **d.** nutrients.

9. Amino acids make up
   **a.** proteins.
   **b.** fats.
   **c.** water.
   **d.** carbohydrates.

10. Your body needs proteins for
    **a.** malnourishment.
    **b.** insulation.
    **c.** energy.
    **d.** growth and repair.

**FILL IN Write the term that best completes each sentence.**

11. Many chemical reactions that take place in the body are controlled by __________.
12. Gastric juice contains pepsin, __________, and mucus.
13. Bile is produced in the __________.
14. The __________ releases digestive juices into the small intestine.
15. When food is swallowed, it enters the __________.
16. A weakened condition that results from a lack of a certain nutrient is called a __________.

## Concept Challenges TEST PREP

**WRITTEN RESPONSE** **Answer each of the following questions in complete sentences.**

1. **EXPLAIN:** Is the action of bile on fat part of mechanical digestion or chemical digestion? Explain.
2. **INFER:** What role does the large surface area of the small intestine play in absorption?
3. **EXPLAIN:** Why is absorption important?
4. **HYPOTHESIZE:** Why do you think low-carbohydrate "liquid diets" are unhealthy?
5. **APPLY:** What would you eat before an athletic competition, a bowl of spaghetti or a steak? Explain.

**INTERPRETING A DIAGRAM** **Use Figure 14-28 to answer the following questions.**

6. What is the function of the part labeled *A*?
7. What letter indicates a organ that has no known function?
8. What letter indicates where gastric juice is produced?
9. What is the function of the part labeled *E*?
10. What does letter *F* represent?

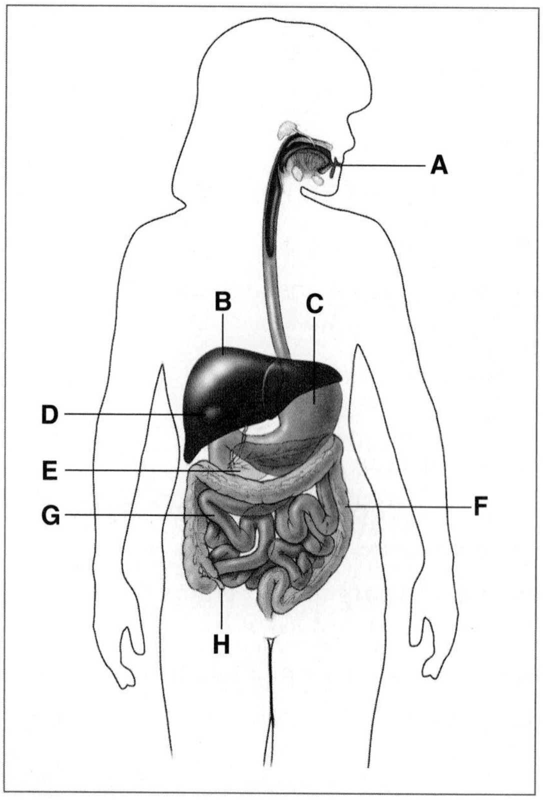


▲ **Figure 14-28** The digestive system

# Chapter 15 Transport in the Body

▲ **Figure 15-1** The oxygen these swimmers need is transported through the body by the circulatory system.

All of the cells in the human body require oxygen and nutrients to function. These materials need to be transported to the cells. Waste products from the cells have to be taken away. During activity such as swimming, muscle cells require more oxygen than usual. Oxygen is transported by blood, which is pumped throughout the body by the heart.

▶Why do you think it is important for the heart to be able to adapt to the changing needs of the body?

## Contents

# 15-1 What is the circulatory system?

### *Objective*

Describe the circulatory system and its functions.

### *Key Terms*

**circulation:** movement of blood through the body

**closed circulatory system:** organ system in which blood moves through vessels

**hormone** (HAWR-mohn)**:** chemical substance that regulates body functions

**Circulation** Most large cities have a complex network of railroads, highways, and subways. This transport system is necessary for people to get around and for materials to go into and out of the city. Your body also has a transport system. It is your circulatory system. The circulatory system transports, or moves, blood throughout the body. The movement of blood through the body is called **circulation.**

1 DEFINE: What is circulation?

**The Circulatory System** Your circulatory system is made up of your heart, blood vessels, and blood. The blood vessels form a closed circulatory system. All vertebrates, including fish, birds, and humans, have a closed circulatory system. In a **closed circulatory system,** the blood moves through blood vessels. The arteries are connected to the veins by capillaries. The arteries, veins, and capillaries form a large network of tubes that form a continuous closed system.

2 LIST: What makes up your circulatory system?

**Jobs of the Circulatory System** The main job of the circulatory system is to transport various materials. However, the circulatory system has many other jobs as well.

- **Transport of Food and Oxygen** The circulatory system transports nutrients from the small intestines to the cells of the body. It also delivers oxygen from the lungs to the cells of your body. A compound called hemoglobin in red blood cells carries the oxygen.
- **Transport of Wastes** The circulatory system carries away wastes and byproducts of cellular processes. One important byproduct is carbon dioxide.
- **Protection** Another job of the circulatory system is protection. Certain cells in your blood called white blood cells defend your body against invading microorganisms. This helps the body fight disease.
- **Transport of Hormones** The circulatory system carries chemicals called **hormones.** Hormones carry chemical "messages" from one part of your body to another part of your body.
- **Regulation** The circulatory system helps regulate your body temperature. Blood distributes heat evenly around your body. This is important for all warm-blooded animals, including humans.

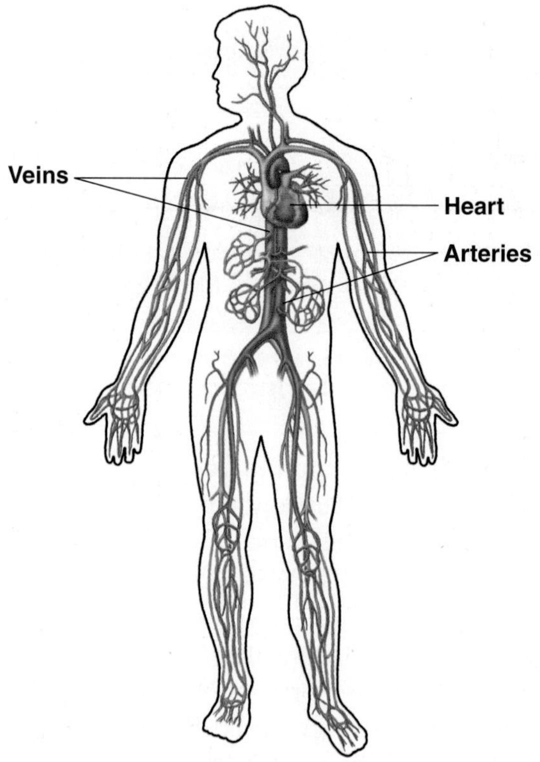


▲ **Figure 15-2** The circulatory system transports materials throughout the body.

3 LIST: What are some jobs of the circulatory system?

## CHECKING CONCEPTS

1. The circulatory system __________ blood and oxygen to all parts of the body.
2. Arteries, veins, and capillaries form a __________ circulatory system.
3. Carbon dioxide is a __________ that is removed from the body by blood.
4. Chemical "messengers" that are carried in the blood are called __________.
5. The job of __________ blood cells is to fight disease.

## THINKING CRITICALLY

6. INFER: Why is the human circulatory system called a closed system?
7. RELATE: How is the circulatory system like a network of highways?

## Web InfoSearch

**Artificial Hearts** In July 2001, a major advancement in medical science was made. The world's first wire-free artificial heart was implanted into a patient. This type of procedure could help thousands of patients who have been waiting years for a natural heart to be donated.

**SEARCH:** Use the Internet to find out more about artificial hearts. Write a report that describes different kinds of artificial hearts, how they work, and how they can help patients. Start your search at www.conceptsandchallenges.com. Some key search words are **artificial heart** and **mechanical heart.**

## *How Do They Know That?*

### BLOOD TRANSFUSIONS

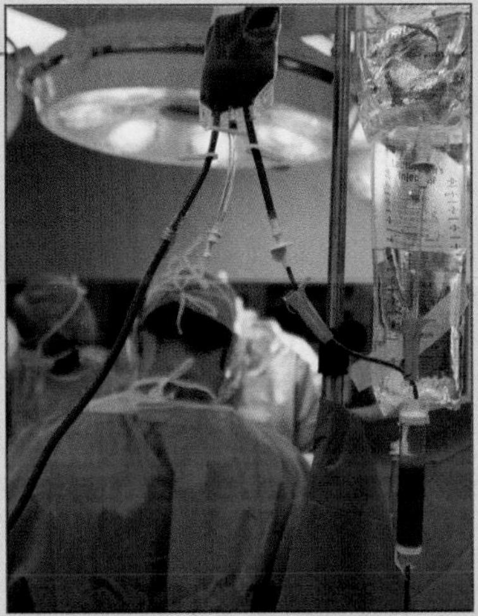

▲ **Figure 15-3** Blood during a transfusion

One of the most important parts of the circulatory system is blood. Blood transports all of the nutrients needed by the body to survive. The circulatory system cannot function properly without the correct amount of blood moving throughout the body. Sometimes, due to an injury or disease, people need blood that has been donated by other people. This blood is delivered to the patient in a process called a transfusion.

One scientist, Charles Drew, led the way for more effective blood transfusions. Drew was an American doctor who concluded that plasma could be used in blood transfusions instead of whole blood. Plasma is the liquid part of blood. Using plasma in blood transfusions has two advantages. Whole blood stays fresh for only about one week. Plasma can last for a longer period of time. Plasma can also be used in a transfusion for any blood type.

Drew did most of his research at Columbia University in New York City between 1938 and 1940. Drew's research was very important for his time. During World War II, Drew set up blood banks in the United States to collect plasma. The blood plasma was then sent to the American armed forces who were fighting in other countries. The blood plasma that was collected saved many lives.

**Thinking Critically** What are the advantages of using plasma in blood transfusions?

# 15-2 What are the parts of the heart?

*Objectives*

Describe the heart. Explain how blood moves through the heart.

*Key Terms*

**atrium** (AY-tree-uhm), *pl.* **atria:** upper chamber of the heart

**ventricle** (VEHN-trih-kuhl)**:** lower chamber of the heart

**septum:** thick tissue wall that separates the left and right sides of the heart

**valve:** thin flap of tissue that acts like a one-way door

**A Muscular Organ** The central organ of the circulatory system is the heart. The heart is a muscular organ about the size of your fist. It is located in the chest cavity behind the sternum, or breastbone.

The function of the heart is to pump blood. The heart is divided into four parts, or chambers. There are two upper and two lower chambers. Each upper chamber of the heart is called an **atrium.** The atria receive blood. The lower chambers are called **ventricles.** The ventricles pump blood out of the heart. The walls of the ventricles are thicker than the walls of the atria. This is because the ventricles need to work hard to pump blood to all parts of the body.

**1** IDENTIFY: How many chambers does the heart have?

**Blood Flow in the Heart** Look at Figure 15-4. You can see that the heart is divided into two sides—a left side and a right side. A thick tissue wall separates the two sides of the heart. This tissue wall is called the **septum.**

Blood flows into the atria of the heart. When the atria are filled with blood, they contract. This motion pumps the blood into the ventricles. Once the ventricles are filled with blood, they contract. This motion pushes the blood out of the heart. The strong muscles of the ventricle walls give the heart enough force to send blood to all parts of the body.

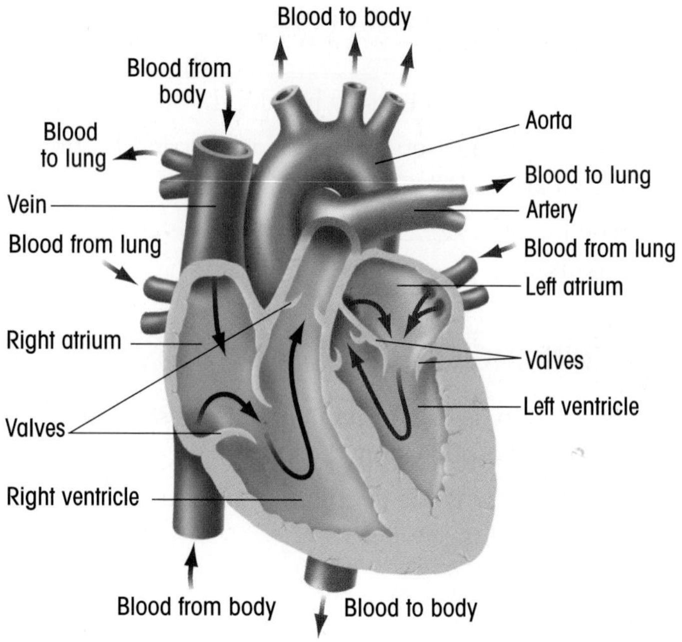


▲ **Figure 15-4** Trace the flow of blood through the heart.

**Go Online**
**active art**
**For:** The Heart activity
**Visit:** PHSchool.com
**Web Code:** cep-4031

**2** SEQUENCE: Trace the flow of blood from the time it enters the heart until it leaves the heart.

**Heart Valves** Inside the heart, there are four valves. A **valve** is a thin flap of tissue. It acts like a one-way door. The valves keep the blood moving in only one direction. Blood is supposed to flow only from the atria to the ventricles. The valves are located between the atria and the ventricles. If the blood tries to flow backward, the valve shuts. There also are valves between the ventricles and the blood vessels. As blood leaves the ventricles, it passes through the valves.

**3** IDENTIFY: What keeps blood from flowing backward in the heart?

**Heartbeat** Your heart will beat over 2 billion times in your lifetime. Your heartbeat is the rhythm of your heart as it pumps blood. A stethoscope (STEHTH-uh-skohp) is an instrument doctors use to listen to your heartbeat. If you were to listen to it, you would hear a lub-dub sound. The lub-dub sound is made by your valves opening and closing. When the valves between the atria and ventricles snap shut, they make a lub sound. When the valves between the ventricles and blood vessels snap shut, they make a dub sound.

4 **DEFINE:** What is a stethoscope?

## CHECKING CONCEPTS

1. The heart is a __________ organ.
2. The __________ divides the heart into left and right sides.
3. The upper chambers of the heart are called __________.
4. The __________ pumps blood out of the heart.
5. The heart has __________ valves.
6. The sound of your heartbeat is caused by the opening and closing of __________.

## THINKING CRITICALLY

7. **INFER:** What do you think would happen if a valve were damaged?
8. **HYPOTHESIZE:** What might cause your heartbeat rate to increase?

## BUILDING MATH SKILLS

***Calculating*** If a person's heart beats 80 times a minute, how many times would it beat in 10 minutes? Calculate the number of heartbeats in an hour, a day, a week, a month, and a year.

## *Science and Technology*

### HEART VALVE REPLACEMENT

When heart valves do not work properly, the heart cannot pump blood effectively, and the body cells may not receive enough blood to supply their need for oxygen and nutrients. Surgeons may be able to repair damaged heart valves, or they may replace them. The faulty valve is carefully removed, and a new valve is attached in its place.

▲ **Figure 15-5** Synthetic valves are used to replace damaged heart valves.

Doctors use several kinds of replacements for damaged heart valves. They may transplant a human heart valve obtained from an organ donor. Valves taken from pig hearts or constructed from cow tissues can also be used. Mechanical heart valves, made from materials such as stainless steel or other materials, may also be used. Valves made of human or other animal tissues are less likely to be rejected by the body, but they are not as durable. Over a period of years, they may break down and have to be replaced. Mechanical heart valves are very durable, but blood clots tend to form on them and can cause a heart attack or stroke. Patients with these valves must take drugs to prevent clotting throughout their lives.

**Thinking Critically** How could a blood clot that formed on a mechanical heart valve cause a heart attack or stroke?

# 15-3 What are blood vessels?

## *Objective*

Describe the three kinds of blood vessels.

## *Key Terms*

**artery** (AHRT-uhr-ee): blood vessel that carries blood away from the heart

**vein** (VAYN): blood vessel that carries blood back to the heart

**capillary** (KAP-uh-ler-ee): tiny blood vessel that connects arteries to veins

**aorta** (ay-AWR-tuh): largest artery in the body

**Blood Vessels** Blood moves through a closed system of tubes called blood vessels. The human body has three kinds of blood vessels. The **arteries** are blood vessels that carry blood away from the heart. Blood vessels that carry blood back to the heart are **veins.** Veins and arteries are connected by tiny blood vessels called **capillaries.**

1 **NAME:** Name the three kinds of blood vessels.

**Arteries** As the heart beats, it pumps blood through the arteries at high pressure. The arteries must be strong to be able to handle this pressure. Arteries have thick muscular walls that prevent the arteries from bursting. The largest artery in the body is the **aorta.**

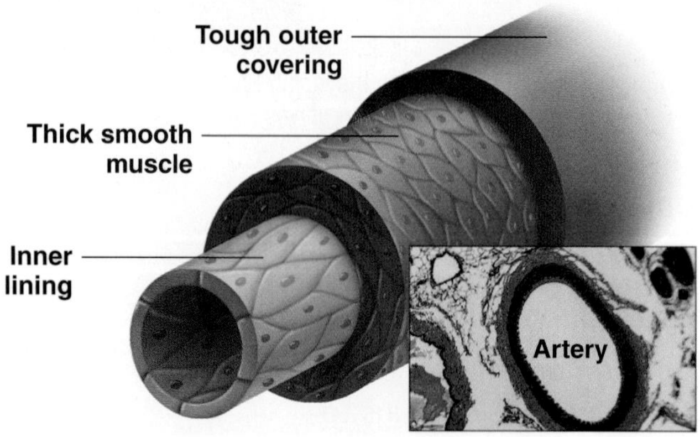


▲ **Figure 15-6** Arteries have thick muscular walls.

2 **LIST:** What are some characteristics of arteries?

**Pulse** As your heart beats, it pushes blood through the arteries in spurts. With each spurt of blood, a beat can be felt. The beat you feel is your pulse. You can feel a pulse wherever an artery is close to the skin's surface. Your pulse rate and heartbeat are the same.

3 **IDENTIFY:** Can you feel your pulse in a vein, artery, or capillary?

**Veins** Veins have thinner walls than arteries do. Blood pumps through the veins at less pressure than it does through arteries. The blood flow through veins is not as forceful as it is through arteries. The contraction of muscles in veins keeps the blood flowing. Some veins also have valves that keep the blood from flowing backward.

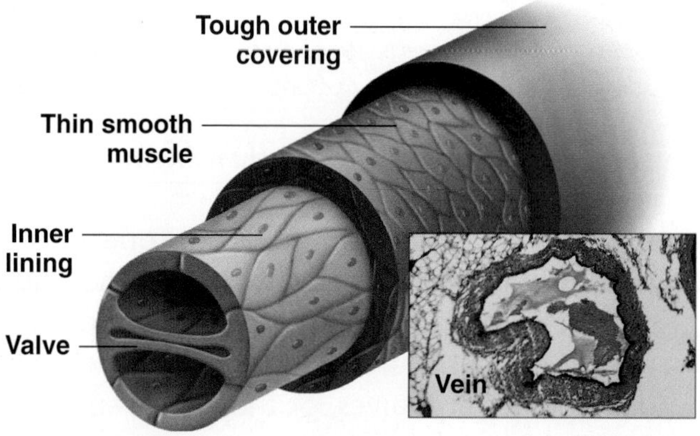


▲ **Figure 15-7** The walls of veins are thinner than those of arteries.

4 **EXPLAIN:** Why are the walls of veins thinner than the walls of arteries?

**Capillaries** Capillaries have walls that are only one cell thick. Blood cells travel through capillaries in a single file. Look at the diagram in Figure 15-8. In the capillaries, blood and body cells exchange nutrients and waste. For example, carbon dioxide and waste products move from body cells into the blood through capillaries. Food and oxygen in the blood move through the capillaries into the body cells.

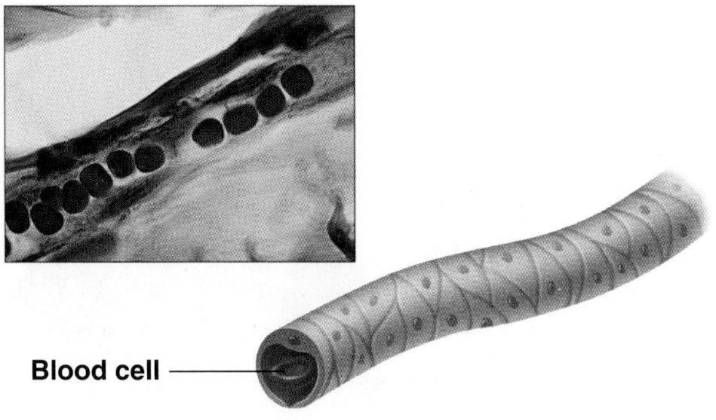


▲ **Figure 15-8** Capillaries are only wide enough for blood cells to pass through one at a time.

5 **DESCRIBE:** What happens in capillaries?

## ✓ CHECKING CONCEPTS

1. How many types of blood vessels are found in the human body?
2. Through which vessel is blood pumped at a greater pressure?
3. In what areas of the body can you feel your pulse?
4. How is blood prevented from flowing backward in a vein?

## ✓ THINKING CRITICALLY

5. **CONTRAST:** What are the differences between arteries and veins?
6. **INFER:** Why do you think a pulse cannot be detected in a vein?

### Web InfoSearch

**High Blood Pressure** Blood pressure is a measure of the force of blood on the arteries. High blood pressure causes the heart to overwork. Over time, high blood pressure causes the arteries and the heart to weaken.

**SEARCH:** Use the Internet to find out more about high blood pressure. Write a report about the possible prevention and treatment of high blood pressure. Start your search for information at www.conceptsandchallenges.com. A key search word is **high blood pressure.**

## *Hands-On Activity*

### MEASURING PULSE RATE

*You will need a clock or watch with a second hand.*

1. Sit quietly for 2 minutes.
2. Have a partner take your pulse for 30 seconds by placing his or her middle and index fingers over the inside of your wrist. Multiply this number by 2 to find your heart rate per minute. Record your answer.
3. Stand up for 2 minutes. Repeat Step 2.
4. Jog in place for 2 minutes. Repeat Step 2.
5. Rest for 2 minutes. Repeat Step 2.

▲ **STEP 2** Have a partner take your pulse.

#### Practicing Your Skills

6. **ANALYZE:** How did your pulse change when you stood up?
7. **ANALYZE:** How did your pulse change when you jogged?
8. **ANALYZE:** What effect did exercise have on your heart rate?

# 15-4 What is blood?

## *Objective*

Describe the different parts of blood.

## *Key Terms*

**plasma** (PLAZ-muh)**:** liquid part of blood

**hemoglobin** (HEE-muh-gloh-bihn)**:** protein found in red blood cells that carries oxygen

**platelet** (PLAYT-liht)**:** piece of cell that is involved in blood clotting

**transfusion:** transfer of blood from one person into the body of another person

**Blood** Blood is a fluid tissue. You have about five liters of blood in your body. Blood makes up about nine percent of your body weight.

Blood is a mixture. It has a liquid part and a solid part. Scientists use a centrifuge (SEHN-truh-fyooj) to separate blood into its two parts. A test tube filled with blood is spun around in the centrifuge. The solid part of the blood is forced to the bottom of the test tube. The liquid part of the blood remains on top.

1 **DEFINE:** What is a centrifuge?

**Plasma** The straw-colored liquid part of blood is called **plasma.** It is made up mostly of water. Digested nutrients, dissolved vitamins, and minerals are found in plasma. Hormones and waste products from the cells of the lungs and kidneys are also dissolved in the plasma.

2 **LIST:** What are some things found in plasma?

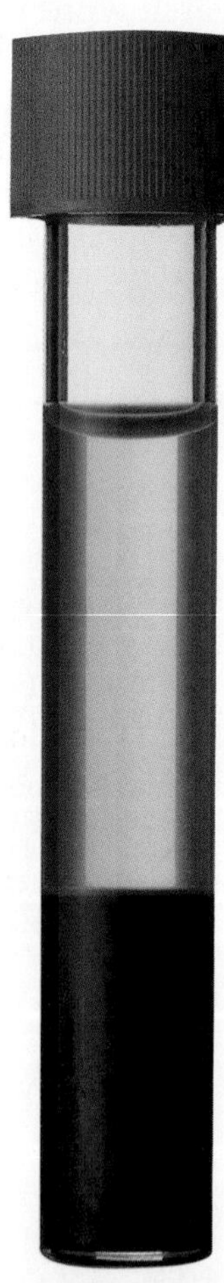

▲ **Figure 15-9** Blood will separate into layers after it has been centrifuged.

**Red Blood Cells** Red blood cells are different from any other cell in the body because they have no nucleus. This means that they cannot divide. Because red blood cells do not reproduce themselves through cell division, they have to be continuously replaced. A typical red blood cell will function for about 120 to 130 days. Then, it has to be replaced. Red blood cells are made in the bone marrow of long bones.

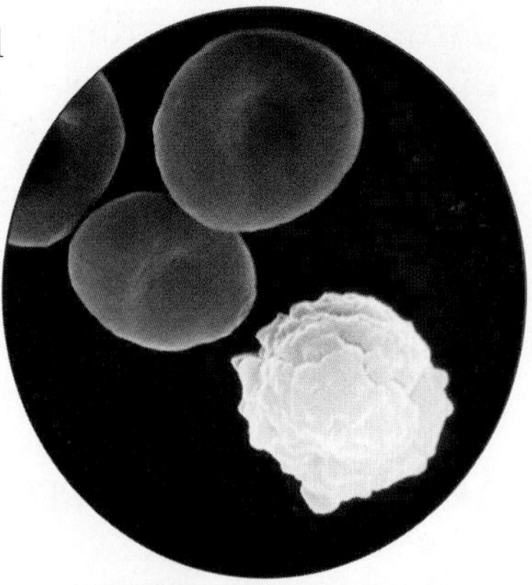

▲ **Figure 15-10** Red and white blood cells

The job of red blood cells is to carry oxygen. Red blood cells contain a compound called hemoglobin. **Hemoglobin** is an iron-containing protein that carries oxygen. Up to four molecules of oxygen can attach to one molecule of hemoglobin. The color of blood can vary depending on the amount of oxygen its hemoglobin molecules are carrying. Blood with the maximum amount of oxygen is usually a brighter red than blood carrying less oxygen.

3 **DEFINE:** What is the function of hemoglobin?

**White Blood Cells** White blood cells are larger than red blood cells. They also have a different shape than red blood cells. White blood cells have an irregular shape and a rough surface. They have a nucleus and can function for many years. There are several different kinds of white blood cells.

White blood cells defend the body against foreign substances. By destroying bacteria and other microorganisms, white blood cells help fight disease. There are many more red blood cells than white blood cells. For every white blood cell, there are about 600 red blood cells.

4 **DESCRIBE:** What does a white blood cell do?

**Platelets** Have you ever cut yourself? What happens to the wound? Soon after you cut yourself, a clot forms. Clotting is controlled by platelets. **Platelets** are tiny, colorless pieces of cells. When tissues are injured, many platelets clump together near the wound and form a temporary plug. Then, the blood produces a chemical that forms long sticky threads. These threads form a net that traps red blood cells. This lump of red blood cells and sticky threads hardens and becomes a clot. The clot prevents the body from losing any more blood. White blood cells in the clot will attack bacteria to help prevent infection.

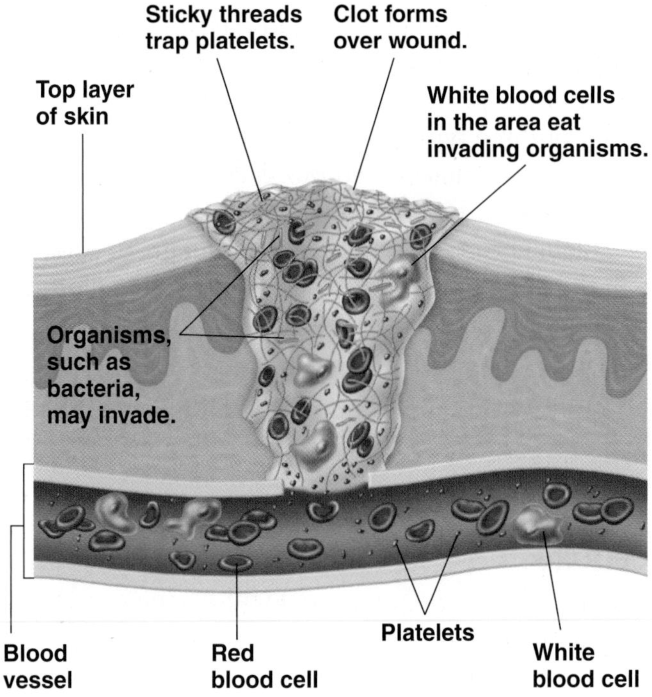


▲ **Figure 15-11** Platelets help the blood form clots.

**5** EXPLAIN: How does a clot form?

**Blood Types** The four major blood types are A, B, AB, and O. Your blood type depends on a specific chemical signal on the red blood cells in your blood. Scientists have labeled two different chemical signals, A and B. People with the A signal have blood type A. People with the B signal have blood type B. Some people have both signals—they have blood type AB. Others have neither the A nor B signal—they have blood type O.

You should know what your blood type is in case of an emergency. Your blood type determines what type of blood you can receive in a transfusion. A **transfusion** is a transfer of blood from one person to another. If you do not know your blood type, ask your doctor.

| BLOOD TYPES | | |
|---|---|---|
| Blood Types | Can Get Blood from | Can Give Blood to |
| A | O, A | A, AB |
| B | O, B | B, AB |
| AB | A, B, AB, O | AB |
| O | O | A, B, AB, O |

▲ **Figure 15-12** Your blood type determines what types of blood you can give and get for transfusions.

**6** IDENTIFY: If a person has type AB blood, what type of blood can that person receive in a transfusion?

## ✓ CHECKING CONCEPTS

1. Red blood cells do not have a __________.
2. The liquid part of blood is called __________.
3. Blood gets its red color from __________.
4. Platelets help the body to form __________.
5. Type __________ blood indicates that there are no signals on the red blood cells.

## THINKING CRITICALLY

6. PREDICT: What would happen if there were no platelets in the blood?
7. EXPLAIN: Why is it important to know your own blood type?

### Web InfoSearch

**Artificial Blood** The Food and Drug Administration has approved use of some forms of blood substitutes. Using artificial blood can help doctors during blood shortages. Each type of artificial blood has its advantages and disadvantages.

**SEARCH:** Use the Internet to find out more about artificial blood. Write your findings in a report. Start your search at www.conceptsandchallenges.com. A key search word is **artificial blood.**

# LAB ACTIVITY
# Observing Blood Cells

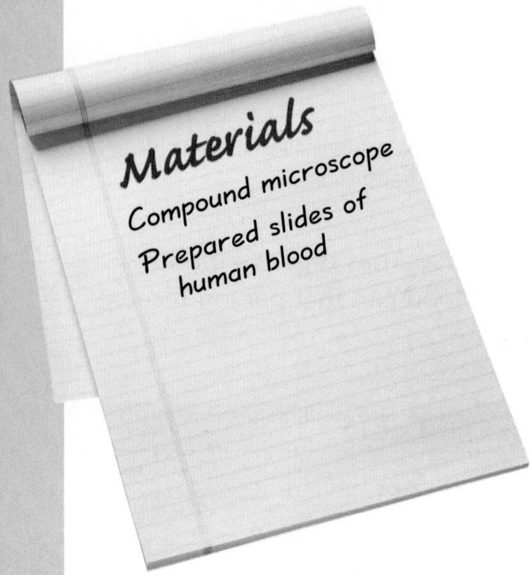


## *BACKGROUND*

Blood is a liquid connective tissue. It carries oxygen and nutrients to your body's cells and it carries away byproducts. Blood contains a liquid part and a solid part. The liquid part is plasma, which makes up about 55 percent of the blood. The remaining 45 percent is composed of three types of cells: red blood cells, white blood cells, and platelets. Red blood cells are the most numerous. White blood cells defend the body against disease. Platelets are tiny, colorless fragments of cells made in the bone marrow. They are involved in clotting.

## *PURPOSE*

In this activity, you will examine the solid part of blood. You will use a microscope to observe different types of blood cells.

## *PROCEDURE*

1. Obtain a prepared slide of red blood cells from your teacher. Make sure the low power objective is in place. Place the slide on the stage of the microscope. Secure the slide in place with the stage clips.
2. Copy the chart in Figure 15-16 onto a sheet of paper. Use the low power objective lens to observe the slide. Use the coarse and fine adjustments to focus the image. Examine the blood under low power. Record your observations in your table. Then, draw what you see on a sheet of paper. Be sure to include the power of magnification.
3. Switch to the high power objective lens. Observe the same slide of red blood cells under high power. Record your observations in your table. Draw what you see on a separate sheet of paper.
4. Using the same slide, try to find platelets. If you need to move the slide, switch to low power first. After you find a few platelets, switch back to high power. Record your observations in your table. Make a drawing of the platelets on a sheet of paper.

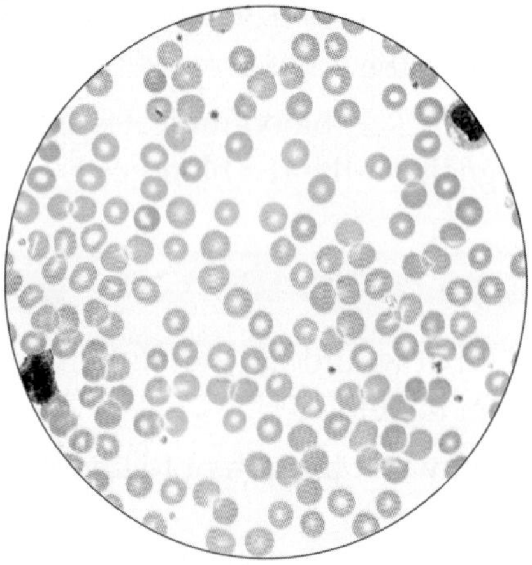

▲ **Figure 15-13** Red blood cells at low magnification

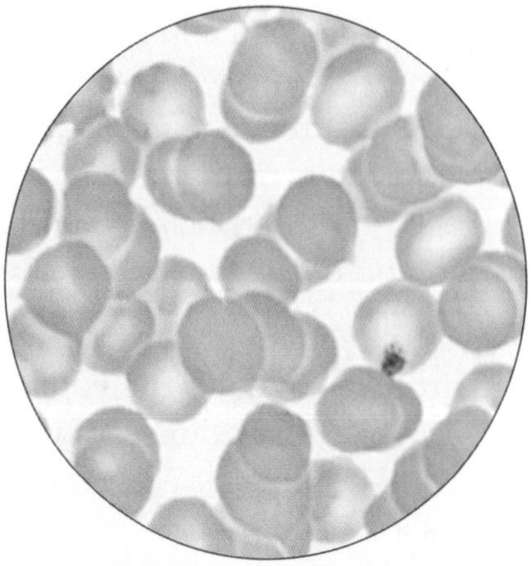

▲ **Figure 15-14** Red blood cells at high magnification

5. Now, try to find a white blood cell. You may use the same slide or get a different slide from your teacher. Observe the white blood cell under low power first; then switch to high power. Record your observations in your chart. Make a drawing of the white blood cell also.

6. Try to find other types of white blood cells. Observe as many as you can under low and high power. Record your observations in the table. Make drawings of each white blood cell you observe.

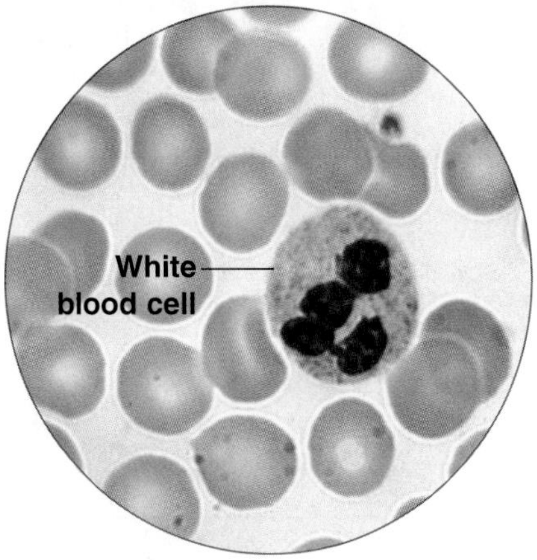


▲ **Figure 15-15** A white blood cell at high magnification

| Type of Cell | Low Magnification | High Magnification |
|---|---|---|
| Red blood cell | | |
| Platelet | | |
| White blood cell | | |

▲ **Figure 15-16** Copy this chart onto a separate sheet of paper.

## *CONCLUSIONS*

1. **OBSERVE:** Does the red blood cell have a nucleus? Does the white blood cell have a nucleus?

2. **CONTRAST:** In what other ways are red and white blood cells different from each other?

3. **CONTRAST:** How does the shape and size of platelets differ from the other blood cells?

4. **RELATE:** How are the shapes of each of the blood cells related to their functions?

# 15-5 What happens to blood as it circulates?

## *Objective*

Describe what happens to blood as it circulates.

## *Key Term*

**pulmonary** (PUL-muh-ner-ee) **artery:** artery that carries blood from the heart to the lungs

**Exchange of Substances** The flow of blood throughout the body is quite simple. Blood is pumped from the left ventricle into the aorta. The aorta is the largest artery in the body. Blood that enters the aorta carries food and oxygen to the body cells.

Once the aorta leaves the heart, it branches into many smaller arteries. These arteries divide again and again until they form capillaries in all the body tissues. Substances are exchanged through the walls of the capillaries. Food and oxygen pass out of the blood in the capillaries and into the body cells. At the same time, carbon dioxide and other wastes or byproducts pass from the body cells into the blood in the capillaries. Look at Figure 15-17 to trace the flow of blood throughout the body.

1 IDENTIFY: Where are materials exchanged between the blood and the body cells?

**Return to the Heart** Once the exchange of substances has taken place, the blood must be returned to the heart. The capillaries in the body tissues join to form small veins. Blood containing carbon dioxide and other wastes are carried in the veins to the left atrium of the heart. Before it can be sent out to the body tissues again, the blood must get a fresh supply of oxygen. It also must get rid of its carbon dioxide. To do this, the blood must be sent to the lungs.

2 NAME: To what part of the heart does blood containing wastes and byproducts return?

**Heart and Lung Circulation** Once the blood is received in the right atrium, it passes into the right ventricle. The right ventricle pumps blood into the pulmonary artery. The **pulmonary artery** carries blood from the heart to the lungs. The pulmonary artery has two branches. One branch goes to each lung. In the lungs, the pulmonary arteries divide many times until they form capillaries. As blood passes through these lung capillaries, it picks up oxygen and gets rid of carbon dioxide. The carbon dioxide is then exhaled from the body.

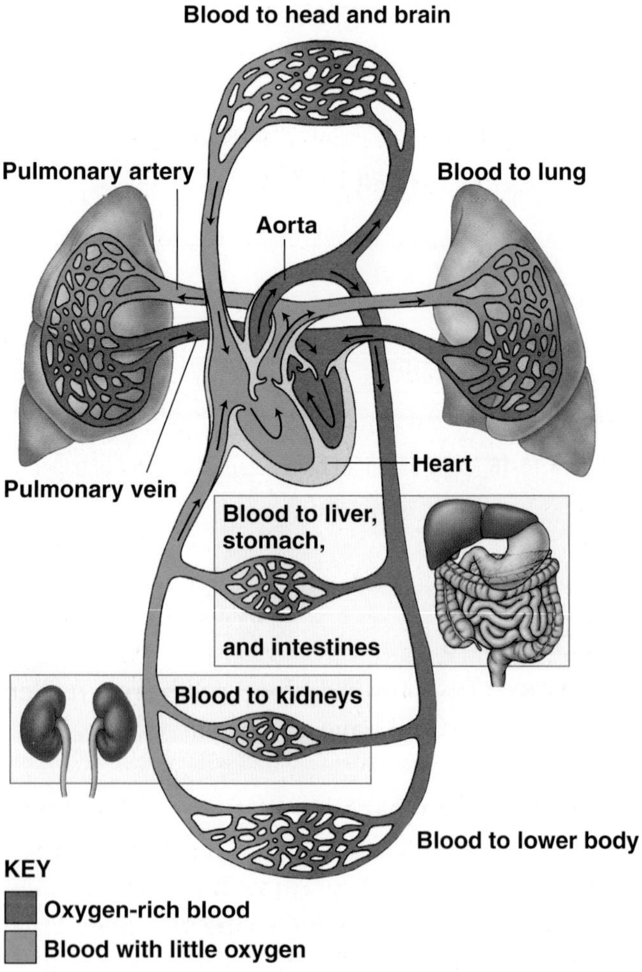


▲ **Figure 15-17** Circulation in the body takes place in two parts or loops.

Once the blood has picked up a fresh supply of oxygen, it is ready to be circulated through the body again. The capillaries in the lungs join together to form veins. The pulmonary veins carry the blood from the lungs to the left atrium of the heart. The left atrium pumps blood into the left ventricle. The left ventricle pumps blood throughout the body.

**3 IDENTIFY:** Where does the blood pick up oxygen and get rid of carbon dioxide?

## ✓ CHECKING CONCEPTS

1. Blood is pumped through the __________ to the lungs.
2. Arteries divide many times until they form __________.
3. Blood picks up oxygen in the __________.
4. Blood is returned to the heart through __________.
5. Materials are exchanged between the blood and the body cells through the walls of __________.
6. Blood is carried to the lungs by the __________.
7. Blood leaving the right atrium passes into the __________.

## THINKING CRITICALLY

8. **SEQUENCE:** Develop a flowchart that illustrates the flow of blood through the body and lungs.
9. **INFER:** What changes take place in the blood as it circulates?

## BUILDING LANGUAGE ARTS SKILLS

***Building Vocabulary*** You can sometimes infer where an artery carries blood to just by knowing its name. Some of the major arteries of the body include the carotid artery, the femoral artery, the bronchial artery, the brachial artery, the renal artery, and the coronary artery. Use library references to look up the meaning of each of these words. Find out where each of these arteries carries blood to in the body.

## *Integrating Physical Science*

**TOPIC: elements in blood**

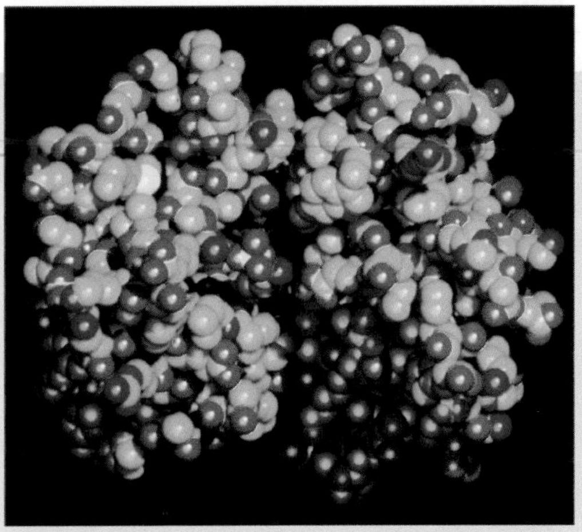

▲ **Figure 15-18** Hemoglobin is a complex molecule made up of proteins and iron.

### IRON IN HEMOGLOBIN

Hemoglobin is the red protein in red blood cells that moves oxygen from your lungs to all the cells of your body. Almost one-third of red blood cells is hemoglobin. When hemoglobin is carrying oxygen, it is called oxyhemoglobin. When hemoglobin has given up its oxygen, it is known as deoxyhemoglobin. Oxyhemoglobin is bright red. Deoxyhemoglobin is much darker.

The element in hemoglobin that is attracted to oxygen is iron. Atoms in iron bond, or combine, with atoms in oxygen. Iron oxidizes well, which means it reacts easily with oxygen. Evidence for the oxidation of iron can be seen when metal is left out and rusts. By oxidating iron, hemoglobin in red blood cells carries oxygen. The rest of the hemoglobin is a twisted pretzel-like protein chain that surrounds the iron. Scientists know the exact structure and shape of hemoglobin by studying X-ray patterns of the molecule after it has been turned into a crystal.

**Thinking Critically** Which type of hemoglobin do you think is found in arteries, oxyhemoglobin or deoxyhemoglobin?

# 15-6 What is heart disease?

## *Objective*

Identify types of heart disease and their causes.

## *Key Terms*

**atherosclerosis** (ath-uhr-oh-skluh-ROH-sis): buildup of fat deposits on artery walls

**coronary** (KAWR-uh-ner-ee) **artery:** artery that carries blood and oxygen to the tissues of the heart

**heart attack:** failure of a part of the heart due to a lack of blood and oxygen

**Heart Disease** Almost one third of all deaths in the United States are caused by heart disease. Heart disease affects both the heart and the blood vessels. Some kinds of heart disease are genetic, or passed from parent to offspring. If someone in your family has heart disease, there is a chance that you also may develop heart disease. Other kinds of heart disease are the result of a person's lifestyle and environment. Figure 15-19 lists some of the factors that contribute to heart disease.

| FACTORS CONTRIBUTING TO HEART DISEASE | |
|---|---|
| Age | Gender |
| High blood pressure | Physical inactivity |
| Family history | Smoking |
| Obesity | Drinking alcohol |
| High cholesterol levels | |

▲ **Figure 15-19** Heart disease may be caused by several different factors.

**1** **INFER:** What are some ways you can prevent heart disease?

**Atherosclerosis** In one kind of heart disease, fatty substances coat the inside walls of the arteries. One of these fatty substances is cholesterol. Cholesterol is found in animal products. As fat builds up in an artery, the opening becomes narrower. The artery walls may also harden and thicken. This condition is known as **atherosclerosis.** This may result in higher blood pressure and other problems related to the circulatory system.

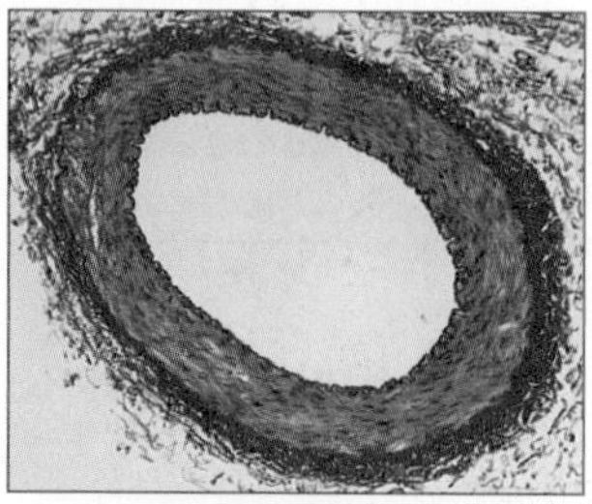

◀ **Figure 15-20** This photo shows a healthy artery.

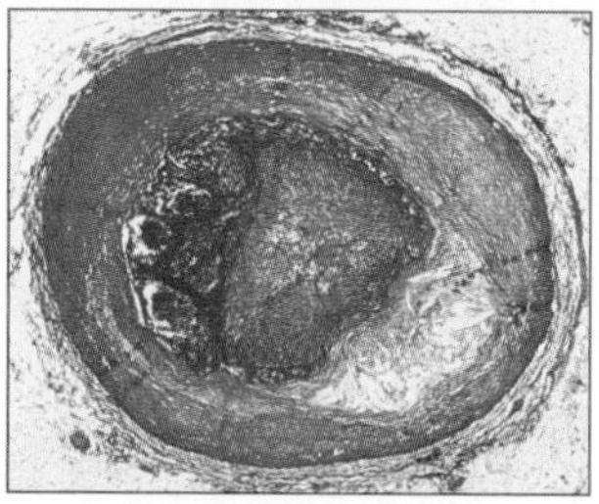

◀ **Figure 15-21** This photo shows an artery clogged by fatty deposits.

**2** **EXPLAIN:** What is atherosclerosis?

**Heart Attack** Like other body cells, the cells of the heart need food and oxygen. Heart cells also need to get rid of waste materials and byproducts. The heart has its own system of blood vessels to take care of these needs. This system is called the coronary system. **Coronary arteries** carry oxygen and blood to the heart muscle.

Atherosclerosis may make the openings in coronary arteries narrower. Coronary arteries can also be blocked by a blood clot. Either form of blockage stops blood and oxygen from reaching the muscles of the heart. The affected part of the heart cannot do its work. This condition is called a **heart attack.** A person having a heart attack usually feels a dull, crushing pain in the chest. Heart attacks often are fatal.

**3** **DESCRIBE:** What is a heart attack?

## ✓ CHECKING CONCEPTS

1. About one third of all deaths in the United States are caused by __________.
2. The __________ arteries carry blood and oxygen to all parts of the heart.
3. A blockage in a coronary artery can cause a person to suffer a __________.
4. A fatty substance that can coat the inside walls of arteries is __________.

## THINKING CRITICALLY

5. **HYPOTHESIZE:** Does the width of an artery increase or decrease as a person ages?
6. **HYPOTHESIZE:** What do you think you can do to reduce the chance that you will be affected by atherosclerosis later in life?
7. **ANALYZE:** Which of the factors listed in Figure 15-19 can be controlled?
8. **EXPLAIN:** Pick three factors in Figure 15-19. How can you lower your risk of getting heart disease for each of the three factors chosen?

### Web InfoSearch

**Pacemakers** The heart sends out electrical signals that keep all four chambers beating in a familiar rhythm. If this electrical signal is not working properly, the heart loses its rhythm. Doctors must then implant a mechanical pacemaker to keep the heart beating normally.

**SEARCH:** Use the Internet to find out more about pacemakers. Write a report comparing the body's natural pacemaker to mechanical pacemakers. Start your search at www.conceptsandchallenges.com. Some key search words are **pacemaker, heart,** and **heart disease.**

## *People in Science*

### CARDIOLOGIST

Cardiologists are doctors who treat patients with heart problems. The field of cardiology is considered a medical specialty, not a surgical one. However, cardiologists often work closely with heart surgeons. Cardiologists may also perform tests, prescribe drugs, and monitor patient progress.

Dr. Mark Blum is a cardiologist. He has been treating patients with heart conditions for 18 years. He specializes in disorders of the coronary arteries. Dr. Blum works with a team of other health-care professionals. This team may include family doctors, surgeons, technicians, and nurses. Together the team diagnoses problems of the heart. They may also help patients recover from heart attacks or other related conditions.

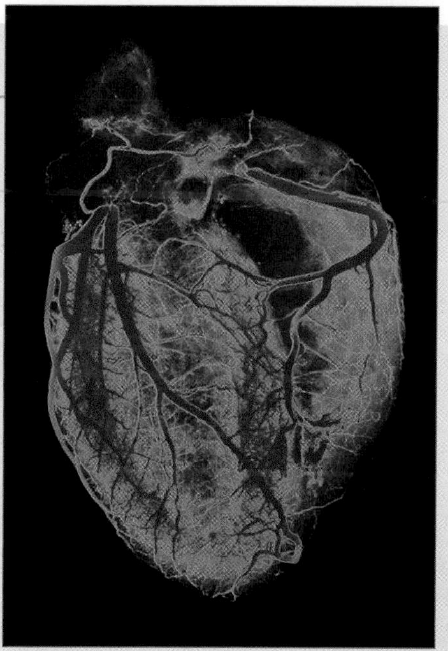

▲ **Figure 15-22** Cardiologists study the human heart.

According to Dr. Blum, a student interested in becoming a cardiologist should work in a hospital or clinic to get an idea about what the job requires. He also feels students need to be hardworking and committed to learning in order to succeed.

**Thinking Critically** Why do you think it is important that cardiologists, surgeons, nurses, and technicians work together?

*Integrating Health Technology*

# THE Big IDEA

## How is technology used to treat cardiovascular disease?

About 12.4 million people have coronary heart disease. Heart disease is a factor in seven out of 10 deaths each year in the United States.

Technology is the application of science to produce things that make life better. Technology can be simple or advanced. A stethoscope is not complex, but it is a very important technological tool. Doctors use it to listen to the heartbeat. An abnormal heartbeat can signal a problem.

Today, doctors have many advanced tools to help them find and correct heart problems. An ultrasound uses sound waves to create an image of the heart. An electrocardiogram shows the electrical activity of the heart. First done in 1977, angioplasty is now a common way for doctors to open clogged arteries.

Technology in heart medicine has reached a new frontier. Robots, under the control of surgeons, fix heart valves. New blood vessels grow from genetic material injected into the heart. An artificial heart provides hope for patients waiting for transplants.

Medical technology has helped saved the lives of many people with heart disease. Look at the boxes of text that appear on this page and the next. They point out some devices used by heart doctors today and others that may become common in the future. Follow the directions in the Science Log to learn more about "the big idea."✦

### Defibrillator

Sometimes the heart quivers instead of beating and pumping blood. This irregular heartbeat can be fatal. An electrical shock can reset the heart's rhythm. The device that delivers this shock is called a defibrillator. In an emergency, an external defibrillator is used on the outside of the chest. Some patients have one placed inside their chest. This is called an implantable cardioverter defibrillator. It resets the heart if it beats too fast or quivers.

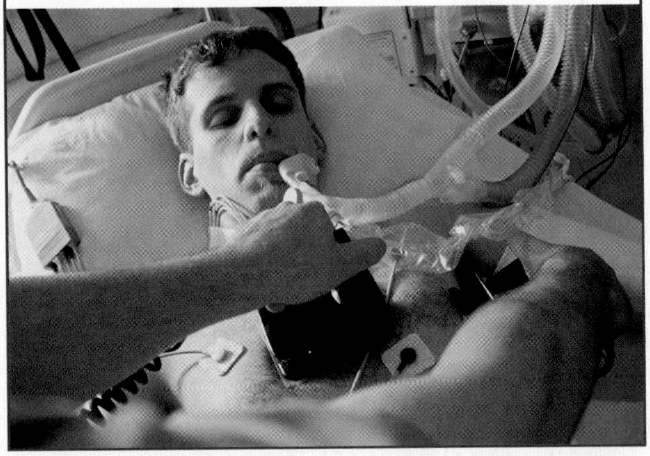

### Angioplasty

Angioplasty is used to open blocked arteries. Fat deposits called plaque block arteries. A special catheter is inserted into the coronary artery. The catheter has a balloon attached to it. The balloon inflates inside the artery. The plaque is pressed against the artery wall. In laser angioplasty, bursts of laser light sent through the catheter break down the plaque. The opened artery improves blood flow to the heart.

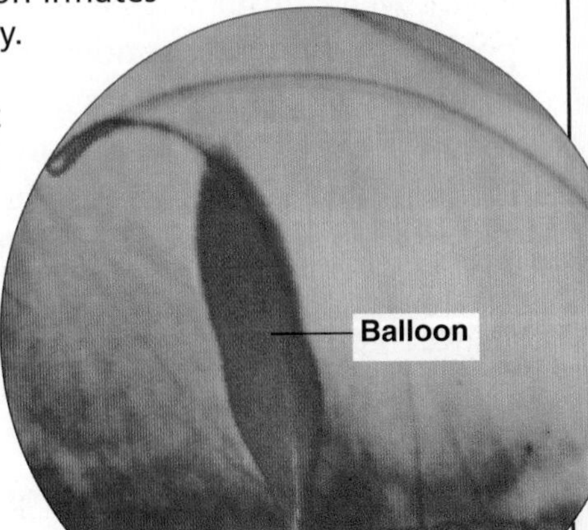

### Arteriogram

An arteriogram is a picture of the arteries. A long, hollow tube called a catheter is inserted into an artery. It is threaded through the aorta into one of the coronary arteries. A dye is injected into the tube. A special X-ray shows the dye moving through the arteries. It reveals places where the artery is clogged.

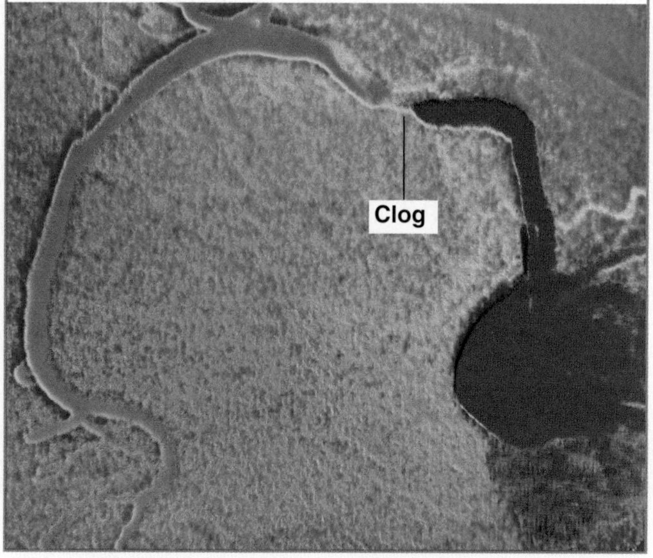


### Artificial Heart

An artificial heart is designed to replace a diseased heart. Most early models were large and clumsy. They had to be connected to an outside power source. They failed terribly. The first self-contained artificial heart was recently developed. It fits inside the chest. No tubes or wires stick out. It must be tested on many patients to see how well it works and to see if it is safe.

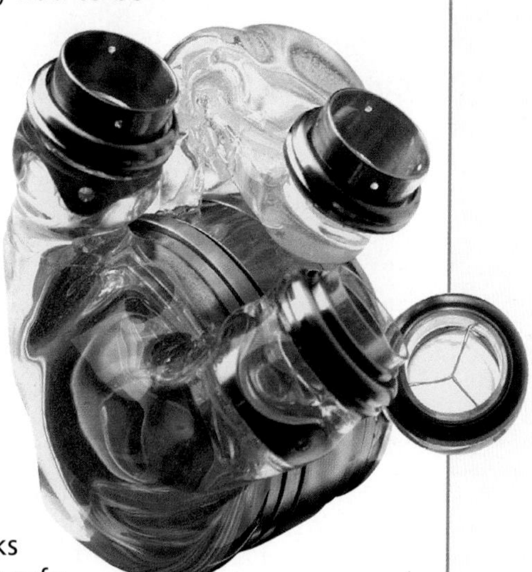

### Robotics

A few surgeons are using robots to repair mitral valves and for other open-heart surgery. The robotic arms can grip, cut, and sew arteries and valves. Surgeons view the heart on a video monitor. They control the robot's movements with joysticks and foot pedals. Robotic surgery requires a relatively small incision. This allows for a faster recovery.

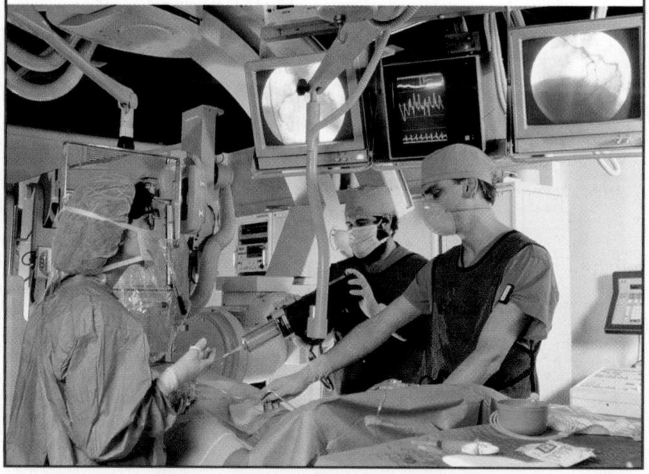

**WRITING ACTIVITY**

*Science Log*

Look at the photos on these two pages. Do you know anybody who has had heart problems? In your science log, research and write about a technology that is used to help heart patients. Describe the benefits of this medical technology. Start your search at www.conceptsandchallenges.com.

# Chapter 15 Challenges

## Chapter Summary

### Lesson 15-1

- **Circulation** is the movement of blood through the body. In a **closed circulatory system,** blood travels within a system of blood vessels.
- The circulatory system transports food and oxygen, and it carries away wastes and byproducts such as carbon dioxide.
- The circulatory system protects your body from disease, carries **hormones,** and regulates body temperature.

### Lesson 15-2

- The heart is divided into **atria** and **ventricles.** The **septum** is a thick tissue wall that separates the left and right sides of the heart.
- Heart **valves** prevent blood from flowing backward.

### Lesson 15-3

- **Arteries** have thick muscular walls and are strong and elastic. **Veins** have thin walls and valves to keep blood flowing toward the heart.
- **Capillaries** are where the exchange of oxygen, carbon dioxide, food, and wastes takes place between the blood and body cells.

### Lesson 15-4

- Blood is a fluid connective tissue. **Plasma** is the liquid part of blood.
- Red blood cells transport oxygen and give blood its color.
- White blood cells destroy germs and help fight disease.
- **Platelets** form clots, which prevent the body from losing blood.

### Lesson 15-5

- As the blood is circulated around the body, it picks up nutrients and oxygen and gets rid of wastes and byproducts, such as carbon dioxide.

### Lesson 15-6

- **Atherosclerosis** is a condition in which fat deposits build up on the walls of arteries.
- **Coronary arteries** carry blood to the heart.
- A **heart attack** occurs when part of the heart does not receive blood and oxygen.

## Key Term Challenges

aorta (p. 360)
artery (p. 360)
atherosclerosis (p. 368)
atrium (p. 358)
capillary (p. 360)
circulation (p. 356)
closed circulatory system (p. 356)
coronary artery (p. 368)
heart attack (p. 368)
hemoglobin (p. 362)
hormone (p. 356)
plasma (p. 362)
platelet (p. 362)
pulmonary artery (p. 366)
septum (p. 358)
transfusion (p. 362)
valve (p. 358)
vein (p. 360)
ventricle (p. 358)

MATCHING **Write the Key Term from above that best matches each description.**

1. cell parts that control clotting
2. protein in red blood cells that carries oxygen
3. liquid part of blood
4. movement of blood through the body
5. transfer of blood from one person to another
6. thick wall of tissue that separates the left and right sides of the heart
7. flap of tissue that prevents blood from flowing backward

FILL IN **Write the Key Term that best completes each statement.**

8. When it reaches the lungs, the __________ divides into two branches.
9. Blood is pumped out of the heart by the __________.
10. Blood vessels with thick muscular walls are __________.
11. The upper chambers of the heart are the __________.
12. The blood vessels that carry blood back to the heart are the __________.
13. The largest artery is the __________.
14. The exchange of food, oxygen, and wastes takes place through the __________.

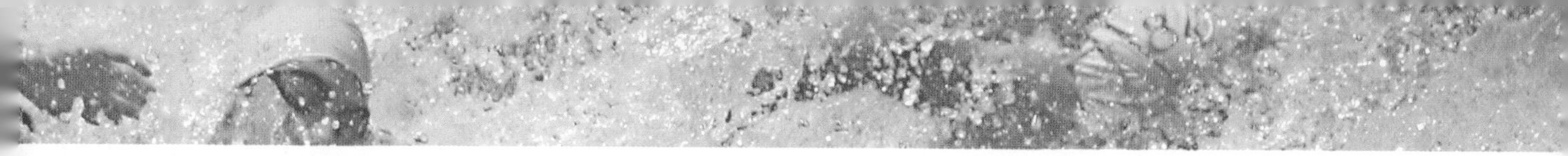

## *Content Challenges* TEST PREP

MULTIPLE CHOICE **Write the letter of the term or phrase that best completes each statement.**

1. The heart is divided into four
   a. valves.
   b. chambers.
   c. atria.
   d. ventricles.

2. The instrument doctors use to listen to your heartbeat is a
   a. stethoscope.
   b. telescope.
   c. thermometer.
   d. centrifuge.

3. When blood is pushed through the arteries, the resulting beat felt at the skin's surface is your
   a. blood pressure.
   b. artery.
   c. pulse.
   d. contraction.

4. The blood vessels through which blood flows at high pressure are
   a. arteries.
   b. veins.
   c. capillaries.
   d. valves.

5. The tiniest blood vessels are
   a. arteries.
   b. veins.
   c. capillaries.
   d. valves.

6. Disease-causing germs within the body are destroyed by
   a. red blood cells.
   b. hemoglobin.
   c. platelets.
   d. white blood cells.

7. The substance that gives red blood cells their color is
   a. plasma.
   b. carbon dioxide.
   c. iron.
   d. platelets.

8. The circulatory system is made up of the heart, the blood vessels, and
   a. oxygen.
   b. hormones.
   c. blood.
   d. enzymes.

9. The main job of the circulatory system is
   a. regulation of temperature.
   b. transport of blood.
   c. protection against disease.
   d. exchange of substances.

10. In the lungs, blood picks up oxygen and gives off
    a. hormones.
    b. food.
    c. oxygen.
    d. carbon dioxide.

TRUE/FALSE **Write *true* if the statement is true. If the statement is false, change the underlined term to make the statement true.**

11. The structures that prevent blood from flowing backward in the heart are called valves.
12. Blood flows from the atria to the ventricles, then back into the body.
13. The walls of arteries are thinner than the walls of veins.
14. With each heartbeat, a pulse can be felt in a capillary.
15. Scientists use a stethoscope to separate blood into liquid and solid parts.

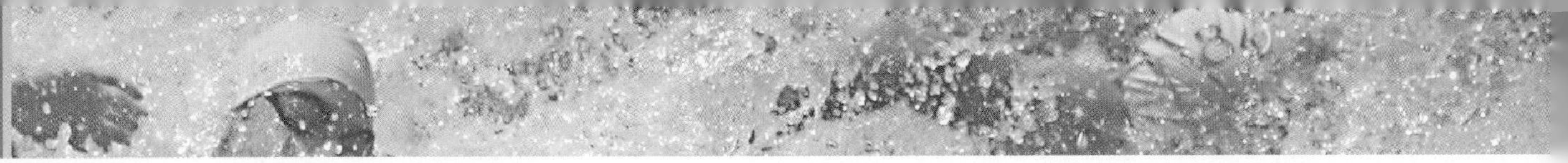

## Concept Challenges TEST PREP

**WRITTEN RESPONSE Complete the exercises and answer each question in complete sentences.**

1. **SEQUENCE:** Describe the complete flow of blood starting from where it leaves the heart to where it enters the heart once again.
2. **DESCRIBE:** Describe the process of blood clotting.
3. **PREDICT:** What happens to the number of white blood cells in your body when you become sick? Why?
4. **INFER:** Explain how the circulatory system provides protection for the body. Give several examples for your answer.

**INTERPRETING A DIAGRAM Use Figure 15-23 to answer the following questions.**

5. What is represented by letter *A*?
6. What is represented by letter *B*?
7. Where is the septum located?
8. Where is the aorta located?
9. What is the job of the aorta?
10. Which letter represents the part of the heart that receives blood from the lungs?
11. In which direction does blood flow in the heart?
12. What blood vessels carry blood to the left atrium?
13. Is blood leaving the right ventricle carrying more oxygen or more carbon dioxide?
14. Is blood carried from the heart to the lungs by a vein or an artery?

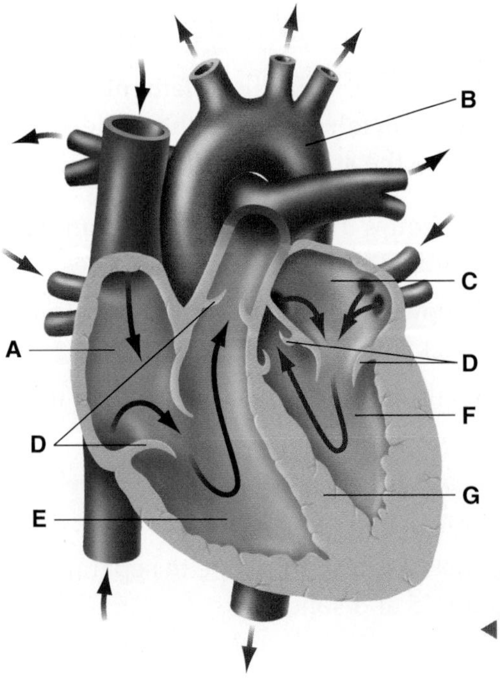


◀ **Figure 15-23** The human heart

# Chapter 16 Respiration and Excretion

▲ **Figure 16-1** Hiking is a demanding physical activity.

Have you ever been outside when the air was so cold you could see your breath? All humans breathe. Breathing is important for cellular respiration, which releases energy from food. When you breathe in, you take in oxygen. This oxygen is used in cellular respiration. When you breathe out, you get rid of water and carbon dioxide. Breathing out is part of excretion, or the removal of waste products from the body. When you see your breath on cold days, you are seeing some of the waste products of respiration.

►Why do you think you breathe harder when you are engaged in a physical activity?

## Contents

# 16-1 What is the respiratory system?

## *Objective*

Describe the parts of the respiratory system.

## *Key Terms*

**trachea** (TRAY-kee-uh)**:** windpipe

**bronchus** (BRAHN-kuhs), *pl.* **bronchi:** tube leading to the lungs

**alveolus** (al-VEE-uh-luhs), *pl.* **alveoli:** microscopic air sacs in the lungs

**larynx** (LAR-inks)**:** organ located on top of the trachea that contains the vocal cords

**The Respiratory System** Each time you breathe in, your lungs fill with air. The lungs, tubes, and passageways through which air moves in your body make up the respiratory system. The job of this system is to take oxygen into the lungs and to get rid of carbon dioxide and water.

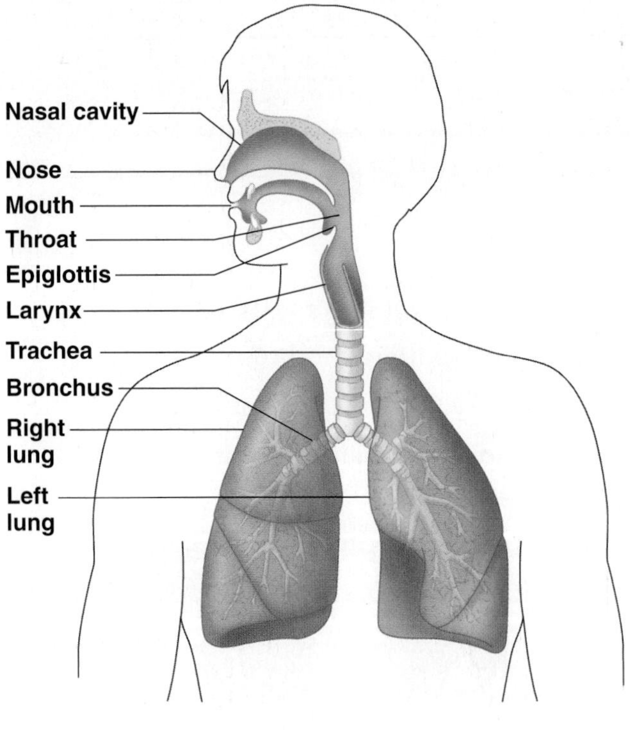


▲ **Figure 16-2** The respiratory system

**1 ANALYZE:** What are the waste products of respiration?

**Passages to the Lungs** Air enters your body through your nose and mouth. Then, air moves into your throat and enters the **trachea,** or windpipe. The trachea is a tube about 10 cm long. The end of the trachea divides into two smaller tubes. These tubes are the **bronchi.** Each bronchus extends into a lung.

**2 OBSERVE:** How many bronchi are there?

**Lungs** The lungs are the main organs of the respiratory system. In the lungs, the bronchi divide many times. The tubes become smaller and smaller. At the ends of the smallest tubes are microscopic air sacs. These air sacs are called **alveoli.** Each lung contains about 150 million alveoli.

**3 NAME:** What are the main organs of the respiratory system?

**Larynx** At the top of the trachea is an organ called the **larynx.** It is made up of cartilage. The human larynx contains two thin folds of skin called vocal cords. During normal, quiet breathing, the vocal cords are relaxed. However, when you speak, your vocal cords tighten. As you breathe out, air passing over the vocal cords causes them to vibrate and produce sounds.

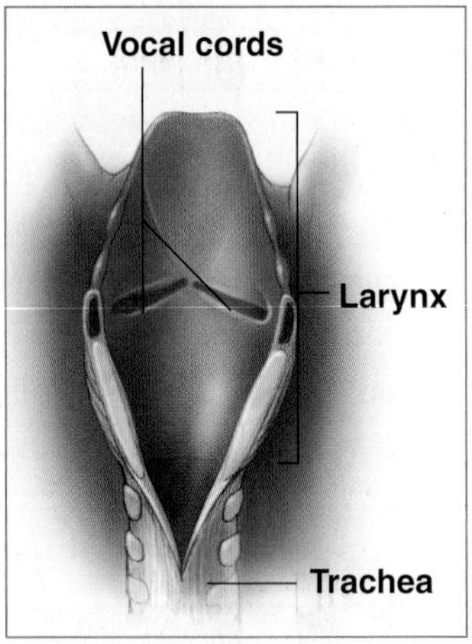


▲ **Figure 16-3** The vocal cords are in the larynx.

When you swallow, a flap of tissue called the epiglottis, automatically closes the larynx. This prevents food and liquid from entering the windpipe. If food or water does enter the windpipe, the cough reflex usually forces the material out.

**4 INFER:** Why do you think that you should not talk while you are eating?

## CHECKING CONCEPTS

1. The organ system that helps you breathe is the __________.
2. Microscopic air sacs in the lungs are called __________.
3. The windpipe branches into two tubes called __________.
4. The main organs of the respiratory system are the __________.
5. Air enters the body through your mouth and __________.

## THINKING CRITICALLY

6. **COMPARE:** The windpipe, bronchi, and branches of the bronchi are sometimes called the bronchial tree. How is the arrangement of these structures similar to the arrangement of a tree?
7. **SEQUENCE:** Place the following words in order to show how air moves through the respiratory system.

| | | |
|---|---|---|
| **a.** trachea | **c.** bronchi | **e.** lungs |
| **b.** nose | **d.** throat | **f.** alveoli |

## HEALTH AND SAFETY TIP

***Asthma*** Many people suffer from asthma (AZ-muh). Asthma usually is caused by an allergy to airborne particles. The muscles react by getting narrower. Air cannot pass easily into and out of the alveoli. Particles in the air can also cause the lungs to produce mucus. Breathing becomes very difficult. Drugs prescribed by a doctor often are used to help relax muscles in the air tubes, allowing them to open up.

## *People in Science*

### RESPIRATORY THERAPIST

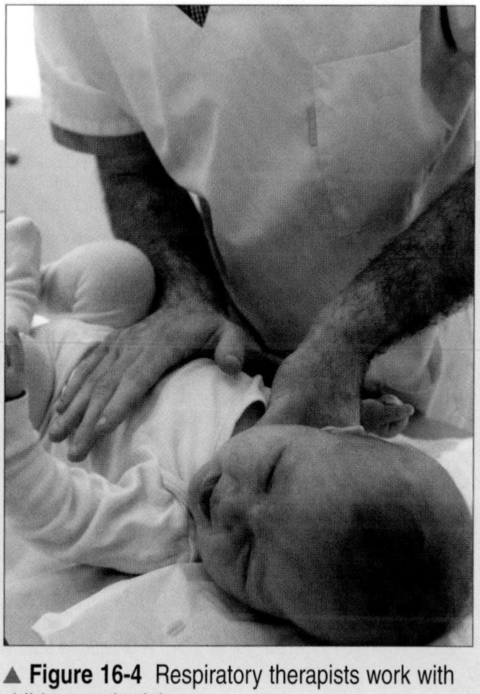

▲ **Figure 16-4** Respiratory therapists work with children and adults.

People sometimes have trouble breathing because of lung or heart disease. Helping people breathe more easily is the job of respiratory therapists. They work with other medical specialists to figure out why patients have trouble breathing. They use special equipment, such as breathing machines and oxygen monitors. They give medications to help people with asthma and other breathing problems.

Steven Sittig is a medical specialist who works with children. He does respiratory therapy while riding in a rescue helicopter. When he gets a call on the job at Mayo Medical Transport in Minnesota, Sittig has 15 minutes to get into a helicopter and take off. The helicopter has the medical equipment and medication needed for moving a patient quickly and safely to a hospital. It is Sittig's job to make sure that his patient is breathing well during the flight. Some patients are very young infants, while others are as old as sixteen.

To become a respiratory therapist, Sittig earned a two-year college degree, specializing in science. Then, he passed a nationwide exam to become a registered respiratory therapist. He also passed another national exam to become a pediatric specialist, which allows him to treat children.

**Thinking Critically** Why do you think respiratory therapists need specialized training to work with children?

Go Online
*active art*
**For:** The Breathing Process activity
**Visit:** PHSchool.com
**Web Code:** cep-4041

# 16-2 What are breathing and respiration?

## *Objectives*

Compare breathing and respiration. Explain the process of breathing.

## *Key Terms*

**respiration** (rehs-puh-RAY-shuhn)**:** process of carrying oxygen to cells, getting rid of carbon dioxide, and releasing energy

**diaphragm** (DY-uh-fram)**:** sheet of muscle below the lungs

**inhale:** to breathe in

**exhale:** to breathe out

**Comparing Breathing and Respiration** Breathing is the process by which air is taken into the body. It is a mechanical process. When you breathe in, oxygen is carried to your lungs. It is not carried to your cells. Breathing does not release energy for your body to use.

Carrying oxygen to your cells, getting rid of carbon dioxide, and releasing energy is called **respiration.**

Respiration is a chemical process. It has three parts.

- **External Respiration** During external respiration, oxygen and carbon dioxide are exchanged between the lungs and the blood.
- **Internal Respiration** During internal respiration, oxygen and carbon dioxide are exchanged between the blood and the cells of the body.
- **Cellular Respiration** Cellular respiration is the chemical process by which energy from food molecules is released by cells. Carbon dioxide and water are given off as byproducts.

1 **CLASSIFY:** Is breathing a chemical or mechanical process?

**The Diaphragm** Below the lungs, there is a sheet of muscle called the **diaphragm.** Look at the position of the diaphragm in Figure 16-5. The diaphragm helps you breathe. It works with the ribs and rib muscles. Many body parts work together to help you breathe.

2 **LIST:** What parts of the body work together to help you breathe?

**Inhaling** When you **inhale,** or breathe in, your rib muscles contract, causing the ribs to move up and out. The diaphragm moves downward, away from the lungs. The space inside the chest becomes larger. Because of this, there is less air pressure in the lungs than outside the body. The outside air pressure causes air to rush into the lungs. The lungs fill with air and expand.

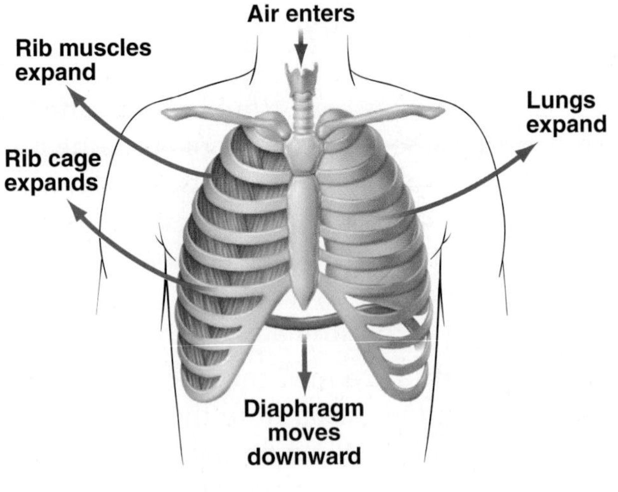


▲ **Figure 16-5** Inhaling

3 **DEFINE:** What does the word *inhale* mean?

**Exhaling** When you **exhale,** or breathe out, the rib muscles relax, causing the ribs to move down and in. The diaphragm relaxes and moves upward, toward the lungs. The space inside the chest becomes smaller. Because of this, the air pressure in the lungs is greater than the air pressure outside the body. Air moves out of the lungs. The lungs deflate and take up less space in the chest.

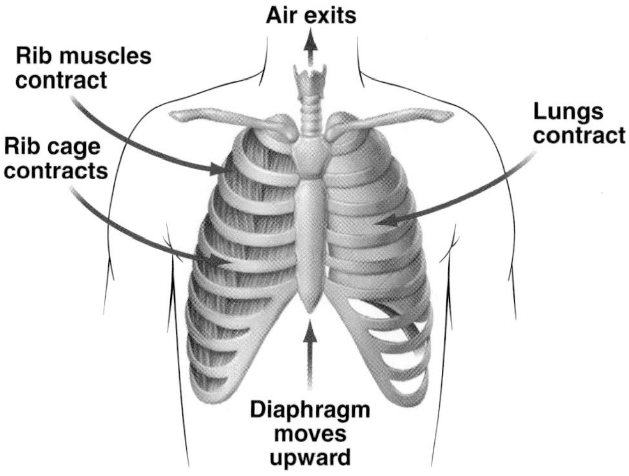


▲ **Figure 16-6** Exhaling

**DESCRIBE:** What happens to the size of the space in the chest when you exhale?

## CHECKING CONCEPTS

1. How does the diaphragm move when you exhale?
2. What is breathing?
3. Does breathing release energy?
4. What are the waste products of cellular respiration?
5. What happens to the space inside your chest when you inhale?

## THINKING CRITICALLY

6. **SEQUENCE:** List the steps your body goes through to get oxygen into your bloodstream.
7. **ANALYZE:** What body systems allow you to breathe?
8. **APPLY:** How are breathing and respiration related?

## INTERPRETING VISUALS

*Use Figures 16-5 and 16-6 to answer the following question.*

9. **ANALYZE:** Look at the red and blue arrows in each diagram. What is the relationship between the directions in which they point? Tell how they explain the actions of inhaling and exhaling.

## *Hands-On Activity*

### EXERCISE AND BREATHING RATE

*You will need a watch or clock with a second hand.*

1. Breathe in and out normally. Have your partner count the number of breaths you take in 1 minute. Record the number of breaths.
2. Jog in place for 20 seconds. Then stop. Have your partner count the number of breaths you take in 1 minute. Record this number.
3. Jog in place for 40 seconds. Then stop. Have your partner count the number of breaths you take in 1 minute. Record.
4. Change places with your partner and repeat the activity.

▲ **Figure 16-7** Have your partner count the number of breaths you take in 1 minute.

#### Practicing Your Skills

5. **MEASURE:** How many breaths did you take in a minute at rest? After 20 seconds of jogging? After 40 seconds of jogging?
6. **COMPARE:** How did your breathing rates compare to your partner's breathing rates?
7. **INFER:** What effect does exercise have on breathing rate?

# LAB ACTIVITY
# Modeling Breathing

**Materials**

Straw
Rubber sheet
Plastic cup with a hole in the bottom
Balloon
Rubber band
Wire
Rubber cement

### *BACKGROUND*

You are always breathing. When you inhale, you breathe in fresh air. When you exhale, you breathe out used air. The diaphragm is a sheet of muscle that helps you breathe. It is located just under your lungs. The diaphragm moves up and down to change the amount of space in your chest. This changes the amount of air pressure in your chest. It is the changing air pressure that forces air in and out of your lungs.

### *PURPOSE*

In this activity, you will make a simple model that shows how you breathe.

### *PROCEDURE*

1. Place a small balloon on the end of the straw. Wrap some wire around the neck of the balloon so that it will not slip off the straw.

2. Push the drinking straw through the hole in the bottom of the plastic cup. Then pull the straw back so that the balloon goes up into the cup, just above the hole.

3. Seal the space around the straw with rubber cement. Allow it to dry.

4. Cover the mouth of the cup with a rubber sheet. Use a rubber band to hold the sheet tightly in place.

▲ **STEP 1** Wrap wire around the neck of the balloon.

▲ **STEP 3** Seal the space around the straw with rubber cement.

5. Copy the data chart in Figure 16-8 onto your own paper. Then, use your thumb and forefinger to grasp the rubber sheet at its center. Pull the sheet out a little bit. Watch the balloon. How did you change the space inside the cup. What happened to the balloon? Write your observations in your data chart.

6. Use your forefinger to push the rubber sheet a little bit in toward the balloon. Watch the balloon. Write your observations in your data chart.

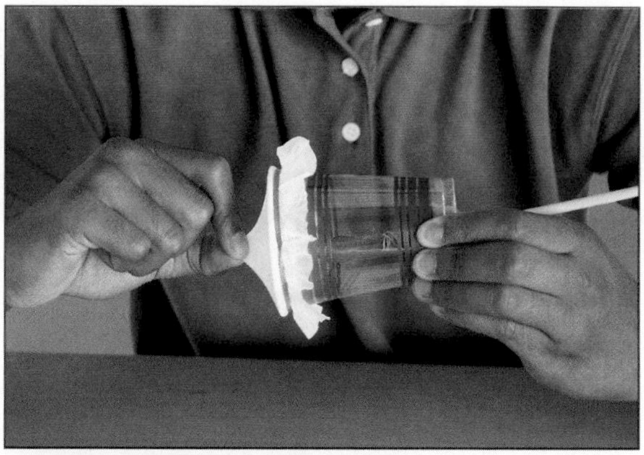

▲ **STEP 5** Pull the sheet out.

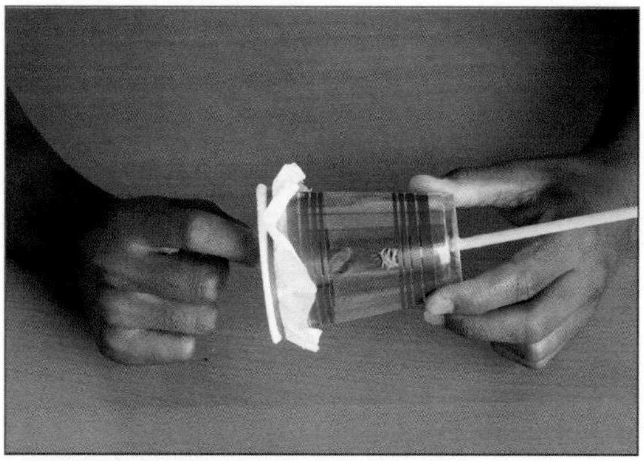

▲ **STEP 6** Push the sheet in.

| Action | Change in Amount of Space Inside Cup | Change in Air Pressure | Change in Balloon |
|---|---|---|---|
| | | | |

▲ **Figure 16-8** Copy this chart onto a sheet of paper.

### *CONCLUSIONS*

1. APPLY: What did the balloon in this experiment represent?

2. APPLY: What did the rubber sheet in this experiment represent?

3. ANALYZE: When you pushed the rubber sheet in, did you model exhaling or inhaling?

4. EXPLAIN: How does your diaphragm help you breathe?

# 16-3 What happens to air before it reaches the lungs?

## INVESTIGATE

### *Modeling Filtering Hairs*

**HANDS-ON ACTIVITY**

1. Your teacher will give you a small dish filled with water.
2. Sprinkle about one teaspoonful of pepper over the surface of the water.
3. Gently run a popsicle stick over the water. How much pepper did you pick up?
4. Repeat Step 3 with a toothbrush. How much pepper did you pick up?

**THINK ABOUT IT:** What do you think caused the difference in the results?

### *Objective*

Explain how air is cleaned, warmed, and moistened as it moves through the respiratory system.

### *Key Terms*

**mucus** (MYOO-kuhs)**:** sticky liquid produced in the nose and windpipe

**cilia** (SIHL-ee-uh)**:** tiny hairlike structures

**Filtering Air** You normally breathe through your nose. The air that you inhale contains dirt and dust particles. These particles may be harmful to the lungs. Inside your nose, there are many hairs. These hairs filter out and trap many dust and dirt particles.

**1** INFER: Why do you think that it is better to breathe through your nose than through your mouth?

**Mucus** The cells inside the nose and windpipe produce a sticky liquid called **mucus.** Mucus lines the inside of the nose and windpipe. Dust, dirt, bacteria, and other harmful particles stick to the mucus. Mucus stops many particles from reaching the lungs. Mucus also keeps the tissues of the respiratory system from drying out.

**2** EXPLAIN: What are the two jobs of mucus?

**Cilia** **Cilia** are tiny hairlike structures. Your trachea and nose are lined with millions of cilia. The cilia move back and forth, pushing mucus toward the back of the throat. Trapped particles are pushed along the throat with the mucus. Some mucus with its trapped particles is swallowed.

▲ **Figure 16-9** Cilia

Sometimes mucus and the particles stuck in it can irritate the lining of your nose. When this happens, you respond by sneezing. A sneeze is a burst of air. Sneezing blows harmful particles out of the nose.

**3** NAME: Where are cilia located in the respiratory system?

**Warm, Moist Air** Sometimes the air you inhale is cold and dry. When the air enters your body, it is warmed by heat from the body. Remember humans are warm-blooded. Your body temperature is about 37°C, except when you have a fever. Air that enters the lungs has been warmed in your nose and throat. The body also adds water vapor to the air you inhale. The air is made moist as it moves through the nose and trachea. Air reaching the lungs is warm and moist. Warm, moist air prevents damage to the lungs.

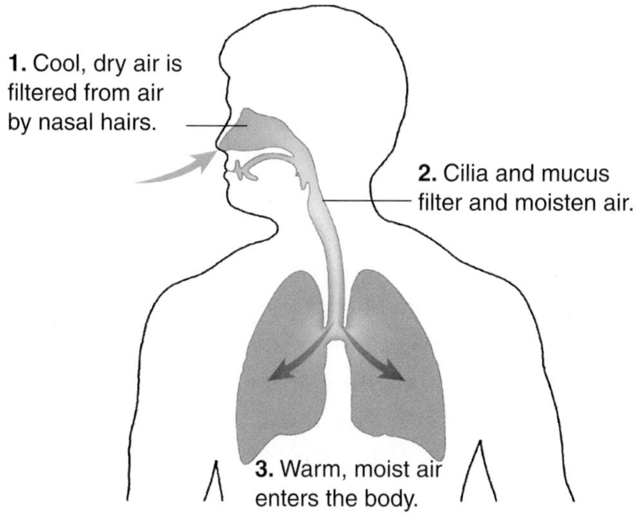


▲ **Figure 16-10** Air is filtered and warmed before entering the lungs.

4 **INFER:** Why do you think it is better for air to be filtered and warmed before it reaches the lungs?

## CHECKING CONCEPTS

1. A burst of air that blows harmful particles out of the nose is a __________.
2. The trachea is lined with tiny hairlike structures called __________.
3. Air that enters the lungs is warm and __________.
4. The sticky liquid that traps harmful particles in the respiratory tubes is __________.
5. You normally breathe through your __________.

## THINKING CRITICALLY

6. **EXPLAIN:** How is the air you breathe in changed before it reaches the lungs?
7. **DIAGRAM:** Develop a flowchart that traces the pathway of air from the nose to the lungs. List each organ the air passes through. Beneath each organ, identify how air passing through the organ is changed.

## *Real-Life Science*

### PROTECTING THE RESPIRATORY SYSTEM

Some chemicals found in the environment can weaken a person's respiratory system. Automobile fumes, smoke, chalk dust, and other common air pollutants are known dangers. Serious damage can occur after prolonged exposure to air pollutants. Workers in occupations that produce air pollutants are at the highest risk for respiratory illness. Coal miners and construction workers fall into this category.

Asbestos (eh-SPEH-stahs) is a material that was used in the past to insulate buildings. Inhaling asbestos fibers can cause lung diseases. Today, asbestos is being removed from buildings to eliminate the danger.

▲ **Figure 16-11** Workers removing asbestos must wear special protective gear.

Another disease that affects the lungs is miner's asthma. Miner's asthma is caused by the inhalation of quartz dust. Quartz dust is usually created during dynamiting in mining. Prolonged exposure to asbestos or quartz dust can cause scar tissue to form in the lungs. There are federal regulations to protect workers from respiratory diseases. Coal companies, for example, are required to provide air masks with filters to miners.

**Thinking Critically** Why do you think there is usually a large number of cases of asthma in cities?

# 16-4 How does oxygen get into the blood?

## *Objectives*

Explain gas exchange in the lungs and between the blood and body cells. Compare the gas makeup of inhaled air and exhaled air.

**Oxygen in the Air** Air is a mixture of gases. It is made up mostly of nitrogen and oxygen. Your body cells need oxygen to carry out respiration. Oxygen enters the lungs in the air you inhale. One of the jobs of the lungs is to take in oxygen from the air.

| PERCENTAGE OF GASES IN THE AIR | |
|---|---|
| **Gas** | **Percentage** |
| Nitrogen | 78.00 |
| Oxygen | 21.00 |
| Argon | 00.90 |
| Carbon dioxide | 00.03 |
| Other | 00.07 |

▲ **Figure 16-12**

**1 ANALYZE:** What percentage of air is made up of oxygen?

**Alveoli** The alveoli are where gases are exchanged in the lungs. Alveoli are shaped like a bunch of grapes. They have very thin walls and are surrounded by many capillaries. Capillaries are very tiny blood vessels. Red blood cells move through the capillaries in single file.

The most important part of respiration is the exchange of the gases oxygen and carbon dioxide. In the lungs, oxygen and carbon dioxide are exchanged between the alveoli and the blood. Oxygen molecules pass through the walls of the alveoli into the capillaries. The oxygen molecules attach to the red blood cells. At the same time, carbon dioxide molecules pass from the blood through the capillary walls into the alveoli.

How does this exchange of gas take place? Fresh air in the alveoli has a high level of oxygen and a low level of carbon dioxide. Blood in the capillaries surrounding the alveoli is low in oxygen and high in carbon dioxide. These differences in concentration of gases allow for diffusion, or movement across cell membranes, to take place. The oxygen diffuses, or moves out, of the alveoli into the capillaries. At the same time, carbon dioxide diffuses from the capillaries into the alveoli.

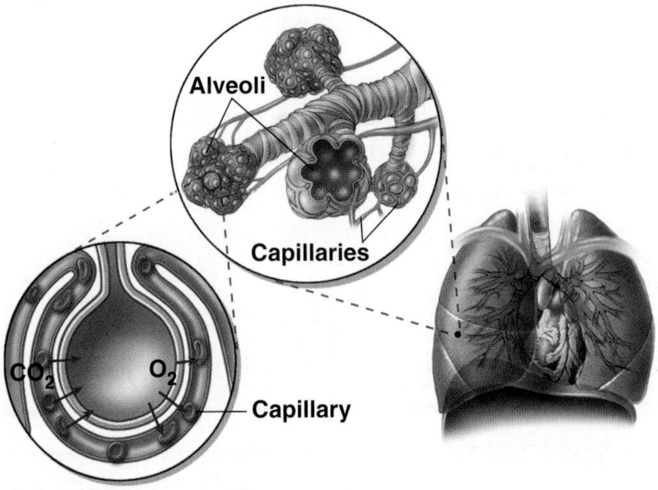


▲ **Figure 16-13** The alveoli

**2 DESCRIBE:** What happens to oxygen molecules in the lungs?

**Gas Exchange in Cells** Once oxygen is picked up by the blood in the lungs, it is brought to body cells. Then, oxygen and carbon dioxide are exchanged between the body cells and red blood cells. Oxygen moves from the red blood cells into the body cells. Carbon dioxide moves from the body cells into the capillaries. The carbon dioxide is carried back to the lungs by blood cells, where it can be exhaled.

**3 DESCRIBE:** What happens to carbon dioxide molecules in the body cells?

**Air In and Air Out** The gas makeup of the air you breathe in is different from the gas makeup of the air you breathe out. Inhaled air contains more oxygen than does exhaled air. Exhaled air contains more carbon dioxide than does inhaled air. Exhaled air is different because oxygen in the air is absorbed by the lungs. In addition, your cellular respiration adds carbon dioxide to air exhaled. Water vapor is also added to the air you exhale.

4 ANALYZE: Why is there more carbon dioxide in exhaled air than inhaled air?

## CHECKING CONCEPTS

1. What is air?
2. Where are gases exchanged in the lungs?
3. What are capillaries?
4. How is carbon dioxide removed from the body?
5. Does inhaled air contain more oxygen or more carbon dioxide than exhaled air?
6. Does exhaled air contain more oxygen or more carbon dioxide than inhaled air?

## THINKING CRITICALLY

7. INTERPRET: How much of the air is made up of nitrogen?
8. INFER: Which percentages would most likely be contained in inhaled air?
   **a.** 78 nitrogen, 21 oxygen
   **b.** 78 nitrogen, 17 oxygen
9. INFER: Which percentages would most likely be contained in exhaled air? How do you know?
   **a.** 21 oxygen; 0.03 carbon dioxide
   **b.** 17 oxygen; 4 carbon dioxide

## BUILDING MATH SKILLS

***Graphing*** A graph is a good way to organize and present information. Use the percentages of the gases contained in air shown in Figure 16-12 to make a circle graph of this data. Make sure you include a title, labels, and units. Add together the gases that make up less than one percent of air. Label these "Other" in your graph.

## *Hands-On Activity*

### ANALYZING EXHALED AIR

*You will need safety goggles, a shallow piece of glass, such as a watchglass or petri dish, 50 mL of limewater, a beaker or glass, and a straw.*

1. Breathe out onto the watchglass. Record your observation.
2. Add the 50 mL of limewater to the beaker or glass. Limewater is used to test for carbon dioxide. If carbon dioxide is present, the limewater becomes cloudy.
3. Put the straw into the limewater. Gently blow bubbles through the straw into the glass of limewater.
   ⚠ CAUTION: Do not inhale while the straw is in the limewater. Do not drink the limewater.

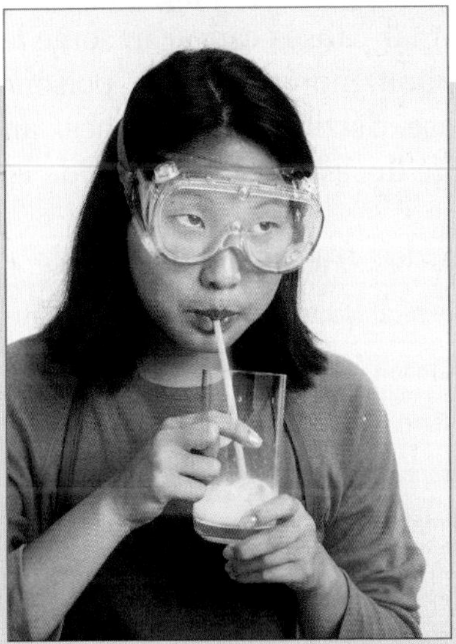

▲ **STEP 3** Blow bubbles into the limewater. Do not inhale.

**Practicing Your Skills**

4. OBSERVE: What forms on the watchglass? Where did it come from?
5. INFER: What happens to the limewater when you bubble exhaled air into it? Explain your answer.
6. INFER: What does this tell you about the air you exhale?

# 16-5 How does tobacco affect the body?

### *Objective*

Explain the effects of tobacco on the body.

### *Key Term*

**nicotine** (NIHK-uh-teen): stimulant found in tobacco

**Tobacco** Tobacco contains more than 100 chemical substances. When tobacco burns, many new substances are formed. All of these substances are taken into the body with the tobacco smoke. One of the harmful substances in tobacco smoke is nicotine. **Nicotine** is a stimulant drug that causes both physical and mental addiction. Tars and carbon monoxide are other harmful substances found in tobacco smoke. When inhaled, tar coats the lining of the lungs. Experiments have shown that tar causes cancer in some laboratory animals. Carbon monoxide is a poisonous gas that may cause dizziness, headaches, and drowsiness. In large doses, carbon monoxide is fatal.

| SOME CHEMICALS IN TOBACCO | |
|---|---|
| **Chemical Name** | **Other Uses** |
| Acetone | Nail polish remover |
| Arsenic | Rat poison |
| Carbon monoxide | Car exhaust fumes |
| Formaldehyde | Preserving dead bodies |
| Methanol | Rocket fuel |
| Nicotine | Insecticides |

◀ **Figure 16-14**

**1** **IDENTIFY:** What are three harmful substances found in tobacco smoke?

**Effect on Breathing** The air tubes in the lungs are lined with cells. These cells have tiny hairlike structures called cilia. The cilia beat back and forth to push mucus from the lungs toward the throat. Foreign substances trapped in the mucus get pushed out of the lungs. Smoking causes the cilia to stop working. Without the action of the cilia, mucus collects in and blocks the air tubes. This trapped air causes the air sacs, or alveoli, to break. With fewer air sacs at work, less oxygen flows into the lungs with each breath. Less carbon dioxide is released from the body with each exhalation. The smoker must breathe harder and more often to get enough oxygen.

**2** **EXPLAIN:** What effect does smoking have on the cilia in the air tubes of the lungs?

**Illnesses** When the cilia stop beating, foreign substances remain trapped in the lungs. There, these substances may cause infection and disease. Smokers are more likely to get heart disease, cancer, and lung disease than nonsmokers. Emphysema (ehm-fuh-SEE-muh) is a lung disease in which the air sacs are destroyed. This leads to a poor exchange of oxygen and carbon dioxide between the lungs and the bloodstream. Smokers have a higher death rate from these diseases than do nonsmokers. Compare the healthy lung on the left in Figure 16-15 with the smoker's lung on the right.

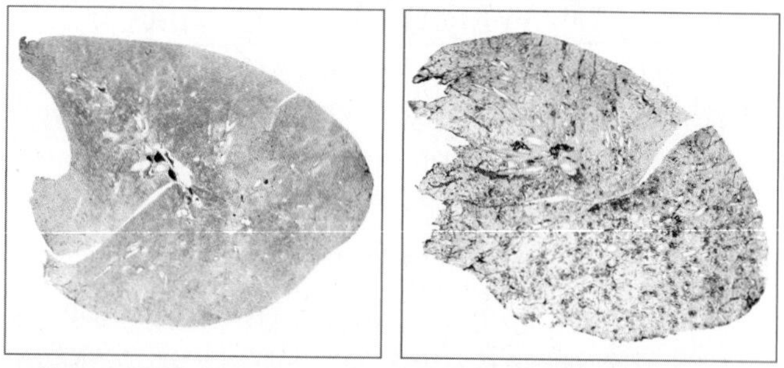

▲ **Figure 16-15** The photo on the left is the healthy lung of a nonsmoker. The photo on the right is the diseased lung of a smoker.

Smoking also places a great strain on the heart. With fewer air sacs in the lungs, the blood gets less oxygen. The heart must work harder to supply enough blood to the body cells. This raises blood pressure. Nicotine also makes the blood vessels narrow. The heart must work harder to pump the blood through the smaller openings. This puts an even greater strain on the heart.

**3** **DESCRIBE:** What effect does nicotine have on blood vessels?

**Secondhand Smoke** Researchers have discovered that tobacco smoke can also affect nonsmokers. For example, children living with smokers are twice as likely to have respiratory problems as children living with nonsmokers. Due to the dangers of secondhand smoke, or the smoke from a burning tobacco product, smoking is banned in many public places. Other public places are required to provide a nonsmoking section.

4 **DEFINE:** What is secondhand smoke?

## CHECKING CONCEPTS

1. Nicotine, carbon monoxide, and ___________ are examples of harmful substances found in tobacco smoke.
2. When cilia in the air tubes stop beating, ___________ collects and blocks the tubes.
3. Nicotine makes blood vessels ___________.
4. Smoking puts a great strain on the ___________.

## THINKING CRITICALLY

5. **INFER:** What effect would cigarette smoking have on a person's ability to exercise?
6. **HYPOTHESIZE:** Nicotine is an addictive drug. Why do you think it may be difficult for a person to quit smoking?

## BUILDING WRITING SKILLS

***Writing to Persuade*** When you write to persuade, you try to get someone to agree with your point of view. Create an antismoking pamphlet to persuade people about the dangers of smoking.

## *Real-Life Science*

## EFFECTS OF SMOKING ON THE HUMAN BODY

You already know that smoking can cause heart and lung disease. You know that nicotine is addictive. Studies show that along with these diseases, there are outward signs of smoking on the human body as well.

Did you know that people who smoke are five times more likely to develop wrinkles earlier than nonsmokers are? The chemicals in smoking can weaken a person's bones. As a result, smokers are more likely to break their bones than nonsmokers are.

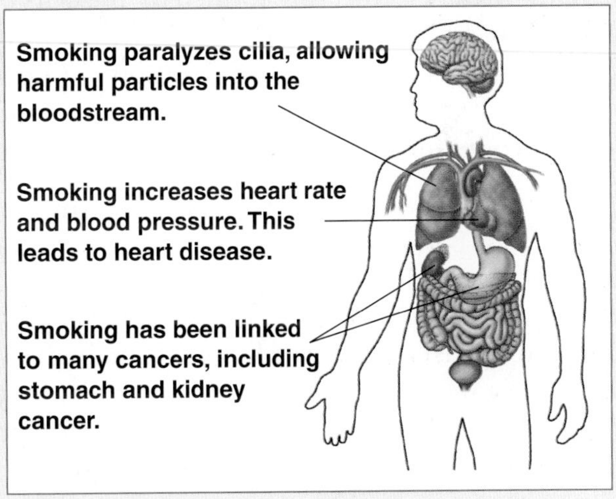


▲ **Figure 16-16** Smoking can damage the entire body.

Smoking damages the inside of the human body as well. Smoking has been linked to several different forms of cancer, including some forms of leukemia, cancer of the larynx, esophageal, lung, kidney, pancreatic, stomach, and urinary cancers.

Despite the information about tobacco's effect on the body, an estimated 48 million people in the United States continue to smoke each year. More than 400,000 of those people will die from cigarette-related illnesses.

**Thinking Critically** Why do some people who smoke look older than nonsmokers who are the same age?

# 16-6 What is the excretory system?

### *Objective*

Explain how waste products are formed and removed by the body.

### *Key Terms*

**excretion** (ehks-KREE-shuhn)**:** process of removing waste products from the body

**kidney:** excretory organ that removes waste products from the blood

**ureter** (yoo-REET-uhr)**:** tube that carries liquid waste from the kidneys to the bladder

**bladder:** excretory organ that stores liquid wastes

**Forming Waste Products** Foods are combined with oxygen in your cells. As the food is used by the body, heat and other kinds of energy are produced. The energy released is used by the body to carry out its life processes. When the foods are used to produce energy, waste products are formed.

Many waste products are formed by the cells of your body. Carbon dioxide and water are byproducts of cellular respiration. Other byproducts made by the cells are salts and nitrogen compounds. Heat also is a waste product.

1 LIST: What are some waste products formed by your body?

**Excretion** The many waste products formed by your body must be removed from your body. If these waste products build up in your body, they will be harmful to you. The process of removing waste products from the body is called **excretion.**

2 DEFINE: What is excretion?

**The Excretory System** Removing waste products from the body is the job of the excretory system. It is made up of many different organs. The lungs are part of the excretory system. You know that the lungs get rid of carbon dioxide and of water. The **kidneys** also are organs of the excretory system. They get rid of liquid waste and dissolved solids. The largest organ of the excretory system is your skin. It gets rid of liquid waste and salts and helps you get rid of extra heat.

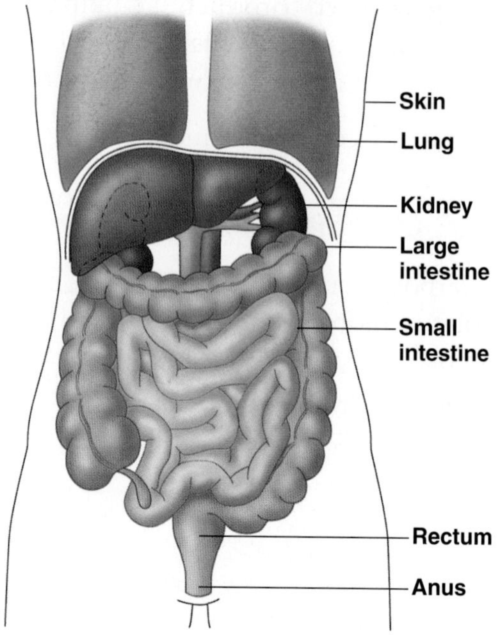


▲ **Figure 16-17** The excretory system

3 LIST: What are three organs of excretion?

**Liquid Waste** Much of the liquid waste in blood is removed by the kidneys. This liquid is collected. It then flows through the **ureters** into the **bladder.** From there, the liquid waste is excreted through the urethra.

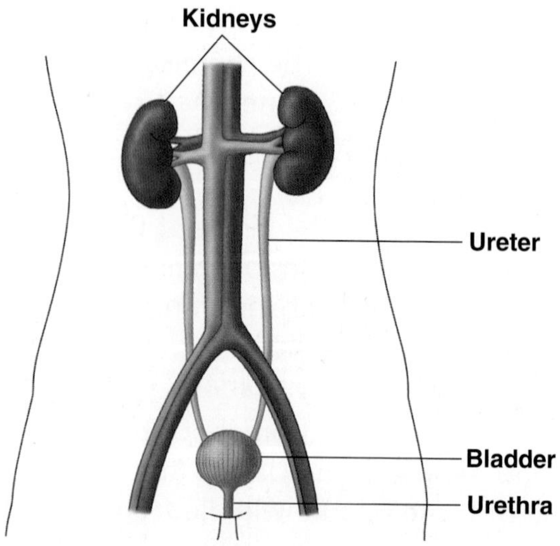


▲ **Figure 16-18** Liquid waste is removed by the kidneys.

4 DEFINE: What is the job of the bladder?

**Solid Wastes** Some parts of the foods that you eat cannot be digested. They cannot pass through the villi. Undigested foods form waste. This waste moves along in the small intestine. It enters the large intestine. Water is removed from the waste in the large intestine, shown in Figure 16-17. As water is removed, the waste becomes solid. The solid waste moves along in the large intestine and into the rectum. From there, the solid waste is excreted through the anus (AY-nuhs).

5 **DESCRIBE:** What is the job of the large intestine?

## CHECKING CONCEPTS

1. What are the waste products of cellular respiration?
2. What is excretion?
3. What does the excretory system do?
4. What does skin do?
5. What is the job of the large intestine?
6. How does solid waste leave the body?
7. How do liquid wastes leave the body?

## THINKING CRITICALLY

8. **CONTRAST:** How is the excretory system different from the respiratory system?

## INTERPRETING VISUALS

*Use Figures 16-17 and 16-18 to answer the following questions.*

9. Which organs in the diagrams excrete liquid waste?
10. Which organ in the diagrams is used to rid the body of excess heat?
11. Through which organ is solid waste excreted?

## Science and Technology

### USING SOUND TO BREAK APART KIDNEY STONES

Mineral compounds that are not excreted by the body can build up and form kidney stones. Kidney stones form inside the kidneys. Large kidney stones can completely block the passage of liquid waste from the kidneys. The liquid waste then backs up into the kidneys. Waste products can quickly destroy kidney cells.

Doctors use X-rays or ultrasound images to diagnose kidney stones and find out exactly where they are. The hard minerals in the stones show up just as clearly as bones in X-ray pictures. Ultrasound imaging bounces sound waves off structures inside the body to form pictures.

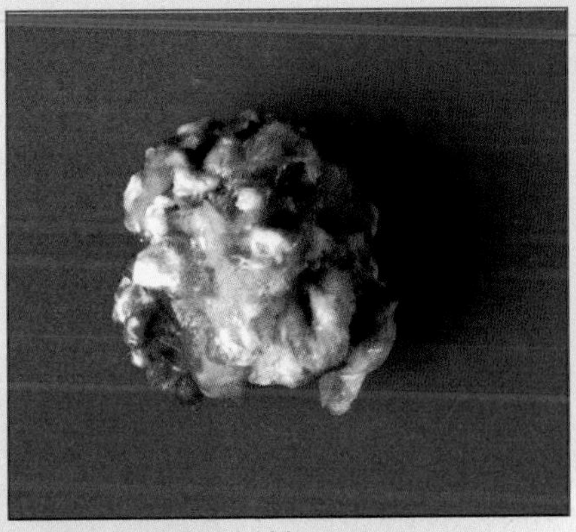

▲ **Figure 16-19** A kidney stone

Some kidney stones will pass out of the body if the patient drinks a lot of water to help push them along. Surgery used to be the only way to get rid of larger stones, but now doctors can use a new method. Lithotripsy sends high-pressure shock waves into the kidneys. The energy from the shock waves produces cracks in the edges of the kidney stone. When new waves hit the stone, the kidney stone breaks into smaller pieces. Eventually the kidney stone may break down into sand-size particles, which can pass out easily with the liquid waste.

**Thinking Critically** If you had a kidney stone, would you rather have it removed by surgery or by lithotripsy? Explain.

# 16-7 How do the kidneys work?

***Objective***

Describe how the kidneys act as a filtering system for the blood.

***Key Terms***

**urine** (YOOR-ihn)**:** liquid waste formed in the kidneys

**urea** (yoo-REE-uh)**:** nitrogen compound formed as a waste product

**nephron** (NEHF-rhon)**:** filtering structure of the kidneys

**The Kidneys** Most people have two kidneys. Each kidney is about 10 cm long. The kidneys are located just above your waist. One kidney is behind your liver. The other is behind the stomach. The main job of the kidneys is to remove waste products from the blood.

**1** IDENTIFY: What is the main job of the kidneys?

**Liquid Waste** Like the skin, the kidneys help the body get rid of liquid wastes. The liquid waste formed in the kidneys is **urine.** Urine is mostly water, but it also contains other materials, including many salts. Some of these salts give urine its yellow color. Urine also contains urea. **Urea** is a waste product formed when proteins are used by the body. It is a nitrogen compound.

**2** NAME: What is the liquid waste formed in the kidneys called?

**Nephrons** The inside of each kidney is made up of millions of tiny tubes called **nephrons.** Nephrons are filtering structures in the kidneys. They remove wastes from blood. Each nephron has a small cup at one end. This cup is called Bowman's capsule. Many coiled capillaries are found inside each capsule. Blood flows through the capillaries. Water and other materials are filtered out of the blood here. These materials move through the walls of the capsule and into the nephron.

How do the nephrons filter waste products from the blood? As you read each step below, look at the nephron in Figure 16-20.

- Blood enters the nephron.
- In the nephron, the blood passes into a cluster of capillaries in Bowman's capsule.
- Water, salts, urea, and nutrients are forced out of the capillaries and into Bowman's capsule.
- In the coiled part of the tube, any nutrients pass back into the blood. Excess water, salts, and urea remain in the last part of the tube, called the collecting duct.

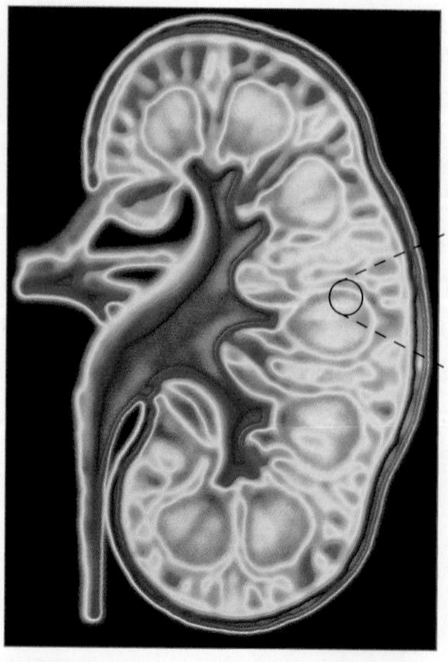

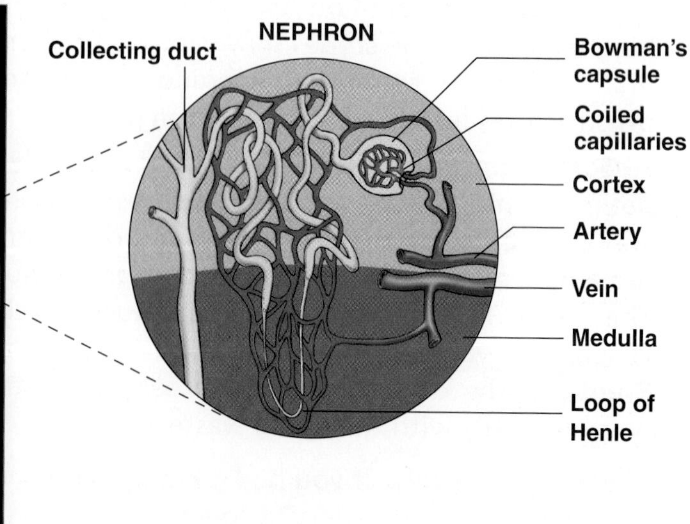


**Figure 16-20** ▶ The kidneys filter liquid waste out of blood. The photo on the left shows a CT scan image of a kidney.

- The filtered blood returns to the heart. The water, salts, and urea are carried out of the kidney as urine.

**3** **SEQUENCE:** How do materials get into the kidney tubes?

**Excretion of Urine** Urine forms in the collecting duct. Then it moves into the hollow, middle part of the kidney. Urine passes out of the kidneys through the ureters. Urine collects in the bladder. Urine passes out of the body through the urethra.

**4** **INFER:** What happens to urine when it leaves the kidney?

## CHECKING CONCEPTS

1. Urea is a __________ compound.
2. Most people have __________ kidneys.
3. The kidneys help to get rid of __________ wastes.
4. The liquid waste formed in the kidneys is __________.
5. Urine leaves the kidneys through the __________.
6. Urine leaves the body through the __________.

## THINKING CRITICALLY

7. **MODEL:** Develop a flowchart that traces the path of urine from the kidneys out of the body.
8. **INFER:** What element do you think is present in all proteins?
9. **APPLY:** What happens to nutrients that are removed from the blood in the kidneys?

## BUILDING MATH SKILLS

***Calculating*** Blood filters through the kidneys at a rate of 125 mL per minute. How many milliliters filter through the kidneys in an hour? A day?

## *Science and Technology*

### DIALYSIS

A field of study that uses engineering concepts to design machines that help or replace diseased organs is called biomedical engineering. Biomedical engineers have developed a machine that acts like a kidney. The machine is called a dialysis (dy-AL-uh-sis) machine. People who have lost their kidneys or have kidney damage are kept alive by using a dialysis machine.

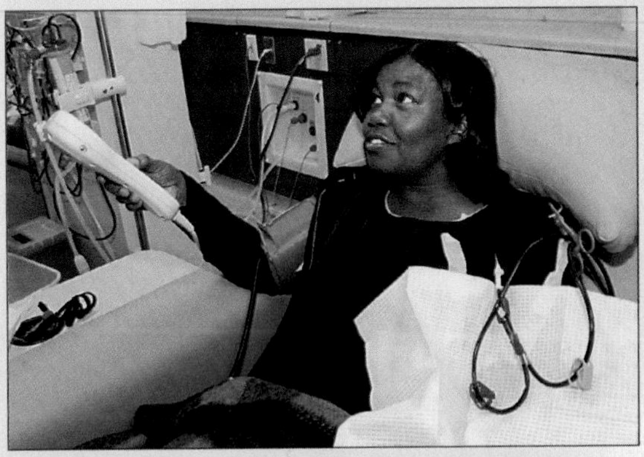

▲ **Figure 16-21** A patient with kidney damage can use a dialysis machine while waiting for a transplant.

A patient is connected to the machine by a tube. The tube is connected to an artery in the patient's arm. Blood from the artery flows from the tube into the dialysis machine. The machine filters the patient's blood, removing waste materials. The blood then flows out of the machine through a tube connected to a vein in the patient's arm.

Many people use a dialysis machine three times a week. However, depending on how serious kidney damage is, some patients may need to use the machine every two days.

**Thinking Critically** How can biomedical engineering help people with diseases?

# 16-8 How does the skin remove wastes?

## INVESTIGATE

### *Observing Evaporation and Cooling*
**HANDS-ON ACTIVITY**

1. Hold two fingers in front of your mouth. Blow on them. Record if one finger feels cooler.
2. Dip one finger in water. Blow on the wet finger and a dry finger. Record which feels cooler.
3. Wet a cotton ball with isopropyl alcohol. Wet one finger. Blow on the wet finger and a dry finger. Record which feels cooler.
4. Wet one finger with water and one finger with isopropyl alcohol. Blow on them. Record which feels cooler.

**THINK ABOUT IT:** Which finger felt cooler? Explain why you think it felt cooler.

### *Objectives*

Identify the layers and some of the structures of the skin. Explain why the skin is an organ of excretion.

### *Key Terms*

**dermis:** inner layer of skin

**epidermis** (ehp-uh-DUR-mihs)**:** outer layer of skin

**perspiration** (pur-spuh-RAY-shuhn)**:** waste water and salts that leave the body through the skin

**pore:** tiny opening in the skin

**evaporation** (ee-vap-uh-RAY-shuhn)**:** changing of a liquid to a gas

**The Largest Organ** The skin is the largest organ of the human body. It covers the entire outside of your body. The main function of skin is to cover and protect the body. The skin is made up of two layers. There is an outer layer and an inner layer. Skin also contains blood vessels, nerves, and other tissues.

1 **OBSERVE:** Look at Figure 16-22. Which is thicker, the outer layer or the inner layer of skin?

**Epidermis** The outer layer of skin is called the **epidermis.** The epidermis covers and protects the body. It is made up of living and dead skin cells. The dead skin cells are replaced constantly by the living skin cells beneath them. Each time you scrape the surface of your skin or wash, thousands of dead skin cells are carried away.

2 **INFER:** Why do you think skin cells are constantly being replaced?

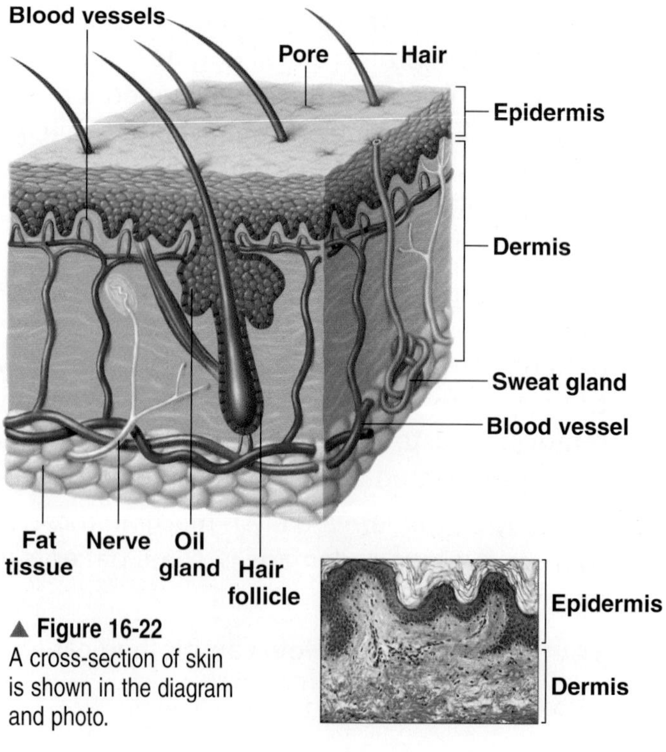


▲ **Figure 16-22**
A cross-section of skin is shown in the diagram and photo.

**Dermis** The inner layer of the skin is called the **dermis.** The dermis is a living layer of skin. The dermis is much thicker than the epidermis. The dermis has many different structures in it.

Hair follicles are one structure in the dermis. Each hair on your body grows from a hair follicle. Oil glands are located near the hair follicles. Oil glands produce oil, which softens and moistens the skin. Nerve endings and many tiny blood vessels are also located in the dermis.

3 NAME: What are three structures found in the dermis?

**Perspiration** Some waste water leaves your body through your skin. This waste water is called **perspiration,** or sweat. Perspiration is made up of waters and salts.

◀ **Figure 16-23** Perspiration cools the body.

4 DEFINE: What is perspiration?

**Sweat Glands** The dermis also contains many sweat glands. A sweat gland is a coiled tube surrounded by capillaries. Water molecules in the blood pass through the walls of the capillaries into the sweat gland. Each sweat gland extends to a tiny opening in the skin called a **pore.** Waste water leaves the sweat gland through the pore.

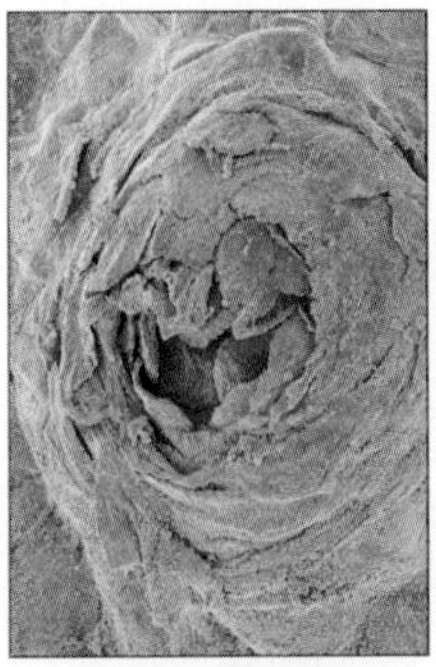

▲ **Figure 16-24** The surface of your skin has openings like this called pores.

5 DESCRIBE: What is a sweat gland?

**An Air-Conditioning System** Your body has a built-in cooling system. When it is very hot, do you sweat? Do you sweat after you exercise or do heavy work? Perspiration, or sweating, helps your body "cool off." The evaporation of perspiration from your skin cools the body. **Evaporation** is the changing of a liquid to a gas. As perspiration evaporates, it removes heat from your body.

6 PREDICT: Are you likely to perspire if your body temperature drops below 37°C? Explain.

## CHECKING CONCEPTS

1. The outer layer of skin is the __________.
2. Hair follicles, oil glands, and nerve endings are located in the __________.
3. A sweat gland is a coiled tube surrounded by __________.
4. Perspiration leaves the body through __________ in the skin.
5. The changing of a liquid to a gas is called __________.
6. Evaporation of perspiration helps to __________ the body.

## THINKING CRITICALLY

7. INFER: When you are cold, you shiver. What do you think shivering does for the body?
8. HYPOTHESIZE: Why do you think it is important to take in more salts when the weather is hot?

## DESIGNING AN EXPERIMENT

*Design an experiment to solve the following problem. Include a hypothesis, variables, a procedure, and a type of data to study.*

PROBLEM: During which types of activities from the list below does your body perspire more heavily?

**a.** jogging
**b.** playing basketball
**c.** climbing stairs
**d.** walking
**e.** dancing
**f.** jumping rope

Integrating Health

# THE Big IDEA

## What happens when the body overheats?

Humans are warm-blooded organisms. This means that our bodies try to keep a constant body temperature, no matter the temperature outside of it. Your body systems work together to maintain a temperature of 37°C. The systems involved in temperature control include your skin, excretory system, respiratory system, and endocrine system.

Sometimes your body temperature rises in response to fighting a virus or bacteria. This is called a fever. When you have a fever, you will sweat to get cool. If you sweat a lot, the kidneys may filter less water out of the blood. However, you should drink liquids to replace the lost water and salts. With a high fever, you may breathe faster, which cools you and gets rid of extra carbon dioxide. Usually, a fever can be controlled with medicine.

Your body temperature also rises slightly during exercise. The same kinds of system changes that occur during a fever will help cool you when exercising. If you exercise in very hot weather, however, it can be dangerous. Heat illness happens when the body is heated beyond the control of normal systems. If your body loses too much water because of sweating, you may get dehydrated. This means the amount of liquid in your blood is less than it should be. When this happens, all of your body systems react!

With heat exhaustion, your body systems cause you to feel faint or collapse. This makes you STOP what you are doing. Fast shallow breathing and fever are symptoms. You need to drink liquids, replace lost salts, and get cool. It is important to prevent a more life-threatening illness called heat stroke.

Look at the illustrations and text on these pages. They show the dangerous steps that lead to heat stroke. Follow the directions in the Science Log to learn more about "the big idea." ✦

### 1 Sweating Leads to Dehydration

Working or exercising in hot weather makes you sweat a lot. When you sweat a lot, you have to drink to replace the fluids and salts leaving your body. If you do not, you can become dehydrated. You may also become overheated.

### 2 Blood Volume Decreases

When you are dehydrated the amount of liquid, or plasma, in you blood is decreased. The total volume of blood in your body is less. This means that the circulatory system cannot function properly. To help, the heart works harder, but less blood gets to organs.

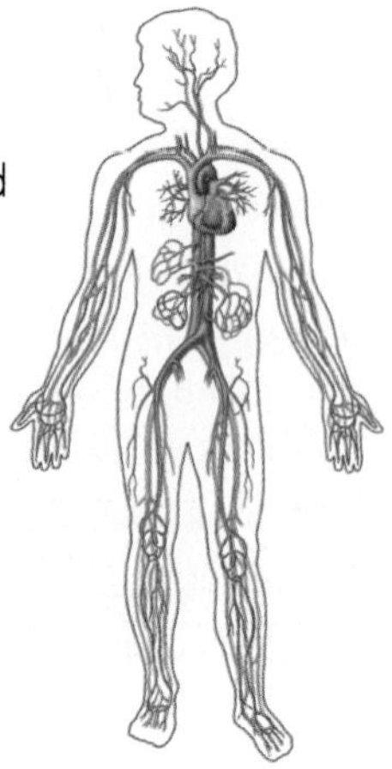

Circulatory system

### 3 Skin Gets More Blood

When you are overheating, your body sends more blood to the skin. This is a way to help cool it. As you sweat, the blood gets cool. However, less blood is going to the other organs.

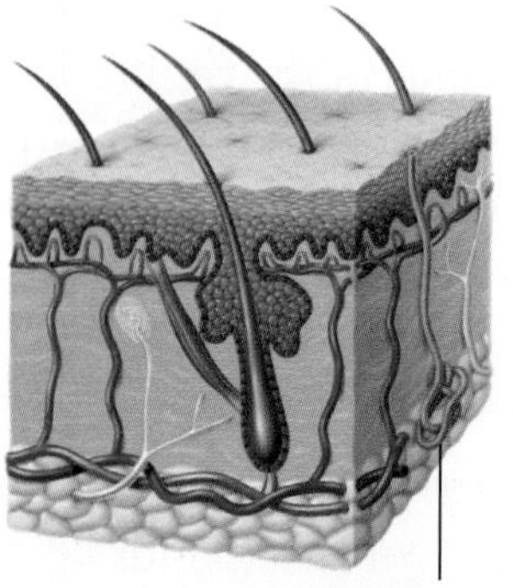

## 4 Carbon Dioxide Builds Up

Cells normally release carbon dioxide into the blood. This happens during gas exchange with blood. When the body is overheating, carbon dioxide builds up in the cells because of the problems with circulation.

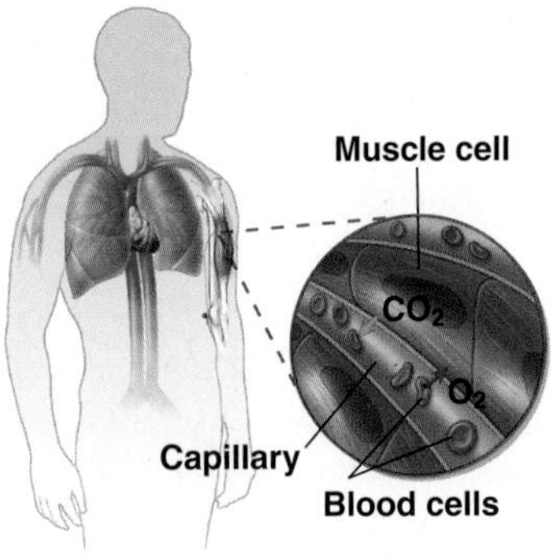


## 5 Breathing Becomes Rapid

Rapid breathing is one way the body responds to overheating. Breathing becomes fast and deep. This decreases the level of carbon dioxide in the blood and increases oxygen. It also cools the body a bit.

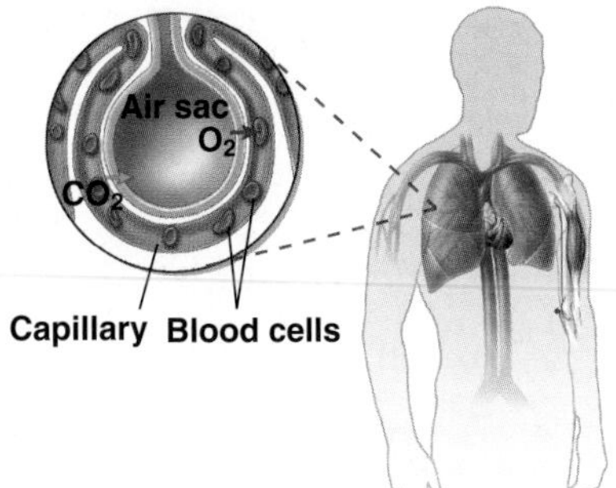


## 6 Kidneys Respond

When the body is dehydrated, the kidneys try to keep more fluids inside the body. When they detect less blood flowing to them, a chemical signal is sent that causes the nephrons to excrete more salts and absorb more water. The urine will be concentrated.

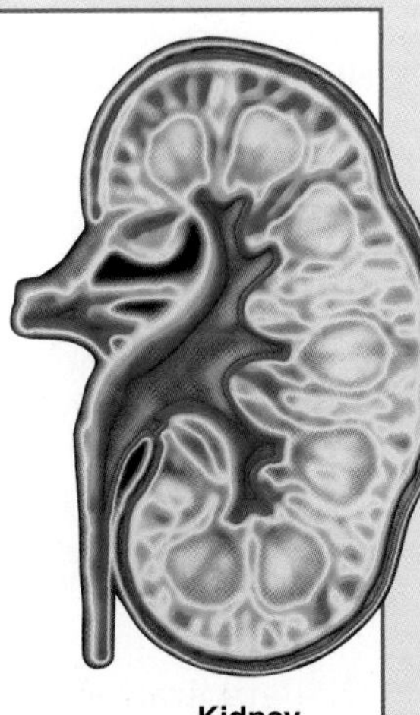


## 7 Heat Stroke Occurs

If the body systems cannot reverse overheating, heat stroke may occur. At this point, the sweating system stops working. The body has no way to cool itself and body temperature rises. One by one, the body systems shut down. Immediate medical treatment is needed to prevent death.

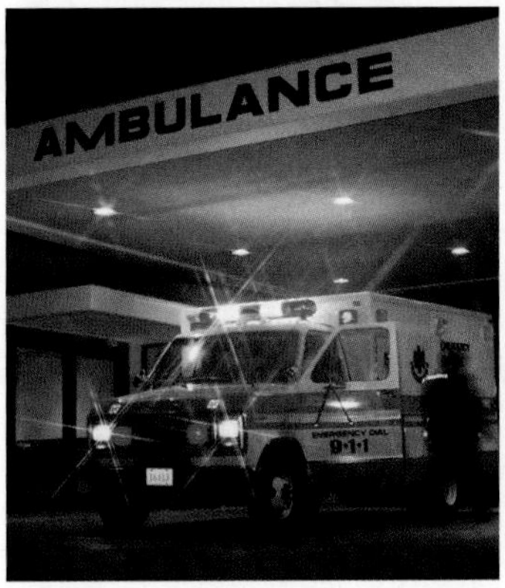


**WRITING ACTIVITY**

### Science Log

Look at the pictures on these two pages. Have you ever felt sick from spending too much time in the heat? In your science log, research heat illnesses and ways to prevent them. Then create a poster that shows how to stay safe in the heat. Start your search at www.conceptsandchallenges.com.

# Chapter 16 Challenges

## Chapter Summary

### Lesson 16-1

- The respiratory system is made up of the lungs, tubes, and passageways through which air moves in the body.

### Lesson 16-2

- **Breathing** is the process by which air enters and leaves the body. **Respiration** is the process of carrying oxygen to cells, getting rid of carbon dioxide, and releasing energy.

### Lesson 16-3

- Hairs in the nose filter dust particles from the air. **Mucus** in the nose and windpipe helps trap harmful particles contained in air. **Cilia** in the windpipe and nose push mucus and trapped particles toward the back of the throat.

### Lesson 16-4

- In the lungs, oxygen and carbon dioxide are exchanged between the **alveoli** and the blood.
- Oxygen and carbon dioxide are exchanged between body cells and red blood cells in the capillaries.

### Lesson 16-5

- Tobacco smoke contains many different kinds of harmful chemicals. Smoking can lead to cancer and heart disease.

### Lesson 16-6

- Carbon dioxide, water, salts, nitrogen compounds, and heat are waste products formed by the body.
- Waste products are removed from the body in a process called **excretion**. The lungs, kidneys, and skin are the three main organs of the excretory system.

### Lesson 16-7

- The main job of the kidneys is to filter wastes from the blood. **Urine** formed in the kidneys leaves the body through the urethra.

### Lesson 16-8

- **Perspiration** is a waste excreted by the skin. It is formed by sweat glands and is excreted through **pores** in the skin.

## Key Term Challenges

alveolus (p. 376)
bladder (p. 388)
bronchus (p. 376)
cilia (p. 382)
dermis (p. 392)
diaphragm (p. 378)
epidermis (p. 392)
evaporation (p. 392)
excretion (p. 388)
exhale (p. 378)
inhale (p. 378)
kidney (p. 388)
larynx (p. 376)
mucus (p. 382)
nephron (p. 390)
nicotine (p. 386)
perspiration (p. 392)
pore (p. 392)
respiration (p. 378)
trachea (p. 376)
urea (p. 390)
ureter (p. 388)
urine (p. 390)

MATCHING **Write the Key Term from above that best matches each description.**

1. microscopic air sacs in the lungs
2. breathe out
3. tube leading into the lung
4. liquid waste excreted by the skin
5. sticky liquid
6. liquid waste excreted by the kidneys
7. process of carrying oxygen to cells, getting rid of carbon dioxide, and releasing energy
8. sheet of muscle below the lungs
9. process by which air is taken into the body
10. filtering structure of the kidney

FILL IN **Write the Key Term from above that best completes each statement.**

11. When you breathe in, you ___________.
12. Tiny hairlike structures called ___________ line the windpipe.
13. The removal of wastes from the body is called ___________.
14. The changing of a liquid to a gas is called ___________.
15. Perspiration leaves the body through openings in the skin called ___________.

## Content Challenges TEST PREP

**MULTIPLE CHOICE Write the letter of the term or phrase that best completes each statement.**

**1.** The waste products of cellular respiration are
- **a.** water and carbon dioxide.
- **b.** water and oxygen.
- **c.** salts.
- **d.** nitrogen compounds.

**2.** A sweat gland is a coiled tube surrounded by
- **a.** alveoli.
- **b.** mucus.
- **c.** capillaries.
- **d.** cilia.

**3.** Urine passes out of the body through the
- **a.** ureters.
- **b.** urethra.
- **c.** kidneys.
- **d.** urea.

**4.** When you inhale, the
- **a.** ribs move up and out.
- **b.** ribs move down and in.
- **c.** diaphragm moves upward.
- **d.** chest cavity becomes smaller.

**5.** The largest organ of the excretory system is the
- **a.** large intestine.
- **b.** kidney.
- **c.** small intestine.
- **d.** skin.

**6.** Air enters the body through the
- **a.** lungs.
- **b.** skin.
- **c.** nose and mouth.
- **d.** windpipe.

**7.** The windpipe divides into two tubes called
- **a.** alveoli.
- **b.** capillaries.
- **c.** bronchi.
- **d.** ureters.

**8.** Air reaching the lungs is
- **a.** cold and dry.
- **b.** warm and moist.
- **c.** cold and moist.
- **d.** warm and dry.

**9.** Oxygen and carbon dioxide are exchanged between the lungs and the blood during
- **a.** external respiration.
- **b.** internal respiration.
- **c.** cellular respiration.
- **d.** breathing.

**10.** When tobacco burns, it releases harmful substances such as tar, nicotine, and
- **a.** carbon dioxide.
- **b.** carbon monoxide.
- **c.** nitrogen.
- **d.** oxygen.

**11.** The process of removing waste products from the body is called
- **a.** respiration.
- **b.** digestion.
- **c.** evaporation.
- **d.** excretion.

**TRUE/FALSE Write *true* if the statement is true. If the statement is false, change the underlined term to make the statement true.**

**12.** Breathing is a chemical process.

**13.** Inhaled air contains more oxygen than exhaled air.

**14.** Water is removed from wastes in the bladder.

**15.** Perspiration is made up mostly of salts.

**16.** Smoking causes the cilia to stop working.

**17.** Waste water leaves sweat glands through capillaries.

**18.** When particles irritate your nose, you respond by sneezing.

## *Concept Challenges* TEST PREP

**WRITTEN RESPONSE Answer each of the following questions in complete sentences.**

1. **SEQUENCE:** Through what tubes and passageways does air pass from the outside of the body to the lungs?
2. **EXPLAIN:** How do mucus and cilia help you fight infection?
3. **CONTRAST:** What is the difference between breathing and respiration?
4. **RELATE:** How do the respiratory system and circulatory system work together?
5. **COMPARE:** How is the skin like an air-conditioning system?

**INTERPRETING A DIAGRAM Use Figure 16-25 to answer the following questions.**

6. Which two labels represent places where air enters the body?
7. What does letter *F* represent? What is the function of this structure?
8. Which letter represents the structure sometimes called the windpipe? What is the name of this structure?
9. How does the nose help in purifying air?
10. Where are cilia found in the respiratory system?

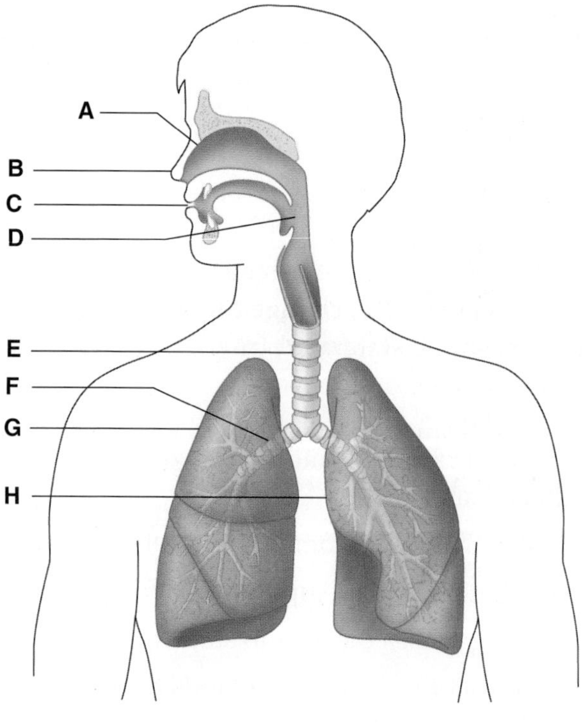


▲ **Figure 16-25** The respiratory system

# Chapter 17 Fighting Disease

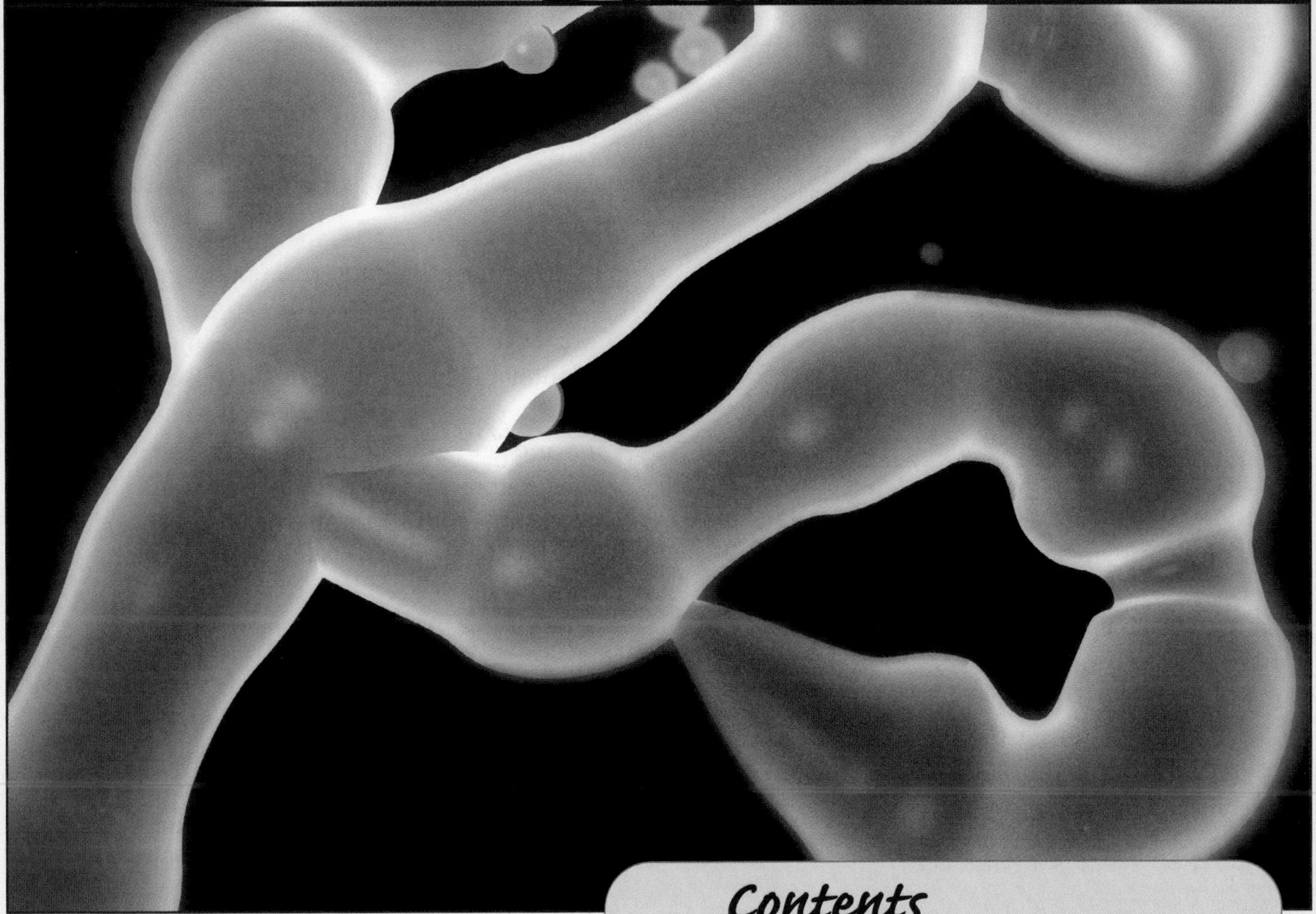

▲ **Figure 17-1** The Ebola virus causes Ebola fever, a disease that can be deadly.

Humans have always been victims of disease. Many diseases, such as the flu, can be passed from one person to another. Other diseases, like cancer, are not contagious. Cures for many human diseases have been found. Many more, including Ebola fever, do not have a cure. More research into these diseases is needed.

►Why do you think research into diseases is necessary?

## Contents

# 17-1 How does the body fight disease?

***Objective***

Identify the ways your body fights disease.

***Key Terms***

**pathogen:** any agent that causes disease

**white blood cell:** blood cell that protects the body against disease

**antigen:** signal molecule that produces an immune response

**antibody:** molecule the body makes to protect itself from disease

**Defense Systems** Your body is under constant attack by agents such as bacteria or viruses. Agents that cause diseases are called **pathogens.** Your body usually can protect itself from illness because it has defenses against disease. These defenses may be physical barriers that actually block the pathogen from entering the body. They may also be chemical defenses that fight the pathogen once it has entered the body.

1 IDENTIFY: What is a pathogen?

**Skin** The skin is a barrier that covers your body. It is made up of several layers of cells. Working together, the layers of the skin act like a wall to prevent pathogens from entering the body. Your skin is your first line of defense against disease.

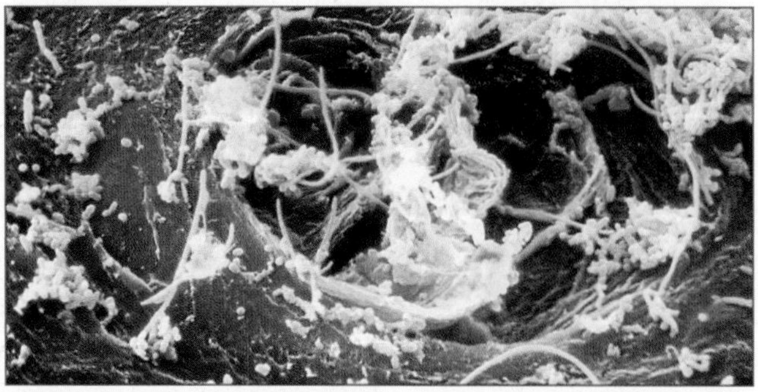

▲ **Figure 17-2** The skin prevents the bacteria, shown in white in this photo, from entering the body.

2 DESCRIBE: How does the skin protect the body?

**Digestive System** Although the skin protects the body from most germs, bacteria and viruses can enter the body through the mouth. The digestive system helps to destroy these agents. Hydrochloric acid in the stomach helps to destroy bacteria and viruses that enter the stomach.

3 EXPLAIN: How does the digestive system help to protect the body from pathogens?

**Respiratory System** Bacteria and viruses also can enter the body through the nose. Hairs in the nose filter the air and trap many small particles. Cilia and mucus in the respiratory system also trap germs before they can enter the lungs. The body gets rid of the trapped particles by sneezing and coughing. Sneezing and coughing force mucus and trapped particles out of the body.

4 EXPLAIN: How does mucus in the nose and windpipe protect the body?

**Circulatory System** When germs get past the defenses of the skin and the digestive and respiratory systems, the **white blood cells** go to work. White blood cells are part of the circulatory system. There are several different kinds of white blood cells, and each works in a different way.

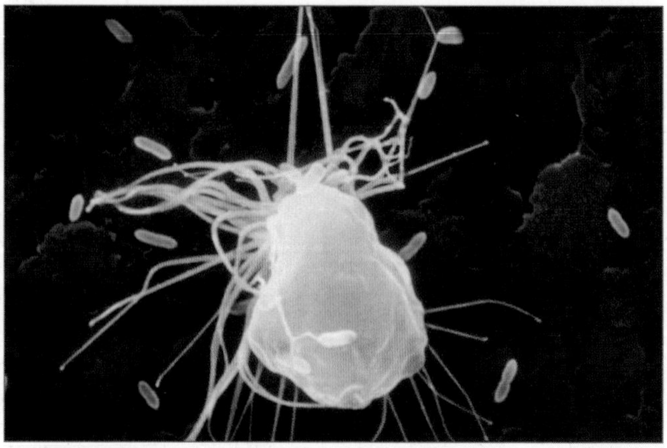

▲ **Figure 17-3** The white blood cell, shown in yellow, is attacking *E. coli* bacteria.

One kind of white blood cell, called a phagocyte, can move and change shape like an amoeba. Phagocytes travel around the body in the bloodstream in search of bacteria or other pathogens. When phagocytes find the pathogens, they surround them. The phagocytes then destroy the bacteria by digesting them.

5 **DESCRIBE:** How do white blood cells help protect the body?

**The Lymphatic System** Other types of white blood cells, called lymphocytes, play a role in fighting disease as well. Special white blood cells can be found in lymph vessels, which are part of the lymphatic system of the body. The lymphatic system is a transport system, like the circulatory system.

The lymphatic system does not transport blood, but a clear fluid called lymph. This system drains excess fluid from tissues and returns it to the circulatory system. The lymphatic system contains many bean-shaped structures called lymph nodes. The nodes filter the fluid before it is returned to the bloodstream. These lymph nodes sometimes get bigger during an infection.

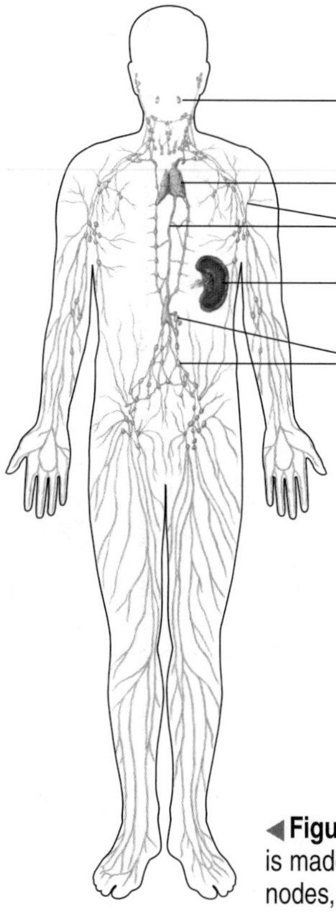


◀**Figure 17-4** The lymphatic system is made up of lymph vessels, lymph nodes, and other organs.

6 **INFER:** Why do you think lymph nodes swell during an infection?

**The Immune System** The body's specific defenses are part of the **immune system.** This system includes several organs that also belong to other systems. The immune system also includes lymph and certain white blood cells. B and T cells are part of this system. These white blood cells are more specific in their attack than the other defenses. They recognize and attack only certain pathogens. These pathogens contain a chemical signal that tells the immune system that it is a foreign substance. These signals are called **antigens**.

Antigens can be whole pathogens or parts of pathogens. They can also be insect venom or pollen. Some white blood cells in the body find foreign substances that contain antigens and produce antibodies. **Antibodies** are molecules that help destroy substances that carry antigens.

7 **EXPLAIN:** What is the function of the immune system?

## ✓ CHECKING CONCEPTS

1. What are two agents that can cause disease?
2. What is your first line of defense against disease?
3. How does the respiratory system defend against disease?
4. How do white blood cells travel?
5. What are antigens?

## THINKING CRITICALLY

6. **INFER:** Tonsils are part of the lymphatic system. Why do you think some people have to have their tonsils taken out?
7. **ORGANIZE:** Make a chart showing how each body system is involved in fighting disease.

## HEALTH AND SAFETY TIP

You can help your body fight disease. Always wash your hands before eating and after using the restroom. You can fight infection by washing a cut and putting a bandage over it. Finally, you can help your body fight disease by eating a proper diet. This keeps your body better prepared to deal with disease-causing substances.

# 17-2 What is immunity?

***Objective***

Explain the difference between natural immunity and acquired immunity.

***Key Term***

**immunity** (ihm-MYOON-uh-tee)**:** resistance to a specific disease

**Resisting Disease** Antibodies protect the body against foreign substances. After these foreign substances are destroyed, many of the antibodies remain. If the same kind of foreign substances enter the body once again, the remaining antibodies destroy the substances before they can do any harm. The body has become resistant to these diseases. This resistance to a specific disease is called **immunity**.

**1** IDENTIFY: What is immunity?

**Types of Immunity** There are two kinds of immunity. One kind is called natural immunity. The other is called acquired immunity. Natural immunity is one that people are born with. Some people have certain kinds of antibodies in their bodies at birth. Natural immunity is your body's natural defense against certain diseases. Acquired immunity is an immunity that people develop, or acquire, at some time during their lives.

**2** COMPARE: What is the difference between natural and acquired immunity?

**Active Acquired Immunity** There are two kinds of acquired immunity. One kind is called active acquired immunity. With this kind of immunity, the body resists a certain disease because it has already developed antibodies against the disease. In most cases, once you have been exposed to certain diseases, your body continues to make the antibodies for that disease. For example, most people who have had chickenpox will not get it again. Their bodies have developed immunity against chickenpox.

**3** EXPLAIN: How do you develop active acquired immunity?

**T Cells and B Cells** T cells and B cells are special white blood cells that are part of the lymphatic system. They are also part of the body's immune system because they help fight disease. T cells identify pathogens by detecting the signal molecules, or antigens. Some T cells then attack and kill the pathogen. They may also kill the damaged body cells that the pathogen has already harmed. Other T cells work by calling the B cells to action. The B cells produce substances that react with the antigens. These substances are called antibodies. Some antibodies cause the antigens to break up or clump together. Then, they can be easily attacked by the phagocyte white blood cells.

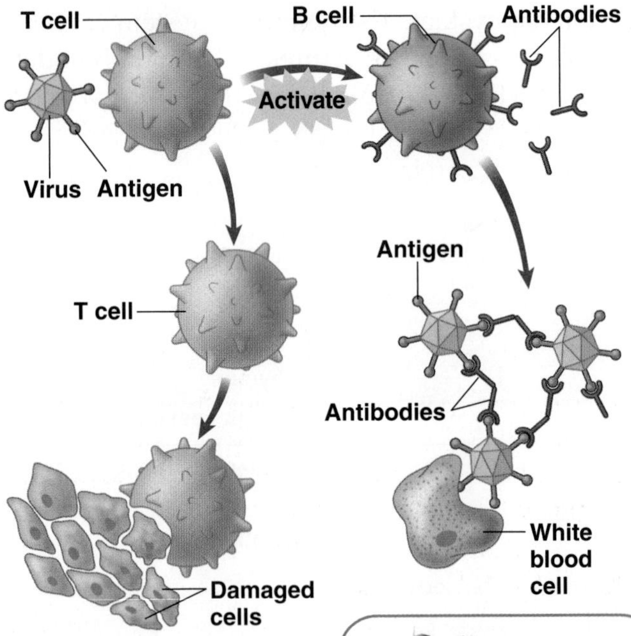


▲ **Figure 17-5** T cells attack some antigens. For others, they signal the B cells to make antibodies.

**Go Online**
*active art*
**For:** Immune Response activity
**Visit:** PHSchool.com
**Web Code:** cep-4052

**4** EXPLAIN: In what ways do antibodies work?

**Passive Acquired Immunity** The second kind of acquired immunity is passive acquired immunity. In this kind of immunity, antibodies are not produced by your body. The antibodies are obtained from somewhere else. You may be injected with antibodies against a certain disease. Then you have passive acquired immunity against that disease. However, this kind of immunity does not last long. Antibodies that are not made by the body usually are destroyed by white blood cells after a short time.

**5** **COMPARE:** Which type of acquired immunity lasts the longest?

**Vaccines** One way of getting immunity is through a vaccine. A vaccine is a serum made from a dead or a weakened form of bacteria or viruses. The serum is injected into the body. Vaccines do not cause you to get the disease. The body responds to the vaccine by making antibodies against the pathogens. The antibodies remain in the body and protect it from the disease. Polio, measles, and mumps have all been controlled by vaccines. The disease smallpox has been completely eliminated because of vaccinations. Scientists continue to try to find vaccines for more diseases.

**6** **EXPLAIN:** How does a vaccine give you immunity?

## CHECKING CONCEPTS

1. A resistance to disease is called __________.
2. Immunity a person is born with is called __________ immunity.
3. Immunity a person develops is called __________ immunity.
4. When a body makes antibodies against a disease, __________ acquired immunity may result.
5. Passive acquired immunity is __________.

## THINKING CRITICALLY

6. **COMPARE:** How are natural immunity, active acquired immunity, and passive acquired immunity similar?
7. **RELATE:** Sometimes a developing baby receives antibodies from its mother. Is this immunity a natural or an acquired immunity? Explain.

## *How Do They Know That?*

### EDWARD JENNER'S DISCOVERY OF VACCINATIONS

The first vaccine was developed and used in 1796 by Edward Jenner, an English doctor. Jenner noticed that many people who worked near cattle got a mild disease called cowpox. He also noticed that these same people did not get the fatal disease smallpox. To find out why, Jenner tried injecting material from cowpox sores into people. Antibodies against cowpox were produced in these people. Jenner found that these same antibodies were able to destroy the smallpox virus. The people did not get smallpox because the cowpox antibodies protected them against smallpox too.

The vaccine Jenner developed was made directly from a pathogen. Today many vaccines are made from inactive parts of bacteria and viruses. The human body responds to these vaccines by making antibodies. Diseases that were once widespread, such as polio, have been almost eliminated due to the creation of vaccines.

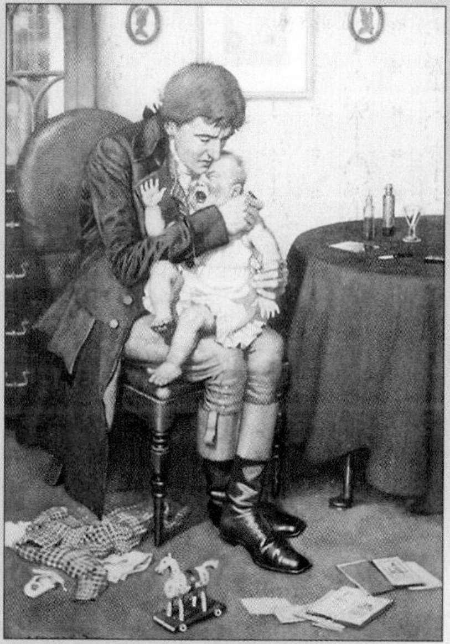

▲ **Figure 17-6** Dr. Jenner gives a child a vaccine against smallpox.

**Thinking Critically** Why do you think the cowpox antibodies prevented people from getting smallpox as well?

# 17-3 What are some bacterial diseases?

### *Objectives*

Describe the causes of different types of disease. Explain how antibiotics are used to fight disease.

### *Key Terms*

**contagious:** can be spread from one person to another

**antibiotic** (an-tih-by-AHT-ihk)**:** chemical made by a living organism that kills bacteria

**Germ Theory** About 150 years ago, Louis Pasteur showed that some diseases are caused by bacteria and other microscopic organisms. The idea that diseases are caused by microscopic organisms, or germs, is called the germ theory of disease.

1 **EXPLAIN:** What is the germ theory?

**Identifying Germs** To fight a disease, one must identify the kind of germ that causes the disease. Robert Koch studied many bacterial diseases. He discovered how to grow bacteria outside a living body. This made it possible to study and find ways of destroying the bacteria. Figure 17-7 lists some common bacterial diseases.

| COMMON BACTERIAL DISEASES | | |
|---|---|---|
| **Disease** | **Bacteria** | **Body Part Affected** |
| Cholera | *Vibrio cholerae* | Small intestine |
| Lyme disease | *Borrelia burgdorferi* | Skin, joints, heart |
| Salmonella food poisoning | *Salmonella* | Intestine |
| Strep throat | *Streptococcus pyogenes* | Upper respiratory tract, blood, skin |
| Tetanus | *Clostridium tetani* | Nerves at synapse |
| Tuberculosis | *Myocobacterium tuberculosis* | Lungs, bones, other organs |

▲ **Figure 17-7**

2 **DESCRIBE:** Why is it important to find the germ that causes a disease?

**Spread of Bacterial Diseases** Cholera, strep throat, and Lyme disease are all examples of diseases caused by bacteria. Most diseases that are caused by bacteria are **contagious.** This means they can be spread from one person to another. Some diseases are spread by coughing or sneezing. If you inhale air that contains the bacteria, you can get sick. Other bacterial diseases, such as Lyme disease, are spread by another living organism. The bacteria that cause Lyme disease are carried by ticks. Diseases can also be spread when people share drinking glasses, utensils, or makeup.

There are other ways that diseases can be spread. Bacteria can be found in foods and in drinking water. To prevent developing a disease from these bacteria, you should wash all foods thoroughly. You should also cook foods, especially meats, properly.

3 **LIST:** What are three ways diseases can be spread?

**Treating Disease** Sometimes your body needs help in fighting off disease. Your doctor may prescribe medicine or you may get an injection. If you are suffering from a disease caused by bacteria, you may be treated with an antibiotic. An **antibiotic** is a chemical substance that kills bacteria.

4 **IDENTIFY:** What is an antibiotic?

**Discovery of Antibiotics** The use of antibiotics to treat disease is a fairly recent discovery. In 1928, Alexander Fleming, an English bacteriologist, was the first person to observe the action of an antibiotic. Fleming was growing bacteria in a dish. He noticed that the bacteria did not grow in a part of the dish where some mold had grown. Fleming guessed that the mold produced a substance that was harmful to bacteria.

Thirteen years later, scientists were able to separate this substance from the same kind of mold. The scientists called this substance penicillin (pen-uh-SIL-in). Penicillin was the first antibiotic.

Since the discovery of penicillin, many other antibiotics have been discovered. Most antibiotics

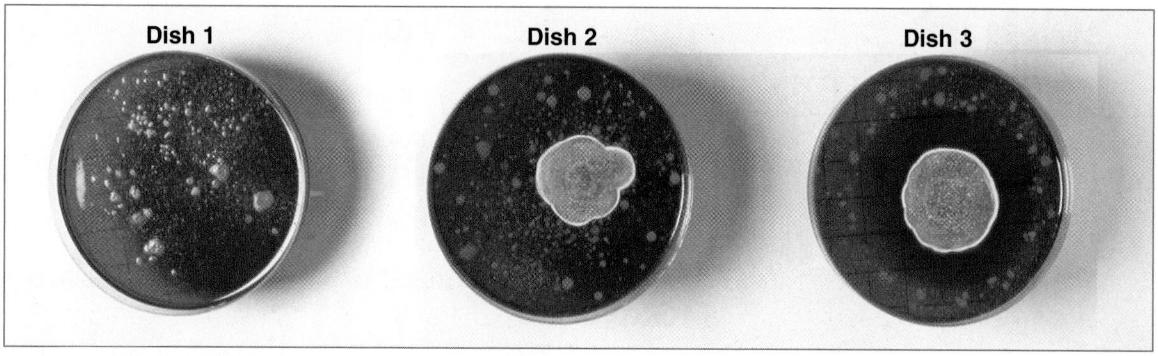


▲ **Figure 17-8** Dish 1 shows the growth of bacteria. Penicillin mold (blue) is growing in Dish 2. In Dish 3, the bacteria around the mold has died.

are produced from molds. Others are made from fungi and bacteria. Certain kinds of plants and animals also produce some types of antibiotics.

5 **EXPLAIN:** How did Fleming discover penicillin?

**How Antibiotics Work** Antibiotics are not all the same. Different antibiotics have different effects on a particular disease. This means that each antibiotic can be used to fight only certain kinds of organisms. For example, penicillin works only against certain bacteria. The penicillin destroys the bacteria and stops them from reproducing. Penicillin does not work against viruses. No single antibiotic can destroy all types of bacteria.

Allergic reactions can be a drawback to the use of antibiotics. For example, some people are allergic to penicillin. If they take this antibiotic, a fever or rash may develop. In severe reactions, they may not be able to breathe. For this reason, it is important to tell the doctor about any drug allergies.

6 **APPLY:** Why is it important to tell your doctor about any drug allergies you might have?

**Overuse of Antibiotics** The overuse of antibiotics has become a concern in the field of medicine. One reason is because antibiotics kill useful bacteria in your body along with the bacteria causing the illness. This is why some antibiotics cause side effects such as intestinal problems.

Another problem with overusing antibiotics is that bacteria can become resistant to the antibiotic. This means that the antibiotic may no longer work against certain bacteria. Resistance can become a problem if an antibiotic is needed for a more serious illness.

For these reasons, many doctors do not prescribe antibiotics as often as they used to. They also ask patients to take all of their antibiotics so that the bacteria in the body are completely destroyed and do not have a chance to form a resistance.

7 **EXPLAIN:** Why should you finish all of the medication given to you by a doctor?

## ✓ CHECKING CONCEPTS

1. The work of __________ showed that diseases are caused by microscopic organisms.
2. Diseases can be spread by __________.
3. The first antibiotic was discovered by __________.
4. Most antibiotics are made from __________.
5. Diseases that can be spread from one person to another are called __________.

## THINKING CRITICALLY

6. **ANALYZE:** What are two diseases that affect the intestines?
7. **INFER:** Why is it important to cover your nose when you sneeze?

## DESIGNING AN EXPERIMENT

*Design an experiment to solve the following problem. Include a hypothesis, variables, a procedure, and a type of data to study.*

PROBLEM: Bacteria can be found in almost every place on Earth. There are bacteria on your desk, on the floor, even on your skin! Bacteria can be collected and grown in petri dishes that contain nutrient bases. Lori wants to know which parts of her school or home have the most bacteria. How can she find an answer?

# LAB ACTIVITY

# Determining the Effectiveness of Antiseptics

**Materials**

10 mL of bacteria sample (*E. coli*), 4 petri dishes with nutrient agar, 3 different mouthwashes, 4 cotton swabs, wax pencil or permanent marker, gloves, safety goggles, apron, antiseptic spray

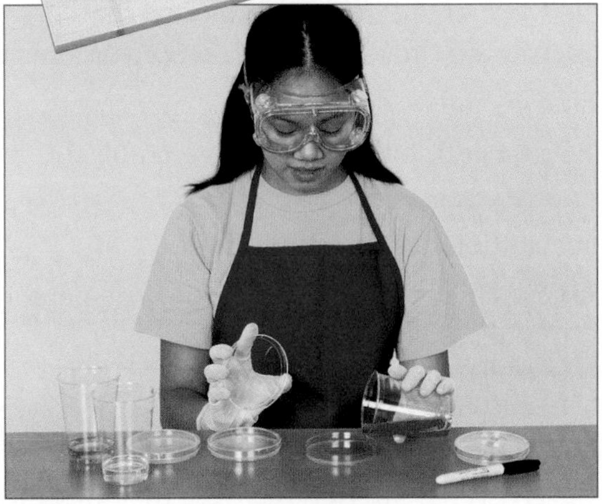

▲ **STEP 4** Pour mouthwash into the third petri dish.

▲ **STEP 6** Rub the cotton swab back and forth across the petri dish.

### *BACKGROUND*

Many diseases are caused by some type of bacteria. Diseases can be spread from one person to another or they can be spread by ingesting contaminated foods or drinking water. Antiseptics are substances that are used to fight harmful bacteria. Mouthwash is a type of antiseptic used to fight bacteria that cause tooth decay. Antiseptics such as mouthwash work by stopping or slowing the growth of bacteria and other microorganisms.

### *PURPOSE*

In this activity you will investigate the effectiveness of several different brands of mouthwash.

### *PROCEDURE*

1. Put on your goggles, gloves, and apron. Label four petri dishes *1* to *4*.
2. Add approximately 10 mL of the first type of mouthwash to petri dish 1. Replace the lid and write the name of the mouthwash on the label.
3. Add approximately 10 mL of the second type of mouthwash to petri dish 2. Replace the lid and write the name of the mouthwash on the label.
4. Add approximately 10 mL of the third type of mouthwash to petri dish 3. Replace the lid and write the name of the mouthwash on the label.
5. Add no mouthwash to petri dish 4. This will be the control sample. Label it *control*.
6. Dip the cotton swab into the bacteria sample. Slowly rub the cotton swab back and forth across the agar in the first petri dish. Be careful not to tear the agar. ⚠ CAUTION: Do not touch any of the bacteria. Using a clean swab each time, repeat for petri dishes 2, 3, and 4.

7. Set the petri dishes aside in a cool, dark place. Keep the lids on the petri dishes at all times.

8. Remove your gloves. ⚠ **CAUTION:** Dispose of your gloves and used swabs in a disposal bag provided by your teacher. Wash your hands with soap and warm water. Clean your workspace with antiseptic spray.

9. After four to six days, return to the petri dishes. Put on gloves before touching the dishes but do not open them. Copy Figure 17-9 into your notebook. Record your observations in this table.

10. Give the dishes and gloves to your teacher for proper disposal. ⚠ **CAUTION:** Do not throw them in the garbage. Wash your hands with soap and warm water.

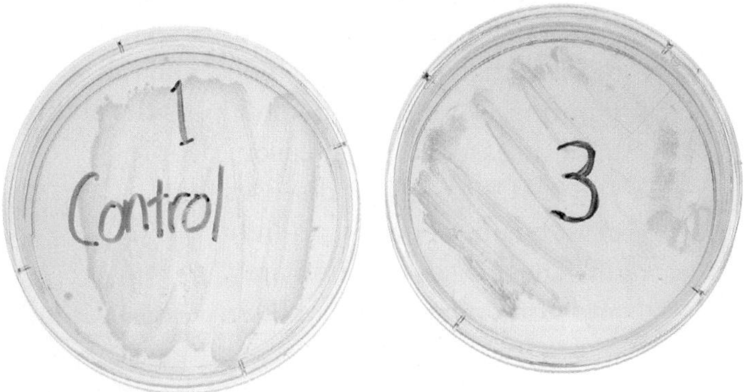


▲ **STEP 9** Observe the petri dishes.

| Petri Dish | Observations |
|---|---|
| 1 | |
| 2 | |
| 3 | |
| 4 | |

▲ **Figure 17-9** Copy this table onto a separate sheet of paper.

## CONCLUSIONS

1. **OBSERVE:** Which petri dish had the most bacterial growth in it? Which had the least bacterial growth?

2. **INFER:** Which antiseptic do you think is the most effective?

3. **ANALYZE:** What factors or variables, besides brand of antiseptic, could have caused the results?

# 17-4 What are some viral diseases?

## *Objectives*

Describe several examples of diseases caused by viruses. Describe the causes and symptoms of AIDS.

## *Key Term*

**AIDS:** viral disease that attacks a person's immune system

**Viral Diseases** Some kinds of disease are caused by viruses. The invention of the electron microscope has helped scientists learn about viruses and diseases. Scientists have discovered that different kinds of viruses attack different parts of the body. Each virus usually attacks only a certain kind of cell or tissue. For example, the viruses that cause warts seem to attack only cells in the skin. Viruses that cause yellow fever attack cells in the liver. Information about how viruses attack the body helps in the fight against the disease the virus causes.

1 **DESCRIBE:** In what way are viruses particular?

**Common Viral Diseases**
Viruses cause many different kinds of diseases. You have probably had several types of viral diseases in your lifetime. The common cold and the flu are both caused by viruses. Other diseases caused by viruses are listed in Figure 17-11.

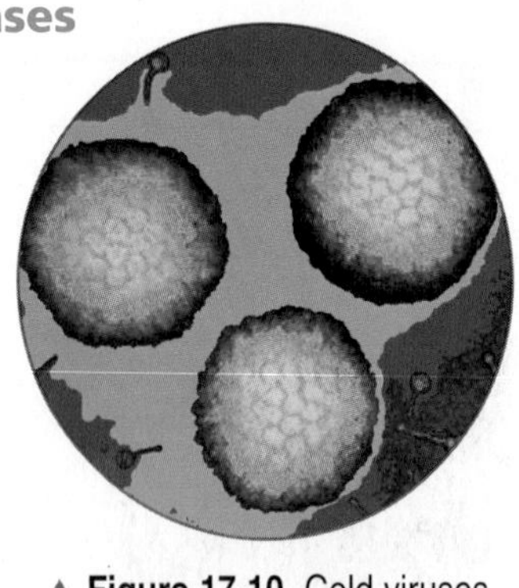

▲ **Figure 17-10** Cold viruses

| VIRAL DISEASES | |
|---|---|
| **Disease** | **Symptoms** |
| Influenza (flu) | Muscle aches, fever, and chills |
| Chickenpox | Skin rash in spots and fever |
| Measles | Pink rash all over the body |
| Mumps | Swollen glands and fever |
| Hepatitis | Jaundiced skin, swollen liver, and loss of appetite |

▲ **Figure 17-11**

There are many different kinds of cold and flu viruses. However, most of them cause the same set of symptoms. These symptoms may include sneezing, coughing, sore throat, headache, and fever.

2 **INFER:** Which body systems does the common cold affect?

**HIV** Viruses cause disease. They are selective in the cells or tissues that they attack. A particular virus, called human immunodeficiency virus (HIV), attacks a person's immune system. The illness caused by HIV is called acquired immune deficiency syndrome, or AIDS. **AIDS** is a viral disease that kills white blood cells in a person's immune system. The person loses the ability to fight disease. For this reason, people with AIDS easily get diseases that most healthy people can fight off. These diseases often are fatal for a person with AIDS.

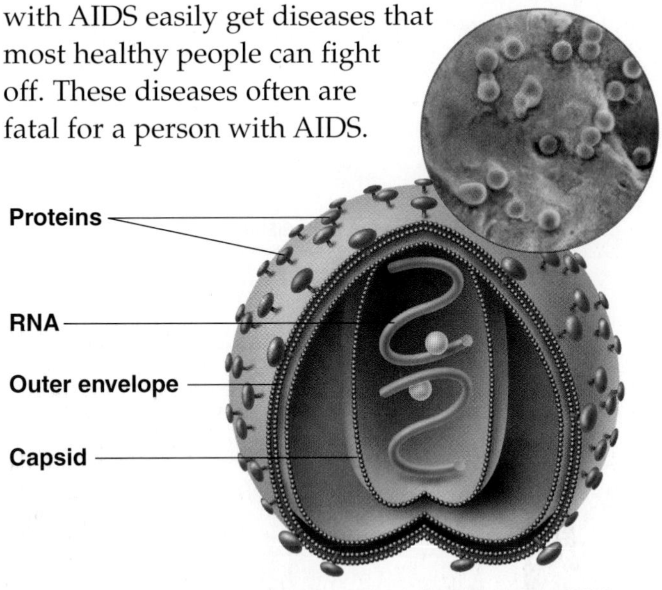


▲ **Figure 17-12** This diagram shows the basic structure of HIV. The photo above shows HIV in pink.

3 **DESCRIBE:** What effect does HIV have on the body?

**Transmission of AIDS** AIDS cannot be transmitted by casual contact. It cannot travel through air, food, or water. People with AIDS have HIV in their blood and body fluids. In order to contract AIDS, you must exchange bodily fluids with an infected person. The virus can enter the bloodstream by sexual contact with someone who has HIV. Another way HIV enters the bloodstream is through a blood transfusion of infected blood.

For this reason, blood banks test donated blood for the HIV virus. Today, it is extremely rare to get HIV from a transfusion given in the United States. You cannot get HIV by donating blood.

4 **EXPLAIN:** How is HIV transmitted?

## CHECKING CONCEPTS

1. The invention of the __________ helped scientists study viruses.
2. Particular kinds of __________ usually attack only certain types of cells and tissues.
3. The common cold and the flu are both caused by __________.
4. HIV attacks the body's __________.

## THINKING CRITICALLY

5. **INFER:** Why do you think the invention of the electron microscope helped in the study of viruses?
6. **PREDICT:** Could a person with AIDS transmit the virus to another person sitting across the room?
7. **INFER:** How does making the immune system stronger lengthen the life of a person with AIDS?

## Web InfoSearch

**Virus Mutations** Many viruses have the ability to mutate, or change their genetic material. This ability to mutate makes studying viruses difficult. It also makes it harder for scientists to find treatments or cures for viral diseases.

**SEARCH:** Use the Internet to find out more about the ability of viruses to mutate. Write a report about how this affects health and medicine. Start your search at www.conceptsandchallenges.com. Some key search words are **virus, viral disease,** and **virus mutation.**

## *Science and Technology*

### TREATMENTS FOR AIDS

HIV is an RNA virus. It causes the disease known as AIDS. The virus attacks T cells, which are a major part of our immune system. Millions of people throughout the world have AIDS.

Researchers are trying to find a vaccine that can help stop the spread of AIDS. Vaccines are dead or weakened forms of viruses that allow the person to build up an immunity to the virus. If an effective vaccine were to be found, the number of new AIDS victims could decrease dramatically. Scientists have developed drugs that can treat the disease to extend the life expectancy of patients. These drugs show promise in the slowing of the disease's progress in the body. However, the virus mutates and evolves so quickly that new drugs must be designed constantly.

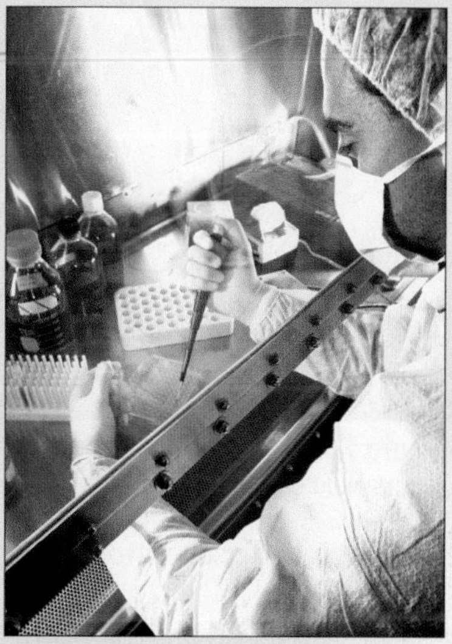

▲ **Figure 17-13** Researchers are trying to find a vaccine for AIDS.

There is no cure as yet for AIDS. The vaccines that exist have not yet been fully tested. People in many nations of the world are now suffering from the HIV virus. More research is needed to find a cure for patients with the disease. For now, education is the best way to stop the disease from spreading to more people.

**Thinking Critically** Why do you think AIDS is such a difficult disease to treat or cure?

# 17-5 What are noninfectious diseases?

*Objective*

Describe several noninfectious diseases and their effect on the body.

*Key Terms*

**tumor** (TOO-muhr)**:** mass or lump of cells

**benign** (bih-NYN) **tumor:** mass of cells that is usually harmless

**malignant** (muh-LIHG-nuhnt) **tumor:** harmful mass of cells that can spread throughout the body

**Noninfectious Diseases** Not all diseases are caused by microorganisms. Those that are not are called noninfectious diseases. They cannot be spread from one person to another. Cancer, Alzheimer's disease, and diabetes are all types of noninfectious diseases. The immune system also reacts to noninfectious diseases.

▲ **Figure 17-14** The cancer cells, shown in pink in this photo, are being attacked by T cells, shown in yellow.

1 **NAME:** What are three noninfectious diseases?

**Cancer** Most cells in the body divide and produce new cells only when necessary. Sometimes new cells grow where they are not needed. Their growth becomes rapid and uncontrolled. The new cells crowd nearby cells and rob them of their nutrients. The new cells form a mass, or lump, called a **tumor.**

There are two kinds of tumors. **Benign tumors** do not spread to other parts of the body and usually are not a serious health problem. **Malignant tumors** are more harmful because they can spread to other parts of the body. As a tumor spreads, it causes harm to the body. The disease caused by the spread of malignant tumors is called cancer.

2 **CONTRAST:** How are benign and malignant tumors different?

**Causes of Cancer** Scientists are not exactly sure what causes cancer to start growing. They do know that certain chemicals increase the chance of getting cancer. Studies have shown that exposure to too much sunlight and X-rays can cause cancer. Scientists believe that certain viruses and hormones also may cause cancer. Research also has shown that people who smoke cigarettes are more likely to get lung cancer than nonsmokers.

3 **LIST:** What are three things that may lead to cancer?

**Alzheimer's Disease** Alzheimer's disease affects the brain. Most people with Alzheimer's develop the disease in their later years. However, it is not a normal part of the aging process. Alzheimer's disease causes memory loss. It may also reduce a person's ability to think and speak clearly. The nerve cells and nerve connections of these patients have been tangled or destroyed. Scientists are still unsure of the exact causes of Alzheimer's disease. Most think that the disease may be caused by many different factors, including genetics.

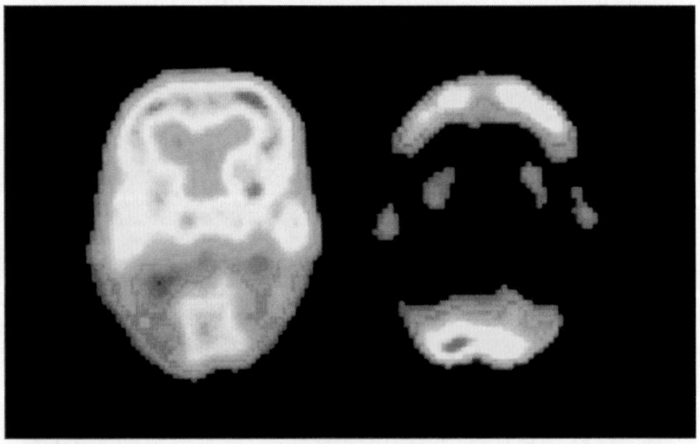

▲ **Figure 17-15** This image shows the brain (left) of a healthy person compared to an Alzheimer's patient (right).

4 **IDENTIFY:** Which body system does Alzheimer's disease affect?

**Diabetes** The pancreas normally produces a hormone called insulin, which regulates the amount of sugar in the bloodstream. If too little insulin is produced, an excess amount of sugar can build up in the blood. This condition is called diabetes mellitus. If untreated, diabetes can lead to kidney failure, blindness, and even death. Most diabetics can control their disease by taking insulin injections and by watching their diet.

5 **EXPLAIN:** How does diabetes affect the body?

## CHECKING CONCEPTS

1. A disease that is not caused by a microorganism is called a __________.
2. A tumor that does not spread to other parts of the body is a __________ tumor.
3. Cancer is the spread of __________ tumors.
4. The hormone __________ regulates the amount of sugar in the bloodstream.
5. Patients with __________ disease may have tangled nerve cells.

## THINKING CRITICALLY

6. **INFER:** Why do X-ray technicians wear lead aprons when taking X-rays?
7. **RELATE:** How is diabetes related to the endocrine, digestive, and circulatory systems?

## HEALTH AND SAFETY TIP

One way to prevent cancer is to avoid the things that contribute to the disease. Not smoking is a way to greatly decrease your chances of getting lung cancer. Wearing sunscreen when outdoors can help prevent developing skin cancer. Eating a healthy diet, with the right amount of vitamins and minerals, can also help reduce your chances of developing cancer. Research cancer using library references or the Internet. Design a health brochure that provides information about cancer prevention.

## *Science and Technology*

### PARKINSON'S DISEASE RESEARCH

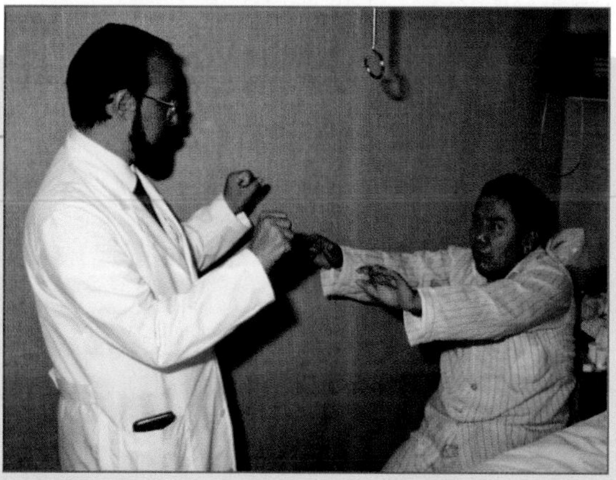

▲ **Figure 17-16** A doctor tests the movement of a patient with Parkinson's disease.

Parkinson's disease (PD) is a disorder of the central nervous system that tends to progress slowly over time. People with PD often have tremors. Their limbs are stiff, their movements are slow, and they may have balance problems. Researchers have discovered that all these difficulties are caused by damage to nerve cells in a small area in the middle of the brain. This results in a decrease in the production of an important chemical messenger called dopamine.

There is no cure for Parkinson's disease although there are a number of treatments. Researchers are working on a new type of drug that helps the brain to rebuild damaged nerve cells. Other scientists believe that injections of neural stem cells, special cells that have the ability to regenerate nerve tissue, may be an effective treatment. Operations in which small areas of nerve fibers are removed from certain parts of the brain can stop tremors. One of the latest advances is deep brain stimulation. A tiny electrode is placed deep inside the brain and stimulates nerve cells. The patient can turn its action on and off with a magnetic control device.

**Thinking Critically** Dopamine is a chemical messenger used by nerve cells in the brain. How can a decrease of dopamine result in problems in the movement of the body?

*Integrating History*

# THE Big IDEA

## How has disease affected us over time?

More than any time in history, people today live longer, more healthy lives. We owe a lot to heroes in medicine. Edward Jenner invented the smallpox vaccine in 1796. In 1977, naturally occurring smallpox was erased from the planet.

Knowledge, effort, and luck play a role in history. Alexander Fleming didn't set out to discover penicillin. The mold grew in his dish of bacteria by accident. Researchers were working on a polio vaccine for many years before Jonas Salk. But with the financial support of a major foundation, Salk got there first.

What is happening in society influences medicine. During the Industrial Revolution, poor living conditions led to many diseases. In the

### Folk Medicine 1400s

Early efforts to fight disease involved magic, faith, and plants. Many modern medicines are based on plants used thousands of years ago. Scientists today are learning more about the power of the mind to help in healing.

### Nursing 1854

Florence Nightingale pioneered the field of nursing. In 1854, she led a group of fellow nurses to Turkey to help wounded British soldiers of the Crimean War. Almost all modern nursing methods can be traced back to her.

### Radiation 1896

Marie Curie was a Polish-born French chemist who studied the radioactive properties of elements. This knowledge would become useful in the development of many types of radiotherapy.

1400 | 1800 | 1860 | 1870 | 1880 | 1890 | 1900

### Smallpox Vaccine 1796

Smallpox killed many people in the 18th century. Cowpox was a form of the disease that affected cattle. Edward Jenner discovered the concept of vaccination. He found that when he gave people small doses of cowpox, they were immune to smallpox.

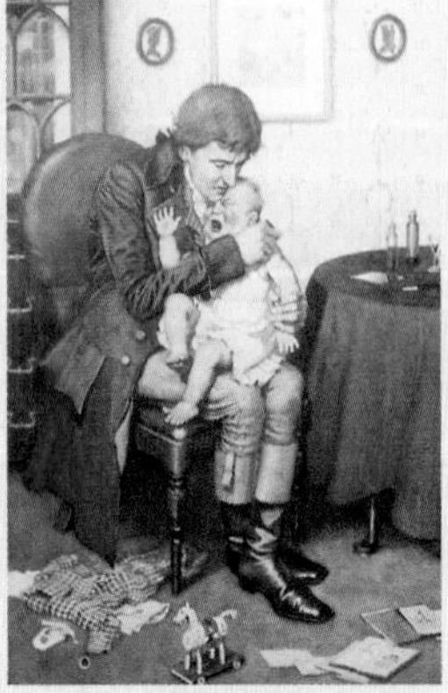

### Germ Theory 1860s–1870s

Germ theory is the idea that specific microscopic organisms cause specific diseases. Louis Pasteur developed this theory and vaccines to prevent diseases. Today, preventing the spread of germs is a very important principle in medicine.

1860s, diseases that killed sheep and silkworms threatened the French economy. Louis Pasteur worked to solve these problems. This work with industry led to important medical discoveries. The desire to treat soldiers in World War II led to mass production of penicillin.

Today, technology is changing at a whirlwind speed. This is fueling amazing advances in the way we detect, prevent, and fight disease.

Look at the timeline on these two pages. It points out important dates in the history of fighting disease. Follow the directions in the Science Log to learn more about "the big idea."✦

**WRITING ACTIVITY**

## Science Log

Look at the timeline on these two pages. In your science log, research and write about a person who played an important role in the history of fighting disease. Tell why you chose that person. Start your search at www.conceptsandchallenges.com.

1930 · 1940 · 1950 · 1960 · 1970 · 1980 · 1990 · 2000

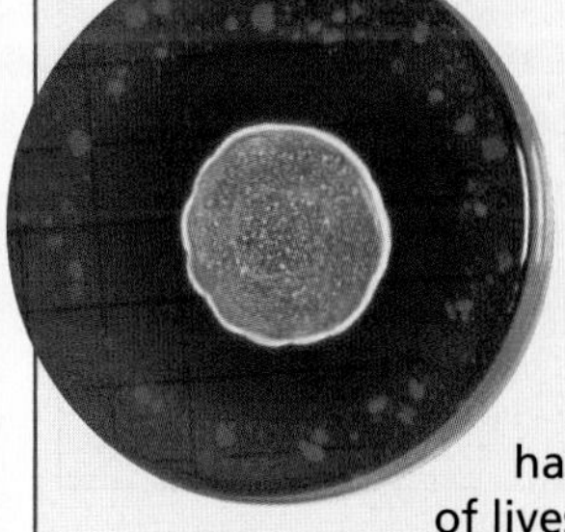

### Penicillin 1928

This lifesaving drug was discovered by Alexander Fleming. This discovery changed forever the way we treat bacterial infections. Penicillin has saved millions of lives.

### Leukemia Drug 1953

Leukemia is a form of cancer that affects the blood. Gertrude Belle Elion invented a drug that has been used to fight leukemia.

### Polio Vaccine 1954

The polio virus causes paralysis. In epidemics in the 1940s and 1950s, thousands of children were crippled each year. Building on the work of other scientists, Dr. Jonas Salk developed a polio vaccine. The disease has been erased in most parts of the world.

### Heart Transplant 1967

Christiaan Barnard was a South African surgeon. He performed the first human heart transplant. Organ transplants save the lives of many people. But donated organs are in short supply.

### Cancer 1971

President Nixon declared war on cancer, and the federal government spends billions of dollars on cancer research. Research led to many advancements in treatment. Still, almost 30 years later, cancer is still the second leading cause of death.

### AIDS Treatment 1996

Doctors began prescribing a new drug treatment for AIDS. It was a combination of three drugs. The number of deaths from AIDS quickly dropped. Scientists continue their search for a vaccine and a cure.

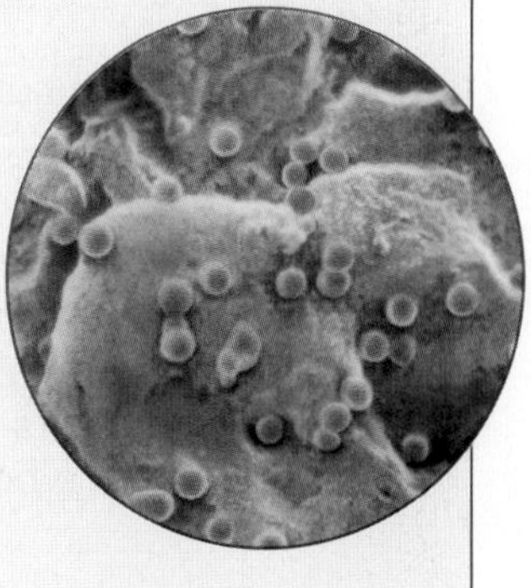

### Human Genome Project 2000

Scientists published the first physical map of the human genome. It is a set of instructions for building each human cell. Researchers now are working on ways to turn this knowledge into new treatments for disease.

# Chapter 17 Challenges

## Chapter Summary

### Lesson 17-1

- The first line of defense against disease is your skin. The defense systems of the body include the respiratory, digestive, circulatory, lymphatic, and immune systems.
- Certain types of **white blood cells** surround and destroy **pathogens** throughout the body.
- The body produces **antibodies** that can destroy foreign substances called **antigens**.

### Lesson 17-2

- **Immunity** is a resistance to a specific disease. There are two kinds of immunity, natural immunity and acquired immunity.
- Active acquired immunity develops after the body has developed antibodies against a certain disease. Passive acquired immunity develops when antibodies are injected into the body.

### Lesson 17-3

- The germ theory of disease states that diseases are caused by microscopic organisms.
- **Antibiotics** are chemical substances that kill harmful bacteria.
- Alexander Fleming was the first person to discover the use of antibiotics to treat disease.

### Lesson 17-4

- Diseases caused by viruses include colds, the flu, and the measles.
- Viruses usually attack a specific kind of cell.
- **AIDS** is a viral disease that kills white blood cells in a person's immune system.

### Lesson 17-5

- Diseases that are not caused by a microorganism are called noninfectious diseases. Alzheimer's disease, cancer, and diabetes are examples of noninfectious diseases.
- A **tumor** is a mass or lump of cells. **Benign tumors** are harmless growths of cells. **Malignant tumors** are tumors that spread to other parts of the body and cause harm.

## Key Term Challenges

AIDS (p. 408)
antibiotic (p. 404)
antibody (p. 400)
antigen (p. 400)
benign tumor (p. 410)
contagious (p. 404)
immunity (p. 402)
malignant tumor (p. 410)
pathogen (p. 400)
tumor (p. 410)
white blood cell (p. 400)

MATCHING **Write the Key Term from above that best matches each description.**

1. cells that protect the body against disease
2. substances produced by white blood cells to help fight disease
3. resistance to a certain disease
4. mass or lump of cells
5. viral disease that attacks a person's immune system
6. microscopic organism that causes disease
7. disease that can be spread from one person to another

IDENTIFYING WORD RELATIONSHIPS **Explain how the words in each pair are related. Write your answers in complete sentences.**

8. benign tumor, malignant tumor
9. antibiotic, bacteria
10. antigen, antibodies
11. white blood cells, immune system
12. vaccine, virus

## Content Challenges TEST PREP

**MULTIPLE CHOICE Write the letter of the term or phrase that best completes each statement.**

**1.** The cells that produce antibodies are called
- **a.** B cells.
- **b.** red blood cells.
- **c.** T cells.
- **d.** antigens.

**2.** A treatment made from dead or weakened viruses is
- **a.** an antibiotic.
- **b.** a vaccine.
- **c.** an antibody.
- **d.** an antivirus.

**3.** AIDS is a disease of the
- **a.** endocrine system.
- **b.** immune system.
- **c.** digestive system.
- **d.** respiratory system.

**4.** Alzheimer's disease affects the
- **a.** digestive system.
- **b.** endocrine system.
- **c.** nervous system.
- **d.** reproductive system.

**5.** Hepatitis usually is caused by a
- **a.** virus.
- **b.** bacterium.
- **c.** fungus.
- **d.** protozoan.

**6.** The disease that results from rapid, uncontrolled growth of cells is called
- **a.** diabetes.
- **b.** Alzheimer's disease.
- **c.** allergies.
- **d.** cancer.

**7.** The system made up of various organs, tissues, and other systems that fight disease is the
- **a.** lymphatic system.
- **b.** immune system.
- **c.** respiratory system.
- **d.** circulatory system.

**8.** The body's first line of defense against disease is the
- **a.** mouth.
- **b.** white blood cells.
- **c.** skin.
- **d.** nose.

**9.** All of the following are caused by bacteria except
- **a.** influenza.
- **b.** viral meningitis.
- **c.** tetanus.
- **d.** strep throat.

**10.** T cells identify pathogens by detecting the signal molecules called
- **a.** antigens.
- **b.** bacteria.
- **c.** germs.
- **d.** lymphocytes.

**FILL IN Write the term that best completes each statement.**

**11.** Louis Pasteur showed that some diseases are caused by __________.

**12.** Some antibiotics cause an __________ reaction.

**13.** Alexander Fleming discovered __________.

**14.** Vaccines are used to acquire __________ immunity.

**15.** Active acquired immunity lasts a __________ time.

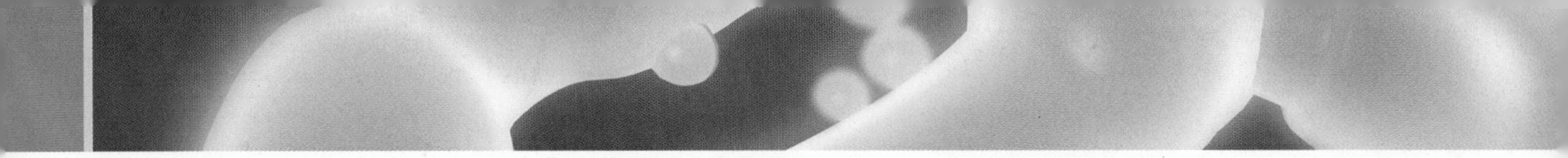

## *Concept Challenges* TEST PREP

WRITTEN RESPONSE **Answer each of the following questions in complete sentences.**

1. **EXPLAIN:** How has the discovery of vaccines helped in the prevention of disease?
2. **INFER:** A person has smoked cigarettes for more than ten years. Do you think it is too late for this person to quit smoking? Explain your answer.
3. **RELATE:** How is good hygiene related to preventing infectious diseases?
4. **INFER:** Why do you think dentists often wear masks and rubber gloves when examining patients?
5. **PREDICT:** If you have already had chickenpox, what are your chances of getting the disease again?

INTERPRETING VISUALS **Use Figure 17-17 to answer the following questions.**

6. What are the symptoms of mumps?
7. Is the disease hepatitis caused by a virus or a bacteria?
8. If you had a loss of appetite, which of the diseases might you have?
9. How are the symptoms of measles and chickenpox similar?
10. How many diseases cause fever?

| VIRAL DISEASES | |
|---|---|
| **Disease** | **Symptoms** |
| Influenza (flu) | Muscle aches, fever, and chills |
| Chickenpox | Skin rash in spots and fever |
| Measles | Pink rash all over the body |
| Mumps | Swollen glands and fever |
| Hepatitis | Jaundiced skin, swollen liver, and loss of appetite |

▲ **Figure 17-17**

# Chapter 18 Control and Regulation

▲ **Figure 18-1** Being part of an orchestra requires a great deal of concentration.

Have you ever played a musical instrument? If you have, you know it takes a great deal of concentration and control. Different parts of your body have to work together to play an instrument. Getting different parts of the body to work together is the job of the nervous system, which includes the brain and sense organs. For example, your ears send the message of sound to your brain, which interprets the sound as music.

▶What other body parts need to work together to play a musical instrument?

## Contents

# 18-1 What is the nervous system?

### *Objectives*

Identify the function of the nervous system. Name the parts that make up the nervous system.

### *Key Terms*

**neuron** (NOOR-ahn)**:** nerve cell

**dendrite** (DEHN-dryt)**:** fiber that carries messages to the nerve cell body

**axon:** fiber that carries messages away from a nerve cell body

**synapse** (SIHN-aps)**:** gap between the axon of one nerve cell and the dendrite of another

**The Nervous System** The nervous system controls all of your body's activities. The nervous system is made up of the brain, the spinal cord, and nerves. Nerves carry information to the spinal cord and brain. Other nerves then carry messages from the brain and spinal cord to the muscles and glands. The muscles and glands carry out the orders of the brain and spinal cord.

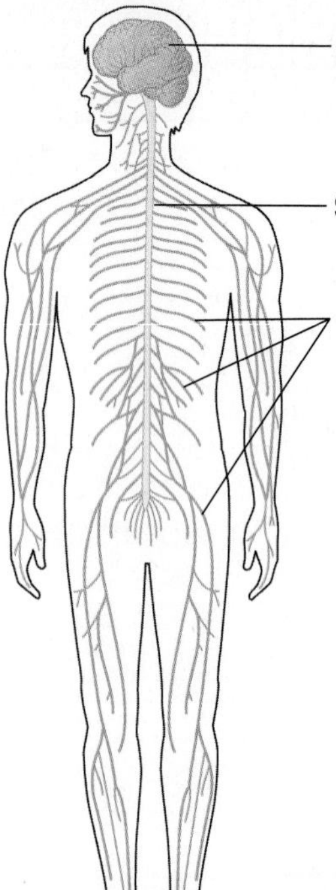


◀ **Figure 18-2** The nervous system

**1 IDENTIFY:** Name the parts of the nervous system.

**The Central Nervous System** Your brain is the control center of your body. The brain is made up of a mass of nervous tissue. The brain is protected by your skull. The spinal cord is made up of many nerves that extend down your back. The spinal cord is protected by the backbone. The brain and spinal cord make up the central nervous system.

**2 NAME:** What structure protects the spinal cord?

**Nerve Cells** There are 31 pairs of nerves that branch out from your spinal cord. These nerves branch many times and extend to all parts of your body. Each of the nerves in your body is made up of nerve cells called **neurons.** Neurons can be either large or small. Some neurons are among the largest cells in your body. In fact, one neuron in your leg can be as long as 1 m.

The job of a neuron is to carry messages. Messages travel through a neuron in only one direction. You can see the structure of two neurons in Figure 18-3.

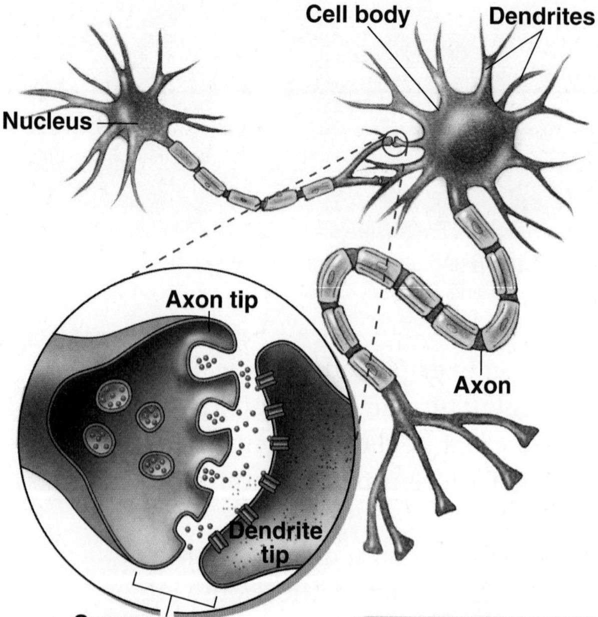


▲ **Figure 18-3** The structure of two neurons

Go Online
active art
**For:** Nervous System activity
**Visit:** PHSchool.com
**Web Code:** cep-4062

The **dendrites** carry messages toward the nerve cell body, or center of the neuron. The **axon** carries messages away from the cell body. The cell body contains the nucleus of the neuron. It contains most of the cytoplasm.

3 **DESCRIBE:** Describe the structure of a neuron.

**Synapses** The axon of one nerve cell normally does not touch the dendrites of the next nerve cell. Usually, there is a small gap between the two cells. This gap is called a **synapse.** Chemicals released by the axon carry messages across the synapse to the dendrites of the next neuron.

4 **DEFINE:** What is the gap between two cells called?

## CHECKING CONCEPTS

1. What is the job of the nervous system?
2. What are the parts of the nervous system?
3. What parts make up the central nervous system?
4. What is a neuron?
5. How many pairs of nerves branch out from the spinal cord?
6. What are the parts of a neuron?

## THINKING CRITICALLY

7. **INFER:** What is the job of nerve tissue?
8. **MODEL:** Draw and label a neuron. Draw arrows on the diagram to show the direction a message travels through the neuron.
9. **PREDICT:** Unlike other body cells, most nerve cells cannot reproduce themselves. What might happen if many of the nerve cells in your hand were destroyed?

## BUILDING LANGUAGE ARTS SKILLS

***Writing Analogies*** When you make an analogy, you are comparing two things that are similar in some way. Write an analogy about how the nervous system is similar to a computer. Your analogy should be at least two paragraphs long.

## *Hands-On Activity*

### MODELING TOUCH RECEPTORS

*You will need a pencil and a paper clip. You will need to work with a partner.*

1. Straighten the paper clip. Then, bend the paper clip until its ends are about 2 cm apart.
2. Ask your partner to close his or her eyes. Gently touch the end of the paper clip to your partner's arm.
3. Ask you partner how many points touched his or her arm.
4. Repeat this three times, each time touching a different part of your partner's arm, hand, and fingers. Also, vary the number of points you use. Record the responses.
5. Repeat Steps 3 to 5 with your partner recording your responses.

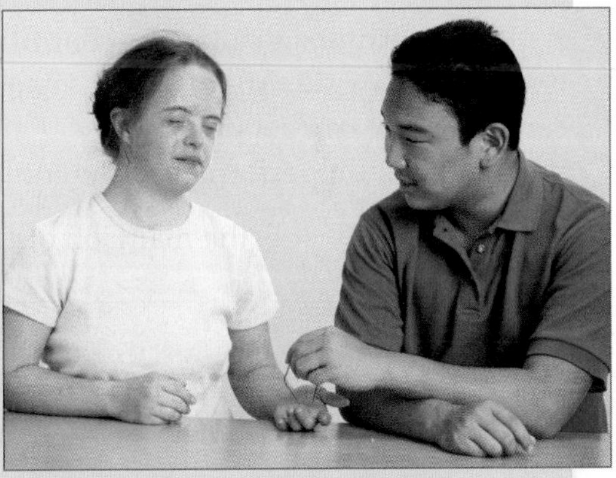

▲ **STEP 2** Gently touch the paper clip to your partner's arm.

**Practicing Your Skills**

6. **INFER:** Were your responses always correct? Explain.
7. **INFER:** Which part of your arm, hand, or fingers was most sensitive? Why do you think this part of your body is so sensitive?

# 18-2 What are the parts of the brain?

### *Objectives*

Identify and describe the functions of the three parts of the brain.

### *Key Terms*

**cerebrum** (suh-REE-bruhm)**:** part of the brain that controls the senses and thinking

**cerebellum** (ser-uh-BEHL-uhm)**:** part of the brain that controls balance and body motion

**brainstem:** bundle of nerves at the base of the brain

**medulla** (mih-DUL-uh)**:** lower part of the brain stem that controls heartbeat and breathing rate

**The Brain** The main job of the brain is to receive, interpret, and react to messages. These messages may come from inside or outside your body. Your brain responds to the messages and then controls all of your body's activities. For example, movement, thinking, breathing, and sleeping all are controlled by your brain.

The brain often is called the control center of the body. It is made up of three main parts: the cerebrum, the cerebellum, and the brainstem. Each part of the brain performs a different function.

**1 EXPLAIN:** What is the main job of the brain?

**The Cerebrum** The largest part of the brain is the **cerebrum.** You can see in Figure 18-4 that the cerebrum makes up more than two-thirds of the brain. One job of the cerebrum is to interpret information from the sense organs. Your sense organs are your eyes, ears, nose, tongue, and skin. A second job of the cerebrum is to control thinking. Your cerebrum is the part of the brain that controls learning, remembering, and making decisions. The cerebrum also controls movement and speech.

**2 EXPLAIN:** What are three jobs of the cerebrum?

**The Cerebellum** The part of the brain located at the back of the brain is the **cerebellum.** The cerebellum is much smaller than the cerebrum. All motor nerve impulses that begin with the cerebrum pass through the cerebellum. Motor nerve impulses are used in movement. The cerebellum adjusts the impulses so your movements are coordinated.

The cerebellum also helps to maintain balance. As your body changes position, the cerebellum receives messages. Then, the cerebellum sends messages out to your muscles. The muscles work to help you keep your balance.

**3 IDENTIFY:** Where is the cerebellum located?

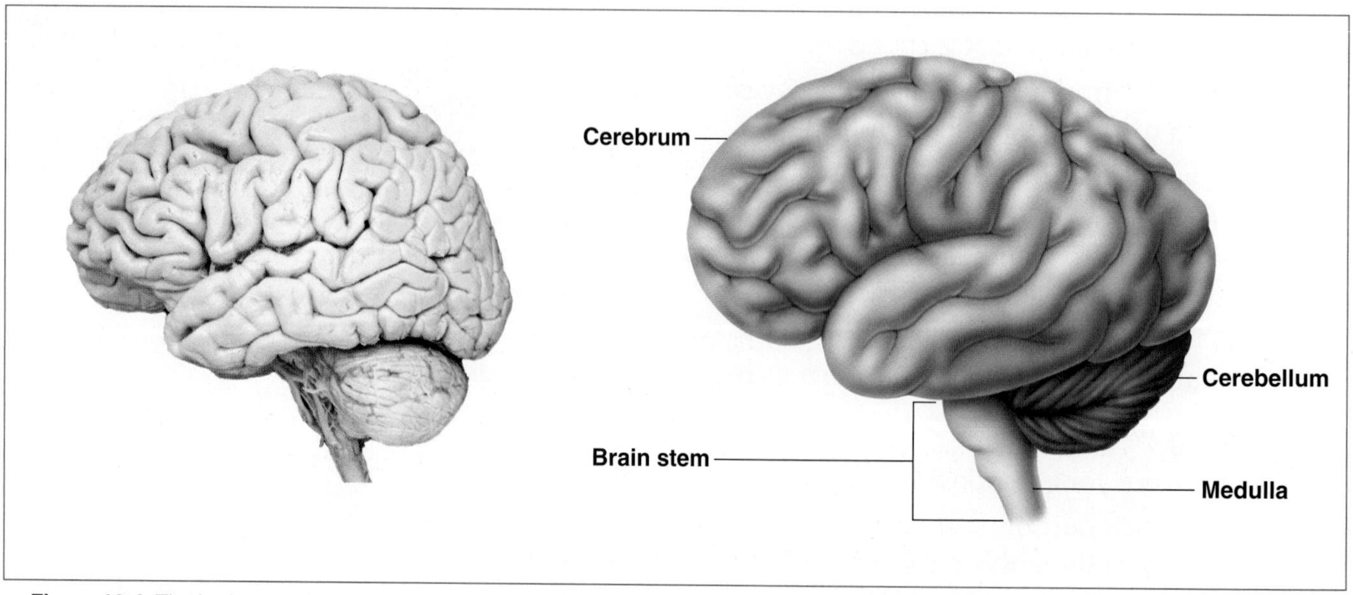


▲ **Figure 18-4** The brain

**The Brainstem** Bundles of nerves that pass from the cerebrum and the cerebellum form a thick stalk at the base of the skull. This is called the **brainstem.** The lower part of the brainstem is called the **medulla.**

The medulla connects the brain to the spinal cord. The medulla controls digestion, breathing, and heartbeat rate. It also controls the activities of many glands.

4 CLASSIFY: Does the medulla control voluntary or involuntary body activities?

**Safety and the Brain** Just like other parts of your body, your brain can suffer injuries. A common injury of the brain is a concussion, a bruiselike injury of the brain that occurs when the soft tissue of the cerebrum bumps against the inside of the skull. Concussions can occur during a car accident, a bad fall, or any other accident in which you hit your head. Some symptoms of a concussion are a headache, dizziness, and loss of consciousness. To reduce your risk of brain injury, wear a helmet when riding a bicycle, skating, or performing other physical activities where you risk hitting your head.

5 DEFINE: What is a concussion?

## CHECKING CONCEPTS

1. What are the three parts of the brain?
2. What is the largest part of the brain?
3. Where is the cerebellum located?
4. Where is the medulla located?
5. What is the main job of the brain?

## THINKING CRITICALLY

*Determine what part of the brain controls the following activities.*

6. You memorize someone's telephone number.
7. You walk to the store.
8. You breathe faster when you run.
9. You smell smoke.
10. You begin to fall but then regain your balance.

## Science and Technology

### TAKING PICTURES OF THE BRAIN

X-rays can take clear pictures of the bones, but soft tissues, such as the brain, do not show up as well. To see images of soft tissues, doctors use a technique known as magnetic resonance imaging, or MRI. This technique involves the use of magnets and radio waves to form pictures of organs. Using MRI, doctors can pinpoint the exact location of tumors in soft tissues.

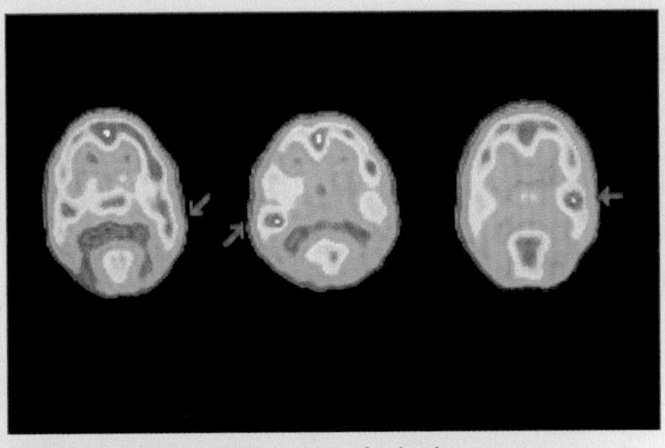

▲ **Figure 18-5** A PET image of a brain

Another technique, called positron emission tomography, or PET, is also used to study body organs, especially the brain. The patient is injected with glucose, a form of sugar. A computer records information about the amount of glucose in the brain. The computer uses this information to make an image showing brain structure and activity. PET is used to diagnose brain tumors and strokes. It is also used to study how the brain reacts to stimuli, such as music.

**Thinking Critically** Why are MRI and PET technologies important?

# 18-3 What are reflexes?

## INVESTIGATE

### Observing Reactions
HANDS-ON ACTIVITY

1. Work with a partner. Have your partner sit so his or her feet do not touch the floor. Your partner should close his or her eyes. Use the side of your hand to gently tap your partner on the knee, just below the kneecap. What happens?
2. Switch places with your partner. Close your eyes. Ask your partner to lightly tap your knee. What happens?

**THINK ABOUT IT:** Could you control your reaction when your partner tapped your knee?

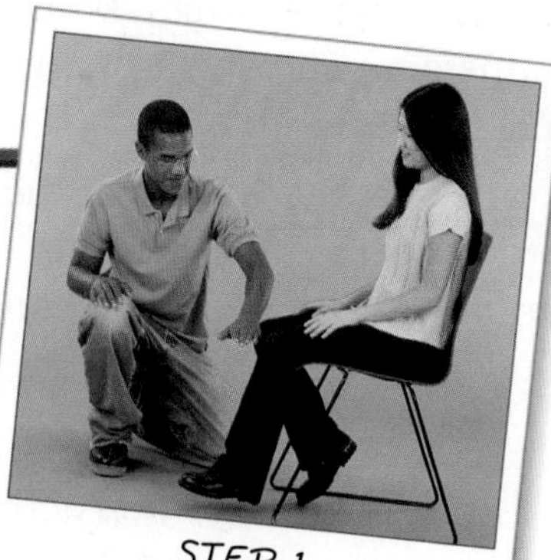

STEP 1

### *Objectives*

Define reflex. Relate reflexes to the stimuli that cause them.

### *Key Terms*

**reflex:** automatic response to a stimulus

**receptor:** part of a nerve cell that receives stimuli from the environment

**reflex arc:** path of a message in a reflex

**Stimuli and Responses** Do you jump at a sudden loud noise? Does your mouth water when you smell food? Do you pull your hand away quickly if you touch something hot? Loud sounds, the smell of food, and heat all are examples of stimuli. A stimulus is something that causes you to react in some way. The reaction to a stimulus is called a response.

1 **RELATE:** How are stimuli and responses related?

**Reflexes** Some responses are simple. You cannot control them. They happen without your thinking about what you are doing. An automatic, or involuntary, response to a stimulus is called a **reflex.**

A reflex usually is a response that protects you in some way. For example, when dust gets into your nose, you sneeze. Dust is a stimulus. Sneezing is the response. Sneezing helps to prevent harmful substances from entering your lungs.

▲ **Figure 18-6** Sneezing is a reflex.

When dirt gets into your eyes, you blink. Your eyes may also water or form tears. Blinking your eyes and forming tears are your body's way of protecting your eyes from harmful substances. Blinking and tearing are examples of reflexes.

2 **APPLY:** Is answering a ringing telephone an example of a reflex? Explain.

**A Reflex Arc** Reflexes usually occur very quickly. One reason reflexes occur so quickly is that they do not involve the brain. Some reflexes are controlled by the spinal cord.

When a reflex takes place, nerves and muscles work together. The stimulus is received by special parts of the nerve cells called **receptors.** Receptors receive stimuli from the environment. Other nerve cells carry a message to the spinal cord. Another nerve carries a message from the spinal cord to a muscle. A muscle causes you to move some part of your body. The message travels along a path formed by nerve cells. This path is called a **reflex arc**. You can trace the path of a reflex in Figure 18-7.

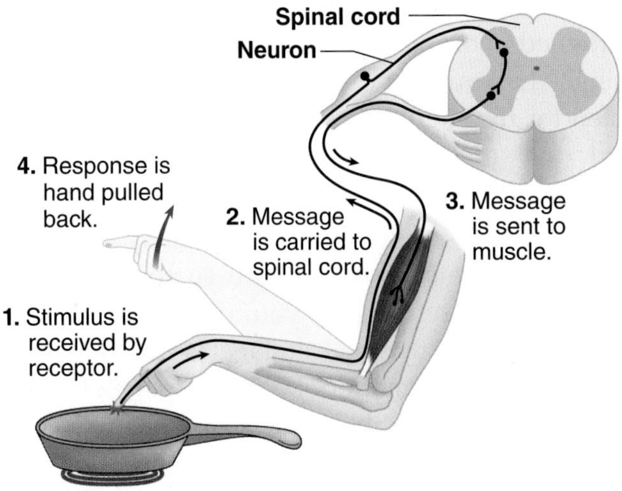


▲ **Figure 18-7** A reflex arc

**OBSERVE:** What is the stimulus in Figure 18-7? What is the response?

## CHECKING CONCEPTS

1. What is a reflex arc?
2. How are stimuli and responses related?
3. What are receptors?

## THINKING CRITICALLY

*Identify the stimulus and response in the following.*

4. You step on a tack and pull your foot away.
5. You blink when a light shines in your eyes.
6. Food in your windpipe causes you to cough.

## DESIGNING AN EXPERIMENT

*Design an experiment to solve the following problem. Include a hypothesis, variables, a procedure, and a type of data to study.*

PROBLEM: How does the size of the eye's pupil relate to the amount of light in a room?

## *Integrating Engineering*

**TOPICS: electronics, bionics, computers**

### TREATING SPINAL INJURIES WITH BIONICS

People that are paralyzed have lost the ability to move certain body parts. This is often due to a spinal cord injury. The degree of paralysis depends on where the injury occurred. A person might be paralyzed from the waist down or from the neck down.

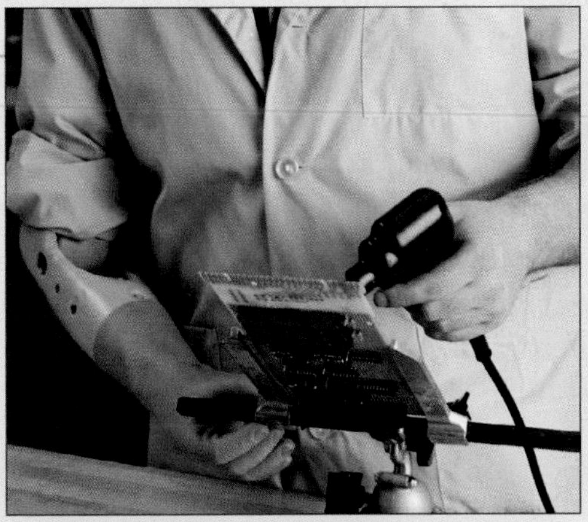

▲ **Figure 18-8** FES and a prosthetic hand allow patients to perform everyday tasks.

A new kind of treatment called functional electrical stimulation (FES) has helped patients who have lost control of their muscles due to paralysis. This technique uses electrodes implanted in the patient's skin to control muscle movement. When combined with a prosthetic hand or arm, this system allows patients to carry out everyday activities such as dialing a phone or writing a letter.

Currently, a movement of the individual must control this type of device. For example, the patient could control the movement of a prosthetic hand by shrugging his shoulder. Engineers are now working on a system that would allow the patient to control a prosthetic limb with their own thoughts. This technology, known as brain computer interface, is not yet perfected. However, researchers hope that in the future, computers and bionics will come together to give patients abilities they never thought possible.

**Thinking Critically** How has engineering helped paralysis patients?

# 18-4 What are sense organs?

***Objective***

Name the five sense organs and their jobs.

***Key Term***

**sense organ:** special organ that receives and processes stimuli from the environment

**Sense Organs** Sound, light, and heat are examples of stimuli. Stimuli are messages your brain interprets. You have special organs that receive and process stimuli from your environment. These organs are the **sense organs.** They are the eyes, nose, skin, ears, and tongue.

1 **NAME:** What are the sense organs?

**Jobs of the Sense Organs** Sense organs work to help you respond to your environment. Sense organs are receptors because they receive messages or stimuli. Each sense organ receives only certain kinds of messages. The eyes are sensitive to light. They help the brain create pictures of things you look at. These pictures are formed by changes in light. The nose responds to different smells. Your skin responds to changes in temperature and pressure. Your skin also responds to pain and touch. Your ears receive sounds from the environment. Your tongue helps you identify different tastes. Each organ senses a different stimulus.

| SENSE ORGANS AND THEIR FUNTIONS | |
|---|---|
| **Organ** | **Sense** |
| Skin | Touch, temperature, pressure, pain |
| Eyes | Sight |
| Nose | Smell |
| Tongue | Taste |
| Ears | Sound |

▲ **Figure 18-9**

2 **DESCRIBE:** What do sense organs do?

**Senses Work Together** Your senses do not work alone. What do you do when you walk into a darkened room? Your hands reach out to touch things that might be in front of you. Your ears listen for the slightest sound. Your eyes search the dark for some sign of light. Your senses work together to help you.

Your senses help you gather many different kinds of information about your surroundings. In this way, your senses help you to learn. Much that you see, hear, taste, smell, and feel is stored in your brain. This information becomes part of your memory. You remember things when you need to use them. Using information gathered by the senses is important for your safety and for all the things you do.

3 **EXPLAIN:** How do the senses help you to learn?

**Taste Buds** Your tongue is covered with receptors called taste buds. Your taste buds can detect four basic tastes: sweet, sour, bitter, and salty. The taste buds that detect each taste are located on different parts of your tongue. Your taste buds cannot taste dry substances. They can only taste substances that are moist. For this reason, foods must be moistened before your taste buds will recognize the food. When the receptor cells in your taste buds are activated, nerve impulses are sent to the brain where they are interpreted as taste.

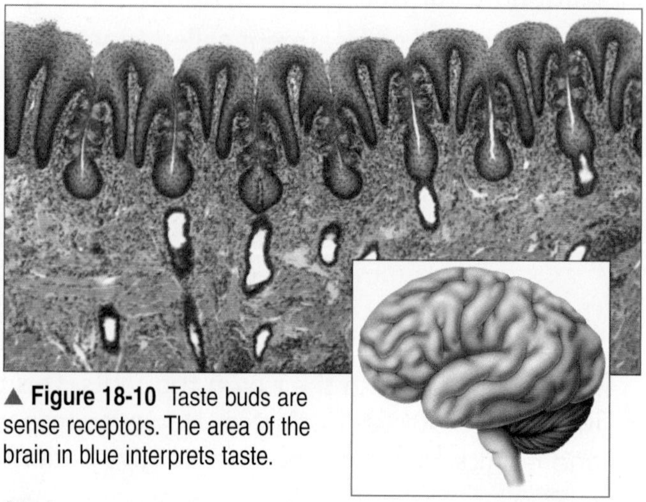

▲ **Figure 18-10** Taste buds are sense receptors. The area of the brain in blue interprets taste.

4 **IDENTIFY:** What organ do you use for taste?

**Smell** The flavor of food is also detected by receptors in your nose. When your nose is blocked, your odor receptors do not function as well. This is why food often tastes bland when you have a cold. Some odor receptors respond to gas molecules. When gas molecules dissolve in the mucus layer inside the nose, the molecules are detected by the odor receptors. Impulses are sent to the brain where they are interpreted as different odors.

▲ **Figure 18-11** Odor receptors in your nose send messages to your brain. The area in the brain in pink interprets smell.

**5** **INFER:** What other sense is related to smell?

**Touch** Your skin is the largest sense organ in your body. Your skin senses touch, pressure, pain, heat, and cold. Each of these sensations stimulates a different kind of sensory receptor in the skin.

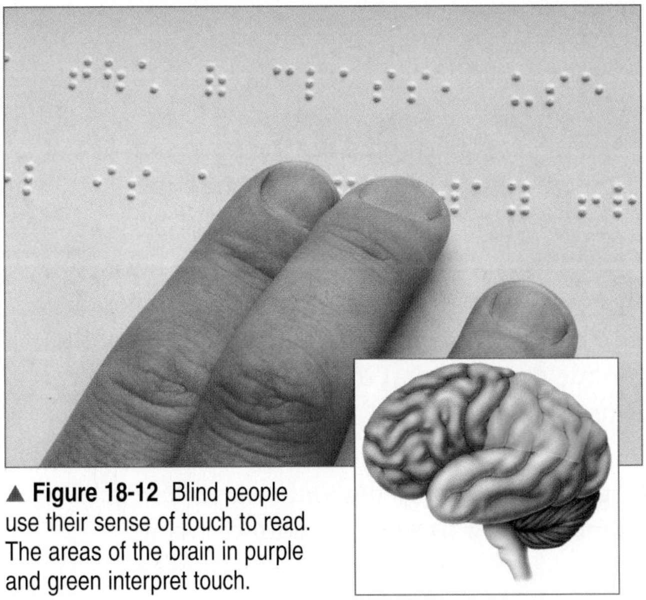

▲ **Figure 18-12** Blind people use their sense of touch to read. The areas of the brain in purple and green interpret touch.

Most touch receptors are found near the surface of the skin. They inform the brain of even the lightest touch. Pressure and pain receptors are found deep within the skin. These receptors alert the brain to dangerous situations in the environment.

Blind people rely heavily on their sense of touch for information. One way that blind people use their sense of touch is by reading Braille. Braille is a series of "letters" made up of a combination of raised dots.

**6** **ANALYZE:** You have more touch receptors in your fingertips than on your back. Why do you think this is important?

## ✓ CHECKING CONCEPTS

*Which sense organ receives the following messages?*

1. pain, temperature, pressure, and touch
2. smells
3. sounds
4. tastes
5. changes in light

## THINKING CRITICALLY

6. **ANALYZE:** How do the senses work together?
7. **RELATE:** How do your senses protect you from danger?
8. **INFER:** How does your body respond to cold temperatures?

### Web InfoSearch

**Braille** The Braille system was developed by the French inventor Louis Braille. Braille lost his sight when he was 3 years old. When he was 15 years old, he developed the Braille system.

**SEARCH:** Use the Internet to find out more about Louis Braille's reading system. Then, make a poster showing the position of dots of your name in Braille. Start your search at www.conceptsandchallenges.com. Some key search words are **Louis Braille** and **Braille system.**

# LAB ACTIVITY
# Identifying Taste Receptors

**Materials**

- Safety goggles
- Colored pencils or markers in four colors
- A glass of water
- 4 cotton swabs
- Sugar
- Lemon juice
- Table salt
- Tonic water

## *BACKGROUND*

Your tongue is covered with taste receptors called taste buds. These receptors can detect whether a substance is sweet, sour, bitter, or salty.

## *PURPOSE*

In this activity, you will be tasting four different substances to determine which area of your tongue has receptors for tasting sweetness, sourness, bitterness, and saltiness.

## *PROCEDURE*

1. Gather the materials needed, shown in Figure 18-13. Copy Figure 18-14 onto a sheet of paper.

2. Put on the goggles. Wet a clean cotton swab in the water. Place the cotton swab in the sugar.

3. Touch your tongue with the cotton swab. Observe what part of your tongue detects the sweetness of the sugar. Shade in this part of the tongue in your drawing.

4. Rinse your mouth with water.

5. Repeat Steps 2, 3, and 4 for the table salt. Use a different color to shade in your drawing.

6. Dip a clean cotton swab in the lemon juice. Touch the swab to your tongue as you did in Step 2. Use a different color to shade in the part of the tongue drawing that detected the lemon juice. Rinse your mouth.

7. Repeat Step 6 using the tonic water. Use a different color to shade in your drawing.

▲ **Figure 18-13** Taste receptors in your tongue can detect sweetness, sourness, bitterness, and saltiness.

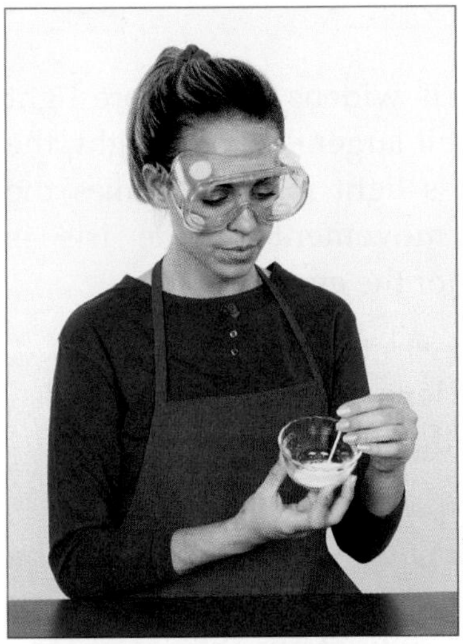

▲ **STEP 2** Place the cotton swab in sugar.

▲ **STEP 3** Touch your tongue with the cotton swab.

▲ **STEP 4** Rinse your mouth with water between each test.

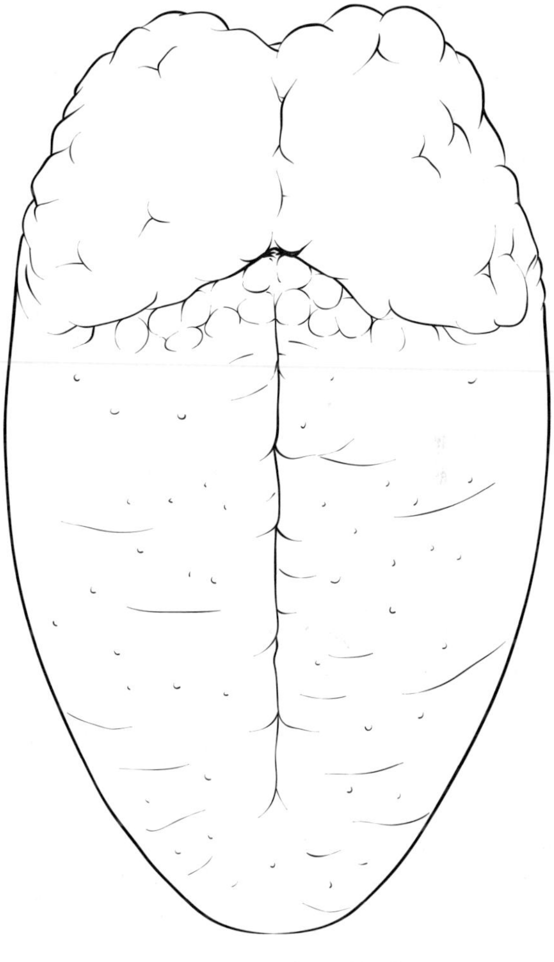

▲ **Figure 18-14** Copy this diagram onto a sheet of paper.

### *CONCLUSIONS*

1. **OBSERVE:** Describe the taste of each substance using the terms salty, bitter, sweet, and sour.

2. **COMPARE:** Look at the drawings made by two of your classmates. How are your drawings the same? How are your drawings different?

# 18-5 How do you see?

### *Objectives*

Name and describe the functions of the parts of the eye.

### *Key Terms*

**cornea** (KAWR-nee-uh)**:** clear covering at the front of the eye

**iris** (EYE-ris)**:** colored part of the eye that controls the amount of light entering the eye

**pupil** (PYOO-puhl)**:** opening in the center of the iris

**lens:** part of the eye that focuses an image on the retina

**retina** (REHT-uhn-uh)**:** part of the eye that receives images from the lens and transmits them to the brain

**The Eyes** The eyes are the organs of sight. The eyes work by responding to light. In order to see an object, your eyes must respond to light from that object. Different parts of the eye work together to send a signal that is produced from the light to your brain. Your brain then receives messages from your eye and interprets what your eyes are looking at, thereby producing a picture.

1 **IDENTIFY:** What kinds of stimuli do your eyes respond to?

**Parts of the Eye** Different parts of the eye work together to help you see. Figure 18-15 shows the parts of the eye. As you read about each part of the eye, locate that part on Figure 18-15.

- **Cornea** The **cornea** is a clear, curved, protective covering at the front of the eye.
- **Iris** Behind the cornea is a round, colored disk called the **iris.** The iris controls the amount of light entering the eye.
- **Pupil** At the center of the iris is a hole called the **pupil**. Light must pass through the pupil to get to the inside of your eye.

In dim light, the iris widens to let more light in. This makes the pupil larger. In bright light, the iris narrows to let less light in. This makes the pupil smaller. The movement of the iris is controlled by muscles of the eye.

- **Lens** After light passes through the pupil, it passes through the **lens** of the eye. The lens is a curved structure that focuses the light entering the eye.
- **Retina** At the back of the eye is the **retina.** The lens of the eye focuses light onto the retina. There are two types of light sensitive receptor cells in the retina, rods and cones. Rods are sensitive to dim light. They can detect only black and white. Cones are sensitive to bright light and allow you to see different colors. When light strikes the rods and cones, nerve signals are produced.
- **Optic Nerve** Nerve signals formed by the retina are carried to the brain by the optic nerve. The brain then interprets the signals it receives from the optic nerve and produces an image or picture.

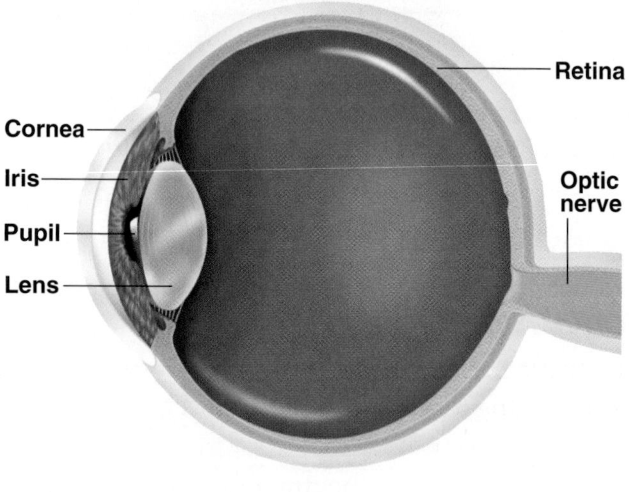


▲ **Figure 18-15** Parts of the eye

2 **SEQUENCE:** List, in the correct order, the parts of the eye through which light passes.

**Protecting the Eyes** The eyes are protected in many ways. The bones of the face extend in front of the eyes. These bones keep large objects from hitting and damaging the eyes. Eyelids and eyelashes help keep small pieces of matter from entering the eyes. Any particles that do reach the eyes usually are washed away by tears. Tears also keep the eyes from becoming too dry.

3 **IDENTIFY:** How do the bones of the face protect the eyes?

## CHECKING CONCEPTS

1. The eyes work by responding to __________.
2. The clear covering at the front of the eye is the __________.
3. Pupil size is controlled by the __________.
4. Light is focused on the part of the eye called the __________.
5. Nerve signals from the eye are carried to the brain by the __________.

## THINKING CRITICALLY

6. **APPLY:** What color are the pupils of your eyes? What color are your irises?
7. **RELATE:** What structure of the eye forms images on the retina?
8. **INFER:** What are some activities or jobs that would require protective eyewear?

## BUILDING SCIENCE SKILLS

***Applying Concepts*** Two problems often corrected with eyeglasses are myopia and astigmatism. Use library references to find out what these problems are and what features eyeglasses must have to correct them. Take a class poll to see how many students wear corrective lenses. Do they have myopia or astigmatism?

## *Hands-On Activity*

### ANALYZING OPTICAL ILLUSIONS

*You will need a metric ruler, tracing paper, and a pencil.*

1. Look at Figure A. Which line appears longer?
2. Look at Figure B. Which arc is longer?
3. Look at Figure C. Which post is tallest?
4. Measure and record the length of each line in Figure A.
5. Trace the top arc in Figure B on a sheet of tracing paper. Place the top arc over the bottom arc. Describe your observation.

#### Practicing Your Skills

6. a. **OBSERVE:** Which line looked longer than the other? b. **MEASURE:** How long is each line?
7. **ANALYZE:** Are the arcs the same size?
8. a. **OBSERVE:** Which post looked shortest? Which looked tallest? b. **MEASURE:** How tall is each post?
9. **EXPLAIN:** Why was your eye fooled by the optical illusion in each figure?

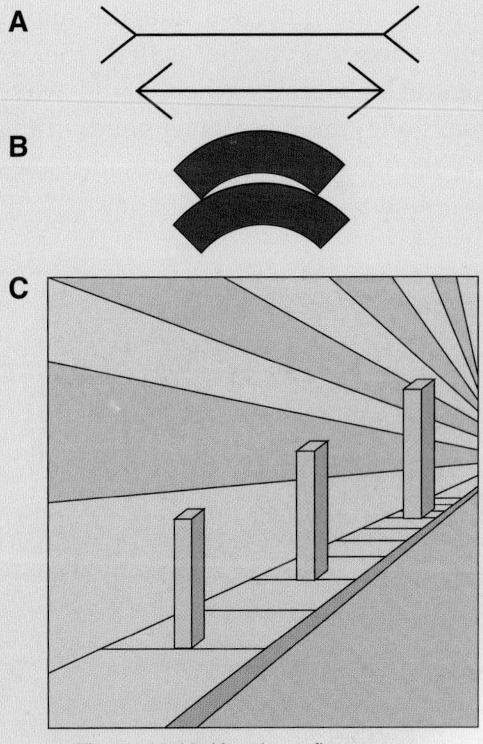


▲ **Figure 18-16** Use these figures to complete the activity.

# 18-6 How do you hear?

*Objective*

Describe the jobs of the main parts of the ear.

*Key Terms*

**eardrum:** sheet of tissue that vibrates when sounds strike it

**cochlea** (KAHK-lee-uh)**:** part of the ear that changes vibrations into nerve signals

**The Ears** The ears are the organs of hearing. The three sections of the ear are the outer ear, the middle ear, and the inner ear. Each part of the ear has a different job. As you read about how the ear works, locate each part in Figure 18-17.

The outer ear acts like a funnel to gather sound. The larger the outer ear, the more sound it can gather. Rabbits have larger outer ears than humans. This is one reason why rabbits have better hearing than humans.

Between the outer ear and the middle ear is a thin sheet of tissue called the **eardrum.** The eardrum vibrates when sound waves hit it. The ear bones are three small bones in the middle ear. When the eardrum vibrates, it makes the ear bones vibrate.

A coiled structure called the **cochlea** is located in the inner ear. The cochlea receives the vibrations of the ear bones.

**1** STATE: What makes the ear bones vibrate?

**Sound Waves** When someone speaks to you, sound waves are formed. The sound waves are different for each word. These sound waves travel in the air and are gathered by your outer ear. They make your eardrum vibrate. Your ear bones also vibrate. The vibrations are different for each word. The cochlea changes these vibrations into nerve signals. Then the signals are carried by the auditory nerves to the brain. The brain interprets the signals so that you can understand what they mean.

**2** EXPLAIN: How do sound signals get from the ear to the brain?

**What You Hear** Some sounds are too low pitched to hear. The sounds are not detected by the cochlea. No signal is sent to the brain. You hear nothing. Other sounds are too high pitched to hear. The cochlea cannot change these sounds into nerve signals. You do not hear anything.

**3** EXPLAIN: Why are certain sounds not detected by the ear?

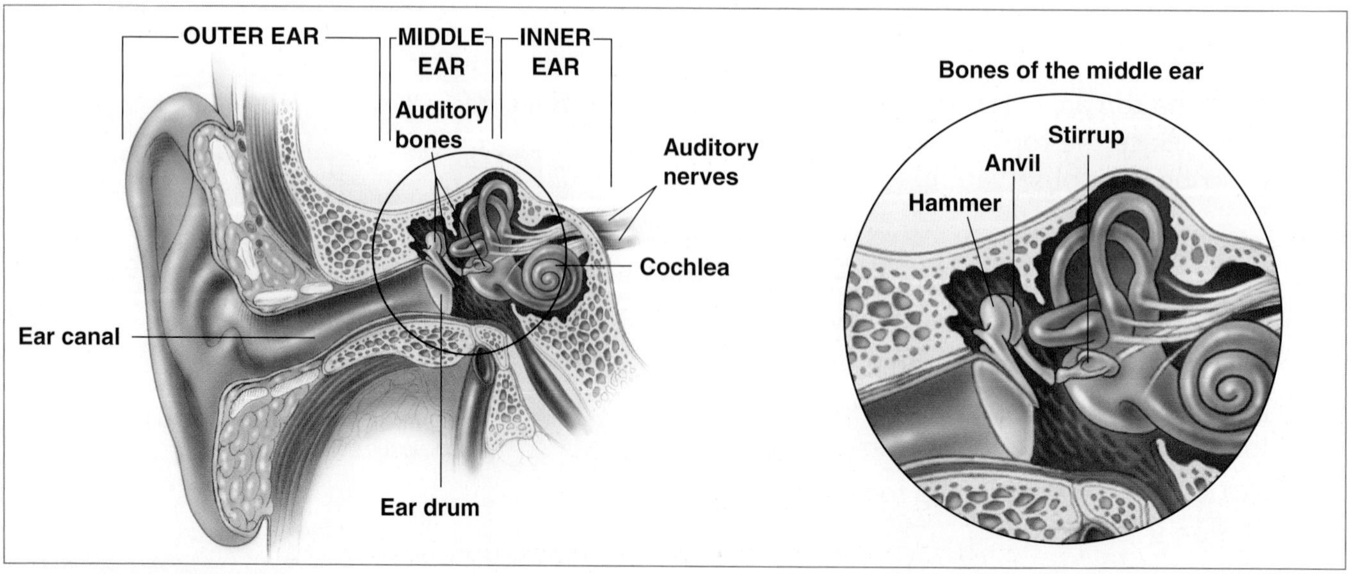


▲ **Figure 18-17** Parts of the ear

**Hearing Aids** Anything that stops part of the ear from working can cause deafness. Each part of the ear is needed for good hearing. Sometimes the ear can be damaged but still work a little bit. This is partial deafness. Sometimes deafness is caused by an infection of the ear bones. After the infection, the bones may no longer be able to vibrate.

Partial deafness can be often corrected by using hearing aids. Hearing aids are like small amplifiers that fit near or into the ear. They make sounds louder, so even damaged parts of the ear may vibrate.

4 **EXPLAIN:** What are hearing aids?

## ✓ CHECKING CONCEPTS

1. The sense organs of hearing are __________.
2. The three main sections of the ear are __________.
3. The cochlea receives the vibrations of the ear bones and changes them to __________.
4. Ear vibrations changed to nerve signals are sent to the __________.

## THINKING CRITICALLY

5. **APPLY:** How do a rabbit's large ears help it to hear?
6. **HYPOTHESIZE:** Why can't we hear certain kinds of sounds?
7. **INFER:** What is the brain's role in hearing?

### Web InfoSearch

**Hearing in Animals** Many animals can hear higher-pitched sounds than humans can. Many animals also can hear lower-pitched sounds than humans can.

**SEARCH:** Use the Internet to find out more about hearing in other animals. Write your findings in a report. Start your search at www.conceptsandchallenges.com. Some key search words are **hearing** and **ears.**

## *Integrating Physical Science*

TOPICS: sound waves, frequency, amplitude

### PITCH AND FREQUENCY

Sound is a form of energy that makes molecules vibrate. Sound waves can move through solids, liquids, or gases.

The number of waves produced by a vibrating sound source each second is called the frequency. Frequency is measured in units called hertz. A sound's frequency determines its pitch, or how high or low it sounds. Animals such as bats, dogs, and dolphins can hear very high-pitched sounds, which humans cannot hear. Elephants communicate over long distances by making low-pitched sounds, which humans also cannot hear.

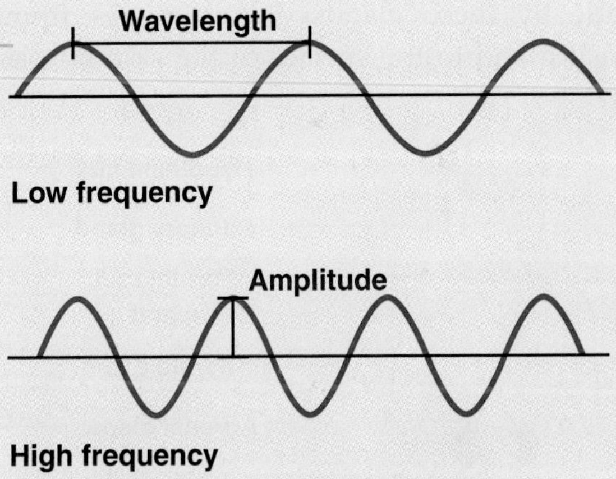


▲ **Figure 18-18** The frequency of a sound wave determines its pitch.

When sound waves vibrate, each molecule moves back and forth from its original position. The farther it moves, the greater the amount of energy flowing through the sound waves and the louder the sound seems. The greatest distance the vibrating molecules move from their original position is called the amplitude of the vibration. A sound wave's amplitude determines how loud the sound is. Loudness is measured in units called decibels.

**Thinking Critically** Why do you think other animals can hear pitches humans cannot?

# 18-7 What is the endocrine system?

## *Objective*

Describe the function of the endocrine system.

## *Key Terms*

**gland:** organ that makes chemical substances used or released by the body

**exocrine** (EHKS-oh-krihn) **gland:** gland that has ducts

**endocrine** (EHN-doh-krihn) **gland:** gland that does not have ducts

**hypothalamus** (hy-poh-THAL-uh-muhs)**:** part of the brain that tells the pituitary gland to release certain chemicals

**Glands with Ducts** A **gland** is an organ that makes substances used or released by the body. Some glands have ducts, or tubes. These are called **exocrine glands.** Substances made by these glands leave the gland through the ducts. Your skin has many sweat glands. Perspiration, or sweat, is made by these glands. Sweat moves from the sweat gland to the surface of the skin by passing through a duct. Salivary glands also have ducts. Saliva passes from the salivary glands into the mouth through these ducts.

1 **NAME:** What are two glands that have ducts?

**Endocrine Glands** Some glands do not have ducts. They are called **endocrine glands.** Substances made by endocrine glands pass from the glands directly into the bloodstream. The blood vessels then carry the substances to the parts of the body where they are needed.

2 **IDENTIFY:** How do substances made by endocrine glands get to other parts of the body?

**The Endocrine System** There are 10 main endocrine glands in the human body. Together, these glands make up the endocrine system. Eight of the glands that make up the endocrine system are shown in Figure 18-19.

3 **OBSERVE:** Where are the adrenal glands located?

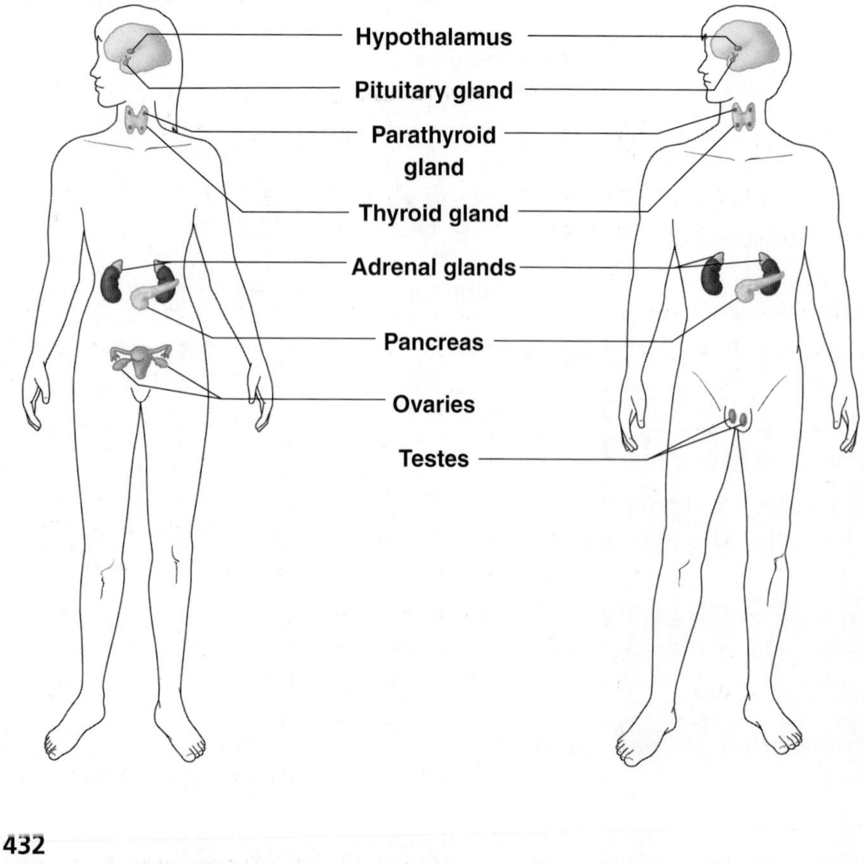


**Figure 18-19** The endocrine systems

**Control of Body Functions** The job of the endocrine system is to help control bodily functions. Each gland in the endocrine system has a different job. The way each gland works is similar to the way a thermostat and a furnace work. If the temperature of a room goes down, the thermostat signals the furnace to turn up the heat. The "thermostat" of the body is the **hypothalamus.** If the hypothalamus senses a need for a certain chemical substance in the body, it stimulates the pituitary gland to produce a chemical. This chemical sends a message to one of the other endocrine glands.

4 **STATE:** What is the function of the endocrine system?

## CHECKING CONCEPTS

1. An organ that makes substances used or released by the body is called a __________.
2. Glands that do not have ducts are called __________ glands.
3. The substances made by endocrine glands are carried by __________ to other parts of the body.
4. Sweat glands are __________ glands.
5. There are about __________ endocrine glands in the body.

## THINKING CRITICALLY

6. **CONTRAST:** What is the difference between an endocrine and an exocrine gland?

## INTERPRETING VISUALS

*Use Figure 18-19 to answer the following questions.*

7. **OBSERVE:** What endocrine glands are found only in males?
8. **OBSERVE:** Where is the pituitary gland located?
9. **IDENTIFY:** Which glands are found in pairs in the body?
10. **INFER:** The prefix *para-* means "by the side of." Based on this information, where do you think the parathyroid gland is located?

## *Real-Life Science*

### EMERGENCY GLAND

Adrenaline is a chemical that is released by the adrenal glands. In times of stress or excitement, the hypothalamus sends a message that triggers the adrenal glands. This releases adrenaline. This surge of adrenaline enables a person to "fight" or "flee" in high-stress times. Scientists believe this response helped early humans to survive in the wild.

An example of adrenaline at work is when a person rescues someone. At that time, the body's heartbeat speeds up, breathing increases, muscles contract, the digestive system shuts down, and blood clots faster. After the emergency has passed, the body returns to normal operations.

The adrenal glands can also be activated by long-term stress, such as pressure from school or a job. This stress can cause artery blockages, which can lead to a heart attack. Long-term stress can cause nervous system disorders, such as headaches and high blood pressure.

**Thinking Critically** How can the endocrine system affect the other systems in your body?

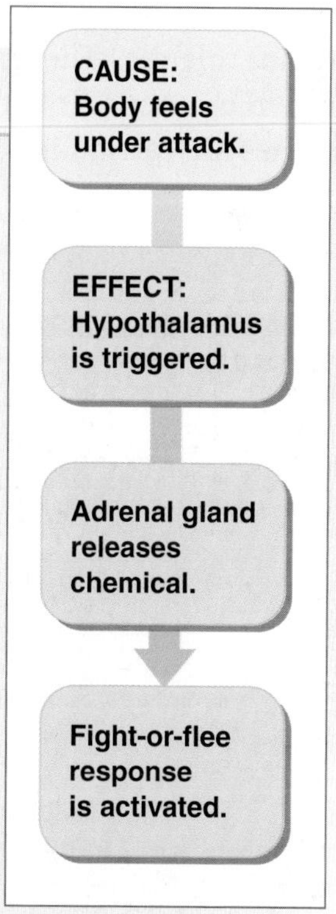


▲ **Figure 18-20** The fight-or-flee response

# 18-8 What are hormones?

## *Objectives*

Define hormones. Explain some of the jobs of hormones.

## *Key Terms*

**hormone** (HAWR-mohn)**:** chemical substance that regulates body functions

**target cell:** cell that responds to a hormone's chemical structure

**Hormones** The chemical substances made by the endocrine glands are called **hormones.** Hormones affect many of your body's functions. For example, growth hormone, which is made by the pituitary gland, controls how fast and how much you grow.

What activates hormones? When the hypothalamus senses the need for a specific hormone in the body, it stimulates the pituitary gland. The pituitary gland then releases its hormones. These hormones activate other endocrine glands. These glands, in turn, release their own hormones into the bloodstream. Because hormones are carried in the bloodstream, they can control tissues and organs far from the glands that produced them.

Not all hormones affect all tissues and organs. Instead, hormones only affect tissues and organs with specific target cells. **Target cells** respond to a hormone's chemical structure. Hormones travel throughout the body until they find the target cell that responds to them.

1 **DEFINE:** What is a hormone?

**Jobs of Hormones** Growth hormone is only one of many hormones made by your body. Hormones may speed up a body function or slow it down. Other hormones do other jobs. Insulin (IHN-suh-lihn) is a hormone made by the pancreas. Insulin is needed to keep a balanced amount of sugar in the blood. Still other hormones regulate other glands. Figure 18-21 shows some of the different endocrine glands, the hormones they produce, and what each hormone does.

2 **INFER:** What do you think would happen if a person had too much growth hormone?

| HORMONES AND WHAT THEY DO | | |
|---|---|---|
| **Gland** | **Hormone** | **Job of Hormone** |
| Adrenal | Adrenaline | Controls muscle reaction and raises heart rate and blood pressure |
| Ovaries | Estrogen and Progesterone | Controls physical and reproductive development in women |
| Pancreas | Insulin | Controls blood sugar levels |
| Parathyroid | Parathyroid hormone | Controls the amount of calcium and phosphorus in the blood |
| Pineal | Melatonin | Helps regulate pituitary gland |
| Pituitary | ACTH | Controls the release of hormones from the adrenal glands |
| Pituitary | Growth hormone | Controls the growth of bones; controls metabolism |
| Testes | Testosterone | Controls physical and reproductive development in men |
| Thymus | Thymosin | Controls the growth of certain white blood cells |
| Thyroid | Thyroxine | Controls rate of metabolism and of body growth |

◀ **Figure 18-21** Different glands produce different hormones.

**Reproductive Hormones** Some hormones control the development of reproductive organs. The glands that control reproductive organs are different in men and women. Men have glands called testes (TEHS-teez). The testes produce a hormone called testosterone (tehs-TAHS-tuhr-ohn). Females have glands called ovaries (OH-vuh-reez). Ovaries produce hormones called estrogen (EHS-truh-juhn) and progesterone (proh-JEHS-tuhr-ohn).

3 STATE: What hormone do the testes produce?

## CHECKING CONCEPTS

1. A chemical substance that regulates body functions is called a __________.
2. Insulin is made by the __________.
3. The two endocrine glands that produce substances that develop reproductive organs are testes and __________.
4. Testes are glands found only in __________.
5. Ovaries are glands found only in __________.

## THINKING CRITICALLY

6. EXPLAIN: How are insulin and blood sugar level related?
7. APPLY: What is the job of growth hormone?
8. CLASSIFY: Which hormones are found in both males and females? Which are found in only one gender or the other?
9. INFER: What health problems might someone have if the pituitary gland produced too much or too little growth hormone?
10. ANALYZE: What hormone is needed to release adrenal hormones?
11. ANALYZE: What gland produces thymosin?

## BUILDING LANGUAGE ARTS SKILLS

***Using Prefixes*** The pancreas is part of the digestive system. It is also an endocrine gland that secretes the hormone insulin. It is the only part of the human body that can be considered an endocrine and exocrine gland. Use a dictionary to discover the meaning of the prefixes *endo-* and *exo-*. Then, find out why the pancreas is considered both an endocrine and an exocrine gland.

## *How Do They Know That?*

### TREATING DIABETES WITH INSULIN

▲ **Figure 18-22** Frederick Banting

If too little insulin is produced by the pancreas, an excess of sugar builds up in the blood. This condition is called diabetes mellitus. Without proper treatment, this can lead to blindness, poor circulation, and even death. Until 1921, however, scientists did not know how to increase the amount of insulin in diabetics.

In 1921, Canadian scientist Frederick Banting and medical student Charles Best isolated the part of the pancreas that produces insulin. They extracted insulin from the pancreas of a dog. They then tested it on dogs whose pancreases had been removed. These dogs were diabetics. When the dogs received injections of insulin, they recovered from their diabetes. Banting and Best's discovery led to a treatment for millions of people living with diabetes.

In 1923, Banting received a Nobel Prize in physiology and medicine for his work. Upset that Best was not honored for his contribution, Banting shared his award equally with Best.

**Thinking Critically** How did Banting and Best's work improve life for diabetics?

### Integrating Art

# THE Big IDEA

## How do we respond to artistic expression?

Is music just sound, created by vibration? Are poems just words that we read or hear? Are paintings just strokes of color on a canvas? Or are they much more?

We experience art and we react to it. This ability is possible because of our nervous system. Our sense organs take in the messages. Different parts of the brain process these messages. However, the brain does not process all sensory stimuli the same way. Imaging technology shows different levels of activity in the brain when a person hears music as compared to other sounds. The brain treats music without words differently than music with lyrics.

An experiment published in 1993 seemed to show that listening to classical music could improve memory. The idea became very popular. One state gave out classical music CDs to every new mother. The research was later found to be flawed.

Scientists have learned which parts, or lobes, of the brain are involved in each of the senses. Brain research has come far, but it does not answer key questions about art. How does art create strong emotions? Why do we like one work but not another? Many artists and art lovers are in no hurry to learn these answers. Enjoying art is enough.

Look at the boxes of text that appear on this page and the next. They point out some art forms and how we sense them. Follow the directions in the Science Log to learn more about "the big idea."✦

### Crafts and Touch

Pottery, textiles, and furniture can be beautiful to look at. These art forms are also tempting to touch. To appreciate them, we want to feel the shape and the texture of the pot, the smoothness of the wood, or the softness of a silk kimono. The parietal lobe interprets touch.

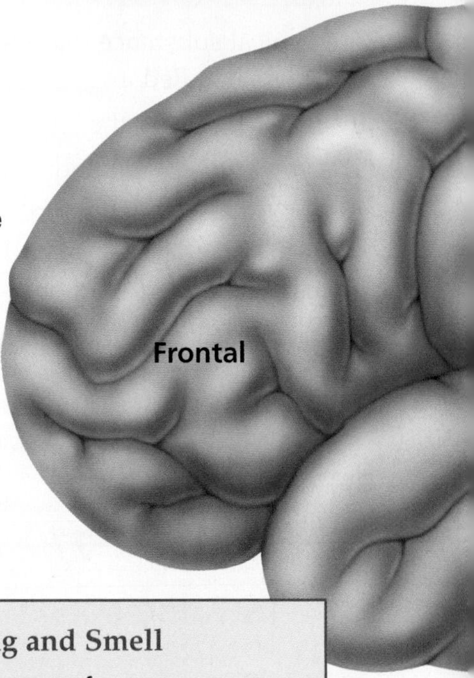


**Figure 18-23** ▶
The brain is divided into sections called lobes. The lobes involved in each form of art are labeled.

### Floral Arranging and Smell

For many years the art of flower arranging has dealt primarily with color. A new trend has developed in recent years, however. Florists and home gardeners are now paying a lot more attention to smell when creating arrangements. Florists can build arrangements that use flowers with specific types of smell, such as sweet, spicy, and fruity smells. They can also create arrangements that relate to the smells of the season. Examples of flowers with very distinct smells are lilac, hyacinth, sweet pea, and peony. The temporal lobe interprets smell.

### Culinary Arts and Taste

Culinary art is the art and science of good eating. Many chefs are creative artists. The kitchen is their art studio. Of course, they want to create food that tastes good. But they pay attention to other things, too: how it looks, how it smells, and how it feels inside your mouth. The parietal lobe interprets tastes.

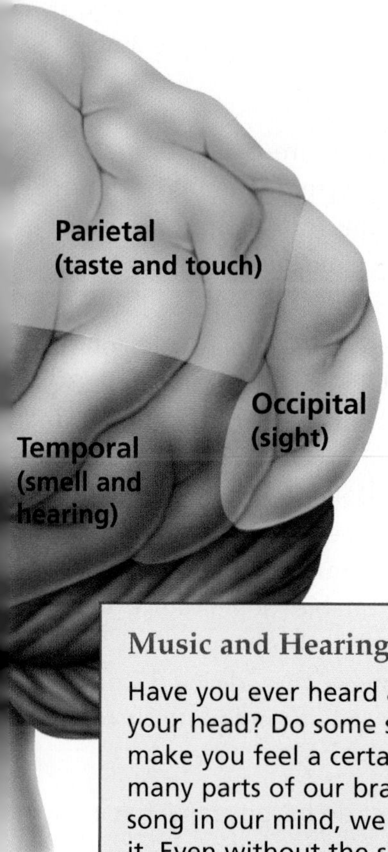


### Painting and Sight

The artist George Seurat used a technique called pointillism. He painted dots of different colors next to each other. The color the brain sees is different from the dots. For example, when a red dot is next to a green dot, the brain sees yellow. This is called optical mixing. Scientists understand how our eyes and brains work together to see art. The occipital lobe interprets sights. It is harder to know how we decide what paintings we like and don't like.

### Music and Hearing

Have you ever heard a song over and over in your head? Do some songs or types of music make you feel a certain way? Music affects many parts of our brain. When we hear a song in our mind, we are creating an image of it. Even without the sound, the temporal lobe reacts. The emotional power of music is not yet fully understood.

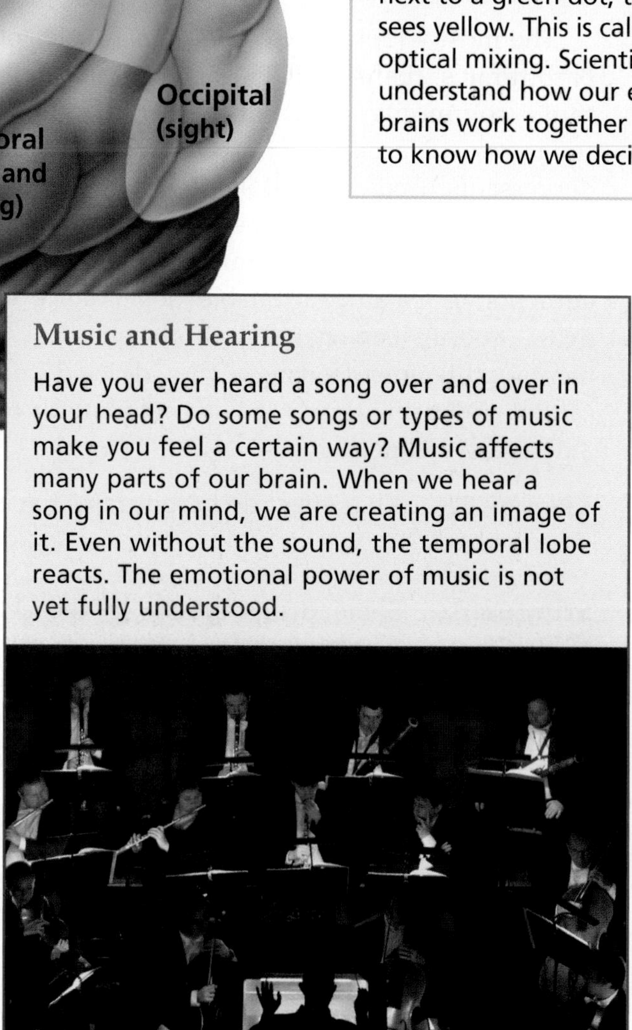

**WRITING ACTIVITY**

**Science Log**

Look at the arts illustrated on these two pages. Which kind of art interests you? In your science log, research and write about one work of art. Describe how you experience this work and how it engages your senses. Start your search at www.conceptsandchallenges.com.

# 18-9 How do some drugs affect the body?

### Objective

Describe the effects of some drugs on the body.

### Key Terms

**drug:** a chemical substance that causes a change in the body

**depressant** (dee-PREHS-uhnt)**:** drug that slows down the central nervous system

**addiction:** uncontrollable dependence on a drug

**stimulant** (STIHM-yuh-luhnt)**:** drug that speeds up the central nervous system

**hallucinogen** (huh-LOO-sih-nuh-juhn)**:** drug that causes a person to see, hear, smell, taste, and feel things in an altered way

**inhalant:** everyday product that is inhaled and used as a drug

**Drugs** A **drug** is a chemical substance that causes a change in the body. Some drugs cause a physical change in the body. Some drugs cause changes in behavior. Drugs can be injected into the body or they can be inhaled, swallowed, or placed on the skin. Many drugs produce abnormal changes that stress the body.

1 **DEFINE:** What is a drug?

**Drugs for Medical Use** There are two types of drugs for medical use. Drugs that can be bought only with a doctor's written permission are called prescription drugs. Antibiotics are an example of prescription drugs. Before writing a prescription, your doctor considers your illness, age, medical history, and your body frame. A prescription should be used only in the way your doctor prescribes it.

Some medical drugs, such as aspirin and antacids, can be bought without a doctor's prescription. These are called over-the-counter drugs.

2 **EXPLAIN:** Why shouldn't you use a drug prescribed for someone else?

**Misuse of Drugs** The improper use of a drug is called drug abuse. There are many ways that drugs can be abused. For example, using too much of a drug or using a drug for the wrong reasons are forms of drug abuse. The use of illegal drugs is also drug abuse. The consequences of drug abuse are listed in Figure 18-24 on page 439. Many times prolonged drug abuse leads to death. Sometimes death can occur after only one use of a drug.

3 **INFER:** Why do you think some people abuse drugs?

**Depressants** **Depressants** are drugs that slow down the central nervous system. They slow down the heartbeat and breathing rate. Large amounts and abuse of depressants can cause a person to go into a coma or even die.

The most widely abused depressant is alcohol. Barbiturates (bahr-BIHCH-uhr-ihts) are depressants commonly used in sleeping pills and sedatives. Narcotics (nahr-KAHT-ihks) are depressants used as painkillers. If barbiturates or narcotics are used over a period of time, the user may develop an **addiction** to the drug. An addiction is an uncontrollable dependence on a drug. People can develop both physical and mental addictions to drugs. The addicted person cannot stop using the drug without going through a period of sickness.

4 **DESCRIBE:** What effect do barbiturates have on the body?

**Stimulants** Some drugs speed up the action of the central nervous system. These drugs are called **stimulants.** In many ways, the effects of stimulants are the opposite of those of depressants. Stimulants speed up a person's heartbeat and rate of breathing. Cocaine is a commonly abused stimulant. Crack is a purified form of cocaine that is extremely dangerous. You may be surprised to learn that caffeine also is a stimulant. Caffeine is found in coffee, tea, cola, and chocolate.

| POSSIBLE SIDE EFFECTS OF ILLEGAL DRUGS | |
|---|---|
| **Depressants** | **Hallucinogens** |
| Sleepiness<br>Respiratory problems<br>Inability to concentrate<br>Coma<br>Death | Increased heart rate and blood pressure<br>Difficulty sleeping<br>Loss of muscle coordination<br>Seizures<br>Heart and lung failure<br>Violent behavior |
| **Stimulants** | **Inhalants** |
| Increased heart rate and blood pressure<br>Difficulty sleeping<br>Respiratory problems<br>Stroke<br>Violent behavior<br>Heart attack<br>Death | Stomach pains<br>Nosebleeds<br>Damage to liver, lungs, and kidneys<br>Brain damage<br>Involuntary urination<br>Irregular heartbeat<br>Death |

▲ **Figure 18-24** Dangers of drug use

Amphetamines (am-FET-uh-meens) also are known as "uppers" or pep pills. Sometimes, doctors prescribe amphetamines to treat some nervous-system disorders. Other times, amphetamines are used to prevent drowsiness. When amphetamines are abused, they can cause violent reactions, convulsions, and even death.

5 CONTRAST: How does the effect of a stimulant differ from the effect of a depressant?

**Hallucinogens** Some drugs change the way a person receives information through the senses. For example, they cause a person to see, hear, touch, smell, feel, and taste things in an altered way. These drugs are called **hallucinogens.** Hallucinogens often make a person feel panicky or threatened. For this reason, people who take hallucinogens often are dangerous to themselves and others. LSD and PCP are two commonly abused hallucinogens.

Marijuana is the most widely abused illegal drug in the United States. It comes from a plant and is usually smoked. Marijuana has mind-altering effects. It also slows down the activity of the central nervous system. For this reason, sometimes marijuana is also classified as a depressant.

6 EXPLAIN: What effect do hallucinogens have on the body?

**Abusing Poisons** Some drugs are products people use every day, such as hair spray, spray paint, glue, or gasoline. Some people inhale these products because of their strong vapors, or smells. Everyday products that someone inhales and uses as a drug are called **inhalants.** Inhalants are often stimulants. Some of the vapors in inhalants stay in the body for a long time. Inhalants can break down myelin, the protective covering of some nerve cells. This can cause immediate damage to the brain. Inhalants also cause serious damage to the liver and kidneys. Inhalants are poisons and can cause death.

7 DEFINE: What are inhalants?

## ✓ CHECKING CONCEPTS

1. What are two types of drugs with medical uses that you can buy over the counter?
2. What effect do depressants have on the body?
3. What group of depressants often are used as painkillers?
4. What effect do stimulants have on the body?

## THINKING CRITICALLY

5. INFER: What effect does coffee have on the central nervous system?
6. RELATE: Which drug, a barbiturate or cocaine, would most likely make a person feel wide awake? Explain your answer.

### Web InfoSearch

**DARE** Many communities have drug abuse prevention programs, such as DARE (Drug Abuse Resistance Education). In these programs, police officers visit classrooms and inform students of the dangers of drug abuse.

**SEARCH:** Use the Internet to find out about drug abuse prevention programs in your community. Then, make a poster encouraging students to stay off drugs. Start your search at www.conceptsandchallenges.com. Some key search words are **DARE, drug prevention,** and **drug abuse prevention.**

# 18-10 How does alcohol affect the body?

*Objective*

Describe the effects alcohol has on the body.

*Key Terms*

**cirrhosis** (suh-ROH-sihs)**:** liver disorder that may be caused by the excessive use of alcohol

**alcoholic** (al-kuh-HAWL-ihk)**:** person who is dependent on alcohol

**Ethyl Alcohol** One of the most commonly abused drugs is ethyl (ETH-uhl) alcohol. Ethyl alcohol is the alcohol that is in beverages such as beer, wine, and whiskey. Alcohol is a very dangerous drug. Most people think that alcohol is a stimulant. However, alcohol is a depressant. It slows down the action of the central nervous system.

1 EXPLAIN: What effect does alcohol have on the body?

**Alcohol and the Brain** The amount of alcohol present in the bloodstream is called Blood Alcohol Concentration (BAC). The effect of alcohol on the body increases as the Blood Alcohol Concentration increases.

▲ **Figure 18-26** Drinking impairs driving skills.

When people drink alcohol, their body systems slow down. They think and react more slowly. Their movements become clumsy.

2 INFER: Why do you think it is dangerous for a person who has been drinking to drive a car?

**Alcohol and the Body** Alcohol affects many organs of the body. If a person does not drink very much, or very often, the effects of alcohol wear off after a period of time. However, if the drinking continues over a period of time, the body can be harmed. The liver can be greatly affected by

**BLOOD ALCOHOL CONCENTRATION (BAC) AND ITS EFFECTS**

| Drinks per Hour* | BAC (Present) | Effects |
|---|---|---|
| 1 | 0.02 – 0.03 | Feeling of relaxation |
| 2 | 0.05 – 0.06 | Slight loss of coordination |
| 3 | 0.08 – 0.09 | Loss of coordination; trouble talking and thinking; legal intoxication in most states |
| 4 | 0.11 – 0.12 | Slower reaction time; lack of judgment |
| 7 | 0.20 | Difficulty thinking; loss of motor skills |
| 14 | 0.40 | Unconsciousness; possible vomiting |
| 17 | 0.50 | Deep coma; possible death |

*Based on a male weighing 120 lbs

◄ **Figure 18-25**

alcohol. Large amounts of alcohol taken over a long period of time can destroy the liver tissues. The liver then loses its ability to carry out its functions. This condition is called **cirrhosis.** Cirrhosis of the liver often leads to death.

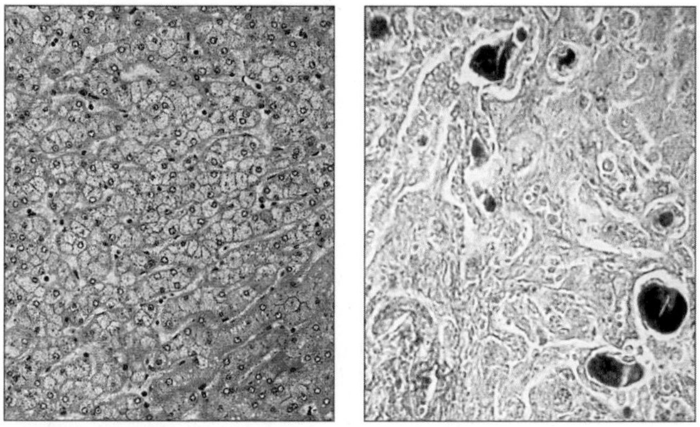

▲ **Figure 18-27** The liver on the left is healthy. The liver on the right has cirrhosis.

**3 IDENTIFY:** What is cirrhosis of the liver?

**Alcoholics** Alcohol is addictive for some people. These people drink more and more alcohol as time goes by. They become dependent on alcohol. A person who cannot control his or her drinking of alcohol is called an **alcoholic.** Alcoholism is a disease because it causes harmful changes in body organs. Many alcoholics get help from groups such as Alcoholics Anonymous or AL-ATEEN. There are also support groups for family members of alcoholics.

**4 DESCRIBE:** What is an alcoholic?

## CHECKING CONCEPTS

1. What kind of alcohol is in alcoholic drinks?
2. What effect does alcohol have on body systems?
3. How does a person act after drinking alcohol?
4. What effect does drinking over a long period of time have on the body?
5. What is a person who is dependent on alcohol called?

## THINKING CRITICALLY

6. **RELATE:** A person drinks a glass of wine every night before dinner. Is this person an alcoholic? Explain your answer.

## *Real-Life Science*

### BREATHALYZERS

Drinking alcohol seriously impairs a person's ability to drive. So, it is very important for law enforcement officials to be able to give drivers a test to determine if they have been drinking alcohol and how high their BAC is. It would be impossible for law enforcement officials to take a blood sample from every driver they suspect of being drunk. Instead, they use a device called a breathalyzer to measure the amount of alcohol in a driver's breath.

▲ **Figure 18-28** Breathalyzers measure the amount of alcohol in a person's blood.

How do breathalyzers work? Alcohol is not digested. Instead, it is absorbed into the bloodstream. As blood flows through the lungs, some of the alcohol leaves with the air that is exhaled. Since the amount of alcohol in the breath depends on the amount of alcohol in the blood, a breathalyzer can be used to find the BAC amount in a person's blood.

**Thinking Critically** How do breathalyzers help keep people safe?

# Chapter 18 Challenges

## Chapter Summary

**Lesson 18-1**

- The nervous system controls all of the body's activities. It is made up of the brain, the spinal cord, and nerves.

**Lesson 18-2**

- The main job of the brain is to receive, interpret, and react to messages from inside and outside the body.

**Lesson 18-3**

- Any action that causes a response is a stimulus.
- An automatic response to a stimulus is called a **reflex.** The path of a message in a reflex is called a **reflex arc.**

**Lesson 18-4**

- The **sense organs** are the eyes, nose, skin, ears, and tongue. Sense organs are used to receive stimuli from the environment.

**Lesson 18-5**

- Different parts of the eye work together to help you see. The main parts of the eye are the **cornea, iris, pupil, lens, retina,** and optic nerve.

**Lesson 18-6**

- The ears are the sense organs of hearing. The main parts of the ear are the outer ear, the ear bones, and the **cochlea.**

**Lesson 18-7**

- A **gland** is an organ that makes substances used or released by the body.
- The job of the endocrine system is to help control body functions.

**Lesson 18-8**

- **Hormones,** produced in **endocrine glands,** control many of the body's activities.

**Lesson 18-9**

- A **drug** is a chemical substance that causes a change in the body. People who use drugs can become addicted to them.

**Lesson 18-10**

- Alcohol slows down body systems.

## Key Term Challenges

addiction (p. 438)
alcoholic (p. 440)
axon (p. 418)
brainstem (p. 420)
cerebellum (p. 420)
cerebrum (p. 420)
cirrhosis (p. 440)
cochlea (p. 430)
cornea (p. 428)
dendrite (p. 418)
depressant (p. 438)
drug (p. 438)
eardrum (p. 430)
endocrine gland (p. 432)
exocrine gland (p. 432)
gland (p. 432)
hallucinogen (p. 438)
hormone (p. 434)
hypothalamus (p. 432)
inhalant (p. 438)
iris (p. 428)
lens (p. 428)
medulla (p. 420)
neuron (p. 418)
pupil (p. 428)
receptor (p. 422)
reflex (p. 422)
reflex arc (p. 422)
retina (p. 428)
sense organ (p. 424)
stimulant (p. 438)
synapse (p. 418)
target cell (p. 434)

MATCHING **Write the Key Term from above that best matches each description.**

1. clear covering at the front of the eye
2. changes vibrations into nerve signals
3. receives stimuli from the environment
4. controls heartbeat and breathing rate
5. makes chemical substances used or released by the body
6. carries messages away from a nerve cell

IDENTIFYING WORD RELATIONSHIPS **Explain how the words in each pair are related. Write your answers in complete sentences.**

7. endocrine gland, hormone
8. axon, dendrite
9. cerebellum, cerebrum
10. reflex, reflex arc
11. response, stimulus
12. alcoholic, cirrhosis

## Content Challenges TEST PREP

**MULTIPLE CHOICE Write the letter of the term or phrase that best completes each statement.**

**1.** The lens of the eye focuses images on the
**a.** cornea.
**b.** pupil.
**c.** iris.
**d.** retina.

**2.** Insulin is made by the
**a.** pituitary gland.
**b.** pancreas.
**c.** ovaries.
**d.** thyroid.

**3.** The smallest part of the brain is the
**a.** medulla.
**b.** cerebrum.
**c.** cerebellum.
**d.** skull.

**4.** Adrenaline controls
**a.** muscle reaction.
**b.** growth.
**c.** the amount of calcium in the blood.
**d.** blood sugar levels.

**5.** The cochlea is found in the
**a.** outer ear.
**b.** middle ear.
**c.** inner ear.
**d.** eardrum.

**6.** The "thermostat" of the body is the
**a.** cerebrum.
**b.** hypothalamus.
**c.** pituitary gland.
**d.** cerebellum.

**7.** The nervous system is made up of the brain, the spinal cord, and
**a.** muscles.
**b.** glands.
**c.** nerves.
**d.** the skull.

**8.** The largest cells in the body are
**a.** axons.
**b.** dendrites.
**c.** hormones.
**d.** neurons.

**9.** Drugs that cause people to see things that do not exist are
**a.** sleeping pills.
**b.** barbiturates.
**c.** depressants.
**d.** hallucinogens.

**10.** Cirrhosis of the liver can be caused by
**a.** inhalants.
**b.** alcohol.
**c.** hallucinogens.
**d.** stimulants.

**TRUE/FALSE Write *true* if the statement is true. If the statement is false, change the underlined term to make the statement true.**

**11.** Estrogen and progesterone are produced by the ovaries.

**12.** The amount of light entering the eye is controlled by the cornea.

**13.** The ear responds to light waves.

**14.** The brain is connected to the spinal cord by the medulla.

**15.** The path of a message in a reflex is called a synapse.

**16.** Reflexes are controlled by the brain.

**17.** Growth hormone is made by the pituitary gland.

**18.** Alcohol is classified as a depressant drug.

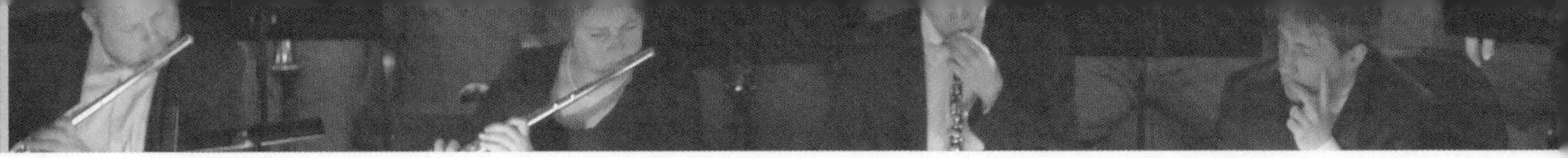

## *Concept Challenges* TEST PREP

**WRITTEN RESPONSE** **Answer each of the following questions in complete sentences.**

1. **APPLY:** How do reflexes help an organism survive?
2. **COMPARE:** How is the eye like a camera?
3. **COMPARE:** How is the spinal cord like a tree trunk?
4. **EXPLAIN:** How do the nervous system and the endocrine system work together?
5. **INFER:** How do you think a drug addiction affects a person's life?

**INTERPRETING A DIAGRAM** **Use Figure 18-29 to answer the following questions.**

6. What does thyroxine control?
7. What are two pituitary hormones?
8. What hormone is needed to regulate the pituitary gland?
9. What gland produces insulin?
10. What minerals are affected by parathyroid hormone?
11. What health problems might a person have if that person's thymus gland produced too little thymosin?
12. What three things does adrenaline control?

| HORMONES AND WHAT THEY DO | | |
|---|---|---|
| **Gland** | **Hormone** | **Job of Hormone** |
| Adrenal | Adrenaline | Controls muscle reaction and raises heart rate and blood pressure |
| Ovaries | Estrogen and Progesterone | Controls physical and reproductive development in women |
| Pancreas | Insulin | Controls blood sugar levels |
| Parathyroid | Parathyroid hormone | Controls the amount of calcium and phosphorus in the blood |
| Pineal | Melatonin | Helps regulate pituitary gland |
| Pituitary | ACTH | Controls the release of hormones from the adrenal glands |
| Pituitary | Growth hormone | Controls the growth of bones; controls metabolism |
| Testes | Testosterone | Controls physical and reproductive development in men |
| Thymus | Thymosin | Controls the growth of certain white blood cells |
| Thyroid | Thyroxine | Controls rate of metabolism and of body growth |

◄ **Figure 18-29**

# Chapter 19 Reproduction & Development

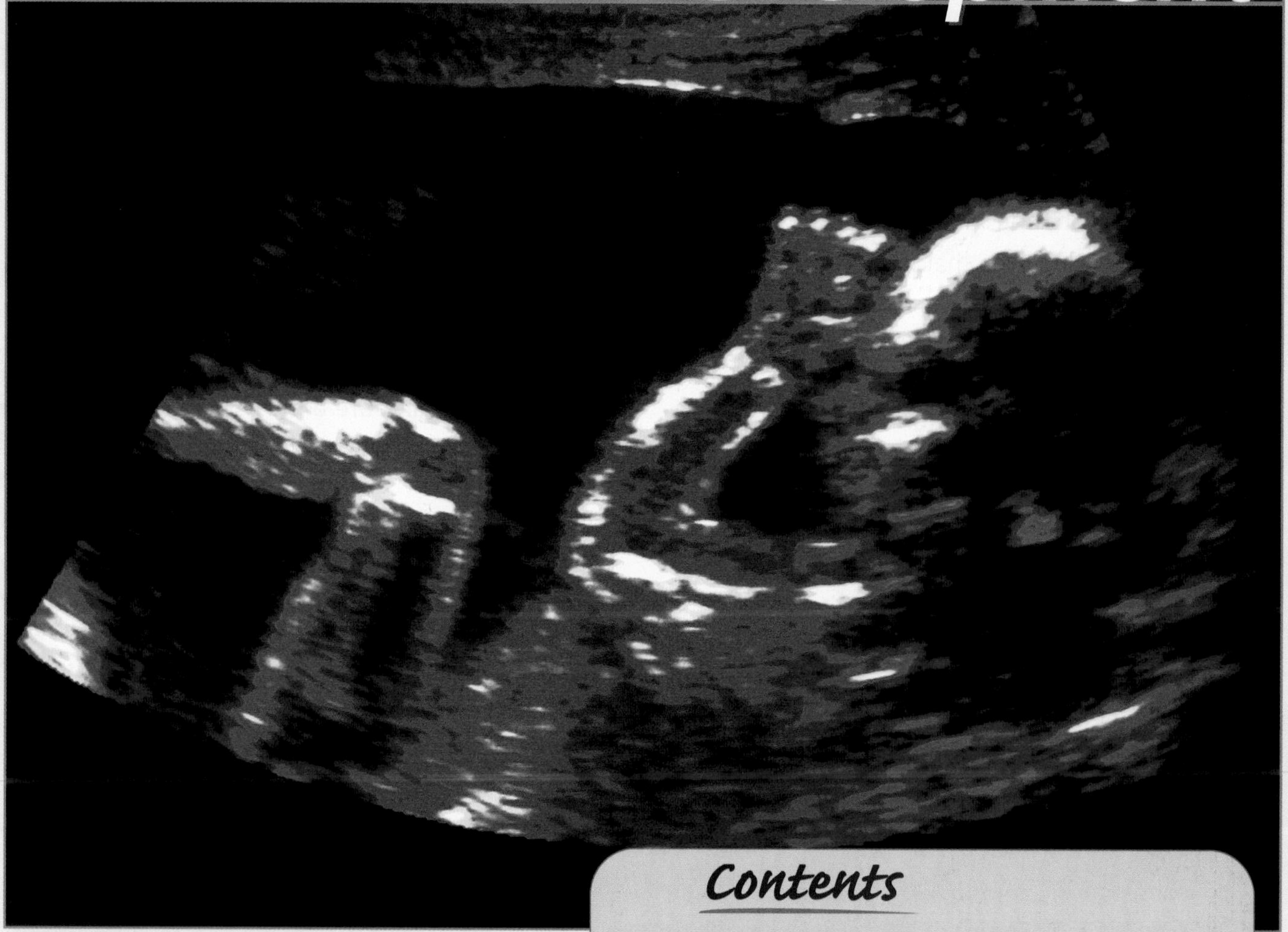

▲ **Figure 19-1** This is an ultrasound picture of a fetus in its sixth month of development.

In what ways have you changed since you were an infant? You can probably think of many. You changed in even more ways during the time before you were born. A human fetus develops inside its mother over a nine-month period. During this time, a complex series of changes takes place. From one cell comes a whole new organism, made up of about 75 trillion cells, each with different functions.

► What do you think are some of the changes a newborn baby goes through?

## Contents

# 19-1 What are the parts of the female reproductive system?

*Objective*

Describe the female reproductive system.

*Key Terms*

**ovary:** organ of the female reproductive system that produces hormones and eggs

**progesterone:** hormone that prepares the uterus for pregnancy

**estrogen:** hormone that helps regulate the menstrual cycle

**oviduct** (OH-vih-dukt)**:** long tube between the ovary and the uterus

**uterus** (YOOT-uhr-uhs)**:** organ in which an embryo develops

**cervix** (SUHR-vihks)**:** narrow end of the uterus

**vagina** (vuh-JY-nuh)**:** birth canal

**Reproductive Systems** Most systems of the body are the same in males and females. This is not true of reproductive systems. The male and female reproductive systems are different. All the organs of the female reproductive system are located inside the body. In the male reproductive system, some organs are inside the body, while others are located in a pouch on the outside of the body. The main job of both the male and female reproductive systems is to produce offspring.

1 **COMPARE:** How is the reproductive system different from other body systems?

**Ovaries** The **ovaries** are the main organs of the female reproductive system. Ovaries are egg-shaped structures. Females are born with two ovaries. One ovary lies on each side of the female's body.

The ovaries contain two different kinds of cells. One kind produces the hormones **progesterone** and **estrogen**. Progesterone helps prepare the uterus for pregnancy. Estrogen helps regulate a woman's menstrual cycle. The other kind of cell produces eggs. Eggs are female reproductive cells.

2 **DESCRIBE:** What do the ovaries produce?

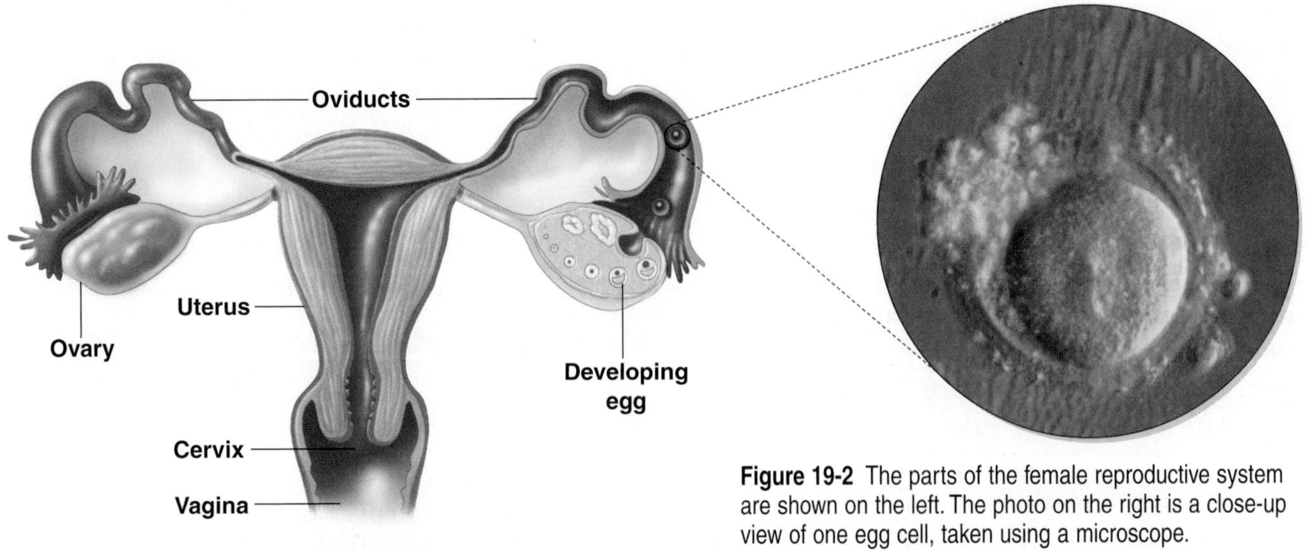


**Figure 19-2** The parts of the female reproductive system are shown on the left. The photo on the right is a close-up view of one egg cell, taken using a microscope.

**Pathway of Eggs** Study the female reproductive system shown in Figure 19-2. A long tube called an **oviduct** lies near each ovary. The oviduct carries eggs to the uterus. The **uterus** is a hollow organ with thick, muscular walls. This is where an embryo develops.

The lower end of the uterus is narrower. This part of the uterus is called the **cervix**. The cervix connects the uterus to the **vagina**. The vagina is the opening through which a baby passes during birth. The vagina is also called the birth canal.

3 **EXPLAIN:** What is the function of the oviduct?

## CHECKING CONCEPTS

1. Which organs of the female reproductive system produce hormones?
2. What are female sex cells called?
3. What is the long tube that carries an egg from the ovary to the uterus?
4. What is the narrow end of the uterus?
5. What is another name for the vagina?

## THINKING CRITICALLY

6. **RELATE:** Through which structures of the female reproductive system does a baby pass?
7. **INFER:** The walls of the uterus are flexible and can expand and contract. How does this help a developing embryo?
8. **INFER:** Why is the vagina also called the birth canal?

## BUILDING LANGUAGE ARTS SKILLS

***Applying Definitions*** Look up the meaning of the prefix *ovi*. Then look up the meaning of the word *duct*. Relate these definitions to the function of the oviduct. List and define several other terms that contain these word parts.

## *Science and Technology*

### TREATMENT OF OVARIAN CYSTS

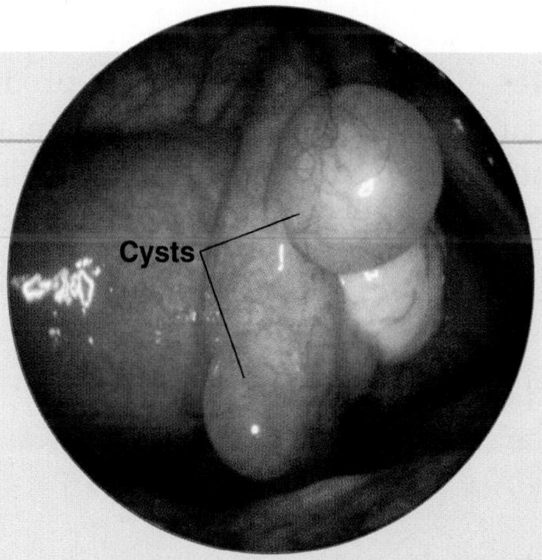


▲ **Figure 19-3** Ovarian cysts can be removed by laparoscopy.

An ovarian cyst is a fluid-filled sac or a round, baglike membrane in the ovary. Some ovarian cysts form quite normally every month. They contain an egg that is ripening, or getting ready to be released to travel through an oviduct to the uterus. After the egg is released, the cyst normally shrinks and disappears within one to three months.

Sometimes the cyst releases the ripening egg but does not shrink. Instead, it may grow as large as a baseball. A sonogram, or a picture made by using sound waves, can be used to determine whether a cyst is a fluid-filled sac, an infection, or a tumor. Perhaps the growth may even be a cancerous tumor. Most ovarian cysts are not cancerous.

Cysts can be removed by surgery. Often this procedure is done by laparoscopy, an operation in which a very small incision is made and a laparoscope is inserted. A laparoscope is a lighted viewing tube that is like a flexible telescope. If tests show that the cyst is cancerous, both ovaries and the uterus may have to be removed.

**Thinking Critically** If ovarian cysts form normally every month, why might a doctor want to follow up with another examination or a sonogram when one is found?

# 19-2 What are the parts of the male reproductive system?

## *Objective*

Describe the male reproductive system.

## *Key Terms*

**testis,** *pl.* **testes:** organ of the male reproductive system that produces hormones and sperm

**scrotum** (SKROHT-uhm)**:** pocket of skin that protects and holds the testes

**testosterone** (tehs-TAHS-tuhr-ohn)**:** hormone produced in the testes

**epididymis** (ep-uh-DID-i-mihs)**:** coiled tube that stores sperm

**urethra** (yoo-REE-thruh)**:** tube that carries urine, and sperm for males, outside of the body

**The Testes** The organs of the male reproductive system that produce hormones and sperm are the **testes**. The testes are egg-shaped structures located outside the body cavity. The testes rest in a pocket of skin called the **scrotum**. The organs of the male reproductive system are shown in Figure 19-4.

1 IDENTIFY: What are the organs that produce hormones and sperm?

**Testosterone** Two kinds of cells are located in the testes. One type produces **testosterone**, a hormone that controls the development of secondary sex characteristics. In a male, these characteristics include a deeper voice and the growth of body hair.

Testosterone also causes male sex cells to develop inside the testes. Male sex cells are called sperm. Sperm are stored in a coiled tube called the **epididymis.** One end of the epididymis connects to the testes. The other end connects to a longer tube that extends upward into the body cavity from the testes.

2 DESCRIBE: What substances are produced inside the testes?

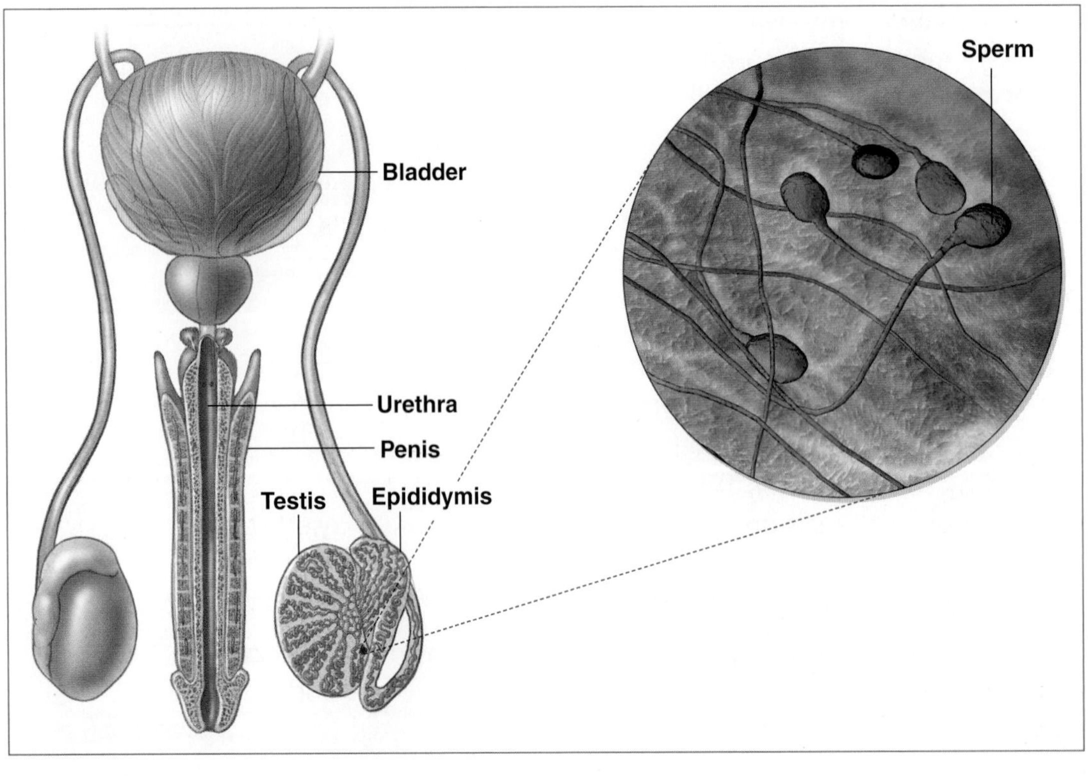


◀ **Figure 19-4** The male reproductive system is shown on the left. The photo on the right shows several sperm cells.

**The Urethra** The **urethra** is part of the excretory system. Urine made in the kidneys travels from the bladder to the outside of the body through the urethra. The urethra is surrounded and protected by the penis.

In males, the urethra performs another job. It is the passageway through which sperm leave a male's body. For this reason, the urethra is considered to be a part of the male reproductive system as well.

3 **EXPLAIN:** Why is the urethra part of two different body systems in males?

## CHECKING CONCEPTS

1. The organs of the male reproductive system that produce hormones and sperm are the __________.
2. The testes are suspended within a pocket of skin called the __________.
3. One kind of cell in the testes produces the hormone __________.
4. Male sex cells are called __________.
5. In males, both sperm and urine leave the body through the __________.
6. The testes produce both testosterone and __________.

## THINKING CRITICALLY

7. **COMPARE:** How is the shape of the testes similar to the shape of the ovaries?
8. **RELATE:** To what two male body systems does the urethra belong?

## BUILDING SCIENCE SKILLS

***Organizing Information*** When you organize information, you put the information in some kind of order. A table is one way to organize information. Make a table that describes the parts of the male reproductive system. Include a description of the function of each part in the table.

*Real-Life Science*

## SEXUALLY TRANSMITTED DISEASES

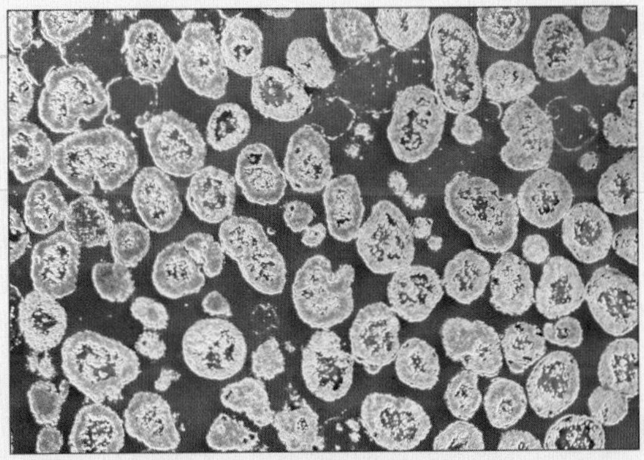

▲ **Figure 19-5** Many sexually transmitted diseases are caused by bacteria such as these Gonorrhea.

A disease that can be passed from one person to another is called a contagious disease. Some contagious diseases are spread by pathogens. Pathogens are harmful microscopic organisms such as bacteria and viruses.

A few contagious diseases are spread through sexual contact with an infected person. These diseases are called sexually transmitted diseases. The pathogens that cause sexually transmitted diseases can live only inside a human body. Outside the body, these pathogens die. Sexually transmitted diseases are not spread by casual contact.

Gonorrhea (gahn-uh-REE-uh) and syphilis (SIHF-uh-lihs) are two sexually transmitted diseases. These diseases usually are treated with penicillin or other antibiotics. Many cases of gonorrhea and syphilis are cured through early diagnosis and treatment.

AIDS is also a sexually transmitted disease. HIV, the virus that causes AIDS, attacks an infected person's immune system, so the person cannot fight the disease. There is no known cure for AIDS.

**Thinking Critically** How can a person avoid getting a sexually transmitted disease?

# 19-3 What is the menstrual cycle?

*Objective*

Describe the menstrual cycle.

*Key Terms*

**puberty** (PYOO-burh-tee)**:** time at which a person becomes sexually mature

**menstrual** (MEHN-struhl) **cycle:** monthly cycle of change that occurs in the female reproductive system

**ovulation** (ahv-yuh-LAY-shuhn)**:** release of a mature egg from the ovary

**menstruation** (mehn-stroo-AY-shuhn)**:** process by which blood and tissue from the lining of the uterus break apart and leave the body

**Menstrual Cycle** When a female is born, her body contains all the egg cells she will ever have. However, the eggs are not mature, or fully developed. The eggs do not begin to mature until the female reaches puberty. **Puberty** is the time at which a person becomes sexually mature. Puberty generally begins between the ages of 10 and 14. In females, puberty is often marked by the beginning of the **menstrual cycle.** The menstrual cycle is a monthly cycle of change that occurs in the female reproductive system. Look at Figure 19-6 as you read about the cycle.

1 IDENTIFY: What is the menstrual cycle?

**Ovulation** The menstrual cycle occurs every 28 to 32 days. It is triggered by the release of hormones in the female reproductive system. These hormones come from both the reproductive system and several glands of the endocrine system. They work together to regulate the menstrual cycle.

One hormone causes an egg to mature in an ovary. Another hormone causes the walls of the uterus to thicken and the supply of blood to the uterus to increase. This happens so that if an egg cell becomes an embryo, the uterus will be ready to support the growth and development of the embryo.

Yet another hormone triggers ovulation. **Ovulation** occurs when a mature egg leaves an ovary and travels into an oviduct.

2 EXPLAIN: What triggers ovulation?

**Menstruation** After an egg is released from the ovary, it travels through an oviduct. If the egg does not meet sperm in the oviduct, it begins to break apart. The amount of hormones in the reproductive system decreases. This causes the thickened walls of the uterus to also break apart. About 14 days after ovulation, **menstruation** occurs. Menstruation is the process by which blood and tissue from the uterus break apart and leave the body.

Soon after menstruation, a new egg begins to mature in the ovary. The menstrual cycle is repeated. The cycle is continuously repeated well into adulthood. For most females, the menstrual cycle continues until about age 50.

3 IDENTIFY: At about what age does the menstrual cycle stop occurring?

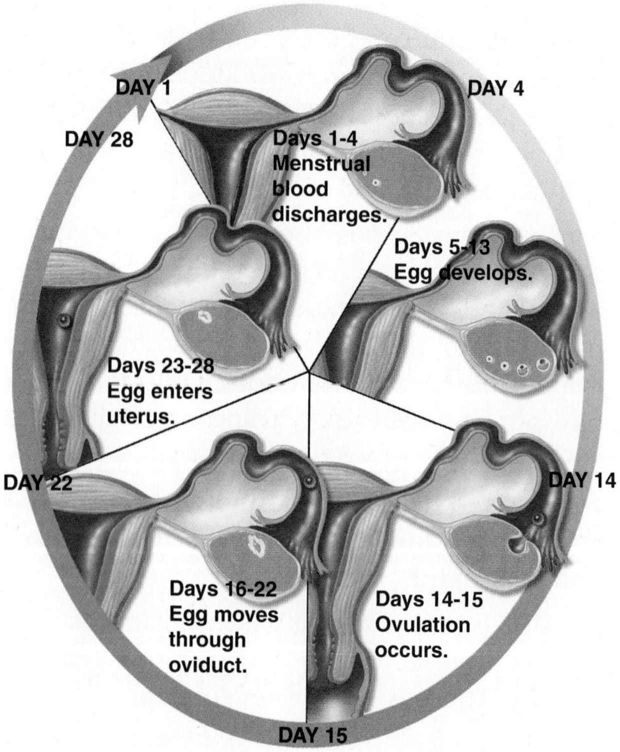


▲ **Figure 19-6** The menstrual cycle takes about 28 days to complete.

## CHECKING CONCEPTS

1. A person becomes sexually mature during __________.
2. A female is born with all the __________ cells she will have in her lifetime.
3. The series of monthly changes in a female's reproductive system is called the __________.
4. Ovulation is triggered by the release of __________ into parts of the reproductive system.
5. During __________, blood and tissue from the uterus are released from the body.
6. A mature egg moves from an ovary into an oviduct during __________.

## THINKING CRITICALLY

7. **COMPARE:** What effect do hormones have on the development of sex cells in the female reproductive system?
8. **INFER:** Why is the thickening of the uterus important to reproduction?

## INTERPRETING VISUALS

*Use Figure 19-6 to answer the following questions.*

9. On what day of the menstrual cycle does ovulation take place?
10. On what day does menstruation take place?
11. At what stage is the lining of the uterus the thickest?
12. If it is day 20 of the cycle, what might be happening?

## How Do They Know That?

### GRAAFIAN FOLLICLES

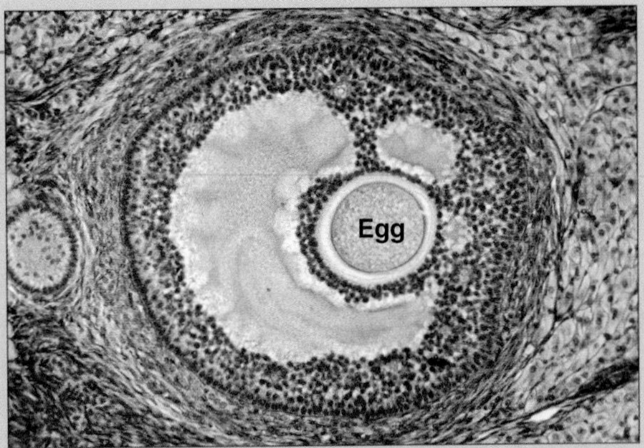

▲ **Figure 19-7** This is a Graafian follicle shown through a microscope.

Reinier de Graaf (1641–1673) was a Dutch physician who lived during the same time as Anton van Leeuwenhoek (1632–1723), the inventor of a powerful, yet simple microscope. Using this microscope, de Graaf observed the large, liquid-filled chambers on the ovary and proposed that their growth was tied to the menstrual cycle. Each of these follicles contained an egg. The follicles were later named after de Graaf and are known today as Graafian follicles.

The Graafian follicle is like a pimple that breaks open on the surface of the ovary. This action releases the egg within a protective layer of cells that surrounds it. The egg breaks free from the Graafian follicle on the ovary about the 14th day of the menstrual cycle. This is called ovulation.

The development of the egg and its Graafian follicle is controlled by hormones from the pituitary gland. The month-long cycle of the Graafian follicle and its functions were important discoveries in human biology.

**Thinking Critically** How do you think the invention of the simple microscope affected studies made by de Graaf and other scientists?

# 19-4 How does fertilization take place?

### *Objective*

Describe how a sperm cell and an egg cell join to form a zygote.

### *Key Terms*

**gamete:** reproductive cell

**fertilization** (fuhrt-uhl-ih-ZAY-shuhn)**:** joining of one sperm cell and one egg cell

**zygote** (ZY-goht)**:** fertilized egg

**Gamete Formation** Before reproduction can take place, special cells called gametes must be formed. **Gametes** are reproductive cells. The male reproductive cells are called sperm. The female reproductive cells are called eggs. Gametes are formed through the process of cell division called meiosis. During the formation of gametes, the number of chromosomes in the cells must be reduced to half of the number of chromosomes in normal body cells. This must occur so that the offspring will receive the same number of chromosomes from each parent. This is an important part of sexual reproduction.

1 **IDENTIFY:** Through which type of cell division are gametes produced?

**Sperm Cells** Sperm cells are microscopic. The largest part of a sperm cell is the round head. The head contains the cell nucleus. A sperm cell also has a long tail. The motion of the tail helps the sperm cell move. This helps the sperm cell to reach the egg.

2 **DESCRIBE:** How does a sperm cell move?

**Mature Egg** During ovulation, a mature egg is released from an ovary. The egg passes into the oviduct. Tiny hairs line the walls of the oviduct. The motion of these hairs moves the egg through the oviduct. Muscles lining the oviduct also help move the egg along.

3 **EXPLAIN:** What causes an egg to move through the oviduct?

**Fertilization** Sperm cells enter the female reproductive system through the vagina. The sperm cells move across the uterus and into the oviduct. Of the millions of sperm cells that enter the uterus, only a few may reach the oviduct.

During ovulation, an egg leaves an ovary and enters the oviduct. If a sperm cell meets an egg cell in the oviduct, **fertilization** can occur. Fertilization is the joining of one sperm and one egg. An egg can be fertilized only after ovulation and only by one sperm.

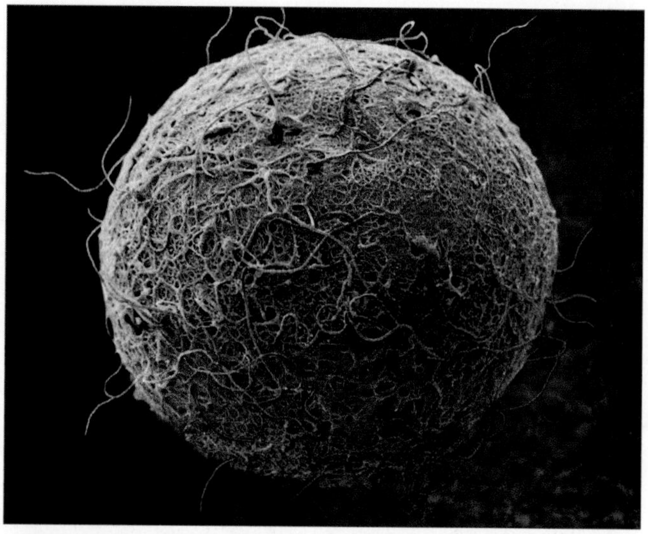

▲ **Figure 19-8** The egg (in yellow) is much larger than the surrounding sperm (in blue).

4 **IDENTIFY:** What is fertilization?

**Zygote** During fertilization, the nuclei of a sperm cell and an egg cell join together. The new cell that results from fertilization is called a **zygote**. A zygote is a fertilized egg. Because the nuclei of the two gametes join, they combine their chromosomes. Human gametes each have 23 chromosomes. This means that after fertilization, the zygote will have 46 chromosomes in its nucleus. The zygote travels down the oviduct and enters the uterus. As it travels, it goes through several cell divisions. See Figure 19-9 on the next page.

1 Zygote

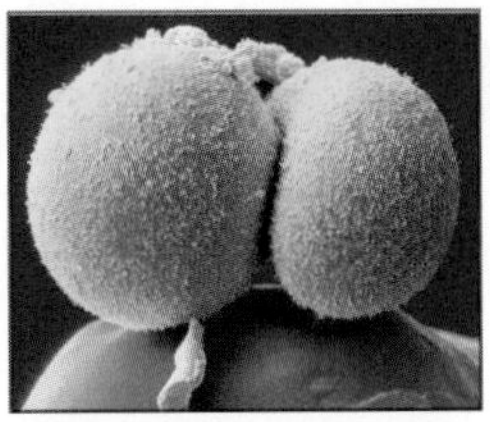

2 Two cells

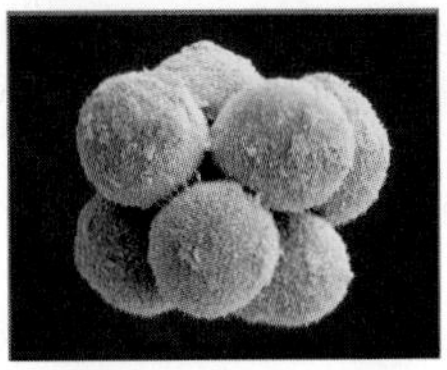

3 Eight cells

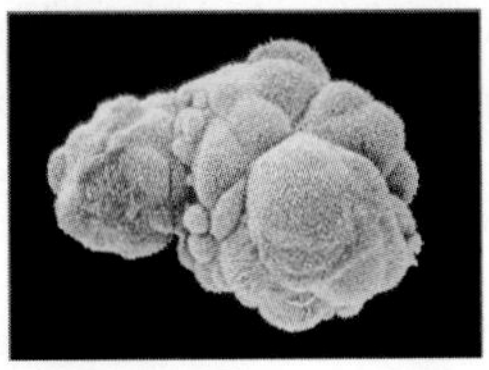

4 Many cells

▲ **Figure 19-9** A zygote goes through several cell divisions as it travels down the oviduct.

5 **EXPLAIN:** What causes a zygote to form?

## ✓ CHECKING CONCEPTS

1. A sperm cell moves due to the motion of its ___________.
2. During ___________, a mature egg leaves an ovary and travels into the oviduct.
3. The joining of a sperm cell and an egg cell is called ___________.
4. The new cell produced by fertilization is called a ___________.

## THINKING CRITICALLY

5. **RELATE:** During which stage of a female's menstrual cycle can fertilization occur? Why?
6. **CONTRAST:** How is the motion of sperm cells and egg cells different?

## BUILDING MATH SKILLS

***Calculating*** Approximately 24 hours after fertilization, the zygote divides into two cells. If the cell divides every 12 hours, how many cells will it have at each of the following time intervals:

**a.** 36 hours
**b.** 2 days
**c.** 3 days
**d.** 4 days

## *Integrating Physical Science*

**TOPIC: chemistry**

▲ **Figure 19-10** Only one sperm is able to get through the egg's cell membrane.

### CHEMICALS INVOLVED IN FERTILIZATION

In order for fertilization to occur, sperm must successfully reach the egg cell. Several hundred million sperm can be deposited in the vagina, but only a small fraction of those actually reach the egg. The challenge does not end there. Sperm cells must also get through the egg cell membrane in order to fertilize it.

During this time, the female reproductive organs secrete several chemicals that change the membrane of the sperm cells. This makes the sperm capable of fertilizing the egg. Although many sperm reach the egg, usually only one will be able to get through the cell membrane of the egg. The sperm that successfully reaches the egg and comes in contact with the egg's membrane will release an enzyme. This enzyme disrupts a section of the egg's protective membrane. The sperm cell is then able to enter the egg cell, and fertilization can take place.

After the first sperm enters the cell, other chemical activities take place. These chemical activities prevent other sperm cells from also entering the egg. These chemicals assure that only one sperm cell fertilizes the egg.

**Thinking Critically** What might the result be if more than one cell were able to fertilize the egg?

# 19-5 How does a human embryo develop?

## *Objective*

Describe the process by which an embryo develops into a fetus.

## *Key Terms*

**embryo** (EHM-bree-oh): developing human organism up until eight weeks of pregnancy

**fetus** (FEET-uhs): term used to describe an embryo eight weeks after fertilization

**placenta** (pluh-SEHN-tuh): organ through which an embryo receives nourishment and gets rid of wastes

**umbilical** (um-BIHL-ih-kuhl) **cord:** structure that connects the embryo to the placenta

**amnion** (AM-nee-uhn): fluid-filled sac that surrounds an embryo

**Implantation** After fertilization, the zygote divides by mitosis. Two cells are formed. These cells are attached to one another. Both of these cells divide to form four attached cells. This cell division continues until a hollow ball of cells is formed. The hollow ball of cells attaches itself to the lining of the uterus. This is called implantation.

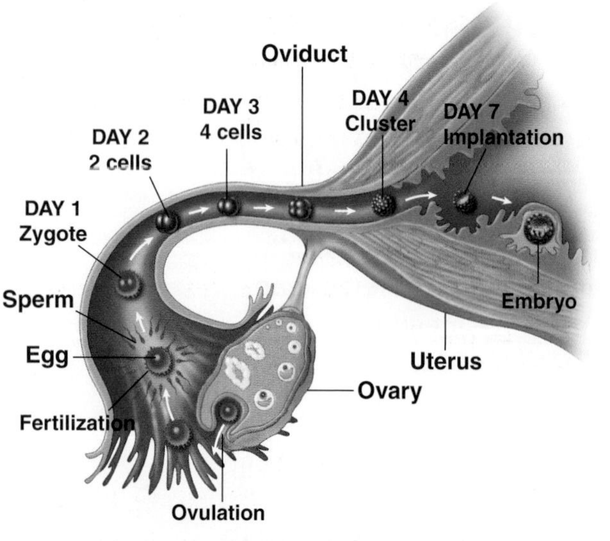


▲ **Figure 19-11** After fertilization, the zygote continues growing before it attaches to the lining of the uterus.

The mass of cells is called an **embryo** until the eighth week of pregnancy. The cells of the embryo will multiply to form tissues and organs.

1 IDENTIFY: What is an embryo?

**Development** After about eight weeks, the embryo has developed a heart, brain, and spinal cord. Eyes and ears also are formed. At about nine weeks, bones form in the skeleton. It is now called a **fetus**. The fetus continues to grow and develop inside the uterus. Between the sixth and the ninth month, the fetus grows very quickly.

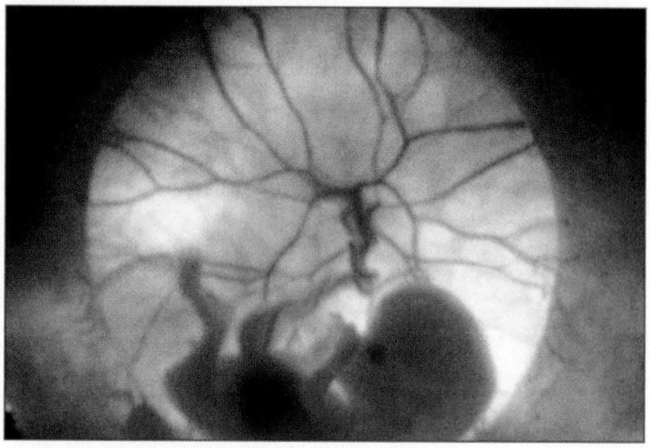

▲ **Figure 19-12** A developing fetus

2 DESCRIBE: When is a developing organism called a fetus?

**Special Structures** During pregnancy, special structures in the mother's body protect and support the embryo as it develops into a fetus. Tissues of the uterus that surround the fetus develop into a thick flat structure called the **placenta**. The placenta is an organ through which the fetus receives nourishment. The fetus also gets rid of wastes through the placenta.

The fetus is attached to the placenta by the **umbilical cord.** The umbilical cord is a thick, ropelike structure. One kind of blood vessel in the umbilical cord carries nourishment from the placenta to the fetus. A different kind of blood vessel carries wastes from the fetus to the placenta. The fetus is surrounded by a clear, fluid-filled sac called the **amnion**. The fluid inside the sac cushions and protects the developing fetus.

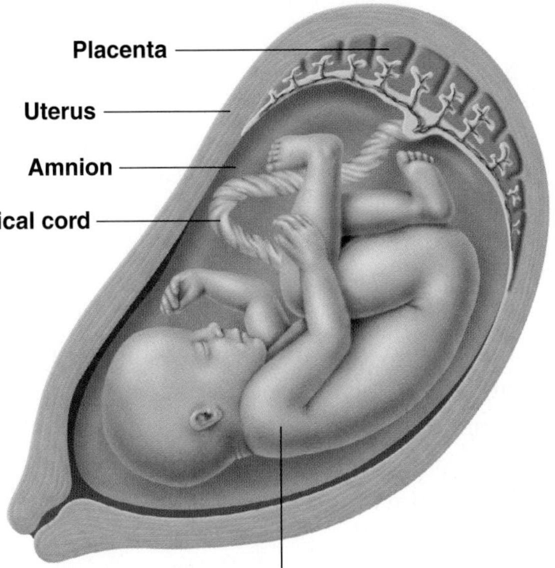


▲ **Figure 19-13** The placenta provides nourishment to the fetus and carries away wastes.

**3 DESCRIBE:** How does a fetus receive nourishment?

**Pregnancy** The period of development of an organism inside its mother's body is called pregnancy. Pregnancy brings about many changes in a woman's body. Most women gain between 10 and 15 kg during their pregnancy. Some women develop back pain and swollen feet as a result of this extra weight. The most common problem associated with pregnancy is a feeling of exhaustion. A woman's body must work harder to meet her own needs as well as those of her baby.

**4 DEFINE:** What is pregnancy?

**Birth** After about nine months, the fetus is ready to be born. The birth takes place in three stages—labor, delivery, and afterbirth. Hormones in the body of both the mother and the fetus trigger the birth process to begin. The muscles of the uterus begin to contract, or squeeze together. This process is called labor. As labor continues, the muscle contractions become stronger and happen more often. Labor may take only a few hours, or may last up to 20 hours or more.

During delivery, the contractions force the fetus out of the uterus and into the vagina. Eventually, the fetus is pushed out of the mother. The fetus usually comes out head first and is still attached to the placenta by the umbilical cord. The umbilical cord is then cut.

A few seconds after birth, the infant begins to cry. Crying helps the infant's lungs to expand so that it can begin to breathe on its own. The location where the umbilical cord attaches to the infant eventually shrinks and becomes the navel, or belly button. After about 10 to 15 minutes, the placenta is pushed out of the mother. This is called the afterbirth.

**5 IDENTIFY:** What are the three stages of childbirth?

## CHECKING CONCEPTS

1. After fertilization, a zygote divides by __________.
2. The umbilical cord connects the embryo to the __________.
3. When the skeleton of an embryo has formed bones, the embryo is called a __________.
4. The embryo receives nourishment and gets rid of wastes through the __________.
5. During labor, muscles in the __________ begin to contract.
6. The place the umbilical cord attaches to eventually becomes the __________.

## THINKING CRITICALLY

7. **INFER:** Why does one type of blood vessel bring nutrients to the embryo while another removes its waste products?
8. **INFER:** Why do you think it is dangerous for a pregnant mother to drink alcohol or smoke?

## INTERPRETING VISUALS

*Use Figure 19-11 to answer the following questions.*

9. At what day is the zygote made up of four cells?
10. On what day does implantation occur?
11. Through which part of the female reproductive system does the zygote travel?
12. To which part of the female reproductive system does the embryo attach?

# LAB ACTIVITY
# Graphing Changes in Fetal Development

## *BACKGROUND*

After fertilization takes place, an embryo forms from one cell, called the zygote. Eventually the embryo develops into a fetus. This process is very complex. During pregnancy, the fetus increases dramatically in size. It must also develop all of the organ systems it will need to survive on its own after birth.

## *PURPOSE*

In this activity, you will use the information in a data table to create two bar graphs representing the stages of fetal development.

▲ **STEP 2** Create a bar graph.

## *PROCEDURE*

1. Study the information in the data table shown in Figure 19-14.
2. Make a bar graph that shows how the length of a fetus changes as it develops.
3. Find the difference between the shortest and longest lengths in the data table. The difference is the total length that is to be represented on the vertical axis. Use this information to determine the length that one box on the axis represents.
4. Label each column along the horizontal axis with the time it represents.
5. Fill in the column above each time label with a bar whose top ends at the appropriate length line.
6. Repeat Steps 1 to 5 on a separate sheet of graph paper to make a second bar graph showing the increase in mass of a developing fetus.

| Average Length and Mass During Fetal Development | | |
|---|---|---|
| Time (weeks) | Length (millimeters) | Mass (grams) |
| 4 | 2.5 | 1 |
| 6 | 9.0 | 2.5 |
| 8 | 30 | 5 |
| 10 | 61 | 14 |
| 12 | 87 | 45 |
| 14 | 120 | 110 |
| 16 | 140 | 200 |
| 18 | 160 | 320 |
| 20 | 190 | 460 |
| 22 | 210 | 630 |
| 24 | 230 | 820 |
| 26 | 250 | 1,000 |
| 28 | 270 | 1,300 |
| 30 | 280 | 1,700 |
| 32 | 300 | 2,100 |
| 34 | 335 | 2,700 |
| 36 | 340 | 2,900 |
| 38 | 360 | 3,400 |

▲ **Figure 19-14** Use this table of average length and mass to make your bar graph.

### *CONCLUSIONS*

1. **OBSERVE:** How long is the embryo at the end of eight weeks of development?

2. **OBSERVE:** Between which weeks does the developing fetus have the greatest increase in length?

3. **ANALYZE:** Does the length of a developing fetus increase in a set pattern? Explain.

4. **RELATE:** Is there a similar pattern between the increase in mass and the increase in length? Explain.

# 19-6 What are the stages of human development?

***Objective***

Identify the stages of the human life cycle.

***Key Terms***

**adolescence:** stage of development in which children experience rapid physical growth

**menopause:** time at which women stop ovulating

**Life Cycle** A developing fetus goes through a series of stages before birth. Some of these changes are listed in Figure 19-15. After birth, a human also goes through a series of stages. The stages of development are called a life cycle. There are five stages in the human life cycle. Certain events take place at each stage of development that make that stage unique.

| FETAL DEVELOPMENT | |
|---|---|
| **Time from Fertilization** | **Major Developmental Changes** |
| 1 week | Cluster of cells have implanted into the lining of the uterus. |
| 4 weeks | Spinal cord and brain begin to form. Eyes and ears form. Limb buds appear. |
| 8 weeks | Muscles and bones develop. Blood vessels move to permanent locations. |
| 16 weeks | Face begins to look "human." The brain develops further. |
| 32 weeks | Nervous system develops further. Fetus greatly increases in size. |

▲ **Figure 19-15**

**1** IDENTIFY: What is a life cycle?

**Infancy** The earliest stage of human life is called infancy. Infancy begins at birth and ends at age 2. Infants show several innate behaviors such as crying, sucking, and grasping. This stage of life is marked by a rapid increase in size. The muscles and nerves of the infant also develop quickly. Mental skills develop and the infant begins to interact with its surroundings. At about 7 months, infants can usually hold their heads up, roll over, or even crawl.

By age 1, most infants are able to walk and speak a few words. Between the ages of 1 and 2, children become much more aware of their surroundings. They become curious about their environment. They also learn that certain behaviors cause a reaction from their parents.

▲ **Figure 19-16** At about 7 months, infants are crawling and holding up their heads.

**2** EXPLAIN: What are some of the developmental changes that take place during infancy?

**Childhood** Childhood usually is defined as the period between ages 2 and 12. During childhood, muscle development allows more complex activities. Children become more independent and are able to feed and dress themselves. Children also develop better coordination. This allows them to participate in activities such as sports or playing an instrument. Mental abilities also increase. Children become much better at expressing themselves verbally at this stage. Most children learn to read and write during this stage of development.

**3** DESCRIBE: What are some of the changes a person goes through during childhood?

**Adolescence** Between the ages of 11 and 14, most young people go through a period of rapid physical change. This state is called **adolescence**. The beginning of adolescence is called puberty. During puberty, the reproductive organs develop. These organs release hormones that cause growth spurts. Adolescents grow taller and gain weight during this period. Males may experience a change in their voices. They may also develop a more muscular build and facial hair. Females usually develop breasts and larger hips during this stage. Adolescents of both sexes develop the ability to reproduce.

4 **EXPLAIN:** What causes rapid growth spurts during puberty?

**Adulthood** Adulthood is the stage at which the physical growth of the human body is complete. The growth process usually stops between the ages of 18 and 21. Muscle development and coordination reach their peak during early adulthood. Between the ages of 30 and 50, muscle tone and agility may decrease. As a result people in this stage may have to work harder to "stay in shape."

Women between the ages of 45 and 55 experience a developmental change called **menopause**. During this time, ovulation stops and menstruation occurs less often. Usually by age 55, menstruation stops completely.

5 **IDENTIFY:** What is menopause?

**Later Years** Later years, or the beginning of the aging process, occur at different times in different people. People who have exercised regularly and eaten a balanced diet all of their lives may stay active into their late 70s or early 80s.

◀ **Figure 19-17** People who exercise may stay active into their late 70s.

The later years of a person's life are usually marked by a decline in muscle strength. People may move more slowly than before or may need help moving. Sense organs such as the eyes and ears may not work as well. The bones of older adults may become brittle and can break more easily. Despite these developmental changes, people are living longer today than ever before. This is probably due to a greater awareness of exercise and nutrition, and also to advances in medicine.

6 **DESCRIBE:** What effects do diet and exercise have on the aging process?

## CHECKING CONCEPTS

1. The earliest stage of human development is called __________.
2. The period between ages 2 and 12 is generally called __________.
3. A person develops the ability to reproduce during the stage called __________.
4. The stage during which the physical growth of the human body is complete is __________.

## THINKING CRITICALLY

5. **COMPARE:** Compare muscle development during infancy and the later years.
6. **RELATE:** At what stage is a person most likely to first put together a jigsaw puzzle?

### Web InfoSearch

**Speech Development** Between the ages of 4 and 6 months, infants begin to babble or repeat sounds like "mamama" and "papapa." Infants from all over the world, even deaf infants, sound very much the same. Babbling infants even make sounds that are not part of their native languages.

**SEARCH:** Use the Internet to find out more about speech development in humans. Make a chart that describes the stages in language development. Start your search at www.conceptsandchallenges.com. Some key search words are **language development**, **speech development**, and **babbling**.

*Integrating Technology*

# THE Big IDEA

## How has technology improved life at various stages?

Americans are living longer, healthier lives. The average person born in 1900 lived about 47 years. A century later, the average lifespan is almost 77 years.

Medical technology helps improve health at every stage of life. Diagnostic tests, such as ultrasound, help monitor the progress of babies in the womb. Surgeons operate on babies in the first days of life. Vaccines have all but erased many fatal childhood diseases.

Drugs and devices help us prevent, detect, and fight disease. Many cancers can be treated if found early. Screening tests, such as mammograms, help find it. Many types of surgery now require only tiny slits in the skin. This reduces the risk of infection and speeds recovery.

About 35 million people are over age 65. By 2050, that figure will double to 70 million. Much research today is focused on staying healthy in old age. Imaging technology is helping scientists study brain activity. Eventually, they hope to develop drugs that will delay the onset of Alzheimer's disease.

Look at the boxes of text that appear on this page and the next. They point out ways in which technology improves health at every stage of life. Follow the directions in the Science Log to learn more about "the big idea." ✦

### Prenatal Ultrasound

Ultrasound technology uses sound waves to create images. During pregnancy, it shows the size and position of the baby. Some doctors use ultrasound to diagnose a serious heart defect before birth. The defect requires three surgeries. The first operation occurs in the first week of life. A study found that babies diagnosed in the womb had a better chance of surviving the first surgery.

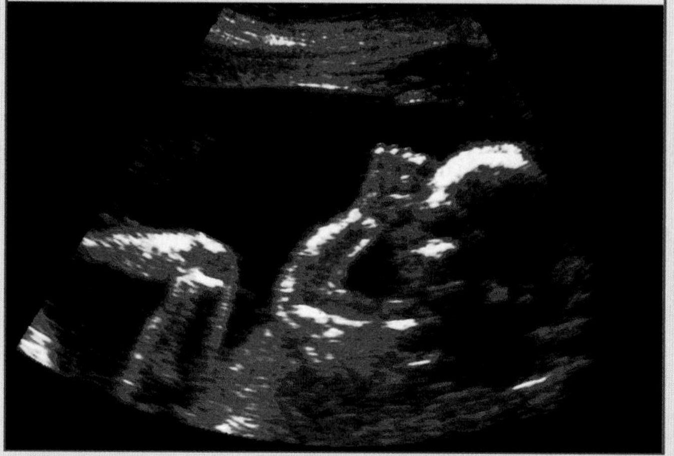

### Childhood Vaccinations

Until vaccines were widely available, many children died from common childhood diseases. Others became blind, deaf, or brain damaged. After vaccines were developed, death rates from polio, measles, and whooping cough fell dramatically. Children today are vaccinated against 11 diseases.

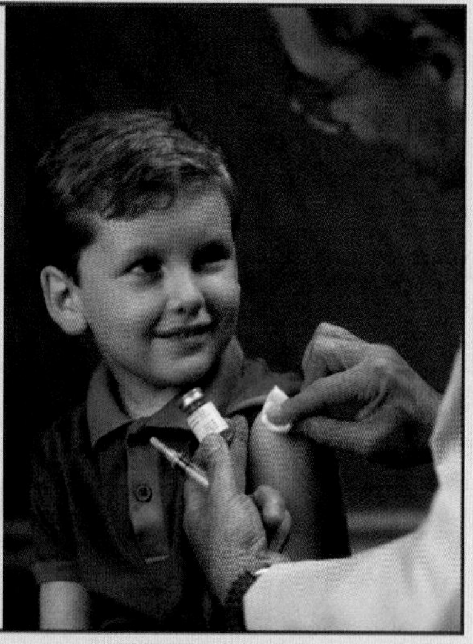

### Laser Eye Surgery

Lasers have become an important tool in the field of eye surgery. Doctors can now dramatically improve a patient's vision using lasers, with few negative side effects. Lasers are used to reshape the cornea and focus images on the retina correctly. They can also be used to treat patients with cataracts, a disease of the eye common in middle aged people.

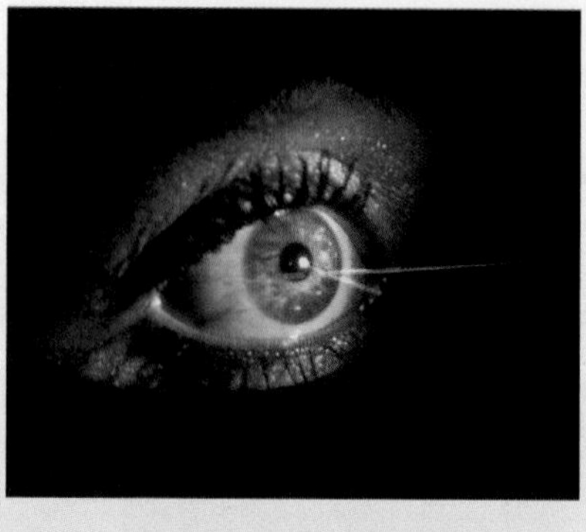

## Infant Monitoring

Premature birth is the leading cause of infant death. Special hospital units that treat premature babies have saved many lives. These units are equipped with technology designed for the tiniest humans. They include special machines to monitor heart rate, breathing, and other body functions.

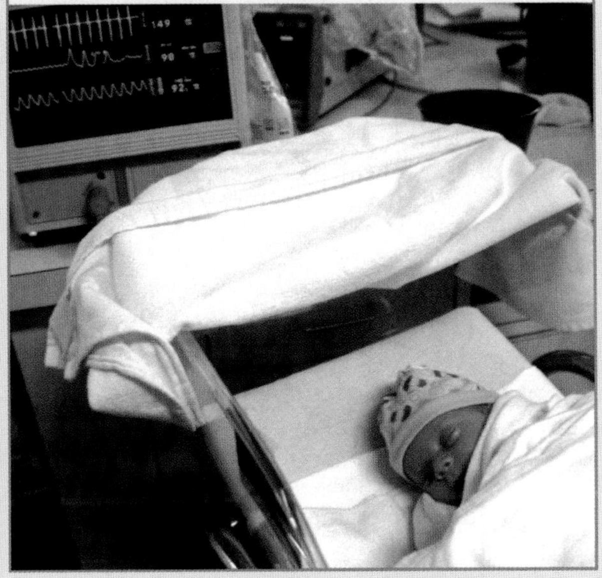

## Safety Equipment

Injuries kill more adolescents than all diseases combined. The technologies most important for adolescent health are often not used in the doctor's office. They are things like seat belts and helmets. These are simple solutions that can save lives, but too often they don't. Why? Adolescents are far less likely than any other age group to wear seat belts, and many don't wear helmets during dangerous activities.

## Hip Replacement Surgery

Problems with the hip joint are common occurrences for people over the age of 65. An artificial hip replaces the ball and socket joint that connects the leg bone to the hip bone. The new hips are made of materials that provide an easy, gliding motion. Researchers continue to develop better surgical techniques and new materials that will help increase the success rate of hip replacement surgery.

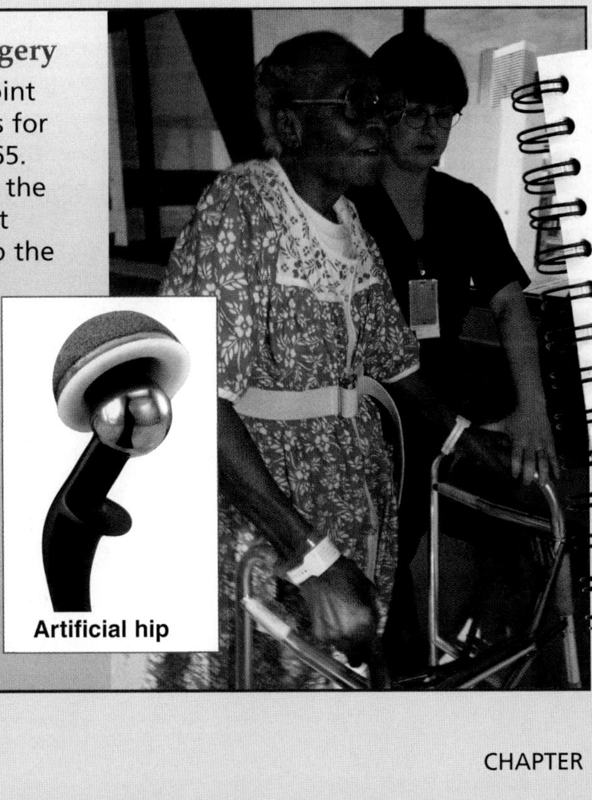

Artificial hip

**WRITING ACTIVITY**

### Science Log

In your Science Log, research and write about one life-saving technology. Describe why it is important at a particular stage of life. Start your search at www.conceptsandchallenges.com.

# Chapter 19 Challenges

## Chapter Summary

### Lesson 19-1

- The **ovaries** of the female reproductive system produce hormones and eggs.
- An **embryo** develops inside the **uterus.** The **vagina** is the passageway through which a baby moves during birth.

### Lesson 19-2

- The **testes** are the organs of the male reproductive system that produce hormones and sperm.
- In males, both urine and sperm leave the body through the **urethra.**

### Lesson 19-3

- **Puberty** is the time when a person becomes sexually mature. The **menstrual cycle** is a series of changes in the female reproductive system that occurs about once a month.
- During **ovulation**, a mature egg leaves an ovary and travels to the **oviduct.**
- The process by which blood and tissue leave the uterus is called **menstruation.**

### Lesson 19-4

- **Fertilization** occurs when a sperm cell and an egg cell meet. The new cell produced by fertilization is called a **zygote.**

### Lesson 19-5

- An embryo is a hollow ball of cells attached to a wall of the uterus.
- An embryo receives nourishment and rids itself of wastes through the **placenta.** The **umbilical cord** connects an embryo to the placenta. The **amnion** cushions and protects the developing embryo.
- Birth takes place in three stages—labor, delivery, and afterbirth. Birth usually occurs after nine months of development.

### Lesson 19-6

- The stages of development in humans are called the human life cycle.
- During **adolescence,** a person goes through a period of rapid physical change.
- Adulthood is the stage at which the physical growth of the body is complete.

## Key Term Challenges

adolescence (p. 458)
amnion (p. 454)
cervix (p. 446)
embryo (p. 454)
epididymis (p. 448)
estrogen (p. 446)
fertilization (p. 452)
fetus (p. 454)
gamete (p. 452)
menopause (p. 458)
menstrual cycle (p. 450)
menstruation (p. 450)
ovary (p. 446)
oviduct (p. 446)
ovulation (p. 450)
placenta (p. 454)
progesterone (p. 446)
puberty (p. 450)
scrotum (p. 448)
testis (p. 448)
testosterone (p. 448)
umbilical cord (p. 454)
urethra (p. 448)
uterus (p. 446)
vagina (p. 446)
zygote (p. 452)

MATCHING **Write the Key Term from above that best matches each description.**

1. hollow organ in which an embryo develops
2. process by which blood and tissue from the uterine lining breaks apart and leaves the body
3. clear, fluid-filled sac that protects the developing embryo
4. developing human organism up until eight weeks of pregnancy
5. organ of the male reproductive system that produces hormones and sperm
6. long tube between an ovary and the uterus

FILL IN **Write the Key Term from above that best completes each statement.**

7. The organs of the female reproductive system that produce eggs are the __________.
8. Sperm is carried to the outside of the body through the __________.
9. The release of a mature egg from the ovary is called __________.
10. The hormone that controls the development of male characteristics is __________.
11. The __________ often is called the birth canal.
12. The __________ connects the uterus to the vagina.

## Content Challenges TEST PREP

**MULTIPLE CHOICE Write the letter of the term or phrase that best completes each statement.**

1. In females, puberty begins with the start of
   a. diffusion.
   b. fertilization.
   c. menstruation.
   d. pregnancy.

2. Muscular strength begins to decrease during
   a. infancy.
   b. adolescence.
   c. adulthood.
   d. old age.

3. The release of an egg is called
   a. fertilization.
   b. ovulation.
   c. menstruation.
   d. pregnancy.

4. The structure through which the developing fetus receives nourishment is the
   a. amnion.
   b. uterus.
   c. birth canal.
   d. placenta.

5. Fertilization in humans takes place in the
   a. vagina.
   b. uterus.
   c. ovary.
   d. oviduct.

6. Sperm and testosterone are produced in the
   a. ovaries.
   b. scrotum.
   c. testes.
   d. urethra.

7. The ovaries produce all of the following except
   a. eggs.
   b. progesterone.
   c. estrogen.
   d. testosterone.

8. The most rapid physical changes take place in humans during
   a. childhood.
   b. adolescence.
   c. adulthood.
   d. old age.

9. The narrow end of the uterus is called the
   a. vagina.
   b. cervix.
   c. oviduct.
   d. ovary.

**TRUE/FALSE Write *true* if the statement is true. If the statement is false, change the underlined term to make the statement true.**

10. Once bones form in the skeleton, the embryo is called a fetus.
11. The urethra carries waste between the embryo and the placenta.
12. The process by which blood and tissue leave the uterus is called fertilization.
13. The growth process in humans ends at adolescence.
14. Eggs are female sex cells.
15. An egg can be fertilized by many sperm.
16. The clear fluid-filled sac surrounding the embryo is called the placenta.
17. A zygote undergoes cell division until a hollow ball of cells forms.
18. People develop the ability to reproduce during adulthood.

## *Concept Challenges* TEST PREP

**WRITTEN RESPONSE** **Answer each of the following questions in complete sentences.**

1. **COMPARE:** How are the functions of the testes and ovaries similar?
2. **INFER:** Why do you think it is important for a pregnant woman to avoid alcohol, tobacco, and drugs?
3. **IDENTIFY:** How do you think you can slow down the effects of aging?
4. **HYPOTHESIZE:** What would happen if the placenta became detached from the fetus?
5. **INFER:** Why do you think the regular monthly changes in females is called a cycle?

**INTERPRETING A DIAGRAM** **Use Figure 19-18 to answer the following questions.**

6. **IDENTIFY:** What organ is represented by letter *A*?
7. **NAME:** Which event is taking place at letter *B*?
8. **IDENTIFY:** What structure is represented by the letter *D*?
9. **IDENTIFY:** Which letter represents the point at which the zygote becomes an embryo?
10. **EXPLAIN:** What is the role of the organ labeled *F* in the female reproductive system?

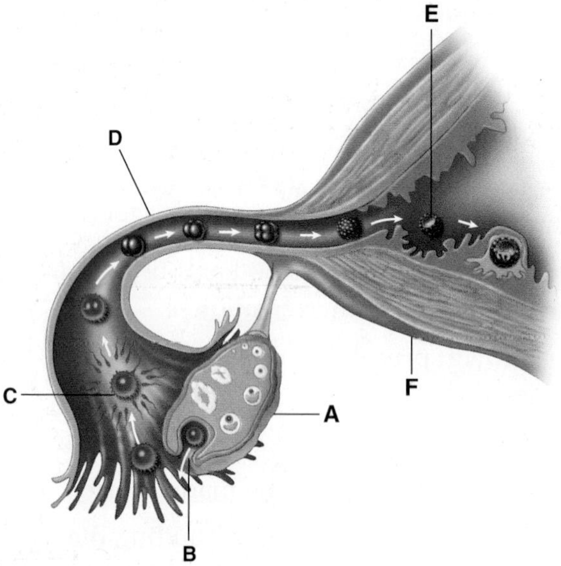


▲ **Figure 19-18**

# Appendix A Metric System

## The Metric System and SI Units

The metric system is an international system of measurement based on units of 10. More than 90 percent of the nations of the world use the metric system. In the United States, both the English system and the metric system are used.

The *Système International*, or SI, has been used as the international measurement system since 1960. The SI is a modernized version of the metric system. Like the metric system, the SI is a decimal system based on units of 10. When you want to change from one unit in the metric system to another unit, you multiply or divide by a multiple of 10.

- When you change from a smaller unit to a larger unit, you divide.
- When you change from a larger unit to a smaller unit, you multiply.

| METRIC UNITS | | |
|---|---|---|
| LENGTH | SYMBOL | RELATIONSHIP |
| kilometer | km | 1 km = 1,000 m |
| meter | m | 1 m = 100 cm |
| centimeter | cm | 1 cm = 10 mm |
| millimeter | mm | 1 mm = 0.1 cm |
| AREA | SYMBOL | RELATIONSHIP |
| square kilometer | $km^2$ | 1 $km^2$ = 1,000,000 $m^2$ |
| square meter | $m^2$ | 1 $m^2$ = 1,000,000 $mm^2$ |
| square centimeter | $cm^2$ | 1 $cm^2$ = 0.0001 $m^2$ |
| square millimeter | $mm^2$ | 1 $mm^2$ = 0.000001 $m^2$ |
| VOLUME | SYMBOL | RELATIONSHIP |
| cubic meter | $m^3$ | 1 $m^3$ = 1,000,000 $cm^3$ |
| cubic centimeter | $cm^3$ | 1 $cm^3$ = 0.000001 $m^3$ |
| liter | L | 1 L = 1,000 mL |
| milliliter | mL | 1 mL = 0.001 L |
| MASS | SYMBOL | RELATIONSHIP |
| metric ton | t | 1 t = 1,000 kg |
| kilogram | kg | 1 kg = 1,000 g |
| gram | g | 1 g = 1,000 mg |
| centigram | cg | 1 cg = 10 mg |
| milligram | mg | 1 mg = 0.001 g |
| TEMPERATURE | SYMBOL | |
| Kelvin | K | |
| degree Celsius | °C | |

▲ **Figure 1**

| COMMON METRIC PREFIXES | | | |
|---|---|---|---|
| micro- | 0.000001 or 1/1,000,000 | deka- | 10 |
| milli- | 0.001 or 1/1,000 | hecto- | 100 |
| centi- | 0.01 or 1/100 | kilo- | 1,000 |
| deci- | 0.1 or 1/10 | mega- | 1,000,000 |

▲ **Figure 2**

| METRIC-STANDARD EQUIVALENTS | |
|---|---|
| **SI to English** | **English to SI** |
| LENGTH | |
| 1 kilometer = 0.621 mile (mi) | 1 mi = 1.61 km |
| 1 meter = 1.094 yards (yd) | 1 yd = 0.914 m |
| 1 meter = 3.28 feet (ft) | 1 ft = 0.305 m |
| 1 centimeter = 0.394 inch (in.) | 1 in. = 2.54 cm |
| 1 millimeter = 0.039 inch | 1 in. = 25.4 mm |
| AREA | |
| 1 square kilometer = 0.3861 square mile | 1 $mi^2$ = 2.590 $km^2$ |
| 1 square meter = 1.1960 square yards | 1 $yd^2$ = 0.8361 $m^2$ |
| 1 square meter = 10.763 square feet | 1 $ft^2$ = 0.0929 $m^2$ |
| 1 square centimeter = 0.155 square inch | 1 $in.^2$ = 6.452 $cm^2$ |
| VOLUME | |
| 1 cubic meter = 1.3080 cubic yards | 1 $yd^3$ = 0.7646 $m^3$ |
| 1 cubic meter = 35.315 cubic feet | 1 $ft^3$ = 0.0283 $m^3$ |
| 1 cubic centimeter = 0.0610 cubic inch | 1 $in.^3$ = 16.39 $cm^3$ |
| 1 liter = 0.2642 gallon (gal) | 1 gal = 3.79 L |
| 1 liter = 1.06 quarts (qt) | 1 qt = 0.946 L |
| 1 liter = 2.11 pints (pt) | 1 pt = 0.47 L |
| 1 milliliter = 0.034 fluid ounce (fl oz) | 1 fl oz = 29.57 mL |
| MASS | |
| 1 metric ton = 0.984 ton | 1 ton = 1.016 t |
| 1 kilogram = 2.205 pounds (lb) | 1 lb = 0.4536 kg |
| 1 gram = 0.0353 ounce (oz) | 1 oz = 28.35 g |
| TEMPERATURE | |
| Celsius = 5/9(°F – 32) | Fahrenheit = 9/5°C + 32 |
| 0°C = 32°F (Freezing point of water) | 72°F = 22°C (Room temperature) |
| 100°C = 212°F (Boiling point of water) | 98.6°F = 37°C (Human body temperature) |
| Kelvin = (°F + 459.67)/1.8 | Fahrenheit = (K × 1.8) – 459.67 |

▲ **Figure 3**

# Appendix B The Microscope

## Parts of the Microscope

One of the most important tools in biology is the microscope. A microscope enables scientists to view and study objects or structures not visible to the unaided eye. The compound microscope is used most often in biology classes.

A compound microscope has two or more lenses. One lens is located in the eyepiece. The eyepiece lens usually has a magnification of 10×. An object viewed through this lens would appear 10 times larger than it would look with the unaided eye.

The second lens is called the objective lens. Compound microscopes may have many objective lenses. Most compound microscopes, however, have two objective lenses. Each objective lens has a different magnification. The magnification is printed on each objective lens.

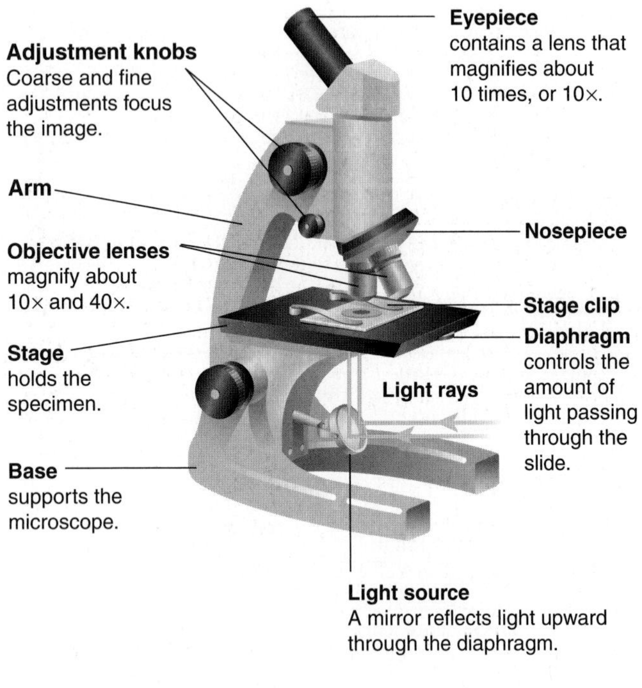


▲ **Figure 4** A compound microscope

## Calculating Power of Magnification

When you use a microscope, you must determine the total power of magnification. To find the total magnification of a microscope, use the following equation.

$$\text{eyepiece lens magnification} \times \text{objective lens magnification} = \text{total magnification}$$

For example, if the eyepiece lens has a magnification of 10× and the objective lens has a magnification of 10×, the total magnification would be 100×. Looking at an object under this total magnification, you would be seeing the object 100 times larger than the object would look with the unaided eye.

A microscope is a delicate, but relatively uncomplicated, tool. Before you try to use a microscope, however, you should know the parts of a microscope and what each part does. Study Figure 4 to learn about the parts of the microscope and their functions.

### HEALTH AND SAFETY TIP

1. ⚠ CAUTION Always carry a microscope with two hands. Place one hand under the base and one hand holding the arm.
2. ⚠ CAUTION Use caution when handling glass slides— they can break easily and cause injury.
3. ⚠ CAUTION Be careful when handling electric cords and plugging them in.
4. ⚠ CAUTION Be careful when handling light bulbs. After using a microscope, the light bulb may be hot to the touch.

## Hands-On Activity

### USING A MICROSCOPE

*You will need a microscope, a slide, a cover slip, and material to be examined. You may also need an eye dropper or pipette and some type of stain.*

1. Place the material to be examined on a clean slide. If you are examining a liquid, use an eye dropper or pipette.
2. You may need to add 1–2 drops of water or liquid stain. Follow the directions in the lab or your teacher's instructions.
3. Carefully place one edge of the cover slip onto the slide, next to your sample. Gently lower the cover slip so that it covers the sample.
4. You may need to clean up excess liquid from the slide. To do this, place a small piece of tissue or paper towel next to the edge of the cover slip.
5. Now you are ready to observe your slide under the microscope! Always begin by using the lowest power objective lens.
6. Make sure the sample is centered over the opening in the stage.
7. Slowly move the slide back and forth or up and down while looking through the eyepiece.
8. Focus using the coarse adjustment knob first and then the fine adjustment. ⚠ CAUTION! Never use the coarse adjustment when you are on high power.
9. Make sure there is enough light coming through the opening in the stage. To adjust the amount of light, turn the diaphragm.

▲ **STEP 2** Add two drops of water to the slide if

▲ **STEP 8** Focus the microscope.

### Practicing Your Skills

10. **OBSERVE:** Draw what you see at low power.
11. **COMPARE:** What details can you see at high power?
12. **ANALYZE:** How does a microscope help you to learn more about something?

# Appendix C The Classification of Life

This appendix gives the taxonomic classification based on a six-kingdom system. Other classification systems have been suggested but are not yet formally recognized. Classification continuously changes as new information about organisms is discovered. Common names are given in parentheses next to the scientific names. Because of the large amount of organisms, not all groups are listed. *Note: The term *division* is used by many scientists in place of *phylum* for the plant and fungi kingdom.

## KINGDOM ARCHAEBACTERIA

*Mostly one-celled organisms without membrane-bound organelles that live in extreme conditions*

This kingdom includes thermoacidophillic bacteria, which live in very high temperatures; methanogens, which produce methane gas; and salt-loving bacteria.

## KINGDOM EUBACTERIA

*Mostly one-celled organisms without membrane-bound organelles*

This kingdom includes cyanobacteria, or blue-green bacteria; planctomycetes, a group of bacteria found in water; and some pathogens, including *Salmonella,* which can cause salmonella poisoning, and *Vibro,* which can cause cholera.

## KINGDOM PROTISTA

*Mostly one-celled organisms that have organelles and may move freely*

- Animal-like Protists
  - Phylum Rhizopoda (amoeba)
  - Phylum Ciliophora (paramecium)
- Plantlike Protists
  - Phylum Chrysophyta (golden algae)
  - Phylum Euglenophyta (euglena)
- Funguslike Protists
  - Phylum Myxomycota (slime mold)
  - Phylum Oomycota (water mold)

## KINGDOM FUNGI

*Many-celled organisms that are heterotrophic and reproduce by spores*

- *Division Zygomycota (bread mold)
- Division Ascomycota (yeast, truffles)
- Division Basidiomycota (mushrooms)

## KINGDOM PLANTAE

*Many-celled organisms that are autotrophic and have cell walls*

- Division Bryophyta (mosses, liverworts)
- Division Pterophyta (ferns)
- Division Coniferophyta (conifers)
- Division Cycadophyta (cycads)
- Division Ginkgophyta (ginkgos)
- Division Anthophyta (flowering plants)

## KINGDOM ANIMALIA

*Many-celled organisms that are heterotrophic and lack cell walls; most animals have complex tissues and can move freely*

- Phylum Porifera (sponges)
- Phylum Cnidaria (hydras, jellyfish)
- Phylum Platyhelminthes (flatworms)
- Phylum Nematoda (roundworms)
- Phylum Annelida (segmented worms)
- Phylum Mollusca (mollusks)
- Phylum Echinodermata (echinoderms)
- Phylum Arthropoda (arthropods)
- Phylum Chordata (chordates)
  - Subphylum Vertebrata (vertebrates)
    - Class Agnatha (jawless fish)
    - Class Chondrichthyes (cartilaginous fish)
    - Class Osteichthyes (bony fish)
    - Class Amphibia (amphibians)
    - Class Reptilia (reptiles)
    - Class Aves (birds)
    - Class Mammalia (mammals)

# Appendix D Science Terms



## Analyzing Science Terms

You can often unlock the meaning of an unfamiliar science term by analyzing its word parts. Prefixes and suffixes, for example, each carry a meaning that comes from a word root. This word root usually comes from the Latin or Greek language. The following list of prefixes and suffixes provides clues to the meaning of many science terms.

| WORD PART | MEANING | EXAMPLE |
|---|---|---|
| a- | not, without | abiotic |
| aero- | air | aerobic |
| anti- | against | antibodies |
| bi- | two | biceps, binary fission |
| bio- | life | biotechnology, biology |
| carn- | meat, flesh | carnivore |
| chemo- | of, with, or by chemicals | chemosynthesis |
| chlor- | green | chloroplasts |
| cyt- | cell | cytoplasm |
| -derm, derm- | skin, covering | echinoderm, dermatology |
| di- | twice, double | dicot, disaccharide |
| eco- | environment, habitat | ecosystem, ecology |
| ecto- | outer | ectoderm, ectotherm |
| endo- | inside | endospore, endoskeleton |
| epi- | on, on the outside | epidermis, epiphyte |
| exo- | outside | exocrine, exoskeleton |
| -gen | produce, generate | pathogen, antigen |
| geo- | earth | geologic, geographic |
| hemo- | blood | hemoglobin |
| hydro- | water | hydroponics, hydrophilic |
| -itis | disease of | appendicitis, dermititis |
| leuko- | white | leukocyte |
| -logy | study of, science of | biology, zoology |
| mono- | one | monocot, monosaccharide |
| -ose | carbohydrate | glucose, cellulose |
| photo- | light | photosynthesis, phototropism |
| -phyll | leaf | mesophyll |
| -phyte | a plant | bryophyte, anthophyte |
| -scope | instrument for viewing | microscope |
| syn- | to put together, with | synthetic, photosynthesis |
| thigmo- | touch | thigmotropism |
| trans- | across | transpiration |
| trop- | turn, respond to | tropism |
| uni- | one | unicellular |

▲ **Figure 5**

# Glossary

Pronunciation and syllabication have been derived from *Webster's New World Dictionary*, Second College Edition, Revised School Printing (Prentice Hall, 1985). Syllables printed in capital letters are given primary stress. (Numbers in parentheses indicate the page number, or page numbers, on which the term is defined.)

| PRONUNCIATION KEY | | | | | |
|---|---|---|---|---|---|
| Symbol | Example | Respelling | Symbol | Example | Respelling |
| a | amber | (AM-bur) | ks | thorax | (THAWR-aks) |
| ah | molecule | (MAHL-ih-kyool) | oh | embryo | (EM-bree-oh) |
| aw | absorption | (ab-SAWRP-shuhn) | oi | joint | (JOINT) |
| ay | adaptation | (ad-uhp-TAY-shuhn) | oo | asexual | (ay-SEK-shoo-uhl) |
| eh | energy | (EHN-uhr-jee) | sh | circulation | (sur-kyoo-LAY-shuhn) |
| ee | ecology | (ee-KAHL-uh-jee) | u | urine | (YUR-ihn) |
| f | phloem | (FLOH-em) | uh | data | (DAYT-uh) |
| g | gamete | (GAM-eet) | y, eye | biome, iris | (BY-ohm), (EYE-ris) |
| I | specialization | (spesh-uhl-ih-ZAY-shuhn) | z | organism | (AWR-guh-nihz-uhm) |
| j | genes | (JEENZ) | zh | diffusion | (dih-FYOO-zhuhn) |
| k | Calorie | (KAL-uh-ree) | | | |

## A

**abdomen** (AB-duh-muhn): third section of an insect's body (p. 220)

**absorption** (ab-SAWRP-shuhn): movement of food molecules from the digestive system to the blood (p. 346)

**active transport:** movement of materials through a membrane using energy (p. 50)

**adaptation** (ad-uhp-TAY-shuhn): trait that helps an organism survive in its environment (pp. 98, 290)

**addiction** (uh-DIHK-shuhn): uncontrollable dependence on a drug (p. 438)

**adolescence:** stage of development in which children experience rapid physical growth (p. 458)

**AIDS:** viral disease that attacks a person's immune system (p. 408)

**alcoholic** (al-kuh-HAWL-ihk): person who is dependent on alcohol (p. 440)

**allele** (uh-LEEL): one of two or more forms of a particular gene (p. 70)

**alveolus** (al-VEE-uh-luhs), *pl.* **alveoli:** microscopic air sac in the lung (p. 376)

**amber:** hardened tree sap (p. 100)

**amino acid:** building block of proteins (p. 330)

**amnion** (AM-nee-uhn): fluid-filled sac that surrounds an embryo (p. 454)

**amphibian** (am-FIHB-ee-uhn): animal that lives part of its life in water and part on land (p. 232)

**angiosperm** (AN-jee-oh-spuhrm): type of vascular, flowering plant (p. 164)

**annelid** (AN-uh-lid): type of worm with a segmented body (p. 206)

**antenna** (an-TEHN-uh), *pl.* **antennae:** structure used for touch, taste, and smell (p. 220)

**anther:** part of the stamen that produces pollen (p. 184)

**anthropology** (an-throh-PAHL-uh-jee): science that deals with the study of human beings (p. 110)

**antibiotic** (an-tih-by-AHT-ihk): chemical made by a living organism that kills bacteria (p. 404)

**antibody** (AN-tih-bahd-ee): molecule the body makes to protect itself from disease (p. 400)

**antigen:** signal molecule that produces an immune response (p. 400)

**aorta** (ay-AWR-tuh): largest artery in the body (p. 360)

**aroheabacteria** (ar-KEE-back-teer-eeya): the most ancient tpe of simple, single-celled organisms on Earth (p. 134)

**artery** (AHRT-uhr-ee)**:** blood vessel that carries blood away from the heart (p. 360)

**arthropod** (AHR-throh-pahd)**:** animal with an exoskeleton and jointed legs (p. 216)

**asexual** (ay-SEHK-shoo-uhl) **reproduction:** reproduction needing only one parent (pp. 32, 192)

**atherosclerosis** (ath-uhr-oh-skluh-ROH-sis)**:** buildup of fat deposits on artery walls (p. 368)

**atom:** smallest part of an element (p. 19)

**atrium** (AY-tree-uhm), *pl.* **atria:** upper chamber of the heart (p. 358)

**autotroph** (AW-toh-trahf)**:** an organism that can make its own food (pp. 20, 178)

**axon:** fiber that carries messages away from a nerve cell body (p. 418)

## B

**bacillus** (buh-SIHL-uhs), *pl.* **bacilli:** rod-shaped bacterium (p. 136)

**bacteriophage** (bak-TIHR-ee-uh-fayj)**:** virus that infects bacteria (p. 128)

**B cell:** special white blood cell that produces antibodies (p. 402)

**behavior** (bee-HAYV-yuhr)**:** way in which living things respond to stimuli (p. 24)

**benign** (bih-NYN) **tumor:** mass of cells that is usually harmless (p. 410)

**bile:** green liquid that breaks down large droplets of fat into smaller droplets of fat (p. 346)

**biome** (BY-ohm)**:** large region with a characteristic climate and plant and animal communities (p. 264)

**bladder:** excretory organ that stores liquid wastes (p. 388)

**blade:** wide, flat part of a leaf (p. 176)

**brainstem:** bundle of nerves at the base of the brain (p. 420)

**bronchus** (BRAHN-kuhs) *pl.* **bronchi:** tube leading to the lungs (p. 376)

**bryophytes** (BRY-uh-fyts)**:** group of plants that do not have transport tubes (p. 154)

**budding:** kind of asexual reproduction in which a new organism forms from a bud on a parent (p. 148)

**bulb:** underground stem covered with fleshy leaves (p. 192)

**byproduct:** something produced in addition to the main product (p. 22)

## C

**Calorie** (KAL-uh-ree)**:** unit used to measure energy from foods (p. 350)

**cap:** umbrella-shaped top of a mushroom (p. 144)

**capillary** (KAP-uh-ler-ee)**:** tiny blood vessel that connects arteries to veins (p. 360)

**capsid** (KAP-sid)**:** protein covering of a virus (p. 128)

**carbohydrate** (kahr-boh-HY-drayt)**:** nutrient that supplies energy (p. 328)

**carbon cycle:** repeated movement of carbon between Earth's atmosphere and organisms (p. 294)

**carcinogen:** substance that causes cancer (p. 87)

**cardiac** (KAHR-dee-ak) **muscle:** type of muscle found only in the heart and major blood vessels (p. 320)

**carnivore:** consumer that eats only animals (p. 278)

**carrier:** organism that has a recessive gene for a trait but does not show the trait (p. 82)

**carrying capacity:** largest population size that can be supported by the available resources of an area (p. 262)

**cartilage** (KAHRT-uhl-ihj)**:** tough, flexible connective tissue (pp. 230, 310)

**cell:** basic unit of structure and function in living things (pp. 18, 40)

**cell division:** process by which cells reproduce (p. 56)

**cell membrane** (MEHM-brayn)**:** thin structure that surrounds a cell (p. 42)

**cellular respiration** (rehs-puh-RAY-shuhn)**:** process by which a cell releases energy from food molecules (p. 22)

**cellulose** (SEHL-yoo-lohs)**:** carbohydrate made up of many sugar molecules that forms most of the cell wall of a plant cell (p. 46)

**cell wall:** thick, outer layer that surrounds the cell membranes of plants and some simple organisms (p. 46)

**centromere** (SEHN-troh-meer)**:** point of a chromosome where two parts meet (p. 70)

**cerebellum** (ser-uh-BEHL-uhm)**:** part of the brain that controls balance and body motion (p. 420)

**cerebrum** (suh-REE-bruhm)**:** part of the brain that controls the senses and thinking (p. 420)

**cervix** (SUR-vihks)**:** narrow end of the uterus (p. 446)

**characteristic:** quality or property that defines or classifies something (p. 18)

**chemical digestion:** process by which large food molecules are broken down into smaller food molecules (p. 342)

**chitin** (KY-tihn)**:** hard material that makes up the exoskeleton of arthropods (p. 216)

**chlorophyll** (KLAWR-uh-fihl)**:** green material in chloroplasts that is needed by plants to make food (pp. 46, 178)

**chloroplast:** organelle in a plant cell that contains chlorophyll (pp. 46, 178)

**chordate** (kawr-DAYT)**:** animal with a notochord at some time during its development (p. 228)

**chromatin:** threadlike material that makes up a chromosome (p. 56)

**chromosome** (KROH-muh-sohm)**:** cell part that determines what traits a living thing will have (p. 56)

**chyme** (KYM)**:** thick liquid form in which food leaves the stomach (p. 344)

**cilium** (SIHL-ee-uhm), *pl.* **cilia:** tiny, hairlike structure (pp. 138, 382)

**circulation** (sur-kyoo-LAY-shuhn)**:** movement of blood through the body (p. 356)

**cirrhosis** (suh-ROH-sihs)**:** liver disorder that can be caused by the excessive use of alcohol (p. 440)

**classification** (klas-uh-fih-KAY-shuhn)**:** grouping things according to similarities (p. 118)

**climate:** average weather in an area over a long period of time (p. 264)

**climax** (KLY-maks) **community:** last community in a succession (p. 268)

**closed circulatory system:** organ system in which blood moves through vessels (pp. 206, 356)

**cnidarian** (nih-DER-ee-uhn)**:** invertebrate animal with stinging cells and a hollow central cavity (p. 204)

**coccus** (KAHK-uhs), *pl.* **cocci:** spherical-shaped bacterium (p. 136)

**cochlea** (KAHK-lee-uh)**:** part of the ear that changes vibrations into nerve signals (p. 430)

**cocoon** (kuh-KOON)**:** protective covering around the pupa (p. 222)

**codominance:** pattern of inheritance in which both alleles of a gene are expressed (p. 78)

**cold blooded:** having a body temperature that changes with the temperature of the surroundings (p. 230)

**commensalism:** relationship between two different kinds of organisms in which one benefits and the other is unaffected (p. 288)

**communication:** sharing information (p. 8)

**community:** all the populations that live in a certain place and can interact with one another (p. 258)

**compact bone:** mostly solid, dense part of a bone (p. 312)

**competition:** struggle among organisms for resources in an ecosystem (p. 284)

**compound:** substance made up of two or more different elements (pp. 19, 58)

**condensation:** changing of a gas into a liquid (p. 292)

**conditioned response:** learned behavior in which a new stimulus causes the same response that an old one did (p. 249)

**conifer** (KAHN-uh-fuhr)**:** tree that produces cones and has needlelike leaves (p. 162)

**connective tissue:** tissue that holds parts of the body together (p. 306)

**conservation** (kahn-suhr-VAY-shuhn)**:** wise use of natural resources (p. 270)

**constant:** something that does not change (p. 11)

**consumer** (kuhn-SOOM-uhr)**:** organism that obtains food by eating other organisms (p. 278)

**contagious:** can be spread from one person to another (p. 404)

**controlled breeding:** mating organisms to produce offspring with certain traits (p. 88)

**controlled experiment:** experiment in which all the conditions except one are kept constant (p. 11)

**cornea** (KAWR-nee-uh)**:** clear covering at the front of the eye (p. 428)

**coronary** (KAWR-uh-ner-ee) **artery:** artery that carries blood and oxygen to the tissues of the heart (p. 368)

**cotyledon** (kaht-uh-LEED-uhn)**:** leaflike structure inside a seed that contains food for the developing plant (p. 164)

**cytoplasm** (SYT-oh-plaz-uhm)**:** gel-like substance inside the cell where most of the cell's activities take place (p. 42)

## D

**data** (DAYT-uh)**:** information you collect when you observe something (p. 3)

**daughter cell:** new cell produced by cell division (p. 56)

**decomposer** (dee-kuhm-POHZ-uhr)**:** organism that breaks down the wastes or remains of other organisms (p. 278)

**deficiency** (dee-FIHSH-uhn-see) **disease:** disease caused by the lack of a certain nutrient (p. 332)

**deforestation:** excessive cutting of forests (p. 294)

**degree Celsius:** metric unit of temperature (p. 6)

**dendrite** (DEHN-dryt)**:** fiber that carries messages to the nerve cell body (p. 418)

**dentin:** spongy substance below the enamel of the tooth (p. 342)

**depressant** (dee-PREHS-uhnt)**:** drug that slows down the central nervous system (p. 438)

**dermis:** inner layer of skin (p. 392)

**diaphragm** (DY-uh-fram)**:** sheet of muscle below the lungs (p. 378)

**dicot:** flowering plant with two cotyledons, or seed leaves, in its seeds (p. 164)

**digestion** (dih-JEHS-chuhn)**:** process of breaking down food so that it can be used by living things (pp. 22, 340)

**DNA:** large molecule contained in chromosomes (p. 68)

**domain:** very broad classification group (p. 120)

**dominant** (DAHM-uh-nuhnt) **gene:** gene whose trait always shows itself (p. 72)

**drug:** a chemical substance that causes a change in the body (p. 438)

## E

**eardrum:** sheet of tissue that vibrates when sounds strike it (p. 430)

**echinoderm** (ee-KY-noh-duhrm)**:** spiny-skinned animal (p. 210)

**ecology** (ee-KAHL-uh-jee)**:** study of the relationship between living things and their environments (p. 256)

**ecosystem** (EE-koh-sihs-tuhm)**:** group of communities interacting with each other and the nonliving parts of their environment (p. 258)

**ectotherm:** animal whose body temperature changes with its environment; cold-blooded animal (p. 230)

**egg cell:** female reproductive cell (pp. 66, 246)

**element:** simple substance that cannot be broken down into another substance (p. 58)

**embryo** (EHM-bree-oh)**:** undeveloped plant or animal (p. 186); developing human organism up until eight weeks of pregnancy (p. 454)

**emulsification** (ee-mul-suh-fih-KAY-shuhn)**:** process of breaking down large droplets of fat into smaller droplets of fat (p. 346)

**enamel:** hard, outer covering of a tooth (p. 342)

**endangered species** (ehn-DAYN-juhrd SPEE-sheez)**:** species of living organisms in danger of becoming extinct (p. 298)

**endocrine** (EHN-doh-krihn) **gland:** gland that does not have ducts (pp. 308, 432)

**endocrine** (EHN-doh-krihn) **system:** organ system that includes all the glands of the body (pp. 308, 432)

**endoplasmic reticulum** (ehn-doh-PLAZ-mihk rih-TIHK-yuh-luhm)**:** small network of tubes inside a cell that substances move along (p. 44)

**endoskeleton** (ehn-doh-SKEHL-uh-tuhn)**:** skeleton inside the body (p. 200)

**endospore:** inactive bacterium surrounded by a thick wall (p. 136)

**endotherm:** vertebrate whose body temperature remains about the same; warm-blooded animal (p. 238)

**energy:** ability to do work or cause change (p. 54)

**energy pyramid:** way of showing how energy moves through a food chain (p. 282)

**environment** (ehn-VY-ruhn-muhnt)**:** everything that surrounds an organism and acts upon it (p. 256)

**enzyme** (EHN-zym)**:** protein that controls chemical reactions in the body (p. 342)

**epidermis** (ehp-uh-DUR-mihs)**:** outer, protective layer of the leaf (p. 176); outer layer of skin (p. 392)

**epididymis** (ehp-uh-DID-ih-mihs)**:** coiled tube that stores sperm (p. 448)

**epiglottis** (ehp-uh-GLAHT-ihs)**:** flap of tissue that prevents food from entering the windpipe (p. 340)

**epithelial** (ehp-ih-THEE-lee-uhl) **tissue:** tissue that covers and protects parts of the body (p. 306)

**era:** division of geologic time; subdivision of an eon (p. 112)

**esophagus** (ih-SAHF-uh-guhs): tube that connects the mouth and the stomach (p. 340)

**estrogen:** hormone that helps regulate the menstrual cycle (p. 446)

**eubacteria** (YOO-back-teer-eeya): simple single-celled organisms that live nearly everywhere in the world (p. 136)

**evaporation** (ee-vap-uh-RAY-shuhn): changing of a liquid to a gas (pp. 292, 392)

**evolution** (ehv-uh-LOO-shuhn): process by which organisms change over time (p. 98)

**excretion** (ehks-KREE-shuhn): process of removing waste products from the body (pp. 22, 388)

**exhale:** to breathe out (p. 378)

**exocrine** (EHKS-oh-krihn) **gland:** gland that has ducts (p. 432)

**exoskeleton** (ehks-oh-SKEHL-uh-tuhn): external skeleton (p. 200)

**extensor** (ehk-STEHN-suhr): muscle that straightens a joint (p. 316)

**extinct** (ehk-STINKT): no longer found as a living species (p. 100)

**extinction:** disappearance of all members of a species (p. 108)

**extremophile** (ex-TREEM-uh-file): an organism that ives under extreme environmental conditions (p. 134)

## F

**fermentation:** process by which a cell releases energy from food without using oxygen (pp. 54, 144)

**fertilization** (fuhrt-uhl-ih-ZAY-shuhn): joining of the nuclei of a male and a female reproductive cell; joining of one sperm cell and one egg cell (pp. 184, 246, 452)

**fetus** (FEET-uhs): term used to describe an embryo eight weeks after fertilization (p. 454)

**fibrous** (FY-bruhs) **root system:** root system made up of many thin, branched roots (p. 172)

**filament:** stalk of the stamen (p. 184)

**flagellum** (fluh-JEHL-uhm), *pl.* **flagella:** whiplike structure on a cell (p. 134)

**flexor** (FLEHKS-uhr): muscle that bends a joint (p. 316)

**food chain:** way of showing how the energy from food moves through populations of organisms in a community (p. 280)

**food web:** way of showing how food chains are related (p. 280)

**fossil** (FAHS-uhl): remains or traces of a once-living organism (p. 100)

**fossil fuel:** nonrenewable energy source formed from the remains of plants and animals that lived and died long ago (p. 294)

**fracture:** crack or break in a bone (p. 312)

**frond:** leaf of a fern (p. 158)

**fruit:** mature ovary and its seeds (p. 186)

**fungus** (FUN-guhs), *pl.* **fungi:** plantlike organism that lacks chlorophyll (p. 124)

## G

**gamete** (GAM-eet): reproductive cell (pp. 66, 452)

**gastric juice:** juice produced in the stomach that contains mucus, pepsin, and hydrochloric acid (p. 344)

**gender:** sex of a person or other organism (p. 80)

**gene splicing** (SPLYS-ing): moving a section of DNA from the genes of one organism to the genes of another organism (p. 92)

**genes** (JEENZ): parts of a chromosome that control inherited traits (p. 70)

**genetic engineering** (juh-NEHT-ihk ehn-juh-NIR-ing): methods used to produce new forms of DNA (p. 92)

**genetics** (juh-NEHT-ihks): study of heredity (p. 64)

**genus** (JEE-nuhs): classification group made up of related species (p. 120)

**geologic** (jee-uh-LAHJ-ihk) **time scale:** record of Earth's history based upon types of organisms that lived at different times (p. 112)

**germinate** (JUR-muh-nayt): to grow from a seed into an embryo plant (p. 190)

**gestation** (jehs-TAY-shuhn): time it takes an embryo to fully develop inside its mother's body (p. 246)

**gill:** structure in a mushroom that produces spores (p. 144); organ that absorbs dissolved oxygen from water (p. 230)

**gland:** organ or group of cells that produces and secretes substances used by the body; organ that makes chemical substances used or released by the body (pp. 308, 432)

**glucose:** simple type of sugar (p. 54)

**Golgi body:** organelle that packages and sends materials to other places in the cell (p. 44)

**gram:** basic metric unit of mass (p. 4)

**gravitropism:** plant's response to gravity (p. 194)

**guard cell:** cell that conrols the size of the stoma (p. 48)

**gymnosperm** (JIHM-noh-spuhrm)**:** type of land plant that has uncovered seeds (p. 162)

## H

**habitat** (HAB-ih-tat)**:** place where an organism lives (p. 260)

**hallucinogen** (huh-LOO-sih-nuh-juhn)**:** drug that causes a person to see, hear, smell, and taste things in an altered way (p. 438)

**heart attack:** failure of a part of the heart due to a lack of blood and oxygen (p. 368)

**hemoglobin** (HEE-muh-gloh-bihn)**:** protein found in red blood cells that carries oxygen (p. 362)

**herbaceous** (huhr-BAY-shuhs) **stem:** stem that is soft and green (p. 174)

**herbivore:** consumer that eats only plants (p. 278)

**heredity** (huh-REHD-ih-tee)**:** passing of traits from parents to offspring (p. 64)

**heterotroph** (HEHT-uhr-oh-trahf)**:** organism that cannot make its own food (pp. 20, 178)

**heterozygous** (heht-uhr-oh-ZY-guhs)**:** having two unlike genes for the same trait (p. 72)

**hibernation** (hy-buhr-NAY-shuhn)**:** inactive state of some animals during winter months (p. 24)

**hilum** (HY-luhm)**:** mark on the seed coat where the seed was attached to the ovary (p. 190)

**homeostasis** (hoh-mee-oh-STAY-sihs)**:** process of keeping conditions inside a body constant, no matter the conditions outside the body (p. 20)

**homologous** (hoh-MAHL-uh-guhs) **structure:** body parts that have the same basic structure on different organisms (p. 102)

**homozygous** (hoh-moh-ZY-guhs)**:** having two like genes for the same trait (p. 72)

**hormone** (HAWR-mohn)**:** chemical substance that regulates body functions (pp. 356, 434)

**host:** organism a parasite feeds on (p. 288)

**hybridization** (hy-brihd-ih-ZAY-shuhn)**:** mating two different kinds of organisms (p. 88)

**hydrotropism:** plant's response to water (p. 194)

**hypha** (HY-fuh) *pl.* **hyphae** (HY-fee)**:** threadlike structure that makes up the body of molds and mushrooms (p. 144)

**hypothalamus** (hy-poh-THAL-uh-muhs)**:** part of the brain that tells the pituitary glands to release certain chemicals (p. 432)

**hypothesis** (hy-PAHTH-uh-sihs)**:** suggested answer to a question or problem (p. 10)

## I

**immune system:** body system made up of cells and tissues that help a person fight disease (p. 401)

**immunity** (ih-MYOON-uh-tee)**:** resistance to a specific disease (p. 402)

**imperfect flower:** flower with either male or female reproductive organs, but not both (p. 182)

**inbreeding:** mating closely related organisms (p. 88)

**incomplete dominance:** pattern of inheritance in which alleles from both parents are blended (p. 78)

**infer:** to form a conclusion (p. 8)

**ingestion** (ihn-JEHS-chuhn)**:** process of taking in food (p. 22)

**inhalant:** everyday product that is inhaled and used as a drug (p. 438)

**inhale:** to breathe in (p. 378)

**inherited disease:** disease caused by an inherited gene (p. 84)

**inherited** (ihn-HEHR-ih-tuhd) **trait:** trait that is passed from parents to their offspring (p. 64)

**innate behavior:** behavior an animal is born with (p. 248)

**instinct:** innate behavior that animals perform correctly the first time (p. 248)

**interact:** process of organisms acting upon one another or on the nonliving parts of their environments (p. 256)

**invertebrate** (ihn-VUHR-tuh-briht)**:** animal without a backbone (p. 200)

**iris** (EYE-ris)**:** colored part of the eye that controls the amount of light entering the eye (p. 428)

## J

**joint:** place where two or more bones meet (p. 314)

## K

**karyotype:** organized display of an organism's chromosomes (p. 70)

**kidney:** excretory organ that removes waste products from the blood (p. 388)

**kingdom:** classification group made up of related phyla (p. 120)

## L

**larynx** (LAR-inks)**:** organ located on the top of the trachea that contains the vocal cords (p. 376)

**larva** (LAHR-vuh)**:** immature stage of many animals that usually looks different from the adult form (pp. 222, 234)

**leaflet:** smaller division of a leaf (p. 158)

**learned behavior:** behavior an animal practices and learns (p. 248)

**lens** (LENZ)**:** piece of curved glass or other clear material that causes light rays to come together or spread apart as they pass through (p. 38); part of the eye that focuses an image on the retina (p. 428)

**ligament** (LIHG-uh-muhnt)**:** type of tissue that connects bones (p. 306)

**limiting factor:** condition in the environment that puts limits on the size a population can grow to (p. 262)

**lipase** (LY-pays)**:** enzyme that digests fats and oils (p. 346)

**lipid:** fat (p. 19)

**liter:** basic metric unit of liquid volume (p. 4)

**lysosome** (LY-soh-sohm)**:** small, round structure that breaks down nutrient molecules and old cell parts (p. 44)

## M

**malignant** (muh-LIHG-nuhnt) **tumor:** harmful mass of cells that can spread throughout the body (p. 410)

**malnutrition** (mal-noo-TRISH-uhn)**:** poor nutrition caused by an unbalanced diet (p. 338)

**mammary** (MAM-uh-ree) **gland:** gland that produces milk in female mammals (p. 242)

**mantle:** thin membrane that covers a mollusk's organs (p. 208)

**marrow:** soft tissue inside bones that produces blood cells (p. 312)

**marsupial:** mammal whose young develops in a pouch (p. 242)

**mass:** amount of matter in an object (p. 4)

**mass selection:** crossing plants with desirable traits (p. 88)

**matter:** any substance that has mass (p. 19)

**mechanical digestion:** process by which large pieces of food are cut and crushed into smaller pieces (p. 342)

**medulla** (mih-DUL-uh)**:** part of the brain that controls heartbeat and breathing rate (p. 420)

**medusa** (muh-DOO-suh)**:** umbrella-like form of a cnidarian (p. 204)

**meiosis** (my-OH-sihs)**:** type of cell division that produces gametes (p. 66)

**meniscus:** curved shape of the surface of a liquid in a thin tube (p. 4)

**menopause:** time at which women stop ovulating (p. 458)

**menstrual** (MEHN-struhl) **cycle:** monthly cycle of change that occurs in the female reproductive system (p. 450)

**menstruation** (mehn-stroo-AY-shuhn)**:** process by which blood and tissue from the lining of the uterus break apart and leave the body (p. 450)

**mesophyll** (MEHS-uh-fihl)**:** middle layer of leaf tissue in which photosynthesis occurs (p. 176)

**metamorphosis** (meht-uh-MAWR-fuh-sihs)**:** series of developmental changes of an organism (p. 222)

**meter** (MEET-uhr)**:** basic metric unit of length or distance (p. 4)

**microscope** (MY-kruh-skohp)**:** tool that makes things look larger than they really are (p. 38)

**migration** (my-GRAY-shuhn)**:** seasonal movement of animals from one place to another and back (p. 24)

**mineral:** nutrient needed by the body to develop and function properly (p. 334)

**mitochondrion** (myt-oh-KAHN-dree-uhn), *pl.* **mitochondria:** structure that releases energy for a cell (p. 44)

**mitosis** (my-TOH-sihs)**:** division of the nucleus (p. 56)

**model:** a tool scientists use to represent an object or a process (p. 3)

**molecule** (MAHL-ih-kyool)**:** smallest part of a substance that has all the properties of that substance (pp. 58, 330)

**mollusk** (MAHL-ushk)**:** soft-bodied organism (p. 208)

**molting:** process by which an animal sheds its outer covering (p. 216)

**monocot:** flowering plant with one cotyledon, or seed leaf, in its seeds (p. 164)

**monotreme:** mammal that lays eggs (p. 242)

**mucus** (MYOO-kuhs)**:** sticky liquid (p. 382)

**multicellular:** containing more than one cell (p. 48)

**mutagen:** substance that increases the rate of mutation (p. 86)

**mutation** (myoo-TAY-shuhn)**:** change in a gene (pp. 86, 98)

**mutualism:** relationship between two different types of organisms in which one lives on or in another organism and causes it harm (p. 288)

## N

**natural resource** (REE-sawrs)**:** material found in nature that is used by living things (p. 270)

**natural selection:** survival of offspring that have favorable traits (p. 104)

**nematode** (NEHM-uh-tohd)**:** type of worm with a round body (p. 206)

**nephron** (NEHF-rahn)**:** filtering structure of the kidneys (p. 390)

**neuron** (NOOR-ahn)**:** nerve cell (p. 418)

**niche** (NIHCH)**:** organism's role, or job, in its habitat (p. 260)

**nicotine** (NIHK-uh-teen)**:** stimulant found in tobacco (p. 386)

**nitrogen cycle:** repeated movement of nitrogen compounds between the atmosphere, the soil, and living organisms (p. 296)

**nitrogen fixation:** process of combining nitrogen with other elements to make usable compounds (p. 296)

**nitrogen-fixing bacteria:** bacteria that can use nitrogen in soil to make nitrogen compounds (p. 136)

**nonrenewable resource:** natural resource that cannot be renewed or replaced (p. 270)

**nonvascular plant:** plant that does not have transport tubes (p. 154)

**notochord** (NOHT-uh-kawrd)**:** strong, rodlike structure in chordates that can bend (p. 228)

**nuclear membrane:** thin structure that surrounds and protects the nucleus (p. 42)

**nucleus** (NOO-klee-uhs) *pl.* **nuclei:** control center of a cell (p. 42)

**nutrient** (NOO-tree-uhnt)**:** chemical substance that is needed to carry out life processes (pp. 22, 328)

**nymph** (NIHMF)**:** young insect that looks like the adult (p. 222)

## O

**offspring:** new organism produced by a living thing (p. 32)

**omnivore:** consumer that eats both plants and animals (p. 278)

**open circulatory system:** circulatory system in which blood does not flow constantly through tubes (p. 216)

**organ** (AWR-guhn)**:** group of tissues that work together to do a special job (p. 308)

**organ system:** group of organs that work together (p. 308)

**organelle** (awr-guh-NEHL)**:** small structure in the cytoplasm that does a special job (p. 44)

**organism** (AWR-guh-nihz-uhm)**:** any living thing (p. 18)

**osmosis** (ahs-MOH-sihs)**:** movement of water through a membrane (p. 50)

**ovary** (OH-vuh-ree)**:** in a plant, the bottom part of the pistil that produces seeds (p. 186); in mammals, organ of the female reproductive system that produces hormones and eggs (p. 446)

**oviduct** (OH-vih-dukt)**:** long tube between the ovary and the uterus (p. 446)

**ovulation** (ahv-yuh-LAY-shuhn)**:** release of a mature egg from the ovary (p. 450)

**ovule** (AHV-yool)**:** part of the ovary that develops into a seed after fertilization (p. 186)

## P

**parasite** (PAR-uh-syt)**:** organism that gets its food by living on or in the body of another organism (p. 206)

**parasitism:** relationship between two different kinds of organisms in which one organism lives on or in another organism and causes it harm (p. 288)

**passive transport:** movement of materials through a membrane without the use of energy (p. 50)

**pathogen:** any agent that causes disease (p. 400)

**pedigree:** chart that shows the inheritance of certain traits over several generations (p. 82)

**pepsin** (PEHP-sihn)**:** enzyme that digests proteins (p. 344)

**perfect flower:** flower with both male and female reproductive organs (p. 182)

**periosteum** (per-ee-AHS-tee-uhm)**:** thin membrane that covers a bone (p. 312)

**peristalsis** (per-uh-STAL-sihs): wavelike movement that moves food through the digestive tract (p. 340)

**perspiration** (pur-spuh-RAY-shuhn): waste water and salts that leave the body through the skin (p. 392)

**petal:** white or brightly colored structure above the sepal of a flower (p. 182)

**pharynx** (FAR-inks): tube connecting the mouth to the esophagus; throat (p. 340)

**phloem** (FLOH-em): tissue that carries food from the leaves to other parts of the plant (p. 174)

**photosynthesis** (foht-oh-SIHN-thuh-sihs): food-making process in plants and other organisms that uses sunlight (pp. 54, 178)

**phototropism:** plant's response to light (p. 194)

**phylum** (FY-luhm), *pl.* **phyla:** classification group made up of related classes (p. 120)

**pistil:** female reproductive organ in a flower (p. 182)

**placenta** (pluh-SEHN-tuh): structure through which materials are exchanged between the mother and the developing embryo (pp. 242, 454)

**plankton** (PLANK-tuhn): microscopic organisms that float on or near the water's surface (p. 142)

**plasma** (PLAZ-muh): liquid part of blood (p. 362)

**platelet** (PLAYT-liht): piece of a cell that is involved in blood clotting (p. 362)

**platyhelminth** (plat-uh-HEHL-mihnth): type of worm with a flattened body (p. 206)

**pollen grain:** male reproductive cell of a plant (p. 184)

**pollination** (pahl-uh-NAY-shuhn): movement of pollen from a stamen to a pistil (p. 184)

**pollution:** release of harmful materials into the environment (p. 108)

**polyp** (PAHL-ihp): cuplike form of a cnidarian (p. 204)

**population:** group of the same kind of organisms living in a certain place (p. 258)

**pore:** tiny opening; tiny opening in the skin (pp. 202, 392)

**poriferan** (poh-RIHF-uhr-uhn): invertebrate animal with pores (p. 202)

**precipitation:** water that falls to Earth from the atmosphere (p. 292)

**predation:** relationship in which an organism kills and eats another organism (p. 284)

**predator:** organism that kills and eats another organism (p. 284)

**predict:** to state ahead of time what you think is going to happen (p. 8)

**prey:** organism that is killed and eaten by another organism (p. 284)

**producer** (pruh-DOOS-uhr): organism that makes its own food (p. 278)

**progesterone:** hormone that prepares the uterus for pregnancy (p. 446)

**protein** (PROH-teen): nutrient needed to build and repair cells (p. 328)

**protein synthesis:** process by which proteins are made (p. 68)

**protist** (PROHT-ihst): simple organism that has cells with nuclei (p. 124)

**protozoan** (proht-uh-ZOH-uhn): one-celled, animal-like protist (p. 138)

**pseudopod** (SOO-doh-pahd): fingerlike extension of the cytoplasm (pp. 48, 138)

**puberty** (PYOO-burh-tee): time at which a person becomes sexually mature (p. 450)

**pulmonary** (PUL-muh-ner-ee) **artery:** artery that carries blood from the heart to the lungs (p. 366)

**Punnett square:** chart that shows possible gene combinations (p. 74)

**pupa** (PYOO-puh): resting stage during complete metamorphosis (p. 222)

**pupil** (PYOO-puhl): opening in the center of the iris (p. 428)

## R

**radula** (RAJ-oo-luh): rough, tonguelike organ of a snail (p. 208)

**range** (RAYNJ): area where a type of animal or plant population is found (p. 262)

**receptor:** part of a nerve cell that receives stimuli from the environment (p. 422)

**recessive** (rih-SEHS-ihv) **gene:** gene of a trait that is hidden when the dominant gene is present (p. 72)

**red blood cell:** blood cell that carries oxygen (p. 48)

**reflex:** automatic response to a stimulus (p. 422)

**reflex arc:** path of a message in a reflex (p. 422)

**regeneration** (rih-jehn-uh-RAY-shuhn): ability to regrow lost parts (p. 212)

**renewable resource:** natural resource that can be renewed or replaced (p. 270)

**replication** (rehp-lih-KAY-shuhn): process by which DNA is duplicated (p. 68)

**reproduction** (ree-pruh-DUK-shuhn): process by which living things produce new organisms like themselves (p. 32)

**respiration** (rehs-puh-RAY-shuhn): process of carrying oxygen to cells, getting rid of carbon dioxide, and releasing energy (p. 378)

**response:** reaction to a change (p. 18)

**retina** (REHT-uhn-uh): part of the eye that receives images from the lens and transmits them to the brain (p. 428)

**rhizoid** (RY-zoid): fine, hairlike structure that acts as a root (p. 156)

**rhizome** (RY-zohm): horizontal underground stem (p. 158)

**ribosome** (RY-buh-sohm): small, round structure that makes proteins (p. 44)

**RNA:** molecule used in the making of proteins (p. 68)

**root cap:** cup-shaped mass of cells that covers and protects a root tip (p. 172)

**root hair:** thin, hairlike structure on the outer layer of the root tip (p. 172)

## S

**saliva:** liquid in the mouth that helps in digestion (p. 340)

**scavenger** (SKAV-ihn-juhr): animal that eats only dead organisms (p. 278)

**scrotum** (SKROHT-uhm): pocket of skin that protects and holds the testes (p. 448)

**seed:** structure that contains a tiny living plant and food for its growth; a reproductive cell (p. 162)

**seed coat:** outside covering of a seed (p. 190)

**sense organ:** special organ that receives and processes stimuli from the environment (p. 424)

**sepal** (SEE-puhl): special kind of leaf that protects the flower bud (p. 182)

**septum:** thick tissue wall that separates the left and right sides of the heart (p. 358)

**setae** (SEET-ee): tiny, hairlike bristles (p. 206)

**sex-linked traits:** traits that are controlled by the sex chromosomes (p. 82)

**sexual** (SEHK-shoo-uhl) **reproduction:** reproduction needing two parents (p. 32)

**simulation:** computer model that usually shows a process (p. 3)

**skeletal muscle:** muscle attached to the skeleton that makes movement possible (p. 320)

**skeletal system:** system of bones and cartilage that helps to support and protect the body (p. 310)

**smooth muscle:** muscle that causes movements that you cannot control (p. 320)

**specialization** (spehsh-uhl-ih-ZAY-shuhn): studying or working in only one part of a subject (p. 16)

**species:** group of organisms that look alike and can reproduce among themselves (pp. 98, 120)

**sperm cell:** male reproductive cell (pp. 66, 246)

**spicule** (SPIHK-yool): small, hard, needlelike structure of a sponge (p. 202)

**spiracle** (SPIR-uh-kuhl): opening to an air tube of a grasshopper (p. 220)

**spirillum** (spy-RIHL-uhm), *pl.* **spirilla:** spiral-shaped bacterium (p. 136)

**spongy bone:** part of a bone with many small pores or spaces (p. 312)

**spontaneous generation** (spahn-TAY-nee-uhs jehn-uhr-AY-shuhn): idea that living things come from nonliving things (p. 30)

**spore:** reproductive structure found in fungi and some plants (pp. 144, 156)

**spore case:** structure that contains spores (p. 148)

**sporulation** (spawr-yoo-LAY-shuhn): kind of asexual reproduction in which a new organism forms from spores released from a parent (p. 148)

**stalk:** stemlike part of a mushroom (p. 144)

**stamen** (STAY-muhn): male reproductive organ in a flower (p. 182)

**stigma** (STIHG-muh): top part of the pistil (p. 186)

**stimulant** (STIHM-yuh-luhnt): drug that speeds up the central nervous system (p. 438)

**stimulus** (STIHM-yuh-luhs), *pl.* **stimuli:** change that causes a response (pp. 24, 194)

**stoma** (STOH-muh), *pl.* **stomata:** tiny opening in the upper or lower surface of a leaf (pp. 48, 176)

**striated** (STRY-ayt-uhd) **muscle:** muscle tissue with stripes or dark bands (p. 320)

**style:** stalk of the pistil of a flower (p. 186)

**succession** (suhk-SEHSH-uhn): gradual change in populations of organisms that occurs when the environment changes (p. 268)

**swim bladder:** organ of a fish that allows the fish

to remain at a specific depth in the water (p. 230)

**symbiosis** (sihm-by-OH-sihs): relationship between different species living in close association with one another (p. 284)

**synapse** (SIHN-aps): gap between the axon of one cell and the dendrite of another (p. 418)

## T

**tadpole:** larval stage of a frog (p. 234)

**taproot system:** root system made up of one large root and many small, thin roots (p. 172)

**target cell:** cell that responds to a hormone's chemical structure (p. 434)

**taxonomy** (tak-SAHN-uh-mee): science of classifying living things (p. 118)

**T cell:** special type of white blood cell that attacks antigens (p. 402)

**temperature:** measure of the amount of heat energy something contains (p. 4)

**tendon** (TEHN-duhn): type of tissue that connects muscle to bone (p. 306)

**tentacles:** long, armlike structures (p. 204)

**testis** (TEHS-tihs), *pl.* **testes:** organ of the male reproductive system that produces hormones and sperm (p. 448)

**testosterone** (tes-TAHS-tuhr-ohn): hormone produced in the testes (p. 448)

**theory** (THEE-uh-ree): set of hypotheses that have been supported by testing over and over again (p. 10)

**thigmotropism:** plant's response to touch (p. 194)

**thorax** (THAWR-aks): middle section of an insect's body (p. 220)

**tissue:** group of cells that look alike and work together (p. 306)

**trachea** (TRAY-kee-uh): windpipe (p. 376)

**tracheophytes** (TRAY-kee-uh-fyts): group of plants that have transport tubes (p. 154)

**trait:** characteristic (p. 64)

**transfusion:** transfer of blood from one person into the body of another person (p. 362)

**transpiration:** process by which plants lose water through the stomata in their leaves (p. 292)

**transport:** process of moving nutrients and wastes in a living thing (p. 22)

**tropism** (TROH-pihz-uhm): change in a plant's growth in response to a stimulus (p. 194)

**tube feet:** small structures of echinoderms used for movement and feeding (p. 210)

**tuber:** underground stem (p. 192)

**tumor** (TOO-muhr): mass or lump of cells (p. 410)

**tympanum** (TIHM-puh-nuhm): hearing organ in a grasshopper (p. 220)

## U

**umbilical** (uhm-BIHL-ih-kuhl) **cord:** structure that connects the embryo to the placenta (p. 454)

**unicellular:** containing only one cell (p. 48)

**unit:** amount used to measure something (p. 4)

**urea** (yoo-REE-uh): nitrogen compound formed as a waste product (p. 390)

**ureter** (you-REET-uhr) : tube that carries liquid waste from the kidneys to the bladder (p. 388)

**urethra** (yoo-REE-thruh): tube that carries urine, and sperm for males, outside of the body (p. 448)

**urine** (YOOR-ihn): liquid waste formed in the kidneys (p. 390)

**uterus** (YOOT-uh-ruhs): organ in which an embryo develops (p. 446)

## V

**vacuole** (VAK-yoo-ohl): space in the cytoplasm of a cell that stores different substances a cell needs to survive (p. 44)

**vagina** (vuh-JY-nuh): birth canal (p. 446)

**valve:** thin flap of tissue that acts like a one-way door (p. 358)

**variable:** anything that can affect the outcome of an experiment (p. 11)

**variation** (ver-ee-AY-shuhn): differences in traits among individuals of a species (p. 104)

**vascular plant:** plant that contains transport tubes (p. 154)

**vegetative propagation** (VEHJ-uh-tayt-ihv prahp-uh-GAY-shuhn): kind of asexual reproduction that uses parts of plants to grow new plants (p. 192)

**vein** (VAYN): bundle of tubes that contains the xylem and phloem in a leaf (p. 176); blood vessel that carries blood back to the heart (p. 360)

**ventricle** (VEHN-trih-kuhl): lower chamber of the heart (p. 358)

**vertebra**, *pl.* **vertebrae:** bone that makes up the backbone (p. 310)

**vertebrate** (VER-tuh-briht): animal with a backbone (pp. 200, 228)

**vestigial** (vehs-TIHJ-ee-uhl) **structure:** body part that seems to have no function (p. 102)

**villus,** *pl.* **villi:** fingerlike projection on the lining of the small intestine (p. 346)

**virus** (VY-ruhs): nonliving particle made up of a piece of nucleic acid covered with a protein (p. 128)

**vitamin** (VYT-uh-mihn): nutrient found in foods that is required by the body and is made by other organisms (p. 332)

**volume:** amount of space an object takes up (p. 4)

## W

**warm-blooded animal:** animal having a body temperature that remains about the same (p. 21)

**water cycle:** repeated movement of water between Earth's surface and the atmosphere (p. 292)

**water-vascular system:** system of tubes used to transport water (p. 210)

**white blood cell:** blood cell that protects the body against disease (p. 400)

**woody stem:** stem that contains wood and is thick and hard (p. 174)

## X

**xylem** (ZY-luhm): tissue that carries water and dissolved minerals upward from the roots (p. 174)

## Z

**zygote** (ZY-goht): fertilized egg (p. 452)

# Index

## C

## D

## G



## H

## N



## O

# P

## Q



## R



## S

# Photo Credits

**Photography Credits:** All photographs are by Pearson Education, Inc., John Serafin for Pearson Education, Inc., and David Mager for Pearson Education, Inc., except as noted below.

**Cover:** Life Science
T. Davis/W. Bilenduke/Stone/Getty Images
Siede Preis/Photodisc/Getty Images

**Table of Contents** i Siede Preis/Photodisc/Getty Images; v t Siede Preis/Photodisc/Getty Images; v m Professors Pietro M. Motta & Silvia Correr / Photo Researchers, Inc.; vi t Siede Preis/Photodisc/Getty Images; vi m L. Willatt, East Anglican Regianl Genetics Service/Photo Researchers, Inc.; vi b Bob Ainsworth/Shutterstock; vii t Siede Preis/Photodisc/Getty Images; vii m Dennis Kunkel/Phototake Inc./Alamy; vii b Vadim Kozlovsky/Shutterstock; viii Siede Preis/Photodisc/Getty Images; ix Siede Preis/Photodisc/Getty Images; ix m Karl Shone/Dorling Kindersley Limited; x t Siede Preis/Photodisc/Getty Images; x m CBpix/Shutterstock; x b G.W. Willis/Animals Animals/Earth Science; xi Siede Preis/Photodisc/Getty Images; xii t Siede Preis/Photodisc/Getty Images; xii m Dr. Linda Sannard/Photo Researchers Inc.; xiii t Siede Preis/Photodisc/Getty Images; xiii b Mikael Damkier/Shutterstock; xiv Siede Preis/Photodisc/Getty Images; xvi Siede Preis/Photodisc/Getty Images; xvi Siede Preis/Photodisc/Getty Images

**Front Matter** P001 John Anderson/Alamy; P001 ml MedicalRF/Alamy; P001 mr Kucherenko Olena/Shutterstock; P001 r Siede Preis/Photodisc/Getty Images; P002 l S. Michael Bisceglie/Animals Animals/Earth Scenes; P002 r John Pontier/Animals Animals/Earth Scenes; P003 br Ventura Educational Systems; P003 r Siede Preis/Photodisc/Getty Images; P007 Siede Preis/Photodisc/Getty Images; P009 t Science Source/Photo Researchers Inc.; P009 bl Denis Finnin and Jackie Beckett/ Dorling Kindersley Limited; P009 br WorldFoto/Alamy; P009 r Siede Preis/Photodisc/Getty Images; P010 Timothy Epp/Shutterstock; P011 Siede Preis/Photodisc/Getty Images; P013 Siede Preis/Photodisc/Getty Images

**Chapter 1** P015 PhotoDisc/Getty Images; P016 tl Saied Shahin Kiya/Shutterstock; P016 bl Tom E. Adams/Peter Arnold, Inc.; P016 tr PhotoDisc/Getty Images; P016 br Art Wolfe/Photo Reasearchers, Inc.; P017 t Roger A. Clark, Jr./Photo Researchers, Inc.; P017 b Lawrence Migdale/Photo Researchers, Inc.; P018 Jean Claude Revy/Phototake; P019 PhotoDisc/Getty Images; P020 l Matt Meadows/Peter Arnold, Inc.; P020 r Rod Planck/Photo Researchers, Inc.; P021 Studio Photogram/Bloom Works Inc./Alamy; P022 Oksana Perkins/Shutterstock; P023 Professors P.M. Motta & S. Correr/Science Photo Library/Photo Researchers, Inc.; P024 l Runk/Schoenberger/Grant Heilman Photography, Inc.; P024 r Dan Guravich/Photo Researchers, Inc.; P024 inset George D. Lepp/Photo Researchers, Inc.; P031 t Bridgeman Art Library; b Jim Sugar/Corbis; P033 t Kristian Sekulic/Shutterstock; P033 b E.R. Degginger/Animals Animals/Earth Scenes; P034 PhotoDisc/Getty Images; P035 PhotoDisc/Getty Images; P036 PhotoDisc/Getty Images

**Chapter 2** P037 MedicalRF/Alamy; P039 Natural History Picture Library, London/Getty Images; P040 l Dr. Jonathan Eisenback/Phototake; P040 r Manfred Kage/Peter Arnold, Inc.; P041 AJPhoto/Photo Researchers Inc.; P041 inset Eye of Science/Photo Researchers Inc.; P042 t Ed Reschke/Peter Arnold, Inc.; P042 b Dr. Gopal Murti/Phototake; P043 Ed Reschke/Peter Arnold, Inc.; P044 P. Motta and T. Naguro/Science Photo Library/Photo Researchers, Inc.; P045 Dr. Gopal Murti/Science Photo Library/Photo Researchers, Inc.; P047 l Ed Reschke/Peter Arnold, Inc.; P047 r Ed Reschke/Peter Arnold, Inc.; P048 bl Carolina Biological Supply Company/Phototake Inc./Alamy; P048 tr MedicalRF/Alamy; P048 br SECCHI-LECAQUE/ROUSSEL-UCLAF/CNRI/SPL/Photo Researchers, Inc.; P049 Dr. Jeremy Burgess/Photo Researchers, Inc.; P051 PhotoDisc/Getty Images; P055 Fenghui/Shutterstock; P058-59 bkgd Michael Newman/PhotoEdit, Inc.; P060 MedicalRF/Alamy; P061 MedicalRF/Alamy; P062 MedicalRF/Alamy

**Chapter 3** P063 DBIMAGE/Jupitier Images; P064 t PhotoDisc/Getty Images; P064 b Olive/IML Image Group Ltd/Alamy; P065 Tony Freeman/PhotoEdit, Inc.; P067 Lawrence Migdale/Photo Researchers, Inc.; P068 A. Barrington Brown/Photo Researchers, Inc.; P070 L. Willatt, East Anglican Regional Genetics Service/Photo Researchers, Inc.; P074 Bettmann Archive/Corbis; P074 inset Beata Jancsik/Shutterstock; P072 Archiv/Photo Researchers, Inc./Photo Researchers, Inc.; P080 l CNRI Science Photo Library/Photo Researchers, Inc.; P080 r Doug Martin/Photo Researchers, Inc.; P080 inset Department of Clinical Cytogenetics Addenbrookes Hospital/Science Photo Library/Photo Researchers, Inc.; t Stanley Fellerman/Corbis; P081 inset Department of Clinical Cytogenetics Addenbrookes Hospital/Science Photo Library/Photo Researchers, Inc.; P081 b Richart T. Nowitz/Corbis; P082 Leonard Lessin/Peter Arnold, Inc.; P084 l Eye of Science/Photo Researchers Inc.; P084 r Ken Karp/Omni-Photo Communications; P085 Robin Nelson/Photo Edit; P086 l Kees Van Den Berg/Photo Researchers, Inc.; P086 r Blickwinkel/Hartl/Alamy; P087 Randy Jeide/Shutterstock; P088 l Leonard Lessin/Peter Arnold, Inc.; P088 r Gerard Lacz/Animals Animals/Earth Scenes; P089 Paul Vathis/AP Wide World Photos; P090 l Lisa F. Young/Shutterstock; P090 r Siloto/Shutterstock; P091 l Carolyn A. McKeone/Photo Researchers, Inc.; P091 m M. Hilgert/Okapia/Photo Researchers, Inc.; P091 r Carolyn A. McKeone/Photo Researchers, Inc.; P093 Reuters New Media/Corbis; P094 DBIMAGE/Jupitier Images; P095 DBIMAGE/Jupitier Images; P096 DBIMAGE/Jupitier Images

**Chapter 4** P097 Guillen Photography/Wildlife/Ecuador/Galapagos/Alamy; P098 t Marek Lambert/Shutterstock; P098 b Joe McDonald/Corbis; Tom Bean/Getty Images; P100 l Francis Latreille/Corbis; P100 tr Layne Kennedy/Corbis; P100 br Bob Ainsworth/Shutterstock; P103 James King-Holmes/Photo Researchers Inc.; P104 t Hulton-Deutsch Collection/Corbis; P104 b Jeff Greenberg/Omni-Photo Communications; P105 Mary Evans Picture Library/Photo Researchers, Inc.; P108 Dewitt Jones/Corbis; P109 t Chris Hellier/Corbis; P109 b Ronald C. Modra/Sports Imagery/Getty Images; P110 l Friedrich Saurer/Alamy; P110 m Archivo Iconografico, S.A./Corbis; P110 r John Reader/Science Photo Library/Photo Researchers, Inc.; P111 Bettmann/Corbis; P112 Biophoto Associates/Photo Researchers, Inc.; P114 Guillen Photography/Wildlife/Ecuador/Galapagos/Alamy; P115 Guillen Photography/Wildlife/Ecuador/Galapagos/Alamy; P116 t Guillen Photography/Wildlife/Ecuador/Galapagos/Alamy; P116 bl Friedrich Saurer/Alamy; P116 bm Archivo Iconografico, S.A./Corbis; P116 br John Reader/Science Photo Library/Photo Researchers, Inc.

**Chapter 5** P117 Ilian Animal/Alamy; P118 Michael Viard/Peter Arnold, Inc.; P119 Bryan and Cherry Alexander Photography/Alamy; P121 Fracois Gohier/Photo Researchers, Inc.; P124 Wikipedia; P125 col. 1 Biophoto Associates/Photo Researchers, Inc.; P125 col. 2 Manfred Kage/Peter Arnold, Inc.; P125 col. 3 Robert Planck/Photo Researchers, Inc.; P125 col. 4 Jean Claude Revy/Phototake; P125 col. 5 Michael Evans/PhotoDisc/Getty Images; P128 l Oliver Meckes/Photo Researchers, Inc.; P128 r Lee D. Simon/Photo Researchers, Inc.; P130 Ilian Animal/Alamy; P131 Ilian Animal/Alamy; P132 Ilian Animal/Alamy

**Chapter 6** P133 North Carolina Biological Supply/Phototake Inc./Alamy; P134 Yellowstone National Park/National Park Service/U.S. Department of the Interior; P134 inset BenC/Shutterstock; P135 t Eye of Science/Photo Researchers Inc.; P135 b P. Rona/OAR/National Undersea Research Program/NOAA; P136 l Dennis Kunkel/Phototake Inc./Alamy; P136 m Dennis Kunkel/Phototake Inc./Alamy; P136 r CNRI/Science Photo Library/Photo Researchers, Inc.; P137 Dennis Kunkel/Phototake Inc./Alamy; P138 t Eric Grave/Phototake; P138 b M.I. Walker/Photo Researchers, Inc.; P139 t Stone/Getty Images; P139 b Lynn McLaren/Photo Researchers, Inc.; P139 inset Manfred Kage/Peter Arnold, Inc.; P141 Blickwinkel/NaturimBild/Alamy; P142 t Dennis Kunkel/Phototake Inc./Alamy; P142 b Jeffrey L. Rotman/Peter Arnold, Inc.; P143 t Nick Kurzenko/Alamy; P143 b Tom and Pat Leeson/Photo Researchers, Inc.; P143 b inset

Blickwinkel/NaturimBild/Alamy; P145 Inga Spence/Alamy; P146 t Steve Lupton/Corbis; P146 t inset SPL/Custom Medical Stock Photo; P146 b The Image Bank/Getty Images; P146 b inset Mediscan/Medical-on-Line/Alamy; P147 t David Young-Wolff/PhotoEdit, Inc.; P147 t inset MedicalRF/Alamy; P147 b Catherine Karnow/Corbis; P147 b inset Walter H. Hodge/Peter Arnold Inc.; P148 l J. Forsdyke/Gene Cox/Science Photo Library/Photo Researchers, Inc.; P148 r E.R. Degginger/Photo Researchers, Inc.; P150 North Carolina Biological Supply/Phototake Inc./Alamy; P151 North Carolina Biological Supply/Phototake Inc./Alamy; P152 North Carolina Biological Supply/Phototake Inc./Alamy

**Chapter 7** P153 John Anderson/Alamy; P155 l Enna Van Duinen/Shutterstock; P155 Timothy Epp/Shutterstock; P156 l Carolina Biological Co./Phototake; P156 m Blickwinkel/Jagel/Alamy; P156 r Jozsef Szasz-Fabian/Shutterstock; P157 Doughoughton/Alamy; P158 Dean Pennala/Shutterstock; P158 r R. de Man/Shutterstock; P159 Publiphoto/Photo Researchers Inc.; P162 l PhotoDisc/Getty Images; P162 r Shutterstock; P163 Walter Hodge/Peter Arnold, Inc.; P164 Vadim Kozlovsky/Shutterstock; P166 Lew Robertson/Corbis Premium RF/Alamy; P167 l PhotoDisc/Getty Images ; P167 r Sydney Thomson/Animals Animals/Earth Scenes ; P168 John Anderson/Alamy; P169 John Anderson/Alamy; P170 John Anderson/Alamy

**Chapter 8** P171 Chas/Shutterstock; P172 l Kateryna Potrokhova/Shutterstock; P172 r Bronwen Sexton/Shutterstock; P173 Alexander Studentschnig/Shutterstock; P174 Manfred/Shutterstock; P177 PhotoDisc/Getty Images; P180-181 bkgd Corbis/Jupiter Images; P181 t Dr. Jeremy Burgess/Photo Researchers, Inc.; P181 b Don Mason/Corbis Premium RF/Alamy; P182 Karl Shone/Dorling Kindersley Limited; P183 tl Michael Grant/Alamy; P183 tr Michael Grant/Alamy; P183 br Garth Helms/Shutterstock; P184 Kucherenko Olena/Shutterstock; P185 Barry L. Runk/Grant Heilman Photography, Inc.; P187 t Harry Rogers/Photo Researchers, Inc.; P187 b H. Taylor, OSF/Animals Animals/Earth Scenes; P190 l Eric Gevaert/Shutterstock; P190 r Cathleen Clapper/Shutterstock; P192 Kim Taylor/Jane Burton/Dorling Kindersley Limited; P193 Jacqui Dracup/Garden World Images Ltd./Alamy; P194 Runk/Schoenberger/Grant Heilman Photography, Inc.; P195 t Oksana Perkins/Shutterstock; P195 b Kim Taylor & Jane Burton/Dorling Kindersley Limited; P196 Chas/Shutterstock; P197 Chas/Shutterstock; P198 t Chas/Shutterstock; P198 b Karl Shone/Dorling Kindersley Limited

**Chapter 9** P199 Ingvars Birznieks/Shutterstock; P200 t Gerard Lacz/Animals Animals/Earth Scenes; P200 b Kelpfish/Shutterstock; P201 t Joyce and Frank Burek/Animals Animals/Earth Scenes; P200 b Runk/Schoenberger/Grant Heilman Photography, Inc.; P203 t Clay Wiseman/ Animals Animals/Earth Scenes; P203 b James Watt/Animals Animals/Earth Scenes; P204 l Herb Segars/Animals Animals/Earth Scenes; P204 r Fred Bavendam/Minden Pictures; P205 Mick Hoult/Photoshot Holdings Ltd/Alamy; P206 l Lester V. Bergman/Corbis; P206 r Scott Camazine/Phototake Inc./Alamy; P207 Breck P. Kent/Animals Animals/Earth Scenes; P208 t James Nesterwitz/Alamy; P208 b Fred Bavendam/Minden Pictures; P210 l Ewen Cameron/Shutterstock; P210 r A. Winkler/Arco Images/Alamy; P211 C. Milikins OSF/Animals Animals/Earth Scenes; P212 l Michael Patrick O'Neill/Photo Researchers Inc.; P212 r Tom Adams/Visuals Unlimited, Inc./Getty Images; P213 Scott Johnson/Animals Animals/Earth Scenes; P216 tl Steve Solum/Bruce Coleman Inc./Alamy; P216 bl Victoria McCormick/Animals Animals/Earth Scenes; P216 tr Aamod Zambre/ePhotocorp/Alamy; P216 br James H. Robinson/Animals Animals/Earth Scenes; P217 Fred Whitehead/Animals Animals/Earth Scenes; P218 bkgd Fred Bavendam/Minden Pictures; P218 Siede Preis/PhotoDisc/Getty Images; P219 l Corbis; P219 r Andrew Wood/Photo Researchers, Inc.; P220 Shutterstock; P221 t Noam Armonn/Shutterstock; P221 b Michael Dick/Animals Animals/Earth Scenes; P224 Ingvars Birznieks/Shutterstock; P225 Ingvars Birznieks/Shutterstock; P226 Ingvars Birznieks/Shutterstock

**Chapter 10** P227 PhotoDisc/Getty Images; P228 tl G.I. Bernard/Animals Animals/Earth Scenes; P228 tm Robert Nystrom/Shutterstock; P228 tr Zig Leszczynski/Animals Animals/Earth Scenes; P228 bl Gerry Ellis/Minden Pictures; P228 bm Mitsuaki Iwago/Minden Pictures; P228 br Morey Milbradt/Brand X/Jupiter Images/Alamy; P229 Jessie Cohen, National Zoo/AP Wide World Photos; P230 Zig Leszczynski/Animals Animals/Earth Scenes; P231 Tui De Roy/Minden Pictures; P232 l Zig Leszczynski/Animals Animals/Earth Scenes; P232 m Suzanne L. Collins & Joseph T. Collins/Photo Researchers, Inc.; P232 r George Bryce/Animals Animals/Earth Scenes; P233 t Juan Manuel Renjifo/Animals Animals/Earth Scenes; P233 b Ventura Educational Systems; P235 Mark Smith/Photo Researchers, Inc.; P236 l Michael Dick/Animals Animals/Earth Scenes; P236 tr Steffen Foerster Photography/Shutterstock; P236 br Victoria McCormick/Animals Animals/Earth Scenes; P237 l Michael Bisceglie/Animals Animals/Earth Scenes; P237 m John Pontier/Animals Animals/Earth Scenes; P237 r Tony Phelps/Nature Picture Library; P238 col 1 Bob Blanchard/Shutterstock; P238 col 2 Leisa Hennessy/Shutterstock; P238 col 3 Nancy Tripp/Shutterstock; P238 col 4 Can Balcioglu/Shutterstock; P238 col 5 Chad Littlejohn/Shutterstock; P242 Chris Sargent/Shutterstock; P243 tl Fritz Prenzel/Animals Animals/Earth Scenes; P243 bl Mark Higgins/Alamy; P243 tr Glenda M. Powers/Shutterstock; P244 t Dinodia/Omni-Photo Communications; P244 b Marilyn Kazmers/Peter Arnold, Inc.; P244 t Peter Weimann/Animals Animals/Earth Scenes; P244 b Skip Nall/PhotoDisc/Getty Images; P246 l Jeff Foott/DRK Photo; P246 tr Michael Fogden/DRK Photo; P246 br Mitsuaki Iwago/Minden Pictures; P248 Thomas D. McAvoy/Stringer/Getty Images; P250 l Aleksandr Frolov/Shutterstock; P250 r Karl Shone/Dorling Kindersley Limited; P251 b E. R. Degginger/Animals Animals/Earth Scenes; P252 PhotoDisc/Getty Images; P253 PhotoDisc/Getty Images; P254 PhotoDisc/Getty Images

**Chapter 11** P255 Steve Hamblin/Alamy; P257 Krystyna Szulecka/Alamy; P258 l Corbis; P258 r Frans Lanting/Minden Pictures; P259 Brand X/Jupiter Images; P260 Eric and David Hosking/Corbis; P261 Peter Yates/Science Photo Library/Photo Researchers, Inc. ; P262 Jim Brandenburg/Minden Pictures; P264 Carr Clifton/Minden Pictures; P265 IF Stewart/Shutterstock; P269 Courtesy USDA Forest Service, Mount St. Helens National Volcanic Monument/AP Wide World Images; P270 l Tom Bean/DRK Photo; P270 tr Ales Liska/Shutterstock; P270 br Susan Quinland-Stringer/Shutterstock; P271 PhotoDisc/Getty Images; P272-273 bkgd Ulrike Welsch/Photo Researchers, Inc.; P272 b Steve Taylor/Getty Images; P272 b inset Juniors Bildarchiv/Alamy; P273 Carolina Biological Supply Company/Phototake; P274 Steve Hamblin/Alamy; P275 Steve Hamblin/Alamy; P276 Steve Hamblin/Alamy

**Chapter 12** P277 cbpix/Shutterstock; P279 Immaculate/Shutterstock; P280 tm Dima Kalinin/Shutterstock; P280 tr Lynn Stone/Animals Animals/Earth Scenes; P280 bl Roland Birke/Phototake Inc./Alamy; P283 OAR/National Undersea Research Program; College of William & Mary; P284 l Michael Quinton/Minden Pictures; P284 r Joe McDonald/DRK Photo; P285 Kitch Bain/Shutterstock; P288 l Michael Fogden/DRK Photo; P288 r Bob Cranston/Animals Animals/Earth Scenes; P289 t A. MacEwan, OSF/Animals Animals/Earth Scenes; P289 b David Hay Jones/Photo Researchers Inc.; P290 l Martin Tiller/Shutterstock; P290 r Nigel J. Dennis/Photo Researchers, Inc.; P291 t William R. Hutchinson Jr./Shutterstock; P291 b John Arnold/Shutterstock; P293 Park. A. Surv. OSF/Animals Animals/Earth Scenes; P298 U.S. Geological Survey/Omni-Photo Communications; P299 t David Shaw/Alamy; P299 b Underwood & Underwood/Corbis; P302 cbpix/Shutterstock; P303 cbpix/Shutterstock; P304 t cbpix/Shutterstock; P304 b Roland Birke/Phototake Inc./Alamy

**Chapter 13** P305 Sean Nel/Shutterstock; P306 l MicroScan/Phototake Inc./Alamy; P306 r Dr. Michael Klein/Peter Arnold, Inc.; P307 Jay Drowns/AP Wide World Photos; P309 Custom Medical Stock Photo; P311 l CNRI/Science Photo Library/Photo Researchers, Inc.; P311 r CNRI/Science Photo Library/Photo Researchers, Inc.; P312 A. & F. Michler/Peter Arnold, Inc.; P313 Manfred Kage/Peter Arnold, Inc.; P314 SuperStock/Alamy; P320 tr G. W. Willis/Animals Animals/Earth Scenes; P320 bl Carolina Biological Supply Company/Phototake Inc./Alamy; P320 br Manfred Kage/Peter Arnold, Inc.; P321 Losevsky Pavel/Shutterstock; P322 t Jean Marc Barey/Angence Vandystadt/Photo Rsearchers, Inc.; P322 t inset AllrightImages/face to face Bildagentur GmbH/Alamy; P322 b Ilene MacDonald/Alamy; P322 b inset Photo Researchers, Inc.; P323 Sean Nel/Shutterstock; P323 t inset SIU Biomend Comm./Custom Medical Stock Photo; P323 b Allen Munsie/Alamy; P323 b inset Living Art Enterprises, LLC/Photo

Researchers Inc.; P324 Sean Nel/Shutterstock; P325 Sean Nel/Shutterstock; P325 Sean Nel/Shutterstock

**Chapter 14** P327 MedicalRF/Alamy; P328 l Charles D. Winters/Photo Researchers, Inc.; P328 r E.R. Degginger/Animals Animals/Earth Scenes; P329 Ken Karp/Omni-Photo Communications; P333 Michael Newman/PhotoEdit; P335 Colin Keates/Dorling Kindersley Limited; P339 Professor P.M. Motta, G. Macchiarelli, S.A. Nottola/Science Photo Library/Photo Researchers, Inc.; P343 Steve Jay Crise/Corbis; P345 Bettmann Archive/Corbis; P347 Prof. P. Motta/Dept. of Anatomy/University La Sapienza, Rome/Science Photo Library/Photo Researchers, Inc.; P350 Martha Cooper/Peter Arnold, Inc.; P352 MedicalRF/Alamy; P353 MedicalRF/Alamy; P354 MedicalRF/Alamy

**Chapter 15** P355 Ema/Shutterstock; P357 Barry Slaven, MD, PdD/Phototake Inc./Alamy; P359 Layne Kennedy/Corbis; P360 l Garry DeLong/Alamy; P360 r Garry DeLong/Alamy; P361 Ed Reschke/Peter Arnold, Inc.; P362 l Dorling Kindersley Limited; P362 r Manfred Kage/Peter Arnold, Inc.; P364 t Visuals Unlimited/Corbis; P364 b Manfred Kage/Peter Arnold, Inc.; P365 Carolina Biological Supply Co./Phototake; P367 Leonard Lessin/Peter Arnold, Inc. ; P368 t Chuck Brown/Photo Researchers Inc.; P368 b Biophoto Associates/Photo Researchers Inc.; P369 SPL/Photo Researchers Inc.; P370 t John Anthony Rizzo/Brand X/Jupiter Images/Alamy; P370 b Doug Martin/Photo Researchers, Inc.; P371 tl Simon Fraser/Science Photo Library/Photo Researchers, Inc.; P371 bl Mehau Kulyk/Science Photo Library/Photo Researchers, Inc.; P371 tr Abiomed Inc./Landov; P372 Ema/Shutterstock; P373 Ema/Shutterstock; P374 Ema/Shutterstock

**Chapter 16** P375 Photos.com/Jupiter Images; P377 BSIP/Phototake; P382 Prof. P. Motta/Dept. of Anatomy/University "La Sapienza," Rome/Science Photo Library/Photo Researchers, Inc.; P383 David Hoffman Photo Library/Alamy; P386 l James Stevenson/Science Photo Library/Photo Researchers, Inc.; P386 r James Stevenson/Science Photo Library/Photo Researchers, Inc.; P389 Susan Leavines/Photo Researchers, Inc.; P395 Alfred Pasieka/Science Photo Library/Photo Researchers, Inc.; P391 Jerry Martin/The Daily Home/AP Wide World Photos ; P392 Lester V. Bergman/Corbis; P393 t Moodboard/Alamy; P393 b Susumu Nishinaga/Photo Researchers Inc.; P394 Moodboard/Alamy; P395 bl Alfred Pasieka/Science Photo Library/Photo Researchers, Inc.; P395 tr Corbis Digital Stock; P396 Photos.com/Jupiter Images; P397 Photos.com/Jupiter Images; P398 Photos.com/Jupiter Images

**Chapter 17** P399 MedicalRF/Alamy; P400 l David M. Phillips/Photo Researchers, Inc.; P400 r Dr. Dennis Kunkel/Phototake; P403 Dr. Stanley Burns/Peter Arnold, Inc.; P405 American Museum of Natural History/Dorling Kindersley Limited; P408 l Dr. Linda Stannard/Science Photo Library/Photo Researchers, Inc.; P408 r NIBSC/Science Photo Library/Photo Researchers, Inc.; P409 Will & Deni McIntyre/Photo Researchers, Inc.; P410 l Jean Claude Revy/Phototake; P410 r NIH/Science Source/Photo Researchers, Inc.; P411 David Leah/Science Photo Library/Photo Researchers, Inc.; P412 tl Bridgeman Art Library; P413 bl Dr. Stanley Burns/Peter Arnold, Inc.; P412 tr Bettman/Corbis; P413 br Bridgeman Art Library; P413 tl Will & Deni McIntyre/Photo Researchers, Inc.; P413 bl American Museum of Natural History/Dorling Kindersley Limited; P413 br NIBSC/Science Photo Library/Photo Researchers, Inc.; P414 MedicalRF/Alamy; P415 MedicalRF/Alamy; P416 MedicalRF/Alamy

**Chapter 18** P417 Sergey Petrov/Shutterstock; P420 Corbis Digital Stock; P421 Roger Ressmeyer/Corbis; P422 Mandy Godbehear/Shutterstock; P423 PhotoDisc/Getty Images; P424 Dr. John D. Cunningham/Visuals Unlimited/Getty Images; P425 t Lawrence Manning/Corbis Premium RF/Alamy; P425 b Royalty Free/Corbis; P435 Wikipedia; P436 t Jack Parsons/Omni-Photo Communications; P436 b Jules Frazier/PhotoDiscGetty Images; P437 t John Rizzo Studio, Inc./Foodpix/Jupiter Images; P437 m The Granger Collection New York/The Granger Collection; P437 Sergey Petrov/Shutterstock; P440 Solid Web Designs LTD/Shutterstock; P441 l E.R. Degginger/Animals Animals/Earth Scenes; P441 r O.J. Staats, M.D./Custom Medical Stock Photo; P441 br Custom Medical Stock Photo; P442 Sergey Petrov/Shutterstock; P443 Sergey Petrov/Shutterstock; P444 Sergey Petrov/Shutterstock

**Chapter 18** P445 Michael Damkier/Shutterstock; n/a or not listed; P446 D. Bromhall OSF/Animals Animals/Earth Scenes; P447 Biomedical Communications/Peter Arnold, Inc.; P448 MedicalRF/Alamy; P449 Science Photo Library/Custom Medical Stock Photo; P451 Carolina Biological Supply Company/Phototake; P452 Yorgas Nikas/Getty Images; P453 tl Dr. Yorgos Nikas/Science Photo Library/Photo Researchers, Inc.; P453 tr Dr. Yorgos Nikas/Phototake; P453 ml Dr. Yorgos Nikas/Phototake; P453 mr Dr. Nikas/Jason Burns/Phototake; P453 br David M. Phillips/Photo Researchers, Inc.; P454 Petit Format/Nestle/Science Source/Photo Researchers, Inc.; P458 Melissa King/Shutterstock; P459 Marcel Mooij/Shutterstock; P460 t Michael Damkier/Shutterstock; P460 m Bob Krist/Corbis; P460 b Alexander Tsiaras/Science Course/Photo Researchers, Inc.; P461 tl Popshots/Omni-Photo Communications; P461 tr Neal Graham/Omni-Photo Communications; P461 b ER Productions/Corbis; P461 b inset SIU BIOMED/Custom Medical Stock Photography; P462 Michael Damkier/Shutterstock; P463 Michael Damkier/Shutterstock; P464 Michael Damkier/Shutterstock

**Appendix** P465 Siede Preis/Photodisc/Getty Images; P467 Siede Preis/Photodisc/Getty Images; P469 Siede Preis/Photodisc/Getty Images; P471 Siede Preis/Photodisc/Getty Images; P483 Siede Preis/Photodisc/Getty Images

**Back Cover:** Siede Preis/Photodisc/Getty Images